D1072387

Jamaica Bay

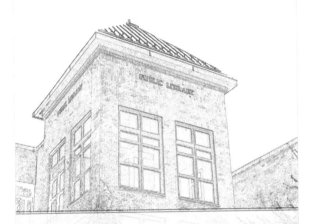

BROOKLYN

THOMAS J. CAMPANELLA

BROO

KLYN

THE ONCE AND FUTURE CITY

PRINCETON UNIVERSITY PRESS | PRINCETON AND OXFORD

Requests for permission to reproduce material from this work
should be sent to Permissions, Princeton University Press

Published by Princeton University Press
41 William Street, Princeton, New Jersey 08540

In the United Kingdom: Princeton University Press
6 Oxford Street, Woodstock, Oxfordshire OX20 1TR

press.princeton.edu

Jacket illustrations: (*front*) "The Steel Globe Tower, 700 Feet High." Lithograph postcard,
Samuel Langsdorf and Company, 1906. Collection of the author. (*back*) Map published in
1907 by August R. Ohman and Co., Library of Congress.

Map on pp. ii–iii: published in 1907 by August R. Ohman and Co.; Library of Congress.

ISBN 978-0-691-16538-7

Library of Congress Control Number: 2018966370

British Library Cataloging-in-Publication Data is available

This book has been composed in Adobe Text Pro, Abolition, and Gotham

Printed on acid-free paper. ∞

Printed in the United States of America

10 9 8 7 6 5 4 3 2 1

In memory of my parents,
Mario and Rose Campanella

And joy suddenly stirred in his soul, and he even stopped for a minute to take breath. "The past," he thought, "is linked with the present by an unbroken chain of events flowing one out of another." And it seemed to him that he had just seen both ends of that chain; that when he touched one end the other quivered.

—CHEKHOV, "THE STUDENT"

CONTENTS

ACKNOWLEDGMENTS

This book took nearly a decade to write; but it was a labor of love and a home-coming too. I began work on it as I found myself returning more frequently to my childhood Brooklyn home to care for my aging parents and—after taking a faculty position at Cornell in 2013—threw myself into the research and writing full time. Like many of Brooklyn's native sons and daughters, I went through a long period of disdain for the place, which had hit rock-bottom by the time I was a teenager. It wasn't until the late 1980s, as a graduate student in the College of Architecture, Art, and Planning at Cornell, that I awakened to the splendor and richness of Brooklyn's urban landscape. This was largely due to the influence of a Brooklynite professor with a passion for history, Leonard J. Mirin, my mentor, friend, and now colleague. Lenny watered seeds of interest in New York's urban past planted years before by my mother and father, who took their boys on countless field trips across the city—to museums and historic sites, Prospect Park, Kennedy Airport, the Brooklyn Heights Promenade, Barren Island and Jamaica Bay, the United Nations, and the vast and humming construction site that was the World Trade Center.

My rediscovery of Brooklyn also tapped deep family roots. My great-grandfather Michael Onorato was the first to cross the East River, bundling his large family out of Little Italy after a cholera outbreak in 1902. He didn't stop until he reached the sea at Coney Island, about as far from Christie Street as you could get and still be in New York City. There he opened a barbershop—Michael's Tonsorial Parlor—on Surf Avenue and long-vanished Oceanic Walk, where one of his customers was George C. Tilyou, fabled founder of Steeplechase Park. This assured that all the barber's children would get summer jobs right next door. My grandmother Mary and her sisters rented out bathing suits in the Steeplechase women's locker room. Aunt Millie went on to nursing school but returned to work alongside showman-physician Martin Couney at his boardwalk baby-incubator exhibit. Three of my great-uncles made Steeplechase their life's work. Vito was the park's plumber, Rocco managed the books, and Jimmy became general manager in 1928—a position he would hold for almost forty years. A voluble man with an omnipresent Palumbo cigar clamped between his teeth, "Jimmy of Steeplechase" became an institution himself on Coney Island. During the Depression he was a one-man WPA, hiring as many out-of-work men as he could afford—including my grandfather. He once hosted an inquisitive Californian who spent a week studying every aspect of the park's spotless, family-oriented operation. That man was Walt Disney, who later tried to recruit Uncle Jimmy to run Disneyland. It turned out that "Jimmy of Steeplechase" meant just that: he would not abandon his beloved park, nor Coney Island, nor Brooklyn.

Uncle Jimmy lived across the street from my grandmother in Borough Park, a few blocks away from his mother and a stone's throw from most of his other siblings. Such snug familial and neighborhood bonds were typical for middle-class New Yorkers of Jimmy's generation. But things unraveled fast after World War II, as their children discovered the automobile and Levittown and life in the suburbs. Many departed the region and state altogether—for New Jersey, Connecticut, Virginia, Washington, California. My parents left their old neighborhoods too, but they didn't go far: my father had a shop to keep—J-C Electric Motors on Sixty-Fifth Street—and was teaching in the public school system. For them, moving up meant moving down the map a smidge—to leafy, tranquil Marine Park, that enigmatic corner of deep-south Brooklyn where, as we will see, European colonists first settled on Long Island. My very first debt of gratitude for this book, then, is owed my much-missed parents, who stuck by Brooklyn as everyone else fled, who not only gave me life itself but launched not one but *two* sons into careers of urban-architectural discovery and wonder. Thank you, Mario and Rose, for never abandoning Brooklyn, so that I could return to make it home again, to discover it afresh, to write this book.

Many others helped make this book happen. First among them is Bob Balder, one of my oldest compatriots and a Cornell colleague who has inspired scores of architecture and planning students as director of our New York City studio. A wellspring of knowledge about Brooklyn and New York alike, Bob has been my interlocutor for countless hours in conversations about the city's architecture, infrastructure, and urbanism. A finer, more loyal friend does not exist. Equally deserving of gratitude is my cousin Michael P. Onorato, a historian himself who—as Jimmy's son—practically grew up at Steeplechase. Michael has published a wealth of primary-source material on Steeplechase over the years, including his father's voluminous daybooks, and patiently answered dozens of questions I had about Coney Island, the Tilyou family, and the Pavilion of Fun that was so tragically destroyed (by Donald Trump's father, as we will see). My good friends and Marine Park neighbors Alyssa Loorya, Malka Simon, and Jane Cowan—founding members of the League of Flatlanders—deserve thanks for their fellowship and kindred passion for Brooklyn's built environment. Alyssa and her husband, Chris Ricciardi, are among the city's most experienced archaeologists, and both contributed greatly to the early chapters of the book.

I hardly know where to begin thanking all my many friends and colleagues who, in one way or another, enriched this book and helped move it toward completion. I owe a great debt of gratitude to my Job-patient editor at Princeton University Press,

Michelle Komie, who helped shepherd this work from vague notion to finished book. My late friend and fellow urbanist Hilary Ballon was the first to read an early draft of this book, and I only wish I could have completed the book in time for her to see it. Adele Chatfield Taylor has long taken a keen interest in my work, both here and at the American Academy in Rome, where I researched the deep roots of Moses-era city park design. Jonathan Kuhn of the New York Parks Department, a living library of knowledge about Gotham's parklands, has been a wonderful friend and colleague. Charlie Denson of the Coney Island History Project took a keen and early interest in my work. My urbanist-historian brother Richard, that veritable Virgil of New Orleans, has been a steady source of advice and expertise.

For all your love, friendship, encouragement, and generosity I also thank Roberta Moudry, Charles Giraudet and Erika Goldman, Jeff Cody, Lee Briccetti and Alan Turner, Tunney F. Lee, Elissa Icso, Vishaan Chakrabarti and Jean Riesman, Vara Lipworth, Antoinette Cleary and my late uncle Tom Cleary, Marina Campanella and my little nephew Jason, Andrew Riggsby and Lisa Sandberg, Charlie and Marcia Reiss, Jessica Wurwarg, Lorna Salzman and her late husband Eric, Eva Salzman and Mitch Corrado, Roy Strickland, Arthur Schwartz and Bob Harned, Kim Evans and David LaRocca, Julie Rutschmann, Inna Yuryev-Golger, Kinga Araya, Sheri Holman, Cathy Lang Ho, C. Adair Smith, Anastasia D'Amato, Wu Nong, and my beloved in-laws Wu Keming and Shao Zhuomin. I owe a special debt of gratitude to my colleague and friend Richard S. Booth, a constant wellspring of wisdom and counsel. Many other colleagues, at Cornell and other institutions, also deserve thanks—including Jeff Chusid, Robert Fishman, John Reps, the late Susan Christopherson, Jenni Minner, Kieran Donaghy, Michael Tomlan, George Frantz, Roger Trancik, Meenu Tewari, Michele Berger and Tim Keim, Phil Berke, Mai Nguyen, Roberto Quercia, Yan Song, Jerold Kayden, Glenn Altshuler, Tina Nelson, Melanie Holland Bell, and Heidi Ingram Berrettini.

I also owe thanks to my wonderful Marine Park neighbors, some of whom have known me since childhood—especially Laura and Richie Allen (and Theresa and Richie, Jr.), Diane and John Taros, Roberta Yasbin and Joe Martino, David and Lisa Newman, Antonio and Celsa Besada, and Jerold and Maxine Weinhaus. Current and former students who helped me with various research tasks over the years include Paige Barnum, Ellen Oettinger, Martin Zeich, Katelin Olson, Daniel Widis, Connie Chan, Imani Jasper, Max Taffett, Daniel Moran, Dillon Robertson, Rhea Lopes, and Gabe Curran. Eric Platt of St. Francis College and I compared our extensive notes on the enigmatic Deborah Moody. Joan Geismar, Bill Parry, and Eymund Diegel helped me unlock the tale of the lost Maryland regiment. Donald and Marguerite Brown and actor Lou Gossett, Jr., shared their firsthand knowledge of the African American community that grew alongside the great racetracks at Gravesend and Coney Island. Allan R. Talbot, Jonathan Barnett, and former planning commissioners Donald H. Elliott and Alex Garvin helped shed light on urban design in New York City during the Lindsay years. Margot Wellington illuminated the precipitous economic decline of downtown Brooklyn in the 1960s. Lois Rosebrooks, former historian of Plymouth Church, graciously hosted my visits to that storied Heights institution. I was fortunate to receive invaluable guidance, support, and advice from

Sharon Zukin, the late Henrik Krogius of Brooklyn Heights, Brooklyn borough historian Ron Schweiger, Jim Abbate and Paul Brigandi, Giovanni Semi, my former neighbor and Brooklyn author David McCullough, the late Marian S. Heiskell, Karl Kirchwey, Kathleen G. Velsor, and Judith M. Wellman.

I consulted a vast array of archival and documentary material in the process of researching this book, at Cornell, Columbia, New York University, the New York Public Library, Brooklyn Public Library, Library of Congress, The Art Institute of Chicago, Brooklyn College, Brooklyn Museum, Brooklyn Historical Society, New-York Historical Society, La Guardia College, the Huntington Library, and the Harry Ransom Center at the University of Texas, Austin. Among the many people who helped me find documentary and photographic material, I thank especially Jeff Roth of the *New York Times*, Marianne LaBatto of the Brooklyn College Library's Archives and Special Collections, Joseph Ditta of the New-York Historical Society, Douglas DiCarlo of the La Guardia and Wagner Archives, and Ivy Marvel of the Brooklyn Collection at the Brooklyn Public Library, who gave me access to a beta version of the full digitized run of the *Brooklyn Eagle* long before it was opened to the public.

Lastly, I wish to thank my life partner and best friend, Wu Wei, for all the love, companionship, and joy she has brought into my life these many years of marriage. I could not have done this without you.

The author's great-grandfather (seated) in front of his barbershop—Michael's Tonsorial Parlor—on Surf Avenue and Oceanic Walk, 1906. Small boy at center is his son, Jimmy, future general manager of Steeplechase Park. Collection of Michael Onorato.

BROOKLYN

INTRODUCTION

What is Brooklyn that thou art mindful of her?
—PSALM 8:4, MODIFIED

This book is about the shaping of Brooklyn's extraordinary urban landscape. Its focus is not the celebrated sites and landmarks of the tourist map, though many of those appear, but rather the Brooklyn unknown, overlooked, and unheralded—the quotidian city taken for granted or long ago blotted out by time and tide. In the pages that follow I hope to breathe fresh life into lost and forgotten chapters of Brooklyn's urban past, to shed light on the visions, ideals, and forces of creative destruction that have forged the city we know today. Spanning five hundred years of history, the book's scope encompasses the built as well as unbuilt, the noble and the sham, triumphs as well as failures—dashed dreams and stillborn schemes and plans that never had a chance. The book casts new light on a place as overexposed as it is understudied. It is not a comprehensive history, nor one driven by a grand thesis, but rather a telling that plaits key strands of Brooklyn's past into a narrative about the once and future city. It is a recovery operation of sorts, a cabinet-of-curiosities tour of the Brooklyn obscure, of the city before gentrification and global fame—that "mythical dominion," as Truman Capote put it, "against whose shore the Coney Island sea laps a wintry lament."

THE QUIVERING CHAIN

Brooklyn may be a brand known around the world, but it is also terra incognita—a terrain long lost in the thermonuclear glow of Manhattan, possibly the most navel-gazed city in the world outside of Rome and the subject of dozens of good books. With some exceptions—the Brooklyn Bridge, Coney Island, the gentrification of

1

Brownstone Brooklyn, and the grassroots struggles to fight poverty and discrim-ination in Bedford-Stuyvesant and East New York—the story of Brooklyn's urban landscape remains largely untold, the subject of only a handful of texts beyond the usual guidebooks and nostalgia-laden compendia of old photographs.[1] Little or nothing has been written about how Gravesend was the first town planned by a woman in America; how Green-Wood Cemetery was not only a place of burial but effectively New York's first great public park; how Ocean Parkway fused a Yankee pastoral idea to boulevard design lifted from Second Empire Paris to create Ameri-ca's greatest "Elm Street"; about how the long-vanished Sheepshead Bay Racetrack became the toast of the thoroughbred world, birthplace of the "Big Apple," and later the launching point of the first airplane flight across the United States; or about how Marine Park was nearly chosen as the site for what ultimately became the 1939 New York World's Fair. We know equally little about the rise and fall of Floyd Bennett Field, New York's first municipal airport and the most technically advanced airfield in the world when it opened; or about the thirty-year political tug-of-war that nearly made Jamaica Bay the world's largest deepwater seaport (complete with the earliest known proposal for containerized shipping); or how a long-forgotten piece of 1920s tax legislation unleashed the greatest residential building boom in American history, one that churned Brooklyn's vast southern hemisphere—much of it farmed since the 1630s—into a dominion of mock-Tudor and Dutch-colonial homes; or the vast urban renewal and expressway projects that Robert Moses unleashed on Brooklyn after World War II, the largest, most ambitious, and most devastating in the United States. All of these are among the subjects of this book.

If this work is about the "onetime futures of past generations," to quote Reinhart Koselleck, it is also about the city today. For the past is a dark moon that tugs at our orbital plane, moving it in barely perceptible ways, exerting—as Pete Hamill has put it—an "almost tidal pull" upon the present and on our lives. The urban landscape has a long memory, an LP record with brick-and-mortar grooves. That which seems long gone is often still about our feet, hidden in plain sight. The urban past is all around us, and it conditions and qualifies the present. The modern city is replete with palimpsests and pentimenti, stubborn stains and traces of what went before, keepsakes that beckon us to unpack and explore and to understand. This book is an excavation, then, and an invitation—to see Brooklyn afresh, to discover that its remotest corners and most familiar places are all layered with memory, alive with meaning and significance. Put another way, it aims to uncover that great cable that links us to the past—what Anton Chekhov described in one of his favorite works, "The Student" (1894), as the "unbroken chain of events flowing one out of another" that leads back from the present. Chekhov's protagonist is a clerical student named Ivan Velikopolsky who relates the story of Saint Peter's denial to a pair of elderly widows on a cold winter's night. Seeing them deeply moved by his telling, Veliko-polsky suddenly understands the enduring power of narrative to convey passion and breathe life into the past: "And it seemed to him that he had just seen both ends of that chain; that when he touched one end the other quivered."[2]

Brooklyn, long-settled western rump of that glacial pile known as Long Island, has been many things to many peoples over the last five hundred years. It was home to the Leni Lenape Nation of Algonquian peoples for at least a millennium by the time Giovanni da Verrazzano cruised its shores in 1524. To European eyes it was virgin terrain, "a fresh green breast of the new world," as Nick Carraway marveled in *The Great Gatsby*—a tabula rasa upon which a whole new script for civilization could be written. It became a rural province of New Netherland until the English named it the West Riding of Yorkshire and, in 1683, Kings County. For the next 150 years this plantation realm fed the rising city across the river, engaging in cultural practices— including chattel slavery—that rendered it closer in spirit to the American South than to New England or the rest of New York. Its quarter closest to Manhattan—the town of Brooklyn proper—became America's first commuter suburb, a ferry ride and a world away from the rush and bustle of "the city." Brooklyn evolved into a tranquil realm of churches and homes where affluent New Yorkers—"gentlemen of taste and fortune"—could raise their families safely away from the chaos of urban life. Others came for eternity, tucked beneath the trees and turf in Green-Wood Cemetery, premier resting place for the silk-stocking set from Brooklyn and New York alike.[3] The teeming masses also came, decanted from the rookeries of the Lower East Side and Harlem to make Brooklyn home and to labor in the factories of Williamsburg and the Fifth Ward—the busiest industrial quarter in North America for nearly a century. Among them were my own immigrant forebears, who left Little Italy for the relative spaciousness and opportunity across the East River.

By the 1880s, the city of Brooklyn was a strapping, self-assured junior rival of New York, with dreams, schemes, and ambitions all its own. This was the Brooklyn that created America's greatest rural cemetery; whose shipyards and factories armed the Union during the Civil War; that commissioned Olmsted and Vaux to create their career masterpiece at Prospect Park; that spanned the East River with the longest suspension bridge in the world; that was Gotham's playground for a generation, where rich and poor alike gathered—at racetracks and turreted seaside hotels, and on the beaches of Coney Island. By the time Roebling's great bridge opened in May 1883, Brooklyn was all of fifty years old. Founded in 1834, it grew like a weed in manure over the next half century, zipping past Baltimore, Boston, New Orleans, and Cincinnati to become the third largest city in America by the Civil War. It swelled from annexation as well as immigration, absorbing Bushwick and the upstart city of Williamsburg in 1855, New Lots in 1886, and the far-flung country towns of Flatbush, Flatlands, Gravesend, and New Utrecht by 1896. Brooklyn thus reached the apogee of its arc, its moment of maximum power and influence. And then, as we will see, everything changed.

THE ALCHEMY OF IDENTITY

How did Brooklyn become itself? What forces have shaped its singular character and identity? Limning the soul of any city—its *genius loci*, to quote Christian Norberg-Schulz, the slippery stuff that gives a place timbre, pitch, and intensity—is no easy feat. It is multivalent, runs deep, and is in a constant state of flux. Brooklyn's place-spirit formed over several centuries and around two principal fulcrums. The first was the land itself. Brooklyn's distinctive topography—of terminal moraine and outwash plain—is a legacy of the last Ice Age, an era that ended some ten thousand years ago. The miles-deep Laurentide ice sheet was a bulldozer of the gods, gouging out the Finger Lakes, grinding down the Adirondacks, and carving the Hudson Valley only to lose its mojo in the vicinity of present-day Gotham. Here it advanced and retreated twice, as if suddenly unsure of its mission, and left in its wake a great pile of scree known today as Long Island. The backbone of this heap—the conjoined Harbor Hill and Ronkonkoma moraines—is Whitman's "Brooklyn of ample hills," a line of elevated ground well charted by place-names: Bay *Ridge*, Brooklyn *Heights*, Park *Slope*, *Prospect* Park, Crown *Heights*, Ocean *Hill*. Below and south of this is the outwash plain, a vast low-slung territory that formed as glacial meltwater and thousands of years of rain flushed much of the high ground toward the sea. The terminal moraine is thus Brooklyn's continental divide, cleaving the borough into two distinct halves: a hilly Manhattan-oriented northern hemisphere, and a broad, low-slung southern hemisphere closer in spirit to Long Island's south shore—a landscape "as flat and huge as Kansas," wrote James Agee, "horizon beyond horizon forever unfolded."[4]

As we will see throughout the book, this ancient glacial binary—terminal moraine and outwash plain—has played a vital role in Brooklyn's growth and development, and remains a key to understanding the borough today. Map the creative class in Brooklyn and you'll see a ghost of glacial history appear before your eyes. North of the moraine, a stone's throw from Manhattan, is the city of rapid gentrification, where elders and the poor are dislodged by implacable market forces—where even a tiny apartment now costs a king's ransom, and nothing, it seems, is not artisanal, batch-made, or cruelty-free. Outwash Brooklyn—basically everything south of a line from Owl's Head Park in Bay Ridge to Broadway Junction at the Queens border—remains a dominion of immigrant strivers and working-class stiffs, of quiet middle-class bedroom communities and the occasional pocket of both wealth (Midwood and Manhattan Beach) and deep poverty (Brownsville and East New York). It is a world scored still by old lines of race, class, and religion, where you can walk for hours without passing a hipster, a Starbucks, or a bar with retro-Edison lightbulbs; where there are entire communities with ties closer to Tel Aviv, Fuzhou, Kingston, or Kiev than to the rest of the United States.

The second fulcrum vital to Brooklyn's singularity among cities is its fateful adjacency to Manhattan Island. The relationship between Brooklyn and New York (composed of Manhattan alone until 1874, when it annexed part of the Bronx) has long been a dynamic and complicated one. To the colonial rulers of New Amsterdam and New York—and to the subsequent American city—Brooklyn was the ideal hinterland: close at hand and yet literally and symbolically a separate place, insulated from the center by a natural moat—the treacherous, fast-moving East River. Conditional proximity, for lack of a better term, made Brooklyn a displacement zone of sorts, a site for peoples and practices untenable in the heart of town—suspect religions, racial outcasts, citizen nonconformists, and, later, dirty industrial operations and morally polluting amusements. In this borderland beyond the gates, new freedoms and liberties were abided because they posed little threat to the sanctum sanctorum.[5] And so it was across the East River, away from New Amsterdam, that an unorthodox religious group—Deborah Moody's Anabaptists (and the Quakers who later joined them)—was permitted to

Northeast coast of Baffin Island, looking toward the Barnes Ice Cap, rapidly vanishing last vestige of the Laurentide ice sheet. Photograph by Ansgar Walk, 1997.

establish a settlement in which religious freedom was guaranteed by law. It was across the river, too, that corrupt Dutch West India Company officials were able to make huge illegal landgrabs, and that slavery was far more deeply embedded than in the progressive core. And yet it was also there that freedmen and slaves escaping north on the Underground Railroad—and blacks fleeing the terror of the Draft Riots—found sanctuary, in the African American settlement of Weeksville and among sympathizers on the very farms in Flatlands that once held men in bondage.

As New York grew, so did Brooklyn. It hatched at the river's edge, eyes fixed on the lodestar city across the way. And just as Manhattan grew north from the Battery, giving the world that enduring binary of *uptown* and *downtown*, Brooklyn began in the north and spread south. Put another way, Brooklyn reversed Manhattan's polarity. Brooklyn north of the terminal moraine hardened into cityscape by about 1915; nearly everything to its south, with the exception of the old rural towns, the amusement district in Coney Island, and a handful of early subdivisions along major axes like Ocean and Fort Hamilton parkways and Flatbush Avenue—Kensington, Ditmas Park, Blythebourne in New Utrecht, Bensonhurst-by-the-Sea, Dean Alvord's Prospect Park South subdivision in Flatbush (with Albemarle Road modeled on Boston's Commonwealth Avenue)—remained in rural slumber for another generation. Not until the great building boom of the 1920s did the metropolitan tide wash across the "broad and beautiful plain," as Henry Stiles called it, of Brooklyn's southern hemisphere. Incredibly, not until the mid-2000s were the last vacant blocks in Brooklyn's deepest south—along Avenue N in Georgetown—finally built up.[6]

From the start, the relationship between Brooklyn and New York was one of reluctant symbiosis. Brooklyn suckled at Gotham's teat, gaining in size and strength by tapping the great city's flows of people, goods, and capital. The radiant glow of New York—flagship American metropolis—fueled Brooklyn's fierce drive and ambition. Like a self-possessed kid who refuses to be bullied by a star older sibling, Brooklyn's civic leaders were driven to match New York drink for drink. It was a competitive relationship of the best sort, with Brooklyn punching above its weight in round after round for most of the nineteenth century. After New York built Central Park, Brooklyn hired the same designers to create an even finer work of landscape art across the river. Land-starved Manhattan could never have a rural cemetery like Brooklyn's Green-Wood, de rigueur for any city worth its salt in the middle years of the nineteenth century. So self-confident was this rising city, so suffused with youthful energy, that it had the moxie to cast a steel-cable net across the East River to catch hold of mighty Manahatta itself. For Brooklyn understood that if it owed its existence to the great city across the way, the reverse was also true. Without Brooklyn, New York would never have become a great metropolis. Land-poor and girdled by water, the island city was "in the condition of a walled town," wrote Frederick Law Olmsted, and would have choked on itself without a vast hinterland across the river.[7] And as Gotham grew, Brooklyn became ever more vital to its existence. Brooklyn fed New York, took its trash, decanted its masses, housed its workforce, manufactured its goods, and buried its dead. At Brighton Beach and Coney Island—that "clitoral appendage at the entrance to New York harbor," as Rem Koolhaas memorably put it—the moral corsets of New York society were loosened.[8] There, all manner of conduct unbecoming—drinking, gambling, whoring—was not only tolerated but well served. Coney Island enabled and sustained Manhattan's hyperdensity by bleeding off the pressures and energy of the metropolitan core, playing id to its massive ego.

WATERSHED 1898

Of course, proximity to Manhattan had its risks. Like an acorn that sprouts too near the great oak from which it fell, it was inevitable that Brooklyn would eventually be eclipsed by the Goliath next door. That moment came on the cold and rainy night of December 31, 1897. As the clock struck twelve, the city of Brooklyn passed into history—extinguished for the greater glory of Greater New York City, what the *New-York Tribune* called "the greatest experiment in municipal government that the world has ever known." While rockets burst over jubilant revelers in Manhattan, Brooklyn's social and cultural elite mourned the demise of their proud independent city—"the moral center of New York," as the *Daily Eagle* ruefully put it. Never had so large and influential a metropolis been so subsumed by a neighboring rival. Consolidation overnight made New York the largest city on earth after London, fulfilling Gotham's "imperial destiny," as Abram S. Hewitt put it in 1887, "as the greatest city in the world."[9]

The mastermind of this forced marriage was Andrew Haswell Green, an extraordinary administrative polymath and political reformer who built many public works, broke the Tweed ring, helped create Central Park, and founded a succession of major institutions—among them the New York Public Library, American Museum of Natural History, and New York Zoological Park (Bronx Zoo). It was in an 1868 memo

"Consolidation Number," an 1897 special edition of the *Brooklyn Daily Eagle* celebrating the coming formation of Greater New York City, with the five boroughs rather improbably represented as virginal maidens. Brooklyn Public Library, Brooklyn Collection.

to the Central Park Commission that Green first sketched out his vision of a future city "under one common municipal government." Consolidation was never a popular movement in Brooklyn, but it had the backing of merchants, bankers, and the powerful real estate industry. It was also supported by that dean of Brooklyn civic life, James S. T. Stranahan, a Green-like spirit who—as we will see—played a formative role in creating Prospect Park and the Brooklyn Bridge. Consolidation was Stranahan's last great campaign (he died just months after its consummation). As the issue came to a head, the Brooklyn Consolidation League and other groups canvassed the city to convince voters that being part of Greater New York would halve Brooklyn taxes, clear its mounting debt, raise property values, and bring about a profusion of public works—including access to Croton water and a much-needed second bridge across the East River. The Consolidation League was checked by the fiercely anti-consolidationist editorial board of the *Eagle*, and by a well-funded group known as the League of Loyal Citizens. Though it included some of Brooklyn's most respected church and civic leaders, the league used scare tactics that alienated many potential supporters. Much of this fearmongering involved race, ethnicity, and religion. The league depicted Manhattan as a whoring Mammon that would contaminate the pure and pious City of Churches. Its vision of Brooklyn was a city of native-born citizens "trained from childhood in American traditions," a white, Protestant motherland with deep Yankee roots that risked being overrun by the swarthy immigrant hordes of the Lower East Side—"the political sewage of Europe," as the Reverend Richard S. Storrs of Brooklyn Heights put it. The Consolidation Referendum was approved by nearly 37,000 votes in New York; in Brooklyn it passed by a mere 277.[10]

FIELD OF DREAMS

Consolidation profoundly altered the genetic code of Brooklyn, as if its DNA had been exposed to a potent source of radiation. But the effects were delayed, like an illness that lay dormant for years before showing signs or symptoms. For most of a generation, Brooklyn's old-guard Protestant elite stayed put and continued to campaign for the improvement of their beloved city—even if it was now a mere borough of Greater New York. To Manhattanite expansionists like Andrew Green, meanwhile, Brooklyn was a vast field of dreams—a tabula rasa onto which all sorts of metropolitan fantasies could be projected. The colonizing gaze hardly troubled Brooklyn's elite; for Greater New York's expansionist plans—its embrace of Brooklyn as a kind of test bed and laboratory for urban experimentation—elided seamlessly with Brooklyn's own ambitions for growth, development, and greatness. This created, from about 1900 to the mid-1930s, a synergy that fueled an extraordinary range of projects and proposals promoted by Brooklyn boosters and metropolitan expansionists alike—two more bridges across the East River, subway lines, a great waterfront park that included the world's biggest sports stadium, a deepwater port larger than anything in Europe, the best airport in North America.

It was also to Brooklyn in this period that, much as its Protestant old guard feared, countless immigrants from across the East River came to find their American Dream. The Manhattan and Williamsburg bridges decanted the overcrowded tenements of

Linked fates: looking east toward Brooklyn from the Woolworth Building, 1916. Photograph by Irving Underhill. Library of Congress, Prints and Photographs Division.

the Lower East Side, channeling tens of thousands of working-class Germans, Scandinavians, Jews, Italians, Poles, and Irish into Williamsburg, Bushwick, Greenpoint, Red Hook, Sunset Park, and the industrial district west of the Navy Yard. By the mid-1920s a residential building boom unprecedented in US history had created a vast tapestry of middle-class streetcar suburbs across Brooklyn's outwash plain, where young families could find "room to swing a cat," as P. G. Wodehouse and Jerome Kern versed it in "Nesting Time in Flatbush." The coming of so many Catholic and Jewish southern and eastern Europeans in this era was a last straw of sorts for Brooklyn's Anglo-Dutch elite. By the late 1920s they were fleeing in droves for the upscale suburbs of Westchester, Long Island, and New Jersey. My mother used to recall how, on walks with her father in the 1930s, she would marvel at the aged Anglo-Dutch widows sweeping the stoops of their glorious brownstones on South Oxford Street; last of their breed, they were relics of a lost world whose families had long ago fled to Scarsdale, Bronxville, or the North Shore.

IN A VASSAL STATE

The Great Depression brought about another inflection point in Brooklyn's evolution. By the mid-1930s, the old order of Anglo-Dutch Brooklyn had largely been supplanted by the borough's surging white-ethnic population. The newcomers were fiercely ambitious in their own right, but also keenly aware of their provisional status in a society still dominated by its white, Anglo-Saxon charter culture. One did not have to travel far to find evidence of just how hated one was as a Jew or Catholic in America: when Al Smith campaigned for the presidency in 1928, there were Klan rallies and cross burnings all over Long Island. Internalizing outsider status can fuel deep anxiety about one's place in the world and breed a sense of self-loathing. In Brooklyn, these immigrant insecurities were validated and confirmed by the borough's own subaltern, "outer" rank *vis-à-vis* mighty Manhattan. By now, the keen competitive stance Brooklyn once had with its East River rival—its eagerness to beat Manhattan at its own game—had greatly diminished. Consolidation robbed Brooklyn of not only its independence, but much of its moxie and optimism. After World War II, the once-proud city had developed a gnawing inferiority complex. Brooklyn began to see itself as colonized terrain, a vassal state forever in Manhattan's shadow. It was the eternal underdog—feisty and bombastic and yet consumed by a chronic sense of inadequacy, a Fredo Corleone of cities. The enduring symbol of this subaltern realm was, of course, the Brooklyn Dodgers—a club defeated in six out of seven World Series matchups with the New York Yankees, and that finally triumphed in 1955 only to double-cross their fans by departing for sunny California two years later. The "Dodger betrayal" became a bitter trope for all the crushed hopes and failures of postwar Brooklyn and its white-ethnic social order.

Of course, self-loathing is generally returned with gleeful interest by the world. Brooklyn became the punching bag of cities, the butt of jokes, an object of ridicule that the rest of America could look down its long WASP nose at. Brooklyn's husky patois—*dawg* for "dog," *pitchuh* for "picture," and of course *cawfee*—was mocked from stage and screen. Rapidly vanishing now, it was something to wrap one's ears about. I remember an aunt telling a story at my grandmother's Borough Park dinner table when I was a child—something involving an "earl." Confused—I thought she was referring to English royalty—I tugged my father's sleeve and whispered, "*Dad, who is this earl?*" Rarely heard today, *earl* was how working-class Brooklynites of a certain age pronounced "oil." Conversely, the word "earl" itself would have been pronounced *oil*, which recalls the great Rogers and Hart song "Manhattan," made famous by Ella Fitzgerald, in which a love-struck boy and *goil* marvel at the city's romantic allure. But the ridicule could be brutal, and always the most withering came from the high cultural elite—the same class that now stumbles over itself for a Park Slope brownstone, whose trust-funded children have colonized the industrial wastes of Red Hook and Bushwick. Exeter-and-Harvard-educated James Agee, on a failed 1939 assignment for *Fortune* magazine, ventured bravely across the East River to discover in Brooklyn "a curious quality in the eyes and at the corners of the mouths, relative to what is seen on Manhattan Island: a kind of drugged softness or narcotic relaxation," much the same look "seen in monasteries and in the lawns of sanitariums." And though possessing something of a center ("and hands, and eyes, and feet"), Brooklyn was in Agee's view mostly "an exorbitant pulsing mass of scarcely discriminable cellular jellies and tissues; a place where people merely 'live.' "[11]

To Truman Capote, Brooklyn was a benighted realm filled with "sad, sweet, violent children," homeland of the Philistine mediocrity, the man who "guards averageness with morbid intensity." He called Brooklyn a "veritable veldt of tawdriness where even the *noms des quartiers* aggravate: Flatbush and Flushing Avenue, Bushwick, Brownsville, Red Hook." Any mention of it brought forth "compulsory guffaws," he mused, for Brooklyn was the nation's laughingstock. "As a group, Brooklynites form a persecuted minority," he wrote in 1946; "their dialect, appearance and manners have become . . . synonymous with the crudest, most vulgar aspects of contemporary life." Capote heaped plenty of highbrow scorn on Brooklyn, but even he recoiled at just how cruel all this mirth making at the borough's expense could be. The teasing, which "perhaps began good-naturedly enough, has turned the razory road toward malice," he observed; "an address in Brooklyn is now not altogether respectable." He also understood the borough's vast complexity better than most. To Capote, Brooklyn was "terribly funny," but also "sad brutal provincial lonesome human silent sprawling raucous lost passionate subtle bitter immature perverse tender mysterious." Capote moved to Brooklyn not long after penning those lines, renting an apartment in the Willow Street home of his friend—set designer and former February House denizen Oliver Smith. "I live in Brooklyn," Capote wrote in perhaps the greatest backhanded compliment ever paid a city—"By choice."[12]

Often the most bitter vitriol came from the borough's own, to whom success was a measure of distance gained from their native place. My mother could be scornful of family and friends who stayed put in her old neighborhood by the Brooklyn Navy Yard. Indeed, the mark of arrival was to leave. "The idea," wrote Pete Hamill, "was to get out."[13] Henry Miller reviled the Bushwick and Williamsburg of his youth, describing Myrtle Avenue as "a street not of sorrow, for sorrow would be human and recognizable, but of sheer emptiness: it is emptier than the most extinct volcano . . . than the word God in the mouth of an unbeliever." Down this grim way "no miracle ever passed, nor any poet, nor any species of human genius, nor did any flower ever grow there, nor did the sun strike it squarely, nor did the rain ever wash it." See Myrtle Avenue before you die, he implored, "if only to realize how far into the future Dante saw." Age did nothing to diminish Miller's odium. In a 1975 documentary, the octogenarian author recalled his birthplace as a "shithole . . . a place where I knew nothing but starvation, humiliation, despair, frustration, every god damn thing—nothing but misery."[14] Such deep loathing for one's birthplace and cradle created a population that, as we will see, tolerated some of the most egregious acts of urban vandalism in postwar America. Place-hatred does not breed a culture of civic activism or preservation, especially when it's fused with poverty. This is one of the reasons why city officials were able to raze unopposed most of the blocks south of the Navy Yard for the largest single housing project in American history; and why Robert Moses was able to bulldoze the Brooklyn-Queens Expressway across Red Hook and Williamsburg with nary a whimper from the locals, when a similar project in the Bronx—the Cross Bronx Expressway—raised howls of opposition from the people of East Tremont, who loved their neighborhood and fought bitterly to save it.

It may well be that Brooklyn's strange alchemy of ambition and self-loathing is precisely why it has churned out more raw talent than any other city in America. The sons and daughters of Brooklyn were hungry, straining at the harness, eager to prove themselves to a cynical, mocking world—or at least to that exalted realm across the East River, the very incarnation of worldly power, wealth, and splendor. And they did just that. There is no quarter of modern life in America that Brooklyn's

Cover of the 1954 Dodger's *Yearbook*, envisioning a dream that would never happen—not in Brooklyn, at least. Collection of the author.

gifted offspring have not touched or transformed. And there were plenty of offspring to go around: it is often said that a quarter of all Americans can trace their family ancestry through Brooklyn. Even a partial list of luminaries born or raised in this crossroads of the world is dazzling: Aaliyah, Woody Allen, Darren Aronofsky, Isaac Asimov, zoning pioneer Edward Murray Bassett, Pat Benatar, Mel Brooks, William M. Calder (father of daylight saving time), Al Capone, Shirley Chisholm, Aaron Copland, Milton Friedman, George and Ira Gershwin, Rudy Giuliani, Doris Kearns Goodwin, Arlo Guthrie, Lena Horne, the Horwitz brothers of Three Stooges fame, Jay Z, Jennie Jerome (Winston Churchill's mother), Michael Jordan, Alfred Kazin, Harvey Keitel, Carole King, C. Everett Koop, Spike Lee, Jonathan Lethem, housing pioneer William Levitt, Vince Lombardi, Norman Mailer, Arthur Miller and Henry Miller, Zero Mostel, Eddie Murphy, The Notorious B.I.G., Rosie Perez, Norman Podhoretz, Nobel physicist Isidor I. Rabi, Lou Reed, Buddy Rich, Joan Rivers, Chris Rock, Carl Sagan, US senators Bernie Sanders and Chuck Schumer, Jerry Seinfeld, Beverly Sills, Nobel economist Robert Solow, Barbara Stanwyck and Barbra Streisand, George C. Tilyou, John Turturro, Mike Tyson, Wendy Wasserstein, Walt Whitman, the Beastie Boys' Adam Yauch.

High view of downtown Brooklyn, 1962. Photograph by Thomas Airviews. Collection of the author.

Brooklyn reached its peak of population in the immediate wake of World War II—a conflict it played no small part in winning (seventy thousand workers at the Navy Yard churned out seventeen warships between 1940 and 1945, including some of the most powerful ever built). But the winds of fortune changed fast. As we will see, a confluence of internal and external forces—the collapse of industry and loss of factory jobs, the lure of the suburbs, surging street crime, a breakdown of social order—began pulling Brooklyn apart. By the mid-1970s, when I was a child growing up in Marine Park, Brooklyn had been brought to its knees. Wracked by a cacophony of social ills, Brooklyn—indeed, most of New York—was a city under siege. More than half a million residents had fled the borough by then, panicked by its changing demographics, spooked by the boogeyman of race, paralyzed by legitimate fears of violent crime. The serial loss of anchor institutions—the *Brooklyn Eagle* (1955), the Dodgers (1957), Ebbets Field (1960), Steeplechase Park (1964), the Navy Yard (1966)—convinced them that the borough's best years were behind it. And so they left, abandoning some of most glorious residential urbanism in North America for car-dependent suburbs, trading townhouses and Tudor-castle apartments for stick-built ranch homes in subdivisions shorn of street life and far from the centers of culture—pawning, in effect, the family jewels for a car and a cardboard box. It would remain for their children and grandchildren to find a path back and rediscover the extraordinary place they had left behind.

CHAPTER 1

THE NATAL SHORE

There is toward the sea a large piece of low flat land . . .
overflowed at every tide.
—JASPER DANCKAERTS AND PETER SLUYTER, 1679

Amidst the leafy quietude of East Thirty-Fifth Street in Marine Park, far from the
hipsters or the merchants of twee, there is a spectacle as unique and unlikely as a
Hollywood stage set. The Hendrick I. Lott house is one of New York City's most
extraordinary survivors, a virtually unaltered keepsake from Gotham's distant past
that sits among its upstart neighbors like an old cat sleeping in the sun. The house
occupies a spacious lot, but it once commanded an empire of earth that swept south
and west from Kings Highway to Jamaica Bay. Canted a few degrees off the street grid
as if in protest of municipal edict, the Lott house is among the oldest homes in New
York and a superlative example of Dutch American vernacular architecture that—
unlike most other colonial holdouts in the city—has sat on the same foundation
for over two hundred years. Incredibly, the Lott house was occupied by the same
family until 1989—the longest tenure of any in New York City history. I remember
well its elderly last occupant, Ella Suydam, a librarian at Eramus Hall High School,
who would wave to us boys as we gaped, wide-eyed, at the "country house" in the
middle of town. Suydam, a neighborhood character who swept her porch in a 1930s
fur coat, was—incredibly—the great-great-great-great-granddaughter of Johannes
Lott, who built the east section of the house in 1719, the year my favorite childhood
book was published, Daniel Defoe's *Robinson Crusoe*.

The long-rural southern hemisphere of Brooklyn was brought into Gotham's
pale in the 1920s, as the city grew south and east in its most exuberant era of expansion. Municipal water and sewer infrastructure had only just been extended to
this part of town—service that, combined with a roaring economy and a ten-year

The Hendrick I. Lott House, c. 1720. Photograph by Alyssa Loorya, 2017.

tax holiday, stoked an unprecedented frenzy of residential development. Fields first plowed in the seventeenth century now brought forth a last great crop of mock-Tudor homes. This remarkable metamorphosis—from countryside to cityscape almost overnight (subject of chapter 13)—is well documented thanks to a twenty-six-year-old aviation entrepreneur named Sherman Fairchild, whose fledgling Fairchild Aerial Survey Company had photographed every inch of Manhattan in 1922 with a fast new camera of his own design. The images were tiled together to produce a map twenty inches wide and more than eight feet long. The following year, Fairchild was commissioned by city engineer Arthur S. Tuttle to do the same for all of New York. By the summer of 1924 his camera plane had flown nearly three thousand miles back and forth over the city, snapping some twenty-nine hundred images of the five boroughs from an altitude of ten thousand feet. These were assembled into a great mosaic to produce an eight-by-twelve-foot aerial portrait of the Big Apple—the first comprehensive photographic map of any city in the world. It revealed, among other things, the hungry grid of metropolis about to consume the old Lott farm—Brooklyn's last rural landscape. Fairchild's camera planes came not a moment too soon; for the very next year—1925—was the last that Johannes Lott's rustic spread would be tilled. Sherman Fairchild's photomosaic thus captured in the wink of a mechanical eye a two-hundred-year-old pastoral realm at the very end of its days.[1]

Lott was a pioneer, to be sure, but hardly the first European in this vernal corner of the New World. Flatlands had been colonized for close to a century by now, and had been home to Native Americans for untold centuries before that. At the northern boundary of Lott's land was an old Indian crossroads, the present-day junction of Flatbush Avenue and Kings Highway. Heavily trafficked thoroughfares today, they still roughly follow ancient alignments, which explains why both roads look like random rips in the urban fabric on a map of the city. At the juncture of

Brooklyn's last rural landscape on the verge of urbanization, 1924. From a citywide photomosaic map produced by the Fairchild Aerial Camera Corporation for city engineer Arthur S. Tuttle. Lionel Pincus and Princess Firyal Map Division, The New York Public Library.

these trade routes was once the Canarsee Indian settlement of Keskaechqueren or Keskachauge (Keskachoque in "modern Long Island nomenclature"), a principal council site of the tribes of western Long Island and possibly the seat of Penhawitz, a powerful, peaceable sachem and friend of the Dutch. One of several chieftaincies scattered across Long Island at the time of European contact, the Canarsee lived in semipermanent settlements made up of small matrilineal family groups. They drew sustenance from land and water—gathering chestnuts, fishing, hunting, and harvesting shellfish; cultivating maize, beans, pumpkins, and squash. They were part of the Leni Lenape Nation of Algonquian peoples that once occupied much of the northeast coast, and whose place-names—Gowanus, Hackensack, Manhattan, Passaic, Rockaway, Weehawken—are the toponymy of daily life in metropolitan New York.[2]

Keskachauge was on the edge of a broad expanse known as the "Plains" or the "Great Flats," which extended north to about where Brooklyn College is today. It was the largest of three such plains in the area that were among the few natural prairies east of the Allegheny Mountains.[3] These long-vanished grasslands were surrounded by woods, but treeless except for an occasional ancient oak or pine tree. In places, they were planted to maize by the Canarsee. They were formed in part by the centuries of periodic burning by Native Americans to facilitate travel, clear underbrush for camps and cultivation, kill off ticks and fleas, and increase the forest-edge habitat favored by game animals—turkey, grouse, quail, deer, rabbits.[4] We recall these miniature prairies today in the name given this part of Long Island

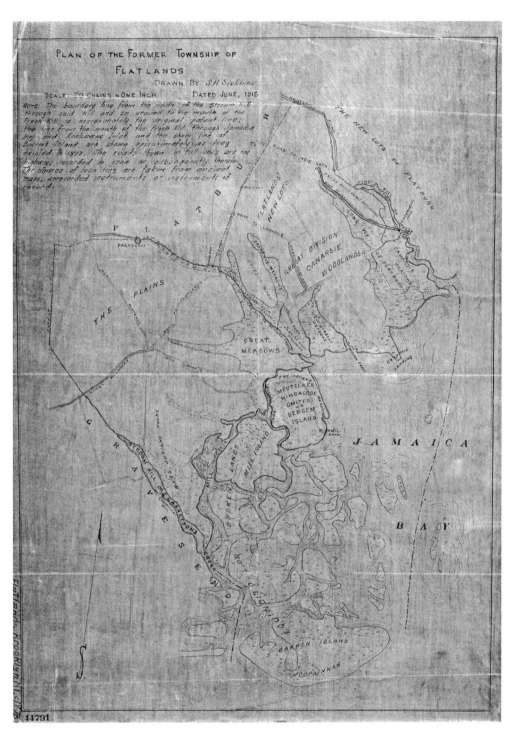

Plan of the former township of Flatlands showing the plains or Great Flats, Baes Jurians Hooke, and the "Stroom Kill or Garretsons Creek." Drawn in 1873 by S. H. Stebbins using early records. Lionel Pincus and Princess Firyal Map Division, The New York Public Library.

by the English—*Flatlands*. Something of their character may be gleaned from a description by Timothy Dwight of the larger Hempstead Plain, farther east on Long Island (a tiny fragment of which may still be seen between Nassau Coliseum and the Meadowbrook Parkway). Then serving a grueling term as president of Yale College, Dwight took a series of extended autumn journeys through New York and New England in the 1790s, one of which covered the length of Long Island. Dwight found the Hempstead Plain to be "absolutely barren" in some places, but elsewhere covered by "a long, coarse wild grass" or thinly forested with pine or shrubby oaks ("the most shrivelled and puny that I ever met with"). Except for peninsular intrusions of forest into the plain, the terrain was relieved only by occasional clusters of trees such as the Isle of Pines—which "at a distance," he noted, "resembles not a little a real island."[5]

Keskachauge appears on the earliest surviving map of New Netherland—the remarkable Manatus Map of 1639. The document—produced by either the Dutch cartographer Johannes Vingboons or colonial surveyor Andries Hudde—was found hanging on a wall at the Villa Castello near Florence and later moved to Michelangelo's Biblioteca Medicea Laurenziana. The nearly identical "Harrisse Copy"—a detail of which is reproduced here—is held by the Library of Congress.[6] On the map, Keskachauge is shown just east of "Conyné Eylant," marked by a longhouse noted as the habitation typical of "de Wilden Keskachaue"—the "savages" of Keskachauge.[7] We don't know what this structure looked like, but it was likely similar to an Indian longhouse several miles to the west at Nieuw Utrecht described in a remarkable document discovered in an Amsterdam bookshop in 1864—a travel journal by two

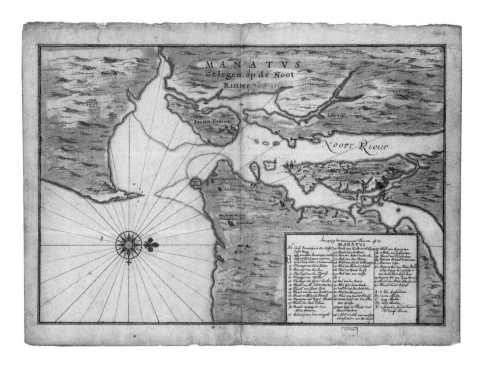

Manatvs gelegen op de Noot Riuier (Manatus Map), 1639. Library of Congress, Geography and Map Division.

visiting missionaries from Friesland, Jasper Danckaerts and Peter Sluyter. While riding along the marshy shore near today's Fort Hamilton, the pair heard the sound of pounding, and discovered nearby an elderly Indian woman "beating Turkish beans [maize] out of the pods by means of a stick."

> We went from thence to her habitation, where we found the whole troop together, consisting of seven or eight families . . . Their house low and long, about sixty feet long and fourteen or fifteen feet wide. The bottom was earth, the sides and roof were made of reed and the bark of chestnut trees; the posts, or columns, were limbs of trees stuck in the ground, and all fastened together.

The roof ridge of the longhouse was left open half a foot the entire length of the structure, allowing smoke to escape from cooking fires below. These were built "in the middle of the floor," noted the men, "according to the number of families which live in it, so that from one end to the other each of them boils its own pot, and eats when it likes." The Keskachauge longhouse was probably located at the headwaters of "a certaine Kill or Creeke coming out of the Sea"—a tidal estuary of Jamaica Bay known as Weywitsprittner to the Indians, the Strome Kill to the Dutch, and Gerritsen Creek today.[8]

The Strome Kill is Brooklyn's natal stream. Once extending as far north as Kings Highway, it was the longest of the many tidal inlets that scored the outwash plain above Jamaica Bay, so cleaving the landscape that the Dutch called it *breukelen*— "the fractured lands." As Daniel Denton observed in 1670, such "Christal streams" on Long Island's south shore not only teemed with fish—"Sheeps-heads, Place,

"Ryder's Pond and Old Cedar," 1899. This photograph by Daniel Berry Austin was taken from the west bank of Gerritsen Creek below present-day Whitney Avenue. Daniel Berry Austin photograph collection, Brooklyn Museum/Brooklyn Public Library, Brooklyn Collection.

Pearch, Trouts, Eels, Turttles"—but ran "so swift, that they purge themselves of such stinking mud and filth" and were thus unlikely to harbor "fevers and other distempers."[9] The cultural history of the Strome Kill may date back some fifteen hundred years, when post–Ice Age sea levels stabilized and the modern coastline of Long Island began to take form. As Frederick Van Wyck speculated in 1924, the tidal estuary "probably contains more undisturbed traces of the Indians than are to be found in any other part of Brooklyn, possibly in any other part of the city of New York." It was on the western shore of the Strome Kill that a Canarsee Indian village and wampum works known as Shanscomacoke once stood. Evidence of long occupation of this place by Native Americans came to light slowly in the nineteenth century. Farmers found arrowheads on the beach; vast shell banks or "middens" were revealed by tides and erosion. When Avenue U was constructed at the turn of the nineteenth century, human skeletons were unearthed in graves filled with still-sealed oyster shells—meant, perhaps, as sustenance in the afterlife.[10]

It was around this time that an amateur archaeologist named Daniel Berry Austin began digging at Gerritsen Creek. Austin was an accomplished photographer with a day job at Standard Oil, but his real passion was the indigenous history of Long Island. Equal parts hoarder and scientist, Austin amassed a breathtaking collection of artifacts over his lifetime. He crammed more than ten thousand items into his modest home on East Fourteenth Street in Midwood, some fifteen hundred of which were from sites in Brooklyn alone. This included several skeletons stored—quite literally—in his closet. One of these probably came from the vicinity of Avenue U and Burnett Street, where Austin discovered a dozen graves each spaced thirty-five feet apart from one another. Sometime later, just to the north, Austin and his two young sons stumbled upon perhaps the most extensive prehistoric site ever unearthed in New York City. They dug up hundreds of arrowheads, stone tools, pottery shards, and animal bones later determined to date mostly from the Late Woodland period—a period that ended a thousand years ago. But Austin excavated carelessly, failing to note relative depth or location of artifacts and thus scrambling forever the archaeological record. Still, if not for him, knowledge of Shanscomacoke might have been lost altogether. For in the 1930s, the entire site north of Avenue U was buried under many feet of sand and soil. What remains of this ancient place today lies beneath the ball fields and turf of Marine Park, especially its western half, south of Fillmore Avenue and Junior High School 278. Austin's hoard was scattered to the winds after he died. Fortunately, some of it passed to a prominent Long Island naturalist named Roy Latham, who later gifted the artifacts to the tiny Southold Indian Museum. They remain there today, across the road from an astronomical observatory named, oddly enough, for the grandniece of Indian fighter George Armstrong Custer.[11]

Austin was not the only one bewitched by this spectral corner of the city. So, too, was Frederick Van Wyck, a New Yorker of old Dutch stock whose cousin was the bumbling first mayor of Greater New York, Robert A. Van Wyck (whom we'll meet in chapter 10). A broker by trade, Van Wyck had the time and money to indulge a lifelong passion for history and the arts. Several of his books were illustrated by his wife, Matilda Browne, a landscape painter who had studied with Thomas Moran.

Austin's macabre display of human skeletal remains exhumed from the west side of Gerritsen Creek c. 1900, close to present intersection of Avenue U and Burnett Street. Daniel Berry Austin photograph collection, Brooklyn Museum/Brooklyn Public Library, Brooklyn Collection.

Like many men of his generation, Van Wyck was dismayed by the decline of Anglo-Dutch New York and the churning Babel that his city was becoming. Each wave of immigrants from Ellis Island seemed to send him on ever-deeper recovery missions into the past. A man literally out of time, Van Wyck came to dwell "mentally and physically in the New York of a bygone era," engrossed in the creation narrative of his city and social class—a real-life Diedrich Knickerbocker, narrator of Washington Irving's satirical *History of New-York*. But obsessions of the creative sort often bear prized fruit. In 1924, Van Wyck published an extraordinary treatise on Brooklyn's earliest history, entitled *Keskachauge*. Nearly eight hundred pages long, it is one of the most voluminous and assiduously researched works of local history ever published in the United States. In it, Van Wyck argued that the Strome Kill and its uplands—a peninsula called Baes Jurians Hooke, heart of the Marine Park neighborhood today—might well have been Gotham's Plymouth Rock.

First contact, in Van Wyck's view, may have taken place as early as 1609. On September 3 that year, Henry Hudson and the crew of the *Half Moon* swung up the coast around Sandy Hook and "came to three great Rivers." One of these was Raritan Bay, the other the Narrows, and the third Rockaway Inlet (then much farther east than it is today). A journal kept by Hudson's mate, Robert Juet, indeed tells of an attempt to enter the "Northermost" of these "rivers," but that shoals and sandbars and "ten foot water" forced the ship back. As Van Wyck saw it, "Hudson's first intention on the afternoon of September third was to go into Jamaica Bay." This meant that, however briefly, the *Half Moon* "probably came head on in the direction of Flatlands," and that its crew could well have ended up making landfall at the mouth of the Strome Kill. He imagined that "every member of the tribe . . . must have seen the strange object that loomed up on the horizon about three o'clock that afternoon, headed straight for the entrance to the bay. These Indians and their chiefs would have been more than mortal if they had not followed with the closest scrutiny every move the stranger made that afternoon until darkness came."[12] Van Wyck also argued that crew members left behind by Dutch trading ships in 1614 and 1615 to dispose of goods might have "wintered at Keskaechqueren, under the protection of the great chief Penhawitz"—thus making Flatlands possibly "the oldest place of white abode in Greater New York." Van Wyck further conjectured that the Strome Kill was the haven where Cornelius Hendricksen and the crew of the *Onrust* wintered in 1616. The *Onrust* (Restless) was the first ship built in the Americas, whose modest draft allowed it to navigate waters too shallow for the *Half Moon*. Hendrickson—and Adrian Block before him—used the craft to explore much of the Connecticut and Long Island coastlines, leading some to call it America's first research vessel.[13]

Even if Van Wyck was wrong about all this—about Hudson and wintering traders and the hunkered crew of the *Onrust*—Keskachauge was certainly settled by 1636, a full decade before the village of Breuckelen on the waterfront at Fulton Street. It was thus among the first permanent settlements in New Netherland and the earliest place colonized by Europeans on Long Island. That summer, several major land conveyances were made to the Dutch by a delegation of Canarsee led by chiefs Penhawitz and Kakapetteyno—in exchange for "certain merchandise" and purportedly with the blessing and "consent of the community." The first was made to Wolphert Gerritsen and Andries Hudde for "the westernmost of the flats called *Kestateuw*."[14] The smaller middle and eastern prairies (known, respectively, as Castuteeuw and Casteteuw) were conveyed to two Dutch West India Company agents still in their twenties—Jacobus van Corlaer, first commissary of wares; and Wouter van Twiller, who had replaced Pieter Minuit as director general of New Netherland three years earlier.[15] Hudde was a surveyor from Amsterdam; Gerritsen had been a baker in the Utrecht town of Amersfoort before sailing to New Netherland in 1625. A forebear of the Roosevelt clan, he was recruited to run a farm in lower Manhattan before striking out for Keskachauge. All told, some thirty-six hundred acres were conveyed by Penhawitz and Kakapetteyno, who almost certainly did not realize that the transactions would forever alienate their people from the land. For the eager and ambitious Van Twiller—satirized as corpulent, bumbling "Walter the Doubter" by Washington Irving (who confused the youth with his father)—the Casteteuw land grant was just another investment in an impressive portfolio that included most of Red Hook, a tobacco plantation in Greenwich Village, and the islands known today as Wards, Randalls, Roosevelt, and Governors (the last a reference to Van Twiller himself). Though he had no interest in homesteading, he seems to have "caused" several structures to be erected on his land at Casteteuw.[16]

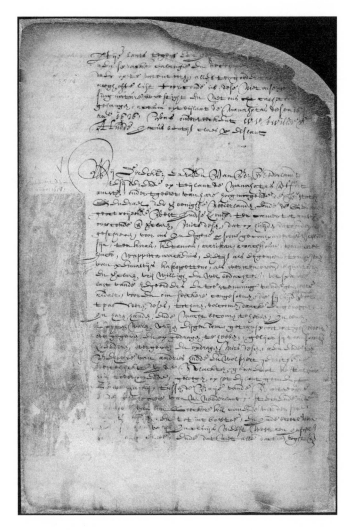

Patent of Andries Hudde and Wolphert Gerritsen van Couwenhoven for a tract of land on Long Island, June 16, 1636. The deed conveys to the colonists the "westernmost of the flats called Keskateuw . . . on the island called Sewanhacky [Long Island]." New York State Archives—Dutch colonial patents and deeds, 1630–1664 (Series A1880, Volume GG).

One of these has miraculously survived to the present—the Pieter Claesen Wyckoff House at Ralph Avenue and Clarendon Road. With its medieval massing and steep-sloped roof, the Wyckoff house is a true envoy from Gotham's deepest past— the oldest building in New York City, one of two or three oldest structures in all New York State and the very first building designated by the Landmarks Preservation Commission when it was founded in 1965. Across the street from a car wash, a salvage yard, and a geriatric diaper supplier called Elderwear (which Google Maps shows, incorrectly but appropriately nonetheless, as occupying the Wyckoff House itself), the building hovered on the edge of destruction for decades, and was known locally in the 1980s as America's oldest crack house. It is today a lovingly managed house museum, thronged by schoolchildren on field trips. Wolphert Gerritsen, the oldest and most experienced of the group, was the only one to take the whole settlement business seriously. He erected a house and barn at the northeast corner of Flatbush and Kings Highway and called his spread the "Bouwery of Achterveldt"—literally the farm beyond the plains. Hudde, too, erected a number of buildings, including a tobacco barn and what may have been the old "Sand Hole House," razed in 1889, that stood on the north side of Kings Highway at East Thirty-Fifth Street. Gerritsen's Achterveldt appears on the Manatus Map, placed just north of an inlet—in all likelihood Gerritsen Creek—and keyed to an index by the number 36. Just below and to the left of this is a small building that is likely the Pieter Claesen Wyckoff house, which would have been about a year old by the time the map was drawn. Though Hudde left for New Amsterdam in 1638 to become the colony's first surveyor general, he held on to his farm, leasing it in 1642 for an annual rent of "two hundred lbs. of well cured tobacco." Gerritsen remained at Achterveldt for the rest of his life. By the 1660s, it had become a vibrant rural village named Nieuw Amersfoort, after Gerritsen's Old World hometown. With the ascendence of English rule in 1664, Nieuw Amersfoort became the town of Flatlands.[17]

What made this place so vital to the Dutch was not good soil but mollusk shells, or—more precisely—the tiny tubular beads drilled by the Indians from quahogs, whelks, and periwinkles known as *wampum*. Wampum had long been used for ceremonial purposes by the coastal Algonquians, but with the arrival of trade-obsessed Europeans, it gained a powerful new role as legal tender—and not only for trade with the Indians. Town records indicate that "wampum was exchanged for a wide

Pieter Claesen Wyckoff House, c. 1652. Historic American Buildings Survey photograph by E. P. MacFarland, 1934. Library of Congress, Prints and Photographs Division.

range of goods and services between 1647 and 1660," writes Lynn Ceci, and "wages in wampum were paid to cowherders and carpenters, and to a schoolteacher or laborer."[18] As the specie's value soared, Canarsee Indian settlements at Narriock (Sheepshead Bay), Massabarkem (Gravesend), Muskyttehool (Paerdegat Basin), Equendito (Barren Island), Shanscomacoke, and—especially—Winnipague (Bergen Beach) became the leading wampum production centers on Long Island. Located at the headwaters of the Strome Kill and linked by trade routes to the East River and Long Island, Keskachauge became a busy entrepôt—the "Wall Street of the Indians," as Van Wyck called it—especially after the fur trade was thrown open by the Dutch in 1639. Wampum was "the source and mother of the beaver trade," the precious lucre that both Dutch and English bartered a range of goods for—cloth, tools, guns, spirits, tobacco—and then carried north to exchange for beaver pelts from the Mahican and Mohawk peoples. The fur was ultimately shipped to Europe and sold at great profit, mostly to be pressed into felt for men's hats. Scholars have hypothesized that it was wampum—not agriculture or town founding—that led to the initial acquisition of coastal sites like Keskachauge and the Strome Kill by the Dutch; these were, after all, the mints of the coin of the New World realm. This countered orders by the Dutch West India Company to find productive farm and pasture lands to sustain the colony, which was experiencing frequent food shortages and "near starvation" by 1633.[19]

Wolphert Gerritsen was involved in just such wampum speculating. He had been deputized in January 1630 to help an Amsterdam pearl and diamond merchant named Kiliaen van Rensselaer build a New World empire trading wampum and pelts. Van Rensselaer was a founder of the West India Company, but it seems his real ambition was fattening his larder at company expense. He also happened to be Director General Wouter van Twiller's uncle. Several months after hiring Gerritsen, Van Rensselaer secured a vast patroonship on the upper Hudson River, a thousand-square-mile domain anchored by Fort Orange and the fur-trade boomtown of Beverwijck—literally "beaver district" (later named Albany). With the Strome Kill at one end and Beverwijck at the other, Van Rensselaer had his hands in two of the three fur-trade cookie jars. These machinations made him fabulously rich. They also got many of his cronies in trouble. In a March 1651 letter to Peter Stuyvesant, West India Company directors blasted Van Rensselaer's minions and ordered the new director general to guard against unauthorized landgrabs like those at Keskachauge—where "very few improvements in regard to settling, cultivating, tilling or planting have been made." They called out Van Twiller for having greedily "stretched out his hand for the two flats on Long Island," and castigated Gerritsen and Hudde for not settling "the fiftieth part" of their expansive tract.[20] The following year, in July 1652, an ordinance was passed prohibiting men "covetous and greedy of land" from "directly or indirectly . . . buying or attempting to obtain any Lands from the Natives." Keeping such valuable land locked up prevented the "Planting of Boweries" and thus "delayed and retarded" the fruitful peopling of New Netherland. They also voided all previous acquisitions of land, including "both the small Flats on Long Island claimed by the former Director Wouter van Twiller" and "the Great Flat . . . with the lands adjacent claimed by Wolphert Gerritsen and Andries

Hudde."[21] This annulment would cast a three-hundred-year cloud of doubt over the actual ownership of all this land. The Gerritsen-Hudde tract, especially, was the focus of a running legal battle that eventually pitted descendants of both families against Robert Moses and the city of New York—a latter-day Jarndyce versus Jarndyce that the *Brooklyn Eagle* described as "the most intricate trial in the annals of the Brooklyn Supreme Court."[22]

Beaver pelts and wampum belts became lodestars of Indian life, too, but with far more malevolent effects. With their intimate knowledge of the coast and its shellfisheries, the Canarsee were well positioned to exploit the rising value of wampum. But it was a Faustian bargain. Prior to European contact, the Algonquian peoples led a peripatetic existence—living "rudely and rovingly," as one observer put it, "shifting from place to place."[23] Even coastal tribes like the Canarsee stayed only part of the year at the shore, typically in summer. As fall approached, they moved inland where there was plentiful wood for fires and game animals to provide meat, fat, and furs for warmth. With the new system of trade, life became more sedentary; seasonal shore camps like Shanscomacoke became permanent or semipermanent villages, a change revealed to archaeologists by dramatic increases in shell detritus and more extensive burial grounds. Ancient patterns of life were scuttled for wampum, and

Detail of beaver and wampum in the Seal of New Netherlands, 1623. Cast iron roundel by Rene Paul Chambellan, 1931, one of five designs he created for the West Side Elevated Highway. Photograph by author.

a once proudly self-sufficient society gradually sank into a state of almost total de-
pendence on Dutch and English trade.[24] And then the whole rodent-based economy collapsed: overhunting caused beaver populations throughout the Northeast
to crash, bringing the entire trade triangle down with it (wampum lingered; it was
manufactured on Long Island into the 1870s to seal treaties with Indians on the
Western frontier). Twilight came fast for the Canarsee, their long day ending with
dispossession and death from war and "raging mortal Disease." Keskachauge was
deserted as early as 1640, at the outbreak of the bloody Governor Kieft War. These
first people of the American land quietly vanished "as noiselessly as the morning
mists," wrote J. Thomas Scharf, "disappear before the advancing day." In 1670 Daniel
Denton eulogized: "To say something of the *Indians*, there is now but few upon the
Island . . . how strangely they have decreast by the Hand of God." The last Canarsee
Indian was said to have died in 1832, buried in a shroud sewn by an old Dutch friend.[25]

Our earliest eyewitness account of the Strome Kill uplands was penned in 1679
by Danckaerts and Sluyter, and describes a landscape strikingly similar to Holland.
"There is toward the sea a large piece of low flat land," they wrote, "which is overflowed at every tide . . . mirry and muddy at the bottom, and which produces a
species of hard salt grass or reed grass." This was mown for hay, they noted, "which
cattle would rather eat than fresh hay." The men were delighted to find the uplands
around the Gerritsen estuary "entirely covered with clover in blossom, which diffused a sweet odor in the air for a great distance." They described the region as "low
and level without the least elevation," but indented with waterways "navigable and
very serviceable for fisheries."[26] On the Strome Kill itself they came upon a "gristmill driven by the water which they dam up in the creek." This structure, one of the
earliest industrial buildings on the Eastern Seaboard, was erected by the Gerritsen
clan between 1670 and 1686, when it appears in the Dongan Patent. Rebuilt several

Cord-marked pottery shard, Late Woodland period (500–1000 CE), from west bank of Gerritsen Creek.
Recovered in a 1979 excavation by the Brooklyn College Archeological Field School. Photograph by Frederick A. Winter.

times, it was the very essence of sustainability: water penned back at high tide behind a rockpile dam was discharged as needed through a sluiceway, turning a drive wheel that powered the millstones via wooden gears and shafts and leather beltings. The plant produced flour for Washington's army and was pressed into similar service by Lord Cornwallis to feed his men before the Battle of Brooklyn, until Samuel Gerritsen—perhaps tired of being miller-in-the-middle—disabled it by contriving to "lose" the millstones, at least according to local lore. Operating into the 1890s, the faded red mill was a local landmark—a picturesque ruin, its big wheel motionless yet still "giving forth a musical swish as the water boils below." Tragically, it burned to the ground on the night of September 4, 1935. A night watchman and police patrolman on-site the night the mill burned claimed to have seen nothing. The mill was being restored by the Parks Department at the time, and plans for a total restoration as a working mill museum by architects Aymar Embury II and H. B. Guillan had just been completed. Though nothing remains of the mill except for a pair of stone posts that held the sluice gate, the tidal dam can still be seen at low tide just below Burnett Street at Avenue V.[27]

Samuel Gerritsen's daughter, Elizabeth, married into the Lott family in 1799. That year, Hendrick I. Lott, Johannes's grandson and heir to the plantation, was busy erecting a substantial addition to the 1720 house. He had plenty of help. A 1792 inventory of the Lott farm lists no fewer than twelve enslaved African Americans—six men and six women—who undoubtedly helped construct the magnificent Dutch-Federal house on what is today East Thirty-Sixth Street. Slavery was an essential element of New York life in the seventeenth and eighteenth centuries. As historian Shane White writes, New York was "the center of the heaviest slaveholding region north of the Mason-Dixon line." Only Charleston, South Carolina, surpassed New York in the total number of enslaved residents. And no place in the state had more slaves per capita than Kings County, where one in three residents was in bonded servitude—"a ratio that would not have been out of place in the South." This was especially the case in Dutch towns like New Utrecht, where 75 percent of white households owned slaves, or Midwout (Flatbush), where African Americans constituted 41 percent of the population in 1790. By this time, Kings County was supplying a lion's share of meat, vegetables, grains, fruits, and other farm products consumed by the surging city across the river. Proximity to urban markets made many Dutch families prosperous, fertilizing their fortunes as the manure they hauled from Gotham's streets and stables fertilized their fields. Kings County became a land of lush and verdant bounty. "I remember no spot," recalled Timothy Dwight, "where the produce of so many kinds appeared so well . . . the wheat, winter barley, flax, and oats, are remarkably fine." Indeed, "wherever the country was cultivated," he observed, "its face resembled a rich garden." But Dwight ignored a vital aspect of the scene. However thorough a portrait his *Travels* are of New York and Long Island two hundred years ago—pages of meticulous observations on the manners and customs of Long Island folk, and the geography, flora, and fauna of the region—he says nothing about the system of human bondage that created the pastoral scenes he so admired, about the forgotten souls who tilled the soil and helped feed the rising metropolis through its long childhood and adolescence.[28]

Gerritsen tide mill, 1914. Photograph by George S. Ogden. Brooklyn Museum/Brooklyn Public Library, Brooklyn Collection.

Archaeologist Alyssa Loorya photographing a channeled stone pier that held the sluice gate of Gerritsen tide mill, Marine Park. Photograph by author, 2016.

Dwight was not the only one to gloss over this aspect of Kings County life and labor. Most nineteenth-century accounts of Brooklyn's past depict slavery in a warmly nostalgic light, pruning it carefully from uglier manifestations of slavery elsewhere in the world. "This race for more than a century and a half," wrote Gertrude Lefferts Vanderbilt of African Americans in 1899, "formed part of the family of every Dutch inhabitant of Kings County. Speaking the same language, brought up to the same habits and customs, with many cares and interests in common, there existed a sympathy with and an affection between them and the white members of the household such as could scarcely be felt toward the strangers who now perform the same labor under such different circumstances." To Vanderbilt and her circle, slavery in early New York was "fundamentally different, and *better*," writes Craig Steven Wilder, "than slavery in the Southern colonies"—so much so that they effectively "recast the Knickerbocker-Yankee enslavement of Africans as the single kindest act that one group of people ever visited upon another." Yet documentary evidence does suggest that the lot of slaves in New Netherland was not as cruel or repressive as in the West Indies or on the plantations of the South, that the position of free blacks was better there than perhaps anywhere else in the New World. As Edgar MacManus has argued in *A History of Negro Slavery in New York*, the Dutch had little interest in creating a racialized caste system of the sort that would develop in the West Indies or the American South; for "neither the West India Company nor the settlers," he writes, "endorsed the specious theories of Negro inferiority used in other places to justify the system." The liberties enjoyed by free blacks in New Netherland bear this out. They could own property and serve in the militia (Jews could do neither); they could own white servants and intermarry with whites, and "were accepted or rejected by the community on their own merits as individuals." Enslaved blacks had the same standing as whites in a court of law, and with a system of "half-freedom" that allowed conditional release, bondage in the colony was often like a severe form of indentured servitude. There were indeed no slave uprisings in New Netherland, and the fact that the Dutch armed their bondsmen to fight enemies indicates a certain degree of trust. All told, MacManus concludes, "master-slave relations were good . . . and generally free of the corrosive hatred which in other colonies helped to create brutal systems of repression." It was only later, after the institution of harsher English controls over slaves—including a separate judicial system and legal code for bondspeople—that slavery in the city and its hinterlands began to take on its more egregious aspects.[29]

Kindly or not, Brooklyn's Dutch settlers practiced chattel slavery and prospered at the expense of men and women squeezed for their labor and deprived of freedom. They had the greatest need for labor in the preindustrial city, and thus became New York's "largest and most dedicated slave owners"—more deeply engaged in extracting labor from bound Africans than any other ethnic group in the city's past.[30] Even if later anti-Dutch sentiment greatly exaggerated their sins (so avaricious were the Knickerbockers, opined a visiting Frenchman in the 1790s, that "they almost starve themselves, and treat their slaves miserably"), the truth remains that the pious Calvinists of Kings County not only "owned Africans," writes Wilder, but "advertised for runaways, auctioned human beings, and exhibited the violence, hypocrisy, and

James Ryder van Brunt, *Van Brunt Homested*, c. 1865. Brooklyn Museum, Bequest of Miriam Godofsky.

immorality that people who systematically exploit other people eventually must display." These "Little Masters," as Wilder calls them, practiced an intimate form of slavery, but one no less morally repugnant than those of greater scale and brutality elsewhere. Many of these men would become vocal opponents of abolition and emancipation. They formed a Southern planter class in miniature—less systematically violent than their Virginia brethren, perhaps, but just as "committed to a way of life premised upon the domination of other people."[31] Those who excused slavery in Kings County vis-à-vis the industrial-scale enslavement of Africans in the plantation South failed to see that scattering the population of bondspeople so thinly "impaired black family development, increased the possibility of sale of kinfolk, and exacerbated conditions for escape among isolated young men and women." And scores of men and women did indeed become "blacks who stole themselves." One of these was a sixteen-year-old boy named Jack who ran away in July 1783 from Jeromus Lott, who posted "5 Guineas Reward" for his return. Johannes H. Lott's youngest son, he was not a kindly soul. A loyalist during the Revolution and "notorious for his cruelty to our prisoners," Lott and two of his slaves were kidnapped by a band of New Jersey patriots in 1781, who hustled the trio to a whaleboat waiting in the Gerritsen marshes. The men were taken to New Brunswick, where Lott was "compelled . . . to ransom his negroes." Jack escaped from Lott again in May 1784. That he bore an iron collar around his neck marked with the initials "JL" tells of a darker truth than what Gertrude Vanderbilt and her fellow gentry allowed to flow from their treacle-dipped pens.[32]

Kings County in the eighteenth century was among the least free places in New York State, its enslaved population quadrupling between 1703 and 1790. The heavily agricultural towns south of the terminal moraine—Flatbush, Flatlands, Gravesend, and New Utrecht—were akin to the coastal-plain counties of Virginia and North Carolina, where most of the big slaveholding plantations of those states were located. While the Lotts owned a mere fraction of the slaves that worked a typical Virginia plantation at the time, they were nonetheless among the largest slaveholders in Kings County. As noted earlier, Hendrick Lott owned a dozen bonded men and women in 1792. And then, sometime before 1810, all of Lott's slaves were freed. As it is unlikely that so large a group of enslaved men and women would have been able to buy their freedom all at once, Lott almost certainly chose to emancipate his slaves. Federal census records indicate that he then hired most back as paid laborers; some would remain in his employ into the 1840s. Only an elderly woman, for reasons unknown, was kept on in bondage. Why Lott would choose to suddenly free his bondspeople is a puzzle—he left no diary or letters to explain himself. Voluntary manumission was not unknown among slaveholders at this time. In fact, while the slave population of both New York and Kings County increased steadily all through the eighteenth century, census returns show a sudden drop in both places between 1800 and 1820. In Kings County, the number of enslaved residents fell by almost half—from 1,506 to 879. Manumissions were also up sharply: in New York City there were a mere 36 recorded manumissions between 1791 and 1800, and 260 between 1801 and 1810. This was due not to a sudden outbreak of goodwill among slaveholders, but to a piece of legislation—the Gradual Manumission Act of 1799. It stipulated that all children of slave women born after July 4 that year were to be free, though they must remain indentured to their masters until the age of twenty-five (for women) and twenty-eight (for men). As Shane White writes, it was not until 1810 that "the full impact of the act was felt in the city," with the number of New York slaveholders falling by more than 25 percent from 1800—"the lowest number recorded in the city in any of the first three federal censuses." However extraordinary Lott's decision appears to us, it was fully in step with the evolving state of slavery at the time.[33]

The Gradual Manumission Act clearly signaled the coming of emancipation. While some slave owners would hold on to their chattel to the bitter end, others saw the writing on the wall and set their slaves free. Such decisions likely also involved agency and action on the part of the bondspeople themselves. As White has put it, "Once it was certain slavery would eventually end, slave owners became more susceptible to pressure from their slaves and often agreed to arrangements whereby slaves were liberated in consideration of a number of years of trouble-free service or cash or both."[34] Indeed, Lott's manumitted slaves stayed and worked for the family long after being granted freedom—a fact typically attributed to loyalty and affection, but that was more likely simply part of the deal. And yet manumission literally involved letting go of an investment. Such an action—the willful reduction of one's own capital—begs an explanation. Lott no doubt surmised that full emancipation was on the horizon, but he could not have known it would happen in 1827, the year slavery was abolished in New York State. In other words, freeing his slaves circa 1810 deprived his three children of a substantial inheritance. So it is possible,

"A true and perfect Inventory of the Goods, Chattles [*sic*], & Credits of Johannes Lott," 1792, beginning with a list of his twelve slaves, five of whom—Syrus, Sam, Hannah, Poll, and Jacob—were children. Collection of Robert Billard.

at least, that other factors account for Lott's action—that perhaps he manumitted his slaves because he believed it was the right thing to do. Indeed, Lott family lore suggests that Hendrick might have been an early abolitionist. The evidence is thin. We know that he was a member of the Flatlands Dutch Reformed Church, buried in its churchyard at East Fortieth Street and Overbaugh Place; and that manumission was considered "a meritorious act in the eyes of God." But it is unclear whether Lott was pious enough to let faith overrule financial interest.[35]

Moreover, faith of the Dutch Reformed sort did not imply charity on the racial front. The Dutch Reformed Church was perhaps the least progressive of the Protestant sects in New York and long vacillated on whether to allow Africans into its fold. The learned and popular minister Henricus Selyns, who served congregations in New Amsterdam and Long Island, instructed enslaved Africans in the faith, but would not baptize a baby if he suspected its parents "wanted nothing else than to deliver their children from bodily slavery, without striving for piety and Christian virtues." Indeed, baptism of the bonded became a matter of great controversy. Some ministers came down forcefully on the side of the angels. Godefridus Udemans, writing in 1638, argued that a Christian was faith bound to free any slaves who converted to his faith; for if they were willing "to submit themselves to the lovely yoke of our Lord Jesus Christ . . . Christian love requires that they be discharged from the yoke of human slavery." But colonial empires are built on greed and grim expedience, not Christian kindness. Slave owners in seventeenth-century New Netherland, fearful of the losses conversion might entail (not to mention that it might "give the Negroes ideas about liberty and freedom"), discouraged missionary work among their slaves. The matter was eventually settled in 1706, out of church and not by the Dutch, but by the English colonial legislature of New York, which made it completely legal, if not moral, for a Christian to be enslaved. All told, "there was little to admire," writes church historian Gerald De Jong, "regarding the attitude of the Dutch Reformed Church toward slavery in colonial America."[36]

Manumission of the Lott slaves has seeded stories that Hendrick's house provided refuge for runaway slaves—that it was, in other words, a way station or depot on the Underground Railroad. Lott descendants alive today recall hearing stories as children that fugitives were given sanctuary on the farm—"that ships came quietly in the night to shore," recalls one family member, "and the people who were part of the Underground Railroad would shepherd the slaves into the house." Of course, tales like this envelope nearly every antebellum house, church, and tavern this side of the Mason-Dixon line. Were a nickel set aside for each property rumored to be part of the Underground Railroad, the federal debt could be paid off in a day. It is not surprising that many would claim connection to this heroic chapter in American history, for reasons of collective sin cleansing if nothing else. The Underground Railroad is an epic part of our national mythology, as hopeful as it is hopelessly misunderstood. Only in recent years has the traditional narrative of the Railroad as the infrastructure of white magnanimity given way to a more nuanced view of its fractal-like complexity—and greater agency accorded freedom-seekers themselves in its actual operation. The very nature of the Underground Railroad—secretive, spontaneous, always in the shadows—makes it a notoriously difficult subject to research. It is virtually impossible to test the veracity of claims like those of the Lott family. The best we can do is expose them to the light of analysis, marshaling evidence from geography, historical context, and archaeology. Is it possible that the Lotts helped spirit enslaved African Americans to freedom? In a word, yes. To start, there is no question that Kings County played a central role in helping move escaped slaves north in the nineteenth century—especially after the draconian Fugitive Slave Act of 1850. Henry Ward Beecher's Plymouth Church in Brooklyn Heights—a topic of chapter 10—was widely hailed as the "Grand Central Depot" of the Underground Railroad. Though he was hardly blameless himself, Beecher's thunderous oratory did as much for American abolitionism as did his sister Harriet Beecher Stowe's novel *Uncle Tom's Cabin*. Kings County was also home to Willis Augustus Hodges, a free black Virginian who ran an antislavery newspaper in Williamsburg, and abolitionist orator James W. C. Pennington sought refuge in Brooklyn after escaping bondage in Maryland. The latter went on to become the first African American to study at Yale, and later helped integrate streetcar lines in both Brooklyn and New York City.[37]

The rural southern half of Kings County was a far less tolerant place. And yet there were exceptions. During the Draft Riots of 1863, blacks fleeing mob violence in Brooklyn and across the East River were hidden in an ancient windmill on the John C. Vanderveer farm, between Canarsie Lane and the long-vanished Paerdegat pond. It was a good place to take refuge. Built in 1804, the mill was a fortress of strength, with a stone foundation and oak timbers twenty-eight feet high and nearly three feet thick. It was being used as a barn at the time, the great sails having been wrecked in a storm decades earlier. Like the Gerritsen tide mill, the Vanderveer plant was also lost to fire, burning on the night of March 4, 1879, in a spectacle of destruction that sent up "showers of sparks . . . like gold-dust sprinkled on a cloth of blue." The geography of the outwash plain may itself have aided bids for freedom. The marshy shore of Jamaica Bay, with its reed-choked serpentine estuaries, would have offered a hidden backdoor entry into Brooklyn and New York City for fugitives coming by boat from New Jersey and points south. The Lott farm included most of the secluded north bank of Gerritsen Creek, the largest tidal estuary on the bay and navigable by ships as far as the mill dam (Van Wyck recalled "sloops of twenty-four tons burden, and in one case thirty tons" making trips in the 1870s between the Gerritsen mill and New York City, "before either Mill Creek or the Strom Kill had been dredged"). At the east end of the dam was Kimball Landing, from which an old Indian path—known as Lott's Lane or the Strome Kill trail—led to Flatlands village, literally passing between the Lott house and its stone kitchen building. In other words, freedom-seekers could have been ushered to the house in swift and total secrecy. We know that tidal estuaries similar to Gerritsen Creek were used for just such purposes farther out on Long Island, where a network of sympathetic Quaker Meetings offered sanctuary to runaways. One was the Jerusalem River, known today as Bellmore Creek, which led to a settlement of free blacks near present-day Wantagh known as The Brush. This place, nestled amidst the larger Quaker community of Jerusalem, was also a waypoint and destination for freedom-seekers coming out of New York and Brooklyn. By the 1830s there was an African Free School there and later an African Methodist Episcopal Zion Church. In its burial ground nearby—itself now buried in a Levitt subdivision at about 1460 Oakfield Avenue—were interred the remains of several men who fought in the Civil War with the Twentieth and Twenty-Sixth regiments of the United States Colored Troops.[38]

But Gerritsen Creek and the Lott house led to an even greater prize—Weeksville, one of the largest free black communities in the United States. Just four miles to the north, Weeksville developed in the 1830s on the northernmost lands of the old Gerritsen landgrab and soon became a major destination for those escaping bondage from the South. Nearly 45 percent of Weeksville adult residents in 1850 were born below the Mason-Dixon line, many of whom—perhaps most—were former slaves. "Weeksville's proportion of southern-born African Americans," writes Judith Wellman in *Brooklyn's Promised Land*, "was one of the highest of any city in the United States." Only Philadelphia, Pittsburgh, Buffalo, and Cincinnati—all major gateways to freedom—had higher proportions of African Americans born in the South. While many of these people came to Weeksville via New York and Brooklyn, it is very likely that others came up from Flatlands just to the south. Weeksville would have been about an hour's walk or a twenty-minute wagon ride from the Lott house via Flatlands Neck Road and Hunterfly Road (from the Dutch *Aander fly*, or "over to the marshes"). One of Weeksville's earliest residents was himself a former Lott slave, Samuel Anderson, born into bondage in 1810. Anderson's master was Jeremiah Lott, who clearly did not agree that those baptized into the Christian flock deserved emancipation. A devout man and later a preacher himself, Anderson was baptized as a youth and attended services at the Flatbush Dutch Reformed Church, where blacks were required to sit apart from whites in an upstairs gallery—"the men on one side," he recalled, "the women on the other."[39]

Newsprint papered over passageway to hidden attic room, Hendrick I. Lott House. This page, from the *New York Times*, is dated June 10, 1863, about three weeks before the Battle of Gettysburg. Photograph by author, 2013.

The most telling bit of evidence that the Lotts may well have offered sanctuary to fugitive slaves is in the building itself. As a child in the 1960s, Catherine Lott Divis—a direct descendant of Hendrick Lott whose father grew up in the East Thirty-Sixth Street house—was told in hushed tones by her elderly aunts about a secret hiding place on the second floor. "They took me upstairs with great fanfare and solemn tones and showed me the Room," she told the *New York Times* in 2002. At the back of a large closet, behind hatboxes and a rack of clothes, was a small, low door papered over with newsprint from 1862. Behind it was a tiny hidden room; there, Divis was told, fugitive slaves smuggled in by boat would be hidden before continuing on to freedom. "I was not to breathe a word of it," she said; for by her family's unspoken code "if something was a secret in the 1800's it was always a secret." The house had other tales to tell, coaxed into the light by a team of Brooklyn College archaeologists who began studying the house in 1998. Led by Christopher Ricciardi and Alyssa Loorya, the students dug more than seventy trenches on the site, patiently sifting through several tons of excavate. They uncovered the foundations of the old plastered-brick kitchen house, razed around 1927 to make way for East Thirty-Sixth Street, and over the four-year project period unearthed thousands of pottery shards, glass and ceramic fragments, pipe stems, toys (including several haunting doll heads), clam and oyster shells, and other faunal remains—the detritus of long and prosperous habitation by scores of women, men, and children.[40]

Yet the most extraordinary discovery at the Lott house was not underground but overhead. One afternoon, a project assistant bumped her head on the ceiling in the eighteenth-century lean-to addition close to East Thirty-Sixth Street. The ceiling appeared to give way. Loorya and Ricciardi grabbed a ladder and flashlights. In the ceiling they found a covered hatch, behind which were the truncated remains of a staircase. The stairs apparently once continued to the ground and led to the second floor of the 1720 house, where a door had long ago been sealed off. Climbing up, the

Corncob talisman discovered beneath the floorboards of Lott House garret room. Photograph by Alyssa Loorya, 1999.

pair discovered twin garret rooms in the attic space on either side of the stairs. The rooms were low and small, about ten feet square and at most four feet high. The doors to the garret rooms had been removed but lay close by. Centuries-old candle-wax was splattered all about. When Loorya and Ricciardi took up some floorboards, they discovered something truly astonishing—an assortment of objects that had been placed carefully beneath each entrance before the floorboards were nailed down. On the north side was a pelvis bone from a sheep or goat, an oyster shell, a small pouch tied with hemp, and an eighteenth-century child's shoe. On the south side were several corncobs—one whole, the other snapped in half and set at right angles above and below the first in the form of a cross. What Loorya and Ricciardi had come upon were arrays of religious talismans clearly African in origin. They had discovered the living quarters of at least some of the Lott family slaves. Caches of objects like these were previously known only in the South; never before had anything like this been seen in New York. As Loorya explains, "the objects were meant as defensive talismans against certain malevolent spirits, to create a kind of protective spell for the occupants," and were usually placed "near doors and fireplaces, where spirits were thought to come and go." The crossed corncobs were themselves likely a microcosm of the universe itself, a Bakongo cosmogram in which the horizontal plane—the unbroken cob—was meant to "symbolize separation," says Loorya, "of the world of the living from the realm of the dead." Through the dark of two centuries, visited only by spiders and mice, the crossed cobs consecrate still a small, fraught corner of the world, a simple act of faith by a people far from home.[41]

Ruins of the eighteenth-century Johannes Lott barn near present intersection of Avenue R and East Thirty-Fifth Street in Marine Park. Photograph by Eugene L. Armbruster, 1922. Irma and Paul Milstein Division of United States History, Local History and Genealogy, The New York Public Library.

LADY DEBORAH'S CITY BY THE SEA

For we are as a young tree or little sprout . . .
for the first time shooting forth to the world.
—GEORGE BAXTER ET AL., 1651

Two miles east of Gerritsen Creek is an urban fossil—the remains of one of the oldest planned towns in North America, the first founded by a woman and the first to mandate religious freedom by formal charter. Unlike the Lott house, the sublime order of Gravesend is not evident to an explorer on foot. The streets here appear jumbled and chaotic—some inexplicably short, others set at crazy angles. This is not a particularly charming part of town, not a place where one expects to find a palimpsest from Gotham's deepest past. The F train lumbers noisily over McDonald Avenue, above the body shops and roofing suppliers. A furniture outlet sits on one corner, near a Chinese steel fabricator, a Korean Bible church and a sketchy-looking nightclub. But rise above the ground-plane chaos here and something extraordinary pulls into focus—a tiny four-square grid, cocked at an odd angle from the city grid, a Cartesian insect trapped in urban amber.

It is a monument to a mysterious soul—an enigmatic Englishwoman named Deborah Moody, whose life and ultimate fate have perplexed antiquarians for generations. She was a child of the nobility, born around 1585 to the Dunch family of Priory Manor, Little Wittenham, in the county of Berkshire. Her mother was Deborah Pilkington, daughter of the bishop of Durham; her father, Walter Dunch, had been a member of Parliament during the reign of Elizabeth I. Oliver Cromwell may have been a relative by marriage on her father's side. In 1606 Dunch married a nobleman named Henry Moody, later granted peerage as a baronet by King James I. The couple made their home at Moody's estate, Garsdon Manor in Wiltshire, a short walk from the ancient Avebury stone circle—less famous but arguably more

Deborah Moody's vernal grid. In this 1924 aerial photograph, traces of Gravesend's original radiating field boundaries can still be seen. Only one remains today, preserved in the form of Lake Place west of the town center. Lionel Pincus and Princess Firyal Map Division, The New York Public Library.

significant than its sister UNESCO World Heritage site at Stonehenge. By 1608 the couple had two children, Henry and Catherine. Sir Henry died in 1629, leaving a large fortune. After being widowed, Deborah Moody moved several times and eventually took up residence in London. This transience ran her afoul of a statute limiting the length of time a person could remain away from his hereditary home. It was no trifling matter; for in April 1635 Moody was summoned by the Court of the Star Chamber, which met in secret and was known for harsh and draconian rulings. The court found "Dame Deborah Mowdie" guilty and gave her forty days to get back home to Wiltshire—"in the good example necessary to the poorer classes." It has long been assumed that around this time Moody also began espousing dangerously radical ideas about religion, becoming a convert to Anabaptism, a heretical creed in England. As Austin P. Stockwell put it in 1884, Moody evidently "chafed under the unlawful restraints of such a civil and ecclesiastical despotism" and in 1639 left England for the presumed freedom and tolerance of America. If this was indeed her motivation for taking leave of Albion—recent scholarship suggests otherwise—she was soon to be disappointed.[1]

Some twenty thousand Puritans emigrated to the Massachusetts Bay Colony between 1629 and 1640, many of whom settled in a chain of coastal towns north of Boston. Deborah Moody was among them. Exactly when she set foot in the New World is unclear, but by early 1640 she had made her way to Saugus, and on May 13 gained approval from the Massachusetts General Court to purchase a spread of several hundred acres known as the Swampscott farm. The transaction left her

Neolithic henge and stone circles, Avebury, Wiltshire, close to Deborah Dunch's childhood home, Avebury Manor (upper left). Photograph by Detmar Owen, 2017.

nearly bankrupt—she was "almost undone," wrote Thomas Lechford in 1641, "by buying Master Humphries farm." Moody joined the Puritan congregation in nearby Salem, a place whose own date with history was fast approaching. It was there that Moody became "imbued with the erroneous idea," as chronicler Alonzo Lewis put it in 1844, "that the baptism of infants was a sinful ordinance." The whole issue of the validity of infant baptism may strike us as ecclesiastical hairsplitting. Anabaptists argued that nowhere in scripture was such a practice sanctioned, and that for baptism to have any meaning, the individual undergoing the rite must possess some minimal understanding of its implications. In their view, to offer a whimpering infant—wholly ignorant of right and wrong—admission to the Kingdom of Heaven was blasphemous. Why not also baptize the barnyard cat? Most Protestants opposed the Anabaptist position, as did the Roman Catholic Church—hardly surprising given the high rate of infant mortality at the time. Moreover, Anabaptists had a bad reputation. In 1534, a group of them in Münster had attempted to establish a theocracy, advocating the use of force to bring about the New Jerusalem predicted in scripture. Fear that all Anabaptists were hotheaded radicals led to severe persecution of the sect in Europe; tens of thousands were martyred, often by drowning. To Winthrop and the Massachusetts Puritans, Anabaptism was right alongside Quakerism as one of the "damnable heresies" threatening their New World project. Moody, who was said to have "imbibed" her Anabaptism from Roger Williams, founder of the Rhode Island Colony, soon learned just how deep this antipathy ran.[2]

The Puritan clerisy was in no mood for theological magnanimity in 1640, especially involving a woman. Only several years earlier, Anne Hutchinson had stirred up a hornet's nest for mocking the pious "learned Scollers" and professing Antinomianism—a belief that faith alone determined one's salvation, not obedience to some compulsory code of moral law. To Winthrop, Hutchinson posed a grave threat to his "Modell of Christian Charity." She was arrested in 1637, convicted of heresy, and banished from the Massachusetts Bay Colony. Hutchinson—an inspiration for Hester Prynne in Nathaniel Hawthorne's *Scarlet Letter*—made her way to Rhode Island and then New Netherland, where she settled at Pelham Bay in the Bronx. Hutchinson's life among the Dutch was brief; she was murdered, along with several of her children, by a band of Siwanoy Algonquins in August 1643. Now Winthrop had another Jezebel on his hands. On December 14, 1642, after several reprimands, Moody was arrested and arraigned with two other women at the Quarterly Court in Salem, for "houldinge that the baptizing of Infants is noe ordinance of God." Winthrop then enacted a decree calling for the immediate expulsion of Anabaptists, accusing them of subverting Puritan rule and even questioning the "lawfulness of making war." They were, he wrote, "incendiaries of the Commonwealth, and the infectors of persons in matters of religion . . . troublers of churches in all places where they have been." Now anyone who condemned or opposed baptizing infants risked being banished to the wilderness like the scapegoat of the Israelites. And speaking out on the matter was hardly necessary; Winthrop's ordinance made clear that even persons who "purposely depart the congregation" during a baptism would be arrested for sedition. Thus facing expulsion from Massachusetts Bay, Moody took off on her own, striking west for New Netherland in early 1643. "My Lady Moody," mourned the Reverend Thomas Cobbett of Saugus, "is to sitt down on Long Island, from under civil and church watch." Nor would she go alone: a large group of fellow worshippers from Salem and neighboring congregations joined her—all of whom, Winthrop railed, Moody had "infected with Anabaptism." And yet Winthrop admitted a begrudging admiration for this thorn among his New World roses—"My Ladye Moodye," he called her, "a wise and anciently religious woman."[3]

New Netherland—booming, profane, and lusty—was a world away from the black-frocked severity of Puritan Massachusetts. Effectively a free-trade zone established by the Dutch West India Company, its first order of business was business. The burgeoning provincial capital of New Amsterdam, at the southern tip of Manhattan, was a medley of ethnicity, race, and creed—"a polyglot community, a confusion of tongues and people drawn from all over the world."[4] It was as tolerant of difference and dissent—within reason—as the Puritan theocrats were not. An eclectic array of freemen, slaves and indentured servants, merchants, seamen, and traders gathered on the cobbled streets of embryonic Gotham, mixed with an even more motley assemblage of "losers and scalawags," as Russell Shorto has put it, "waiting around for the winds of fate to blow them off the map." It was here that Deborah Moody and her Anabaptist band came to build a new life. They were not only tolerated but warmly welcomed, for very practical reasons. The director of New Netherland, Willem Kieft, couldn't care less when a baby was baptized. What he needed were permanent settlers, pious or not, who would make the desert bloom, feeding New Netherland and turning it into a lasting colony. Traders and merchants made for a thriving entrepôt, but without a stable base of agrarians New Netherland would never sustain itself or grow. And here was a whole band of farmers and artisans, a little village in the making! All they needed was some land, which Kieft had more of than he knew what to do with. In June 1643 Moody was issued a patent for a large tract of land near Coney Island, a place far removed from New Amsterdam just in case the English newcomers caused trouble. Kieft named the place Gravesend, not for the English port city, but 's-Gravenzande, his birthplace on the Maas River delta in Holland.[5]

The newcomers threw themselves into the long work of settlement. But there was trouble in the land. Willem Kieft was possibly the worst chief executive ever to rule the future New York City, an impulsive tyrant whom Washington Irving satirized as "William the Testy"—a waspish tinhorn prone to "valorous broils, altercations and misadventures." Only months before Moody's arrival, Kieft touched off a bloody conflict with local Indians after they resisted his attempts to squeeze them for tribute. When his Council of Twelve Men—the first representative democratic body in the Dutch colonies—balked at endorsing a plan of war, he simply dissolved it and forbade the men to meet. In February 1643 Kieft sent troops to attack a refugee encampment of Weckquaesgeek and Tappan Indians near today's Jersey City, killing eighty people. "Young children, some of them snatched from their mothers, were cut in pieces before the eyes of their parents," wrote David de Vries, Kieft's former council chief; "other babes were bound on planks and then cut through, stabbed and miserably massacred so that it would break a heart of stone." De Vries was sickened by the slaughter, which he described as "a disgrace to our nation." Kieft, on the other hand, thanked the men for this "deed of Roman valor." In retaliation, Algonquin warriors carried out a series of equally brutal raids throughout the region in subsequent months, including the one that killed Anne Hutchinson at Pelham Bay. By the time "Kieft's War" was over in the fall of 1645, hundreds of colonists and some sixteen hundred Indians had been killed. Trade was at a standstill and farms lay idle, immigration had all but ceased, and many settlers left the colony altogether; those remaining were on the verge of mutiny. All told, it was a very bad time to be coming on board.[6]

Indeed, Moody's fragile encampment was attacked repeatedly in its first year at Gravesend, forcing her band to seek refuge at nearby Nieuw Amersfoort. Eventually the settlers erected stout enough dwellings and a defensive stockade that enabled them to repel marauders. Yet survival seemed precarious, so much so that Moody contemplated returning to Massachusetts. In the aftermath of Hutchinson's murder in the fall of 1643, she wrote John Winthrop to ask his advice. It is not known whether he responded, but upon learning of her query, John Endicott—deputy governor of the Massachusetts Bay Colony—penned a missive to Winthrop himself in which he advised against allowing Moody back, unless she signal repentance and "leave her opinions behinde her"—for "shee is a dangerous woeman," he warned, and "it is verie doubtefull whither she will be reclaymed." Endicott then added—one imagines with a sudden shudder of dread—"*The Lord rebuke Satan the adversarie of our Soules*" (author's italics). Hostilities between the Dutch and the Indians eventually cooled, and on December, 19, 1645, Governor Kieft issued the Gravesenders a new and more robust patent to the land that had been their tenuous home for more than two years now. In it, Kieft granted "ye Honoured lady Deborah Moody" and her associates "a certaine quantitie or p'cel of Land, together with all ye havens, harbours, rivers, creeks, woodland, marshes. . . . uppon & about ye Westernmost parte of Longe Island." The settlers were to "injoye & pocesse" this land with full authority "to build a towne or townes with such necesarie fortifications as to them seem expedient." But the most remarkable passage came next, for in it Kieft stipulated that the Gravesenders were to both govern themselves—to "erect a bodye pollitique" and make "such civill ordinances as the Major part of ye Inhabitants . . . shall thinke fitting for theyr quiett & peaceable subsisting"—and enjoy "free libertie of conscience . . . without molestation or disturbance from any Madgistrate or Madgistrates or any other Ecclesiasticall Minister that may p'tend jurisdiction over them." Deborah Moody's Gravesend settlement thus became only the second in America founded on principles of religious freedom, established nine years after Roger Williams founded Providence Plantation as a haven from religious persecution. But Gravesend was the very first to legislate religious freedom in its founding charter. In this, Moody's town was five years ahead of the Toleration Act that mandated religious tolerance in Lord Baltimore's Maryland colony, and twelve years ahead of the seminal Flushing Remonstrance.[7]

What kind of place was Gravesend circa 1645? It was wild, to be sure, much of it heavily wooded and home to wolves, bear, and possibly the long-extinct Eastern elk. It was flushed by seaborne winds, scored with tidal creeks, on the edge of a bay teeming with fish and crabs. But it was not a howling wilderness. In a letter to John Winthrop's son, George Baxter described the land Kieft allotted his group as "a place not yet settled on Long Island, and so commodious that I have not seene or knowne a better." In fact it had long been inhabited by Native Americans, and though the exact spot chosen for the new town had never been settled, it was a junction of two old Indian paths—one, today's McDonald Avenue, ran south to the sea from the Mechawanienk trail (Kings Highway); the other, Gravesend Neck Road, led east to the Strome Kill and Shanscomacoke. There were also at least two other Europeans in the immediate area; for Kieft had granted, in 1639, a two-hundred-acre plantation in the vicinity to a Moor named Anthony Jansen van Salee. Van Salee, known as "the Turk," was a character every bit as memorable as Deborah Moody, whom he came to know well. His father had been a notorious privateer on the Barbary Coast, a convert to Islam, and ruler of a short-lived city-state called Salé in what is now Morocco. Van Salee was born in Cartagena, Spain, in 1607 and spent time in North Africa and Amsterdam before coming to New Netherland around 1630. He and his salty German-born wife, Grietje Reiniers, were renegades of a different sort, and exiles too: the pair was ordered to leave New Amsterdam after repeated legal disputes, financial trouble, and quarrels with clergy over their libertine ways. The original litigious New Yorker, van Salee was in court more than he was home, hauled in for—among other things—aiming a loaded pistol at slave overseers of the Dutch West India Company and passing off a dead goat as payment for a debt. The angry Moor was derided as a drunk and denounced as a rogue and "horned beast." At Gravesend, the unrepentant couple evidently got along well enough with Deborah Moody, though the boorish van Salee fought constantly with her Oxford-educated poet son. In the first of several legal actions, Henry Moody dragged van Salee into court after the latter stormed his house, calling him names and abusing his servant with "evil language." Aside from their shared traits of grit and gumption, it's unlikely that the pious Lady Moody and Grietje Reiniers would have had much to bond over.

Reiniers had been an Amsterdam barmaid before turning to prostitution, a line of work she evidently kept up after marrying van Salee. She regularly provoked moral outrage in New Amsterdam with her licentious behavior, no easy thing in the raffish colony. When some sailors called her a "two pound's butter whore," she hiked up her skirt, slapped her rump and shouted "Blaes my daer achterin"—"Kiss my ass," roughly translated.[8]

Deborah Moody was America's first woman town planner; for in this primeval place she etched an exquisite diagram for spatial order: four squares of four acres each, aligned to the cardinal points of the compass and scored by streets running north-south and east-west—the ancient Roman *cardo* and *decumanus* on New World soil. It was only the second town in Anglo-Dutch America planned as a precisely surveyed grid, "laid out," as nineteenth-century chronicler Nathaniel S. Prime opined, "with a great deal of taste." From its center an array of lot lines were plotted, like spokes of a wheel, to create "triangled" home lots for each of the settler families. Communal pasture land and woodlots lay beyond. As a diagram, the Gravesend plan is one of the most striking in American history—an essential mark of human will on the land, reaching outward across space as if to tap the very life force itself.[9] But this was no dreamy Utopia. Given the political situation of New Netherland at the time, the first order of business here was sanctuary and safety. The tight four-square layout made Gravesend easy to defend, aided by a stockade of sharpened timber stakes—a "fence of pallisadowes of six footes." Close scrutiny of the plan reveals—at each of the four corners—guard posts in the form of tiny vestigial bastions. The radial bloom of planting fields, too, so evocative of a flower in the sun, was itself the result of expedience and pragmatism. Not only could such an array be quickly surveyed from a single station point, but the triangular fields enabled settlers to work their own holdings as close in or as far from the secure town center as the threat of attack necessitated—in time of conflict huddling close to the nest; in time of peace moving outward into a progressively expanding realm. Gravesend may have been founded by a devout noblewoman seeking religious freedom, but it began in a time of war, even surveyed by a military officer—James Hubbard, one of Moody's original patentees and the town's first constable or "schout." Like most English surveyors at the time, Hubbard was trained in the martial arts; and rectilinear town plans—easy to lay out and easy to defend—had been a mainstay of military science since the gridded *castra* of ancient Rome.[10]

But the Gravesend plan may have drawn upon a yet more lofty source of inspiration. Deciphering its hidden code requires tracing Moody's journey from Massachusetts to New Netherland. We do not know her exact itinerary, but can be fairly certain the voyage was made by ship and took the group around Cape Cod, past Nantucket and Martha's Vineyard into the protected waters of Long Island Sound, where they dropped anchor at New Haven. That this place would be of special interest to Moody is clear, for it had been founded only five years earlier by another Massachusetts émigré, John Davenport. As a settlement of religious exiles in a wild landscape, New Haven appears to have been the template for Moody's own encampment in the wilderness. Like Moody, the "Moses of New Haven," as Cotton Mather called Davenport, had clashed with the Puritan clerisy over infant baptism, taking

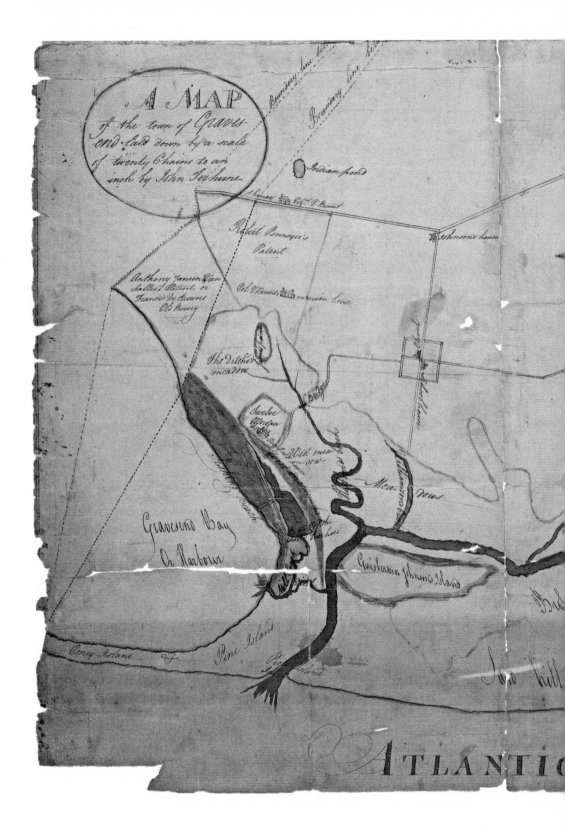

John Terhune map of Gravesend, c. 1674. The town center is just left of center; Gerritsen Creek and tide mill to right of compass rose. New York State Archives—Survey maps of lands in New York State, 1711–1913 (Series A0273–78, Map #429).

Boundary line between Terhune's
House of the Abm Bruen & Holland

Holland

Garritson's Mill

Shoom hill or Garritson's Creek

Part of

Flatlands

Mea — dows

Flag point

from the want of a fish instrument
the inaccuracy of methods without one
we decline making any observations on
the variation of the needle but find on a
map of part of this town made in the
year 1674 that the needle varied
from the Meridian from the north
to the East Six degrees & that
the which were then laid out
S 3.30 W than now. Lg 96 W.

Grove creek

Plumb Island

Cove

or Marsh

Plumb Island
Inlet

OCEAN

an even stricter line than Moody—that the sacrament should be administered only to the infant children of full church members. Davenport yearned to establish a more orthodox Puritan colony than Massachusetts Bay, and eventually struck out with a large following to found a holy city on the Connecticut shore. His orthodoxy extended to the landscape itself; for in Davenport's hands the Bible became a kind of planning manual used to guide the very design of his holy city. In the summer of 1638, Davenport and surveyor John Brockett began laying out at New Haven one of the most extraordinary town plans in colonial America—a great nine-square grid based on descriptions of the New Jerusalem in the Old Testament. John Winthrop might have been a pious man, but the layout of his "City upon a Hill" at Boston was anything but inspired; Davenport's "Bible Commonwealth," on the other hand, carried the word of God out of the meetinghouse and into the streets—literally.[11]

Ideal cities—all square with a temple sanctuary in the center—are described in several places in the Bible, but the most detailed are in the book of Ezekiel; there, Davenport observed, "Christ hath given his People a perfect pattern."[12] Chapter 40, for example, provides an exhaustive description of the Holy Temple of the Israelites, stipulating a temple 500 cubits on a side (approximately 750 feet) and giving precise measurements for even alcoves, courtyards, and door jambs. By the early seventeenth century, many of these passages had become the subject of biblical "commentaries," often illustrated with reconstructions of the plans described within. One of the earliest, by French theologian Sébastien Castellión in 1551, illustrated the Temple of Jerusalem described in Ezekiel 40 as a nine-square grid; another, by Jesuit scholar Juan Bautista Villalpandus, published in 1604 and widely reproduced, included drawings of a nine-square encampment of the Israelites with a temple in the center. It is virtually certain that Davenport—a learned theologian who had studied at Oxford—would have known of these illuminated commentaries. Though he took some liberties in transcribing Ezekiel to Yankee soil—*each* of Davenport's nine New Haven squares, for example, is roughly 500 cubits on a side, as if each itself worthy of temple status—New Haven could well have been laid out by the Hebrew prophet himself. Barely five years old, the town would have been very much a work in progress in the summer of 1643 when Moody came ashore, its essential design clear to see.

She was not there very long. Despite their shared status as Massachusetts émigrés, Moody and Davenport hardly saw eye to eye on matters religious. An orthodox Puritan, Davenport had played a key role in prosecuting Anne Hutchison only several years before in Boston, and may well have considered Moody a radical heretic too. Indeed, the good woman appears to have stirred up a hornet's nest in the short time she was at New Haven. The controversy involved her friend Anne Lloyd Eaton, the wellborn widow of Thomas Yale (grandmother of Elihu, future namesake of Yale College), whose second husband was Davenport's close friend and Oxford classmate Theophilus Eaton, first governor of Connecticut. How Eaton and Moody first met is unknown, but they evidently knew each other from London, and it is probable that Moody stopped at New Haven specifically to see her. There they discussed the issue of baptism, and Eaton asked Moody to lend her a recently published book—Andrew Ritor's 1642 *Treatise of the Vanity of Childish-Baptisme*. Eaton read the book in secret, concealing it from her husband and minister Davenport, but shared it with several

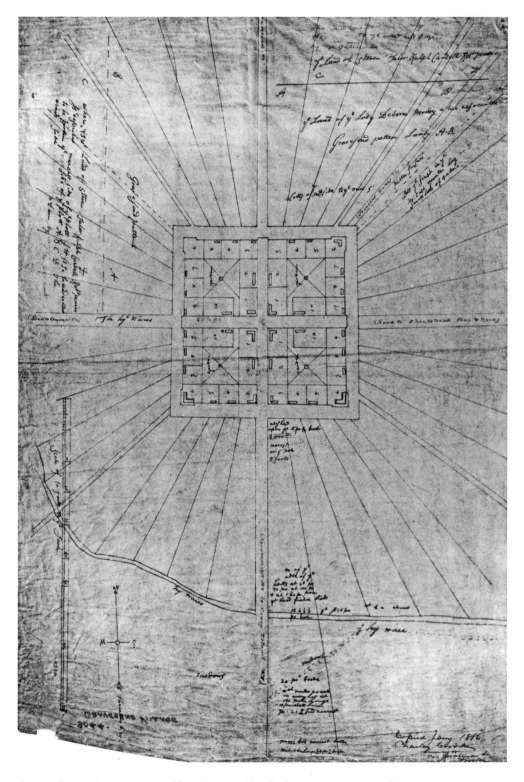

Gravesend town plan, c. 1645, copied from the original by Charles Crooke in 1886. Brooklyn Historical Society.

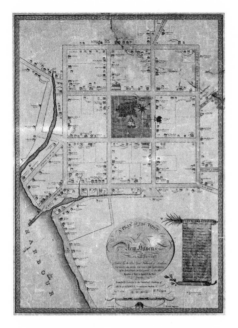

A Plan of the Town of New Haven With all the Buildings in 1748, James Wadsworth. Engraving by T. Kensett, 1806. Library of Congress, Geography and Map Division.

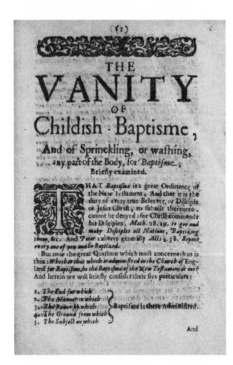

Andrew Ritor's *Treatise of the Vanity of Childish Baptisme*, 1642. British Library.

other women in the community. At worship one Sunday not long after, Eaton suddenly arose from her front-row pew and walked out of the meetinghouse. In the weeks that followed she began absenting herself from baptisms and services generally. When several congregants demanded an explanation for such reprehensible behavior by the governor's wife, Eaton told them that she had come to doubt the validity of baptizing infants. This prompted Davenport to borrow the borrowed book in order to prepare a series of sermons disproving Ritor, demonstrating that baptism had indeed "come in the place of circumcision, and is to be administered unto infants." Unmoved by months of lectures and admonition and refusing to repent, Eaton was censured and excommunicated. The episode rocked New Haven and wrecked Eaton's marriage (poor Theophilus was evidently "denied conjugall fellowship" for not defending his wife). Moody was long gone by the time all this unfolded, but it is likely that Davenport or Theophilus Eaton had indeed learned she was proselytizing in New Haven and hastened her on her way. For as antiquarian Nathaniel Prime put it in 1845, Moody came into "new difficulties" in Connecticut, "having made some converts to her new opinions."[13]

But Lady Moody appears to have carried off to New Netherland a token of this Yankee New Jerusalem. On a bold venture of settlement herself, she would have been keenly aware of the town-making groundwork so evident at New Haven at the time, the still-fresh lot lines and newly surveyed streets. A measure of Gravesend itself provides the most compelling evidence of a Connecticut connection; for Moody's four-square Gravesend grid is precisely the size of each of New Haven's nine constituent squares; if superimposed, Gravesend would snap perfectly into the center of Davenport's holy matrix, originally the market-place or public square and long known as the Green. If you walk beneath the "el" on McDonald Avenue from Village Road South to David's Bread at the corner of Village Road North ("World Famous Rye Bread") you'll have gone just over five hundred Babylonian cubits—almost precisely the length of Ezekiel's Temple. It was as if Moody had carried off a cutting of New Haven to plant on Long Island (ironi-cally, Gravesend and several other coastal English towns were all briefly annexed to Connecticut in 1662, shortly before the English took over faltering, credit-starved New Netherland). The distinctive pattern of planting fields at Gravesend—arrayed about a quadrangular nucleus—may have also been inspired by New Haven. There, a number of roads radiated outward from the nine-square grid, the most direct means of moving between village and hinterland. There is no evidence suggesting the planting fields were themselves arrayed spoke-like about the center; that the town was bounded east and west by creeks would alone have made such a pattern unworkable. Instead, planting lots were laid out *between* the radiating roads, creating the distinctive "cobweb" form of streets that surrounds New Haven today, to the annoyance of many drivers.[14]

If New Haven did indeed provide Moody and Hubbard a germ of inspiration for the Gravesend plan, the latter improved on a number of its elements. New Haven's radiating avenues and streets—Broadway, Prospect, Whitney, State, and Grand to the north and east; Chapel, Legion, Davenport, and Washington to the west and south—converge only roughly upon the town center, whereas the field boundaries at Gravesend, many of which later became roads, did so with mathematical precision. Superior execution is also evident in the town center. The house lots within each of New Haven's squares were laid out in a seemingly haphazard pattern, while those at Gravesend were fastidiously placed about the perimeter, each with its own garden plot. More telling still is how open space was provided in each plan. At New Haven the central square was set aside as the Green, while at Gravesend shared open space was provided at the center of each quarter. These were initially used for the safekeeping of livestock, but over time they took on a variety of communal uses—one for the town hall, others for the school and a meetinghouse, and the fourth for the burial ground, which still exists today. Finally, it appears that Davenport's sixteen-acre units proved to be impractically large; for as early as 1802, most of the nine New Haven squares had been further subdivided, into four-acre squares just like those at Gravesend.[15]

As a town founded by a woman seeking freedom of worship, with a codified guarantee of "free libertie of conscience," Gravesend not surprisingly would become a haven for other religious dissenters fleeing persecution. In the 1650s it had begun to attract a number of Quakers, who found that the Gravesenders' own experience with religious intolerance "fitted them to take kindly," wrote chronicler A. P. Stockwell, "to the peculiar principles of that society." Certainly there were strong commonal-ities between Quakerism and Anabaptism. Both claimed an individual relationship to God, rather than one mediated or brokered by an organized church. They were a community of "fellow believers or brothers" in faith. This is codified in the town plan. As Nathaniel Prime noted in his *History of Long Island*, the original plan for

Gravesend contained "no designated site for a house of worship," nor is any mention made of such a structure in early town records. A 1657 report on the status of New Netherland's churches claimed that, rather than holding traditional services, the Gravesenders would read to one another, often in each other's homes. The Religious Society of Friends had been founded in England around 1647 by George Fox, the eldest son of a Leicestershire weaver who sought a more essential relationship with Christ, unmediated by ordained clergy or exacting interpretations of scripture. A powerful speaker, Fox was imprisoned numerous times for blasphemy and at one point was nearly condemned to death (it was in mockery of Fox's exhortation that one should "tremble at the world of the Lord" that the term Quaker came about).[16]

In June 1657 a party of English Friends, led by a magnetic young preacher named Robert Hodgson, crossed the Atlantic and visited Gravesend en route to Rhode Island. It was there—reputedly at Lady Moody's own house—that the first Quaker meeting in America took place. Hodgson also visited Hempstead on Long Island, where he discovered that the magnanimity of Gravesend was the exception rather than the rule. There, while meditating in an orchard, Hodgson was arrested by a Dutch magistrate and sent to prison in New Amsterdam. Willem Kieft might have been a troublemaker, but religious freedom flourished under his administration. His replacement, Peter Stuyvesant, was mean and illiberal on matters of faith, a partisan of the Dutch Reformed Church who barred Lutherans from worshipping, called Jews a "deceitful race," and reserved special hate for "the abominable sect of the Quakers." He decided to make an example of the twenty-three-year-old Hodgson, sentencing him to pay a hefty fine or "work two years at a wheelbarrow with a negro." When he refused to pay, he was chained to a wheelbarrow and sent off to repair a section of the city wall with a slave, who was later forced to whip Hodgson when he refused to work. Stuyvesant then had the young man hung by his hands and beaten within an inch of his life. He was eventually released, but not before Stuyvesant passed an ordinance, in July 1657, that made it illegal for anyone in the colony to host a Quaker in his home.[17]

Not even Gravesend was safe now. Indeed, the first man hauled to New Amsterdam for violating the ordinance was Gravesend town clerk John Tilton, who "dared to provide a Quaker woman with lodging."[18] It was Stuyvesant's growing intolerance of religious diversity that led the citizens of Flushing to draft their Remonstrance that October, precursor to the provision of religious freedom in the US Bill of Rights. Not long after, in the winter of 1660, the doomed Mary Dyer preached at Gravesend on a last hopeful mission before returning—against all warnings—to Boston, where she had been condemned to death some months earlier but given a last-minute reprieve at the gallows. This time the ruthless John Endicott had Dyer hanged on Boston Common—killed, incredibly, by a sect of religious fanatics that had crossed the Atlantic to escape persecution. By this time, Gravesend had developed a reputation as an American "Mecca of Quakerism"; poet Gertrude Ryder Bennett called it "one of the most important Quaker colonies in the New World." Even the revered Quaker prophet George Fox spent time there. Fox sailed to America in 1671 (ironically, his ship was chased one night by a man-of-war from Salé, the Barbary outpost once ruled by Anthony Jansen van Salee's father). After stopping briefly in Barbados and

Jamaica, he sailed north to Maryland in early 1672, and traveled thence on horseback up the coast to Middletown, New Jersey. From there Fox and his party were taken by boat across the Lower Bay, landing at Coney Island and making it to Gravesend by nightfall. Fox "tarried that night" in town before moving on—accompanied by a number of Gravesend Quakers—to Flushing and Oyster Bay, where a four-day "Half Year's Meeting" was held. Fox again passed through Gravesend in July 1672, attending there "three precious meetings."[19]

Of course, the American city best known for its Quaker heritage is Philadelphia, founded by William Penn in 1682. It was the third and largest settlement in the Anglo-Dutch colonies laid out in precision form—as a great four-quarter gridiron stretched between the Delaware and Schuylkill rivers. Could it be that Lady Moody's little grid, each quarter endowed with a square of its own, was the germ of this landmark plan? Even a casual glance at the Penn scheme reveals a layout that fuses elements of both New Haven and Gravesend, with a dominant central space (later filled by City Hall) surrounded by smaller squares in each of the four quadrants. Was Philadelphia the grand culmination of a westward transit of a spatial design idea, from New Haven to Gravesend to the City of Brotherly Love? We know that many Gravesend Quakers migrated west as Dutch intolerance grew, and even after the English took over the colony in 1664. Some settled in Monmouth County, New Jersey; others in Burlington and neighboring towns in West Jersey, the vast province—about half the present Garden State—acquired by a group of Quaker investors, including Penn, in 1677. We also know that Fox, who had been to Gravesend twice, was a friend of Penn's and visited William and his wife Gulielma at their Rickmansworth home upon returning from the American colonies in 1673. Penn therefore would surely have known of Lady Moody's sanctuary from religious persecution. Perhaps Penn thus also learned from Fox of Gravesend's unique plan and its New Haven roots—and that he and his surveyor general, Thomas Holme, had Lady Moody's vernal scheme in mind when they drafted plans for Philadelphia.[20]

Unfortunately for Brooklyn partisans, evidence suggests otherwise. It turns out that Penn and Holme were not on the same page, so to speak, when it came to laying out the Quaker city. It was Holme, not Penn, who authored the signature grid, for the latter had in mind a very different, more pastoral arrangement for Philadelphia. Penn was hardly an urbanist—and for good reason: he had lived through two horrific back-to-back events in London that would have driven even Jane Jacobs to the suburbs—the Great Plague of 1665 and the Great Fire of 1666. In both cases, extreme urban density, crowding, and congestion hastened the spread of death and destruction. The very last things William Penn wanted in his New World colony were Old World urban hazards. As he famously put it in a letter, he meant Philadelphia to be not a city but a "greene country towne which will never be burnt, and always be wholesome." It would occupy a series of parallel hundred-acre "strip lots," each 825 feet wide and a mile deep, extending down to the Delaware River. Rather than a tight, nucleated settlement between the rivers, Penn's Philadelphia would have been little more than "an extension of the countryside," a rustic realm laid out along a sixteen-mile stretch of riverfront. Houses for the colonists would have been placed squarely in the center of each immense lot, not arrayed about urban squares. Indeed,

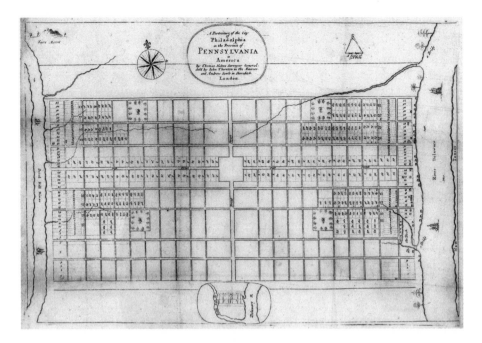

Thomas Holme, *A Portraiture of the City of Philadelphia*, 1683. Collection of Historic Urban Plans, Ithaca, New York.

in such a nonurban scheme "residential squares would have been a superfluity," writes historian Sylvia D. Fries. Penn had dreamed up a subdivision of McMansions, not a city. And the centerpiece of his river-strip scheme? Not a great central space, teeming with markets and life, but a house—Penn's very own "scituation," his grand manor, set on a three-hundred-acre estate.[21]

It was the reality of the vast Pennsylvania site—its topography and the fact that much of it was already in private hands—that eventually put the kibosh on Penn's plan, leading Holme toward a more compact, urban scheme for the highest, driest available land. As for sources, it appears Holme's looked not to Gravesend or New Haven, but to the Old World—London's residential squares or possibly Richard Newcourt's post-1666-fire proposal for rebuilding London, a gridiron with a nearly identical array of internal squares. He may even have had in mind Sir Thomas Phillips's 1611 plan for the crown settlement of Londonderry, the first planned town in Ireland, where Holme spent some years. But Lady Moody may have had some westward influence yet. As part of his grand plan, Penn envisioned an array of agricultural villages in the hinterlands around Philadelphia—nucleated settlements where "virtuous industry and righteous tranquility" might take root. He described two different methods of land division for these rural towns, the second of which—a central square surrounded by a radial bloom of planting fields—bears a striking resemblance to Gravesend. There, a taut union of field and hearth would assure, Penn wrote, "that the Conveniency of Neighbourhood is made agreeable with that of the land." Though his regional vision for Philadelphia was only partially realized, two townships northeast of the city proper—Newtown and Wrightstown—were

Thomas Holme, *A Map of the Improved Part of the Province of Pennsilvania in America*, 1695. Note the hub-and-spoke layout of Wrightstown and Newtown, center-right side of map. Library of Congress, Geography and Map Division.

laid out in such starburst form. On the 1720 "Mapp of ye Improved Part of Pensil-vania in America," they appear like embroidered stars winking in a patchwork quilt. Though few traces of colonial Wrightstown survive, several routes around Newtown today—Swamp, Durham, Eagle, Washington Crossing, and Twining roads—clearly originated with the old pattern of radial field boundaries.[22]

And what of Gravesend and the "American Dido" who founded it? After Willem Kieft's War ended in late 1645, peace settled over the land and Gravesend prospered for decades. The town appeared to have a bright future ahead of it. The land, after all, was blessed with fertile soil and plentiful timber and game; the seas adjoining abounded with fish, its bays and creeks thick with waterfowl, crabs, and shellfish. It was a com-modious place indeed, as George Baxter had so enthusiastically related to Winthrop the Younger in 1644—so hospitable that Gravesend's founders and Dutch officials alike were confident that the embryonic settlement would soon be a boomtown. In a report to the Dutch West India Company in 1651, Gravesend officials Baxter, James Hubbard, Nicholas Stillwell, and several other signatories envisioned a grand urban future. "We are as a young tree or little sprout now, for the first time shooting forth to the world," they wrote, but "which if watered and nursed . . . may hereafter grow up a blooming Republic." Geography, too, seemed in Gravesend's favor, at first flush at least. The town was on a bay, close to the head of the Narrows and a short haul to both the docks of New Amsterdam and the open sea. But in fact Gravesend Bay was fatally flawed—too shallow to accommodate large seagoing vessels. As merchant ships grew in size and draft, they could no longer drop anchor at Gravesend, dimming its prospects of future port-city fame. "And so," wrote Peter Ross in his 1902 *History of Long Island*, "the idea of building a 'city by the sea,' which in extent, wealth, and busi-ness enterprise, should at least rival New Amsterdam, was reluctantly abandoned."[23]

Nonetheless, Gravesend was eventually designated one of three official ports of entry on Long Island by the English—perhaps because it was there that Richard Nicolls anchored his men-of-war on August 18, 1664, to land the forces that would demand Peter Stuyvesant surrender the Dutch colony. By then, Gravesend's loyalties had been divided for years, its fortunes rising and falling with the affairs of state between England and Holland, the world's two major, oft-clashing colonial powers at the time. In 1654, with the start of the first Anglo-Dutch War, Stuyvesant's council decided to stop calling on the Gravesenders to defend or even help repair the fort at New Amsterdam, "so as not to 'drag the Trojan horse' within the city's walls."[24] Later that year some fifty Englishmen attended a clandestine meeting in Gravesend, fueling rumors that there was mischief afoot against the Dutch. The prime suspect was George Baxter, one of Moody's original Yankee band and Stuyvesant's English secretary. That year Baxter presented a "Humble Remonstrance" to the director general, complaining of the many officers and magistrates he had appointed "without the consent or nomination of the people."[25] Baxter along with James Hubbard had been elected officers of Gravesend town, in open defiance of Stuyvesant's order that all such appointments be reviewed by him. Baxter was summarily dismissed and later arrested for hoisting the English flag above Gravesend, pledging loyalty to Lord Protector Cromwell, and "reading seditious papers to the people." For this he languished in a brig for months until Henry Moody pleaded for his release, after which he returned to England and began lobbying for an all-out invasion of the Dutch colony. As Martha Lamb put it in an 1877 history, Long Island—and especially Gravesend—was "one continual source of anxiety to the men in power at New Amsterdam."[26]

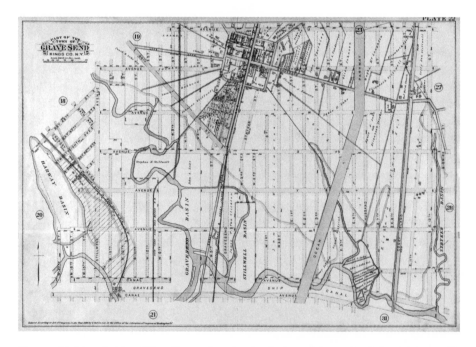

Plate 22 of Robinson's *Atlas of Kings County*, 1890, showing Gravesend overrun by Gotham's hungry grid. Lionel Pincus and Princess Firyal Map Division, The New York Public Library.

Once the English took over, of course, special favor fell upon the erstwhile Trojans of Gravesend. New Netherland became the Province of Yorkshire, split into three ridings. Gravesend was made the seat of the "West Ryding of Yorkshire upon Long Island," which included all of Brooklyn, Staten Island, and part of Queens. Its tenure as an administrative capital lasted until 1683, when Kings County was formed. Remarkably, Gravesend would remain an independent town until 1894, when it was annexed by the city of Brooklyn, thus ending 250 years of independence. As for the fate and final resting place of Deborah Moody, it remains an enduring mystery. She appears to have died in 1658 or 1659. By some accounts she had become a Quaker herself and led a contingent of settlers to Monmouth County, New Jersey. Others claim she passed on peacefully, an elder matriarch in the town of her founding. It may well be that Moody rests—fitfully perhaps, what with the F train rumbling noisily overhead—in an unmarked grave in the cemetery that still occupies the southwest quadrant of her four-square grid, across the street from a construction company, Mama's Restaurant Supply, and a place called Russian Shoppe. If this "dangerous woeman" ever had a headstone there, it has long been lost, stolen, or eroded to illegibility. Her four-square monument endures, however, defiant in a sea of change, a 350-year-old relic of a long-vanished world.[27]

CHAPTER 3

DEATH AND THE PICTURESQUE

Let's talk of graves, of worms, and epitaphs . . .
—SHAKESPEARE, *RICHARD II*

More than a century and a quarter would pass before the winds of history blew once more through Lady Deborah's vernal town—winds that filled the sails of a much fiercer envoy from Albion: the largest and most powerful naval invading force since the Spanish Armada. It came on a balmy summer day in late June 1776—a fleet of 130 warships and nine thousand men under the command of British general William Howe. Dropping anchor off Sandy Hook, just weeks after the bloodshed of Bunker Hill, the fleet was paying no social call. "In the van were big British ships of the line," writes David Hackett Fischer, "cleared for action with red gunports open, batteries run out, and huge white battle ensigns streaming in the breeze." Then came transports loaded with fighting men, advancing "at a majestic pace, as if nothing in the world could stop them." A private with the fated Maryland Line, Daniel McCurtin, watched in awe: "I thought all London was afloat," he wrote. Howe's ships then sailed through the Narrows to moor off Staten Island, where the troops disembarked. They were soon joined by an even larger force led by Howe's older brother, Admiral Richard Howe. By the third week of August nearly 500 ships and 30,000 soldiers had arrived to put down the American rebels—until then "the largest projection of seaborne power," writes Fischer, "ever attempted by a European state."[1]

The gathered storm made landfall at Brooklyn. On the morning of August 22, flatboats packed with 4,000 British regulars under the command of General James Grant were launched from Staten Island, landing near Fort Hamilton—a place then known as Denyse's Ferry. A second force led by Sir Henry Clinton rowed into Gravesend Bay, coming ashore at De Bruyn's landing—about the present

James Wallace, *The Phoenix and the Rose engaged by the Enemy's Fire ships and Galleys on the 16 August, 1776*, engraved by Dominic Serres, 1778. National Archives at College Park, George Washington Bicentennial Commission Series (Record Group 148).

intersection of Twentieth Avenue and Twentieth Drive (where Fred Trump would one day build hundreds of homes on filled land). By noon some 15,000 troops had arrived, under the protective cover of battery fire from a phalanx of warships—the HMS *Rainbow, Phoenix, Rose, Thunder*, and *Greyhound*.[2] The guns sent a wave of fear over the land. Farmers fled with their livestock, crowding country lanes ahead of the troops. Slumbering villages were awakened with a jolt. General Howe established his headquarters at New Utrecht, Lord Cornwallis at Gravesend. From there, Hessian colonel Carl von Donop was dispatched with his grenadiers to a position at Flatbush, where they skirmished with a band of colonists just south of the present Dutch Reformed Church. He was soon joined by additional Hessian and British brigades led by Wilhelm von Knyphausen and Philip de Heister. There were now 22,000 enemy troops on the ground; Kings County's population had quadrupled in a matter of days. The infant American nation, having boldly declared its independence not two months before, was about to have its mettle tested. Major General George Washington's ragtag army barely numbered 8,000 men—"imperfectly organized, insufficiently equipped, largely composed of unreliable militia, without adequate artillery, and without any cavalry."[3] Gathered against them was the world's most proficient, best-equipped fighting force. The Declaration of Independence had been signed in ink in Philadelphia; it would now be signed in blood.

As night fell on August 26, American militiamen on the hills above Flatbush—the great glacial moraine running from the Narrows to Jamaica and beyond, a "natural breastwork" that was Washington's first line of defense—could plainly see what lay in store for them.[4] From the "impenetrable shadow of the woods which crowned the summit and slopes," wrote Henry Stiles, "these few regiments of raw, undisciplined troops awaited the coming of their foe, whose tents and camp-fires stretched along the plain beneath them, in an unbroken line, from Gravesend to Flatlands."[5] Shortly before nine o'clock, the summer skies nearly dark, Howe and his generals—Clinton, Lord Percy, and Lord Cornwallis—made their move. De Heister was ordered to the Flatbush pass, and Grant dispatched to head north from the Narrows to engage the American right flank at Gowanus. Both were mere diversions; for Howe's real objective—the plan was actually Clinton's, accepted only reluctantly by his superior—was to send his main army through the unguarded easternmost pass over the morainal ridge at Jamaica. The troops, bivouacked along the Kings Highway, withdrew quietly, banking their fires and leaving tents in place. Thus were Washington's spies tricked, for all through the night the enemy camp had "every appearance of actual occupation." All seemed quiet on the southern front.

It was, of course, anything but. With the summer sky now finally dark, Clinton's battalion of light infantry set out for the village of New Lots, followed closely by Percy, Cornwallis, and Howe with the main force of some 10,000 troops and fourteen pieces of field artillery. At about midnight, just beyond the Flatbush road (Church Avenue), they struck off on a northeast bearing, moving ghost-like over field and forest "so silently that their footfalls could scarcely be heard at ten rods' distance."[6] Two miles by the crow, at a roadhouse called the Rising Sun (present junction of Broadway and Jamaica Avenue), the army swung to the left and began ascending the terminal moraine. Nowhere along the route did they encounter resistance. Clinton had anticipated at least a skirmish as the men crossed a soggy bottom by Keuter's Hook (the head of Fresh Creek, near today's Betsy Head Memorial Playground). "To his surprise, the place was found to be entirely unoccupied," wrote Stiles, "and the country open to the base of the Bushwick hills." Nor did anyone confront them on the Jamaica Pass—"a winding defile, admirably calculated for defence"—where the British expected a sharp fight. By dawn Clinton and his men were in full possession of the high ground. From there they moved swiftly on to the

Hayward and Lepine, *Battle Pass, Valley Grove*, c. 1866. Brooklyn Museum, Dick S. Ramsay Fund.

village of Bedford, now but a stone's throw from the Continental units still hopelessly skirmishing with de Heister's Hessians at the Flatbush pass. Thus was the great trap sprung: Howe had encircled the Americans from behind. General John Sullivan, Washington's junior commander on Long Island, had suspected the British might do just this, but nonetheless was so duped by Howe's feints at Gowanus and Flatbush that he sent no patrols to guard his left flank. "Fatal mistake!" exclaimed Stiles; "The battle was lost before it had been begun." It was Hannibal minus the elephants. The Americans, like the Romans, were blindsided.[7]

If the battle was effectively over, the bloodshed had just begun. While Clinton's army was encircling the Americans from behind, Grant marched some 5,000 men from the Narrows east to the New Utrecht Road—today's Eighteenth Avenue— turning north onto Martense Lane for the Gowanus Heights. The diversionary ma-neuver was to become an all-out assault at the sound of Clinton's signal cannon. Just before midnight, guards from a Pennsylvania regiment led by Colonel Samuel Atlee spotted British soldiers raiding a watermelon patch near a tavern known as the Red Lion Inn. The guards fired on the interlopers from the building, which of course immediately gave away the American front line. Grant then dispatched several hundred troops to attack the tavern, which stood at a sharp bend in the old Gowanus Road at Martense Lane (about where the garage and shops of Green-Wood Cemetery are located today near Fourth Avenue and Thirty-Fifth Street). Informed of this development, General Israel Putnam—Washington's senior commander on Long Island—ordered Brigadier General Lord Stirling to check the British advance. Stirling grabbed two regiments nearest the action—one from Delaware under the command of Colonel John Hazlet and Colonel William Smallwood's First Maryland Regiment, mustered at Baltimore and Annapolis and led that day by Major Mordecai Gist. Shortly after sunrise, Stirling's men ran into Atlee's retreating Pennsylvanians about a half mile north of the Red Lion; not far behind them the British were in hot pursuit. Stirling positioned his 1,500 troops in a long thin line from the marshy flats of Gowanus Bay up the crest of the hills then known as "The Heights of Guana" (running roughly from Third Avenue and Twenty-Third Street east to today's Slope Park at Sixth Avenue and Nineteenth Street). The forces clashed all morning, yet Grant made no bold forward move.

He was waiting, of course, for the signal that Clinton and the main British army had gained the rebel rear. When it came, Grant charged forward while Cornwallis's grenadiers—having routed the Americans fleeing the Hessian assault at Flatbush pass—swept down from the northeast. Stirling was a cornered rat. He ordered most of his troops to evacuate through the Gowanus marshes, while he and the ten Mary-land companies unleashed a furious series of assaults on the British grenadiers. "It was Stirling's hope," writes historian James L. Nelson, "that the Marylanders could both cover the men's retreat and fight their way to safety."[8] They accomplished the first, if barely, a delaying action that saved hundreds of fellow soldiers from certain death or capture. Again and again the Marylanders flung themselves at the British, who were fortified in an old stone farmhouse—the 1699 Vecht-Cortelyou house, reconstructed in nearby Washington Park by Robert Moses (as a restroom) and today the Old Stone House Museum. They were checked mercilessly by a volley of

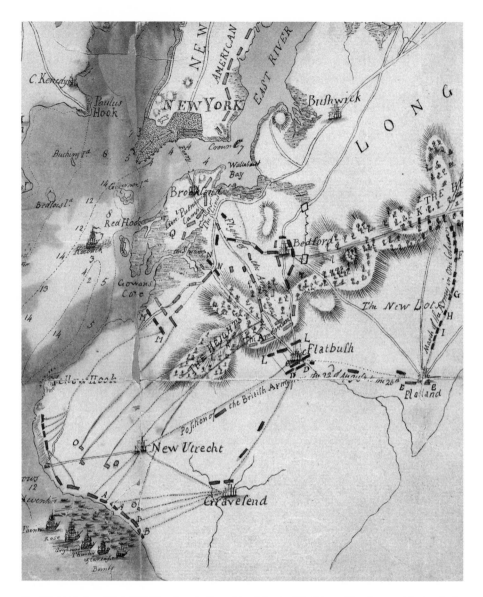

Detail from *A plan of New York Island, part of Long Island, Staten Island & east New Jersey, with a particular description of the engagement on the woody heights of Long Island . . . on the 27th of August 1776*, William Faden, 1776. Lionel Pincus and Princess Firyal Map Division, The New York Public Library.

cannon grape. And yet they persisted, closing ranks and even briefly capturing the stronghold before being repelled again.

As the battle unfolded, Washington watched helplessly from a redoubt just to the north at Fort Ponkiesberg, located about where Trader Joe's is today at 130 Court Street in Cobble Hill (a bronze tablet on the former South Brooklyn Savings Institution marks the spot). At last, with most of his men safely across the creek and en route to Brooklyn Heights, Stirling ordered the Marylanders to fall back and seek shelter as best they could behind American lines. Many never made it. Casualty

J. R. Smith, *Guann's near Fort Swift*, 1817, a sketch of the Gowanus marshes where fighting between British grenadiers and the First Maryland Regiment occurred on August 16, 1776. Library of Congress, Prints and Photographs Division.

estimates have been wildly exaggerated over the years, but of the 800 or so men of the First Maryland Regiment—Smallwood's nine companies and the Seventh Independent Company led by Captain Edward Veazey—a total of about 260 men were killed, captured, or wounded, including 12 officers. New research has put the number of dead at between 25 and 142, far fewer than the traditional counts. Captain Veazey was among them, the highest-ranking officer to die in combat during the Battle of Brooklyn (though two other officers died later of wounds). Most were taken prisoner, which—for ordinary enlisted men—was itself effectively a death sentence. Though Major Gist made it to safety, General Sullivan was captured and Lord Stirling surrendered to the Hessians. Social class saved both men, who were treated "with great civility" by General Howe and even "dined with him almost every day." The privates suffered a much worse fate. Many ended up in the pestilential holds of prison ships riding anchor in Wallabout Bay, where up to 11,000 American combatants would perish over the seven years of the Revolutionary War—more than were killed in all its land and sea battles combined. Thus did Brooklyn become the site of what Kenneth T. Jackson has called "the greatest American tragedy of the eighteenth century."[9]

The Battle of Brooklyn was the largest single fight of the American Revolution, the first after the nation declared its independence and the first that Washington himself commanded. It was a defeat, to be sure, but the best of sorts; for the Americans—and Washington—lived to fight another day. How and why this happened has long been debated. The British could easily have pushed on to storm the works at Brooklyn Heights, crushing the Continental Army and capturing its commander. It was only early afternoon when the Americans began retreating. For

The rebuilt c. 1699 Vecht-Cortelyou house (Old Stone House) in Washington Park, 1940. Historic American Buildings Survey photograph by Stanley P. Mixon. Library of Congress, Prints and Photographs Division.

Howe, the course of action seemed clear. "Six good hours of daylight remained," wrote Charles Francis Adams, "and, after demolishing the commands of Stirling and Sullivan, he should have followed up his success, striking at once and with all his force at Washington himself." Had Howe done so, the war would have ended then and there, the feeble flame of American independence perhaps snuffed out for good. But Howe did not persist. He ordered his army instead to halt and make camp, so infuriating his officers that it "required repeated orders," Howe reported, "to prevail on them to desist." It is not clear why he did this, whether it was simple incompetence—"the dilatoriness and stupidity of the enemy," as one of Washington's generals put it—or because Howe wanted to prevent further bloodshed. Indeed, neither General William Howe nor his seafaring brother Richard were eager to fight a war against the American colonies; they agreed to serve only when pressed by George III. This had to do with their late elder sibling, George Augustus Howe, killed at Fort Ticonderoga during the French and Indian War. To honor the officer, the General Court of Massachusetts funded a memorial in Westminster Abbey. "The younger Howe brothers never forgot that kindness," writes Nelson, "and it shaped their view toward the colonists, which was largely friendly and sympathetic."[10]

That the Americans lived to fight another day was also due to good luck—"almost miraculous good-luck," as Adams put it—involving two providential turns in weather. The first was a change in winds. The prevailing southwest wind typical of late summer in New York would have easily carried the British ships of the line into the East River, cutting Washington's army in half and marooning him on Long Island. But as the battle got under way, the wind began blowing from the northeast.

Against this (and a stiff outgoing tide), the fleet of heavy warships could only struggle in vain. Then came the rain. On the morning after the battle the sky was "lowering and heavy," according to Stiles, "with masses of vapor which hung like a funeral-pall over sea and land." A drenching rain kept men on both sides in their tents and trenches. The fog persisted the following day, August 29, giving Washington the cover he needed to begin evacuating his troops. That night some 9,000 men and arms were moved across the East River in boats crewed by a regiment of sailors and fishermen from Marblehead, Massachusetts—a brilliantly executed maneuver that saved Washington and his army. Howe learned of the mass evacuation from a slave informant sent by a Tory sympathizer, but hours too late; for the emissary was mistakenly dispatched to a unit of Hessians, who couldn't understand what he was saying—they spoke no English—and so detained him until daybreak. By then Washington was long gone. The American cause was still alive.[11]

The Battle of Brooklyn has long been a hushed chapter in America's founding story—a "strange military fiasco," as Adams called it, that never quite fit the glowing national narrative of God-sped exceptionalism. It was worse than a mere defeat, for rather than "inspiriting the defenders of freedom," opined Nehemiah Cleaveland in 1847, "its consequences were depressing and disastrous; and the day was long thought of as a day of mistakes, if not disgrace." That the whole mess was largely Washington's fault also didn't square with patriotic renderings of the sage and brilliant *pater patriae*. Washington's decision to defend New York against Britannia's mighty clenched fist was a strategic error—"hopeless from the start," as Adams put it. What, he marveled, "could have induced Washington, with the meagre resources both in men and material at his command, to endeavor to hold New York against such an armament as he well knew the British could then bring to bear?" One of Washington's more outspoken generals, Charles Lee (namesake of Fort Lee), had warned him that the water-bound city was indefensible against a naval power. "It is so encircled with deep navigable water, that whoever commands the sea must command the town." Lee advised letting it all go. "I would have nothing to do with the islands to which you have been clinging so pertinaciously," he wrote Washington; "I would give Mr. Howe a fee-simple of them." Washington ignored the advice.[12]

Nor did the whole episode cast the future city of Brooklyn in very flattering light. Manhattan-bound antiquarian Peter Ross impugned the residents of "Kings and Queens" for the whole ugly episode; they, unlike their evidently more patriotic betters across the river, "remained callous to the slogan of Liberty" and cared less "whether King or Congress reigned." Even Brooklyn stalwart Henry Stiles had to admit that "the people of Kings County seem to have viewed the approaching storm with perfect indifference," for in them "fear of pecuniary loss and personal inconvenience quite outweighed the more generous impulses of patriotism." The charges were not unfounded. Loyalist sympathies were strong in Kings County—not only in the old English settlement of Gravesend but all across the outwash plain. It was a trio of local Loyalists who guided the British army from Flatlands on the fateful night of August 27, after all. And unlike the patriotic lads from Maryland, Pennsylvania, and Massachusetts, most of the Kings County militia—including commanding officer

Colonel Nicholas Cowenhoven—defected to the British on Staten Island or simply hid from service. Without such friends "even Howe's army," Ross charged, "could not have landed in triumph."[13]

All this has long obscured the Battle of Brooklyn, effectively erasing it from landscape and collective memory alike. Its stain of failure has even eroded appraisals of the strategic importance of the Marylanders' action on that fateful day. In a damning 1957 report to Congress, the National Park Service concluded that the rearguard action of the Marylanders saved only about 700 men at best, did little to restrain General Grant ("cautious by training" in any case), and only briefly sidetracked a small number of enemy troops—"perhaps 3,000 British and Hessians out of a total force of some 19,000 men." The battle was already lost (though the soldiers had no idea of this); all the Marylanders did was snatch "brief glory from the jaws of imminent disaster." In other words, they sacrificed their lives for nothing. Worse, the Park Service concluded that the Marylanders' actions were "not of national significance" and thus unworthy of a monument. "Neither for its influence on the course of the battle, nor as a unique example of heroic military gallantry," the report opined, were the events at Gowanus "comparable to the 'matchless' significance accorded national recognition at Saratoga and Yorktown Battlefields, and at Independence Hall." Brooklyn's great moment of Revolutionary glory was thus dismissed as misguided boosterism.[14]

It has long been assumed that the Marylanders felled in the fighting of 1776 were buried together in a mass grave, the finding of which—Brooklyn's Holy Grail—has preoccupied history buffs for well over 150 years now. The story was propagated by an imaginative antiquarian named Thomas Warren Field, whose 549-page treatise on the Battle of Brooklyn was published in 1869. Moved perhaps by patriotic sentiment in the wake of the Civil War, Field wrote with every stop pulled on his rhetorical organ. "Artillery ploughed their fast-thinning ranks," he dirged of the Marylanders, "with the awful bolts of war; infantry poured its volleys of musket-balls, in almost solid sheets of lead upon them; and, from the adjacent hills, the deadly Hessian yagers sent swift messengers of death into many a manly form." And yet the brave lads were undaunted, closing ranks and turning "their stern young faces to their country's foe." All that's missing from Field's narrative is Moses on high, arms uplifted, speeding the Israelites to victory. Two hundred pages into his tale, Field turns to the fate of the Maryland dead, confiding that "on shore of Gowanus Bay sleep the remains of this noble band." The fallen were interred on "a little island of dry ground" on the farm of Adrian Van Brunt, who "consecrated the spot for the sacred deposit" (Van Brunt actually did not buy the Staats farm for another decade, but we'll let that pass). According to Field, this knoll was situated just east of Third Avenue between Seventh and Eighth streets. To its slopes the dead were carried and "laid beneath its sod, after the storm of battle had swept by." Anticipating skepticism, Field hastily calls in his sole source: "Tradition says that all the dead of the Maryland and Delaware battalions who fell on and near the meadow were buried in this miniature island, which promised at that day the seclusion and sacred quiet which befit . . . the heroic dead."[15]

Like any good fable, Field's narrative rests partly on a foundation of truth. It is correct that much of the fighting on the morning of August 27 took place in and around the Gowanus tidal marshes—not an ideal place to bury bodies. It stands to reason that any interments afterward would have occurred on higher dry ground. And Revolutionary-era maps do show one or two small hummocks rising above the marsh in precisely the area delineated by Field (roughly a quarter mile southwest of the Vecht-Cortelyou house, where many of the casualties took place). Moreover, this elevated ground had long been used as a burial place. John Van Brunt, whose father purchased the Staats farm in 1786, recalled seeing graves there as a youth, some marked with headstones and others evident only by mounded earth. The knoll and its old cemetery were left intact by the Van Brunt family, as some of their number were buried there. Ultimately, however, the hummock fell before the "remorseless surveyor's lines" of urban growth. No matter how altered, it would always be hallowed ground. "The very dust of those streets is sacred," exclaimed Field. "And our busy hum of commerce, our grading of city lots, our speculations in houses reared on the scenes of such noble valor, and over the mouldering forms of these young heroes, seem almost a sacrilege."[16]

Field's account was effectively cast in stone when Henry R. Stiles retold it almost verbatim in his monumental, two-volume *History of the City of Brooklyn*, still the most expansive—if frequently inaccurate—opus ever written about the place. In less than a generation, the mass-grave story had firmly become part of the canon of New York City history. Few doubted its veracity, though the persistent lack of evidence should have given pause. When a tradition is compelling enough, "evidence" of its truth is often willed into being. As Gowanus urbanized in the 1890s, the occasional grave or human bones unearthed by grading and excavation were invariably hailed as proof that the Marylanders were in the 'hood. A 1906 *New York Herald* piece claimed, without a shred of evidence, that the grave site of the Marylanders was destroyed when Third Avenue was cut through the old Van Brunt farm around 1854—a time when "burial trenches . . . still showed plainly" on the east side of the new thoroughfare. Foundation work for the apartment buildings at 423–427 Third Avenue revealed an array of bone sets "laid out in regular, or military, order." More human remains were discovered across Third Avenue some years later during construction of the Collyer Printing plant.[17]

These discoveries helped launch an effort to commemorate the fallen troops. In early 1897 a stone tablet with inlaid bronze lettering was commissioned from the Yale and Towne Company and set in the sidewalk at 429 Third Avenue (paid for with leftover funds raised for the Maryland Monument in Prospect Park). Ironically, the slab was itself later buried—possibly when Third Avenue was widened or repaved in 1915—and thus lost underground just like the men it recalled. By then, the adjacent lots were in the hands of a coal dealer memorably named Henry Wildhack. A German immigrant, Wildhack purchased 429 Third Avenue in 1905 and the adjacent parcel (431) several years later. Both were vacant, the latter still at its original grade seven or eight feet below the street. Wildhack was a history buff and breathed new life into the Marylander story. As he related to the *Brooklyn Eagle* in 1910, a series of graves were "plainly visible" when he first bought the property. "The soldiers had been buried in about fifteen trenches," he recalled, "each about a hundred feet long and extending diagonally from Third avenue to 8th street, in a southeasterly direction."

Henry Wildhack, Jr., with the long-vanished Maryland Regiment tablet at 429 Third Avenue, c. 1910.
James A. Kelly Local History Collection, Brooklyn College Library Archives and Special Collections.

Wildhack tried to persuade city officials to buy the lots for a memorial, but failed and ultimately filled both to street grade. If the hapless Marylanders were ever under this land, they were now buried again, this time beneath an inglorious blanket of clinkers and ash. Wildhack's son confirmed much of this account in an interview forty-five years later. He recalled "playing about the burial trenches . . . as a boy of ten or twelve, and digging through the crest of one of the mounds in the back part of the lot at 431." There, "bones and miscellaneous material" were found. Wildhack, Jr., recalled the grave mounds being "three or four feet wide," each "six or seven feet from the other." He even drew a sketch map of the site and array of mounds.[18]

This was, for many, proof positive of the mass-grave theory. After Wildhack's company closed in 1931, a victim of the Great Depression, the property was acquired by a manufacturer of Red Devil paints—the Technical Color and Chemical Works. The former coal yard was excavated to accommodate several concrete-lined tanks for pigments, lacquers, and thinners. But the tanks extended only seven or eight feet below grade, so it is unlikely that they would have disturbed anything from the Revolutionary era. Indeed, the excavating contractor reported finding no bones or artifacts; he was probably only removing Wildhack's old fill. It wasn't until January 1957 that the first serious archaeological study of the presumed burial ground was made—directed by Columbia University anthropologist Richard B. Woodbury and his graduate student Robert C. Suggs. Supervising the work was Frank Barnes, author of the aforementioned National Park Service report, and James A. Kelly, a schoolteacher and former vaudeville actor whom Mayor Fiorello La Guardia appointed Brooklyn's first borough historian in 1944. Three days into the work, the

Wildhack coal and coke yard, c. 1910. James A. Kelly Local History Collection, Brooklyn College Library Archives and Special Collections.

team had excavated several large pits in the cellar of the former paint factory. They found nothing of value. The search was expanded to include backyards along Third Avenue, which were excavated to a depth of fifteen feet. Still no Marylanders. This was especially exasperating to Kelly, a Gowanus kid who grew up on stories of the lost soldiers. "I can't understand it," he reportedly said; "they should have been here."[19]

That frustrated conviction was because Kelly, like Wildhack and many others before and after, took the mass-grave account as gospel truth, when in fact it was based largely on hearsay and folklore. Field, architect of the tale, had conflated John Van Brunt's confused memories of the Staats family cemetery on the meadow island with his recollection that, according to family tradition, "it had been the burial place of American soldiers who fell in the battle of L. I." Field leaped to the conclusion that not only must a mass grave of Marylanders exist, but it must have been on the little knoll depicted on battle maps as part of the old Staats farm. To complicate matters further, there were *several* old graveyards in this area—including the Van Brunt family's own plot at about Eighth Street and Third Avenue and a slave burial ground close by. Though family members in the Van Brunt cemetery were later exhumed, those buried in the other plots were likely not—especially not if they were "the servile sons of Africa," as Field put it. These graves may explain the bones found now and then as streets were graded and foundations excavated. Some may even have been the remains of fallen colonial fighters. They were not, however, evidence of a mass grave of battlefield dead.

There are several reasons why the mass-burial story is almost certainly false. First, we know from multiple accounts that the fighting in Gowanus on August 27

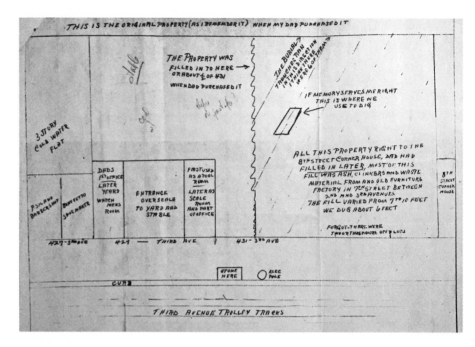

Henry Wildhack, Jr.'s 1957 sketch map of his father's coal and coke yard as it was fifty years earlier. James A. Kelly Local History Collection, Brooklyn College Library Archives and Special Collections.

ranged over a very large area—from the watermelon patch at the Red Lion Inn all the way north to the Vecht-Cortelyou house, a distance of nearly two miles. That ten companies of 800 Marylanders spent the entire chaotic morning glued together as a single unit over this span of ground is preposterous. This was guerrilla warfare, at least on the part of the Americans. Smallwood's Maryland companies split up and converged and ultimately "broke up into separate groups near the close of the battle." The combat dead would therefore have been scattered all about, not clustered in a group. Of course, bodies could have been moved later to a single burial site. But this does not square with either reason or British battlefield practice at the time. Would soldiers in the thick of a hot fight be taken from the front to haul corpses through field and swamp so that men who had just tried to kill them could repose in a neat array? Not likely. As Hunter College anthropologist William J. Parry explained in a 2017 research paper, "The British were distracted both by the construction of siege works, and by heavy rain." The rain, as we have seen, fell for two full days after the battle, after which "both sides withdrew from the battlefield." There was neither the time nor the weather for a coordinated mass interment.[20]

Nor was there the will. Until the Civil War, battlefield dead were rarely "gathered in formal cemeteries, or marked or recorded," notes Parry, especially enemy dead. They may not have even been buried at all—at least at first. Corpses were often deliberately left where they fell to rot, and could remain there for weeks or months. Ambrose Serle, General William Howe's private secretary, noted on September 3 that "the Woods near Brookland are so noisome with the Stench of the dead Bodies of the Rebels . . . that they are quite inaccessible." Decomposing corpses were reported in the field as late as June 1777, a full ten months after the Battle of Brooklyn. And if the bodies of the dead were committed to the ground, it was usually done with great haste and minimal decorum. Graves were typically shallow and unmarked, and thus easily disturbed by groundwater, frost heaving, or animals. In the aftermath of the Battle of White Plains in October 1776, bodies of the dead had been "so slightly buried," observed Connecticut private Joseph Plumb Martin, "that the dogs or hogs, or both, had dug them out of the ground . . . sculls and other bones and hair were scattered about the place." Given the heat and rain of late August 1776, the corpses would have putrefied rapidly, making it all but certain that the fallen Marylanders "would have been buried as close as possible to where they fell," writes Parry, "with the least possible handling." The likelihood that the rotting remains would have been carried from afar for burial in an orderly array is virtually nil. If—and wherever—they were buried, who might have carried out the grim work? Locals pressed into service by the British, most likely, or labor battalions of former slaves who joined the British side in exchange for the freedom promised by Virginia governor Lord Dunmore's "Emancipation Proclamation" of November 1775. What about the mounds and trenches that Henry Wildhack, Jr., played amidst as a boy? Parry suggests that these may have been the traces of a short-lived road, Hammond Avenue, one of four new thoroughfares proposed in 1839 by a committee on streets and squares. Named after Brooklyn street commissioner A. G. Hammond, the road began at Atlantic Avenue and Smith Street and ran south to Twenty-Third Street at Green-Wood Cemetery—a trajectory that took it across the Wildhack lots in precisely the same location and orientation of the presumed burial trenches. Though it's unclear how much of Hammond Avenue was actually built, some of it was probably staked and graded before being closed and struck from maps—in March 1846—by the Brooklyn Common Council.[21]

In the end, the tale of the Marylanders' mass burial was a largely manufactured one—an example of what historian Eric Hobsbawm has called an "invented tradition."[22] Typically formed about a kernel of historical truth, invented traditions enlarge or distort the past to meet specific political needs. They almost always appear in times of rapid social change, especially when a dominant group feels threatened by forces beyond its control. The mass-grave story was simply not part of Brooklyn history until Stiles popularized Field's account in 1867, at a time of unprecedented national trauma and mourning in the United States. No chronicler beforehand mentions a word of the collective burial—an astonishing omission in light of the story's eventual grip on the public imagination. By the end of the nineteenth century, interest in the Marylanders had soared. Keyword analysis of the *Brooklyn Eagle* newspaper archives shows a surge of articles on the topic between 1890 and 1915. This was, not coincidentally, a period of convulsive transformation in both New York City and America at large. In those years some twenty million immigrants entered the United States, mostly from the impoverished countries of southern, central, and eastern Europe. The vastly different religious, linguistic, and cultural backgrounds of these people—Russians, Slavs, *shtetlekh* Jews from the Pale of Settlement, Italian peasants from the Mezzogiorno (including some of my own ancestors)—caused tremendous anxiety among native-born Americans, and the Anglo-Dutch "Old Brooklynites" were no exception: the charter culture of the United States, they feared, would soon be smothered. The antidote? Recover all traces of the hallowed past to recharge and renew it as a means of inoculating one's heritage against the alien Other. If this required the embroidery or embellishment of traditions—or even their outright fabrication—so be it.

Invented or not, romantic tales are hard to kill—especially those about the dead. By 2010, with the Wildhack lots newly capped by a five-story condominium, the search for the Marylanders shifted to a nearby site—a vacant block-wide parcel between Eighth and Ninth streets just off Third Avenue. That *this* site might at last be the fabled mass burial ground was a view aggressively championed by two neighborhood activists—Robert Furman of the Brooklyn Preservation Council and Eymund Diegel, a South African–born urban planner with experience in remote sensing and digital cartography. They had a strong ally right next door, literally: the Michael A. Rawley, Jr. American Legion Post at 193 Ninth Street, whose members were understandably thrilled at the prospect of a major Revolutionary War landmark at their doorstep. Furman and Diegel proposed setting aside the parcel as open space, an effort that received extensive press coverage. In August 2012 the *New York Times* ran a feature article on this latest quest for the lost Marylanders, describing the mass grave as "the archeological equivalent of the Golden City of El Dorado." Not only would a park preserve the site for archaeological work, the pair argued, but it might help slow the snowballing gentrification of Gowanus—already a wild mix of collision shops, Pilates studios, and artisanal bakeries. "In their eyes," wrote the *Times*, the parcel's fate "will determine whether the neighborhood remains a low-rise middle ground that acts as a bridge between Carroll Gardens and Park Slope, or becomes an architectural island, full of the glossy towers . . . that have transformed the Williamsburg waterfront in recent years."[23]

As often happens when passion runs ahead of reason (especially when an agenda of ulterior motives is involved), Furman and Diegel and their supporters began seeing the Marylanders everywhere. Diegel had been mapping lost streams around Gowanus using balloon-borne camera technology shared by a citizen science initiative, Public Lab, which he helped found after the 2010 Deepwater Horizon oil spill. In July 2012 he and several volunteers lofted a camera—a "Canon SD 880 Hello Kitty camera strapped into a recycled organic carrot juice bottle," as Diegel put it—above the Ninth Street parcel. One of his volunteers lay down on the concrete to provide comparative scale. Studying the photographs, Diegel detected a strange repetitive pattern of cracks in the concrete, aligned to a north-south axis and seeming to match the burial trenches described long ago by Henry Wildhack. As the *Times* put it, the cracks suggested to Diegel "that the ground underneath had been disturbed in a way that might be consistent with a grave site."[24] Far more convincing was a digital elevation model he subsequently produced with Jarlath O'Neil-Dunne of the University of Vermont, using a sophisticated remote-sensing technology known as LIDAR (Light Detecting and Ranging). By sending and receiving back a pulsed beam of laser light, this technology permits distances across a surface to be measured or "ranged" with extreme accuracy. Variations as small as a quarter of an inch can be detected, enabling cartographers to create highly detailed models of terrain or surface features.

Diegel and O'Neil-Dunne used public-source LIDAR data to generate a color-coded elevation model that revealed what they described as "an intriguing pattern of human shaped bumps." Of all the many sketches, maps, and drawings put forth over the decades in quest of the Marylanders, this is easily the most powerful and the most haunting, and it's not clear why Diegel and Furman back-grounded it in favor of the somewhat clownish balloon-cam work.

Eymund Diegel (right) with his "Over My Dead Body" balloon-mapping team at the Ninth Street lot. Photograph by Sara Dabbs, 2012.

Propelled by such convincing imagery, the story of the search for the Mary-landers spread far beyond Brooklyn. In June 2014 Diegel and his team were invited to present their study—cleverly titled "Over My Dead Body"—to President Barack Obama at Public Lab's inaugural White House Maker Faire. They even sent a balloon camera aloft over the Rose Garden. By then, he and Furman had begun describing the Marylander site as "America's First Veteran's Cemetery" and even planned an international design competition for a commemorative park—the Marylander Green—which would be linked to the Old Stone House at Washington Park

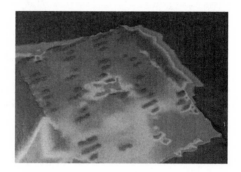

LIDAR model by Jarlath O'Neil-Dunne and Eymund Diegel of the Ninth Street lot, showing terrain microanomalies. Courtesy of Eymund Diegel.

and other area sites via a Gowanus Canal Revolutionary Trail and Greenway. It was an admirable initiative, but one built on a shaky foundation. Nonetheless, Diegel and Furman drew many to their cause, including—of all people—the erstwhile captain of the Starship *Enterprise*, Patrick Stewart. The knighted actor's enormous prestige and personal gravitas served as a public relations godsend. In February 2017, the actor led *GQ* reporter Caity Weaver to the vacant lot while regaling her with the tale of the ill-fated regiment ("sounding like a narrator," she noted, "the History Channel could not afford"). "It's worth making, I think, a bit of a fuss of," he said.[25]

And then it all came to an end. In May 2017 the New York City School Construction Authority bought the site for a proposed kindergarten at 168 Eighth Street. Within weeks, the State Historic Preservation Office formally requested an archaeo-logical survey—a requirement for almost all city construction projects. A consulting firm was contracted, AKRF Associates of New York. Digging began at once. Eight trenches, evenly spaced across the site, were excavated to depths of seven to ten feet. At the eastern end of trench five several potentially significant features were uncovered—a brick cistern, a stone well, and a privy—along with evidence of a buried ground surface. These deserved greater study, and so that September the central portion of the site was further excavated—this time to as much as fourteen feet below the surface. The results were disappointing. The privy, well, and cistern, along with a plethora of other artifacts—filled post holes, old ash pits, iron pipe, broken liquor bottles, and burned animal bone (waste from an old ink factory on the site)—dated back only to the nineteenth and early twentieth centuries. Undisturbed subsoil was encountered close to the surface, meaning the site was never extensively filled. More to the point, "no evidence of human remains or grave shafts was observed anywhere within the Phase 2 work area," according to the study's lead archaeologist, Elizabeth D. Meade, making it "exceedingly unlikely that intact 18th century archeological sites or human remains are located on the project site." Against cold, hard evidence like this even the most compelling tales must fall. Diegel's LIDAR imagery, it turns out, revealed nothing more than pavement anomalies, while the pattern of cracks detected with the balloon-cam rig were likely just caused by rusted, swollen reinforcement bar in the concrete. And yet Diegel remains committed to the idea of a mass Marylander grave of some sort, even if not on the Ninth Street site. "I feel the jury is still out," he told me recently; for even if a single mass burial site is unlikely, "there would still have been some piling up of bodies," he says, "meaning probably several mass graves in soft marshy soil areas."[26]

If the Maryland dead never found peace together in consecrated ground, consecrated ground ultimately came to them. For by the mid-nineteenth century much of the battlescape of August 1776 had been transformed into a vast burial ground. This "silent city of the dead," christened Green-Wood Cemetery, was the third and greatest example of a Franco-American invention of the romantic era—the "rural" cemetery. Created a generation before the arrival of Frederick Law Olmsted and Calvert Vaux, it drew upon the same design tradition that would be used for Central and Prospect parks—the so-called English school of "landscape gardening" that formed in the early eighteenth century in reaction to the French neoclassical tradition. Theorists and practitioners like Lancelot "Capability" Brown (who waxed lyrical about the "capabilities" of an estate to potential clients) and his disciple Humphry Repton set about composing landscapes evocative of the romantic landscape paintings then in vogue—scenes of classical antiquity, idyllic ruins, and the Italian *campagna* by Claude Lorraine, Nicholas Poussin, and Salvatore Rosa. Garden design was turned on its head; the spatial discipline of the French baroque—rigid geometries, unyielding symmetry, anchored sightlines—fell in favor of a studied informality, a great tousling of form and space that emulated the seeming "chaos" of nature. The straight was made crooked, the smooth made rough. Terraces became hillocks; walls were replaced by the "ha-ha," a trenched barrier tucked behind a berm from manor-house view. Trees, once planted in bosques and allées, were now set in scruffy clumps—"like dumplings," snarked Norman T. Newton, "floating in a sea of sauce." This was nature perfected for the enlightenment of man, or so its admirers thought.[27]

If such a curated rustic landscape so pleased the living, perhaps it could also comfort the dead—or at least those who mourned them. It was in France—at Père Lachaise Cemetery on the eastern outskirts of Paris—that this idea of eternity-in-a-garden first took form. Named after the father confessor of Louis XIV, Père Lachaise opened in 1804 as a secular alternative to the hideously overcrowded church burial grounds in the center of Paris. Far from the city and not consecrated by the Catholic Church, Père Lachaise languished at first. It was a clever marketing move—"seeding" the cemetery with the exhumed remains of two exalted Frenchmen, Molière and Jean de la Fontaine—that stoked interest in the place among the Paris elite. Within a generation, Père Lachaise had become *the* place to go when you went. Its grave roll is a catalog of French history—Balzac, Callas, Chopin, Proust, and Edith Piaf are all buried there (so are Oscar Wilde and American rocker Jim Morrison). It also became a popular pleasure ground, where families could picnic and promenade on Sundays among the illustrious dead. It was on the rural outskirts of Boston, about a mile west of Harvard Yard, that this French idea first took hold in America. Mount Auburn Cemetery was the brainchild of a Boston physician and botanist named Jacob Bigelow, who became a vocal advocate of modern "sepulture" after an 1820s revival of *ad sanctos* or churchyard burials in Boston. Prevailing medical theory at the time blamed a variety of dread diseases on the poisonous exhalations or "miasmas" thought to emanate from congested city graveyards. A rural cemetery not only offered a solution to a public health menace, but indulged Bigelow's long-standing interest in trees and plants. It also reflected changing perceptions of death, less burdened now by Calvinist notions of worms and damnation—of "gloomy vaults and silent aisles," as Washington Irving wrote of Westminster Abbey—and charged instead with a redemptive yearning to celebrate the lives and deeds of the deceased. Why, Irving asked in *The Sketch Book of Geoffrey Crayon*, "should we thus seek to clothe death with unnecessary terrors, and to spread horrors round the tomb of those we love? The grave should be surrounded by every thing that might inspire tenderness and veneration for the dead; or that might win the living to virtue."[28]

Backed by the newly established Massachusetts Horticulture Society, Bigelow arranged the purchase of a seventy-two-acre woodland tract above the Charles River known as "Sweet Auburn." There an "ornamented rural cemetery" was consecrated in September 1831, laid out by Bigelow himself and engineer Alexander Wadsworth. With its hills and dales and century-old trees, "Sweet Auburn" needed little to become a paragon of the picturesque. Here "the beauties of nature should, as far as possible, relieve from their repulsive features the tenements of the deceased," Bigelow wrote, and, "at the same time, some consolation to survivors might be sought in gratifying . . . the last social and kindred instincts of our nature." Of course, it would not do for Boston's Brahmins to have such an exquisite place to spend eternity and not New Yorkers, whose city—even in the 1830s—had three times the population and tenfold the ambition of Boston. It was Henry E. Pierrepont, scion of Brooklyn's most prominent family, who took up the cause on behalf of Gotham. Son of Hezekiah Pierrepont—creator of Brooklyn Heights—the younger Pierrepont visited Mount Auburn in 1832, returning "with the desire awakened that New York and Brooklyn should have a similar establishment . . . not unworthy of their greatness." He spent the following year in Europe visiting the historic cemeteries and *campi santi* of France and Italy. While away, Pierrepont was appointed chair of the Board of Commissioners charged with laying out streets for the new city of Brooklyn. It was in this role, ironically, as Brooklyn's master of the urban grid, that Pierrepont gained the authority to set aside land for a cemetery. He initially tried to buy the same Van Brunt farm later said to hold the fallen Marylanders. When the Van Brunts refused to sell, Pierrepont looked instead to a sprawling tract of high ground just to the south, on the Heights of Guana that saw so much fighting in 1776. The land— "beautifully diversified by hill and valley" and encompassing "a variety and beauty of picturesque scenery . . . seldom to be met with in so small a compass"—included Kings County's highest point, Mount Washington. Rising some 220 feet above sea level and affording spectacular views of the harbor and New York beyond, it would eventually be renamed Battle Hill.[29]

Pierrepont and a group of wellborn Brooklynites chartered their cemetery as a joint-stock corporation on April 11, 1838, and spent most of the next ten months wresting a 175-acre site from multiple, often avaricious, landowners. The grounds were very nearly called Necropolis. But the name was deemed too classical for a romantic landscape, and much too urban. After all, this was a *rus* to counter the fevered *urbs*. "Necropolis," it was decided, "*savours* of *art* and *classic refinement*, rather than of *feeling*, and herein is our objection. A Necropolis should be an architectural establishment, not a shady forest. Besides, a Necropolis is a mere depository for *dead bodies*—ours is a *Cemetery . . . a place of repose*." And so it was named Green-Wood instead, a landscape whose "visible associations," wrote trustee David B. Douglas,

Rudolph Cronau, *View from Greenwood Cemetery, Brooklyn*, 1881. Brooklyn Museum, Gift of Gerold Wunderlich.

"are intended to be exactly what its name implies—*verdure, shade, ruralness, natural beauty*; every thing, in short, in contrast with the *glare, set form, fixed rule* and *fashion* of the city."[30] A civil engineer who had cut his teeth on the Croton Aqueduct and the Brooklyn-Jamaica railroad, it was Douglas who oversaw the long work of coaxing a landscape garden from the wild Gowanus heights. It was the first expression in New York of an English landscape aesthetic—the picturesque—that would reach a zenith with the urban parks of the Olmsted era. Adumbrated by the English aesthetic theorists William Gilpin and Uvedale Price, the picturesque differed from the sublime or the beautiful by its emphasis on "roughness." As Gilpin explained in a 1792 essay, picturesque design—on canvas or on the ground—required snapping the line of beauty, interrupting the "*smoothness of the whole*":

> Turn the lawn into a piece of broken ground: plant rugged oaks instead of flowering shrubs: break the edges of the walk: give it the rudeness of a road: mark it with wheel-tracks; and scatter around a few stones, and brush-wood; in a word, instead of making the whole *smooth*, make it *rough*; and you also make it *picturesque*.[31]

The first improvements at Green-Wood—a simple rail fence around the cemetery's perimeter and a road "passing through its most interesting portions"—were made the summer of 1839. The first interment, of a man named John Hanna, came the following September. By then the cemetery's metamorphosis was well under way. Writing in 1841, the pioneering plantsman and landscape designer Andrew Jackson Downing—America's first authority on spatial improvement—predicted that Green-Wood would inevitably eclipse Mount Auburn as the greatest garden cemetery in the United States. "In size it is much larger," he noted in the *Gardener's Magazine*, "and if possible exceeds it in the diversity of surface, and especially in the grandeur of the views. Every advantage has been taken of the undulation of surface, and the fine groups, masses, and thickets of trees, in arranging the walks; and there can be no doubt, when this cemetery is completed, it will be one of the most unique in the world." All told, Downing conjectured, America's new rural cemeteries were "the first really elegant public gardens or promenades formed in this country" and "the only places . . . that can give an untravelled American any idea of the beauty of many of the public parks and gardens abroad."[32]

As odd as it may sound to us, the rural cemeteries of Boston, Philadelphia, and New York were thronged from the start—not by the dead or their mourners but by the living, ordinary people yearning for trees and fresh air, an afternoon's relief from the pressures and congestion of urban life. Once Green-Wood's main road opened, on July 4, 1839, word got out fast that a place of great beauty "had been added to the scanty privileges of New York and Brooklyn," related Cleaveland; "and Green-Wood soon became a place of considerable resort." By the 1860s, only Niagara Falls was drawing more visitors annually than Green-Wood. Twenty years before Central Park, the cemetery was effectively New York's first great urban playground. "Judging from the crowds of people in carriages, and on foot, which I find constantly thronging Green-wood and Mount Auburn," Downing reported in the *Horticulturalist*, "I think it is plain enough how much our citizens, of all classes, would enjoy public parks on a similar scale." Indeed, the immense popularity of Green-Wood and its predecessors—Mount Auburn and Philadelphia's Laurel Hill Cemetery—would spark an urban parks revolution that, by the end of the century, profoundly transformed the form and structure of the American metropolis.[33]

If Brooklyn provided Manhattan a model for its greatest park, it received—in caskets and coffins—the isle's illustrious dead. Many a Knickerbocker recoiled at the thought of spending eternity in the provinces, much as Mayor Ed Koch would cantankerously do a century later. When Trinity Church contemplated purchasing a large plot at Green-Wood, it nearly caused a riot among the congregation—native Manhattanites who were "shocked at the idea of being taken over the water, or of being buried anywhere except on that same rock-ribbed isle." Instead, the church acquired a small burial ground on the Upper West Side (where Koch was buried in 2013). That changed soon enough; as Green-Wood's fame spread, it became the location of choice for Gotham's aristocracy to spend eternity. By 1842, lonely John Hanna had been joined by 133 other dead men and women. A decade later there were some 26,000 souls interred at Green-Wood, a peaceful population nearly equal to that of the Bronx and Queens at the time. This included fresh burials as well as "removals from other grounds," among them members of the Van Brunt family interred atop their salt marsh knoll. If any men from the First Maryland were buried with the Van Brunts, they may well now also rest at Green-Wood—"Beneath the verdant and flowery sod," Cleaveland rhapsodized in full Victorian mode; "beneath green and waving foliage—amid tranquil shades, where Nature weeps in all her dews, and sighs in every breeze, and chants a requiem by each warbling bird."[34]

John Bachmann, *Bird's Eye View of Greenwood Cemetery*, 1852. Library of Congress, Prints and Photographs Division.

CHAPTER 4

YANKEE WAYS

A system of grounds . . . designed for the recreation of the
whole people of the metropolis.
—FREDERICK LAW OLMSTED AND CALVERT VAUX, 1866

If Brooklyn gave New York its first de facto urban park in Green-Wood Cemetery,
it had to wait another generation for a great, truly public playground of its own.
Prospect Park was not the first large urban park of nineteenth-century America—
Manhattan got that, of course—but it was the finest of its age, the crowning achievement of the same creative polymath who gave us Central Park. Frederick Law Olmsted was a wanderlusting Yale dropout from Hartford who, before the age of forty,
had sailed to China, apprenticed with farmers in Connecticut and upstate New York,
run an experimental spread of his own that his father bought for him on Staten Island, Tosomock Farm, edited *Putnam's*, and published three books of his own—one
of which, *A Journey in the Seaboard Slave States* (1856), galvanized the abolitionist
movement and thus helped change the course of history. Restless and churning
with ambition, Olmsted was the product of a patrician lineage—reaching back to
the Puritans and filled with Revolutionary heroes (including one who died on a
prison ship in Wallabout Bay)—that augured distinction in some profession, if not
greatness. That this would come in a field of his own making, *landscape architecture*,
few could have presaged before 1855. Olmsted had no formal degree in architecture
or the design arts, knew little about plants beyond those he farmed, and studied
engineering only briefly with a Massachusetts divinity student who taught surveying
to pay the rent. Olmsted knew only that he wanted to do *something*, and something
good. "I want to make myself useful in the world," he confided to classmate Frederick
Kingsbury in 1846, "to make others happy."[1]

Olmsted's formal education may have been haphazard, but the peripatetic youth read voraciously, devouring Emerson, Ruskin, Lowell, Timothy Dwight's *Travels in New-England and New-York*, William Gilpin's *Forest Scenery*, and *An Essay on the Picturesque* by Uvedale Price—the latter two of which he would later force on all who came to work in the Olmsted office, to be read "seriously, as a student of law would read Blackstone."[2] And before even books was the landscape itself. Olmsted developed a keen and probing eye, tutored on long childhood jaunts through field and forest with his parents—"really tours," he later wrote, "in search of the picturesque" that took him to some of the most scenic places in New England and New York. "I had been driven over most of the charming roads of the Connecticut Valley and its confluents," he recalled of his boyhood years, "through the White Hills and along most of the New England coast." Olmsted became a critical observer of place and landscape, absorbing lessons that no school could have provided at the time (there were no landscape architecture programs then; the first, at Harvard, would be founded by his son in 1900). "I took more interest than most travelers do in the arrangement and aspect of homesteads," he wrote, "and generally in what may be called the sceneric character of what came before me."[3]

Olmsted eventually gained the confidence to make "modest practical applications" of the lessons he absorbed over the years—"applications . . . to the choice of a neighborhood, of the position and aspect of the homestead, the placing, grouping and relationships with the dwelling of barns, stables and minor outbuildings." He found that even the humblest rural compound could gain from wise spatial planning—"that even in frontier log cabins," he wrote, "a good deal was lost or gained of pleasure according to the ingenuity and judgment used in such matters." There were also, Olmsted reasoned, "lines of outlook and of in-look," the shaping of views by adding or removing plant material, the importance of "unity of foreground, middle ground and back ground" and the choreography of overall scenic effect—both from without and "within the field of actual operations." Trees, too, were muses from earliest youth. One of Olmsted's fondest childhood memories was seeing a towering column of American elms that his elderly grandfather, Benjamin Olmsted, had planted as a child in the 1760s. Marveling at how once-scrawny whips could become such giants, the boy yearned to set out elms of his own. "I wanted my father to let me help him plant trees and he did," Olmsted wrote, "but they were not placed with sufficient forecast and have since all been cut down."[4]

Forecast—not merely sufficient, but prescient, even prophetic—would be the leitmotif of Olmsted's long and fruitful career. It began in earnest in September 1857, when he applied for the superintendent job to build a "central park" in the middle of Manhattan. Apprised of the political nature of the project and its Board of Commissioners, Olmsted pulled all the strings he could, fortifying his application with "a number of weighty signatures"—including those of Peter Cooper and Washington Irving. Even so, he barely made the grade. The project engineer, a gifted but jinxed West Point graduate named Egbert Ludovicus Viele, took an immediate dislike to the wellborn Yankee. When Olmsted called to present his qualifications, Viele made him wait most of an afternoon before trying to dodge out of the office. The tenacious Olmsted followed Viele to his streetcar, finally having a chance to plead his case in front of the weary commuters—only to have Viele tell him he preferred to hire a "practical man." Nor was the board much swayed by Olmsted, who won its approval by just a single vote—cast by a commissioner opposed to the candidate but impressed nonetheless with his endorsement from the great fabulist. With Viele as his boss, Olmsted gradually shaped the park's army of laborers—all of whom owed their jobs to graft and were accustomed to doing little work—into an effective field force. Thus far, the vast project had been guided by Viele's survey and site plan. But the Viele plan was a holdover from the first Central Park Commission, a body appointed by Mayor Fernando Wood and subsequently dissolved. The present commission, answering to the governor, chose to wipe the slate clean. They were quietly encouraged in this by a young English architect named Calvert Vaux, who had worked with the Hudson Valley landscape designer Andrew Jackson Downing until the latter's tragic death in 1852. Downing had spent years advocating for a great New York park, and Vaux felt duty bound to make sure its design met his late friend's high standards. He was fiercely critical of the Viele plan, pointing out that it would be "a disgrace to the City and to the memory of Mr. Downing to have this plan carried out." Vaux's campaign was successful: in October 1857 the commissioners tossed the Viele plan and announced a competition for a new park design. Vaux, keen on entering the contest himself but unfamiliar with the site, wisely sought to partner with Olmsted, whom he had met through Downing. Olmsted initially declined the invitation out of respect for Viele, who was enraged that his plan—prepared at his own expense—had been unceremoniously scuttled (he later sued the city and was awarded damages). Olmsted changed his mind only after Viele "took occasion to express, rather contemptuously, complete indifference as to whether Mr. Olmsted entered the competition or not." Thus did the hapless Viele help make himself the Salieri to Olmsted's Mozart.[5]

Olmsted and Vaux worked nights and weekends on their entry at Vaux's Gramercy Park home, where family and friends were enlisted to help with the drawing. That Olmsted knew the rocky site so well proved invaluable, for he was able to clarify details of topography missing from the survey maps provided to competitors. To further inform their proposal, Olmsted and Vaux would rove the vast site "together by moonlight to discuss features of the plan, with the land before them." Their proposal, the "Greensward," was completed just hours before the deadline, the last entry to be submitted. Olmsted and Vaux won the competition, of course, their plan selected from a field of more than thirty submissions. Its genius was its unity, conceived as a whole and orchestrated like a symphony. "The Park throughout," wrote Olmsted and Vaux, "is a single work of art, and as such subject to the primary law of every work of art, namely, that it shall be framed upon a single, noble motive, to which the design of all its parts, in some more or less subtle way, shall be confluent and helpful." Their park was charged with a simple twofold purpose: to boost the physical health of city dwellers—especially the poor and working classes—with "pure and wholesome air, to act through the lungs"; and to inoculate New Yorkers against the presumed moral ills of urban life by treating them with a distillate of nature, a concentrated dose of rural landscape. It would work by providing "objects of vision" that countervailed "those of the streets and houses," bringing remedial relief "by impressions on the mind and suggestions to the imagination." As Olmsted explained, the prevailing purpose of the park was

> to supply to the hundreds of thousands of tired workers, who have no opportunity to spend their summers in the country, a specimen of God's handiwork that shall be to them, inexpensively, what a month or two in the White Mountains or the Adirondacks is, at great cost, to those in easier circumstances.

And the need for such a prophylaxis would only increase; for "the time will come," Olmsted foretold, "when New York will be built up, when all the grading and filling will be done, and when the picturesquely-varied, rocky formations of the Island will have been converted into formations for rows of monotonous straight streets, and piles of erect buildings." Only then, with the city grown up all around Central Park, surrounding it with "an artificial wall, twice as high as the Great Wall of China," would its role as a mighty green antidote to the metropolis be fulfilled.[6]

This notion that cities are best paired with nature, that the artifice of *urbs* should be annealed by *rus*, is one of the founding principles of American urbanism. Its roots run deep, to the Founders themselves. Most were literate, landed gentlemen, well tutored in the classics, who looked to Europe as the arbiter of all things civilized but nonetheless regarded its great cities as something best kept away from America's vernal shores. They believed that cities were antithetical to the American democratic experiment, that the new republic would flourish best if its citizens lived close to the land, each peaceably tilling his own soil. As John Adams explained in 1786, "a people living chiefly by agriculture, in small numbers, sprinkled over large tracts of land ... are not subject to those panics and transports, those contagions of madness and folly, which are seen in countries where large numbers live in small places." Urbanism of the Old World sort—especially of industrializing London and Manchester, with their grim factories and exploited workers—must be avoided at all costs. No one made this case more forcefully than that Lord of Monticello, Thomas Jefferson, to whom farmers were angels in overalls. "Those who labour in the earth," he wrote in *Notes on Virginia*, "are the chosen people of God, if ever he had a chosen people." To Jefferson, agrarians kept alive the moral flame of civilization. "The mobs of great cities," on the other hand, "add just so much to the support of pure government," he wrote, "as sores do to the strength of the human body."[7]

In the Jacksonian era, a hefty dose of nationalism was added to this mix. In its wild beauty and seeming infinite abundance, American nature came to be regarded as a defining element of national identity—a possession at least equal in value to the Old World's vast legacy of cultural achievement. "If we have neither old castles nor old associations," wrote Downing, "we have at least, here and there, old trees that can teach us lessons of antiquity, not less instructive and poetical than the ruins of a past age." By now, American cities were growing—Jefferson and Adams notwithstanding—like weeds in a field of manure, making it more urgent than ever that hallowed "rural values" be sustained in the face of urbanization, that the chimera of "Nature's Nation" be sustained. New strategies were contrived to bring town and country into harmonious union, to temper the city with a tincture of nature. Nothing seemed to accomplish this more effectively than planting forest trees on city streets—and not just any tree, but that fast-growing denizen of the lowland woods, the American elm. The tree, *Ulmus americana*, had long been a presence in the New England landscape, and was planted in rows on roads and lanes in the Connecticut River valley as early as the 1780s. But it wasn't until the 1840s, as a "new craving for spatial beauty" swept across the region, that the practice of planting street elms became institutionalized and spread throughout New England.[8]

The drivers of this movement were improvement societies founded by civic-minded townsfolk to carry out a variety of betterment and beautification projects. They were inspired by the same romanticism that gave us the rural cemeteries, and fortified by popular writing on horticulture and landscape improvement by Downing and others. But the village and town improvers were also responding to something darker—the effects of economic decline. With the region's rocky soils and harsh winters, farming in New England was never easy. After the Erie Canal opened in 1825, its agriculturalists were suddenly competing with upstate New York and eastern Ohio, fertile regions now plugged in to New York City. Eastern markets were soon flooded with cheap produce, sending New England's rural economy into a tailspin. Many Yankee farmers headed west themselves, while the best and brightest youth of its towns and villages left for the region's booming cities. "What is it that is coming over our New England villages, that looks like deterioration and running down?" asked Berkshire minister Orville Dewey; "Is our life going out of us to enrich the great West?" Perhaps, the improvers reasoned, the youth might stay if the townscape were made newly appealing. The village improved and enhanced might "instill in the youth that love of beauty and morality which would enable him to withstand the attraction of urban wealth and vice." Spatial beauty, in other words, could be weaponized to counter the toxic effects of a failing economy.[9]

The almost universal activity of the early village improvement societies was planting elms, a fact attested to by the name of the first such group in New England—the Elm Tree Association of Sheffield, Massachusetts. Yankee improvers chose the elm for a number of reasons: it was easily obtained in any lowland forest, transplanted easily, grew like a rocket, and was tough as nails—at least in an age before asphalt, buried utilities, and Dutch elm disease. But more than anything, it was the extraordinary beauty of the American elm that made it such a universal favorite, endowed with formal and aesthetic properties—a high spreading crown, a fountain-spray tumble of branches and limbs, small leaves that allow dappled sunlight to reach the ground—that made it ideal for street and city use. These qualities were identified early on by European botanical explorers. The Milanese botanist Luigi Castiglioni, who traveled extensively in North America in the 1780s, described the American elm as "remarkable for the beauty of its branches, which are numerous, very wide-spreading and pendant"—features that made it "preferable to the European for . . . avenues and other ornamental plantings." A French contemporary, François André Michaux, admired the elm's "long, flexible, pendulous branches, bending into regular arches and floating lightly in the air." He allowed that while the sycamore might exceed it in girth and "amplitude of its head," the elm possessed "a more majestic appearance . . . owing to its great elevation, to the disposition of its principal limbs, and to the extreme elegance of its summit." This, wrote Michaux, was "the most magnificent vegetable of the temperate zone."[10]

An immense American elm on the Elmwood Farm in Conway, New Hampshire, 1930. The tree was planted as a one-inch whip by Leavitt Hill in 1780, and was for many years the largest in New England. Photograph by Ernest Henry Wilson. Photographic Archives of the Arnold Arboretum, Harvard University.

The New England of Olmsted's youth was a paradise of elms. The tree was so extensively planted throughout the region, so celebrated in its literature and art, that it had become an abiding symbol of New England—a sylvan counterpoint to the whitewashed church steeple. "In no other part of the country," wrote Charles Sprague Sargent of the Arnold Arboretum, "is there a tree which occupies the same position in the affection of the people as the Elm does in that of the inhabitants of New England." Brooklyn's Henry Ward Beecher, firebrand minister of Plymouth Church, was a lot more effusive: "The Elms of New England! They are as much a part of her beauty as the columns of the Parthenon were the glory of its architecture." To him, elms were "tabernacles of the air" that consecrated the profanest street. "We had rather walk beneath an avenue of elms," he confessed, "than inspect the noblest cathedral that art ever accomplished." The queen of New England's elm-tossed towns was New Haven. By the 1850s it had become as famous for its trees as for Yale College, exemplary of a uniquely American kind of city—a city in harmony with nature, where *rus* and *urbs* were one. Its pièce de résistance was Temple Street,

Temple Street, New Haven, c. 1865. New Haven Colony Historical Society.

on the New Haven Green. Though the thoroughfare was named for its three houses of worship, its cloistral elms ultimately stole the show—overshadowing the churches both literally and figuratively. As the trees matured to form a great vaulted roof overhead, the street became a temple itself—"a temple not built with hands, fairer than any minster." New Haven was a must-see stop on the American grand tour. Emmeline Wortely, a visiting Englishwoman, noted that the "profusion of its stately elms" made New Haven "not only one of the most charming, but one of the most 'unique' cities I ever beheld." Charles Dickens visited New Haven on his celebrated 1842 tour of the United States. He praised the city's "rows of grand old elm-trees," which seemed "to bring about a kind of compromise between town and country; as if each had met the other half-way, and shaken hands upon it."[11]

Elm Street was a Yankee invention, but it hardly stayed put. It was sped afield by the same "westward transit of New England culture," in the words of Whitney Cross, that diffused so many Yankee traditions—from jack-o'-lanterns and Thanksgiving to the Cape Cod house.[12] The spread of the urban elm forest tracked closely that of the New England diaspora. Upstate New York was directly in its path, and by the late nineteenth century its principal cities—Albany, Syracuse, Rochester,

Buffalo—were as heavily elmed as those in New England. So too hundreds of towns and cities across the Midwestern states. New York City, with its Dutch heritage and polyglot culture, proved more resistant. Certainly *Ulmus americana* could be found in the city's parks, but the tree never quite entered the cultural bloodstream the way it had in New England. There is but a single "Elm Street" within the bounds of New York City today—hidden on the north shore of Staten Island—while two others were long ago lost to name changes. A mile-long Elm Street once ran through the Bushwick section of Brooklyn but was made an extension of Hart Street sometime before 1898. Another Elm Street extended from Chambers Street to Broome Street in Manhattan, most of which was renamed Lafayette Street around 1900. Only a tiny (treeless) fragment survived near City Hall, but even that was later rubbed out—rechristened Elk Street by Mayor Fiorello La Guardia to honor his fraternal lodge. Queens has Elmhurst, of course—contrived by a real estate developer in 1897—while Elm Avenue in Flushing was not laid out until the 1920s. There is a short Elm Place in the Fordham section of the Bronx, and an even shorter one in Brooklyn (all of 370 feet long). Historically, the greatest concentration of street elms on Long Island was in those Anglo east-end towns—Bridgehampton, Sag Harbor, East Hampton—originally settled by Yankees and closer in spirit to New England than to New York.

Species aside, both New York and Brooklyn lagged behind New England in planting public trees—and in taking up the causes of betterment and beautification generally. As late as 1891, the enchantingly named Tree Planting and Fountain Society of Brooklyn could describe that city's sylva as "creatures of chance, with little taste in selection and less care in planting." On the other hand, what trees New Yorkers did set out in parks and public ways suggests a more catholic attitude about species relative to New England, with its single-minded passion for the native elm. Indeed, one of the most popular street trees in nineteenth-century New York was a Chinese species, the ailanthus or Tree of Heaven (*Ailanthus altissima*). Frederick Van Wyck, chronicler of Keskachauge whom we met in chapter 1, recalled fifty-foot-tall ailanthus trees on "all the residential side streets, and also up Fifth Avenue" in Chelsea in the 1860s.[13] In Greenwich Village, ailanthus trees "formed the principal umbrage" of Washington Square Park, as related by the narrator in the 1880 Henry James novel *Washington Square*. Its day in the sun was short, however; for the very plantsmen who popularized the ailanthus were soon demonizing it as a foul-smelling alien. The denunciations could be meanly racist: Andrew Jackson Downing called the ailanthus a "petted Chinaman" with the "fair outside and the treacherous heart of the Asiatics."[14] It was our Connecticut Yankee, Frederick Law Olmsted, who made the American elm part of the New York scene. A more fitting emissary could hardly be found; for not only was Olmsted a child of the Connecticut River valley—birthplace of "Elm Street" in America—but he had elms in his blood, so to speak. The name Olmsted, which first appears in the Domesday Book of the County of Essex in 1086, is a variant of *Elmsted*, a parish in the Hundred of Tendring from which the Olmsted clan hailed. As explained in a 1912 genealogy on the Olmsted family, *Elmsted* is a Saxon name that literally means "the place of Elms," evidently because the landscape there was once "remarkable for the growth of trees of that kind." In New York, Olmsted would re-create New Haven's Temple Street—"grandest arch of trees on the globe"—in the Central Park Mall. And in Brooklyn, as we will see, he would lay out the longest elm-lined streets in America.[15]

The man who lured Olmsted and Vaux across the East River is one of the unsung heroes of New York's urban landscape—James S. T. Stranahan. Stranahan is to Brooklyn what Andrew Haswell Green was to Manhattan. Green, whom we met in the introduction, drafted the 1897 consolidation plan that created the Greater City of New York—an initiative that had Stranahan's full backing. As comptroller of the Central Park Commission, Green had authority over the entire park project. He was a deeply principled public servant who defended the park from plunder at the hands of "political harpies ready to pounce on it at the slightest relaxation of vigilance." But Green was also obstinate and humorless, intolerant of dissent, and unable to "delegate plenary powers to subordinates . . . and refrain from dictatorial interference in the details of their work." First among his victims were Olmsted and Vaux, whose constant quarrels with Green ultimately led both men to sever ties with the project. Brooklyn was a very different story. The political culture there was, if anything, even more crooked than New York's. But in Stranahan, Olmsted and Vaux found both a public official with the mettle to keep graft at bay and a patron who understood the importance of artistic freedom. From the start, their relationship was one of mutual esteem and admiration. To Stranahan, Olmsted and Vaux were "the ablest landscape architects in this or any other country."[16]

A native of Peterboro, New York, Stranahan moved to Brooklyn in 1845 to find his fortune with the Atlantic Dock Company, developer of Brooklyn's first deepwater port (in present-day Red Hook). He subsequently served as an alderman and was elected to Congress in 1855. Four years later, legislation passed in Albany authorizing "the selection and location of certain grounds for Public Parks" in the city of Brooklyn. After a lengthy process in which citizens were "invited to submit their opinions," three principal sites were chosen by a commission—one on the Queens line in Ridgewood that included a reservoir then used for Brooklyn's water supply (today's Highland Park); a second in Bay Ridge that afforded "magnificent views of the bay" (now Dyker Beach Park and Golf Course); and a third on the moraine near Flatbush known as Prospect Hill, where much of the Battle of Brooklyn took place. The commissioners pointed out that parks at these three locations,

James S. T. Stranahan monument, Prospect Park, 1891. Sculpted by Frederick William MacMonnies on a pedestal by Stanford White. Photograph by author, 2018.

chained together by a "grand drive or carriage road," would create an amenity far greater than the sum of its parts—"a public attraction unsurpassed . . . in the world." This, as far as I am aware, is the very first mention of a *system* of parks and open space in the United States—an idea Olmsted himself would run with first in Brooklyn, as we will see, and later in Buffalo (1868) and Boston (1878).[17]

Though not their official charge, the 1859 commissioners were clearly also searching for a single major site for a park like the one then under way in Manhattan. And while "no single location for a great central park, suitable both to the present state and future growth of the city, presented itself," the commissioners concurred with public opinion that Prospect Hill—with its rolling meadows, old-growth woods, and "commanding views of Brooklyn, New York, Jamaica Bay, and the Ocean beyond"— would do well for the purpose. On April 17, 1860, an act was passed in Albany "to lay out a Public Park and a Parade Ground for the city of Brooklyn." A second commission was appointed, with Stranahan as its president. Its charge was to give Brooklyn a great landscaped park like the one in Manhattan—"a public place to be known as Prospect Park." This is, of course, a wonderful example of bantam-weight Brooklyn jabbing at its mighty next-door neighbor—Gotham's second city eagerly straining to upstage the first. What no one anticipated, least of all Stranahan and the Board of Commissioners of Prospect Park, was that the Brooklyn project would end up the greater of the two parks—indeed the finest and most visionary work Olmsted and Vaux would ever create. But they were not, alas, the first to be hired for the job. In a redux of the drama that had played out earlier in Manhattan, it was the ubiquitous Egbert Ludovicus Viele whom Stranahan first brought on to execute both a survey and a ground plan for the vast Brooklyn site.[18]

But Viele once again failed to rise to the occasion, producing an artless and uninspired piece of work. Ostensibly looking to the site's "natural topographical features" as a basis for improvement, he applied "the skillful hand of UNPERCEIVED ART" to make nature's "blended beauties . . . more harmonious." This meant, Viele lectured, "the cautious pruning of trees, the nice distribution of flowers and plants of tender growth, the introduction of the green slope of velvet lawn." Ever the engineer, Viele spent six pages discussing drainage details, and another five on "theories of manuring." But his real flaw was accepting the park site as given, with hundred-foot-wide Flatbush Avenue piercing its heart, instead of recognizing that it would be fatal to his very own declaration of the park's purpose—"as a rural resort, where the people of all classes, escaping from the glare, and glitter, and turmoil of the city, might find relief for the mind." Split like Solomon's baby, Viele's Prospect Park would have in reality been two middling parks forever divided by a busy urban thoroughfare. It's not clear whether Viele simply lacked the vision to anticipate that Flatbush might be more than a country lane, or if—soldier before all—he was just following orders. Viele was a complicated soul, a man of old Dutch stock proud of his trace Iroquois ancestry, despite having eagerly fought in the Indian Wars. Ironically, he was Olmstedian in many ways—a politically astute sanitary reformer who helped create New York's first Board of Health; a naturalist who could write lyrically about spiders and moths ("little messengers of the night"); a proficient engineer who conceived the Harlem Ship Canal. Viele's spectacular 1865 *Sanitary and topographical map of the*

Detail of Egbert L. Viele, *Sanitary and topographical map of the City and Island of New York*, 1865. The New York Public Library.

City and Island of New York is still consulted on major building projects. But as Viele himself often put it, he was a "practical man" who approached the world as an engineering problem and lacked "the springing imagination," as M. M. Graff put it, "that distinguishes an artist from an artisan." He had minimal knowledge of aesthetics, and his plans for both the New York and Brooklyn parks lacked any sense of spatial structure, hierarchy, or sequence—elements vital to a large urban landscape.[19]

Thankfully Brooklyn was spared a Viele park, this time by the winds of history. The Civil War began three months after Viele submitted his Prospect Park plan. He answered the first call for volunteers, tendering his resignation to the Board of Commissioners to take command of Company K of the Seventh New York Militia. Viele's war service was distinguished. He helped open the Potomac River to Washington, served as military governor of Norfolk, Virginia, and participated in the siege of Fort Pulaski on the Georgia coast—defended, ironically, by a distant Southern kinsman of his Central Park nemesis, Confederate colonel Charles Hart Olmstead.[20] Viele returned to Brooklyn after the war only to find that Calvert Vaux had been there already. Stranahan had been unsatisfied with Viele's plan and reached out to Vaux; the men met in early January 1865. Vaux immediately began lobbying Olmsted—who had taken an ill-starred job in California managing the land holdings of the Mariposa Mining Company—to join him back in New York for this exciting new commission. He delivered a preliminary report to Stranahan and the park commissioners in February, and was hired that June to draft a new plan for the park. Begged, cajoled, and bullied by Vaux, Olmsted returned from the West Coast that November. Their Prospect Park report was delivered in January 1866.

Contrary to Viele's approach, their very first point was that the "inconvenient shape" of the site—particularly its "complete bisection . . . by a broad and conspicuous thoroughfare"—effectively made a great park impossible. "It is obvious that this division," they wrote, "must seriously interfere with the impressions of amplitude and continuous extent" vital to any urban parkscape. Their first recommendation, then, was that the entire site east of Flatbush Avenue—the area today encompassing the Botanic Garden, Brooklyn Museum, and Brooklyn Public Library—"be abandoned for park purposes." They then urged the commissioners to extend the park by acquiring additional lands south of the original site—a "broad plain, overlooked on the park side by the highest ground in the vicinity" that they suggested would be ideal for a lake. Turning to the park's internal design, the partners sketched out a theoretical basis for their proposal. "A scene in nature is made up of various parts," they explained, each with an "individual character and its possible ideal." Mere imitation of nature would never suffice, nor could chance alone be relied upon to gather in harmony "the best possible ideals of each separate part." Design, however, could very well bring it about. "It is evident," they asserted, "that an attempt to accomplish this artificially is not impossible," so long as it was predicated on "a proper study of the circumstances." "The result," they added, "would be a work of art." All this predictably set off the volcanic Viele more, who accused Olmsted and Vaux of once more copying his work and attempting "to defraud me of the credit due for the first conception of the Park and its plan of improvement."[21]

Unlike the rocky, soil-bare Central Park site, the three-hundred-acre spread in Brooklyn needed little coaxing to become a lush pastoral landscape. Their objective again was to create a place that provided a sense of escape from the "cramped, confined and controlling circumstances of the streets of the town"—that conveyed to the city dweller *a sense of enlarged freedom.* The park would deliver recuperative benefits for both body and mind—giving the lungs "a bath of pure sunny air" while granting the mind "rest from the devouring eagerness and intellectual strife of town life." Pulling this off required scenery of "tranquilizing and poetic character," which Olmsted and Vaux created using the same tripartite arrangement of space employed at Central Park—"three grand elements of pastoral [*sic*] landscape." These included a hilly district "shaded with trees and made picturesque with shrubs" and reminiscent

Future site of Prospect Park lake, c. 1866. Photographer unknown / Museum of the City of New York. X2010.11.14264.

of mountain scenery (like the Ramble in Central Park); a lake district on the low plain south of the original site boundary; and, most importantly, a meadow district with a broad expanse of turf configured by grading and the judicious addition or removal of trees to conceal its full extent from immediate view. This, reasoned the designers, would impel the visitor forward by appealing to that natural desire to discover what lies just beyond the bend. "The observer, resting for a moment to enjoy the scene . . . cannot but hope for still greater space than is obvious before him," Olmsted and Vaux explained; "The imagination of the visitor is thus led instinctively to form the idea that a broad expanse is opening before him." The keen awareness of space and sequence, wholly lacking in Viele's work, is what truly distinguishes the Olmsted and Vaux scheme for Prospect Park. Their spatial genius is nowhere more powerfully evident than at the approach to the park from Grand Army Plaza. The idea was Vaux's, clearly noted—"Principal natural entrance from Brooklyn"—on a rough sketch sent to Olmsted in California. From the street one is delivered into the park via a narrowing path to Vaux's Endale Arch. Its vaulted brick tunnel, dark and close, creates a palpable—and unsettling—sense of compression. But it is fleeting: at the far end is a window of daylight; one spies a glimpse of green. As you hasten through Vaux's venturi, the floodlit opening progressively dilates, until you are delivered with a sudden, almost orgasmic sense of release into the Long Meadow. The vast space unspools before you, peopled with strollers and picnickers, curving seductively out of sight and beckoning you forward into its full embrace.[22]

This deployment of landscape as an elixir for the harried city dweller was, of course, decades premature for Brooklyn. The vast majority of Kings County in the 1860s was agricultural hinterland, and would remain so for years to come. It took no little vision to anticipate a day when Brooklyn would be thickly settled urban terrain. Of this Olmsted and Vaux had little doubt: Brooklyn would ultimately need Prospect Park to serve the same check-valve functions that Central Park did for New York. "We regard Brooklyn," they wrote, "as an integral part of what to-day is the metropolis of the nation, and in the future will be the centre of exchanges for the world." Until then, however, Brooklyn's civic leaders needed their new park to perform an almost opposite set of duties. If Central Park tempered urbanism with a dose of the rural, Prospect Park was meant—initially at least—to introduce a note of urban spatial order and sophistication to an anarchic rural hinterland. It would help make Brooklyn more civilized, more urbane; more like Manhattan. Just like its New York equivalent, Prospect Park would cultivate "cheerful obedience to law" among the people, while advancing their "health, strength, comfort, morality, and future wealth." But it would also prevent Brooklyn from "sinking into the character of a second-rate suburb of the greater city." The great park would boost Brooklyn's stock value, offering—in Stranahan's words—"strong inducements to the affluent to remain in our city, who are now too often induced to change their residences by the seductive influences of the New York park."[23]

Prospect Park is a masterpiece of landscape design that would never have happened without Calvert Vaux. But it was Olmsted who looked past the park to see it as the engine of something greater still. Vaux makes no mention of extending the park's civilizing reach in his early plans or correspondence with Stranahan. Only

Frederick Law Olmsted and Calvert Vaux, *Design for Prospect Park in the City of Brooklyn*, 1870. From William G. Bishop, *Manual of the Common Council of the City of Brooklyn* (1871).

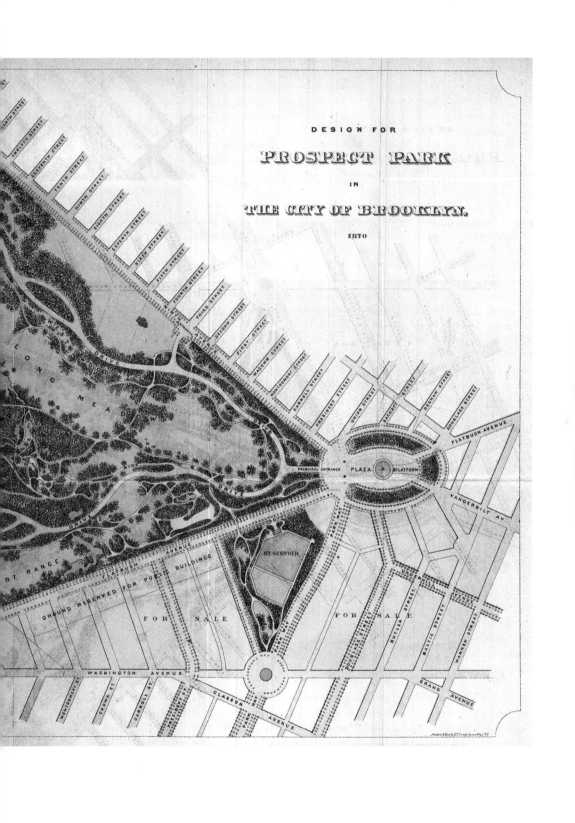

DESIGN FOR

PROSPECT PARK

IN

THE CITY OF BROOKLYN.

1870

after Olmsted returns from his California junket do we begin to see the park described in terms of planning the larger metropolis. Unlike Central Park, a capsule of
rusticity locked in the city grid, Olmsted saw Prospect Park as the core of an open
space system whose green tendrils would reach across Brooklyn and Queens and
even back over the East River to Central Park—a "system of grounds . . . designed for
the recreation of the whole people of the metropolis and their customers and guests
from all parts of the world for centuries to come." The idea was first sketched out in
Olmsted and Vaux's 1866 report to the Prospect Park commissioners. On the accom-
panying plan, they show a road stubbed out from the park's southern entrance—the
start of a "shaded pleasure drive," picturesque in character and free of commercial
"embarrassments." Olmsted did not specify the route of this drive, except to say
that its destination should "unquestionably be the ocean beach." And that was not
all. "It has occurred to us," he added, that "a similar road may be demanded in the
future which shall be carried through the rich country lying back of Brooklyn, until
it can be turned . . . so as to approach the East River, and finally reach the shore at or
near Ravenswood." Olmsted is even more vague as to where this "grand municipal
promenade" would start, except that it would branch off the first drive somewhere
south of the park. The most logical place for this—which Olmsted almost certainly
had in mind—is Kings Highway, the ancient Indian trading path that played such
a crucial role in the Battle of Brooklyn. In any case, at Ravenswood—just east of
Roosevelt Island in Long Island City—the drive could "be thrown" via bridge or
ferry over the East River to hook up with "one of the broad streets leading directly
into the Central Park." The twenty-mile loop would allow a carriage to be "driven
on the half of a summer's day," wrote Olmsted, "through the most interesting parts
both of the cities of Brooklyn and New York [and] through their most attractive
and characteristic suburbs." The *Eagle* was more expansive, noting that Olmsted's
"grand highway of intercourse"—from Prospect Park to East New York and then
"over a suspension bridge at Blackwell's Island into Central Park"—would "unite in
one common interest the two finest parks on the American continent."[24]

Over the next two years, Olmsted's ideas on Prospect Park's "suburban connections" evolved into no less than a treatise on the future of Brooklyn. This was
presented to Stranahan and the commissioners in January 1868, and published
two months later with a typically long-winded Victorian title—*Observations on the
Progress of Improvements in Street Plans . . . with Special Reference to The Park-Way
Proposed to be Laid Out in Brooklyn*. Prefaced by a fourteen-page discourse on the
history of urban form, Olmsted's exposition argued that Brooklyn could seize its
future by planning for the vast population growth that would invariably come its
way. Manhattan, waterbound and thus "in the condition of a walled town," would
soon run out of land to build on. "Brooklyn is New York outside the walls," wrote
Olmsted, where there was "ample room for an extension of the habitation part of the
metropolis upon a plan fully adapted to the most intelligent requirements of modern
town life." The key to bringing this about was those shaded pleasure drives first discussed in 1866—what Olmsted now termed *parkways*. Extrusions of the park itself,
the parkways would "extend its attractions" across new terrain while also serving as
structural elements to guide street layout and residential development. The scenic

thoroughfares—upon which "driving, riding, and walking can be conveniently pursued in association with pleasant people"—would create, like freshets in the desert, valuable real estate wherever they ran. "The further the process can be carried, the more will Brooklyn, as a whole, become desirable as a place of residence."[25]

For all his inventive genius, the parkway was not sui generis Olmsted, but rather an idea he adapted from Continental precedents. Olmsted had been sent to Europe by the Board of Commissioners of Central Park in September 1859, and spent the next two months touring parks and public works in Liverpool, London, Paris, Brussels, and Dublin. Olmsted was most impressed by what he saw in Paris, where his host was Jean-Charles Adolphe Alphand, the brilliant engineer who had helped Georges-Eugène Haussmann transform Paris under Napoleon III. Introduced to Alphand by a former Central Park commissioner who had retired to France, Olmsted spent ten days in Paris "examining as carefully as practicable . . . all its pleasure-grounds and promenades." The visit "opened his eyes," writes Elizabeth Macdonald, "to the prospect of landscape architects acting as city planners, and he brought this vision to Brooklyn." Olmsted visited the Bois de Vincennes and the gardens of Versailles, and made no fewer than eight trips to the Bois de Boulogne. He also toured the Avenue de l'Impératrice (today's Avenue Foch), which had opened five years earlier to connect the Bois de Boulogne to the Place de l'Étoile. The commodious avenue was 430 feet wide, with separated bridle paths, carriage drives, and walkways in the center, and bordered by hundred-foot landscaped strips and service roads on either side. This road, and Unter den Linden in Berlin—with its central carriageway and twin pedestrian malls—were examples of what Olmsted termed the "fourth stage of street arrangements." They were both source and departure point for Olmsted's next, presumably ultimate stage of street design—the parkway—to

Vue de l'Avenue du bois de Boulogne, c. 1854. State Library Victoria, Australia.

consist of a "central road-way, prepared with express reference to pleasure-riding and driving," flanked on the inner sides by "ample public walks" and, beyond those, "ordinary paved, traffic road-ways" along which villas and homes would be built. The twin pedestrian malls would be planted with triple rows of "trees . . . of the most stately character."[26]

Olmsted envisioned three great parkways radiating outward from Prospect Park—one running east toward Queens before turning north to the East River at Ravenswood; one extending southwest to Bay Ridge and Fort Hamilton; and one running straight south to Coney Island. This infrastructure would not only make for long pleasure drives, but unlock Brooklyn's urban future by irrigating a vast field for residential development of the choicest sort—a "continuous neighborhood . . . of a more than usually open, elegant, and healthy character." This would give Brooklyn something its island-bound rival was unlikely to get anytime soon; for, as Olmsted pointed out, Andrew Green had already dismissed the idea of laying out "fanciful" avenues north of Central Park. The parkways would give Brooklyn "special advantages as a place of residence," wrote Olmsted, "to that portion of our more wealthy and influential citizens, whose temperament, taste or education leads them to seek . . . a certain amount of rural satisfaction in connection with their city homes." As the *Eagle* predicted, the parkway neighborhoods would "enjoy every advantage of city life . . . and yet be isolated from city traffic, surrounded by luxuriant foliage and enjoy all the pleasures and felicities of rural retirement. They will be in short, a perfect *rus in urbe*." Olmsted's parkway plan was the most ambitious open space system yet proposed for an American city, and "represented," writes Elizabeth Macdonald, "a city-planning vision of a type and scale never before imagined." Though based on a European model, the vast scale and reach of Olmsted's parkways, their function as scaffolding for orderly urban growth—even the idea of joining scattered parks and open spaces into a single metropolitan system—were all unprecedented and "formed a wholly new urban design vision."[27]

The plan gathered little dust. Legislative authority for constructing Olmsted's parkways was secured within several years, and—despite legal challenges from affected landowners—construction on the first drive was well under way by the end of 1872. Variously called Sackett Street Boulevard, Jamaica Park Way, East Parkway, and ultimately *Eastern Parkway*—it was created by widening Sackett Street to 210 feet and running it over the rural countryside east of Prospect Park toward the Queens boundary. A first short segment opened in March 1874, from Grand Army Plaza to Washington Avenue, and by December the drive was complete to Ralph Avenue in Brownsville. That month, the commissioners announced the sale of hundreds of prime building lots—"elegant sites for private residences"—fronting the new drive. Then, after just two miles, Olmsted's projected twenty-mile metropolitan loop petered out, for years ending abruptly "on the brow of a forbidding hill." And while it was later extended—first to Stone Avenue (Mother Gaston Boulevard) and ultimately to Bushwick Avenue at the Cemetery of the Evergreens—the parkway east of Ralph Avenue hardly deserves the name. It was built simply as a wide urban thoroughfare, with few of the landscape amenities that so distinguished the Olmsted original. Ironically, truncated Eastern Parkway

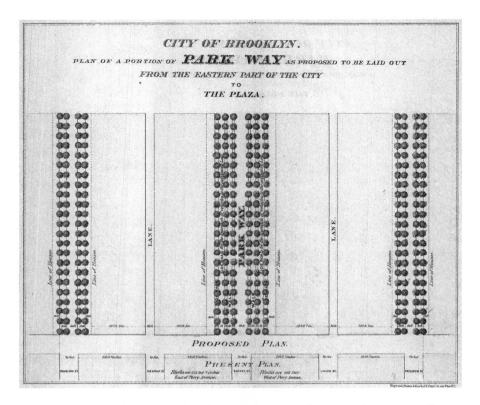

Frederick Law Olmsted and Calvert Vaux, plan view of a portion of Eastern Parkway. From William G. Bishop, *Manual of the Common Council of the City of Brooklyn* (1868).

would be effectively extended a generation later as a new form of parkway—a *motor* parkway that would put Brooklyn within easy reach, not of Manhattan, but of the sandy pleasures of Long Island.[28]

It was another giant of American urbanism, Daniel H. Burnham, who urged that Eastern Parkway be extended across the morainal backbone of Long Island all the way to Montauk Point. As we'll see in chapter 10, Burnham visited New York as a guest of the Brooklyn Committee on City Plan in December 1911, just months before his death. "If you are going to inaugurate city planning in Brooklyn," he said at the time to *Eagle* correspondent Frederick Boyd Stevenson, "you ought to include all Long Island from the East River to Montauk Point." Burnham envisioned "fine streets and boulevards . . . running the entire length and breadth of your beautiful island." As if to conjure Robert Moses, still years away from the start of his legendary career as New York's master builder, Burnham advised that "one man should have all these plans in charge, so they would dovetail one into another and form a perfect, a continuous whole." Burnham's words fell not on dry sand. Within months, an All Long Island Planning Movement was launched, complete with a slogan—"All for One and One for All"—and chock-full of committees of "representative men" from Brooklyn, Queens, and a dozen Long Island towns. Though it was preoccupied with building a "Central Island Boulevard" from Brooklyn to the South Fork—a "splendid and continuous thoroughfare without a break"—the All Long Island Planning

Yankee elms on Eastern Parkway at Nostrand Avenue, 1914. William D. Hassler Photograph Collection, New-York Historical Society.

Movement remains the first step toward coordinated regional planning in metro-politan New York. An extension of Eastern Parkway through the Cemetery of the Evergreens—designed by Andrew Jackson Downing and Brooklyn's second rural cemetery—was approved in 1908 by the state legislature, but there was no money for moving hundreds of bodies from the path of the road. In 1913, the Topographical Bureau of Queens presented a "Grand Central Boulevard" running from Brooklyn across Cypress Hills Cemetery and Forest Park to join William Vanderbilt's Long Island Motor Parkway at the Nassau County line. It was designed with twin thirty-six-foot carriageways separated by a forty-two-foot median and configured in a series of curves "to fit the topography of the country." Though World War I put an end to these plans, the idea of extending Eastern Parkway across Long Island was revived in the 1920s and eventually realized as the Interboro (Jackie Robinson), Grand Central, and Northern State parkways—all built by Burnham's "one man," Robert Moses.[29]

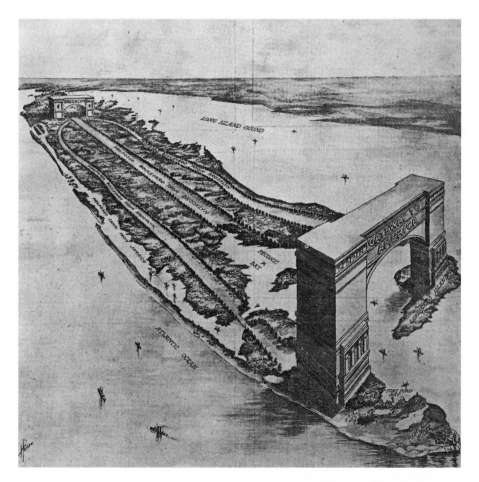

"Gateway to America": Eastern Parkway claims Long Island on behalf of Imperial Brooklyn. From *Brooklyn Daily Eagle* Development Series, April 26, 1912. The three trunk roads cartooned here foreshadowed the Northern State Parkway, Long Island Expressway, and Southern State Parkway. Brooklyn Public Library, Brooklyn Collection.

If Eastern Parkway barely made it to the Queens line, at least it was built. The parkway Olmsted projected from Prospect Park to the Narrows would never see the light of day—at least not in the magnificent form he had in mind. Fort Hamilton Parkway would begin from the southern entrance of the park, today's Machate Circle, and run southwest through the town of New Utrecht. At Seventy-Eighth Street, the south end of Kathy Reilly Triangle today, a second drive would split off, running west along Bennett's or Van Brunt's Lane (Seventy-Ninth Street) to meet the bay at Van Brunt's dock, near the present Seventy-Ninth Street playground on Shore Road. The main road would continue south for its namesake fort, where Olmsted advised that land be secured "for a small Marine Promenade . . . overlooking the Narrows and the Bay." Joining the points was Shore Road, which ran south from the ferry pier at Bay Ridge Avenue around Fort Hamilton to the Dyker marshes. A bill to authorize construction of Fort Hamilton Parkway was introduced at Albany by Senator Henry C. Murphy on March 25, 1869. Though no immediate action was taken, by 1872 Franklin Avenue—which ran along the southern boundary of Prospect Park (Parkside Avenue today)—had been renamed Fort Hamilton Avenue and extended west as Olmsted had suggested. The new road became a parkway by executive fiat—and in name only—in August 1892. This was a wishful christening; for the "parkway," a mere one hundred feet wide between building faces, was not even close to the expansive boulevard Olmsted had in mind, with a carriageway flanked by tree-lined malls and service roads. Now under the jurisdiction of the Parks Department, Fort Hamilton Parkway yet languished; in 1895 it was described as little more than a "mud slough through nearly its entire extent." The following year, however, it was finally upgraded from the park to Sixtieth Street, and to Seventy-Ninth Street by late 1897. And though the *Eagle* now called it a "splendid boulevard," it still hardly deserved the title *parkway*.[30]

By this time, an exciting new possibility had arisen: to connect Fort Hamilton Parkway to the shore via not Seventy-Ninth Street but a new parkway running between Sixty-Sixth and Sixty-Seventh streets. This landscaped drive—initially called Bay Ridge Parkway (a confusing choice, as a thoroughfare of that name had already been approved to replace Seventy-Fifth Street)—would swing south around the bluff where Owl's Head Park is today, improving the old shoreline route to Fort Hamilton and—foreshadowing the Belt Parkway by a generation—possibly on to Coney Island. Shore Road, dating back to the early eighteenth century, was a diamond in the rough—unpaved with steep grades and washed-out gullies, but affording splendid views of the harbor, Staten Island, and lower Manhattan. Given proper "artistic treatment," opined the *New-York Tribune*, it might well become "one of the finest drives in the world," a scenic perch looking out upon "a constantly changing sea-picture." A parkway in place of Shore Road had first been advocated by James Stranahan, so it was only appropriate that the man tapped to create it was Stranahan's old friend and colleague Frederick Law Olmsted. In June 1892 the aging landscape architect was engaged by the Public Driveway and Parkway Commission of Kings County, chaired by former Brooklyn park commissioner Elijah R. Kennedy. Olmsted visited the Bay Ridge site with his son, John Charles, in late December that year. He came to regard the Bay Ridge Parkway as one of the most important projects in the office.

The final plan was delivered in January 1895, just months before Olmsted, his mental state deteriorating rapidly, was forced to retire from active practice. It was Olmsted's last parkway, and among the very last projects he personally oversaw.[31]

Kennedy hoped the pleasure drive would be "a broad, splendid avenue down close to the water" like London's Victoria Embankment on the Thames, or "such as Paris, Pisa, Florence, Rome, Naples and other cities have built down closer to their water sides." Closer to home, he predicted that Bay Ridge Parkway "would easily surpass New York's Riverside Drive." Indeed, Olmsted's drive was laced with planting beds, with a tree-lined carriageway, a sixteen-foot pedestrian mall, and a twenty-foot-wide bicycle path. Sweeping from high bluffs to the shore, it was "a waterside boulevard," the *New-York Tribune* opined, "such as . . . no other city in the world can boast of." Construction was well along by the end of 1897. Beyond the scope of Olmsted's commission but essential to connecting Bay Ridge Parkway to Prospect Park was a nine-block run from Owl's Head to Fort Hamilton Parkway. Title to the required land was in city hands by 1902, and by August the first section—from Fourth Avenue to Colonial Road—had opened. Set in a wide reservation, the drive wound downhill toward Olmsted's road, passing under two "substantial and not wholly inartistic stone bridges" carrying Third Avenue and Ridge Boulevard overhead. Brooklyn's great chain of parkways was nearly complete, and the Bay Ridge drive would be its pièce de résistance—"one of the most notable landscape features of Greater New York" and an attraction "worth a trip," effused the *Eagle*, "across the continent to see." But a chain is only as strong as its weakest link, and for the Bay Ridge Parkway that link was a painfully short last extent of unbuilt road from Fourth Avenue to Fort Hamilton Parkway. By 1897 the commission was out of cash and canceled plans to cover these last few blocks. Enthusiasm for the project waned after Consolidation; then came the world war. The land sat idle for twenty years. By the 1920s, Bay Ridge was home to a large, politically engaged Norwegian community. Keen on securing its vote for the 1925 election, Mayor John F. Hylan directed the Parks Department to use the idled parkway corridor for a memorial to Norse explorer Leif Ericson and "the hardy race of Northmen who . . . fearlessly sailed the Atlantic." Improved in the Moses era, Leif Ericson Park is today a centerpiece of Brooklyn's fast-growing Chinese community. At its western end, the old Bay Ridge Parkway—Shore Road Drive—emerges from a lush green trough to melt back into the street grid.[32]

If Eastern Parkway was only partially realized according to Olmsted's plan, and Fort Hamilton Parkway botched altogether—today "a major pedal-to-the-metal truck route," as *Forgotten New York*'s Kevin Walsh calls it—Ocean Parkway was built almost precisely as the Connecticut Yankee envisioned it in 1868. The five-and-a-half-mile drive was constructed in two sections: from the park to the so-called Prospect Park Fair Grounds at Kings Highway, an early amusement ground and racetrack; and from Kings Highway to Coney Island. Work on the latter ended in 1876, and that November the parkway's full five-mile length was opened to the public, "by whom it was quickly appreciated," reported Stranahan and his commissioners, "and utilized as a delightful, convenient and substantial thoroughfare to the ocean." Ocean Parkway made Brooklyn "the first American city," wrote an admiring

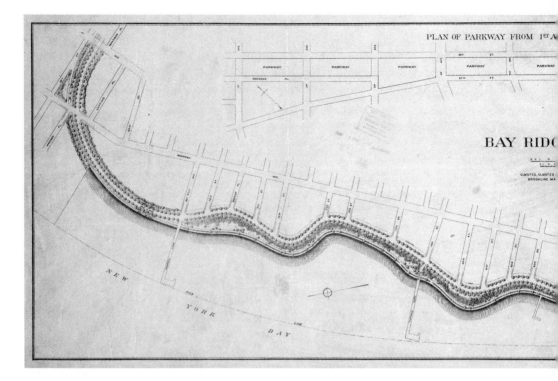

Plan of Bay Ridge Parkway, Olmsted, Olmsted and Elliot, Brookline, Massachusetts, 1895. Lionel Pincus and Princess Firyal Map Division, The New York Public Library.

critic, "to establish a recreative route between the interior and the sea." Running between the city and the great seaside playground of Coney Island, Ocean Parkway was popular from the start—almost *too* popular. The center roadway, seventy feet wide, was paved with twelve inches of fine gravel "from which all stones of large size were excluded," its surface "carefully shaped and rolled until a proper bond was secured." This smooth surface allowed for the fastest operation of carriages— Phaetons, Demi-Landaus, Rockaways—anywhere in New York. The traffic, which thronged the road on a fine summer weekend, moved according to unwritten rules, at least at first. There was no dividing line; drivers kept to the right, then as now, though the travel lanes expanded or contracted according to traffic volume—a vernacular, swarm-source form of zipper-lane or "barrier transfer" technology used on major commuter routes today. "In the mornings and early afternoons, when most carriages were heading toward Coney Island," writes Macdonald, "the southward flow took up much of the roadway," while in evenings, with the great throng heading home, "the northward flow predominated." From the start, farmers and teamsters were also tempted to use Ocean Parkway's fine carriageway, though most stayed on the side roads. Pleasure drivers were incensed by the heavy commercial vehicles, which rutted the pavement and vexed their good nostrils with the smell of cow shit and coal dust. Prohibiting such traffic from the central road—"business wagons of every kind, whether heavy or light, including trucks"—was first suggested in 1884 and made law by 1896. This practice was extended into the automobile age: the

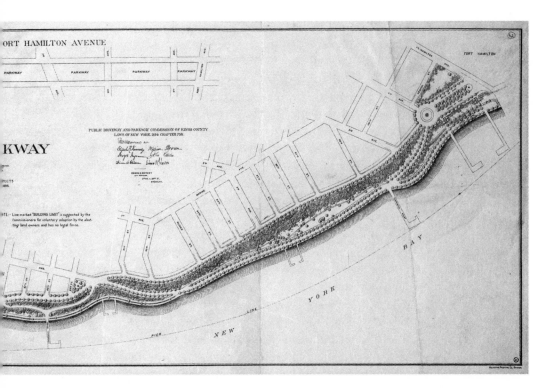

motor parkways of the 1920s and 1930s in Westchester and Long Island all similarly banned trucks and buses, and still do today.[33]

Ocean Parkway also gave us the very first dedicated bicycle lane in America. By 1890, bicyclists—or "wheelmen," as they were known at the time—had become so numerous on the parkway that the Brooklyn Park Commission required riders to register at the superintendent's office at the Litchfield Villa and wear a conspicuous numbered badge on their left breast. Bicycling was an elite pastime, and the city's many wheelmen clubs supported these codes not only to promote their sport as a respectable activity but to filter out the riffraff. "Requiring bicyclists to register," writes Macdonald, "was an effective way of discouraging lower-class people . . . from riding on the parkways." Then, in 1894, park commissioner Frank Squier consented to a petition from Brooklyn's well-organized bicycling clubs to create a special bike lane along the parkway's western mall. The Parks Department provided the labor to build the track, and the wheelmen raised the $3,500 needed to purchase the finely crushed bluestone for its surface. The Ocean Parkway bicycle path opened on a perfect summer day in June 1895, with a three-division parade organized by the Good Roads Association. The procession began at Eastern Parkway and Bedford Avenue, led by a military escort from the Thirteenth and Twenty-Third infantry regiments and followed by a bicycle division of the Brooklyn Police Department—the first bike-mounted police unit in the country. They wound around Grand Army Plaza and into Prospect Park before heading down Ocean Parkway for Coney Island. Some ten thousand "wheelmen and women" rode past the reviewing stand at Newkirk Avenue, representing fifty-eight bicycle clubs and unions—from the

Whirling Dervishes to the Harlem Wheelmen (with their "very jaunty air"). Carriages, horses, and even pedestrians were prohibited from the new path. Bicyclists were forbidden to coast, had to keep below twelve miles per hour—"scorchers" would be arrested—and had to "keep their feet upon the pedals . . . at all times." The bike path was too popular. The more fanatical wheelmen—forebears of the Lycra-clad jackasses who slap tourists on the Brooklyn Bridge today—complained of women and children clogging the path, which turned into a "mudway" after the smallest thunderstorm. They demanded that the rule banning wheelmen from the main carriageway—"a very ungraceful attempt to discriminate"—be rescinded. Instead, a second bike path—on the east side of Ocean Parkway—was opened the following summer to even greater fanfare. The *New York Times* estimated the spectators at more than 100,000—"stretching along the entire length of the boulevard . . . a fat line of enthusiastic people, five deep on either side."[34]

The next time you find yourself traffic bound in an Uber on Ocean or Eastern parkways, recall that these arterials were conceived not just as transportation infrastructure, but as instruments of urban order projected across the countryside. Essential to their civilizing mission was to inject into the "chaos" of rustic space a perfected, idealized symbol of American nature. As we've seen, the regimented rows of forest trees that lined Olmsted's parkways were not merely ornamental but a vaccination against the presumed enervating effects of the impending metropolis— the great wave of urban development that, by 1930, had swamped Brooklyn's last

Opening day parade, Coney Island cycle path, Ocean Parkway, 1896. Edgar S. Thomson photograph collection, Brooklyn Museum/Brooklyn Public Library, Brooklyn Collection.

working farms in a flood tide of brick and mortar. To both ruralize the cities and urbanize the country was, paradoxical as it seems, the double lodestar of Olmsted's long career—"the supreme *desiderata*," as *Putnam's Monthly* put it, "of a higher civilization." Olmsted's Brooklyn parkways, planted six trees across, were veritable forest corridors. Some eight thousand trees were set out on Ocean and Eastern parkways by 1880, almost certainly the single largest coordinated street tree-planting campaign in nineteenth-century America. They included a robust mix of native and introduced species, even occasional "exotics" like weeping willow, which was used on Ocean Parkway near the sea owing to its reputed tolerance for salt. But far and away the most numerous species was the American elm. Requests for proposals made in the fall of 1872 for Eastern Parkway called for 550 sugar maples (*Acer saccharum*); 550 box elder trees (*Acer negundo*); 245 Norway maples (*Acer platanoides*); 245 European elms (*Ulmus campestris*); 232 European lindens (*Tilia x europaea*); 192 tulip trees (*Liriodendron tulipifera*); and nearly 2,500 American elms—significantly more, in other words, than all the other species combined. Olmsted appears to have used the maples and lindens for the outermost row of trees, along the service lanes. For the main carriageway and malls he used only American elms, as nearly every old photograph clearly shows. Thus did this Connecticut Yankee, child of a land of elms, give Brooklyn the mightiest Elm Street of all.[35]

CHAPTER 5

WHIP, SPUR, AND SADDLE

After the race was over,
After Diablo won,
After your pockets were empty
You by the bookmakers stung . . .
—DITTY FROM BROOKLYN HANDICAP OF 1893

Just a few blocks east of Ocean Parkway at Avenue W, where Olmsted's grand avenue bends for its final run to the sea, there is a church whose congregants believe, like Lady Moody, that only mindful adults should be let into the kingdom of God. The First Baptist Church of Sheepshead Bay, founded in 1901, is set midblock amidst a hodgepodge of homes, an ashlar stone edifice with steeple tower and courtyard close. It is one of four very different houses of worship on East Fifteenth Street between Gravesend Neck Road and Avenue X, a homey strip of urban turf tucked beneath the embankment of the old Brighton Beach Line. The neighborhood is a rainbow of diversity, where elderly Italians and Sephardic Jews mix with recent immigrants from south China, Pakistan, Central America, and the former Soviet Union. Century-old row houses and wooden bungalows linger next to new Chinese infill condos, with their stainless-steel railings and telltale potted squash vines. Across the street and just below First Baptist is the Pentecostal Mission Rey de los Reyes. Closer to the Neck Road subway station is a handsome modernist building—the Brooklyn Chinese Christian Church, led by a youthful minister who claims his father invented orange beef. Between is the Burmese Masoeyein Sāsanajotika Buddhist Temple, whose saffron-robed monks are often seen in the produce section of the Stop & Shop around the corner. From their modest sanctuary—a wood-frame bungalow behind a chain-link fence—comes the ethereal lilt of chanted sutras, drifting into the street to mingle with birdsong and rumbling trucks.

It's hard to say whether it is the Baptists or the Burmese Buddhists who are the greater anomaly in this part of town. There are only a handful of Buddhist temples in all Brooklyn—the Dorje Ling Buddhist Center on Gold Street, with its alarming ketchup-and-eggs paint job; West Temple on Eighth Avenue in Sunset Park. And while Baptist churches are plentiful, most—both the storefront sort and those in grand old edifices—are in neighborhoods far north of Gravesend. Indeed, mapping the Baptist churches in Brooklyn yields an accurate spatial portrait of the borough's African American community. The Baptist Church in America is largely a Southern institution, where it is far and away the largest Protestant denomination. A northern faction split off in 1845 over slavery, which white Southern Baptists overwhelmingly supported. Even today, the Southern Baptist Convention is 94 per-

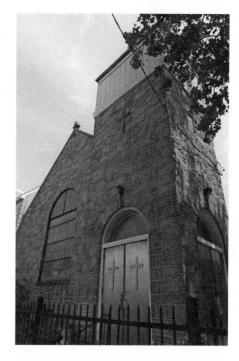

First Baptist Church of Sheepshead Bay. Photograph by author, 2014.

cent white. Black Baptists in the South formed their own churches and, as many moved north after Reconstruction, established new congregations in Baltimore, Philadelphia, Newark, and New York. In New York City even today, the Baptist church is a black institution; most congregations are in Bedford-Stuyvesant, Crown Heights, Brownsville, and East Flatbush. What, then, explains the presence—and for nearly 120 years—of the First Baptist Church of Sheepshead Bay, its flock so far from the main pastures of African American culture in New York City?

As discussed in chapter 1, the black presence in Kings County dates back to the very earliest days of New Netherland. Africans lived in Gravesend, too, since at least 1651, when its English founding fathers petitioned Dutch authorities to allow them to charter "some ships in Holland" to bring in more settlers, especially indentured servants. Failing that, would the good directors consent to sell them "Negroes or Blacks" to answer the manpower shortage? The men—Deborah Moody's name is conspicuously absent, one hopes because of the good woman's moral objection to slavery—pointed out that doing so would bring the company "double profits . . . from what we shall pay for those Negroes."[1] But the African Americans who built First Baptist had little to do with this far-off past. They came instead with horses, thoroughbred horses, to be exact, and the long-vanished tracks on which they ran—an infrastructure that once made southern Brooklyn synonymous with horse racing around the world. Washboard-flat agricultural land is the stuff of equine dreams, and Long Island had this in spades on its vast outwash plain. Racing thoroughbreds is quintessential English sport, and among the first things the

British did once Peter Stuyvesant signed over his colony was build a racetrack—the Newmarket course at Salisbury, about where the Garden City Hotel stands today in Nassau County. Opened in 1665 on the Hempstead Plains, it was the first such track in America (Long Island hasn't been without one since). Racing came early to Kings County, too, with matches and foxhunts at Ascot Heath on the Flatlands plains. It provided a range of diversions for New York's colonial masters, including races for women with prizes—"a Holland smock and chintz gown, full-trimmed"—going to the winners. A tavern nearby, Charles Loosley's King's Head, provided "Breakfasting and Relishes"—and plenty of ale—to huntsmen and punters.[2] The Union course, America's first earthen track (Ascot Heath was turf) opened in Queens in 1821, followed by the nearby Eclipse and Fashion tracks (where baseball's first all-star game was played in 1858). After the Civil War, the Long Island racing scene moved to Jerome Park in the Bronx before settling, as we will see, in deep-south Brooklyn.[3]

In the last two decades of the nineteenth century, the beaches east of Coney Island became a favored playground of the Gotham elite. Three grand resort hotels—the Manhattan Beach, Brighton Beach, and Oriental—opened there by 1880, connected to the rest of the city by rail and streetcar lines. At these sumptuous places guests feasted on Long Island duckling, baked bluefish, and Jamaica Bay oysters; enjoyed light opera; and danced to the music of John Philip Sousa, Patrick Gilmore, and Carlo Cappa. Scores of the city's wealthiest families summered there, and exclusive clubs like the University and the Union League made it their seasonal home. The first, largest, and most resplendent of the great hotels—by some accounts the most elegant hotel in the United States—was the Manhattan Beach, a towered, turreted, veranda-wrapped pile that opened in the summer of 1877. Designed by

The Brighton Beach Hotel, 1903. Detroit Publishing Company Photographic Collection, Library of Congress, Prints and Photographs Division.

J. Pickering Putnam—a graduate of the École des Beaux-Arts—the Manhattan was a breathtaking sight on a bright summer day, sprawling splendidly over six hundred feet of beachfront, its banks of windows bedecked and aflutter with striped canvas. It was all the brainchild of Austin Corbin, the brilliant, ruthless tycoon and Harvard Law graduate who created the modern Long Island Rail Road and was described in 1889 as belonging to "that tribe of human monsters who prey upon poor men, who combine the natures of hog and shark . . . who are never more pleased than when they are bleeding those who are brought within reach of their 'devil-fish' grasp." When he wasn't fleecing farmers or immigrants (in one extraordinary scheme, he convinced the mayor of Rome to send Italian peasants to sharecrop a plantation he wrangled from the family of South Carolina secessionist senator John C. Calhoun), Corbin busied himself hating Jews—banning them from his hotels and founding, in 1879, the American Society for the Suppression of the Jews. What irony that his namesake street today—Corbin Place in the Manhattan Beach neighborhood—is home largely to Russian and Sephardic Jews, most of whom frankly couldn't care less about Corbin and his grim society. In typically pragmatic New Yorker fashion, the residents rejected an initiative some years ago to change the street name; it was simply not worth all the hassle and expense.[4]

Such a great gathering of wealth in a horse-powered age meant a ready market for the Sport of Kings. Impromptu horse races were already being run on Sundays along Ocean Parkway. Entrepreneurs soon stepped up to meet demand. The first of several racetracks to open in Brooklyn was the Brighton Beach, established in 1879 by William A. Engeman. This was followed by a world-class track at Sheepshead Bay, developed by the posh Coney Island Jockey Club. Six years later a third establishment was opened at Gravesend by the Brooklyn Jockey Club. The three courses drew vast crowds of New Yorkers to the Brooklyn shore, rich as well as poor. The influx helped fuel a building boom in Coney Island, culminating in the 1897 opening of Steeplechase Park, where the chief attraction—appropriately enough—was a gravity-powered "coaster" ride known as the Steeplechase Horses. The relationship between the tracks and the hotels was especially symbiotic; on a big race day "more than 10,000 people would crowd the verandas and walks" of the Manhattan Beach Hotel alone, "either to celebrate their winnings or to dissipate regret for their losses." This vortex of leisure and recreation soon transformed southernmost Brooklyn into America's paramount playground—or, as the *Brooklyn Eagle* put it with characteristic restraint in 1880, the "grandest watering place on the face of the earth."[5]

Warren R. Walker, "At the Steeplechase," 1902, which the songwriter dedicated to George C. Tilyou. Music Division, The New York Public Library.

William Engeman brought racing to the New York masses. Engeman was a colorful character, born in New York City in 1841 to German immigrant parents. As a teenager he worked as a newsboy and shipwright before striking out for the West, where he crewed a Mississippi lumber raft, brokered cattle in Texas, led wagon trains over the Sierra as a government scout (befriending Buffalo Bill Cody along the way), and sold mules to the Union army during the Civil War. He returned to New York in 1868 a rich man, opening a restaurant in downtown Brooklyn followed by the Ocean Hotel in Coney Island, complete with a pier—Coney's first—to receive excursion boats from Manhattan. It was as a guest at the Ocean that Austin Corbin was inspired to build the Manhattan Beach Hotel on a site just east. Not to be outdone, Engeman erected a vast bathing pavilion the very next year, aiming to exploit the new popularity of saltwater bathing among the city's middle classes. Drawing on his Mississippi experience—and having observed how "the sad waves hurled all sorts of debris on the beach"—Engeman floated lumber from Gowanus Canal on old Erie barges, cutting them loose on an incoming tide. The waves dashed the boats to pieces, but the payload washed up on his beach right where it was needed. Engeman's stick-built palace, four hundred feet long with accommodations for twelve hundred bathers, was begun on May 9, 1878, and completed a mere seven weeks later.[6]

Engeman later sold half his ocean property to a group of investors who erected there Brooklyn's second great beachfront resort, the Brighton Beach Hotel (Corbin would build the last of the trio in 1880, the grand, Moorish-themed Oriental Hotel). Three stories high with 174 rooms, the Brighton Beach boasted flush toilets and a sewage system with tanks to filter wastewater before it was discharged into Coney Island Creek—ostensibly "free from any offensive odor, and pure." The settled-out solid waste was periodically removed in blocks and sold to local farmers as manure. In time, beach erosion threatened to wash the immense complex into the sea, and in April 1888 the entire structure—all six thousand tons of timber and trim—was jacked up, set on rails, and tugged six hundred feet inland by a team of locomotives. "Simultaneously six throttles were thrown open—first gradually, then to their full," reported a *New York World* correspondent; "The music of the guy ropes and tackle was weird and Wagnerian; then the tug of war began." The great throng of spectators held its collective breath as the locomotives strained against the load. "For a moment, and a moment only, they tugged in vain, their immense drive wheels revolved with perceptible swiftness; then, as if with a mighty effort, they forged ahead." It was the largest building moved in nineteenth-century America, and without breaking a single window pane or mirror.[7]

Engeman, too, moved inland, trading surf for turf and founding—in 1879—the Brighton Beach Racing Association. On a large plot just north of the Ocean Hotel that year he unveiled his greatest project yet—a racetrack known as the Brighton Beach Fair Grounds. The track was built even faster than his bathhouse; an army of some five hundred construction workers completed the project in a mere thirty days. But Engeman clearly had his doubts about the viability of the venture, and "built the grandstand," writes sports historian Steven Riess, "so it could easily be converted into a row of cottages if his investment failed." Of one thing he was sure—getting to the track would be easy; for no fewer than six railways, including predecessors of

The 174-room Brighton Beach Hotel, set on twenty railroad tracks, is pulled from the shore by a team of locomotives, April 1888. Library of Congress, Prints and Photographs Division.

the Culver, Sea Beach, and Brighton lines—today's F, N, and B/Q trains—connected it to the rest of Brooklyn and New York, as did Ocean Parkway and an assortment of steamboats and ferries. While not as posh as Jerome Park—then New York City's premier track, home of the American Jockey Club—Brighton Beach had a faster and more spacious course (the Jerome track had an odd goggle shape). Its simple twin grandstands could accommodate thirteen thousand spectators, with room for an additional thirty thousand standees.[8]

In short order, Brighton Beach was running more events than any other track in the nation, earning Engeman well over $100,000 a year. His trick was simply to service a neglected market of working-class bettors and racing enthusiasts— something most other tracks, especially Jerome Park, eschewed. Brighton Beach was the "people's track," and from the start it drew a large and remarkably polyglot crowd. A snarky *Detroit Journal* correspondent described it as made up of "Negro stablemen, Irish saloonkeepers, French barbers, German tailors, Scandinavian boarding house runners . . . canal boatmen, waiters, hackmen, bootblacks [and] English visitors." The teeming crowd was peppered with "crooks of every variety" and full of men "elbowing their way in and out, smoking cheap cigars, drinking quantities of beer and betting all they are worth on every race." There were women too. These were hardly the posh ladies of Jerome Park, but rather "a strange lot" opined the *Journal* reporter, now putting his very life at risk; "hard-featured, coarse and repulsive creatures dressed in gorgeous red or blue satin gowns, with their slim fingers loaded with showy rings, and their hair bleached to a sickening shade of yellow."[9] The *New York Times* found the plebian crowd's enthusiasm for gambling more abhorrent than the women. A sanctimonious 1885 editorial described Brighton Beach as "the pesthole of race-track gambling in this neighborhood." There, "the clerks and cashiers and office boys of the city are drawn into the fever of betting on races, and many a petty theft and serious embezzlement may be traced directly to the demoralizing influence of that track and its evil surroundings."[10] Nor was the populist attraction a particularly accommodating place for horses. In its inaugural season, an average of two horses were killed weekly in accidents at Brighton Beach, prompting a sobriquet for the course—the Coney Island Slaughter House. The *Times* called it "The Track to Kill a Horse." In a five-day period in September 1879, three steeds had to be put down after breaking legs and shoulder bones at the track—including an old campaigner named Egypt whose injury was so sickening that "the most hardened in the crowd . . . turned away." A police officer put the unfortunate beast out of its misery, firing "a friendly bullet into his brain."[11]

But the racing elite also had its eyes on deep-south Brooklyn, especially as one of its brightest lights, Leonard W. Jerome, lost management control of the Bronx track he had built and named. Just a week after the Brighton Beach Fair Grounds opened, Jerome and a group of youthful, fabulously wealthy racing enthusiasts founded the Coney Island Jockey Club. In addition to Jerome—the "King of Wall Street" and grandfather of a five-year-old boy named Winston Churchill—the investors included August Belmont, Jr., financier and founder of the Interborough Rapid Transit Company; railroad magnate William K. Vanderbilt; Alexander Cassatt, soon to be president of the mighty Pennsylvania Railroad; tobacco heir Pierre Lorillard IV; and Wall Street stock mogul James R. Keene. This was a gathering of souls with the power and money to quite literally move mountains, and they meant to build a temple to their sport that would be the envy of the racing world. When Engeman reneged on his offer to sell them his Brighton Beach track, Jerome built a new one instead on a forested 112-acre site nearby—between Ocean Parkway and Gerritsen Creek. In late January 1880 an army of workers, led by Jerome's brother Lawrence, began clearing the old-growth hickory, oak, and elm. "Hundreds of trees were felled," reported the *Eagle*, "hundreds of stumps . . . drawn from the ground and burned." The dark woods were rent open to the sunlight, looking "as if Aladdin had been around with his genii and his wonderful lamp."[12]

The Coney Island Jockey Club's Sheepshead Bay Racetrack opened to the public in early June 1880. Built on the deep sandy loam of Brooklyn's outwash plain, it was "the pearl of New York racing" and the best track yet in the United States. The course was fast, laid out as "a splendid ellipse, so constructed as to give a long and easy sweep on the turns," and a vast improvement over the contorted Jerome Park course. The new grandstand was a spectacle in itself, two stories tall and made of brick and iron, with a large central pavilion and lesser ones at each end. It gave patrons a broad view of the Atlantic while shielding them from the glare of the sun during races. And Sheepshead Bay only got better with time, its wealthy owners plowing nearly all profits back into the increasingly large and lavish facility. From the initial 112 acres, the complex expanded to 200 acres in 1884, when the main track was extended to a mile and a furlong—the longest in North America. By 1902 the Sheepshead Bay Racetrack had grown to 500 acres. It was hailed the "American Ascot," and considered the only course in the United States equal to the celebrated tracks of England and Europe—Newmarket, Ascot, Longchamp in Paris, Frendenauer in Vienna—turf itself soon vanquished by the Coney Island Jockey Club when Lorillard's Iroquois won two major British races and Keene's Foxhall won the Grand Prix de Paris in 1881. To the somewhat biased *Brooklyn Eagle*, Sheepshead Bay eclipsed "anything of its kind in the United States" and was very likely "the finest race course of the world." It was also the nation's richest racetrack, grossing more than any other New

View of the racecourse of the Coney Island Jockey Club, Hatch Lithographic Company, 1880. Library of Congress, Prints and Photographs Division.

York course at the turn of the century and in 1907 becoming the first in America to rake in over $1 million.[13]

By the 1900s, major race days at Sheepshead Bay attracted crowds of fifty thousand people, far more than what Ebbets Field would see a generation later. It was an upmarket crowd, with the price of grandstand admission more than double that at Brighton Beach. The new track became a favorite with society women, who often attended in parties—dressed to the nines and joyously unaccompanied by men. They appreciated the splendor of Sheepshead Bay, a track so exquisite that "no such place as these beautiful grounds," opined the racing periodical *Spirit of the Times*, "were ever even dreamed of by Ponce De Leon." The women also liked the order and discipline of the crowd, a quality attributed to the presence of "argus-eyed detectives" from the fabled Pinkerton agency. In 1884 the Coney Island Jockey Club inaugurated the Suburban Handicap, the first of several annual races for which Sheepshead Bay would become renowned. Run in early June, the "Great Suburban" marked the opening of the Sheepshead Bay racing season. It was a major event on the New York society calendar, drawing scores of Gotham's power brokers and "best families" to the wilds of Brooklyn, many of whom delayed their summer leave-taking to the mountains or sea until the race was run. The Suburban even set style standards for the city. "The costumes on the grand stand," observed the *Tribune*, "create the particular edicts of fashion which are to be followed by the elect for the season."[14]

The Futurity Stakes, first run on Labor Day 1888, was the highlight of autumn at Sheepshead Bay and heralded the end of racing season. So named because the competing two-year-old steeds were nominated at birth or even before, the Futurity was the biggest prize in American sports and awarded some of the largest racing purses of the nineteeenth century. The inaugural Futurity broke all club attendance records, thronged by a "surging, noisy, good-natured" crowd that hailed from every quarter of the city. The wellborn mixed with the low, men who ran Wall Street with those who swept it. "Millionaires and beggars, touts and dudes," observed the *New York Times*, were all briefly equalized by the thunder of hooves. There were drawling horsemen from the "great breeding States" of Kentucky, Virginia, and Tennessee on hand to see the horses they bred compete. And there were women, too, the *Times* estimating as much as one-quarter of the crowd. The doyennes of New York society basked in the gaze of men bewitched and bothered by their silk-and-satin finery, their faces "bronzed and burned" from the summer's sojourns. No one thought to count the heads, but catering records reveal that a great repast was consumed. The feast included 500 gallons of clam chowder, 12,000 pounds of lobster, 600 soft-shell crabs, 25 spring lambs and 50 racks of ribs, 960 chickens and 500 squabs—all that and the kitchen still fell short of demand. From the bars and taps, meanwhile, poured forth a great river of drink: 250 kegs of lager, 380 cases of champagne, 5 barrels and 40 cases of whiskey, 30 barrels of ginger ale, and 600 boxes of soda water and sarsaparilla. The first Futurity was worth almost $40,900, and the 1890 race had a purse of nearly $70,000, prompting the *Los Angeles Herald* to call it "the most valuable event run for in this country . . . probably in the world." The Sheepshead Bay Racetrack, along with those at Brighton Beach and Gravesend, made Brooklyn the racing capital of the United States for a generation. This is how Brooklyn gave New York City its greatest nickname. If the Old South was the wellspring of thoroughbred racing, New York City was its biggest trophy; or, as a long-forgotten African American stable hand once put it, the "big apple." The reference, invoking a favorite treat of horses, was overheard by a turf scribe named John J. FitzGerald, whose *Morning Telegraph* racing column eventually made the "Big Apple" a beloved moniker for New York City, even if its very core—then as now—was Brooklyn.[15]

Of course, all this play was also work. An immense labor force was needed to run the great hotels, bathing pavilions, restaurants, beer gardens, dance halls, saloons, and betting parlors. Thousands of waiters, cooks, cleaners, footmen, drivers, and musicians found employment between surf and turf, especially in summer months, not to mention the vast army of card sharks, whores, and hustlers that preyed on the summer crowds. The Manhattan Beach Hotel alone employed some five hundred workers at peak season. The racetracks relied on a particularly skilled and specialized array of workers—grooms, trainers, farriers, hotwalkers, stable hands, and stall cleaners. With each new racetrack the population of the surrounding areas swelled; Gravesend alone grew from fewer than twenty-two hundred residents in 1870 to nearly seven thousand in 1890. The Sheepshead Bay track had a race-season worker population of more than a thousand by 1902. Many lived on-site and found employment among the sixty-odd stables in and around the complex. These were not city people, for the most part, but men and women from the horse country of the American South—Virginia and the Carolinas, Kentucky, Tennessee. And unlike the majority of others employed around Coney Island, most were African American. They were former slaves and the sons and daughters of slaves. Far from Harlem, the heart of African American life in New York City at the time, they formed an especially tight community of their own, turning a handful of streets in Gravesend and

Sheepshead Bay into a little Southern town. It was a town full of soul, but had no place to sing or pray. That changed in 1899, when a black Virginian named Maria J. Fisher appealed to William Engeman's son and heir for a parcel of land nearby on which to erect a house of worship. Fisher made a living selling baked goods at the Brighton Beach track, and her request moved the Engeman family to donate a pair of parcels on East Fifteenth Street. There Mother Fisher erected what would become the soul of Sheepshead Bay's African American community. For a builder she had no choice but to hire the kid brother of notorious John Y. McKane, a ward boss who ran Gravesend like a feudal estate. The Concord Baptist Church on Duffield Street in downtown Brooklyn, founded by abolitionists and still one of the foremost African American congregations in New York, sent pastor George O. Dixon to lead the new flock. Thus did Mother Fisher's First Baptist Church of Sheepshead Bay become the first black house of worship south of Prospect Park, and one of the first and few churches in all New York to have an integrated congregation.[16]

But African Americans did more than just groom and clean horses; they also rode them—and fast. Long before the Civil War, black jockeys gained renown for their skill and daring in front of audiences both black and white, from New Orleans to Virginia. As the war ended thoroughbred racing throughout much of the Deep South, the sport retreated to the bluegrass country of Kentucky, then occupied by federal troops. Kentucky became the epicenter of thoroughbred racing and breeding in the United States, and by the 1880s its horses and jockeys—many of whom were African American—were winning on tracks up and down the Eastern Seaboard.

Mother Maria J. Fisher with Fanny Brown and Bertha Greene, 1927. Collection of Donald Brown.

Black jockeys from the Bluegrass State dominated the thoroughbred scene for a generation. They helped usher in the golden age of racing in America, the nation's first great spectator sport. Racing drew far larger crowds at the time than even baseball, and the highest-paid athlete in the United States in the 1870s was an African American jockey from Lexington named Ike Murphy. At the first Kentucky Derby in 1875, nearly all the jockeys at the starting gate were African American, and black riders won more than half of the first twenty-eight derbies. Murphy himself won the Kentucky Derby three times—in 1884, 1890, and 1891—and was earning $20,000 a year a mere decade after Emancipation. The winner of the Coney Island Jockey Club's inaugural Futurity in 1888—one of the greatest races of the nineteenth century—was jockeyed by an African American named Shelby "Pike" Barnes, while the second-place horse was under the command of another black jockey, Tony Hamilton. So celebrated was the race that Currier and Ives issued a print of Barnes and Hamilton charging toward the finish line, possibly the earliest depiction of black athletes in American media.[17]

Of course, the prominent role of African Americans in racing was hardly due to some lost gene of racial tolerance in society at large. Blacks became illustrious jockeys because they were highly skilled athletes, but also because the job of jockeying defaulted to them. The prevailing belief for many years was that thoroughbred horses effectively "rode themselves," and that the jockey was just along for the ride. In other words, the jockey didn't matter. Jockeying was also dangerous, and like most dangerous work in nineteenth-century America, it was left for blacks to do. As David Wiggins has argued, jockeying was known as "nigger work," which was more than enough to keep whites away. Not until well after the Civil War, as racing became more sophisticated, was the jockey's vital role in a race recognized. The rising stock value of jockeying soon made it a well-paid line of work; and in no time black riders were battling to stay in the saddle. A year after being feted for winning the lucrative 1890 Futurity, Tony Hamilton was vilified as an opium-addled drunk and a "muckle-headed negro." The best black jockeys held their own, for a time. Then came the Panic of 1893 and the series of recessions it triggered. "As the economy collapsed and American racing shrank," writes Ed Hotaling, "the fight for the dwindling number of jobs turned more vicious, and blacks were pushed out at an accelerated rate."[18]

By the turn of the nineteenth century, African American jockeys had effectively been purged from a sport they helped make a national pastime. As the *New York Times* observed, "the decline of the negro jockey has been so apparent since the season of 1900 opened that even the casual racegoer has had an opportunity to comment upon it." While many racing fans assumed that black jockeys had disappeared simply because "old-time favorites of African blood had outgrown their skill," the real reason was a deliberate campaign to shut them out. White riders have simply "drawn the color line," reasoned the *Times*, "and wish to free the jockeys' room from the presence of the blacks." Track gossip suggested that the jockeys were not alone in this chicanery—that they were "upheld and advised" by influential turfmen and horse owners, possibly even the powerful Jockey Club itself, formed in 1894 to set national standards for the sport. If a stable or owner ran a black jockey in defiance of the unspoken ban, "concerted action by all the white boys" would assure the defeat of his horse. This often involved violence. As Charles B. Parmer writes, white jockeys "literally ran the black boys off the tracks." Typically, they would surround a black rider and force him to slow down and lose a race, or gang up against him on the rails, where he could be lashed with a whip and even thrown off his mount. The last great black American jockey was Jimmy Winkfield. "Wink," as he was known, won the Kentucky Derby in 1901 and 1902, but left the country after jumping contract at the rain-soaked 1903 Futurity. The prominent stable owner he double-crossed vowed at Sheepshead Bay that Wink would never ride again in the United States. The Lexington, Kentucky, native left for Europe soon after and by the next spring was in czarist Russia, home to a third of the world's equine population at the time. Before long, the self-exiled black American was winning races in Budapest, Hamburg, Vienna, Warsaw, Moscow, and St. Petersburg. Wink became the toast of Russia, gaining celebrity and wealth until the Bolshevik Revolution forced him to seek refuge in France. He returned to the United States when the Nazis seized his stables, finding work on a WPA road gang. He returned to France after the war, and stayed the rest of his life.[19]

By the time Winkfield left for Russia, American racing itself was increasingly under siege, subjected to a purge that threatened not only jockeys but the entire racing establishment in New York State. The target was not horse racing per se, but betting on the outcome of races, a ubiquitous feature of racing since the earliest days of the sport. Gambling was the purr in the race-day cat, and a track without betting was like a bar without drinks. In due time both fell into the gun sights of moral reformers, with consequences as unfortunate as they were unforeseen. Oddly, organized efforts to abolish horse-race gambling in the United States began with the hotly contested 1876 presidential race between Rutherford B. Hayes and Samuel J. Tilden, in which immense sums were wagered on the vote. Betting on elections was common at the time, but because the outcome of the Hayes-Tilden race was not settled for months, it played havoc with the gambling market. This led the next session of the New York State Legislature to ban "pool-selling," collecting bets in a common fund to be divided among the winners. The result was the Anti–Pool Room Law of 1877. Like the temperance movement that led to the Eighteenth Amendment and Prohibition, the Anti-Pool Law was championed by progressive elites, clergymen, and establishment institutions like the *New York Times*, a strident advocate of "public morals and public decency."[20]

Predictably, the new law slashed attendance at racecourses—Jerome Park, especially, where turnout for the 1877 season was the lowest in its history. But it was unevenly enforced at tracks and off. In Saratoga the new regulations were honored mostly in the breach, and of course any ban in New York was a great boon for New Jersey, where Hoboken's notorious poolrooms were especially busy taking bets on seemingly any competitive event. Even in New York City, poolrooms downtown and in "Gambler's Paradise" near Madison Square continued with only occasional, well-announced raids by reluctant police. With the perpetual threat of a real crackdown looming and tired of losing millions to outside wagering, the American and Coney Island Jockey clubs lobbied hard for a law that would allow betting at tracks but not off. The result was the Ives Act of 1887, which permitted gambling only at

The futurity race at Sheepshead Bay (1888), Currier & Ives, 1889. Library of Congress, Prints and Photographs Division.

L. Maurer. N.Y.
1888.

authorized tracks between May and October; anywhere else, pool selling or book-making was a felony. But shielded by Tammany Hall and allies in the police force and local courts, the poolrooms continued to flourish, despite increased raids by police and Pinkerton agents hired by racetracks. In 1899 a vast poolroom trust was uncovered that implicated the city's top cop, William "Big Bill" Devery, the man who later helped bring the Yankees to New York. Even the city's mayor at the time, Robert Van Wyck, was in on it.[21]

Given the severe moral tone of America in the late nineteenth century, it was perhaps inevitable that an outright ban on horse-race gambling, on course or off, would eventually come. To crusaders like mutton-chopped Anthony Comstock—founder of the New York Society for the Suppression of Vice and self-proclaimed "weeder in God's garden"—gambling in any form imperiled the character and well-being of young, working-class men, the backbone of urban industrial society. A ban on wagering, they argued, was for the good of both hearth and nation. Many Americans agreed. In 1893 racetrack gambling was criminalized in New Jersey, effectively banishing racing from the Garden State for fifty years. In Chicago, the Washington Park and Hawthorne tracks closed by 1896, victims of an antigambling campaign led by Mayor Hempstead Washburne. Though both would later open again, racing was effectively banned statewide in Illinois in 1905. That same year racetrack gambling was criminalized in Missouri by Governor "Holy Joe" Folk, closing tracks in St. Louis and Kansas City and spurring the rise of baseball as the dominant spectator sport. Nationwide, antigambling legislation devastated the thoroughbred racing industry; of the 314 tracks in the United States in 1897, only 20 were still operating by 1908.[22]

That year the bell tolled, too, for the turfmen of New York and Kings County. Until then, Brooklyn had repelled the best efforts of reformers to end gambling there. Unlike the patrician *New York Times*, its paper of record—the *Brooklyn Eagle*—initially supported racetrack betting, arguing that grown men "ought to be free to amuse themselves in any way they see fit," so long as they did not hurt others. Gravesend's notorious political boss, John McKane, had only tepid interest in enforcing New York gambling laws at the three tracks in his jurisdiction. The tracks themselves applied all manner of creative maneuvering to circumvent gambling laws, leading police and prosecutors in a great game of cat and mouse. In 1885, for example, the Coney Island Jockey Club introduced a scheme in which punters made a monetary "contribution" to owners of the finest, fastest horses; the cash was then pooled and divided among the winners as before. But even tough and scrappy Brooklyn and its trio of tracks proved no match for a crusading constitutionalist from the Adirondacks named Charles Evans Hughes. Born in Glens Falls in 1862, Hughes studied law at Columbia and, after a decade of practice in New York, joined the Cornell law faculty at the tender age of twenty-nine. In 1906 he ran as a Republican for the governorship of New York State, defeating publisher William Randolph Hearst on a platform of progressive social reform. As New York's chief executive, he pushed for voting reform and workmen's compensation, passed legislation to limit campaign contributions and increase the powers of the state's public service commissions, and won passage of the Moreland Act, which armed his office to investigate any state board or agency. Hughes famously rejected an appeal to commute the death sentence of

Chester Gillette, whose 1906 murder of his pregnant lover on an Adirondack lake was fictionalized by Theodore Dreiser in *An American Tragedy*.[23]

But the biggest fight of his governorship was against gambling and the racing industry. By any reckoning, it should not have been a struggle at all. In 1895 New York voters had amended the state constitution to include an all-out ban on "pool selling, bookmaking, or any other kind of gambling." But a loophole had been created, largely at the behest of the state's powerful, politically connected racing interests. This was the Percy-Gray Law, which created a state racing commission—the first in American sports—but effectively neutered the constitutional prohibition on gambling by threatening nothing more than a wrist-slap for most track violations. The only penalty for placing a bet was forfeiture of the wagered amount, to be recov-

Charles Evans Hughes walking to his office from Union Station, Washington, DC, c. 1913. Photograph by Harris & Ewing. Library of Congress, Prints and Photographs Division.

ered through civil action, and so long as there was no written record of the bet—no "exchange, delivery or transfer of a record, registry, memorandum, token, paper, or document of any kind"—criminal penalties could not be imposed. Within months of taking office, Governor Hughes charged aides to study the constitutionality of Percy-Gray, and in January 1908 introduced a package of antigambling legislation to impose criminal penalties—including stiff prison sentences—for gambling on or off the track. The legislation was named for the two Republicans who introduced it on the governor's behalf, Senator George Bliss Agnew and Assemblyman Merwin K. Hart. Hughes then launched a campaign to get the legislation passed, backed by a broad coalition of church and civic groups and the Citizens' Anti–Race Track Gambling League. Even the seventy-thousand-member Grange lent its weight, persuaded by a $250,000 appropriation to state agricultural societies that Hughes had cleverly written into the bill. The racing crowd fought back mightily. Jockey clubs and bookmakers ponied up $500,000 in secret funds to defeat the bill. Leading turfmen—Whitney, Keene, Belmont—traveled to Albany to testify against Agnew-Hart, arguing that an industry employing thousands would be destroyed if the bill were approved. After months of acrimonious debate, the legislation passed easily in the assembly but was defeated by a razor's margin in the senate.[24]

Hughes was not finished, however. But before introducing his legislation again, he called a special election to fill a vacant senate seat he knew would be won by a Republican. With the narrowest of margins now his, he called the legislators back into session. The Agnew-Hart bill again passed the assembly and came to the senate floor on June 10. Moments before the vote was called, legislators were stunned to see the chamber doors open and Brooklyn senator Otto G. Foelker wheeled, semiconscious, to his desk by two men. Foelker had just undergone surgery for appendicitis and was roused out of bed to make the vote, against the pleas of his wife and doctor. Hughes had ordered an express train from New York to stop specifically for him at Staatsburg, where he was recuperating. Foelker was so ill he collapsed upon arrival at Albany. But he cast the deciding vote all the same, delivering a great victory for Hughes, who lauded Foelker's actions as "most heroic and worthy of the same praise that we give to distinguished service on the battlefield." Boston minister Adolf A. Berle of the Shawmut Congregational Church was more effusive. "What a spectacle is this for Americans!" he gushed; "A poor son of Germany, an immigrant . . . a baker's apprentice, who by hard work and self-denial gains an education and place in the state government, and who while the money princes of New York and the whole race track fraternity of gamblers and corrupters hold out prizes . . . risks life and all that life means to be carried to the state capitol to help save the honor of a sovereign state and maintain the majesty of the law."[25]

Foelker probably cringed at this eruption of purple prose. As a Brooklyn resident—he lived on Bedford Avenue in today's Clinton Hill—he certainly had reason to steer clear of Coney Island for a while. For nowhere was the impact of the new antigambling legislation more immediate or devastating than at Brooklyn's trinity of racetracks. When the law went into effect on June 12, 1908, it wasn't clear at first how strenuously it would be enforced, or whether there were loopholes to exploit. Because the law was aimed at professional gamblers and required written record of a wager for conviction, oral bets and private betting by individuals were allowed, so long as these used credit rather than cash. Gamblers, amateur and professional, were certainly present when the various tracks opened for the season, but oral betting proved cumbersome; what wagering took place was furtive and the atmosphere generally tense and edgy. The city's ironfisted police commissioner, Theodore A. Bingham, instructed his men to break up groups of two or more persons, even if they were just talking about the weather. On opening day at Sheepshead Bay on June 19, the Coney Island Jockey Club obtained an injunction to keep Bingham from harassing its elite patrons. He sent an army of three hundred men to hover menacingly nonetheless, worrying the punters like wolves watching sheep. Once the bookmakers learned of Agnew-Hart's permeability, they "took corresponding liberty," observed the *Times*, "but with police keenly alert for offenses that would come under the interpretation of the law."[26]

Of course, the constant threat of arrest spoiled the festive air of meets and ravaged track attendance. Race enthusiasts who liked to pepper the day's outing with a harmless bet or two now risked arrest, while professional bookmakers simply stayed in town to ply their trade under the table. Track crowds were substantial enough in the spring of 1908, but that autumn it became clear that Agnew-Hart was taking a toll. William A. Engeman, Jr., who was arrested in July for letting bookies operate at Brighton Beach, canceled outright the fall meet and put the entire property on the market the very next month. Sheepshead Bay was drawing only a thousand or so spectators to races by the end of September. The Coney Island Jockey Club posted a staggering loss of $350,000 that season, when normally it would turn a profit of $400,000 from just its Suburban and Futurity races. Then, in early 1910, a suite of legislation known as the Agnew-Perkins bills passed in Albany to tighten the screws on racetrack gambling, closing the oral betting loophole and—in an especially draconian move—making track management and trustees personally responsible for bookmaking on the premises. This kicked the threat of arrest and prison upstairs into the executive suite. Now the industry had its back against the wall.[27]

On Independence Day that year, just weeks after Agnew-Perkins became law, a surprisingly large crowd turned out for the Lawrence Realization Stakes, closing event of the Coney Island Jockey Club's season. It was a cool summer day and the gala atmosphere in the grandstands "put the regulars in mind of conditions four or five years ago," before crusader Hughes clouded race-day skies. In the steeplechase feature, a horse named Bird of Flight hit the fourth jump and fell to the track crumpled and twitching, so badly injured that it had to be shot in full view of the crowd. It was an omen of sorts, for that day would be the very last of horse racing at Sheepshead Bay—crown jewel of New York tracks, the plumpest and most succulent big apple of all. By early September 1910 all three of Brooklyn's great thoroughbred courses had closed. They would never open again. The defenders of moral order prevailed, but their victory was a costly one. Thousands of employees lost their jobs. Trades and businesses that provided the racing industry's vast support infrastructure took a blow, sending shock waves through the state economy. Not even rural New York was immune, as the numerous agricultural societies throughout the state were now deprived of a major revenue stream from a special tax on track profits. With so few affluent New Yorkers trekking to the Brooklyn shore, the area quickly lost its upmarket cachet. One after another, the great seaside hotels closed—the Manhattan Beach in 1911, the Oriental in 1916, with the Brighton Beach lingering until 1924. On the world map of track and turf, a bright American light flickered and went dark; Brooklyn's brief, bountiful age of bridle leather was over.[28]

The Brighton Beach Hotel being demolished, July 1924. Photograph by Eugene L. Armbruster. Irma and Paul Milstein Division of United States History, Local History and Genealogy, The New York Public Library.

CHAPTER 6

THE ISLE OF OFFAL AND BONES

Waft, waft, ye summer breezes,
  Barren Island's fearful smell . . .
—BROOKLYN DAILY EAGLE, SEPTEMBER 1, 1897

In September 1887 the famed thoroughbred Lucky B was stricken by equine meningitis at the Sheepshead Bay Racetrack. Its grieving owner—millionaire California developer Elias "Lucky" Baldwin—revealed that his namesake steed would be buried in the Coney Island Jockey Club's equestrian cemetery, where the steed's remains would mingle with those of several other turf luminaries—the $29,000 filly Dew Drop, felled by stomach cancer; Vera, star of the stable of R. Porter Ashe (scion of the founding family of Asheville, North Carolina), whose neck was snapped in a fall. The fate of these priceless thoroughbreds was far kinder than what awaited Gotham's vast army of workhorse nags, the lowly beasts of burden that were the city's primary source of motive power well into the 1920s. The destiny of these and other creatures lost and spent was a remote corner of New York City known as Barren Island. Many miles and a world away from the centers of metropolitan life, the shifting sea-swept isle was a realm of literal fire and brimstone—the setting of dark tales that made children hug tight their dogs and elders bring in the cat. Each year there, tons of slaughterhouse offal and tens of thousands of horses and other animals—rats and cats and dogs, cows, goats, even an executed circus elephant—were cut, boiled, pressed, and burned into the afterlife, in a grim and sprawling tryworks that eventually became the largest waste-processing and "reduction" complex in the world. It was Golgotha by the Sea, smelled long before seen, the "Place of Awful Stenches."[1]

Barren Island was called *equan-tah-ohke* by the Canarsee Indians—"broken lands"—Anglicized as *Equendito*. It was conveyed to Samuel Spicer and John Tilton in May 1664 by two Canarsee tribesmen—Wawamatt Tappa and Kacha-washke—in exchange for a kettle, coats and shirts, a gun, powder and lead, and "a quantity of Brandie wine, already paid," and excepting "one half of all such whale-fish that shall by wind and storms be cast upon the said Island." On early maps, the island appears as a roughly triangular spit of sand on the southwest edge of Jamaica Bay. Its uplands were originally forested with Atlantic white cedar, but before 1820 the island was apparently "destitute of trees, producing only sedge, affording coarse pasture"—a state that no doubt helped mutate the Dutch 't Beeren Eylandt (Bearn Island) into Barren Island, which itself appears on maps as early as 1731. It was fringed to the north by creek-carved salt marshes and exposed to the Atlantic on the south—a place known as Hoopaninak by the Canarsee and later named Pelican Beach. It wasn't until about 1890 that natural sand deposition had extended Rockaway Peninsula to the west past Barren Island, shielding it from the sea and creating the present geography of Jamaica Bay. The diurnal action of strong tides flushing the vast bay had carved a deep channel along the island's east bank; an 1844 coastal survey indicates depths of up to forty feet a stone's throw from shore. This allowed relatively large vessels to dock right up against the island, the only one so accessible in the area.[2]

Barren Island was used by Native Americans for hunting and fishing, but no evidence has ever been found of permanent settlement. Nor did its succession of early European owners use it for more than grazing livestock and harvesting salt hay. It was not until the end of the eighteenth century that the first substantial structure appeared—a "rude house at the east end," according to antiquarian chronicler Anson Dubois, "where fishermen and sportsmen were entertained." Constructed by Nicholas Dooley, self-styled "King of the Island," the building stood as late as the 1880s. Lost souls and flotsam were often brought to Dooley's door. In 1807 a fisherman found a little girl wandering the marsh, a piece of fat pork in one hand, a sea biscuit in the other. Like the "whale-fish" that would wash up on the beach, she had no name, no identification. The child was taken to the house and eventually became part of the Dooley family, raised as Julia Ann. Years later the woman was reunited with her mother, who recognized her daughter by a half-moon birthmark on her leg. Julia Ann, it turns out, had been kidnapped and left on the beach by a sailor her father, a prominent New York businessman, had double-crossed. Smugglers and pirates came to Barren Island, too, with the requisite buried treasure. In 1830, a Philadelphia-bound brig from New Orleans carrying cotton, sugar, and $54,000 in Mexican silver was commandeered by its crew. The mutineers killed the captain and mate and set sail for Long Island. Nearing the shore, they scuttled the ship and made way to land in two rowboats. One sank; the other reached Pelican Beach, where the surviving men buried their loot. They were soon caught, two of them later tried and hanged on Bedloes Island. The story, embellished over the years, was revived in the 1870s when the *Times* reported that a fisherman attempting to retrieve a lost anchor off Barren Island snagged a sailor's chest bound with iron straps and filled with nearly $5,000 in coins so firmly fused together by time and tide that "hammer and chisel had to be used to separate them."[3]

The remoteness and isolation of Barren Island—hinterland of a hinterland—made it a natural candidate for the city's official quarantine station, and even led to its

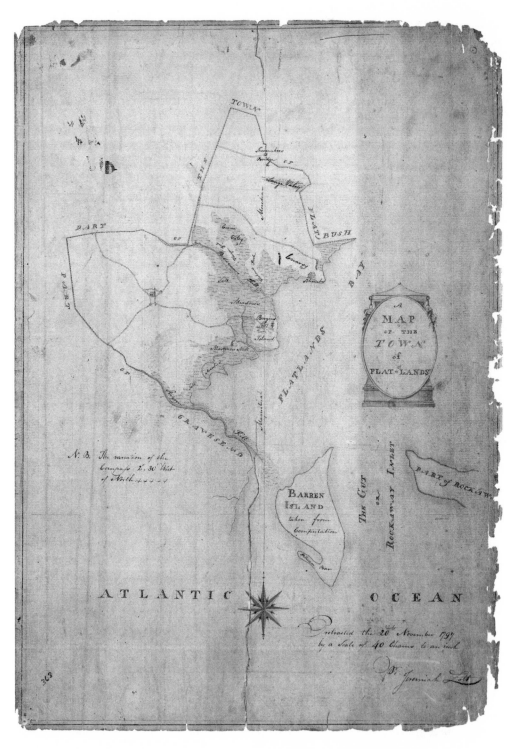

A Map of the Town of Flat-Lands, 1797, showing Barren Island and Pelican Bar in lower-right quadrant. New York State Archives—Survey maps of lands in New York State, 1711–1913 (Series A0273–78, Map #368).

designation in 1867 as a temporary post for patients arriving via "cholera vessels, or others infected with epidemic diseases." Plans for a permanent hospital complex on the island were scuttled, however, after health commissioners learned firsthand on a field trip just how inaccessible the place was; "the surf, it would appear, only permits of the approach of small boats in exceptionally fine weather." Paradoxically, it was this inaccessibility and isolation that led to the island's industrial development, attracting processes too noisome or polluting to be tolerated in the city proper. The opening of the first such plant brought this far-off wild place into the pale of metropolis. It was Lefferts R. Cornell, a distant relative of the founder of Cornell University, who launched this formative chapter in the island's history, securing in 1855 a contract to collect and dispose of "all the night-soil, garbage, and dead animals" from the streets of New York and Brooklyn. Cornell erected a small plant on the island's east bank, where carcasses were processed into a fertilizer ingredient he shipped to his London investor—the Nitro-Phosphate Company, whose "Patent Blood Manure" offered farmers an alternative to rapidly diminishing supplies of Peruvian guano. The product was "composed of Bones dissolved with sulfuric acid," described a contemporary advertisement, "to which is added about 1,500 lbs. of pure Blood to every ton of the Manure." The *Agricultural Gazette* praised Nitro-Phosphate's artificial manure "as nearly perfect, whether for roots or corn." It won accolades at the 1862 International Exhibition in London, where—coincidentally—Charles Babbage introduced his "analytical machine," progenitor of the modern computer. But Cornell soon had competition. William B. Reynolds opened a similar plant a year or so after Cornell, whose city contracts he eventually bought out. He and his two partners—including Charles Pratt, founder of Pratt Institute and one of John D. Rockefeller's original Standard Oil trustees—shipped their fertilizers as far away as Prussia, where they were prized by vintners in the Rhine valley. Thus, perhaps, did the souls of New York's nameless nags and curs return home in bottles of Spätburgunder and Riesling.[4]

Many of these creatures—dogs, especially—had been spirited off well before their time. Until the mid-nineteenth century, dogs in New York City roamed the streets with complete freedom, often biting people and causing nightly mayhem with their howls and barking. Eventually public outrage grew to the point that laws were passed requiring dogs to be muzzled and authorizing the capture and dispatch of any left unrestrained on the street. Driving the new legislation was fear of rabies, known then as hydrophobia; for "no animal-borne illness," writes historian Jessica Wang, "struck a greater sense of terror in humans." The disease was thought to be most prevalent in summer months, and "ordinances authorizing the collection and disposal of unmuzzled dogs eventually became an annual summer ritual." In Brooklyn, citizens were authorized to kill any unmuzzled dog running free on the street. Broadsides would go up toward the end of June, "announcing to the boys that the season has come again when stealing dogs may be legitimately reckoned as the largest source of income." With a fifty-cent reward on their heads, it was "profitable to steal and indeed raise pups for the New-York market." Some found grim humor in this annual rite of canine catching. In August 1855 the *New York Times* lampooned a

"Distressed Widow" who appeared at the newspaper's offices one day seeking help in finding a lost King Charles spaniel. Mrs. Sob-easy, as the columnist called her, was advised to visit the new city pound. There, a worker confessed to the widow and her escort that with "lard . . . so high now and venison scarce," dogs had become prized for more than companionship. Thousands of Rovers, Spots, and Fidos had already been turned in for cash that summer by heartless, enterprising urchins. Some were retrieved by their owners—for a fee, of course. Others were given a one-way ride to Jamaica Bay; for the real money was in selling the animals to tryworks operators like Cornell and Reynolds. Of some thirty-six hundred dogs collected by the city pound that summer, only four hundred were redeemed. The rest? "We put them in a big box," explained the pound man, "and let on the Croton water till they are drownded . . . I tell you, ladies, it's very doleful to hear 'em howl out of their box when the water's comin' in, all in different voices so." He tried to spare the distraught pair further details; but the widow was persistent: "You spoke of Barren Island, my good man; I suppose that is the Cemetery where they are buried? Is there any ferry to the place?" Alas there was not, he allowed, but then assured her "that it was a very romantic place for a dog to rest in, after his life's labors were ended . . . the ocean is always performing a dirge."[5]

However numerous, city dogs were small and scrawny. The real prize in the "reduction" trade was the horse. With the urban horse today relegated to the occasional police mount or pulling contested Central Park carriages, it is difficult to picture the mammoth role this living machine played in the economy and daily life of American cities prior to 1920. By the end of the nineteenth century there were

W. A. Rogers, *At the Dog Pound—The Rescue of a Pet.* From *Harper's Weekly*, June 16, 1883.

some 130,000 horses in Manhattan alone, with tens of thousands more in Brooklyn and Queens. Horses hauled much of the city's passenger traffic and nearly all of its freight (an 1885 study revealed that nearly eight thousand horse-drawn vehicles passed the corner of Broadway and Pine Street in lower Manhattan on a typical day). The animals supported a vast network of trades, including blacksmith shops, wheelwrights, and saddle makers. With the introduction of the "horsecar" in the 1830s, they even helped expand the footprint of the city. Essentially a carriage on rails, the horsecar might not seem like revolutionary technology, but the minimal friction of steel on steel enabled a fourfold increase in a horse's pulling power. This allowed operators to carry a larger payload per animal and thus charge lower fares, which increased ridership and led companies to expand their systems. Because these lines required a costly up-front investment in track, routes were "sticky" and not easily changed. To real estate developers, this was a bankable asset. Wherever the horsecar lines went, houses followed, driving residential development outward from the city center along corridors served by the new mode of transit.[6]

The urban horse produced an avalanche of waste—an average of 50 pounds of manure per animal every day (about 7 tons a year). New York's horses thus churned out an astonishing 1.8 billion pounds of dung annually, the equivalent in weight of twenty *Iowa*-class battleships. Manure was a rich source of fertilizer, of course, and local farmers carted off much of it. But it was heavy, consisting mostly of water, and difficult to move in quantity. As farms were forced farther out by the spreading city, and with lighter, more potent fertilizers increasingly available—like those manufactured at Barren Island—city stables couldn't give the stuff away. It was simply not worth moving, and thus often piled up on streets and empty lots, bathing blocks in barnyard stench, attracting rats, and breeding biblical clouds of flies. The deluge created a public health menace that became one of the most fretted-over city-planning issues at the time. Horses also aged, sickened, and died in large numbers every year—especially when a deadly contagion tore through the horse population, such as the Great Epizootic of 1872, an outbreak of equine influenza that ground transportation to a halt throughout the northeastern states. The dead were collected from street and stable, hauled to a Hudson River pier, and loaded for Barren Island on scows or an aged schooner known as the "horse boat." There the animals would render their last service to humankind through a process of reduction that began as soon as the boat docked. The carcasses were lifted from the deck, skinned, and gutted, and the flesh was cut off and carted to a boiler house. As the *Brooklyn Eagle* described it in 1861, the carrion was then "placed in large boilers, and boiled until every particle of fat is taken from it." As anyone who has made bone broth or chicken stock knows, heat breaks down fat molecules, which rise to the surface. Skimmed off and congealed, the horse fat was sold to chandlers to make soaps and candles (Gotham's horses, in death, helped illuminate the very shops and homes they trotted past in life). Bones were carved into buttons, combs, and knife handles or burned to make "bone black," used as a pigment and as a filter in the sugar-refining process. Hides were salted down and sold to tanners; hooves were rendered for glue. To paraphrase Chicago meatpacking magnate Gustavus Swift, everything of the horse but its snort was put to good use.[7]

The Close of a Career in New York, c. 1900. Detroit Publishing Company Photographic Collection, Library of Congress, Prints and Photographs Division.

In theory, at least. The early Barren Island carcass processors used crude equipment in hastily built structures, and were not very efficient extractors of value from the city's expired animals. Bad weather, shipping delays, worker shortages, and market fluctuations played havoc with operations—especially those on fixed city contracts. If there was a glut on the island, or if demand for products fell, carcasses would simply be dumped en route, fouling the shores of the upper and lower bay and forcing those seeking the delights of the water's edge "to give up the pleasure," noted the *Times*, "because of the hideous objects that floated on the waves." Barren Island itself was strewn with the detritus of death. In May 1866 Jackson S. Schultz, head of the newly formed Metropolitan Board of Health—the first such municipal authority in the United States—made an inspection tour of the island in response to complaints about horrific odors voiced by the residents of Gravesend, two miles distant. He discovered there "thousands of dead animals lying under the sun . . . sending forth a highly offensive stench." He also learned that these creatures, though dead, had yet a disconcerting ability to wander; for the carcasses were "washed away by every high tide, and . . . becoming bladders, float up and down along the shore." Wind and waves would push the grim flotsam into a small cove on the west side of Barren Island, which still carries the doleful name Dead Horse Bay. In an era before municipal consolidation, multiple parties would often be paid to remove the same wandering carcass that New Yorkers had already paid a contractor to dispose of. Washed up at Bay Ridge, the animal would be carted afresh to a Brooklyn collection pier only to be dumped again and surface next perhaps on Staten Island. "As a general rule, one funeral is deemed sufficient for a human being," clowned the *New York Times*, "but when a New-York horse 'shuffles off' . . . three of the most enlightened counties in the state give him each a separate funeral, and spend money *ad libitum* to do honor to his remains." Indeed, "no death in the Republic causes more trouble or anguish than that of the New-York horse."[8]

Other creatures, too, were made part of Barren Island's baleful menagerie. In 1880 alone, more than 8,000 dogs ended their days on the isle, in the process destroying "more intelligence, more faithfulness and more common sense," lamented the *Times*, "than ever bothered some of their persecutors." Nine years later, the vast rendering and fertilizer works of P. White and Sons—heir to the Cornell operation—processed a staggering 23,765 cats and dogs, along with more than 7,000 horses, 2,565 cows and calves, 699 sheep, 171 goats, 26 hogs and pigs, 461 barrels of poultry, and 125 barrels of rabbits. Also boiled off that year were three deer, a bear and an alligator. But the most unusual creature rendered to its essence on Barren Island was a thirty-year-old Asian elephant named Pilot. Captured in Ceylon (Sri Lanka) around 1870, the animal was acquired by a London investor, but sold after stomping his keeper "into an unrecognizable and shapeless mass." The elephant's buyer was American circus pioneer P. T. Barnum, who shipped the beast with his trunk chained to his belly and his legs so tightly fettered that he could move only inches at a time. Once in the United States, the elephant manifested still worse behavior—especially, it seems, after being upstaged by the beloved gentle giant, Jumbo, largest circus elephant in American history. Pilot bruised attendants, killed dogs, broke loose in Bridgeport, Connecticut, and struck a keeper unconscious with his trunk at Madison Square Garden. Brutally shackled and beaten after yet another incident, the animal became crazed with rage, battering down a chimney and bellowing so loudly that he could be heard for blocks around Madison Square. Barnum's partner, James A. Bailey, ordered the elephant killed—an extraordinary move given his value. It took three shots of a .48 caliber navy revolver to get the job done. A team of twenty "white-aproned and bloody-armed butchers" then descended on the carcass, and "before midnight proud Pilot was in small pieces" (the animal's stall mate, Gipsey, was so traumatized by the butchery that she refused to eat for days afterward). A leg was claimed by a veterinary college, the tusks turned into billiard balls; but most of Pilot was loaded on Charon's boat for Barren Island, "to be rendered into glue, buttons and other substances." This was an especially harsh fate for a circus elephant, even a murderous one. When another Barnum and Bailey killer pachyderm, Albert, was executed by a New Hampshire firing squad for crushing his keeper, his remains were sent to the Smithsonian. But Pilot's "long career of wickedness," as one reporter put it, was deemed deserving of exile to the dreaded isle.[9]

Fish, by the tens of millions, were also rendered more useful to humanity on Barren Island, which became a major processing center for Atlantic menhaden in the decade following the Civil War. The oily, nutrient-rich fish had been used by Native Americans for centuries as a fertilizer for maize, a practice adopted by early New England colonists. In his 1637 *New English Canaan*, Thomas Morton noted that a thousand fish were used to fertilize a single acre of land, which "thus dressed will produce and yeald so much corne as 3 acres without fish." The name *menhaden* was in fact derived from the Narragansett *munnawhatteaûg*, which meant "that which manures." In New York, the fish was more commonly known as mossbunker, from the Dutch *marsbanker* (maasbanker), a species of Atlantic mackerel it resembled. Oddly, the silvery pelagic was first described for science in 1799 by one of America's first great architects, Benjamin Henry Latrobe. An English émigré, Latrobe supervised construction of the US Capitol and—among many other commissions—designed the east and west colonnades at the White House. He was also an accomplished amateur naturalist who researched digger wasps and the geology of Virginia. Latrobe gave the toothless plankton-eater a delightfully menacing name—*Brevoortia tyrannus*—because of a small parasitic isopod or fish louse often found in its mouth. The louse, which Latrobe named *Oniscus praegustator*, "fares sumptuously every day," he observed, though he couldn't quite tell whether the freeloader was there "by force, or by favor." A good patriot, he chose the former: "The oniscus resembles the minion of a tyrant," wrote Latrobe; "for he is not without those who *suck* him." The architect thus named his hapless autocrat *tyrannus*.[10]

By whatever name, the fish was as numerous as the stars of heaven—a pelagic passenger pigeon that darkened the seas the way great flocks of the doomed bird once blacked out American skies. The physician-naturalist Samuel L. Mitchill described the "prodigious numbers" of menhaden in New York waters in 1814: "From the high banks of Montock" [*sic*], he wrote, "I have seen acres of them purpling the waters." In 1819 a Newport sea captain sailed through a single school off New England that stretched two miles wide and a staggering forty miles long. Unlike the passenger pigeon, which market hunters blasted toward extinction, the titanic menhaden shoals were unmolested by man as they migrated up the coast each spring. Relatively flavorless and full of bones, the fish was seldom eaten, and after the colonial era its utility as a fertilizer was largely forgotten. It was rising demand for oil, for lighting and lubricating America's Industrial Revolution, that led to a rediscovery of the species—this time as little silver oil wells. The high oil content of menhaden transformed *Brevoortia tyrannus* from a runt of the sea into one of its most profitable resources. By the 1880s, nearly five hundred million pounds of menhaden were being harvested every year—more than all other fish species combined, including cod, mackerel, salmon, herring, shad, and Great Lakes whitefish. Boiled, skimmed, and pressed from the fish, the oil was favored by coal miners as headlamp fuel, and used to manufacture rope, mix paint, and curry leather. The inexpensive fish oil was used to cut more costly lubricants, such as linseed oil, and in its purest form was even marketed for cooking as olive oil. Menhaden might be mere foodstuff for a sperm whale, but it soon beat out its predator in the American marketplace. The oil extracted from the annual menhaden haul in the 1870s exceeded by some 200,000 gallons that harvested from whales. Indeed, Latrobe's little tyrant helped finish off the dying whaling industry and thus may well have helped save its colossal nemesis from extinction. By the end of the century, prey had usurped predator; for what was often sold as whale oil for lamps and lubricant was mostly menhaden oil.[11]

It was certainly a lot easier to get oil from a small fish than from a fifty-ton cetacean. On Barren Island at least four plants were engaged in this malodorous and

MENHADEN (BREVOORTIA TYRANNUS)

Sherman Foote Denton, *Menhaden (Brevoortia Tyrannus)*. From Denton, John L. Ridgway, and Louis Agassiz Fuertes, *Fish and Game of the State of New York* (1901).

messy work by the 1880s, including Barren Island Menhaden, the E. Frank Coe Company, and the Hawkins Brothers Fish Oil and Guano Company of Jamesport—the largest processor in the state. Each had its own fleet of fishing boats that would use purse seines to harvest fish in the New York bight. Once the boats docked, the menhaden would be bailed out of the hold in buckets. They would be chopped up and dumped into great wooden vats partially filled with water, steamed hard for an hour, then "punched and broken up" and simmered for five hours. The water and oil would then be drawn off and the broken fish or "residuum" drained and cooled for many hours more. It would then be placed in perforated iron vessels and run under hydraulic presses to wring out every last drop of water and oil. The remaining "cheese" was moved to dry in the sun on wooden platforms covering two or three acres, then packaged for sale as "fish guano." The Barren Island plants would run twenty-four hours a day in summer, boiling through some two million menhaden every week. In the fall, when the fish were fattest, as much as six gallons of oil could be extracted per thousand fish. Though not as valuable as the oil, menhaden guano was rich in phosphates and nitrogen. It was widely used to amend the stony, depleted soils of New England and those of sandy Long Island, enabling farmers to keep productivity in step with soaring demand from the region's growing cities.[12]

The Barren Island workforce consisted of a polyglot mix of mostly single men—black and white, immigrant and native born. African Americans from Virginia and Delaware worked the fish plants, while Prussians, Swedes, and English, Irish, and Swiss immigrants dominated the rendering works. Most lived in company boarding-houses, some with only ship hammocks for sleep. They only rarely left the island in warmer months, and travel in winter was almost impossible. With no bridge or causeway to the mainland, it took most of a day to get to Manhattan from Barren Island. The trip involved taking a boat (which ran only in summer) to Canarsie Landing, a railcar to East New York, and a train across Brooklyn to Fulton Ferry. The heady essence of Barren Island industry often went along for the ride. When several employees of the Edward Clark offal works attempted to board a Broadway Railroad car in 1878, the conductor informed them of a rule banning anyone reeking of rendered flesh. But the men were "strong in numbers as well as smells" and boarded the train anyway, giving the poor conductor "a sick and sorrowful time" until he flagged a policeman and had them all arrested. One worker, Thomas Murphy, sued the railroad but lost his case on appeal when the court ruled that the constitutional obligations of a common carrier did not extend to "the transportation of smells." More or less banished from the city they served, Barren Island's workers developed a self-contained community of their own. With ten women and twice as many hogs as men, Barren Island was hardly known for its gentility and grace. A staff writer from the *Brooklyn Eagle* visiting in August 1877 was received like an interloper from another galaxy. A crowd of dogs and children gathered around him as he walked the island's sandy "Main Street," and men so covered in filth that their faces were obscured reached out to feel his clothing. "If the reporter had dropped from the clouds," he wrote, "he could not have created a greater sensation."[13]

Far from the wardens of state, Barren Island also bred lawlessness and anarchy. In early 1874, Frank Swift, who ran the old Reynolds plant on a big city contract, was discovered to be distilling more than horseflesh. At first light on February 9, agents from the new US Bureau of Internal Revenue—tasked with enforcing an 1862 liquor tax to help pay for the Civil War—stormed the island with 120 federal troops. In one of Swift's buildings, windows covered by horse hides, they found "an extensive distillery in full operation," complete with immense vats filled with some fifty thousand gallons of sour mash and molasses. It was one of the largest moonshine operations uncovered in New York City during the "Whiskey Wars" of the 1870s. The agents also boarded an old schooner riding at anchor offshore, which was found to be loaded with kegs. Swift had teamed up with the notorious Brady brothers—barons of the Gotham moonshine trade—and was using the derelict two-master to haul his potent sour mash whiskey from Barren Island to a gin mill at Gold and John streets in the heavily Irish Fifth Ward, Brooklyn's roughest neighborhood (Vinegar Hill today). Clandestine activity of this sort required discouraging the curious visitor to Barren Island, who—upon making landfall—would often be forced back to his boat by members of the notorious Bone Gang that ruled the isle before a permanent police presence was established. At the very least, he would be met by a pack of snarling dogs, animals none too trusting of man (and for good reason; most were escapees from the offal boats). By the 1880s, Barren Island's population had doubled, but its reputation as a closed and clannish, even dangerous place only got stronger. That image was hardly eased by lurid accounts of bodies washed up on the shore. One of these bodies was that of the beautiful, doomed Fanny McKnight, daughter of a wealthy merchant who dropped out of Claverack College on the Hudson to plumb the pleasures of Gotham, where "she appears," sniffed the *New York Times*, "to have led a wild life." On July 26, 1880, McKnight boarded the excursion steamer *Kill Von Kull* for Coney Island but jumped overboard before the vessel reached the Iron Pier—at least according to police. The diamond rings and a large amount of cash she was carrying were never recovered, nor was the gentleman identified whom she was seen talking to just before taking leave of the deck, leading many to conclude that the wayward collegian had been robbed and thrown from the boat.[14]

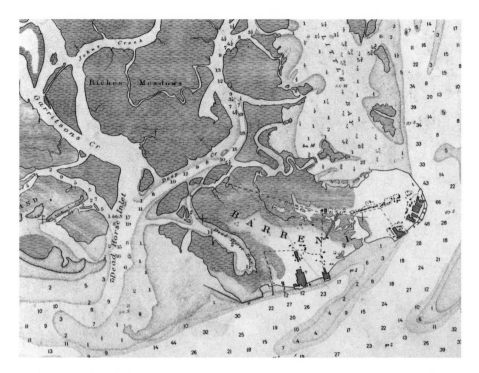

Detail from *Jamaica Bay and Rockaway Inlet* showing the waste treatment and rendering plants and village of Barren Island (center-right), United States Coast and Geodetic Survey, 1911. Lionel Pincus and Princess Firyal Map Division, The New York Public Library.

But what most outraged New Yorkers about Barren Island was not lawlessness or animal cruelty, but fearsome odors—the smell of industrial death. We can only imagine just how bad this must have been, as the olfactory dimension of the urban past is as irretrievably lost as the people who once walked the city's streets. One account from the Civil War era described the vapors of Barren Island as "like nothing on earth," so offensive that "if Jeff Davis would entrench himself behind a line guarded by such effluvia, his position would be impregnable." Another favorably likened the milk-curdling breath of a homeless drunk to "the wind that blows over Barren island." Which of the island's rendering plants committed the most egregious crimes against the nose was hard to say. Many reported several distinctive odors, emanating—in turn—from the rendering plants, the fertilizer works, and the fish-oil factories. Putrefying horseflesh and fish-cheese drying in the sun seemed to produce the most revolting smells of all. These "foul and sickening vapors . . . carried by the wind" became an increasingly fractious political issue as nearby beaches evolved into popular summer resorts, and—especially—as residential development extended south into Flatbush and Flatlands after the city expanded sewer service to the area. The earliest objections came from Gravesend and from seasonal residents of the Rockaways, where the smells were often "so powerful that it is impossible to keep the doors or windows of dwelling houses open."[15]

It was the infamous anti-Semite of Manhattan Beach, Austin Corbin, who organized the first legal battle against the olfactory scourge of Barren Island. In August

1888 his Manhattan Beach Improvement Company brought suit in Brooklyn's supreme court, seeking damages and an injunction against each of the island's principal rendering plants for inflicting grievous harm on the health and welfare of the public. But liberal application of that "popular tranquilizer of politicians, well known as 'palm oil,'" assured that nothing was done to shut down the well-connected contractors. Corbin then called upon his own arsenal of political connections, firing back with a "monster petition" that went straight to Albany and the desk of his buddy Governor David B. Hill. Hill was a conservationist—he signed the legislation establishing what eventually became Adirondack Park—and immediately ordered an investigation into the Barren Island nuisance issue. Testimony was taken from scores of men and women in a hearing before the State Board of Health on November 6, 1890. Counsel for the offal processors did all they could to trip up those testifying, but were "unable to shake the witnesses on one point—that Barren Island and its foul odors was the burden of their lives." Under oath, Charles H. Shelley, manager of Corbin's Oriental Hotel, described the reeking medley of smells carried in the east wind—one "pungent, nauseating," the other so violently offensive that "I have seen all the ladies on the piazza of an evening," he related, "leave us in consequence." The smells were so fearful in the summer of 1886, Shelley recalled, that hotel guests circulated a petition in protest. Another witness—Philip P. Simmons, who summered at Rockaway Park right in the path of winds from Barren Island—testified that "exceedingly pungent" stenches often made his wife and daughters nauseated, and one August night the fumes were so noxious that "every member of my family was waked up by the smell." Fenwick Bergen blamed his "malarial fever" on the island's ill winds and told of being "sick at the stomach" from a reeking cocktail of phosphates mixed with "rotten dead fish . . . rotten animals." Others testified of smelling the island as far away as downtown Brooklyn and the Five Towns.[16]

The governor's committee charged with investigating the mess proposed appointing an inspector to make biweekly reports on sanitary conditions at the rendering plants, and outlined a number of remedies for the island's olfactory ills—covering fish kettles, sealing storage buildings, mounting fans to drive noxious vapors into disinfectant baths or back into the furnaces to be burned away. All proved ineffective; for five years later, Corbin was threatening another round of legal action after the dreadful plume from Barren Island had his guests heaving again on the verandas of the Oriental and Manhattan Beach hotels. What finally quieted the much-loathed Corbin was not remedial action but a carriage accident on his New Hampshire estate—one that dashed his brains out on a stone wall. He was thus spared knowing that matters of the nose were about to get even worse back in Brooklyn. The very summer of Corbin's death in 1896, Colonel George E. Waring, newly appointed commissioner of the Department of Street-Cleaning—forerunner of the Sanitation Department—proposed to solve New York's growing "garbage problem" by rendering it into soap grease and fertilizer on Barren Island. Son of a wealthy Westchester manufacturer, Waring studied agricultural engineering in college. He later managed Horace Greeley's experimental farm, led the Thirty-Ninth New York Volunteers (the Garibaldi Hussars) in the Civil War, and helped drive Confederate forces from Missouri with General John C. Frémont. Just before the war he assisted the brilliant, irascible General Egbert L. Viele on the initial grading and drainage work for Central Park, which led to the job that made his career—helping Frederick Law Olmsted and Calvert Vaux implement their competition-winning "Greensward Plan" (Waring was especially proud of having planted the iconic American elms on the Central Park Mall). Waring later designed a municipal wastewater system for Memphis, Tennessee, following a terrible outbreak of yellow fever, the first system in the nation to separate storm water runoff from sewage. He was doing similar work in New Orleans when Mayor William L. Strong tapped him to clean filth-strewn New York.[17]

Cleaning this Augean stable of a city was a Herculean task indeed. Waring whipped the patronage-bloated Department of Street-Cleaning into shape, giving his troops crisp white canvas uniforms, new brooms, and nifty wheeled trash bins designed by his wife. He ended the practice of dumping all the city's refuse in the harbor, where it clogged shipping channels and befouled shores. Now only ashes and street sweepings would sleep with the fishes; dry light refuse—rags, paper, boxes, barrels, and assorted other junk—would be picked clean of usables (tin cans, for example, were melted to make window sash weights) by an army of Italian immigrant "scow trimmers" and incinerated in a Colwell furnace. Organic waste such as kitchen scraps and cast-off food—that "most troublesome element of city refuse . . . known as garbage"—Waring meant to render on Barren Island. There he would have it pressed for marketable grease and oil, or what the *New York Times* later called "unspeakable fats, for uses which it is a delight not to know or even imagine." All this required, of course, that city residents separate trash into three receptacles—one for ashes, another for dry waste, and a third for garbage (a practice recently reintroduced by the Department of Sanitation). The new law was honored mostly in the breach, however, prompting an editorial in the *New York Times* upbraiding the "enemies of civic cleanliness" whose "inveterate habits of slovenliness and negligence" would keep the city steeped in filth. After a bidding war and backroom deals, Waring's big garbage contract was awarded to the New-York Sanitary Utilization Company, based in Philadelphia but backed by a consortium of investors led by the same White family that had operated reduction works on Barren Island for decades (among the backers were infamous Philadelphia boss Dave Martin and Brooklyn politico Patrick H. McCarren, namesake of McCarren Park in Williamsburg). The company began construction at Barren Island in the fall of 1896—not a moment too soon for island residents. Most of the fish works had shut down by this time owing to a crash in the menhaden population. The new plant would not only solve Gotham's garbage problem but employ Barren Island's idled workers.[18]

The twin, side-by-side plants of the New-York Sanitary Utilization Company (the second one was erected to handle a subsequent Brooklyn contract) made it the largest waste-processing works in the world, capable of churning through fifteen hundred tons of garbage a day. It was designed around a state-of-the-art reduction system known as the "Arnold Process." Garbage arriving by scow would be conveyed upward and dropped through chutes into a bank of forty-eight digesters—"perpendicular cooking tanks" each five feet wide and fifteen feet tall and capable of holding ten tons of material. Once full, these would be sealed tight and pumped with steam to cook the garbage for several hours, to break it down and neutralize bacteria. "No offensive odors can escape from the tanks," the company promised, "and unpleasant gases will be conveyed through pipes and thrown in the form of spray upon the fires in the furnaces," thus scrubbing the plant's exhaust and—in theory, at least—rendering it wholly inoffensive to the nose. The contents of the digesters would then be emptied into sheet-iron receiving tanks, the liquids drained off and sent back into the boilers. The waste was then loaded into a series of Boomer & Boschert screw presses and put under several tons of pressure to squeeze out the oil and grease, which was sold for lubricants or soap making. It was next carted by tramcars to the drying room, where a "masticating machine" fed a series of cylindrical, steam-jacketed dryers, each sixteen feet long and equipped with revolving shafts armed with paddles to stir up the detritus. Once dry, the "tankage" or "oil cake" was released into hoppers, and screened, bagged, and marketed as a fertilizer ingredient. A motor room (with two big Corliss engines), pump house, office, storage facilities, and a dining hall for workers rounded out the complex, which struck observers as the very essence of efficient modernity. The Barren Island works, subject of an adoring five-page spread in *Engineering News*—seemed to share little with the ancient and unsavory business of waste, but rather "can only be regarded," wrote engineer William W. Locke, "as a large chemical engineering business requiring the best scientific intelligence for its operation."[19]

Had the writer consulted the plant's operators, another picture would have emerged—of working conditions as infernal as they were hazardous. When the digester tanks were emptied, for example, the hot swill "gushed out with great force, splattering the operators and the floor until the former were hardly recognizable." In 1898 a twenty-four-year-old African American named Robert Wedlock slipped on a wet rail and tumbled headfirst into a cart full of boiled mush as it moved into position beneath a press. Teetering on the edge, Wedlock's shoulder blade was crushed by the descending plate before the operator could shut down the machine. A moment more, reported the *Eagle*, and "his head would have been severed from his body." The worst accident occurred when an overloaded digester exploded, blowing a ten-foot hole in the roof and destroying much of the plant. The massive blast broke windows in nearly every building on Barren Island and echoed across the city. Workers—nearly all blacks and immigrant Poles and Russians—were enveloped in a violent gush of steam and boiling juice, blinding and scalding them and forcing some to leap to safety from third-floor windows. One, Antonio Carditz, was killed by a flying cast-iron boiler door; others were crushed beneath falling timbers and debris. The parboiled victims were saved only when harbor police made two five-mile motorboat dashes across Jamaica Bay to get them to hospital.[20]

The vast Sanitary Utilization facility also looked a whole lot better than it smelled. The effluent that was supposed to be boiled off—a noxious red-brown liquor—was in fact drained to Jamaica Bay, where it helped poison the most famous oyster beds in the United States. Windows meant to be kept closed in plant buildings were opened by workers desperate to ventilate rooms where the temperature soared to "that of a Turkish bath." The critical scrubbing technology was either never installed or simply didn't work, for soon the odors emanating from Barren Island—"pungent, penetrating and sickening"—were worse than ever. Even admiring engineer Locke admitted that the strange burnt-caramel odor from the Barren Island complex was "capable of a range . . . and penetration equal to that of our modern coast defense rifles." And there were more people than ever now in the line of fire—in rapidly developing communities around Jamaica Bay like Bergen Beach, the Rockaways, even Richmond Hill. Complaints came in from communities twelve miles from Barren Island, suggesting an odorshed that took in lower Manhattan, all of Brooklyn, and points as far east as Forest Hills, Rockville Center, and Long Beach. Outrage over the new pollutants was fast and fierce, but not without moments of poetic wit. As a woman named "Kate" versified in a letter to the *Eagle*,

> Waft, waft, ye summer breezes,
>   Barren Island's fearful smell;
> If the officials don't soon stop it,
>   We'll wish them safe in Hell.[21]

Others got straight to the point, dismissing the city's argument "that smells are a part of civilization and that the world would have to return to the savage state and live in the woods to avoid the nuisance." Civic groups denounced the garbage plant's gut-wrenching emanations, reportedly capable of producing a "headache in three minutes." Dr. Samuel Kohn of Arverne in the Rockaways caused mirth at a state Board of Health inquiry by describing the garbage smell as "awfully offal," telling how residents in his community would "suddenly be awakened from a sound sleep with a suffocating, irritating feeling in the throat" and quickly become "seized with nausea." When the flummoxed chairman of the inquiry asked Kohn to recommend a better place for the city's garbage, he suggested—what else?—New Jersey. Waring also testified before the panel, ridiculing complainants as misguided "victims of lively imaginations." He asserted that his pet reduction plant produced no odors offensive "in the proper sense of the word," and described the only smell there as "one like boiling cabbage"—so unobjectionable that "only a supersensitive stomach would be effected even at the factory."[22]

For the next twenty years, the city fought a running battle with state authorities and an increasingly powerful array of civic groups and real estate interests over Barren Island pollution. In 1898 Governor Frank S. Black issued a toothless proclamation ordering an end to the nuisance. The New York State Board of Health threatened to shut operations down if abatement measures were not implemented. The following year, Senator Joseph Wagner and George W. Doughty, a state assemblyman from Queens, introduced a bill on behalf of the Anti–Barren Island League "to remedy the suffering of a great number of residents whose health was alone impaired, but who also suffered financially . . . because of the stenches coming from Barren Island." When word came from Albany on April 26, 1899, that the bill had passed—over an attempted block by Mayor Van Wyck—the Rockaways erupted in jubilation. Newly elected governor Theodore Roosevelt, citing "hundreds of letters begging me to sign," promised to act; "I shall sign the bill," he declared, "no matter what action the Mayor may take." But Roosevelt did not sign the bill. In the interregnum, he was convinced to allow the city time to find an alternative to disposal at Barren Island lest it have a public health crisis on its hands. Roosevelt visited the rendering works himself in July 1899, which convinced him afresh that "the Barren Island nuisance must go." He gave the city a year to find an alternative and instructed Dr. Alvah H. Doty of the Port of New York to explore options. Doty toured Europe searching for a solution and returned convinced that the city needed to build a "public crematory" in which to burn all its trash. He suggested that New York follow Hamburg's lead, where mixed trash was cremated in a sealed furnace, the smoke condensed in water and the clinkers raked out for use in concrete for foundations and street paving. Doty reasoned that several such plants, odorless and inoffensive, could be built at points along the city's waterfront. But the deadline came and went; Roosevelt failed to win reelection, and in March 1901 Doughty quietly withdrew his bill altogether, explaining that he hadn't realized its broad language would put factories out of business all over the city. Around this time, a proposal was made by Brooklyn legislator Jacob D. Remsen to move the Kings County Penitentiary from its aging Crown Heights facility to Barren Island, thereby giving New York a kind of sandy Alcatraz a generation before Rikers became the city's isle of crime and punishment. Remsen's bill passed in Albany but was vetoed by Mayor Robert Van Wyck, partly because it was really the brainchild of a real estate concern—the Prospect Park Improvement Company—trying to boost its position by removing an "incubus upon all the property of the neighborhood." All this time, six scows daily were being towed out from the harbor to dump the city's garbage at sea, much of it driven right back to shore by wind and waves. Without a better solution in hand, the city reluctantly renewed Sanitary Utilization's contract, which of course "found itself in a position of such advantage" that it now demanded a much higher fee and a minimum five-year tenure.[23]

Picnicking among the ruins of the New-York Sanitary Utilization Company plant, 1931. The great chimney can be seen in the background. Photograph by Percy Loomis Sperr. Irma and Paul Milstein Division of United States History, Local History and Genealogy, The New York Public Library.

And so it was a red-letter day for the long-suffering victims of Barren Island when, on May 20, 1906, the Sanitary Utilization Company's sixteen-acre complex burned to the ground. The fire began in the digester building, quickly engulfing the entire plant and torching twenty thousand bags of fertilizer. Only a small fireboat, the *Seth Low*, was on hand to fight the blaze, the plant's own firefighting equipment having been consumed by the flames. As the fire spread, panic broke out among island residents who feared the wind-whipped blaze would soon burn their homes. A *Times* correspondent mocked the immigrant families as they rushed to a hodgepodge evacuation flotilla in the bay, piling "pellmell into the boats, carrying all sorts of household articles with them . . . some of them even took their carpets." In the chaos, several people fell into the water, including a woman "carrying a parrot and a marble clock" who was quickly "dragged out by her husband, who scolded her in Bohemian," forcing her to let the parrot go and drop the clock off the pier. The parrot was rescued by a boy in a rowboat. The dunked woman was soon back, triumphantly dry now and supervising her husband as he fished for her marble heirloom with a hook and sinker. News of the demise of the great odor engine was—quite literally—a breath of fresh air to those downwind, to whom the plant's destruction "seemed like a retributive act of divine Providence." Unfortunately, the Sanitary Utilization Company proved resilient. When the plant burned, the city had no choice but to begin dumping its garbage at sea once again—at least fifty miles out this time (scows would have to round an anchored "stakeboat" before they could release their payload). But fifty miles was not enough—if in fact the tugs were taking the barges that far; for within days, Rockaway residents were howling about the tons of trash fouling the beach at Arverne. Though at least one elected official suggested that Barren Island, cleansed now by fire, be used for a seaside park and convalescent home for the poor, the city had no choice but to implore Sanitary Utilization to rebuild as fast as possible. Within months, a new complex rose phoenix-like from the ashes—bigger, better, and hungrier than ever for Gotham's trash. And now, city residents could point to where their garbage went; for the plant was anchored on the skyline by a tremendous chimney meant to loft noxious exhalations to some distant place beyond city limits, like Nassau County. At 225 feet, it was one of the tallest structures in the United States at the time, and the loftiest on Long Island until the Williamsburg Savings Bank building was completed in 1929. The belching chimney, visible many miles at sea, was used as a navigation aid by mariners and greeted immigrant eyes long before Lady Liberty's torch. The massive concrete cylinder was ugly, lacking even an entasis; but it was a beacon of opportunity nonetheless. If the Mother of Exiles welcomed the newcomers, the chimney put them to work; some headed straight to Barren Island after landing and rarely—if ever—set foot on mainland America.[24]

By the 1900s, Barren Island was home to one of the most polyglot communities on the Eastern Seaboard, with a mostly immigrant population of some fourteen hundred Poles, Italians, African Americans, eastern European Jews, Germans, Irish, and a smattering of native-born Americans. Almost wholly unserved by the city it so vitally cleansed, the island was a throwback to another century. It boasted a hotel and boardinghouses, two churches, a school, dance hall, several bars, a grocery store, butcher, and baker. But Barren Island's streets were unpaved and flooded by spring tides. There was no permanent police presence on the island until 1897, no fire protection, and—ironically—no trash collection; rubbish was simply tossed in the streets for the pigs and gulls. Fruit was scarce, vegetables meager, and meat (often horse) poor in quality. The well water tasted like fish oil and was later found to be so laden with toxins that residents were forced to subsist on collected rain-water. Flies were ferocious and legion; food left unattended for more than a minute would be black with the insects. There were pig wallows and pools of stagnant water that bred clouds of mosquitoes and caused frequent outbreaks of malaria, typhoid, and diphtheria (which residents fought by wrapping their throats with a compress of salt pork and flannel). Infant mortality on Barren Island was twice the city average. Children rummaging through the island's great trash heap—known as "The Klondike"—punctured and cut their feet on rusty nails and tin cans. Industrial accidents averaged two a week and were often catastrophic. And yet there was no hospital, infirmary, doctor, or nurse on the island. Worker cottages were terribly overcrowded, with families often taking in a half dozen boarders to make ends meet. The little hovels—many adorned with desperate gardens struggling in the sand— were arrayed along the island's Main Street, "like a convict settlement," wrote one unsympathetic observer, "or the outdoor wards of a pesthouse." Many island resi-dents and most of its children had never been to the mainland, for not until 1905 was there regular ferry service to Canarsie—and even then only in warmer months. Ice in Jamaica Bay made it difficult for ships to reach the settlement in winter, delaying delivery of mail and often leaving residents critically short of food and medicine.[25]

Barren Island's catalog of ills made it a target of social reformers. The North American Civic League for Immigrants, founded by crusading progressive Fran-ces A. Kellor, carried out some of its earliest programs there, sending operatives on

Catholic church, Barren Island, 1931. Photograph by Percy Loomis Sperr. Irma and Paul Milstein Division of United States History, Local History and Genealogy, The New York Public Library.

"friendly visiting" sorties into the homes of immigrant laborers to convey "American social ideals . . . American standards of living and in general an understanding of the principles behind them." The ministrations were largely altruistic, but not without a political edge. Aiding the isle's workers in this way might well keep them from being exploited by labor agitators or foreign propagandists; for "wretched housing, over-crowding, extortion and lack of water supply and health protection," wrote Kellor, then chief investigator for the New York State Department of Labor, "provide the groundwork for rebellion and sedition" (and "Barren Island," she emphasized, "is a rather strategic point in our coast defenses"). Whatever her ultimate aim, Kellor helped bring a plethora of improvements to Barren Island. An infirmary and milk-and-ice station for mothers was opened under the auspices of the Department of Health, staffed by a trained nurse. A Little Mothers' League was organized to edu-cate girls about child rearing; evening classes were offered on citizenship and home economics; a playground and ball field were constructed to provide children an alternative to rummaging in the dump; youth clubs were launched to counter the pull of saloons. But even before these, Barren Island was not without its richness and beauty. Life blossomed with weed-like vigor amidst the sand and garbage, and nowhere more fully so than at the handsome gray-and-white Public School 120, erected in 1901 and alive with "bright, active little people, in love with nature and the sea by which they are surrounded." And life flourished there in ways scarcely imaginable at the time elsewhere in New York. Not only was Barren Island one of the city's most ethnically diverse communities; it was among the earliest to be racially integrated. A 1901 *Brooklyn Eagle* article about its new school was accompanied by a photograph—captioned "Two of the Scholars"—that epitomized racial optimism in America. In it, two adorable kindergarten girls—one black, the other white—beam for the camera with their arms around each other. Racism spoiled the *Eagle* piece nonetheless, as its author related with salacious censure how "young white women frequently choose negro partners" at the weekly Barren Island dance—and how "the children look on and drink in . . . the seamy side of Barren Island society." Blacks and whites also engaged in collective action, striking against the New-York Sanitary Utilization Company plant in April 1913. Press and engine room operators walked off the job when company officials balked at a requested pay raise, and were soon joined by most of the plant's "500 Polacks and fifty negroes." The facility remained closed for nearly two weeks, until the company brought in two hundred strikebreakers on May 16. The day shift went forward without incident, but it was a Friday—payday—and there was, yet again, nothing for the strikers. Enraged by the scabs and "inflamed by Barren Island liquor," they attacked the arriving night-shift workers, firing revolvers, hurling bricks, and clubbing and kicking them. The seven policemen on-site at the time were quickly overwhelmed. Dozens of workers were injured, and one striker shot by the time the riot was quelled by police called in from the mainland.[26]

The rubbish of the modern world came to Barren Island by the scow-load, while its wonders arrived only in fits of happenstance. It was a brutally cold winter that brought the first motor vehicle to the remote community, nearly a decade before Barren Island was finally joined to the mainland by road. In January 1918 oysterman

Harold Rohde drove a one-ton Maxwell truck over miles of ice to reach the clam cribs he stored on the island. There he was greeted by "droves of wild-eyed children" who begged for a ride and "persisted in hooking their sleds on behind, riding all the way to Canarsie shore." Rohde's Maxwell was burdened with twenty-three hundred pounds of clams on the return trip, making it a wonder indeed that he did not break through the weak sea ice and commit sledders and bivalves alike to the bay bottom. Six months later, Barren Island was blessed by the arrival of another female redeemer, one who brought more joy to the long-scorned isle than a diamond ring pulled from the trash. Jane F. Shaw, a farm girl raised on the edge of the Adirondacks, was already an experienced teacher when the Board of Education tapped her to head P.S. 120. She had taught for many years in city schools—most recently near the Henry Street Settlement in lower Manhattan. To Shaw, Barren Island was anything but. She quickly took command of her new station, staying on-site all week and returning for the weekend to the home she shared in Williamsburg with two sisters—both also educators. Within months of her arrival Barren Island began showing signs of metamorphosis. Well aware that children with chaotic home lives were in no condition to learn, Shaw extended her reach well beyond the classroom, making it her business "not only to teach the children . . . but to go into their homes and help their parents." She had the Red Cross send milk daily during the great influenza pandemic, her boys meeting the police boat at the dock and pushing carts loaded with bottles through heavy sand to the homes of the sick. Trained by a navy physician stationed in Jamaica Bay, Shaw became the island's de facto doctor. Disease became rare, and the rowdiness and disorder long associated with Barren Island vanished as saloons were closed by Prohibition. At the end of the year Shaw would invite her eighth-grade class to tea at her Marcy Avenue home. Many of Shaw's pupils went on to high school, enduring long mainland commutes by foot, trolley, and subway. A decade later, Barren Island had been transformed from the butt of jokes into a model town, the "richest spot on earth," Shaw called it, with a post office and a stigma-free new name: South Flatlands. When the city balked at building a plank road in from Flatbush Avenue, Shaw organized the islanders to construct one themselves. She taught cooking classes in her kitchen, encouraged residents to grow vegetables and raise chickens, ducks, and cows, and turned P.S. 120 into a community center—persuading the Board of Education to outfit it with a radio and movie projector and using her own money to buy a piano.[27]

The New-York Sanitary Utilization Company finally closed its Barren Island plant in 1920, demolishing all but the great chimney a year later. With hundreds of jobs now gone, the island's population plunged. And yet life carried on nearly two decades more, clinging to this spit of sand as the world swirled in change all around it. Flatbush Avenue was extended across Barren Island in 1923, ending the island's isolation and filling many of the salt meadows and creeks with sand dredged from Rockaway channel. A small airstrip was constructed in 1927 by an enterprising young pilot named Paul Rizzo; four years later, New York City would open at Barren Island its first municipal airport (see chapter 12). Then, in March 1936, agents of the city's powerful and ambitious new parks commissioner, Robert Moses, trudged through the sand to deliver eviction notices to the island's four hundred-odd remaining

FLATBUSH AVE, EXTENSION
LOOKING SOUTH TOWARD TOWARD BARREN ISLAND ON LINE OF EXT, 11/20/24 5732

End of an island, November 1924: sand slurry being pumped from Jamaica Bay to extend Flatbush Avenue from Avenue U to Rockaway Inlet, joining Barren Island to the rest of Brooklyn. Edgar E. Rutter photograph collection, Brooklyn Public Library, Brooklyn Collection.

residents, some of whom had lived on Barren Island for forty years. Now they had fourteen days to pack up and leave, to make way for what was planned to be the largest urban playground in the world. "Lady Jane" Shaw knew every one of these men, women, and children; she had attended their every christening, wedding, and funeral; she was their "counselor, dictator, friend and champion." And now she rendered one last service—imploring Moses and other city officials to give her benighted Barren Islanders a reprieve long enough to see her last class graduate. In a letter to Brooklyn borough president Raymond V. Ingersoll, Shaw told of the panic and plight among her flock, invoking the "Exile of the Acadians" popularized by Longfellow's epic poem *Evangeline*. Moved by the plea, Moses granted her request, postponing the deadline to June 30, graduation day. The old school was boarded up the very next morning. The symbolic end of Barren Island came a year later, on March 20, 1937, when the great smokestack of the Sanitary Utilization plant was toppled by dynamite. However handy a landmark for ships and fishermen, it had become a menace to aviators at Floyd Bennett Field. Mayor Fiorello La Guardia, the short-lived airport's biggest booster, set off the charge personally in front of an enormous crowd of spectators. There was a boom and a wisp of smoke, followed by silence. The crowd murmured with confusion. And then, with a gathering roar, the old stack leaned into a fall, crashing onto the sand like a mighty tree trunk. It had been hoped that the chimney's four platinum-plated lightning arrestors—said to be worth thousands of dollars—might be a last gift to the island's Depression-poor residents; but the rods had been removed long before. Jane Shaw was not among those gathered; for the "guardian angel of Barren Island" had bid farewell to her beloved isle three years before, still mourning the loss of the community she loved.[28]

Public School 120, Barren Island, 1931, Board of Education of the City of New York. Irma and Paul Milstein Division of United States History, Local History and Genealogy, The New York Public Library.

A HOUSE FOR THE GOD OF SPEED

. . . we have beaten Rome now.
—EVERARD THOMPSON, 1915

The reek of rendered horseflesh, like the thunder of hooves, was soon just a memory in Brooklyn. But to Sheepshead Bay now came horsepower of another sort. Only weeks after the final Realization Stakes in 1910, inventor-aviator Glenn H. Curtiss of Hammondsport leased the idled racetrack for a two-week air meet. It was the first air show on the East Coast and only the second in the United States. Curtiss, who first flew over Gotham the previous fall during the Hudson-Fulton Celebration, claimed his extravaganza would give New Yorkers "their first view of a real aeroplane contest" and seed interest in the city for commercial aviation. Curtiss had his eye on opening an airport in New York City—"a permanent aviation field within a short distance of the metropolis"—and just a year earlier had moved his base of operations from the Finger Lakes to Mineola; for the table-flat Hempstead plain that the English found so well suited for horse racing made it ideal for airplanes too (it was with Curtiss's approval that the Hempstead Plains Aerodrome opened there in 1912, later named Roosevelt Field). On August 19, 1910, first day of the Sheepshead Bay air meet, a furious wind kept nearly all the fliers grounded. But the next afternoon spectators were thrilled to see Curtiss and his three top students—James Cairn "Bud" Mars, Eugene B. Ely, and Canadian J.A.D. McCurdy—lift into the sky and stack their planes in precise formation. A reporter from the *New York Times* marveled at the planes soaring "like a flock of wild ducks." And then the fliers launched into a race—the first true air race ever held in America (in previous contests, aviators flew individual timed solo runs). As the official program ended and the crowd dispersed at dusk, military brass were shown around the flying machines. Bud Mars took up Captain Harrison S. Kerrick of the US Coast Artillery, while Glenn Curtiss ascended with a young lieutenant from the Twenty-Ninth Infantry named Jacob E. Fickel. Fickel carried aloft a Springfield rifle, and as Curtiss made a low pass over the track, he fired at a three-by-five-foot target on the field below. It was the first gun ever fired from an airplane.[1]

On Sunday a crowd fifteen thousand strong turned out to see the aviators, but a roaring wind forced Curtiss to issue a "wind check" to all. The second round of the Sheepshead Bay "air carnival" began on the afternoon of August 26, with perfect flying weather. Ely started the show, followed by Mars, who had just that morning nearly killed himself flying across the Narrows. Bucking a strong wind that was pushing him out to sea, his aircraft suffered a catastrophic structural failure, plunging a thousand feet into the lower bay, where Mars was picked up by a tug.[2] Now he set the crowd roaring as he skimmed low over the track like a winged thoroughbred. "Mars followed the path of the race horses around the hurdle course," reported the *New York Times*, "touching the earth between the hurdles, and bounding over them with the grace of a dolphin running up out of the sea." Augustus Post thrilled the crowd with a daredevil stunt in which he jumped off his plane while it was skimming the track, ran around to the starboard side, grabbed the wing and swung the entire craft around to a stop in the opposite direction. Ely literally dropped his harbinger of a new age in the very lap of the old, landing his Curtiss biplane on the front lawn of the nearby Manhattan Beach Hotel for a dinner date with his wife. But the truly momentous achievement of the day was lost on the very officials—from the War Department and the US Army—who had the most to gain from it. Radioman Harry M. Horton had set up a wireless transmitter and receiver on the roof of the Sheepshead Bay grandstand the week before, and used it to beam reports of the day's flights to Manhattan. Now he wanted to see whether an airborne unit could successfully relay a message to the base station. He strapped the transmitter in Doug McCurdy's airplane, trailing a long wire behind for an antenna and mounting the telegraph key alongside the steering yoke. McCurdy had trouble at first using it while maintaining control of his ship, but the next day he pulled it off—tapping out a brief message to Horton in Morse code as he circled five hundred feet overhead. McCurdy's dispatch was the first wireless communication between an airplane and the ground. A high-ranking dunderhead from the Signal Corps, Major Samuel Reber, thought the whole affair a waste of time, telling a reporter that the army had already "lost interest in it," and forbidding the press to mention his name in any future stories about the use of radios in airplanes.[3]

The thousands who gathered at Sheepshead Bay for this first great air meet in New York City witnessed an assembly of aviation pioneers whose exploits in coming years would help shape the age of flight. Just weeks after the Brooklyn meet, Eugene Ely became the first aviator to take off from a ship (and, soon after, to land on one). Augustus Post was a writer and ballad-singer with degrees from Brooklyn Polytechnic Institute and Harvard Law School who owned the first automobile in New York City (an electric car, no less). He went on to draft, in 1919, the rules for the New York–Paris competition that Charles Lindbergh would win in 1927. As for Bud Mars, there are likely many New Yorkers with ancestors who actually saw the intrepid flier pilot his Baldwin "Red Devil" biplane—not in Brooklyn, but in the Far

East. In December 1910 Mars left for an extended sojourn in Asia, where he made some 250 flights. These were the very first airplane flights in most of the countries he visited. Their purpose, as Mars quaintly put it, was "to advance the art of aviation in the heathen and semi-heathen countries." Millions watched Mars fly over Manila, Tokyo, Beijing, Tianjin, Singapore, Bangkok, Calcutta, and St. Petersburg. At Osaka he drew a crowd of more than 750,000 people. Mars terrorized Chinese peasants, was cheered by exiles laboring in the czarist mines at Irkutsk, and was deemed both a deity and a devil in the Philippines. In Bangkok, Mars took up the youthful king of Siam, Rama VI, for a spin over the city, and in Japan he trained the nation's first fliers—though perhaps not very well: both of his pupils, officers in the Imperial Japanese Army, died in a plane crash before Mars even got back to the United States.[4]

A year after the Brooklyn track introduced New York City to the aviation age, it served as the launch point of an agonizingly slow and hazardous (sixteen crashes in forty-nine days), but nonetheless historic jaunt across the United States—the first transcontinental flight across America that was—appropriately enough for this first nation of consumerism—also an ingenious advertising ploy for a new soft drink. The adventurer was a dashing young pilot named Calbraith Perry Rodgers. Rodgers was the scion of a large and distinguished family of navy officers. Among his forebears were Captain John Rodgers, who led the recapture of Washington after the British invasion of 1814, and the brother-commodores Oliver Hazard Perry ("Don't give up the ship!") and Matthew C. Perry, who opened Japan to the West. Cal Rodgers had Brooklyn roots too—ancestors George Washington Rodgers and Christopher R. P. Rodgers, superintendent of West Point in the 1870s, were both raised there. Wellborn and wealthy, six-foot-three, and uncommonly handsome, Rodgers seemed to have it all. But a childhood bout of scarlet fever had left him nearly deaf and thus unfit for military service. Denied the naval career that was his birthright, Rodgers cast about for a meaningful vocation. He crewed for millionaire members of the New York Yacht Club, living at the club's posh West Forty-Fourth Street headquarters, raced automobiles, and made news with a mad, one-day dash on a motorcycle from Buffalo to New York City. Introduced to aviation in the spring of 1911, he knew he had found his calling. Rodgers learned to fly at the Wright Flying School in Dayton, Ohio. When his instructor balked at letting him take the training aircraft up for a solo run, he bought it, thus becoming the first civilian to own a Wright biplane.

Within weeks of passing his flight test Rodgers bagged over $10,000 in prize money at the International Aviation Meet in Chicago's Grant Park. He caught the eye there of a savvy showman and promoter named Stewart Ives DeKrafft. DeKrafft had brought a musical comedy, *The Prince of Pilsen*, to Broadway and helped organize the 1910 Glidden Tour—a 2,850-mile promotional motor race from Cincinnati to Chicago "by way of Dallas"—blazing the grueling competition route himself with two other drivers. DeKrafft immediately recognized Rodgers's star potential. The handsome aristocrat might be a novice flier, but he had great courage and a charismatic presence. DeKrafft approached him about competing for the $50,000 prize William Randolph Hearst had offered the first person to fly across the United States in under thirty days. Rodgers assented. DeKrafft soon found a sponsor in J. Ogden

Calbraith Perry Rodgers poses before launching on his star-crossed flight across America, September 17, 1911. Caltech Archives, Theodore von Kármán Collection.

Armour, whose meatpacking company had recently expanded into the soft drink business. In exchange for advertising the company's new grape-flavored Vin Fiz beverage—one rather profoundly unsuitable for long-distance flight, it turned out, given its laxative properties—Armour offered Rodgers $5 for every mile flown east of the Mississippi and $4 for every one west. He paid to outfit a three-car chase train complete with Pullman sleeper, repair shop, onboard chase car, and parts enough to completely rebuild the expedition aircraft—a modified Wright Model B biplane christened the *Vin Fiz Flyer*. They were well used; only a fraction of the original machine would make the full trip. Rodgers's wife, Mabel Graves, was made an honorary "postmistress" to handle letters and postcards carried aloft by her husband, and even had designed a handsome twenty-five-cent semiofficial stamp for the occasion—the first in the world to depict an airplane. Despite its obvious commercial aspect, the flight of the *Vin Fiz* gave Rodgers the sense of mission and purpose he had been seeking for years. When a reporter asked him why he was doing it, he said, "Because everything else I've done was unimportant."[5]

DeKrafft was a skilled publicity man and drummed up enormous press and public interest in the Hearst Prize flight. Rodgers would launch his transcontinental expedition from Sheepshead Bay Racetrack on Sunday, September 17. By early afternoon, the field was crawling with spectators, whom Rodgers and his crew had to fight to keep them from signing his airplane's wings or, worse, trying to pull off a souvenir screw or scrap of fabric. At 4:25 p.m., having finally cleared a path through the mob, the *Vin Fiz* wobbled and bounced its way across the field, the namesake soft drink used to christen this ship still dripping from its skids. The craft became airborne near the present intersection of Bedford Avenue and Avenue X, near today's Bill Brown Playground. As Rodgers climbed over Coney Island, he cast Vin Fiz coupons down to the crowds on the beach below, aiming for the Brooklyn Bridge. He crossed Manhattan at Twenty-Third Street, where thousands had gathered to watch him pass some eight hundred feet overhead. Once across the Hudson he followed the Erie Railroad west across New Jersey and the Southern Tier of New York, picking it out from the maze of tracks in Jersey City by the strips of white canvas—two thousand yards' worth—flagging its rails. He landed at Middletown, New York, at 6:18 p.m. As he took off the next morning, his skids caught a willow, pivoting the plane off course and into a hickory tree. Plane and pilot tumbled thirty-five feet to the ground, flattening a chicken coop and killing a dozen birds. The engine came close to crushing Rodgers, who nearly called the whole thing off. By now his mother had shown up, begging him to cancel the trip. She would tag along until they reached Arizona Territory, quarreling with Mabel the whole way. The *Vin Fiz* repaired, Rodgers got airborne again—to Binghamton and Elmira (where he had another accident), Hornell, Olean, and Salamanca. Just south of there, Rodgers nearly wrecked the craft yet again—three times in seven days—when he snagged a barbed-wire fence taking off from a field.[6]

And thus—a pocket full of stogies and isinglass goggles affixed—did Cal Rodgers make his halting, willy-nilly way to California, winning the hearts of millions of Americans in the process. He was not yet halfway across the country when the Hearst Prize expired, still nineteen days and some two thousand miles from the Pacific, but Rodgers pressed on all the same, surviving yet more brushes with death and blogging all the way—sending dispatches for the national press via his wife and crew. He made it to Chicago by October 8, flew over the Illinois State Penitentiary at Joliet "for the benefit of the prisoners," was forced down by storms and fog in Oklahoma, appeared at the Texas State Fair, raced an eagle to Waco, and crashed a circus in New Mexico territory. Towns all along his route hung up buntings and banners, hoping to entice the intrepid flier down for a stop. Rodgers's longest nonstop flight—133 miles—ended when a connecting rod punctured the engine

Vin-Fiz semiofficial 25¢ stamp on back of envelope. An extreme rarity, examples like this have sold for over $100,000. Courtesy Robert A Siegel Auction Galleries.

crankcase, tearing it to pieces and forcing him down from four thousand feet over the Imperial Valley. But at 4:10 p.m. on November 5, 1911—forty-nine days, thirteen states, and sixteen crashes after leaving Brooklyn—Cal Rodgers and the *Vin Fiz* touched down at Tournament Park in Pasadena, site of the first Rose Bowl. A hysterical mob of twenty thousand people received him like a deity. Overcome with emotion, Rodgers was handed a great bouquet of chrysanthemums and draped in an American flag. When the Yankee airman finally got to the Hotel Maryland, still wrapped in Old Glory, he requested not champagne or even Vin Fiz, but a tall glass of milk. It was the longest airplane flight yet attempted by anyone in the world, more than doubling the previous record—Harry Atwood's twelve-hundred-mile run from St. Louis to New York. Rodgers returned east in January—by train this time—to receive a gold medal at a banquet of the Aero Club of America. A monoplane had been suspended from the ceiling of the rococo Sherry Ballroom for the occasion; the French ambassador was a guest of honor and President William Howard Taft made a brief appearance. The restless Rodgers was soon back in California, planning an even greater conquest—a flight across the Atlantic. But in April that spring, during a routine flight at Long Beach, Rodgers lost control of his craft after playfully chasing a flock of gulls, plunging two hundred feet into the surf. This time the engine landed on his back, breaking Rodgers's neck and killing him instantly. Many years later, his widow revealed that a gull had been found lodged in the plane's control cables.[7]

Cal Rodgers's passion for speed and daring would live on at the Sheepshead Bay Racetrack. Tired of waiting for the crusading governor's antigambling laws to be rescinded, hemorrhaging money on taxes and maintenance of their immense facility, the Coney Island Jockey Club began looking to unload the property. Even as the *Vin Fiz Flyer* was still puttering across the United States, the *Brooklyn Eagle* reported that "no more will thousands of Brooklyn and Manhattan people see the Suburban or Futurity races at Sheepshead Bay racetrack. The place is advertised for sale." It was the first of the great Brooklyn tracks to be put on the market. By December a group of investors had purchased an option on the property, with vague but ambitious plans to develop it into a "high-class residential colony . . . along the lines of Newport," with slips for pleasure craft along Gerritsen Creek. There were also rumors of an aerodrome and sport track that would turn the idled acreage into a motor-sport theme park. But the big deal, "shrouded in considerable mystery," fell through. The track lay largely idle for the next three years, awaiting its fate. It hosted a number of semipro baseball matches, and a Decoration Day outing for the female employees of Macy's; August Belmont stabled his yearlings there. In 1913, the annual show of the Long Island Kennel Club was held at the track, a "fuzzy old English sheepdog" named Brentwood Hero taking the top honors.[8]

But the salesgirls and show dogs would not be coming back. In late 1914, the Coney Island Jockey Club finally sold the 430-acre site. Presiding over the deal was Schuyler Livingston Parsons, the club's last president, whose name was a three-note threnody to the faded glory of old New York. The buyer was a syndicate of New York and Chicago "automobile men" led by James C. Nichols, Standard Oil heir Harry S. Harkness, and famed builder of the Indianapolis Motor Speedway and creator of Miami Beach Carl G. Fisher. Their aim was to build a mammoth motordrome and sporting arena—a "Mecca for Manly Sport." With steeds mechanical, the Sheepshead Bay Speedway would revive the old racetrack's legacy as a rendezvous for New York society.[9] "It is believed by the new promoters," the *New York Times* explained, "that those of wealth and sporting instinct who formerly followed the performances of thoroughbreds have now turned their attention to high-powered automobiles." The speedway would be "second to none in the country," built on a scale to match the ambition of the Empire State—wider and faster than Indianapolis, with a design speed of 130 miles an hour. As many as 200,000 spectators would ultimately be accommodated at the speedway, on the field and in grandstands that would rise as high as a seven-story building. The motoring press had little doubt about demand for all this. As the *Automobile* reasoned, "If Indianapolis with a population of only 233,000 can muster a crowd of 100,000 automobile race enthusiasts, New York City with 5,000,000 people . . . should furnish at least double the attendance which is found each year at the Hoosier speedway." But the great motordrome would be about work as well as play, serving as a "great outdoor laboratory," the *New York Times* observed, "for the perfecting of motor types."[10]

Heading this effort was an experienced sports and entertainment impresario, Everard "Tommy" Thompson, recruited from Yale to be general manager of the Sheepshead Bay Speedway Corporation and to make the old track a motordrome for the new "king sport of America." Thompson had been a music major at Yale and was an old-school Renaissance man. He wrote a baseball column for the *Yale Daily News*, managed ticket sales for the athletics department, and supervised construction of the Carnegie Pool. But he also loved opera and brought major companies to

New Haven for performances. Thompson's greatest contribution was conceiving the unique design and supervising construction of the Yale Bowl, father of all "bowl" stadia in the United States and today a National Historic Landmark. Thompson gathered about him a core of advisers, among them Amos G. Batchelder, an early bicycling advocate, pioneer of the Good Roads Movement, and founding chairman of the American Automobile Association. New York's premier architecture firm, McKim, Mead & White, was initially approached to design the grandstands and other buildings for the speedway complex. So was the prominent theater architect V. Hugo Koehler, designer of the Lyric Theater on Forty-Second Street and the Washington and Lafayette theaters in Harlem.[11]

But the commission went instead to a Brooklyn-born architect who had spent boyhood summers on his grandfather's Flatlands farm—Henry Hornbostel, known to friends as "Horny." A dazzling figure, Hornbostel once rode a bicycle from Brooklyn to Niagara Falls as a teenager and became a national champion bike racer in college. He studied architecture at Columbia and the École des Beaux-Arts in Paris, where he earned the sobriquet *l'homme perspectif* for his uncanny ability to bring renderings to life. By the turn of the century, Hornbostel had built a successful practice in New York, winning commissions as far away as Oakland, California, where he designed the city hall. His impact was especially strong in Pittsburgh, where he spent much of his career and designed over a hundred major buildings—including much of what is today Carnegie Mellon University. Despite a penchant for the neoclassical, Hornbostel was not afraid of steel. Working with commissioner of bridges Gustav Lindenthal,

Laminated pine track and grandstand under construction, Sheepshead Bay Motor Speedway, August 1915. Brooklyn Public Library, Brooklyn Collection.

he brought beauty to some of New York's iconic spans—including the Hell Gate, Williamsburg, and Queensboro bridges. Hornbostel's single completed grandstand at Sheepshead Bay, with a capacity of 30,000, was already among the largest in the world and the first designed for air shows—the cantilevered balcony and roof were set back so that most seats could enjoy an unobstructed view of the sky. And this was just the start; for ultimately 175,000 spectators would find grandstand seats, with standing room for many more on the field. If New York was the new Rome, this would be its mighty coliseum, an arena where modern gladiators met to race their motor chariots. "We have always looked back to Rome for our ideas of magnitude in sport," Thompson told the *Eagle*; "But I think we have beaten Rome now."[12]

Grandstands might seat the ticket-buying throngs, but the soul of a speedway is its track, and for that Fisher and his associates turned to a Missourian named Blaine Heston Miller. Fisher knew Miller well from Indianapolis, where he had recruited the young civil engineer—then still in his twenties—to design his Hoosier speedway. As with that project, Miller's Brooklyn track was no simple earthen loop, but a highly engineered plane, seventy feet wide on the straightaways, stretching to seventy-six feet on the turns. Framed with steel, these were banked or "super elevated" along a parabolic curve, sweeping gracefully upward to nearly the height of a three-story building. This design was far more sophisticated than the simple conical or straight-section turns at the Hoosier track. Miller drew this limber parabolic form from the revolutionary Brooklands track in England, creating turns nearly identical to those used later on the rooftop track at the Fiat Lingotto factory in Turin, designed shortly after the Brooklyn speedway opened. Miller used 3.2 million bricks to pave the Indy roadbed. But for Sheepshead Bay, he turned to wood. A board track was state-of-the-art for motor racing at the time, first used in 1910 for the Los Angeles Motordrome at Playa Del Rey. Wood was labor expensive, prone to rot, and highly flammable, especially if coated with creosote. But it was fast and the drivers loved it. The smooth surface of a well-maintained board track minimized the bone-jarring ride of a hard track that could shake a machine to pieces. It also reduced friction, thus minimalizing the heat that caused tires to blow—often with tragic consequences—on coarser concrete or brick. Three million board feet of Georgia longleaf pine was used for the Sheepshead Bay speedway, another 3.5 million on the grandstand and bleachers. The two-by-four-inch planks, from ten to twenty feet in length, were laid on edge, set on transverse concrete sleepers and nailed together into a great butcher-block roadbed. "To the eye it has the appearance of numberless strands of ribbon," the *Eagle* related, "and when the sun glances on it the picture is almost entrancing."[13]

Building the mammoth playground began in earnest in April 1915. That summer an army of twenty-five hundred men worked around the clock to ready the speedway for an opening race in October. Cement and stone came by barge via Coney Island Creek, while lumber and twenty-five hundred tons of steel came by rail right to the front gates, using the old racetrack spur of the Long Island Rail Road's Manhattan Beach Branch. Wooden forms for poured concrete were recycled from the old racetrack's grandstands. The care and feeding of so many workers in relatively remote Flatlands required the infrastructure of a small town—"our little principality," as

Panorama of Sheepshead Bay Motor Speedway, October 14, 1915. Photograph by Charles E. Stacy. Library of Congress, Prints and Photographs Division.

Blaine Miller called it, complete with dormitories and mess halls. "We have our own grocery store, butcher shop, ice plant, tobacconist shop and clubroom," he explained; "There is a bath house, rough and ready but efficient. A barber shop is in full swing and lathering and scraping go on all day." A carpentry shop, machinists and blacksmiths, a wheelwright, and a motor garage rounded out the complex. The clerical and engineering staff alone consisted of thirty men and women. Ironically, the great course for "manly sport" was first driven by a woman, Nancy Hanks, who steered a high-powered roadster around the sap-scented course while it was still under construction, scattering workers at "better than eighty miles an hour."[14]

The official opening came on Saturday, September 18, 1915, and began not in Brooklyn but across the river and uptown at Columbus Circle. Just after lunch that afternoon, a handful of motorcars headed down Broadway to Fifth Avenue and over the Williamsburg Bridge. The motorcade started small, but hundreds of vehicles joined all along the way, expanding it "like a snowball rolling down hill." By the time the procession reached the speedway gates at Ocean Avenue and Neck Road, it was two thousand vehicles strong—very likely the mightiest motor-vehicle parade ever seen in New York City. Had all these cars headed *back* to Columbus Circle, they would have formed a thirteen-mile convoy (cars at the head would reach Central Park just as those at the tail got going). The parade cars were decked out like Mardi Gras floats, judged for their originality. First prize went to a vehicle draped with white silk bunting, a "flock" of stuffed doves mounted on the hood, as if flying out in front. Another carried a likeness of Mercury, while the African Americans who helped build the speedway—many of them former stable hands and grooms—were forced to endure a blackface farce called *A Coontown Wedding*. After speeches, stage actress and society doyenne Eloise S. Kilborn smashed a bottle of champagne against a concrete wall, raining bubbly and broken glass on the pine planks below: "I hereby christen the Sheepshead Bay Speedway," she declared, "to the God of Speed." But the real star of the afternoon was an Italian racer named Dario Resta, who set a

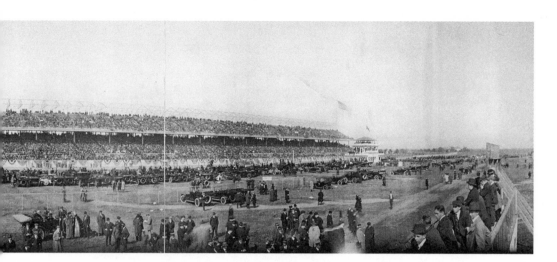

new world speed record in one of the time trials—108 miles an hour—his little blue Peugeot looking "no bigger than a bug" from high in the grandstand. "This is the finest track in the world," Resta declared, "and I have driven on them all." Miller's banked turns were so flawlessly engineered that Resta's car "took them naturally without an effort at the steering wheel." The youthful driver's triumph made it a red-letter day for the city's Italian American community. But the joy was short-lived. Ten days later, on September 27, Vanderbilt Cup champion Harry F. Grant's Maxwell burst into flames as it entered a turn during a trial heat. Grant was able to steer the machine down the embankment, but he suffered terrible burns and later died at Coney Island Hospital.[15]

The tragedy cast a pall over the first big race at the new track, the Astor Challenge Cup. The 350-mile run was conceived expressly for the speedway inauguration. It was initially postponed because of rain; water made board tracks slick as ice. The delay wrecked the speedway's balance sheet, as a workforce of fifteen hundred men and women—including five hundred ushers, all Columbia students—had to be paid nonetheless. The rain took no shine off the $50,000 purse, however, which lured the best drivers in the world to southern Brooklyn—Ralph DePalma, Johnny Aitken, Dario Resta, Eddie Rickenbacker. The race was finally run on October 9, a brilliant fall day. A crowd of sixty thousand spectators jammed the stands, including much of the Gotham smart set—a veritable "outpouring of the beau monde" led, of course, by Vincent Astor, donor of the cup itself. "To name all those in the boxes would be to call the roll of New York's socially elite," noted *Motor* magazine. There were Vander-bilts and Speyers, Parsons, Belmonts, and Iselins—all dressed to the nines, "society decked in its most charming gowns and its most modish millinery . . . reflecting the glory of the sunlight of the perfect October day." The cup and prize money went to Norwegian driver Gil Andersen, who averaged 102.6 miles an hour for the race—a new world record. The Americans claimed victory nonetheless, as both Andersen and runner-up Tom Rooney drove US-made Stutz Bearcats. The European cars were speedier but fell short on endurance—plagued by burned bearings and broken rods and pistons owing to poor engine lubrication. "Yankee Stamina Wins Astor Cup,"

William "Billy" Chandler at Sheepshead Bay Motor Speedway, 1916. George Grantham Bain Collection, Library of Congress, Prints and Photographs Division.

Hospital, Sheepshead Bay Motor Speedway, c. 1915. George Grantham Bain Collection, Library of Congress, Prints and Photographs Division.

proclaimed *Motor*, cheering the "overthrow of the foreign racing supremacy." The Astor Cup was run only one other time—in 1916, shortened by a hundred miles, and won by Indianapolis native Johnny Aitken in a Peugeot (American victory declared again, this time emphasizing the importance of the driver). The resplendent silver cup itself, however, has been in use ever since and is today awarded to winners of the Indy Racing League's IndyCar series.[16]

For many New Yorkers, it was an event in the spring of 1916—the Earth and Air Carnival—that delivered even bigger thrills. It pitted airplane against motorcar—and man against woman—in a two-day festival of speed. Calamity was narrowly averted when one of the billed fliers, DeLloyd Thompson, was nearly killed in a crash on his way to Brooklyn. Thompson had gained celebrity just weeks earlier for having "bombed" Washington and Manhattan—to demonstrate how "absolutely at the mercy of hostile aircraft are the great cities of our country. I could have blown the White House and Capitol off the map." It was instead a petite young "aviatrix" with an Alabama drawl and a thousand-watt smile named Katherine Stinson who won the crowd that weekend. Stinson was the fourth woman to earn a pilot's license in America, the first woman to pilot an airplane in Japan and China, and the original skywriter—her specialty was writing at night with magnesium flares, using her airplane "like a great invisible pen writing in molten fire on the curtain of the night." At Sheepshead Bay the "Flying Schoolgirl" performed the first true aerobatics in New York airspace—inside loops, spiraling dives, Cuban eights—all with smoke pots affixed to the lower wing of her Curtiss airplane. The smoke trails limned against the sky "the graceful course," marveled the *Times*, "of the machine

Starting line of the hundred-mile Harkness Handicap, June 1, 1918, Sheepshead Bay Motor Speedway. George Grantham Bain Collection, Library of Congress, Prints and Photographs Division.

so adroitly handled." Stinson made two daring dives over the speedway, eventually "landing so lightly that the jar of her machine would hardly have shattered a nest of eggs." The highlight of the weekend was Stinson's race against Dario Resta. After circling the track several times, Stinson dipped down to a breathtaking fifty feet above Resta, beating the Italian to the finish by a few yards. Stinson would return many times to Sheepshead Bay, racing another pioneer woman aviator, Ruth Law, in 1917. Unlike many early pilots, Stinson enjoyed a long life, largely because she quit flying in the 1920s, taking up a new career as a mother and architect in Santa Fe.[17]

With storm clouds gathering over Europe, history soon put an end to all this play. Even as the "Flying Schoolgirl" zipped around the pine-plank track, the carnage of World War I was under way. Just a week after the Earth and Air Carnival, the Sheepshead Bay Speedway hosted one of the largest military tournaments ever staged in the United States—a "Big War Show" that brought together ten thousand troops of the New York National Guard under the command of Major General John F. O'Ryan. The Military and Naval Tournament for Adequate National Defense, as it was called, was opened on May 20, 1916, by President Woodrow Wilson—remotely, by his pressing an electric button to signal on-site borough president Lewis H. Pounds to let the war games begin. Getting the troops to Sheepshead Bay was itself meant to be a training exercise—for citizens as much as the guardsmen. It involved, incredibly, a mass "mobilization" using the automobiles of ordinary New Yorkers—"thousands of machines . . . pressed into service" to whisk the weekend warriors from the city's armories toward Flatlands, "to repel theoretic [*sic*] attack and defend the Sheepshead Bay Speedway against invasion." "Nothing like it," a skeptical O'Ryan admitted, "has ever before been attempted in this county." Nor would it be done again, given the specter of frightened citizens steering commandeered cars into an unholy traffic jam (in fact, New Yorkers were asked rather politely to volunteer their vehicles; "We hope," O'Ryan told the press, "that every owner of a motor car in New York will advise [us] of what cars will be available and when they can be called for"). At Sheepshead Bay the troops erected acres of white-canvas tents, staked out an airfield, dug trenches, placed field artillery, and set up a field hospital, mess hall, and command post with radios and telephones. The tournament was meant to both appeal "to the home-loving instincts of all true Americans" and give the public "a lesson in preparedness." But it was also entertainment, with a slate of athletic events, martial music and cavalry race, a "pyrotechnic battleship and blow-up by bomb from aeroplane," and nights "made beautiful by army searchlights and fireworks." But the weekend warriors met with an unexpected foe—the Kings County Sunday Observance League, which threatened legal action if the "mimic war" was anything but very silent.[18]

Two weeks after the big show an assembly of a different sort took place at the speedway—a great rally against the fierce anti-German sentiment that was sweeping America at the time. With the outbreak of fighting in Europe, especially after the sinking of the *Lusitania* by a German U-boat in May 1915—a tragedy that claimed 1,198 lives—anyone with a Germanic name was suspected of divided loyalties, or, worse, of being a spy or saboteur. Vigilantes beat and tarred and feathered hundreds of German immigrants nationwide, and in April 1918 a miner named Robert Paul Prager was lynched by a mob in Collinsville, Illinois. German newspapers were

Aviator Katherine Stinson in front of her Curtiss-Stinson Special biplane at the Sheepshead Bay Speedway, c. 1916. George Grantham Bain Collection, Library of Congress, Prints and Photographs Division.

Katherine Stinson and Italian-English driver Dario "Dolly" Resta rehearse their upcoming "Earth and Air" race at the Sheepshead Bay Speedway, May 1916. George Grantham Bain Collection, Library of Congress, Prints and Photographs Division.

burned. Schools stopped teaching the German language, which was outlawed in some cities and states. Dachshunds were kept indoors for their safety; pretzels disappeared from pubs. Orchestras refused to play Wagner. The *Los Angeles Times* insisted that all German music be banned, claiming it was "symbolical of neither the sunbeams singing among the daisies nor of grand cathedral bells," but rather "a combination of the howl of the cave man and the roaring of north winds." Anti-German sentiment even helped move the country toward Prohibition; for beer was closely associated with Teutonic culture and German Americans owned most of the nation's breweries. Even flier Kay Stinson was caught up in the madness, whispered to be a spy because she was observed chatting with a man whose mother's cook was from Germany. The whole matter was complicated by strong support for the kaiser's war in the upper echelons of German American society. The German press, political organizations, and prominent individuals like Harvard psychologist Hugo Münsterberg all cheered the kaiser. Theodore Roosevelt branded them "sinister, professional German-Americans." Many rank-and-file citizens also supported the kaiser, at least before America entered the war. When Russian troops invaded East Prussia in 1914, the German community in New York—the largest German-speaking population outside of Berlin and Vienna—loosened its collective purse strings. The kaiser himself sent a letter of thanks to "our German-American brothers" from the city, pledging that the ruined town of Ragnit (now Neman, on the Russian-Latvian border) would "be rebuilt as an American city," reported the *Eagle*, "with the streets bearing such American names as New York, Chicago, Philadelphia and Atlanta." Prominent Chicago architect Louis Guenzel—a designer of Prairie-style homes whose partner had trained with Frank Lloyd Wright—volunteered to draft a plan.[19]

The upsurge of hatred and violence against German Americans rattled the community's pro-kaiser leadership enough to motivate them to take a stand. In New York, the German-American Alliance leased the Sheepshead Bay Speedway for a patriotic rally meant to repudiate the charge "that citizens of Teutonic extraction have their hearts across the sea." Huge crowds were nothing new at Sheepshead Bay, but the one that assembled on June 4, 1916—"American

TEUTONS PROCLAIM LOYALTY TO AMERICA

100,000 Gather at Sheepshead Bay Speedway to Celebrate " Liberty Day."

DECLARATION OF PRINCIPLES

Henry Weismann Says He Hopes They Will Be Heard in Chicago ——Patriotic Songs Sung.

Brooklyn Daily Eagle account of the German-American Alliance "American Liberty Day" rally at the Sheepshead Bay Speedway, June 4, 1916. Brooklyn Public Library—Brooklyn Collection.

Liberty Day"—broke all records. The *Times* called it "probably the largest number of persons . . . ever assembled in one place under private auspices." More than 120,000 people filled the grandstands to declare allegiance to "America first, last and all the time." A parade of floats was led by "America, Land of All Nations," with a Mrs. Roemmele of Brooklyn in the figurative role of Columbia, followed by "Peace," with a hundred cornucopia-bearing maidens dancing in its trail. Next was an immense "flag" formed by sixteen hundred schoolgirls marching in columns of red, white, and blue—"said to be the largest American flag of fabric or humanity ever made," according to the *Times*. From the podium, Henry Weismann—president of the German-American Alliance of New York and chief organizer of the rally—denounced those demagogues "sowing the seeds of racial strife and arousing a spirit of shallow jingoism fraught with danger to the country's peace." Weismann, it turns out, was hardly a standard-bearer of moral virtue. As a baker's apprentice and labor activist in his youth, he had helped lead a chapter of the Anti-Coolie League of California, prime instigator of the very racial strife and jingoism he now condemned. And whatever goodwill the big rally generated was itself soon lost. On July 30, less than two months after the Sheepshead Bay gathering, a series of enormous explosions rocked New York Harbor, damaging the Statue of Liberty and blowing out windows in lower Manhattan. German saboteurs had detonated a huge stockpile of munitions staged for shipment to England and France at an offshore depot known as Black Tom Island (now part of Liberty Island State Park). The blasts, heard as far off as Maryland, killed seven and injured dozens.[20]

When America was finally dragged into the great European bloodbath, the Sheepshead Bay Speedway became a mustering ground for troops—this time for real. The weekend war games were over; now two thousand men of Brooklyn's own

Fourteenth Regiment of the New York State Militia gathered there in August 1917 to ready themselves for deployment. Headquartered at the Eighth Avenue Armory in Park Slope, the Fourteenth Regiment had a long history, its abolitionist forebears having distinguished themselves in key battles of the Civil War—Antietam, Gettysburg, the Wilderness. The volunteers bivouacked under Flatlands skies for a month before heading to Camp Wadsworth in Spartanburg, South Carolina, and overseas the next May with the 106th Infantry. Many would come back crippled or maimed, or never return at all. The war sucked in many who once thrilled crowds at Sheepshead Bay. Kay Stinson drove an ambulance in France. Eddie Rickenbacker became a flying ace and war hero, credited with shooting down twenty-six German aircraft. The speedway itself was a distant victim of the conflict. With attendance sharply down, the facility began losing money and soon fell into foreclosure for a huge sum owed its builders, the Coast and Lake Company. In May 1917 Harry S. Harkness—one of the speedway's founders and, as an heir to the Standard Oil fortune, one of the richest men of the age—came to its rescue, buying the complex outright and swearing to manage it personally. He saw to it that the annual police games were staged at the speedway that fall, a benefit that drew a crowd of 100,000 and featured a performance by Enrico Caruso and the Irish tenor John McCormack. But Harkness died less than two years later, sealing the speedway's fate.[21]

There was one last great show before the end, a vast performance of Giuseppe Verdi's *Aida* that not only dwarfed all things before at Sheepshead Bay, but was the single largest operatic production ever staged in the United States—equal in size to the much-ballyhooed production in Shanghai in 2001, promoted (incorrectly) as the largest ever. Conceived as a benefit to raise money for victims of the earthquake that struck a few miles north of Florence on June 29, 1919, it was organized in a matter of weeks by Fortune Gallo of the San Carlo Opera Company, Andrés de Segurola of the Metropolitan Opera, and Italian consul general of New York Romolo Trittoni. Gallo, a self-made immigrant, was a master impresario and the first to popularize grand opera in the United States. His San Carlo touring company was so successful that Gallo eventually settled down in a theater of his own, at 254 West Fifty-Fourth Street in New York—what would later become Studio 54. That the benefit was held at Sheepshead Bay was Tommy Thompson's doing. For all his interest in speed and motor sports, Thompson's first love was music; he had studied music at Yale and directed productions there of *Aida*, *Tosca*, *The Tales of Hoffman*, and *Hansel and Gretel*. He looked forward to bringing "open-air entertainment of a non-sporting character" to the speedway. "Imagine what a wonderful setting could be given to 'Aida,'" he told a reporter; "It would be a performance such as the Khédive of Egypt enjoyed when he had Verdi compose this work . . . raised to the nth power."[22] It was an era of great alfresco productions, beginning with Arturo Spelta and Adolfo Bracale's titanic staging of *Aida* at the foot of the Giza pyramids in 1911. Big outdoor productions of the Verdi masterpiece took place in Buenos Aires in 1917 and Mexico City the following year. In the United States, Spelta and the National Open Air Festival Society presented Verdi's *Requiem* at the Polo Grounds on June 4, 1916, with the New York Philharmonic Orchestra and a chorus of twelve hundred, followed by ambitious productions of *Aida* at Philadelphia's Franklin Field and Ewing Field in San Francisco.

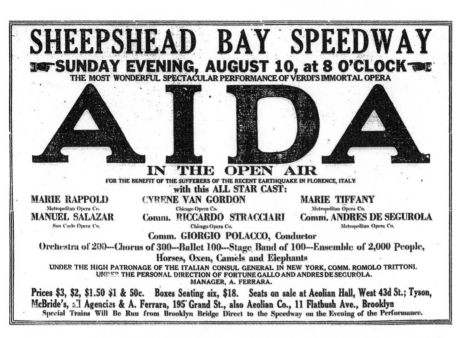

"Aida in the Open Air." Newspaper advertisement for the Speedway production of Verdi's masterpiece—the largest operatic performance ever staged in the United States. From *New York Evening Telegram*, August 3, 1919.

The Brooklyn production exceeded all of these. It featured the Metropolitan Opera's Marie Rappold in the role of Aida, contralto Cyrena van Gordon as Amneris, and Costa Rican tenor Manuel "Melico" Salazar as Radamés. There would be only one performance, on August 17, postponed from the previous week because of a transit strike. A vast stage—120 feet wide and 80 feet deep—was specially constructed for the show. It was solidly built, for it had to support a cast of thousands and a chorus of three hundred men and women. Italian designer Carmine Vitolo created the set, with a pair of fifty-foot lotus-capped Egyptian columns framing the proscenium against a "night-blue sky," one reviewer wrote, "swept by soft airs from over Sheepshead Bay and Coney Island and illuminated by searchlights massed aloft." There were two orchestras with two hundred musicians in all—one onstage and a larger one on the board track below conducted by Giorgio Polacca, who inherited the Metropolitan Opera's baton from Arturo Toscanini. A battalion of 250 Boy Scout ushers arrived late to find a near riot in the grandstands, as patrons scrambled for oversold seats. The triumphal march scene at the end of the second act was the most spectacular ever staged—with five hundred soldiers from the New York State Militia, sixteen horses, four camels, a pair of oxen, and Hattie the elephant from the Central Park Menagerie. More than forty-five thousand people attended the gala performance, ferried home in extra trains when the show finally ended well past midnight.[23]

By the time Aida and Radamés suffered their terrible shared fate, the ground beneath the proscenium was far more valuable than anything that could be raced, flown, or staged above. In early December, with residential development roaring south across Brooklyn, it was announced that the speedway once hailed "the fastest

A last vestige of the Sheepshead Bay Motor Speedway can be seen at the top of this 1931 photograph, with the coming street grid platted over it. Photograph by Fairchild Aerial Surveys, Inc. Collection of the author.

motorcar course in the world" would be demolished for housing. The Swift-McNutt wrecking company of Boston was contracted to dismantle all structures, and over the next ten months they trucked off 27,000 grandstand seats, 50,000 tons of steel, and six million board feet of lumber—enough wood to frame a thousand small houses. The speedway and adjoining land owned by the Harkness estate was 650 acres in all, including nearly a mile of frontage on Ocean Avenue and some 4,000 feet of Jamaica Bay waterfront (adjacent to Plum Beach). It was the largest piece of unimproved land in Brooklyn and—well served by public transit—one of the most valuable parcels of land anywhere on the Eastern Seaboard. In late June 1923 a deal was sealed between the Harkness estate and three of New York's most savvy real estate operators—Charles F. Noyes, Max M. Natanson, and Joseph P. Day. Noyes, a dean of American real estate who later owned the Empire State Building, brought the group together, convinced that the Harkness property was a gold mine. He persuaded Natanson—an experienced Manhattan developer, but with no Brooklyn experience—to plunk down enough cash to make the deal happen. Closing the sale on June 27, 1923, made Natanson the biggest landholder in all of New York City. "In this one transaction," wrote the *Times*, "he has taken over more of the area of New York City than ever was owned at one time by an individual, not excepting the great holdings of old John Jacob Astor." The land was then subdivided into thousands of lots and auctioned off to builders and the public. Noyes and Day plugged the sale hard, buying ads in local newspapers that touted "the New Flatbush," and even reviving an old Edwin French tune—"Down at Sheepshead Bay"—to spread the word.[24]

Day sold lots like popcorn at a matinee—2,000 of them went in just the first two days of the initial auction. At one point he sold a parcel every ten seconds for half an hour. Some 2,500 would-be buyers crowded around the auction tent—their parked cars strung along Ocean Avenue for nearly a mile. Most house lots sold for $300; a valuable corner at the junction of Avenue U and Nostrand Avenue—home of the Brennan & Carr restaurant since the 1930s—sold for three times that. Day held two subsequent auctions in 1923 and 1924, selling a grand total of 9,600 lots. It was the largest real estate auction in New York City history, clearing a cool $3 million in profit for Noyes, Natanson, and Day. Even before the last auction got under way, a ghostly skein of streets was cast over the still-visible traces of the track, like a new painting sketched out over an older one. The blocks quickly filled with the brick and mortar of middle-class life. All traces of the great speedway were soon gone, vaporized into the shifting fogbank of Gotham's past.[25]

"Last farmer." Frank Albanese harvesting a crop of dandelion at long-abandoned Sheepshead Bay Motor Speedway, 1949. Behind him are concrete piers that once held the grandstand. The Sheepshead-Nostrand public housing complex is under construction in the background. Brooklyn Public Library, Brooklyn Collection.

CHAPTER 8

THE STEAMPUNK ORB

Verticality is such a risky business.
—COLSON WHITEHEAD, *THE INTUITIONIST*

The port metropolis once imagined for Gravesend—capital of a "blooming republic" that would stretch from the East River to Montauk Point—obviously never came to pass. But Deborah Moody's old town was destined nonetheless to become a great city by the sea, even if the good woman and her pious votaries could hardly have approved of it. For Willem Kieft's 1645 grant to the Massachusetts Bay émigrés included all of that seaside place later known far and wide as Conyne Eylandt—"rabbit island" in Dutch. The westernmost of a long chain of barrier islands between Long Island's south shore and the Atlantic, it was part of the common lands of the town of Gravesend for over two hundred years. With a thick mane of brush and scored by tidal creeks, the lands were used by townsfolk for pasturing livestock, harvesting salt hay, and hunting waterfowl. Coney was then truly an island; one reached it by fording Coney Island Creek at low tide. Around 1830 a toll causeway was built over the channel—a southward extension of Gravesend's main street, physically joining the old settlement to its future. Soon a small hotel—the Coney Island House—was erected to accommodate visitors. Within a few years a great circular tent pavilion had been built, followed by a wharf, another hotel, and several bathhouses. The trickle of visitors became a flow. On a balmy spring Sunday in 1847, some three hundred coaches and carriages passed through town on their way to the beach. The Gravesenders made a big show of condemning such "wholesale Sabbath-breaking," but in private they rubbed their hands in glee. The world was knocking at the door.[1]

In short order, horsecars and a rail line—the Brooklyn, Bath and Coney Island Railroad—were ferrying carloads of passengers down from the growing city to the north. Around the terminal sprang up beer halls and bathing pavilions. Development quickly spread out from there, until "the entire beach front was thickly studded," noted William H. Stillwell (namesake of Stillwell Avenue), "with these aspirants for public favor." Iron piers were built to receive steamers from New York and New Jersey. Additional rail lines—the Culver and the Sea Beach—brought ever larger waves of New Yorkers to the beach. Vast bathing pavilions soon rose over the sands—Charles Feltman's Ocean Pavilion, Bauer's West Brighton Hotel, the Sea Beach Palace. Towering overhead was the tallest structure in the United States at the time—a three-hundred-foot observation tower recycled from the 1876 Centennial Exposition in Philadelphia. By the 1880s, as many as 100,000 people would descend upon Coney Island on a summer day. Baptist or otherwise, the god of fortune had come to town. Gravesend's common lands were now among the most valuable real estate on the Eastern Seaboard; leases brought in a rich bounty of rents and fees. The old settlement was soon "probably the wealthiest town in the State." Long run by a peaceable gentry descended from the Moody crew, Gravesend was increasingly dominated by one of the more colorful figures in Brooklyn history—John Y. McKane. McKane was a native Gravesender of immigrant Irish stock, a carpenter and builder by trade. The man craved power. He ran successfully for town constable, and was soon made a commissioner of common lands and a Gravesend town supervisor. Before long McKane was also chief of police, commanding a force of 150 men, as well as president of the Town Board, Board of Health, Police Board, and Water Board—each "made up of the same five persons" and all nominated by McKane himself. He was the self-appointed king of Gravesend.[2]

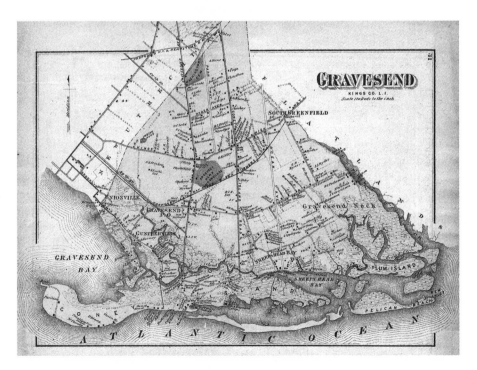

Gravesend and Coney Island, 1873. From F. W. Beers *Atlas of Long Island, New York*. Lionel Pincus and Princess Firyal Map Division, The New York Public Library.

McKane abused all this authority in full-blown Tammany fashion. He was especially adept at lining his pockets through shady deals involving the priceless common
lands. Because he was town supervisor, every lease required his signature, which
was forthcoming only after substantial sums passed into his hands. Though McKane
deserves credit for building Coney Island's first modern infrastructure, his administration was also responsible for turning a once-lovely place for a family outing into
an unholy warren of gambling dens, whorehouses, and assorted other "cheap and
shifty places where the quick-witted huckster caught the nimble dime and nickel of
an ever growing clientele." By the 1890s there were seven hundred saloons in Gravesend, half without a license and nearly all on the island proper. It was this "Sodom
by the Sea" reputation that sequestered the gentry eastward in the clipped and staid
Brighton Beach and Manhattan Beach hotels. Attempts to depose McKane always
ended in failure and ruin. When a new law was passed mandating six election districts
in Gravesend, he ingeniously used the town's seventeenth-century pattern of radial
lot lines to force a sliver of each district through the town hall, enabling him to make
it a personal panopticon from which he could watch voters and intimidate them into
casting ballots his way. Not until 1893 was McKane finally convicted of something that
stuck—election fraud, alas—and sent up the Hudson to Sing Sing Prison. Gravesend
was finally relieved of the Tammany thumb. But it had little time left itself: in 1894
the old town was annexed by the city of Brooklyn, ending 250 years of independence.
The stage was now set for the rise of modern Coney Island. It would be dominated
by a man every bit as ruthlessly ambitious as McKane—George C. Tilyou. Born
in Manhattan but raised on Coney Island, where his parents ran the popular Surf
House restaurant and bathing pavilion, Tilyou made a fortune brokering real estate
when the Gravesend common lands were offered for sale in the 1880s. He caught the
entertainment bug after a honeymoon trip to the World's Columbian Exposition in
Chicago in 1893. There at the Midway plaisance, Tilyou was enraptured by George
Ferris's colossal wheel, which he promptly tried to buy. Rebuffed, he commissioned
instead a half-size replica—billing it nonetheless as the world's largest. Bejeweled with
hundreds of lightbulbs, Tilyou's wheel quickly became the most popular attraction
in Coney Island when it opened in 1894, paying for itself in a matter of months.[3]

But success in Coney Island required constant reinvention. Tilyou owned many
rides, but they were scattered on unconnected parcels over a quarter mile of beachfront. When the renowned open-water swimmer Paul Boyton launched Sea Lion
Park nearby in 1895—by some measures the first modern amusement park in the
world—Tilyou realized that he had to consolidate his attractions into a single compound to which he could charge admission, thereby monopolizing custom while
filtering out the riffraff. He also understood the value of a high-profile superattraction
to draw people in—a kind of "killer app." Boyton's centerpiece was an exhilarating
boat ride called Chute-the-Chutes; Tilyou's was the Steeplechase Horses—the gravity horse race he adapted from an English prototype—that ran on six parallel tracks
over an eleven-hundred-foot course, complete with buglers and attendants dressed
in jockey silk. Steeplechase Park, named for this star attraction, opened in 1897, the
first of Coney Island's three great amusement parks. Steeplechase was larger than Sea
Lion Park and soon eclipsed it in attendance. But Tilyou knew better than to rest on

this success. Always on the prowl for new attractions, he met two entrepreneurs—Frederic Thompson and Elmer "Skip" Dundy—who struck gold with a ride called A Trip to the Moon at the 1901 Pan-American Exposition in Buffalo. Tilyou convinced the men to move this and two other rides to Steeplechase once the fair closed. But the following season was a disaster for Coney Island operators, with rain seventy out of ninety-two days. Attendance was sharply down throughout the amusement district. When it came time to renew their lease, Tilyou told Thompson and Dundy they would have to fork over more rent to keep A Trip to the Moon at Steeplechase. They refused. Boyton, meanwhile, was forced to close Sea Lion Park. The two men leaped at the chance to take over his grounds and strike out on their own.[4]

Tilyou's greed truly backfired; for Steeplechase both lost a major attraction and gained a new competitor. In the spring of 1903, Thompson and Dundy opened their hauntingly beautiful Luna Park, a glittering jewel that made Steeplechase suddenly look frumpy and dull. In creating his park, Thompson realized that more than a mere "collection of individually ingenious rides" was needed to capture the imagination of the public. The challenge was to cast a magical master theme over the entire place, one that made the whole greater than the sum of its parts. Thompson had studied at the École des Beaux-Arts in Paris and used an inventive, highly eclectic style of architecture to spin a richly theatrical setting. The result was a kind of orientalist Columbian Exposition, Chicago's "White City" beheld through an opiate fog—an urbanism of ecstasy and delight rather than order, duty, and civic responsibility. Indeed, if the Columbian Exposition "preached discipline," writes John Kasson in *Amusing the Million*, "Luna Park invited release." Tens of thousands of electric lights transformed Luna's staff-and-plaster buildings into a dazzling apparition at dusk. "Tall towers that had grown dim suddenly broke forth in electric outlines and gay rosettes of color," wrote Albert Bigelow Paine in 1904, "as the living spark of light traveled hither and thither, until the place was transformed into an enchanted garden, of such a sort as Aladdin never dreamed." A second spectacular amusement park, Dreamland, opened in May 1904, topped by a tower so tall and brightly lit it could be seen fifty miles out at sea. Tilyou knew he was in trouble.[5]

It was a desperate need to regain a competitive edge that aligned the orbits of this Brooklyn impresario with an enterprising Missouri tinkerer named Samuel Meyer Friede. Friede, born in 1861, was the youngest son of Meyer Friede, a successful German-Jewish watchmaker and silversmith with a keen interest in civic affairs. The elder Friede was the first Jew to serve in the Missouri state legislature, where he supported the Union cause and was famous for his impassioned response to an anti-Semitic screed by a fellow legislator. Meyer Friede's older boys, Joel and Isaac, followed him into the family business. Samuel, it seems, had his eye on bigger things. Leaving school after only the eighth grade, he worked briefly as a notions and dry goods clerk, and in 1883 married an Italian woman named Christina. The couple's only child, a daughter named Minnie, was born the next year. Marrying outside the close-knit St. Louis Jewish community evidently caused a rift with his father, who wrote Samuel out of his will (Sam filed a partition suit in response). Samuel Friede's first passion was the machine shop. He became a serial inventor, filing in 1885 the first of many patent applications. He designed a portable fare box for streetcars, a

Luna Park, c. 1905—"Electric City by the Sea." Detroit Publishing Company Photographic Collection, Library of Congress, Prints and Photographs Division.

roll-paper cutter, an automatic station indicator for passenger trains, a spring-loaded label holder for drug-store bins, a combination ratchet-and-monkey wrench, an envelope-sealing machine, and a variety of plumbing fixtures, including a "Stop and Waste Cock." But these were mere trifles given Friede's towering ambition. With the turn of the century, as plans took shape for a great world's fair in St. Louis—the Louisiana Purchase Exposition of 1904—Friede saw the opportunity of a lifetime, a chance, perhaps, for this star-crossed son to prove he was a man of consequence. In March 1901 Friede unveiled plans for an iron-and-steel "Giant Aerial Globe" that would rise 555 feet above the city—equal in height to the Washington Monument. Friede promised that the colossal orb would be the fair's biggest attraction—greater in scale and spectacle than the Ferris wheel that stole the Chicago show in 1893.[6]

Friede had already been working on his globe for some eighteen months by this time, aided by Albert Borden, a prominent St. Louis engineer who built several warehouses on the industrial waterfront. As eagerly reported in the press, the orb would feature a vast aerial rotunda at the 325-foot level, enclosed in plate glass and encircled by a "movable platform twenty feet in width." From this, the sightseer would enjoy a commanding view of the exposition grounds. At the very top would be an observatory, crowned with a pair of "gigantic searchlights, as an after-dark feature." Borden rather wildly estimated that the structure would weight forty million pounds and cost $1.3 million to erect. Upwards of thirty thousand people could be accommodated at any given time. The globe was to rise from an elevated spot on the south side of the Forest Park fairgrounds. The remote site, far from the heart of the fair and its midway, makes little sense until seen on a map. And then it all clicks: Friede had positioned his orb on the main axis of the fairgrounds, terminating the sightline from the Plaza of St. Louis and Cass Gilbert's Palace of Fine Arts. The great orb, in other words, would have loomed over the fair's austere neoclassical buildings, a great Yiddish moon looming over the gathered goyim.[7]

By June of 1901, Friede had convinced a prominent St. Louis businessman, Cyrus F. Blanke, to back his globe venture, forming a company capitalized with $1.5 million (more than $40 million today). Partnering with Blanke—founder of the largest coffee-roasting company in America at the time—granted immediate legitimacy to what otherwise might have been dismissed as a joke. Not coincidentally, Blanke happened to serve on both the Board of Directors of the Louisiana Purchase Exposition and its powerful Committee on Concessions—though he eventually resigned the latter post owing to conflict of interest (which the press read as a sign that the globe would win approval and might actually be built). Blanke featured the globe in advertisements, promising to serve "in all this Colossal Structure . . . Faust Blend Coffee"—an appropriate name and choice indeed, as we shall see. He even produced a promotional glass jar in the shape of the globe, a rarity that surfaces on eBay from time to time. But

Blanke's Faust Blend Coffee to be served "In all this Colossal Structure." Advertisement from *Saturday Evening Post*, October 26, 1901.

not everyone was pleased with the Friede-Blanke Aerial Globe, as it came to be called. To composer Emile Karst, president of the city's Franco-American Society, the globe "seems to look dumpy, no matter what its proportions." He feared that the great orb would "scarcely possess the surpassing artistic merits which made the Eiffel Tower world-renowned," though he allowed that "it may be possible to remedy this inartistic defect." Annoyed, Friede told Karst to take the matter up with Eiffel himself. Karst did just that; for as the *Republic* reported on June 22, Mr. Eiffel was asked "for information as to the financial and structural obstacles overcome in the construction of the Eiffel Tower." It is not known whether the great engineer responded. Eiffel might well have been astonished to see Borden's sketch of the globe, for it looked suspiciously like a project by one of his own students.[8]

Alas, the Aerial Globe was no sui generis fruit of Friede's fertile mind but rather something he absorbed wholesale from published renderings of an 1891 project by Biscayan architect Alberto de Palacio y Elissague, who studied engineering in Paris with none other than Gustave Eiffel. Palacio went on to design scores of civic and institutional buildings in his career—including the Crystal Palace and the old Atocha train station in Madrid. He is best known for his unique Puente de Vizcaya Bridge across the Nervión River near Bilbao—the first transporter or aerial transfer bridge in the world, today a UNESCO World Heritage site (a roadbed gondola, slung beneath the structure and loaded with vehicles, is pulled across the span). In 1891 Palacio unveiled plans for a heroic monument to Christopher Columbus in the form of a mammoth globe, 1,000 feet in diameter and rising 1,400 feet from a great iron pedestal that—at 262 feet—was itself no mean structure. Palacio meant the orb for a planned Spanish exhibition marking the four hundredth anniversary of the Columbus voyage—what became instead the rather modest 1892 Exposición Histórico-Americana in Madrid. An early rendering shows the monument hovering over Palacio's Crystal Palace in Buen Retiro Park, site of the Exposición. When it became clear that Spain lacked the resources to erect his colossus, Palacio submitted his drawings to a competition sponsored by the 1893 Chicago World's Columbian Exposition. He walked away with first prize.

Of course, the orb was not built in Chicago either. But Palacio's Eiffelian pedigree and the sheer audacity of his Columbus monument—reminiscent of Boullée's 1784 cenotaph for Isaac Newton—assured it great publicity. An ethereal rendering of the Chicago globe first appeared on the cover of *Scientific American* on October 25, 1890, and was widely reprinted over the next two years—in the Spanish periodical *La Ilustración Española y Americana*, the *British Printer*, the New York–based *Manufacturer and Builder*, and a popular English pictorial called the *Picture Magazine*. In the view, the soaring sphere is cottoned by clouds and hovers over a riverine city—presumably Chicago. Belting the equator is a great balcony, nearly half a mile long and studded with hundreds of cabanas. Its most delightful feature is a spiral cog tramway that winds upward to the polar cap, topped by a meteorological observatory in the form of the *Santa Maria*—"the caravel," the *Manufacturer and Builder* reminded readers, "which carried Columbus to the New World." A corresponding track ran inside the southern hemisphere, taking visitors up to the equator from the great Roman-arched base—where an auditorium, museums, and a "large Columbian library" would be located. The interior of the sphere was to be decorated with the constellations; the oceans and land masses on the exterior traced by lights and "casting over the city torrents of refulgent brilliancy." All in all, this would be "one of the wonders of the world."[9]

[Entered at the Post Office of New York, N. Y., as Second Class Matter. Copyrighted, 1890, by Munn & Co.]

A WEEKLY JOURNAL OF PRACTICAL INFORMATION, ART, SCIENCE, MECHANICS, CHEMISTRY, AND MANUFACTURES.

Vol. LXIII.—No. 17.]
Established 1845.

NEW YORK, OCTOBER 25, 1890.

[$3.00 A YEAR.
WEEKLY.

M. PALACIO'S DESIGN FOR A COLOSSAL MONUMENT IN MEMORY OF CHRISTOPHER COLUMBUS.—[See page 260.]

Cover of October 1890 issue of *Scientific American* with a rendering of Alberto de Palacio's "Colossal Monument in Memory of Christopher Columbus."

Sam Friede's globe, first published in the *St. Louis Sunday Republic* on March 17, 1901, is a shameless duplicate of Palacio's Columbus monument—from the observatory right down the spiral tramway to its Roman-arched steel-frame base. It seems incredible that the St. Louis press, in all their coverage of the Aerial Globe, never figured out that Friede had brazenly pilfered his idea from overseas. Or they may have been well aware of the orb's Latin provenance but chose to keep the matter quiet. What would it profit St. Louis, after all, to point out that local-boy Friede's mighty orb—a Midwestern landmark in the making, an Eiffel tower of the prairie!—was in fact a Spanish import cast aside by that mighty nemesis to the north, Chicago? But Friede was a quick study, and soon his globe bore only passing resemblance to the Palacio scheme. What next appeared in the St. Louis press is a far less literal representation of the earth, an orbital edifice that revealed "the extreme possibilities of steel structural work" and might have actually been buildable. The new globe was also more circumscribed in its cultural pretensions. Stripped of museums and library, the Friede-Blanke Aerial Globe would be instead "a collection of amusements in midair, containing provision for every form of popular diversion from grand opera to vaudeville . . . from pipe organ concerts to a three-ring circus."[10]

But none of this was to be. For reasons obscure, Cyrus Blanke ended his partnership with Friede in the fall of 1901. He is conspicuously absent from a half-page advertisement that ran in the *Republic* in November—promising "A City in the Clouds," with gardens, a coliseum, and music by a "gigantic orchestrion." Listed instead as vice president and treasurer is Frank A. Ruf of the Antikamnia Chemical Company, a maker of habit-forming patent medicines. The next month, in a front-page *Republic* piece just before Christmas, again nary a word is mentioned of Blanke. Did Blanke begin to doubt the legitimacy of Friede's venture, or the sketchy method he devised to finance it—by public subscription, raising capital by selling stocks to the public for a dollar a share? Whatever the reason, Blanke vanishes and—not long afterward—so, too, does the tower itself. After January 1902 the project never appears again in the local press. Friede's St. Louis globe thus had another thing in common with Palacio's orb—neither project ever saw the light of day. Unfazed, Friede was soon back in his shop. He set his sights a bit lower—for a time at least. Inspired by a 1903 competition for an "air yacht," Friede submitted a patent application for an amusement park ride named the Revolving Airship Tower. The contraption featured a rotating tower, sixty-five feet square at the base, that flung four suspended cigar-shaped "airships" outward by centrifugal force. The cars were lifted up the tower by cable and fitted with mirrors, "so that, no matter which way the passenger looks, he sees nothing but a birdseye view of the country." Friede formed a company in Chicago to build the tower and erected a prototype the following year at Chicago's popular Sans Souci Amusement Park, whose general manager—Miles E. Fried—may have been a relative. It was certainly no Aerial Globe; but at least it was real. More importantly, it caught the eye of George C. Tilyou.[11]

It is not known exactly when or how Tilyou and Friede first met—Friede may have sent Tilyou material about his Airship Tower, or, more likely, the two might have crossed paths at the Louisiana Purchase Exposition. But however it happened,

S. M. FRIEDE.
AMUSEMENT APPARATUS.
APPLICATION FILED JUNE 15, 1904.

2 SHEETS—SHEET 1.

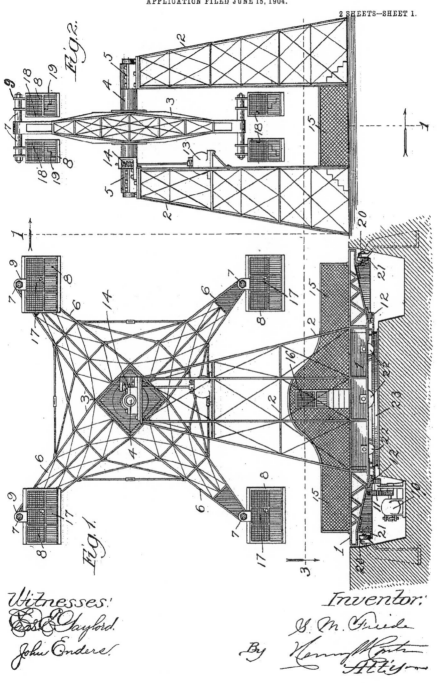

Witnesses:

Inventor:

Samuel M. Friede, illustration for an "Amusement Apparatus," 1906. United States Patent Office.

No. 813,549.

PATENTED FEB. 27, 1906.

S. M. FRIEDE.
REVOLVING AIR SHIP TOWER.
APPLICATION FILED AUG. 7, 1903.

6 SHEETS—SHEET 1.

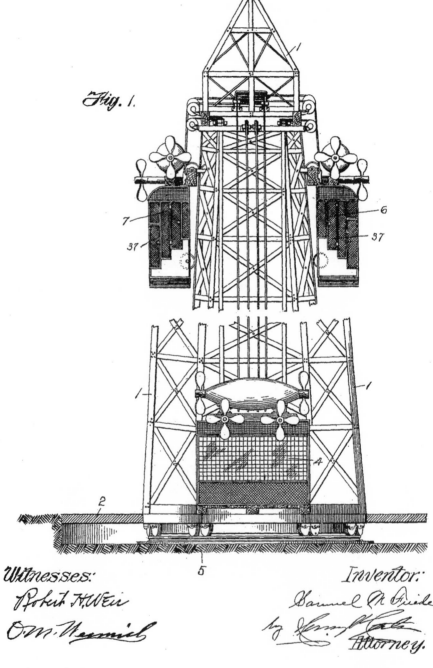

Fig. 1.

Samuel M. Friede, illustration for a "Revolving Air Ship Tower," 1906. United States Patent Office.

they hit it off immediately. For all their differences, the Brooklyn Irishman and the Missouri Jew were equally ambitious and shared a common passion for entertainment. Friede was soon in Brooklyn himself and by November 1904 had incorporated the Revolving Airship Tower Company of New York to erect a second, taller airship tower at Steeplechase Park. He also developed a second ride for Tilyou, the figurative opposite of the Airship Tower—a theatrical piece called Atlantis Under the Sea. Both attractions were in place for the 1905 season and were a great hit with the public. As Edward S. Sears put it in his *Souvenir Guide to Coney Island*, the Airship Tower and Atlantis Under the Sea were "the most striking novelties at Steeplechase . . . the sensations of the season." Sears was especially impressed with the airship ride, which he called the "piece de resistance, so to speak, of Steeplechase Park." The tower was three hundred feet tall—or so Tilyou and Friede claimed—and "with its 15,000 electric lights of alternating crimson and white serves as a fitting landmark for this great pleasure garden." Thus, wrote Sears, despite being "eclipsed and shadowed . . . by the magnificence of its younger rivals," the new rides made Steeplechase shine forth "with a radiance fairly equaling Luna Park and Dreamland." Tilyou was back, and thanks largely to Samuel Meyer Friede.[12]

This success convinced the Missourian that his mighty mothballed orb might take more readily to the sands of seaside Brooklyn than it did to prairie loam. He soon convinced the Steeplechase showman that his globe tower was the "killer app" that would bury Dreamland and Luna Park once and for all. On October 1, 1905, Tilyou offered Friede a twenty-five-year lease for a two-acre parcel within Steeplechase Park, on Surf Avenue between West Seventeenth and West Nineteenth streets. Rent would be $25,000 a year, due quarterly. That January, Friede announced the formation of the Friede Globe Tower Company. With offices at Steeplechase and 27 William Street in Manhattan, the concern was nonetheless registered—nefariously, as will soon become clear—in the state of Arizona. Friede flooded city newspapers with advertisements and published a plush "Red Book" prospectus that was available on request (along with a free six-month subscription to *Industrial Amusement Record*, a perk of rather dubious appeal). A broadside in a January 1906 Sunday edition of the *Sun* offered to the public $250,000 of preferred stock at $10 a share. As an incentive, he would toss in a free share of common stock for every one of preferred stock purchased. A week later, Friede reported that "we have been working night and day making out stock certificates and indorsing [*sic*] checks, and over $50,000 of the stock is already sold and subscribed for to date." Promising stock performance of "100 per cent interest annually," Friede cleverly pitched his capitalization scheme as democracy itself: "We prefer to have 100,000 stockholders with $10.00 each than one stockholder with One Million Dollars"— for the raising of this great building, he claimed, was "an enterprise to be owned by the people, for the people." (This would also, a cynic might point out, spread deception so widely as to make a coordinated legal challenge unlikely.) To reward its common builders, Friede promised an exalted "Hall of Names" in the globe itself. "This marvelous room," he avowed, "will contain the names of every man, woman and child purchasing one or more shares of stock . . . inscribed in alphabetical order on metal plates, to remain for all time to come."[13]

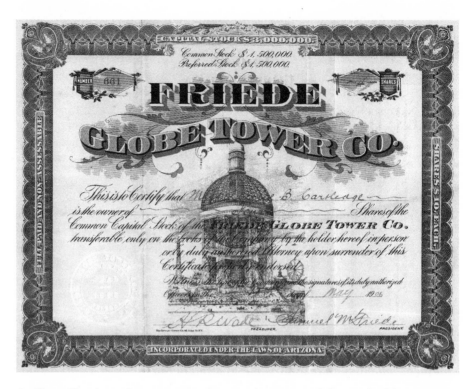

Certificate of four shares of common stock in the name of Louise B. Carsledge, Friede Globe Tower Company, 1906. At $10 a share, Carsledge had invested the 2018 equivalent of about $1,100 in Friede's scheme. Courtesy of David M. Beach, cigarboxlabels.com.

And what, beyond a polished nameplate, would the people's hard-earned pennies buy? All the wonders of the world, it would seem. As Friede's "Red Book" gushed, the new Globe Tower—designed with the prominent New York firm of Cleverdon & Putzel, architects of the Astor Building—was to be quite simply "the most gigantic, unique and permanent amusement structure in the world . . . the greatest building in existence" and "more to America than the Eiffel Tower is to France." From its base just off Surf Avenue (at about where the entrance stairs to MCU Field are today), the titanic gourd would swell to nine hundred feet in girth and loom seven hundred feet above the sand and racket of Coney Island. Some eight thousand tons of steel would go into the globe—"more steel than was used for the construction of the Williamsburg Bridge." The Flatiron and Singer buildings, the Metropolitan Life Tower, would all be "mere pygmies, architecturally speaking, in comparison." A constellation of electric lights would make it "a gigantic tower of fire by night." Inside, visitors would discover a "Department Store of Amusements" filling the orb's 500,000 square feet of floor space—the equivalent of six city blocks. Those arriving by automobile would park beneath the great pedestal base, under which—according to some illustrations—would be a subway station (never mind that ocean water would immediately fill anything more than a few feet below the sand). Riding one of the ten huge elevators ("largest ever built"), visitors would pass an "Aerial Hippodrome" with slot machines and a "Continuous four-ring Circus";

an immense ballroom belted by a mechanical café that crawled the belly of the tower was "equipped with comfortable chairs and tables where a table d'hôte meal is served." Above this would be an "Aerial Palm Garden," with pools, cascades, and statuary and—soaring overhead—"beautifully curved steel arches, 150 feet high" that rose to the Observatory, five hundred feet above the street. From the catwalk promenade there, it would be impossible to see anything of the structure beneath, a sensation "most novel and exhilarating," testified the prospectus, and "suggestive of being suspended, or floating, as it were, in mid-air." At last came the vaunted "Hall of Names" and, above that, a US weather observatory and wireless telegraph station topped by a great flagpole and the world's largest, brightest revolving searchlight. All told, fifty thousand people could fill the mighty colossus at any one time.[14]

Friede called on the public to witness the launch of the Globe Tower on May 30, 1906, promising that "everything possible will be done by the company to make the cornerstone laying a notable event." A crowd of several thousand spectators gathered to hear speeches by Friede and a number of company officers, and hear "celebrated orators" including a retired third-tier judge, E. Y. Bell of New Jersey, who "spoke of the Friede Tower as the eighth wonder of the age and compared it with the Collossus [*sic*] of Rhodes." At five o'clock sharp, a former assemblyman laid the cornerstone on behalf of Brooklyn borough president Bird S. Coler, accompanied by fireworks and music performed by the uniformed Friede Tower Band (led by an Italian of minor fame named Filipo Govarale, of whom we shall hear more in a moment). The cornerstone was evidently equipped with a chamber that held "a facsimile of the company's charter, a menu of the dinner given to the newspaper-men . . . and a set of coins." Afterward, Friede led a large group of his stockholders to Stauch's Casino for a banquet. The guests were likely not informed that their host didn't even have a building permit for the great globe they had just christened. It was not until August 8, 1906—more than two months after groundbreaking—that the Globe Tower finally received the critical permit—"the largest ever issued of its kind," as Friede predictably spun it. A month later he awarded a construction contract to the Alfred E. Norton Company of New York. On Sunday, February 17, 1907, investors saw the first tangible evidence of Friede's promise to build. That afternoon some two thousand New Yorkers—a huge crowd for Coney Island in winter—braved a fierce wind to witness the "setting above ground of the first steel" for the mammoth Globe Tower ("the cold weather," noted the *Brooklyn Eagle*, "did not seem to prevent many women from attending"). Conductor Govarale led the Tower Band, and then "President Friede" addressed the crowd, telling of the work already done—that "600 of the 800 concrete piles needed for the foundation have already been sunk." Each was driven thirty feet deep, and together they would create a bed for the forty-one concrete piers that formed the socles, or pedestals, from which the great steel structure would rise.[15]

But even as the globe began to take shape, Friede's relationship with Tilyou faltered. The project was already far behind schedule—construction was supposed to start in October 1906. Work had been delayed nearly a year, allegedly because of Tilyou's refusal to remove several small buildings that Friede claimed were on his leased parcel. Now, emboldened by the groundbreaking and with many tons

"The Steel Globe Tower, 700 Feet High." Lithograph postcard, Samuel Langsdorf and Company, 1906. Collection of the author.

of steel stockpiled on-site, Friede directed his workers to raze the Steeplechase structures on the disputed boundary. Tilyou responded swiftly. As the *New York Times* reported, once the "tower people" started to tear down the buildings, a Tilyou lieutenant rushed out to stop them, backed by a dozen Steeplechase men—"a force of carpenters, bricklayers, and plumbers." The Coney Island police were called; Friede's construction superintendent was arrested, not once but twice. Tilyou was a powerful man in Coney Island; by virtue of ethnicity alone he could count on the Coney Island reserves as a private security force (Brooklyn's police ranks were nearly all Irish then). Not so the supreme court of Brooklyn, which came down on Friede's side, granting him an injunction to prevent "any further interference on the part of the Steeplechase people." Tilyou had met his match. Indeed, it would later be revealed that Friede had a secret weapon in Borough Hall that made even the mighty George C. Tilyou quake—an ally with power enough to shut down every ride in Steeplechase Park. Tilyou's hand thus stayed, Friede retracted his threat to "shut off the park's view of Surf Avenue" by erecting a tall fence around his site. Friede was rolling now. He placed another big order for Pittsburgh steel on March 31— four thousand tons' worth—enough, reported the *Times*, to "bring the tower up to a height of 350 feet." Friede paid cash in advance, and arranged for a second load of steel—another four thousand tons—to be sent once the first order was received. Work on the concrete foundations was fast nearing completion; things appeared to be quite literally looking up. By now, some two thousand men and women had purchased shares of Friede Globe Tower Company stock. With such concrete proof now on the ground, hundreds more contributors rushed forward with cash in hand. And then it all began to unravel.[16]

When the best-laid schemes of men and mice go awry, it's usually due to misplaced trust. Unbeknownst to Friede, the man he put in charge of all Globe Tower financial matters, Henry Clay Russell Wade, had a very dodgy past. A Canadian dry goods clerk who came to the United States in the 1880s, Wade had been charged with petty theft and "passing queer checks"; later convicted of "running a bucket shop on lower Broadway," he was sentenced to three months in jail. As president of a shady outfit known as Empire Bond and Securities, Wade had conned a Canadian landowner into floating a timber company with bonds backed by his very own Imperial Trustee Company—"a fictitious concern," reported the *New York Sun*, "connected with the bogus 'Hanover Bank of Boston.'" Wade was arrested again, this time for grand larceny, in June 1905, only months before Friede launched his Brooklyn venture. The Missourian blundered into a contract with Empire Bond and Securities to sell Globe Tower stock, making Wade company treasurer in the process. He even encouraged Wade to rent an adjacent office at 27 William Street. Thus Friede not only let the fox into the henhouse; he gave it a knife and fork. Soon enough, Wade began embezzling funds. Friede found out, and in early August 1906 he fired Wade and reported him to the district attorney's office. Indicted, Wade promptly disappeared, only to return the following spring to stun Friede with a countersuit—claiming he was owed $36,000 in unpaid commissions. Incredibly, because the Globe Tower Company was registered in Arizona and thus considered a "foreign corporation," Wade was able to take legal action against it despite being a fugitive himself. On

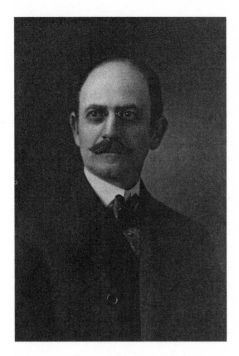

Portait of Samuel M. Friede in his Red Book prospectus for the globular "Department Store of Amusements," 1906. The Huntington Library, Rare Books Department.

April 8, 1907, sheriff's deputies marched into Friede's William Street office to attach the furniture. The company's bank account was frozen, while officers swept down on Steeplechase to seize Friede's stockpiled lumber and steel.[17]

Friede posted bond easily enough, and the attachments were lifted the next day—"SHERIFF RELEASES EIFFEL OF CONEY," shouted the *New York Herald*. But the Missourian was outraged. He attacked the district attorney's office for failing to arrest Wade, and as soon as the sheriff's deputy left his office, Friede "put up notices over the place," the *Herald* reported, "calling Wade by various impolite titles. He pasted epithets above him on the blue prints of the plans of the tower," and called police headquarters demanding to know why Wade—rumored now to be hiding out in Philadelphia—had not been arrested. Friede offered a reward for his capture, and within days Wade was hauled into custody by Pinkerton men and handed over to the police. The arrest made the front page of the *New York Times*. This time Friede accused Wade of having absconded with $15,000—several times the previous sum. Tilyou chimed in, too, charging that Wade had pocketed a check he was meant to deposit. It took real moxie to cheat world-wise men like Tilyou or Friede. The *Brooklyn Eagle* offered a portrait—describing Wade as a "well built, well dressed young man," with "keen, steel blue eyes. His manner is suave, his tongue glib, and those who have had dealings with him say that he is one of the shrewdest promoters it was ever their fortune—or misfortune—to meet." Wade pleaded not guilty, but was convicted of embezzlement and sent to Sing Sing for a lengthy prison term. But he would have his revenge, as we shall see.[18]

The thieving Canadian was hardly the only scoundrel Samuel Friede had on board. A few weeks before the Wade affair exploded, the *Brooklyn Eagle* revealed that a prominent city official, Edward A. Langan, had been appointed vice president of the Friede Globe Tower Company. Langan was chief inspector of elevators for the Brooklyn Bureau of Buildings. Without elevators, the Globe Tower was just a giant steel-framed gourd. Elevators circa 1906 were still a primitive technology, an Achilles heel of the building industry; those in the tower would be the largest and most mechanically complex ever built. It mightily behooved Friede to befriend this man responsible for approving elevators in Brooklyn. But Langan was no pushover; it would take more than a title to "fix" this corrupt and seasoned operator. Soon enough, inspector Langan was making a tidy commission selling shares of Globe Tower Company stock. When pressed by a reporter about this astonishing convergence of duties in a single man, Friede was matter-of-fact, describing Langan as "an energetic, hustling underwriter"—a man "deeply concerned with getting others to invest their funds in the company's securities." Friede further explained—needlessly—that Langan was "an invaluable man to us," who "from his official position . . . knows how to cut a lot of red tape and get straight to the goal, without loss of time, when it comes to our obtaining permits." Moreover, he proved to be an especially effective salesman, "turning in subscriptions by the cartload almost every day." When the reporter asked how "a friend" might go about purchasing Globe Tower stock, Friede replied, "Send him right over to Mr. Langan . . . at the Borough Hall."[19]

Advertisement for Friede Globe Tower stock with photograph of socle piers under construction. From *New-York Tribune*, June 9, 1907.

For a brief time, work on the tower continued despite the gathering scandal. In early summer 1907 Friede ran an advertisement in the *New-York Tribune* that included one of only three known photographs of the Globe Tower structure. In the foreground are nine massive concrete piers, each built over a cluster of concrete piles driven beneath the sand. The nine piers form the foundation for just one of the great socles upon which the mammoth steel-frame pedestal would rest. In the advertisement, Friede explained that there were to be forty-one such piers in all, built atop a grid of eight hundred piles. The foundation photograph appeared in the June 9 issue of the *Tribune*. Eight weeks later disaster struck. In the early morning hours of July 28, a fire broke out in Tilyou's Cave of the Winds. It spread rapidly, burning out of control the whole day and well into evening. By the time it was quelled, Steeplechase Park was a smoldering ruin. The irrepressible Tilyou was quick to market the disaster—famously charging admission to the still-burning wreckage and promising to build a bigger and better Steeplechase atop the ruins. The fire put a decisive end to the poisonous relationship between Tilyou and Friede. In an "Open Letter" in the *New-York Daily Tribune* that fall, Friede bewailed "the many obstacles which have . . . caused considerable delay in the construction of our Gigantic Enterprise," and he sued Tilyou for $245,000 in damages. The men also quarreled over the charred remains of the Revolving Airship Tower, totaled by the fire. In his rush to rebuild, Tilyou had unceremoniously sold off the wreckage to a salvage firm. Furious, Friede sued. Tilyou was served an injunction, but the charges were later dismissed.[20]

With Langan exposed and demand for Globe Tower stock incinerated by the fire, Friede was having serious financial problems—or so he claimed. In January 1908, after two years of punctual payments, Friede failed to make the quarterly rent. Tilyou hauled him into court, and this time the Globe Tower Company was evicted from Steeplechase. By now, Tilyou was working around the clock to get his mammoth 120,000-square-foot Pavilion of Fun finished for the 1908 season; the last thing he wanted on opening day was charred relics of failure. The Globe Tower signs were pulled down easily enough; but the great concrete piers were a lot more difficult to get rid of. They would sit abandoned for more than a year, gathering birdlime and soot. Finally, in February 1909, Tilyou commissioned H. J. Linder and Company to have Friede's foundation literally blasted out of the ground. "EVICTION BY DYNAMITE," the *Eagle* shouted. The steampunk orb, barely yet born, was now no more. And vanished too, it seems, was its erstwhile maker; for Samuel Friede had taken leave of both Brooklyn and America by the time Tilyou blew away the remains of his steampunk orb. The Missourian had never been out of the country before; now he hastily applied for a passport (occupation: "architect") and by the fall of 1908 was off to Europe with his wife and daughter.[21]

Friede was fleeing not only the tower scandal but a second fiasco in its wake. In an attempt to shelter the fugitive stock of the Globe Tower Company, he launched yet another venture—the Coney Island Hippodrome Circus, a swindle built atop a scam (or, as the *Eagle* put it, "the dying gasp of the Friede Globe Tower Company"). The centerpiece this time was a mammoth tent, largest in the world, erected about the steel supports of the aborted orb. Enclosing an area of 77,400 square feet—nearly two acres—it had seats on all sides "in true circus fashion," and could accommodate

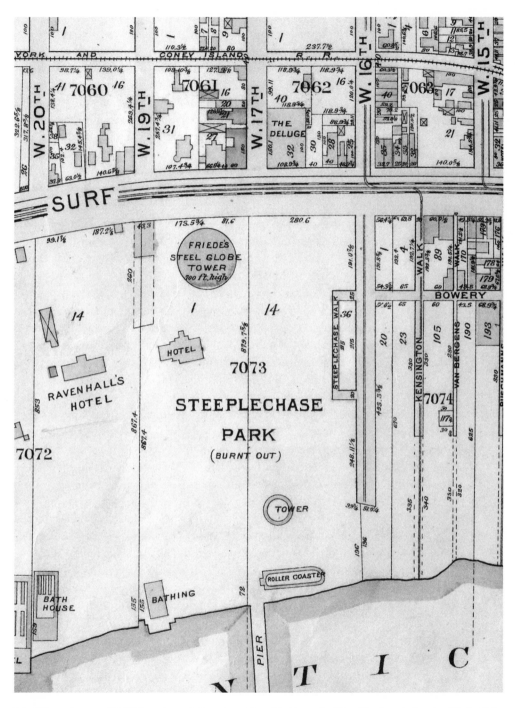

Detail from plate 29 of G. W. Bromley and Company, *Atlas of the Borough of Brooklyn* (1907), showing Friede Globe Tower site amidst burned ruins of Steeplechase Park. Lionel Pincus and Princess Firyal Map Division, The New York Public Library.

an audience of sixty-five hundred, more than Madison Square Garden at the time. The big top was set aglow at night by 250 arc lamps and fifteen thousand lightbulbs. Under it were three rings and two stages, upon which "for three solid hours," anticipated the *New-York Tribune*, "there will not be a minute in which something is not happening." Friede announced that the first hundred unmarried couples at the gate—"sweethearts who are engaged or hope to be"—would be admitted free on its Memorial Day opening, May 30, 1908. On the bill were acts from the American West and England, France, Italy, Russia, and Turkey—the famous Nelson family of aerialists from London, a "death-defying automobile act" by the Devillos, Captain French's Wild West Rough Riders (with "genuine Sioux Indians"). Among the animal acts were Professor Bristol's Troupe of Performing Ponies, John G. Robinson's elephant show from Ohio, and a lion act with Captain Jack Bonavita, a dashing trainer who had lost an arm to a Coney Island cat four years earlier but found subsequent fame commanding—single-handedly—a troupe of twenty-seven lions. Billed as America's first "permanent circus," the Hippodrome lasted all of two days. Expecting to be paid, the two hundred-odd circus employees were treated instead to dinner at a nearby hotel. "When the acrobats and performers returned to the circus lot," reported the *Tribune*, "everything had been sold, and it was explained that the show had been discontinued." In fact, nearly all the equipment—including the great tent, horses, stage props, dozens of wagon cars—was owned by Friede's major partner in the venture—the Bode Wagon Works of Cincinnati, renowned makers of the ornate wagons used by the Ringling Brothers and other circus companies. When the ill-fated circus defaulted on a required payment—on opening day, no less—Albert Bode moved fast to take possession of his property. Much of it had already been carted off to Jersey City, "out of the jurisdiction of the Kings County Sheriff." The slippery Friede had himself exited the picture, having "sold his interest when it became known that the project would fail."[22]

With his family in tow and ill-gotten gain in his pockets (a yearlong sojourn in Europe could not have come cheaply), Friede stayed well away from New York until September 1909. He was thus conveniently out of reach when the nine-lived Henry Wade was released from Sing Sing, singing a tune himself. In late summer 1909 Wade made a series of revelations that kept the city desk hopping despite the August heat. Friede, it turned out, had first run into Langan when he was building the Revolving Airship Tower, and had to "fix" the good inspector with twenty-five thousand shares of stock and $3,000 in cash to get the plans for the Globe Tower through the Brooklyn Bureau of Buildings. Langan was, moreover, the secret weapon Friede used to keep Tilyou in line. Among his responsibilities was assuring the safety of rides at Coney Island. Whenever Friede had trouble with Tilyou, he would call Langan to send an inspector down to Steeplechase; and invariably a grave violation would result. A shuttered ride on a summer weekend was very costly, and not even Tilyou's beloved horse coaster—namesake of Steeplechase—was safe from the Bureau of Buildings' newfound passion for public safety. And just as Tilyou suspected, it was Langan who had had the disputed Steeplechase shacks torn down. "They came to me, the Friede people," Langan recounted under oath; "I advised them to go ahead and tear down the buildings." When Tilyou complained to borough president Coler, matters got even worse. Inspectors swept down on Tilyou like avenging angels, subjecting him to a "systematic pounding" and placing violations "on almost every amusement device in Steeplechase Park with the possible exception of the ocean."[23]

The truth also came out about Langan's uncanny knack for selling Globe Tower stock. He simply forced applicants for building bureau permits or approvals to buy a cartload of Globe Tower stock before he would sign off on anything. "These people," Langan smugly said of his victims, "cannot refuse to buy." According to Wade, the inspector spent at least twenty-five hours a week for six months in his Borough Hall office serving not the people of Brooklyn, but the Globe Tower Company, selling its dubious stock on a 15 percent commission. Langan had also assigned several Bureau of Highways engineers to survey the tower site and stake out the foundation, using the city's rod, transit, and other equipment. Just as damning was Wade's allegation that, as it began to look less and less likely that the globe would ever be built, Friede and three of his officers—including Langan and engineer William J. Burdette—conspired to divide up the cash from sales of Globe Tower Company stock. All told they harvested $345,000, of which $146,000 was paid in sales commissions and engineering expenses; thus some $200,000 was divvied up among the four—making them all rich overnight. And that mighty bank of elevators, largest in the world, the very mechanism by which this titanic "Department Store of Amusements" would function? They hadn't even been designed yet at the time Langan's office approved them. "There were no plans for elevators," engineer Burdette admitted; "If there were, I would have drawn them." Langan's powerful, thoroughly crooked Bureau of Buildings turned out to be the tail that wagged the administration dog. If Friede expressed concern about Coler, Langan would respond, "Leave it to me . . . What I say with Coler goes." The Globe Tower investigation became a central part of a lengthy and often sensational probe into the hopelessly corrupt Coler administration, led by a tenacious young Tammany-slayer named John Purroy Mitchel, then New York City commissioner of accounts, who would later become New York City's youngest mayor.[24]

In all, some two thousand investors—large and small, rich and poor, even schoolchildren—bought shares of Globe Tower stock. "Professional men were just as gullible as the day laborers," wrote the *Eagle*; and it was "as easy to get business men who should have known better to bite at the tempting bait as it was to rope in those who were richer in artistic temperament than in common sense."

Brownie camera photograph of the Globe Tower socles under construction, 1907. Courtesy of Paul Brigandi.

Some Langan had forced to pony up in exchange for building permits; others—like William Stead, a former manufacturer—were lured by promises of titles and other rewards. Stead was made a director in exchange for dropping a cool $10,000 on the venture ($250,000 today). Edwin J. Quinn, Friede's superintendent of construction, called them all "suckers" but was good enough to include himself in that number. Some of those fleeced by Friede and company lost their life savings to the scam; none would ever get a penny back. One such victim was Maestro Govarale of the Globe Tower Band. Govarale enjoyed modest fame as a conductor at the time—the *Brooklyn Eagle* described him as "the famous Italian director." Seduced by Friede's offer to make him a company officer and musical director of the entire enterprise, Govarale invested $5,000 in the tower scheme. But he grew suspicious when Friede would "come around with his wife in automobiles and diamonds," while at every board meeting he would be asked to invest more and more money. He was soon convinced that the tower was a scam and had been from the start. "In my opinion that company was organized to rob people." On the witness stand, he cried that Friede and his henchmen "took my money all . . . all I had saved in twelve years." Govarale was ruined and wished to see Friede "hanging." "Poor Fillipo's dreams were shattered," the *Eagle* lamented; "He is now eking out a commonplace existence by playing music in an uptown restaurant in Manhattan."[25]

Was Samuel Friede's venture a swindle from the start, or did the Missouri tinkerer truly mean to build his titanic orb? It's a question that will likely never be answered. There was probably more than a little good intention at the outset, but it was corrupted by the lure of a quick and easy fortune. Or perhaps Wade and Langan bullied Friede into turning his tower dream into a scam. It's impossible to know when the Rubicon was crossed—perhaps as it became increasingly clear that stock sales would never cover the full cost of erecting the colossus, or that even its very construction might be impossible. In any case, breaking ground for the massive footers and stockpiling tons of steel on-site for all to see—even "fixing" officials like Langan to secure a valid building permit—all became part of an elaborate, very effective ploy to convince skeptics that the project was real. Indeed, "the most active stock-selling period," recounted the *Eagle*, "was while the foundations were being laid, and for some time afterward"; for now even the cautious and skeptical "began to take an interest when they saw the foundations actually going down." George Tilyou had begun openly questioning Friede's good faith in the summer of 1906, when borough president Coler arrived one morning with a crew of workers. They were to inspect the foundation to make sure it complied with the plans filed with the Bureau of Buildings. Those called for pilings to extend at least thirty feet below grade; tests that day revealed they were sunk no more than eighteen feet. The short pilings only fortified Tilyou's conviction that Friede never intended to erect the tower—a charge that was vociferously denied. Tilyou then presented Friede a little challenge: if he would "guarantee the completion of the tower and would get some reliable surety company to go on their bond . . . he would cancel the lease for $25,000 a year and give them a new lease for only $1 a year." In other words, Tilyou offered Friede a fourteen-year lease on a priceless patch of Coney Island for all of $14. No one took him up on the offer.[26]

But even with its mortal remains blown out of the ground, the ill-fated orb lived on in spirit. Years later, a letter to the *Eagle*—"An Iridescent Dream"—lamented the collapse of Friede's "grand enterprise." "I was anticipating its completion with much pleasure," related the correspondent, presumably unstung by the stock swindle, to "enjoy the sensation of being seated on one of its moving platforms, eating a good dinner, smoking a good cigar . . . while being carried slowly around the horizontal equator of this great steel globe." Why not try it again? "It seems to me that it ought to be a good and safe investment," offered this amnesiac, "to build a tremendous steel and concrete building right out in the ocean . . . where they would not have to buy the site or pay rent." But the most enduring legacy of the Globe Tower was Steeplechase Park, version 2.0. George C. Tilyou might have rued the day he ever met Samuel Friede, but he owed the Missourian a debt of gratitude for planting in his head an idea that would make Steeplechase the foremost amusement park in the world. Instead of simply rebuilding his complex after the 1907 fire, Tilyou hired architect Reynold H. Hinsdale to design a monumental steel-and-glass "Pavilion of Fun" in which to house all his rides. The structure, 450 feet long and covering nearly three acres, gave him an immediate competitive advantage over all Coney operators simply by allowing him to open in inclement weather.[27]

Architecturally, the pavilion belonged to another age. Artist Reginald Marsh, who sketched and painted scenes at Steeplechase Park all through the 1930s, regarded it as the "last and greatest example of Victorian architecture in the United States."[28] Similar shed-like structures, framed with cast iron and sheathed in glass, had been erected as early as the 1820s. The Crystal Palace, built for the Great Exhibition of 1851, was the wonder of Victorian London. Victor Baltard's vast Halles de Paris, part of Haussmann's modernization campaign and the setting for Emile Zola's

George C. Tilyou's Pavilion of Fun, its scale wildly exaggerated in this 1908 postcard, brings Sam Friede's "collection of amusements in midair" down to earth. Collection of the author.

Le Ventre de Paris—was the largest market complex of nineteenth-century Europe. It was dwarfed a generation later by the Galerie des machines at the 1889 Exposition Universelle in Paris, the largest vaulted building ever constructed. In the United States, such structures were built in New York in 1853, in Philadelphia for the 1876 Centennial Exposition, and in Jersey City a decade later—the vast terminal shed of the Central Railroad of New Jersey, today a ruin in Liberty State Park.[29] Hinsdale's first proposal for Tilyou—a "Palace of Pleasure"—was a lavish confection straight out of Second Empire Paris. The Pavilion of Fun was sheet cake in comparison, reminiscent in its massing of one of the earliest iron-and-glass shed structures— Gabriel Veugny's 1824 Marché de la Madeleine in Paris. If it broke no new ground as a type, Tilyou's Pavilion of Fun was unprecedented in that it made Steeplechase the first amusement park in the world to bring under a single roof a vast range of amusement rides and attractions. It remained the largest such structure anywhere during its life, surpassed only by the ill-fated Old Chicago mega-mall and indoor amusement complex that opened in the Chicago suburb of Bolingbrook in 1975 (and closed five years later).

Tilyou would be loath to admit that Friede's orb was floating across his sagittal plane as he contemplated the Pavilion of Fun. But even a cursory comparison reveals striking parallels. For all its absurdities, Friede's sphere was probably the first self-contained, self-enclosed theme park ever proposed—certainly it was the first to gain widespread publicity. The Steeplechase shed was a kind of pancaked, economy version of Friede's soaring "Department Store of Amusements." Indeed, Tilyou himself described his Pavilion of Fun as an "Amusement Emporium." And like the star-crossed orb, it was outfitted with a grand ballroom, probably the largest in the city when it opened. It, too, had a palm garden and an observatory, just like the Globe Tower. Tilyou may well have even adopted Friede's business model to help pay for the great building—by incorporating and selling shares of stock. Tilyou had never done this before. Yet now, in February of 1908, he incorporated Steeplechase Park, capitalizing it at $2 million and authorizing the issue of 400,000 shares of stock. A quarter of these he proposed to sell to the public. He was scrupulously transparent and democratic about it, the specter of Friedean fraud no doubt in mind. As the *Billboard* reported, "Many of Mr. Tilyou's friends have urged him to let them into this money-making investment through the organization of a stock company, but Mr. Tilyou has taken the position that he can show no partiality. His friends, he says, are the public, and if he lets any in on such a deal it will be the public or nobody; and if the public it would be through a system of small shares of one or five dollars or so that would enable the poorest of his old patrons to realize well on their investment." He was also swift to share the wealth, declaring an 8 percent dividend in October and sending out "a barrel of checks" to his big and little backers. The master showman also sweetened his stock with something Friede could never offer: each dollar certificate was also an admission ticket to Steeplechase.[30]

In the end, for all the outrage and indignation the Friede Globe Tower hoax provoked, its context must never be forgotten. *This was Coney Island!* The counterfeit palace, an island fantasy built out of smoke, mirrors, and windblown sand, a place where nothing was what it seemed and artful sleights of hand were the coin of the realm. Coney Island had been relieving honest folk of cash and morals since almost the day the Dutch first spied its namesake rabbits. Here was an empire of illusion and altered reality—the "apotheosis of the ridiculous," as Reginald Wright Kauffman put it the very year Tilyou dynamited Friede's footers. The seductions of Coney Island required a temporary suspension of one's faith in fact and veracity. And it was above Coney Island's bewitching mix of reality and the absurd that Samuel Friede floated his marvelous steampunk orb, an apparition that vanished at first light—"a beautiful bubble," eulogized the *Eagle*, "burst before the eyes of a long list of optimistic Brooklyn investors." The Globe Tower was no crime against New Yorkers, no black mark on the good name of Coney Island; it was the undiluted essence of the place, a trick played on the tricksters, the biggest joke of all.[31]

CHAPTER 9

PORT OF EMPIRE

I'd like to take a
Sail on Jamaica
Bay with you,
And fair Canarsie's Lakes we'll view . . .
—ROGERS AND HART, "MANHATTAN"

From the long-vanished footers of the great Globe Tower, it is but a short walk today to the corner of Shell Road and West Sixth Street. Framed by used car lots and a large commercial laundry, the spot is anything but picturesque—a scruffy crossroads on the way to the beach. And yet here one may glimpse, like strata exposed, multiple layers of Brooklyn's past. Shell Road is the southernmost extension of McDonald Avenue, a major commercial artery that plunges down the map from Green-Wood Cemetery through the heart of Gravesend's ancient grid. Beneath the asphalt here (and occasionally peeking through) are the buried rails of the Prospect Park and Coney Island Railroad, a streetcar line that began operating in 1875. Overhead roars the Belt Parkway on its way to the Narrows; above that runs the F train, clattering and screeching. And back on the ground, just beyond the cracked sidewalk and the ailanthus-tree sprouts, is water—the stagnant, bulkheaded terminus of Coney Island Creek. Litter-bobbed and reeking, it is nonetheless a storied channel; for the creek separates Coney from mainland Brooklyn, thus making it an island. It's perhaps best known today for a half-submerged, barnacle-encrusted submarine— the *Quester I*—resting in shallow water just off Calvert Vaux Park. Built in 1970 by a Navy Yard shipfitter named Jerry Bianco, it was part of a mad scheme to raise the Italian ocean liner SS *Andrea Doria* off the Nantucket sea bottom (by injecting its hull with inflatable air bags). In the spirit of Sam Friede, the project was funded by the sale of shares of stock in a company called Deep Sea Techniques. Though the craft won coast guard and navy approval, it capsized upon launch and never got beyond its birth chamber.

Coney Island Creek once plied a meandering course between Gravesend Bay and Sheepshead Bay and was navigable by small craft as late as 1915. Even then it was no enchanting rivulet; the *Brooklyn Standard Union* described it as "a nuisance and eye-sore, winding its noxious way . . . serving no useful purpose whatever." Nonetheless, the creek once hovered on the verge of fame; for its waters were to serve one of the most heroically misguided infrastructure projects ever proposed for New York City—the "Great World Harbor" that would turn Jamaica Bay into the largest port on the seven seas. A stone's throw from Ambrose Channel and the "four-fathom curve"—the isobath or contour indicating the depth at which most coasting vessels will not run aground—Jamaica Bay was touted as America's front door to the Atlantic. As Harry Chase Brearley

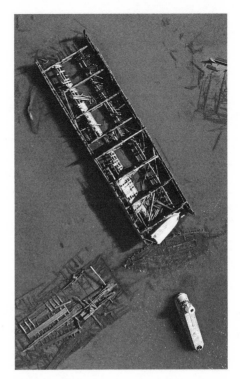

Sunken vessels in Coney Island Creek, 2017. The wreck of the *Quester I* is at lower right. Photograph by author.

observed in his 1914 treatise *The Problem of Greater New York and Its Solution*, the forty-five square miles of Jamaica Bay made it large enough to absorb "the principal portions of the harbors of Liverpool, Antwerp, Hamburg, and Rotterdam . . . without undue crowding." In his view the bay was a godsend for Gotham—"a physical fact of compelling proportions," he wrote, and "one of the dominating geographical features of Greater New York." New Yorkers got a first glimpse of what that geography might become on March 13, 1910. That morning, the *New York Times* ran an article headlined, "JAMAICA BAY TO BE A GREAT WORLD HARBOR," accompanied by a breathtaking aerial view of the port-to-be by the celebrated artist and illustrator Vernon Howe Bailey. In a literal flight of the imagination, Bailey depicted Gotham not from the usual Manhattan vantage, but from seagullian heights far above the rolling surf of Rockaway Beach. In the center of Jamaica Bay a pair of islands sidle up to one another like whale pups in a great amniotic sac. Fringed with cilia-like wharves, the islands resemble mini-Manhattans, progeny of the great city slumbering on the horizon. The projected seaport was as breathtaking as it was visionary. Here the world's merchant fleet would find hundreds of miles of harborage on the edge of America's greatest manufacturing city. On its western edge at Barren Island a series of great piers would be built, each 850 feet wide and 8,000 feet long—bigger than anything in North America at the time. As many as fifty vessels could berth at any one time. The port would be developed in stages; until more room was needed, why not turn the bay's marshy hummocks into a great water park? John Charles Olmsted, stepson of the designer of Prospect and Central parks, suggested just that: a low-slung realm of "lagoons and wooded archipelagos." Harold Caparn, who later helped design the Brooklyn Botanic Garden, envisioned an expansive playground: "Not a conventional park, with lawns and exotic trees and shrubs," he explained, "but a water-park with many and intricate channels intersecting the great level areas of reclaimed marsh, on which all the sports of smooth water . . . may find ample space."[1]

All this struck a chord with New Yorkers worried about Gotham's future as America's leading port city. By the end of the nineteenth century, the city's aging port infrastructure—much of it built before the Civil War—could hardly keep up with the flood of goods pouring into town. New York was the entrepôt through which nearly half of the total foreign commerce of the United States passed annually. The value of goods entering and clearing its port jumped from $620 million in 1875 to $1.2 billion in 1905, while tonnage in foreign trade more than doubled—from 8.73 to 18.9 million tons—in that same period. These concerns gained urgency once the United States began work on the Panama Canal in 1904, for it was widely assumed that seaborne custom would surge once the isthmus was crossed. New port facilities were needed beyond Manhattan, and Jamaica Bay seemed an ideal place to build a seaport equal to the ambitions of the newly consolidated city. Long overshadowed by worldly Manhattan, Brooklyn might well now hold the keys to Gotham's future. As John E. Ruston of the Brooklyn Chamber of Commerce put it, Jamaica Bay was "the potential savior of the commercial pre-eminence of the port of New York." At first flush, it seemed to offer much indeed, with twice the water frontage of Manhattan from Hell Gate to the Battery and up the Hudson to 135th Street. The Coney

The Great Port of Jamaica Bay on cover of a commemorative dinner program, 1912. Buttolph Collection of Menus, Rare Books Division, The New York Public Library.

Island Canal—and an even more ambitious ditch from Jamaica Bay north across Queens to Flushing Bay on Long Island Sound—were deemed essential to this vision; for they would make the World Harbor part of a weather-safe inland passage from the Hudson River to the sea. Because the New York State Barge Canal—the modernized, much-expanded successor to the famed Erie Canal—meets the Hudson just below Albany, these canals would effectively tie the new seaport into a mighty system of inland navigation that, with Lake Erie, would reach some eight hundred miles into the American heartland. Shipments of grain, ore, coal, or lumber could be barged from as far away as Detroit or Cleveland without ever touching land or hazarding open coastal waters. Jamaica Bay would be not only Gotham's portal to the world, but America's.[2]

From above, Long Island resembles a great split-tailed fish, with Prospect Park for an eye and Jamaica Bay a gaping mouth. As we've seen, it was shaped by that great sculptor of New York State—the Laurentide ice sheet that made its last sortie out of the Canadian arctic some twenty thousand years ago. The glacier crept down the map, withdrew, and advanced again, leaving behind Long Island—a sea-swamped moraine pushed forward by the ice and left behind after its last retreat. As the glacier began melting, sand and silt were carried seaward, creating the broad outwash plain of Long Island's south shore. Jamaica Bay was a delta at the mouth of a river of glacial meltwater that subsequently flooded as sea levels rose at the end of the Ice Age. Ocean currents, tidal action, and storms further shape-shifted the sands, eventually extending Rockaway Peninsula—the westernmost end of the sandy archipelago that parallels Long Island's south shore—to create a long, sheltered entrance to Rockaway Inlet. Thus shielded from the fury of the Atlantic, Jamaica Bay developed an extraordinary diversity of plant, animal, and marine life. Upland areas were dominated by sumac, blueberry, holly, and cedars; salt marshes supported a myriad of native grasses and were laced and drained by an array of tidal creeks. The abundance of marine and animal life in and around Jamaica Bay provided sustenance for native peoples long before Hudson's *Half Moon* appeared on the horizon. The name *Jamaica* has nothing to do with the Caribbean island nation (despite Brooklyn's large West Indian population), but—like so many place-names in metropolitan New York—derives from the Lenape word *yemacah*—"place of the beaver."[3]

Tucked behind the sheltering arm of the Rockaways (from the Lenape *Rechqua Akie*) Jamaica Bay fairly leaped off the map as a would-be seaport. Brearley described the bay as "not only shore-enclosed, but vestibuled as well," a harbor whose waters were protected "so thoroughly from the ocean that while a heavy surf may be thundering at the beach, the surface of the bay is scarcely rippled."[4] The frailest craft would find safe shelter within. Exactly who first advocated making Jamaica Bay a great world port is unclear, but it may well have been that Zelig-like Gotham visionary Andrew Haswell Green—the autocrat who helped create Central Park, even as he drove its designers mad. Though nothing of Green's writings on Jamaica Bay survive, we know of his dreams for a port there from a 1909 speech by Joseph Caccavajo—a prominent civil engineer with an interest in city planning. In a lecture to the Brooklyn Allied Boards of Trade and Taxpayers' Associations, Caccavajo related an encounter with an elderly man on a train some eight or nine years earlier

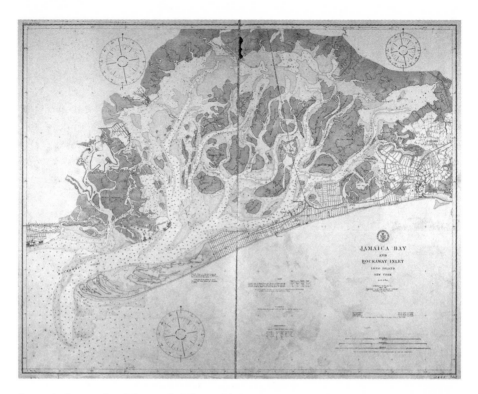

"Not only shore-enclosed, but vestibuled as well." Jamaica Bay and Rockaway Inlet, 1911, United States Coast and Geodetic Survey. Lionel Pincus and Princess Firyal Map Division, The New York Public Library.

(circa 1900). "This old gentleman," he told his audience, "was Andrew H. Green, the father of Greater New York, and I shall never forget the earnest manner in which he told me that I would probably live to see New York City extend north to Dutchess County and east to absorb all of Nassau and a good portion of Suffolk County." Caccavajo was particularly spellbound by Green's prediction that within a generation "Jamaica Bay would be the greatest shipping center in the world . . . connected with the East River and Long Island Sound by a great ship canal across Queens Borough to Flushing Bay" and another "back of Coney Island connecting Jamaica Bay with Gravesend Bay." The octogenarian seemed so certain about the future of the bay and "spoke so enthusiastically of its possibilities," Caccavajo recalled, "that a few days after our meeting I visited Jamaica Bay, and later . . . prepared some preliminary plans for its improvement." Caccavajo's work has since been lost but was likely the earliest scheme for a seaport at Jamaica Bay.[5]

Caccavajo eventually moved on to other things, planning routes for the city's first rapid transit lines. But the seaport scheme soon found an even more passionate promoter in the person of Edward Marshall Grout. Dubbed the "Longheaded Politician" for his shrewdness and scholarly mien, Grout was a New Yorker of old Yankee stock and the prosecutor who put Gravesend autocrat John Y. McKane behind bars. He later became Brooklyn's first borough president and ran successfully for comptroller of the city of New York in 1901 on an anti-Tammany fusion ticket with Seth Low. It was as comptroller that Grout submitted a proposal to the Sinking Fund in 1905 for the development of Jamaica Bay, which awaited only the hand of man, he believed, to become "a commercial and manufacturing Venice, or a Venice of homes, or both." Transforming this vast expanse of "waste land and water" into a great seaport was an idea Grout had been mulling over for years. "My proposition," he wrote, "is that the City should at once take up, formulate and execute a comprehensive scheme for the full development of this property . . . by reclaiming the salt marshes, filling in the shallow parts and hummocks of the bay, bulkheading the islands and shores throughout the entire extent, and opening up such channels between the filled-in lands as may best develop the locality." Creating new land could be done cheaply enough, for filling and bulkheading could be "easily accomplished from the waste products collected by the Department of Street Cleaning . . . and perhaps by the use of the excavated material from future rapid transit subways." By developing Jamaica Bay, Grout concluded, the city would help "furnish here a centering point for great manufacturing interests." Grout could well be suspected of Brooklyn boosterism (he had been the borough's first president, after all). But his real interest was the continued supremacy of New York as a center for shipping, trade, and commerce, particularly the "absolute need of increased water front and dockage facilities in the port of New York at cheap rates."[6]

By the time Grout made his proposal, Jamaica Bay was alive with craft—garbage scows, barges, trollers, fishing skiffs, ferries carrying passengers to and from the Rockaways. But except for ships hauling fertilizer to Europe, it only rarely saw an oceangoing vessel, or even those plying coastal waters. Most goods shipped from Flatlands, Canarsie, and other towns typically went overland to Brooklyn and thence by ferry to Manhattan. The shores of Jamaica Bay were still largely in a wild state, with little more than ferry docks and stilted shacks. Of course, Brooklyn had elsewhere developed an impressive array of port facilities by this time, mostly clustered on the borough's northwest shore along New York Harbor. Many dated to the earliest years of colonization. Merchant vessels were being built in Wallabout Bay in the 1780s, later the site of the Brooklyn Navy Yard. Warehouses, piers, and a ferry terminal were built at the foot of Brooklyn Heights, across from lower Manhattan. Farther south, Erie Basin in Red Hook was developed in the 1850s by William Beard. One of the largest artificial harbors on the Eastern Seaboard, it served as a terminal for grain and other products shipped via the Erie Canal. On the south side of Gowanus Bay was Brooklyn Basin, where Edwin Clark Litchfield's Brooklyn Improvement Company dredged Gowanus Creek into a mile-long canal that received—among many other things—the barge-loads of brownstone used to build Brooklyn's iconic row houses. The canal was lined with lumber, brick, and coal yards. Farther north, on Brooklyn's border with Queens, Newtown Creek Canal stimulated industrial development in Greenpoint and Williamsburg, and was originally meant to be extended south across Bushwick and Brownsville to join Jamaica Bay at Canarsie (both Gowanus and Newtown creeks are Superfund sites and among the most polluted waterways in the United States). By the 1890s these improvements helped make Brooklyn one of America's leading port cities. As Henry R. Stiles enthused, they "attract hither the commerce of the world," granting Brooklyn "supremacy over all other cities on this continent." On the eve of Consolidation, the city's portfo-lio of port and manufacturing facilities gained one last diamond—Bush Terminal, America's first multitenant, intermodal industrial complex. Construction on the vast project began in 1895 and eventually spread over two hundred acres of Brook-lyn's waterfront, just below Sunset Park. Some twenty-five thousand workers were employed in Bush Terminal's shipping, warehouse, and manufacturing plants. In developing his namesake complex, Irving T. Bush exploited the Achilles heel of port operations in Manhattan. For despite its splendid piers and wharves, getting goods into and out of the port had become a time-consuming and costly affair.[7]

But even with Bush Terminal, the Port of New York was at capacity, and the specter of losing trade to competitors made Grout's Jamaica Bay proposal compel-ling indeed. Historically the hub of shipping activity in the city, Manhattan Island is blessed with deepwater portage on both the Hudson and East rivers, allowing oceangoing vessels to tie up a stone's throw from the center of commerce. But what served well in a slower age of sail proved inadequate as ships grew longer and the pace of commerce increased. The city faced a dilemma of abundance. On the eve of the First World War, New York was America's busiest port, handling half of all the foreign commerce of the United States. In 1914 alone, 120 million tons of freight passed through the port by ship and rail. But the very geography that made Manhattan so accessible to the world isolated it from the rest of the country, with serious implications for commerce. The nation's mighty rail network ended in a great ganglion of tracks in Bayonne and Hoboken. "Eight of the twelve railroads on which Manhattan, Brooklyn, Queens and the Bronx depend," wrote William R. Wilcox in a 1920 report that presaged formation of the Port Authority, "are on the New Jersey side of the Hudson." All goods arriving in port had to undergo a grueling transfer process to make it to the railheads, save only those to be consumed in Manhattan or shipped upstate via the New York Central Railroad—the only line with a direct freight connection to Manhattan. The others were forced to lift their goods-filled boxcars by gantry crane onto barges (known as "float bridges" or "car floats") to be tugged—a handful at a time by the venerable New York Dock Railway—to the railheads across the river. Transferring freight between truck, ship, and train created choke points that slowed the movement of freight, drove shipping costs through the roof, and bred all sorts of crime and racketeering. Longshoring—loading and unloading ships—soon accounted for 50 percent of a ship's total expense in moving cargo. This made a large labor force vital to the transshipment process, one that organized into one of the most powerful unions in the city—the International Long-shoremen's Association. The rough, racket-ridden world of the longshoremen—memorably depicted in the Marlon Brando film *On the Waterfront* (actually shot in New Jersey)—was itself largely a function of Manhattan's isolation from the main-land and inadequacy as a modern seaport. "There has never been a loading racket in San Francisco, in New Orleans, in Baltimore or Philadelphia," wrote Daniel Bell in *The End of Ideology*, for "the spatial arrangements of these other ports is such that loading never had a 'functional' significance." Each enjoyed a direct connection to trunk-line railroads, enabling easy transfer of cargo to the nation's rail grid, while none had to struggle with the "congested and choking narrow-street patterns" that made Manhattan's piers so difficult to access. As William R. Wilcox cogently summarized it in a 1920 report, "Our port problem is primarily a railroad problem."[8]

One of the most lucid assessments of New York's looming port crisis was made in 1908 by George Ethelbert Walsh, a writer better known for romances and children's books. In a piece for *Cassier's Magazine*, Walsh pointed out what every longshoreman knew well: "The Island of Manhattan is too full"—not only of people, but "too full of freight traffic. Its streets are arteries through which the life-blood of the nation often stagnates instead of flowing steadily in a limpid stream. From terminal to terminal, and from pier to pier, the great freight stream pours, crossing and re-crossing, and often making wide detours to reach its destination." East side and west, the call from the wharves was for 'room, and more room'!" Studies at the time revealed that all available wharfage in New York would be exhausted in ten or fifteen years. Manhattan was also increasingly fettered in its ability to handle large passenger ships—a situation that came to a head in early 1911 when the War Department refused the city permission to extend its Hudson River steamship piers by two hundred feet. The request was made when the Dock Department learned that two ships of the White Star Line—the *Olympic* and the *Titanic*, each over nine hundred feet in length—would be making maiden voyages to the city within months (the *Olympic* would arrive in June; the *Titanic* sank, of course, en route the following April). The War Department ruled that extending the piers would narrow the channel, impeding navigation on the river and possibly increasing the river's rate of flow—a kind of hydraulic Venturi effect. The permit denial brought joy to Brooklyn,

Brooklyn's working waterfront, 1918, site of Brooklyn Bridge Park today. William D. Hassler Photograph Collection, New-York Historical Society.

for it already boasted the city's longest piers—at Thirty-First and Thirty-Third streets in Bush Terminal, where the Dock Department planned to build several more ranging in length from twelve hundred to seventeen hundred feet. The thousand-foot steamship crisis underscored the need for a modern port; for the "real need," opined the *Sun* in December 1912, "is not merely to meet the emergency of the moment affecting one class of shipping—but to devise and adopt a system of port development that shall preclude forever . . . the possibility of other emergencies."[9]

Grout's proposal for an alternative port at Jamaica Bay gathered little dust. Within months of publication, the Board of Estimate and Mayor George B. McClellan, Jr., formed a Jamaica Bay Improvement Commission. Its exhaustive *Report*, released in the summer of 1907, surveyed a gamut of issues related to Gotham's economic growth—manufacturing output, import and export activity, shipping tonnage, population growth—and the "probable demands" these would place upon the city's port facilities. The commissioners found the port operating at a mere quarter of the efficiency of Antwerp's. Not only was Manhattan difficult to reach; it offered few warehouses close to piers and wharves. This "spatial mismatch" between berth and warehouse caused endless, costly schlepping across town. The Manhattan merchant was "obliged to proceed to some pier or several," reported the commissioners, "secure his consignment of material, truck it over miles of city streets to the warehouse or factory, unpack it, sort it, make it up, repack and again truck it back to the wharves for shipment." They, like Walsh and other analysts, concluded that Manhattan simply could not sustain an upsurge of port activity. Efforts to increase its efficiency—by building, for example, the Chelsea Piers, embellished by the architects of Grand Central Terminal—would only delay the inevitable. Manhattan was maxed out. Indeed, "the City has arrived at that point," they concluded, "where it is necessary for her to reach out and take advantage of the vast amount of water frontage which she possesses in her other boroughs"—such as Jamaica Bay. The Brooklyn press heartily concurred. "If New York continues its great stride," editorialized the *Standard Union*, "much of the growing shipping must go either to Newark Bay or Jamaica Bay and naturally this city wants the latter to have it." Or, as George Walsh put it, "The development of Jamaica Bay into a great basin for the docking of ocean steamers, where deep-sea freight can be transferred directly to cars, would undoubtedly eliminate many of the evils which congest the City and river fronts of to-day."[10]

Adding further weight to arguments in favor of a Jamaica Bay seaport was the upsurge in shipping widely—and hopefully—expected to come with completion of the Panama Canal. It is no coincidence that Grout's proposal was written in 1905, the first full year of American work on the big ditch. The Panama Canal was the moonshot of its age, the most ambitious civilian works project in US history until the Apollo space program. Crossing the Panamanian isthmus had been a dream of seafarers and imperialists since the sixteenth century. It was especially seductive to American merchants, for it would eliminate the treacherous journey around Cape Horn that made traveling by ship between the East and West coasts of the United States a long and costly affair. Cutting across the isthmus halved the distance between New York and Los Angeles. "Canal fever" began spreading as the United States took over control of the project from the French, sped by the Pan-American Union's "Get

The author's grandfather, Giovanni Tambasco (below boom, farthest to the right in pit), on steam-shovel crew excavating the New York State Barge Canal in Madison or Oneida County, New York, 1908. Collection of the author.

Ready for the Panama Canal" campaign. Cities up and down both coasts upgraded their ports for the expected flotilla of canal-borne traffic, even building canals of their own in emulation of the federal effort. New Orleans dug the Industrial Canal between the Mississippi and Lake Pontchartrain; Texas deepened its Houston Ship Channel. New York upgraded the old Erie Canal, an infrastructure that profoundly altered the regional economies of the Northeast in the mid-nineteenth century but by 1900 was as obsolete as a dirt airstrip in an age of jets. The New York State Barge Canal—approved by voters two weeks before the United States and Panama signed the treaty creating the Canal Zone—was meant to modernize and expand the Erie system, deepening and rerouting the original channel and adding three new ones: the Champlain, Oswego, and Cayuga-Seneca canals. Together, the upgraded system formed "a continuous highway for interstate and foreign commerce" spanning eight hundred miles.[11]

However extensive its inland reach, the State Barge Canal would be only as good as its terminal in New York City, its gateway to the world. Gotham was admonished to help ready the Empire State, and not allow complacency and "its colossal egotism" to impede implementing necessary improvements to its port. John Barrett, director general of the Pan-American Union, worried in 1912 that the great metropolis, "overconfident in its magnificent power and position," had not stirred "to make the same effort to get ready for the [Panama] canal or to develop its commerce with Latin America as are Boston, Philadelphia, Baltimore, New Orleans, Los Angeles, and San Francisco." But enhancements were made, however few and slowly. Erie Basin, terminus of the Erie Canal, was upgraded as one of several official Barge Canal stations in the city. The improved basin and adjacent Gowanus Canal could handle, among other craft, the twenty-five-hundred-ton ships of the Pacific Coast Lumber Company, which hauled timber from Oregon and Washington through the Panama Canal and onward to Chicago via the Barge Canal. Soon new canal terminals were under construction on Newtown Creek, Flushing Bay, at Rogers Street in Long Island City, Hallet's Cove in Astoria, Mott Haven in the Bronx, and in Manhattan at West Fifty-Third Street and Pier 6 on the East River. This last facility, at the foot of Coenties Slip (today's Downtown Manhattan Heliport) was the first completed. Described as "immaculate in white paint and with electric lights gleaming along the sides," the facility was opened by Governor Al Smith in October 1919. An even more substantial improvement was made in Brooklyn—a huge grain elevator at the foot of Columbia Street on Gowanus Canal. Previously, the only grain storage facilities in the city were owned by the railroads, mortal enemies of canals. Grain arriving in New York by canal boat was thus forced to sit for days on barges, to the joy of the local vermin population. Industry and city leaders feared that New York was ill prepared to handle the expected surge in Midwest grain shipments once the Barge Canal was completed—that the city would lose the grain trade just as it had earlier lost the cotton and tobacco trades. Gotham's biggest competitor in this was Montreal, which had plenty of grain elevators at its disposal. Montreal built its first storage facility in the 1850s and erected five modern grain elevators between 1900 and 1930. By then its elevator capacity was a staggering eighteen million bushels— enough wheat to make 756 million pounds of pasta (twelve servings of spaghetti for every person in America today). Gotham had fallen hopelessly behind its northern neighbor, prompting frantic action by officialdom and industry. "The crying need," wrote the state's chief engineer, Frank M. Williams, in 1919, "is for an elevator in New York." The New York State Barge Canal Grain Elevator, completed in 1922 with capacity for two million bushels, was the somewhat meager and belated answer to this call. The derelict structure still dominates the Red Hook skyline.[12]

But these terminals in New York City were small and designed to handle primarily domestic trade. For the Barge Canal to really shine—to become infrastructure of global consequence—required a great deepwater seaport, a "general terminal for the accommodation of export trade" that could handle a fleet of oceangoing vessels. As Nelson B. Killmer of the Harbor Protective and Development Association stressed, "success of the export business over the canal" required a separate terminal for seaborne trade in New York City, one segregated from "local and coastwise business" and with "plenty of room where transshipment can be made quickly and cheaply." The Jamaica Bay seaport would give the Barge Canal access to the world, while itself drawing sustenance from the canal's eight-hundred-mile taproot into the American heartland. Consummating this union, however, required not only vast internal improvements to Jamaica Bay (dredging channels, filling marshes, building bulkheads, piers, and wharves), but construction of two crucial last segments of the Barge Canal itself—the Coney Island Canal, from Gravesend Bay to Jamaica Bay, and a considerably longer channel north from Jamaica Bay across Queens to

The derelict New York State Barge Canal grain elevator on the Red Hook waterfront, 2018. Photograph by author.

Flushing Bay. These canals would provide convenient weatherproof connections to the bay from New York Harbor and Long Island Sound. While Jamaica Bay could be accessed by sailing around Coney Island, this open-water route was reliably safe only in summer. Winter months exposed barges and canal boats—craft designed for placid waters, vulnerable to swamping when heavily laden—to the constant menace of storms. The Flushing Canal would similarly make access to Jamaica Bay easier for craft plying the coast from New England, which were forced to either navigate the treacherous Hell Gate or steam all the way around Long Island on open seas. As Noble E. Whitford explained in 1921, Jamaica Bay could never develop into a port of consequence without these links, for "safe water communication was . . . essential, even indispensable to the success of the project." Together, the channels would give canal men "a continuous waterway," noted the *New York Times*, "from the northern part of the State to the principal landing place of the ocean steamers."[13]

Proposed Coney Island Canal linking Gravesend Bay to the Great World Harbor via Sheepshead Bay. From E. W. Spofford, *Views of Picturesque Sheepshead Bay* (1909).

The Coney Island and Flushing canals would be the only segments of the Barge Canal not directly linked to the rest of the system, and the only saltwater canals in New York State aside from a short passage between Shinnecock and Peconic bays built in 1892. Saltwater canals present unique hydrographic challenges owing to the effect of tides, which can vary considerably at opposite ends of the channel. This was only a minor issue with the Coney Island project, which simply improved a natural waterway. It also required no locks to negotiate terrain, and because the Gravesend and Sheepshead Bay sections of Brooklyn were still only thinly settled at the time, land acquisition would be easy. Compared to the Flushing project, making Coney Island Creek a canal was a cakewalk. Indeed, just such an improvement had been floated long before the Jamaica Bay seaport project. In 1864 the Kings County Land Commission proposed a two hundred-foot-wide ship canal to Sheepshead Bay, flanked on both sides by grand avenues a hundred feet wide. But there was one serious problem at Coney Island—the tremendous amount of traffic that would have to be carried across the canal daily to and from America's most popular seaside resort. Tens of thousands of New Yorkers flocked to Coney Island's amusement parks and beaches on a summer day, most via public transit. "If enlarged and made a highway for small craft," complained the *Brooklyn Standard Union* in 1918, "the delays which passenger traffic would suffer . . . would be irritating beyond measure." Costly bridges would be needed all along the channel. Regardless, the canal was authorized by the New York State Legislature in 1919, with an appropriation of $883,000 recommended the following year by the Gravesend–Jamaica Bay Waterways Board to purchase the necessary 400-foot-wide right-of-way. This would enable construction of a channel 250 feet wide and 15 feet deep. As predicted, getting all that beach traffic over the new channel would cost a king's ransom: the bascule bridges recommended by the Waterways Board were estimated at more than $9 million.[14]

Canal Avenue, Coney Island. Photograph by author, 2018.

The Flushing Bay canal presented far more serious engineering and logistical challenges. To begin with, it was four times longer than the Coney Island Canal. Three alignments were studied, each leading north from the vicinity of today's John F. Kennedy International Airport. Two were dropped because of engineering complexity and cost. The route eventually chosen followed Cornell Creek from Jamaica Bay inland toward Baisley Pond (which the long-buried waterway still drains today in a culvert). Prior to airport development, Cornell Creek meandered lazily through the salt marshes toward the bay, making a last slow bend where Concourse C of Terminal 8 stands today (the Swatch Store by Gate 38 sits roughly above the creek's old west bank).[15] From Cornell Creek the canal was to pass near the junction of 109th and Lakewood avenues, and from there run just east and parallel to today's Van Wyck Expressway. It would join the channelized Flushing River—the "small foul river" coursing F. Scott Fitzgerald's valley of ashes in *The Great Gatsby*—about where Willow and Meadow lakes are today in Flushing Meadows Park. The canal was to enter Flushing Bay after crossing the central axis of the 1964 World's Fair, just opposite that stainless icon of Queens, the Unisphere. But even this route meant an uphill battle with Long Island—literally. It does not take much topography to make canal building a challenging and costly exercise. Though the landscape north of Jamaica Bay rises gently for the first few miles, the sandy plain soon lifts to meet the great terminal moraine. At its highest point in Forest Park, the moraine rises more than one hundred feet above sea level—hardly a mountain, but serious elevation nonetheless for a boat road. There was no getting around this geological impediment; any north-south canal would have to go over, through, or under the broad rump of till.[16]

Three build alternatives were investigated. The first—a high-level canal—would rise and fall with the topography and thus require relatively little excavation. But multiple locks would be needed to negotiate the terrain, each requiring costly, temperamental pumps. And because much of the cut would not reach bedrock, the canal bottom would have to be sealed with concrete or "puddle" (a mixture of wet clay), adding further cost. The second option—a sea-level or "open-cut" canal—required only two locks, one at each end, and could rest on bedrock throughout.[17] It was the cheapest of the alternatives, and the one favored by the state engineer. But it was hardly an easy build either; for cutting across Long Island at sea level would necessitate a colossal amount of earthmoving, resulting in a very deep (and thus very wide) cut that meant more land takings and larger bridges to carry streets across it. The third option—a tunnel canal—was estimated at nearly twice the cost of the sea-level route ($21 million, or about $500 million today), though it involved far less disruption of private property or the city's street grid. The tunnel would consist of two parallel conduits, each fifty feet wide and made of steel and reinforced concrete. It would extend from Liberty to Union avenues, constructed with the "cut and cover" method employed on much of the New York City subway system. Added to these terrestrial challenges came one by sea—the dramatic tidal variation between Jamaica Bay and Long Island Sound. Low tide in Flushing Bay occurs some three hours before high tide in Jamaica Bay, with as much as six feet differential in tidal elevation at certain times of the year. This obviously made an unregulated sea-level canal impossible, for it would become a swift-flowing river several hours a day. But even a high-level canal would be subject to powerful diurnal currents. Canals and currents do not mix well, for fast water not only plays havoc with barges, but scours the canal bottom and transports sand that forms hazardous bars. Any of the canal types considered would require tidal locks with double-acting gates at both ends.[18]

Engineers could do little about a tide of another sort—of red brick and mortar—that threatened to quash plans for canals and seaport alike. South Brooklyn and much of Queens were still largely rural in the early years of the twentieth century, but not for long. World War I stoked a roaring national economy that helped unleash the greatest building boom in New York history. Vast sections of rural land were subdivided into streetcar and subway suburbs for the city's prospering middle class. Every brick laid on mortar further diminished the chances that a canal would ever transit the neighborhood, for the immense cost and legal complexities of condemning such land made such a retrofit virtually impossible. And as homes sold, they filled with voters who could bring electoral doom upon any politician who supported unpopular land uses. Aerial photographs of Coney Island show nearly the entire projected canal alignment built up into shops, homes, and apartments by 1924. Though much of Queens was still being farmed at the time, it too was on the verge of development. Pockets of the borough, such as Forest Hills Gardens, had already become sought-after neighborhoods. As early as 1908, residents of Morris Park and Richmond Hill—upscale bedroom communities full of attractive homes—voiced opposition to the projected waterway, fearful "that a freight canal would cause many factories to spring up and injure the districts as home places."[19]

But if canal promoters were in a race against the homebuilders, they also welcomed the anticipated surge of construction, touting it as a major reason itself for building the channel. As the *New York Times* concurred in 1912, "the great importance of the canal lies in the fact that it would provide for the transportation of lumber, cement, coal, and other material into the heart of Queens County and East New York and South Brooklyn, at a cost far below that over present routes of transportation." Indeed, the very first cargo shipped to Jamaica Bay via the New York State Barge Canal was a boatload of 110,000 bricks delivered to the Howard Beach Building Company of Queens. The vanguard barge set out from the Aetna Brick Company in Crescent, New York, a hamlet on the Mohawk River, making its way through Barge Canal Lock No. 6 to enter the Hudson River at Waterford. It passed through New York Harbor some 175 miles later, was towed by the Narrows and Coney Island, and moored at Hawtree Basin on November 6, 1915. You would think the *Lusitania* itself had been resurrected and towed into port; for news of the lowly craft's arrival made every paper in the city. Frederick W. Kavanaugh, president of Howard Beach, reported that shipping via canal was not only faster but cheaper—saving his company more than one dollar per thousand bricks over rail transport.[20]

By the time the brick barge made its sortie, both the Coney Island and Flushing canals were still dreams on paper. The New York State Barge Canal, too, was far from completion, delayed for years by administrative changes, engineering battles, and inept management. By 1914, some $100 million had been expended, with little to show and plenty to explain. "Has State or city benefitted by so much as a dollar?"

asked the *Evening World* in an editorial that October. "On the contrary, Erie Canal traffic has been so hindered and hampered that east-bound tonnage to this city has fallen off more than two hundred thousand tons." Even the mighty Panama Canal, launched the same year and one of the greatest engineering feats of all time, was completed before the New York project. Seas were joined in Panama, under budget and ahead of schedule, "while work on New York's waterway has dragged along with scandalous slowness." This was a particular embarrassment since the Panama Canal was one of the original motivations for both the canal upgrade and the Jamaica Bay seaport itself. Now the long-anticipated surge of trade was about to begin, and New York was still literally in the trenches. The opening of the Panama Canal meant that cargo could be shipped from California to New York and onward to Albany, Buffalo, Chicago, or Cleveland for less than what the railroads would charge to ship direct to final destination. But as Frank S. Gardner of the New York Board of Trade and Transportation admonished, the Barge Canal would have to be finished fast for all this to work in New York's favor. Any further delay could lock the city out of newly forming flows of trade. "If by our own unpreparedness it is diverted into other ports like Baltimore, Norfolk, New Orleans and Galveston," he warned, "it will tend to fix itself in those routes. We can never regain it, and our loss will be very great."[21]

The New York State Barge Canal was finally inaugurated on May 15, 1918, some $70 million over budget and already out of date. In its first full year, the canal operated at a mere 10 percent of capacity, carrying just a million bushels of grain when the much more primitive Erie Canal had hauled thirty million bushels annually decades earlier. Within a generation the Barge Canal was effectively put out of business by the St. Lawrence Seaway, which gave cities on the Great Lakes an easy route to the Atlantic.[22] If all this boded ill for the great seaport plan, its promoters faced even greater challenges of their own. First there was the bay itself. What appeared on maps to be a seaport-in-waiting was in reality full of shoals, shallows, and shifting sand—as Henry Hudson and his crew of the *Half Moon* may have learned that September day in 1609. This was, after all, the glacier's outwash plain, not the deeply scoured troughs it left alongside Manhattan. Jamaica Bay's fatal lack of depth was well known to colonial officials, and their successors would have done well to heed the total absence of positive commentary on the bay in early reports on provincial waters. Like the Dutch before them, the seafaring English knew a good harbor when they saw one, and they saw nothing of the sort in Jamaica Bay. One English writer even described such impassability as protection from marauders. In the first detailed account of New York by an Englishman, Daniel Denton remarked in 1670 that there were several navigable bays on Long Island's north shore, "but upon the South-Side which joyns to the Sea, it is so fortified with bars of sands & sholes that it is a sufficient defence against any enemy." In his 1678 study of navigable waters in the region, Governor Edmund Andros made no mention of Jamaica Bay. A decade later, Governor Thomas Dongan penned an extensive trade report on New York, affirming that in its waters "a thousand ships may ride here safe from winds and weather." On the north side of Long Island, he pointed out, there were "very good harbors . . . but on the south side none at all." William Tryon, provincial governor in the 1770s, was similarly mute on Jamaica Bay when queried about "Principal Harbours, how situated and of what extent." Revolutionary-era charts with soundings for all New York Harbor and the Hudson and East rivers give none for Jamaica Bay—damning evidence indeed of its lack of suitability for maritime use.[23]

Making Jamaica Bay a deepwater port would require a Herculean dredging effort—so much so that General William L. Marshall of the Corps of Engineers, famed canal builder and dredger of Ambrose Channel, remarked that the project "practically amounts to the construction of an artificial harbor." The federal government agreed to dredge the entrance through Rockaway Inlet, along with a thirty-foot channel around the perimeter of the bay—largely owing to the lobbying efforts of Brooklyn congressman Charles B. Law, who later drowned in mysterious circumstances (though not in Jamaica Bay, however shallow). But keeping these lanes open was itself a Sisyphean task, labor quickly undone by powerful currents. Rockaway Inlet, the very gateway to the future seaport, was described in 1910 as "a shallow strait with a sandy bottom, which under the suction of the tides and the pounding of the surf shifts about in a most treacherous manner." The motive power of these waters is well illustrated by the absence of present-day Breezy Point on early maps. Between 1866 and 1911, the western tip of Rockaway Peninsula grew by more than a mile; nearly all of today's Breezy Point community, so devastated by Hurricane Sandy, was ocean before the Civil War. And even if the hydraulics of Jamaica Bay could be made to work, there was the matter of access. Despite the rapid expansion of the city toward its shores after 1900, the bay was still a long haul from the center of life and commerce in New York. More so than Manhattan, this part of Brooklyn was long hampered by problems of transportation that the Coney Island and Flushing canals would do little to remedy. In focusing so much on canals, seaport advocates cast their lot with a technology rapidly approaching obsolescence by the 1920s. The Erie Canal might have been the carotid artery of antebellum America, but it could never match the speed and flexibility of trains or the vast extent of the North American rail network. A seamless connection to the nation's rail grid was increasingly essential to the port's success, and this put Brooklyn at an even greater disadvantage than water-girdled Manhattan. The great trunk railroads might lie like bundled nerve endings beyond Gotham's grasp across the Hudson, but what was far from Manhattan was doubly so from southern Brooklyn. Of course, Brooklyn was not without railroads of its own, but they were internal lines or routes out to Long Island. It was not until 1917 that the New York Connecting Railroad hooked Brooklyn up to the nation beyond, albeit by a long, circuitous route over Hell Gate Bridge and Spuyten Duyvil.[24]

However roundabout, the Connecting Railroad watered many a garden of dreams. John B. Creighton of the Brooklyn League, well aware of the borough's "insular position," was convinced the new line would make Brooklyn "one of the greatest, if not the greatest, manufacturing centre in the United States."[25] A decade later, John Henry Ward proposed a great Union Railroad Terminal at Jamaica Bay served by the Connecting Railroad. Described as "an inland station of huge dimensions," it would bring together "all the great trunk lines of the Metropolis" via a short spur of the Long Island Rail Road that ran from the Connecting Railroad in East New York to Canarsie Pier—the old Brooklyn and Rockaway Beach line. Ward's scheme, published in September 1919, was the most sophisticated treatise yet on the actual

Bronze plaque cast by Paul E. Cabaret and Company for presentation to Congressman Charles B. Law, 1910. The erstwhile "Champion of Jamaica Bay Harbor" drowned in Lake George. Henry Meyer Collection, Othmar Library, Brooklyn Historical Society.

infrastructure needed to make the deepwater port work. Ward was a waterfront development specialist with an office in the old New York Times Building on Park Row and a founding member of the Citizen's Budget Committee. His rail terminal, though promised to be "second to none in the universe," was but a small part of a sprawling complex for ships, trains, and motor trucks he proposed called the Trinity Freight Terminal. This would be the great ganged switchbox powering the Jamaica Bay port, located at the foot of Pennsylvania Avenue, about where the Spring Creek Towers housing estate stands today (formerly Starrett City). Ward was especially interested in the efficient delivery of fresh food and thought it defied logic to serve the city's millions from so crowded a "kitchen" as lower Manhattan. "How absurd it is," he wrote, "to so largely feed more than 8,000,000 people of the Metropolitan area from a section that is so inaccessible and remote, and otherwise so cramped and busy . . . as the section below Canal Street." Indeed, to Ward, this "inadequacy of the present central wholesale foodstuffs market" was not just contributing to the high cost of city living; it was "the great eruptive volcano of causes thereof." Ward's plan called for a dozen "mammoth piers"—450 feet wide and 1,600 feet long—to receive the world's cargo. It would also feature grain elevators, a Central Wholesale Market, abattoirs, an ice plant, coal storage facilities, a dry dock, and ship repair yards. But Ward's most innovative idea, decades ahead of its time, was the "Store-Door Service" he proposed using a fleet of "specially designed and standardized" motor trucks to distribute fresh meats and produce to local markets throughout the city. What made Ward's proposal truly remarkable was the "demountable body" his trucks would be equipped with. Once the truck was fully loaded at the wharf, it would be driven to a rail siding in the terminal, where

> a traveling crane takes the full body off the chassis and puts it onto the flat car destined for the railroad divisional freight station within the freight zone in which the foodstuffs are to be delivered. At the Divisional Railroad Freight Station another traveling crane takes the Motor Truck body . . . off the flat car and puts it on another chassis, and it is at once driven to the store of delivery by only a short haul.[26]

This may sound familiar, for it's the first proposal for modern intermodal containerized shipping, an idea that would revolutionize world commerce by replacing the costly and inefficient "break-bulk" method of schlepping goods between sea and land. Had this one idea of his been adopted, John Henry Ward would have become a very wealthy man. But he buried his "demountable body" stratagem within an otherwise grandiose and unrealistic scheme that was doomed to fail—the puny Connecting Railroad could never have served a world-class seaport; it would have been like using a dime-store extension cord to power a sawmill. The global economy would have to wait some forty more years for containerization to finally make its debut, this time at the hands of a North Carolina entrepreneur named Malcolm Purcell McLean, founder of the mighty Sea-Land shipping line.

In the end, a plan is only as good as the assumptions it is built upon; and those on which the Jamaica Bay dream were based began to vaporize like mist on the morning water. New York in the 1920s might have had the industrial output of Chicago,

Cleveland, St. Louis, and Philadelphia combined, but it was not the city's destiny to remain a mighty manufacturing center. Gotham's age of grease and muscle and working waterfronts faded in the decades after World War II, as the city gradually reinvented itself as a global city dominated by a range of service-sector industries—information technology, banking and finance, education, media, marketing, and publishing—whose raw materials were knowledge and information instead of lumber, coal, or steel. Few indeed in the Roaring Twenties could have anticipated a day when the West Side's swarming wharves would lie idle and rotting, as many were by the 1970s. Today, with the city bustling with creative-class strivers and globe-trotting elites, New York's once-neglected waterfront—from the Chelsea Piers to Brooklyn Bridge Park—has been revived and renewed. Waterfront real estate is now so dear it seems almost inconceivable that it was once used for anything other than upscale condominiums and high-style parks.

There is, of course, still commercial port activity in New York City today—at Red Hook and Sunset Park, and on Staten Island at the Howland Hook Marine Terminal—but the vast majority of port functions long ago migrated to New Jersey, whose mainland perch gave it a tremendous competitive edge over New York. It was far easier to dredge the Newark meadowlands into a deepwater port, after all, than to extend the nation's trunk railroads across two rivers and all of Brooklyn. That New Jersey would one day muscle in on Gotham's trade was something New Yorkers had fretted over since colonial days. In his 1687 report to London, Governor Thomas Dongan complained that reprobate ship captains were running goods to the Jersey shore to avoid paying customs in New York. "Wee are like to bee deserted," he warned, "by a great many of our merchants whoe intend to settle there." His delightful solution? Make "East and West Jersey" part of New York! "To bee short, there is an absolute necessity those provinces and that of Connecticut be annexed." Two centuries later, shippers began migrating across the Hudson to avoid the booming, overcrowded port. In 1908 John Creighton reported that some thirty firms had recently decamped to Newark, "where they can have direct connections with the great trunk line railroads." Harold A. Caparn, in a park proposal for Jamaica Bay's islands, acknowledged that a harbor there would succeed only in the absence of competition from New Jersey. Jamaica Bay might be "eight or ten miles nearer Europe," he noted, but the Newark marshes "could be dredged and filled in the same way and for the same purpose." And unlike isolated Jamaica Bay, a port at Newark would be "on the mainland and in direct communication with all the lines of railroad."[27]

It was on April 30, 1921, that fate threw its weight toward the Garden State. On that day, a compact was signed establishing the Port of New York Authority, the self-supporting public agency known today as the Port Authority of New York and New Jersey. The Port Authority formally sanctioned a long-standing fact—that competition for shipping between New York and New Jersey was wasteful and inefficient, and that the entire region would be better served if its shared waters were managed as a single port. Port Newark, first excavated in 1910, was modernized by the Port Authority after World War II and eventually expanded into today's Port Newark–Elizabeth Marine Terminal. It was here that the first shipment of

Construction of Mill Basin at Avenue U, 1922, the only part of the Jamaica Bay World Harbor to be built. Photograph by Eugene L. Armbruster. Irma and Paul Milstein Division of United States History, Local History and Genealogy, The New York Public Library.

standardized containers was made in 1956, and—two years later—the world's first container terminal opened by Sea-Land. Port Newark–Elizabeth is today the largest port complex on the Eastern Seaboard and was for a time in the 1980s the busiest container port in the world (the spectacular rise of China has since moved Hong Kong to the head of the pack). But big plans generate tremendous momentum and, like a loaded freight train, tend to roll on long after the brakes are applied. Despite the great shift of port activity to New Jersey, dreams lingered on for years at Jamaica Bay. Only weeks before the Port Authority was formed, the *Long Island Daily Press* reported that the channel dredging had advanced enough to allow a fleet of ten freighters—"the first in 300 years, it is said"—to enter the bay, "irrefutable proof that ocean going craft can negotiate the present entrance channel in safety." And later that spring, June 6, 1921, came the long-overdue and now futile symbolic launch of the Jamaica Bay port project. The occasion tapped for this largely political show was the start of dredging in Mill Basin—the first of seven great industrial basins planned for the bay's perimeter. A crowd of several hundred people gathered at Flatbush Avenue and Avenue U to hear speeches by dignitaries including Mayor John F. Hylan, Brooklyn borough president Edward J. Riegelmann, and the youthful president of the New York City Board of Aldermen, Fiorello H. La Guardia. As Mayor Hylan approached the podium, the forty-man Department of Street Cleaning Band—resplendent in starched white—struck up "Yankee Doodle." "The work started today," he proclaimed, "will progress rapidly and will stop only when the Jamaica Bay project is completed." La Guardia praised Jamaica Bay as a "natural harbor" and predicted that its metamorphosis would endow New York with "the greatest port in the world," lamenting only that "it was too long in reaching this day, far too long." When the speeches were over, the fourteen-year-old daughter of the city's commissioner of docks, Murray Hulbert, pressed a button that set off a ship's cannon. As the great boom echoed across the water, "an ungainly dredge boat moved from the shore out into the narrow channel," reported the *Brooklyn Daily Eagle*; "Its chains began to rattle and the long-planned, long-discussed, long-delayed Jamaica Bay project was actually under way."[28]

The author and his brother Richard at construction site of Kings Plaza Mall, Flatbush Avenue and Avenue U, 1971. The site is still zoned for heavy industry, a legacy of the failed port project. Photograph by Rose Campanella, Collection of the author.

THE MINISTRY OF IMPROVEMENT

And I saw the holy city . . . coming down from God out of Heaven.
—REVELATION 21:2

Not all who gazed into Brooklyn's crystal ball saw either steel-ribbed globes or a future of seaports and industry. Some hoped instead that it would remain a quiet retreat from the fevered rush of Mammon, a leafy bedroom city with a skyline spiked by steeples and spires—so many that Brooklyn was long known as the City of Churches. It was in one of these good houses in 1899 that a youthful Chicagoan named Newell Dwight Hillis stepped up to the most famous pulpit in America. The church was the Plymouth on Orange Street in Brooklyn Heights, and like its namesake it was the rock upon which Brooklyn's progressive elite built their house. Plymouth Church had become legendary a generation earlier for its mighty—and mightily flawed—founding pastor, the "Great Divine" Henry Ward Beecher. Though eventually brought down by a sex scandal—the biggest in nineteenth-century America (earning him more headlines than the Civil War)—Beecher at his height was among the most celebrated public figures in the world. So many pilgrims came to hear his thunderous oratory that Sunday ferries from Manhattan were known as "Beecher Boats."

Despite his Calvinist roots, Beecher was a fire-breathing abolitionist who practiced what he preached, turning Plymouth Church into the "Grand Central Depot" of the Underground Railroad by hiding fugitive slaves in its tunneled cellar. He also staged one of the great publicity stunts of the abolition era—mock auctions in which congregants could purchase the freedom of an actual slave. The most famous of these involved Sally Maria "Pinky" Diggs, an enslaved nine-year-old girl from Washington described as "nearly white" by the *Brooklyn Eagle*, "having only one sixteenth of negro blood" (sale of this "interesting chattel," the paper reported, brought $900).[1] Beecher shared his pulpit with many luminaries of the day—Charles Dickens, Ralph

Waldo Emerson, Sojourner Truth, Frederick Douglass, and Mark Twain (whose best-selling *Innocents Abroad* satirized an 1867 grand tour by a group of Plymouth congregants). It was as Beecher's guest at Cooper Union on February 27, 1860, that Abraham Lincoln delivered the speech—a powerful denunciation of slavery and secession—that gained him the Republican nomination and eventually the presidency. Plymouth would remain the only church in New York City that Lincoln ever attended. Beecher still lords over the Orange Street courtyard of Plymouth Church, in a bronze likeness by Gutzon Borglum, sculptor of Mount Rushmore.

Hattie Clarke Smith (left) and Rose Ward Hunt at the Henry Ward Beecher monument, Plymouth Church, 1927. Hunt, formerly Sally Maria "Pinky" Diggs, was the enslaved child whom Beecher "sold" to freedom in a mock auction at the church in February 1860. Smith was in the congregation that day with her father, and the two girls became fast friends. Brooklyn Public Library, Brooklyn Collection.

The Reverend Newell Dwight Hillis thus had outsized shoes to fill upon becoming Plymouth's pastor in the winter of 1899. But he quickly filled them, proving himself a worthy heir to both Beecher and his scholarly and controversial immediate successor, Lyman Abbott. It might seem odd that an institution with such Yankee roots—Beecher and Abbott were both New Englanders, as was most of the original congregation—would choose the son of a small Midwestern town to shepherd its flock. Hillis was born in Magnolia, Iowa, in 1858 and raised on a Nebraska farm; he spent summers preaching to miners in Wyoming and studied theology at Chicago's McCormick Theological Seminary. But Hillis had a pedigree that made him attractive to the Plymouth elect. He was of Puritan stock—"American from core to cuticle"—and the son of the deacon of the Litchfield, Connecticut, church headed by Henry's father, Lyman Beecher, firebrand of the Second Great Awakening (whose granddaughter, Emily Baldwin Perkins, was briefly engaged to Frederick Law Olmsted). Moreover, Hillis was a gifted orator in his own right. His sermons drew ever larger crowds at each of his early church posts—Peoria, Evanston, Chicago. Tall, thatched with a lordly mane of silver hair, Hillis filled the Plymouth tabernacle with a presence that rivaled that of his revered predecessor. One admirer called him "the most irresistible creature that ever lived." Hillis had a keen intellect, a mind "quicker than chain lightning," and a personality both charming and magnetic—reaching toward men "as the charged steel toward scattered needles." He was already a well-published author; his command of theology, history, and the classics made his sermons as erudite as they were spiritual. One of his most ardent devotees, Theodore Roosevelt, called Hillis "the greatest forensic orator in America."[2]

He was not, however, Beecher reheated. Beecher stirred the passions; Hillis appealed to the intellect. The former's oratory was "a mighty battle of the elements," after which came a "glorious calm and the still, small voice of God." Hillis's voice, on the other hand, "never booms," wrote Peter MacFarlane in a 1912 *Collier's* profile. It crackled instead like electricity, setting off sparks and moving "swiftly on, lighting the gloom, kindling the intelligence." If Beecher delivered a punch to the "solar plexus of the soul," Hillis "put a steam-hot towel on the face of conscience," gently opening the pores of "man's moral nature." But Hillis was also a man of action. Within a year of assuming the Plymouth pastorate he picked an Oedipal fight with the Presbyterian clerisy that had trained him. At issue was a core tenet of Calvinism—the doctrine of predestination, specifically a grim passage in the Westminster Confession of Faith holding that while "some men and angels are predestinated unto everlasting life," others are "foreordained to everlasting death." Hillis took exception, declaring, "I would rather shake my fist in the face of the Eternal" than accept the "frightful view" of a cruel and vindictive God. This so outraged his elders at McCormick Seminary that they threatened to try him for heresy. But his Brooklyn Congregational flock backed him fully—one suspects with glee that their brave David had taken on the corn-fed Philistines. Hillis refused to back down. Instead, he resigned from the Chicago Presbytery and demitted himself from the Presbyterian Church—roughly equivalent to giving up tenure. It is no surprise that Hillis would find the notion of "infant damnation," as predestination was often called, so repulsive; he was a reformer at heart, a crusader with steadfast faith in man's capacity to improve—not just his body and soul, but his earthly home. Hillis yearned to make straight the crooked path, to better the city around him, to make Brooklyn a place of beauty, grace, and order.[3]

His first Goliath was Tammany Hall. The fabled political machine had resurrected itself from Boss Tweed infamy in 1897, when Tammany stalwart Robert A. Van Wyck ran against Seth Low for the mayor's office. Van Wyck gave not a single campaign speech but won nonetheless to become the first mayor of consolidated Greater New York. His administration was a circus of corruption and incompetence, though it did succeed in awarding the city's first subway contract. Routinely denounced as a dictator, Van Wyck presided over "probably more administrative scandals," pronounced the *New York Times*, "than any Mayor in the city's history." The Tammany revival stirred reformers to take back City Hall in the fall of 1901, a political cataract into which Hillis jumped a week before the election. His Sunday sermon on October 27 blasted Tammany for making New York "a blot on the world map," dragging the great metropolis into the gutter and leaving "a stench in the nostrils of the other great cities of the world." For Hillis the election was not about jobs or the economy; it was a struggle between darkness and light. What the people needed was moral leadership. Would a future citizen lifted above the city "behold the webwork of government," he asked, "bright with the glow of manhood and integrity?" Or would that airborne judge see instead "a veritable devil's web in which all the threads run out as so many channels along which iniquity can thrill and throb?"[4]

Hillis avowed that there could be no fellowship with Tammany Hall. "Reconciliation of iniquity with virtue," he lectured, "does not ask for the methods of a lawyer; it asks for the methods of a soldier." This was a swipe at Edward Morse Shepard, the respected Brooklyn attorney and reformer who had accepted the Tammany nomination hoping to reform the Democratic Party from within. Many felt, like Hillis, that the dapper blueblood was naive and would be eaten alive by the Tammany tiger (a *Harper's Weekly* cartoon—"A Marriage of Convenience"—showed Shepard at the altar with a veiled tiger bride). Hillis chose his words carefully—Shepard was powerful and a Brooklyn Heights neighbor—but pulled no punches. "If the water in the well is full of typhoid germs," he asked, "can you purify it by putting in a pump painted in soft and esthetic [sic] colors?" Comparing Tammany boss Richard Croker to Beelzebub ("with apologies to Beelzebub"), Hillis concluded that an election victory for Shepard would enthrone "a vicious band of men who have . . . made it impossible for the great lawyer to reform them." Alas, there could be no conciliation here, for "vice and virtue cannot be compromised." Shepard's main rival was fusion candidate Seth Low, then president of Columbia University and a former two-term mayor of Brooklyn. At a Broadway campaign rally for Low, Mark Twain compared Shepard to the edible end of an otherwise rotten banana. The race was close, but enough New Yorkers concurred with Twain to hand Shepard a five-point defeat.[5]

Hillis also extended Henry Ward Beecher's legacy of racial justice into the new century, moved to speak out by comments on the "race problem" by his immediate predecessor at Plymouth, Lyman Abbott. At the time, Abbott was editing the *Outlook*—a popular national news and opinion weekly—and had been lecturing around the country on how blacks and whites "might live together amicably . . . in a community permeated by the democratic spirit." The union he envisioned, however, was hardly an equal one. At a 1901 banquet of the Get-Together Club, Abbott sympathized with the South and commended "the work it has undertaken for the negro." He reminded his audience that if Southern attitudes seemed harsh, Northerners would likely act the same way or worse if the shoes were switched. "Let us get away from the thought that all men have an equal right to vote, to a place in society," he counseled; for it was "a mistaken impression" to regard "the black man as good as the white man." Abbott ended on a "hopeful" note: "We haven't been able to turn the mongrel into the full-blooded collie in a century," he said, "but let us have patience."[6]

Abbott later spoke at a 1903 benefit for Tuskegee Institute at Madison Square Garden, sharing the platform with Booker T. Washington, Seth Low, and the presidents of Columbia and New York universities. In the audience were some of the wealthiest men in America, including Jacob H. Schiff and Andrew Carnegie, who made a large gift to Tuskegee afterward. The keynote speaker was former president Grover Cleveland, who delivered a tough-love soliloquy on "the vexatious negro problem at the South" prefaced by the requisite claim that he was "a sincere friend" of the black race. Cleveland lamented the "racial and slavery-bred imperfections and deficiencies" of African Americans, which neither freedom nor the rights of citizenship "any more purged them of" than it "changed the color of their skin." White Southerners were forced to "stagger under the weight of the white man's burden," he claimed, before echoing Washington's Atlanta Compromise—arguing that blacks "who fit themselves for useful occupations and service" would find "willing and cheerful patronage . . . among their white neighbors" (for it was "at the bottom of life we must begin and not at the top"). Abbott followed Cleveland on the stage, likewise counseling against putting the cart of suffrage before the horse of culture and improvement. "We have tried the experiment of giving to the negro suffrage first and education afterward," he related, "and bitterly had the country suffered from our blunder." The implication was that the right to vote, despite the Fifteenth Amendment, should be withdrawn until some charmed stage of cultural attainment was reached.[7]

In a blistering sermon several weeks later, Hillis reproached Abbott and Cleveland for having "closed the door of hope in the negro's face," arguing that "our fathers founded the Republic upon liberty and equality." Of course, Hillis omitted the inconvenient fact that many of those fathers were slaveholders, and that African Americans were not even legal citizens of the United States after the 1857 Dred Scott decision. He submitted that if ignorance or illiteracy were to cost blacks suffrage, then plenty of white Americans—"the foreign races—Italian, Bohemian, Pole, and Greek"—should also lose the right to vote. Hillis hoped that in their struggle for freedom, Booker T. Washington and other black leaders would not guide themselves by such fickle lodestars as Abbott or Cleveland, whom he likened to "tin weathercocks on the neighboring barns." In the end, the problem of the South was an industrial and economic one, Hillis stressed, "not a political problem to be settled by a political method." Around this time, a chambermaid at an Indianapolis hotel refused to tend to Washington's room, claiming no white woman should have to clean up after a black man. She was summarily fired but received an outpouring of donations, job offers, and even marriage proposals from across the South. The episode made national headlines, to which Hillis added by declaring that if Washington were to visit Brooklyn Heights, he would gladly make up his bed.[8]

But the Plymouth pastor's greatest passion was more grounded, literally, than politics or even matters of the soul. He developed a keen public interest in city planning, joining a raging transit debate in March 1902 with an eager homespun proposal to solve the problem of traffic congestion on the Brooklyn Bridge—a great hoop tunnel linking downtown Brooklyn and lower Manhattan like a wedding band. His "little underground circular railroad" would run trains in both directions and tap the main streetcar and elevated lines of both boroughs. Clockwise from City Hall, the tunnel would pass under the Lower East Side and the East River to the industrial quarter known as Dumbo today, arc southwest toward Borough Hall and downtown Brooklyn, cross Atlantic Avenue near Clinton Street and on to Red Hook. At the foot of Hamilton Avenue it would turn back north to cross the harbor just east of Governors Island, reaching Manhattan at the Battery—precisely the alignment, ironically, that Robert Moses would use decades later for the Brooklyn-Battery Tunnel. Explaining to a *Brooklyn Eagle* reporter that he knew nothing about tunnel work and might well be joining "that company of fools who rush in where engineers fear to tread," Hillis nonetheless plunged into an elaborate exegesis of his scheme, pointing up its elegant simplicity and explaining how it "diffuses and distributes constantly, and makes congestion impossible."[9]

Congestion to Hillis was a sin on the urban soul; it stirred his priestly passions and even led to poetry. On a Sunday afternoon in May 1903 the minister's trolley got stuck in a major jam on the Brooklyn Bridge, causing him to miss a train to a Connecticut speaking engagement. After raging at the empty platform, he sat down and composed a mordant piece of doggerel—"To Hades on a Brooklyn Car." The *New York Herald* praised it and printed it in full. The *Evening Telegram* was less impressed, describing the minister's lines as "a bit off their feet, as if they had been clinging to a strap" and noting that, in any case, Brooklynites needed no trolleys to get to hell—they'd go a faster way. Hillis was also among the many prominent Brooklyn men who spoke out in favor of city bridge commissioner James W. Stevenson's proposal to eliminate the "bridge crush" in Brooklyn by building an elevated loop across the Lower East Side connecting the Manhattan ends of the Brooklyn and Williamsburg bridges. The plan was controversial from the start, pitching long-suffering Lower East Siders against a well-organized array of Brooklyn civic organizations and business interests backed by the *Brooklyn Eagle*'s partisan editorial board. "Loop agitation" reached a fever pitch in 1906, with broadsides flying back and forth across the river. As the *New York Times* weighed it, each side claimed "humanitarian motives, and accused the other of shortsightedness, bad judgment, unpracticality, sectionalism, and other unneighborly qualities." Charles Bunstein Stover, then head of the East Side Civic Club, called the proposal "a brazen and amazing attack on the east side by the people of Brooklyn" that would plunge the Bowery into noise and darkness. Meant to be a temporary fix until the Manhattan

Bridge opened, the scheme was voted down by the Board of Rapid Transit Commissioners in favor of the now-defunct Centre Street Loop Subway. But Brooklyn clamored still for the el, well aware it would be years before the new subway and bridge were completed. At a commission hearing in January 1907 a rambunctious crowd of three hundred Brooklynites—chanting "Loop! Loop! Loop!"—were nearly ejected for their hoots and catcalls. Two weeks later, Hillis and a Brooklyn lawyer with a burgeoning interest in city planning—Edward Murray Bassett—led a rally on Fulton Street to denounce the heartless Rapid Transit Commission. Hillis likened Brooklyn's patience to that of Job, remarking that if he were a cartoonist, he'd draw the borough "as a man trying to swim the East River with a millstone tied about his neck." That spring, the tide seemed to turn briefly when the Dowling Elevated Loop Bill passed the senate before being killed in the assembly, thus putting the whole weary matter finally to rest.[10]

For Hillis, however, this was just the start. In April 1908 the minister spoke at the opening of the Congestion of Population exhibit at the Brooklyn Institute of Arts and Sciences. The brainchild of social reformer Benjamin C. Marsh, the exhibit called attention to the evils—real and imagined—of rapid population growth. At the time, American cities were expanding at an unprecedented pace. Between 1860 and 1910, the urban population of the United States increased sevenfold, with some nine million immigrants arriving from abroad in the first decade of the twentieth century alone. Hillis focused on humanitarian matters, emphasizing the great need for playgrounds and warning that congestion in New York had caused such a surge in the death rate that it would soon match that of the recent San Francisco earthquake and fire. By May, city-planning fever was in the air. That month, Marsh and Frederick Law Olmsted, Jr., held the landmark First National Conference on City Planning in Washington—an event Hillis almost certainly attended. The same weekend the *Brooklyn Eagle* ran a front-page story on a proposed "Grand Gateway to Brooklyn," featuring a great circular "Bridge Plaza" on Flatbush Avenue at about Tillary Street— the imagined junction of the extended Brooklyn and Manhattan bridge alignments. It was meant to give Brooklyn a formal entrance, alleviate the old "bridge crush" problem, and create a symbolic link to Manhattan by opening up views straight up both bridges—consolidation of a visual sort. Designed by Whitney Warren, a graduate of the École des Beaux-Arts who later designed Grand Central Terminal, the scheme was first proposed by the New York City Improvement Commission in its 1907 *Report* to Mayor George B. McClellan. From the extravagant colonnaded space—a Parisian sampler for a gritty town—thoroughfares would radiate traffic across the borough like spokes in a great baroque cartwheel. Flatbush Avenue was extended to the Manhattan Bridge, while new thoroughfares would lead north to the Brooklyn Bridge and east and west to the New York Naval Shipyard and Borough Hall. The *Eagle* praised the commission proposal and "the moral effect of such public works on a community. They excite public pride and an increase of public spirit follows as a consequence." It was a theme Hillis would take up powerfully now from his pulpit.[11]

That following Sunday, Hillis delivered possibly the most eloquent paean to the city ever to shake the rafters of an American church. The first of several sermons he

Portrait of Newell Dwight Hillis at Plymouth Church, c. 1910. Photograph by author.

would deliver on the subject, Hillis's oration began with a haunting passage from the book of Revelation—"And I saw the holy city, the New Jerusalem, coming down from God out of Heaven." Hillis interpreted the text not as idle prophecy but as a mandate for the urban present. The pastoral time of Genesis was over; upon us now was an urban age, a time "when the very word of civilization means the manner of life of men who dwell in cities." The countryside may feed us, but it is the city that draws the generation's brightest souls, tugging at "the heartstrings of a gifted youth as an oasis draws the birds of paradise in from the Sahara with its stifling dust and heat." To Hillis, the metropolis was the great storehouse "into which all the sons of genius bring their treasure." It was the foundry where laws are forged and justice bestowed, the "granary for all the sheaves of intellect, the museum that holds the achievements of artists, investors and travelers . . . the home of music, art and eloquence." And as goes the city, the minister avowed, so goes civilization. "Linger long in the streets of the great capital . . . and there you will find the seeds that will ripen harvests of prosperity, or days of disaster and retribution. What is the future of France? Read that open page named Paris . . . Madrid is making Spain. St. Petersburg is shaping Siberia. As goes New York, so will go the republic."[12]

Hillis soared on the subject of Gotham, which he considered the heart, mind, and soul of America. "Cherishing for our beloved city all the enthusiasm that Dr. Johnson and Charles Lamb cherished for London," he pressed, "let us strengthen our confidence that free institutions will finally burst into their finest flower and fruit in this great metropolis, that will ultimately become the city of beauty, the city of art, architecture and learning, and perhaps, under God, the greatest as well as the most influential city in the world." In a sermon that September—"Life in the Great City"—he described New York as the polestar metropolis of the West. "All the steamships from all the world converge toward this harbor; all the trains . . . run like spokes toward this central spot." Writers might extoll the splendors of world's fairs or expositions; but New York "is a perpetual world's fair, assembling treasures that never could be brought together in an exposition in Paris or Chicago or St. Louis." He also recognized, at a time when nativist sentiment was rising throughout America, that the wellspring of Gotham's genius and vitality was immigration. To the great city came the self-gleaned best and brightest, from both countryside and abroad— women and men who, "like Saul, stood head and shoulders above their fellows in the old home town." The singular truth that immigrants "dared transplanting and think themselves equal to the keen rivalries of the city," argued Hillis, "is in itself an unconscious revelation of their power." New York must always welcome these daughters and sons of ambition; "We need their strength; they have power to found and genius to adorn an empire. We need their enthusiasm; they will freshen our jaded hearts and inspire our worn lives." And all this was symbiotic; for the immigrant, too, "needs the city's wisdom, needs the city's gold, the city's commerce, the city's art, the city's religion."[13]

Gotham was hardly beyond reproach, of course; for just as genius thrives in a great metropolis, so do stupidity, vice, and evil—drawn to its streets as surely as a granary draws vermin. Not for nothing, Hillis reminded his congregants, did Genesis make the first city—Enoch, in the Land of Nod—the domain of fratricidal Cain. It is in the city, Hillis related, "that sin puts on enticing garments, appearing as an angel of light," that mansions are built by greed, whose avenues are "lined with houses that represent avarice and cruel selfishness." Poverty in the city was both a moral and a physical hazard. Hillis reminded his well-heeled listeners that Brooklyn's poorest, most congested district—the old Fifth Ward—lay but a stone's throw from Plymouth Church. He imagined a time when leading citizens would no longer abide such privation in their midst. A rising generation, he predicted, would make a better, more beautiful city. It would condemn sundry private yards and make instead a "common flower garden," transform the empty lots of downtown Brooklyn "into little bowers of beauty"—perhaps even create a grand gateway to the borough at the Brooklyn Bridge. And he looked to a day "when some great architect and artist . . . will plow an avenue 600 feet wide, with a great open esplanade looking upon Wall street, straight to yonder flower-crowned height, Prospect Park, and make it as broad and beautiful as . . . the Champs Elysees." For all its swagger, this was hardly idle rhetoric; Hillis meant to take his message to the streets.[14]

In February 1910 Hillis rallied a large gathering of Heights residents to demand better transit service and a station on a projected subway route that was to pass directly beneath Brooklyn Heights—an extension of the Interborough Rapid Transit Company's West Side line. Comparing the Heights to "a baby with a hemp rope about its neck . . . slowly being strangled to death," he asserted that the community was ignored by City Hall because it had been too mannerly and gracious; now it was time to "get up and do some shouting." They voted to found an advocacy group—the Brooklyn Heights Association—and elected Hillis one of its officers. Soon enough the association wrangled a promise from the city that the Heights would get a subway station all its own—the Clark Street IRT stop below the Hotel St. George, opened in April 1919 and still the deepest station in Brooklyn. The Brooklyn Heights Association would go on to become one of New York's most fabled civic organizations, credited with defeating plans to route the Brooklyn-Queens Expressway through the community in the 1950s and establishing the city's first historic district in 1965. But the minister's vision of improvement ranged well beyond his own neighborhood. In April 1911 Hillis spoke on "The Brooklyn of the Future" at an annual gathering of the Brooklyn League, an event that brought together many of the borough's leading men. Citing trends as alarming as they were inaccurate, Hillis made a number of extraordinary predictions—among others, that the population of Manhattan would reach 12 million by the 1970s, and that of the United States a staggering 800 million. Brooklyn, too, would rank among the world's largest cities by then—at some 10 million residents. Geography, Hillis claimed, made all this possible; for in Brooklyn, "the great ocean takes the tides out twice each day, carrying all filth with it, and pours back the pure, life-giving flood." But getting through the straits of rapid growth called for thorough preparation. "What we need at once," Hillis counseled, "is a great working plan for a city of 10,000,000 people." He imagined a commission of leading men to guide the work, with citizens rallied to the cause by drawings "put on slides and carried through the stereopticon into every ward."[15]

HER MASTERPIECE.

Editorial cartoon on the Boston 1915 Movement. From *Boston Sunday Herald*, April 4, 1909.

That summer, Hillis set off across the Atlantic with his family to visit the Holy Land. During a brief stay in Paris he met a delegation of some eighty men and women from Boston. They were part of an ambitious campaign spearheaded by future Supreme Court justice Louis Brandeis, retail magnate Edward A. Filene, and banker James J. Storrow. The "Boston 1915" movement, as it became known, was inspired by the 1909 Chicago "City Beautiful" plan and sought to establish a metropolitan planning commission for the Boston area. The group was in Paris on a study tour of European cities in advance of two major conferences in Boston the next year—on city planning in April and global trade and commerce in September. The enthusiasm of the Bostonians—especially delegation leader John H. Fahey, whom Hillis later invited to Brooklyn—was infectious; for the minister soon canceled his Holy Land tour to explore Paris and Europe with Fahey's group. It was a conversion on the road to Damascus, for Hillis's pilgrim interest in cities now became an obsession. Returning to Brooklyn with more than twenty books on architecture and city planning, he immersed himself in study. That fall, Hillis launched a series of evening lectures on city planning at Plymouth Church, beginning with an address on England and the Liverpool transport strike of August 1911. In it, Hillis railed against the English factory system and the "industrial feeblings" it was producing—men so frail they could hardly hold a rifle. How very different from Germany! There, Hillis found the youth ruddy cheeked and strapping, their arteries "gorged with red blood." He recoiled at the thought of depleted English workers reproducing, burdening society with "degenerate" offspring and "third and fourth-rate children." Indeed, the "physically unfit," Hillis ventured, "have no right to reproduce." It was an ominous foreshadowing of things to come, as we shall see.[16]

The minister's topic on the evening of October 29 was "What Our People Can Learn from Paris and France." He began mildly enough, praising Parisians for their beaux arts culture: "The great contribution of France to modern society," he remarked, "is the diffusion of the beautiful, until the common life is made increasingly to minister to taste and imagination." He extolled Napoleon III for having the gumption to unleash his brilliant prefect of the Seine—Baron Georges-Eugène Haussmann—on a great campaign of creative destruction that made Paris the envy of the world. Hillis struggled to convey the vast scale of Parisian modernization. "Imagine every building from Columbia Heights on the west, between Orange street and Atlantic Avenue on to the corner of Flatbush and Fulton, leveled to the ground tomorrow."

> And then imagine other houses and stores on one side of Flatbush avenue razed to the ground to make an avenue 1,200 feet wide, until the man who stands on MacMonnies' arch at the entrance of Prospect Park, could look straight down a splendid driveway . . . with noble buildings flanking either side, until the eye rested upon a central arch, crowning the Heights, and looking out on Manhattan island.[17]

Haussmann's wrecking ball kicked up a terrific squall of dust, of course. The poor were made homeless, merchants lost custom, and the populace feared that taxes would rise to Mansart's famous roofs. But in time a great dividend began to flow. Paris boomed, the poor found work, the parks and boulevards thronged with people.

And all this, Hillis told his audience—bending the truth again—was accomplished without factories, foundries, or "chimneys belching smoke." The Parisians had created a vast work of art, a metropolis that "lay like Venus upon the bank of the river." Millions had been spent on the city; billions were now harvested as the world came to savor its delights—"visitors from all nations of the earth, who wish to forget the roar and din and dirt of their own capitals, and rest in the sunshine of the accumulated loveliness and beauty of Paris." Hillis further explained that in France, property rights yield to the greater good; plans for public amenities and improvements were not held hostage by private interests. He then tossed a little bomb at Tammany Hall, claiming it was full of idiots who were tone-deaf to art or beauty. But "stupidity, thank God, cannot live forever," he sighed, hopeful that "apoplexy and diabetes" would soon whisk away to Green-Wood Cemetery such "obstacles to progress and the beautiful."[18]

As the helmsman of one of America's most influential churches, Hillis had a powerful platform from which to preach his city-beautiful gospel. But he also realized that an improvement campaign of the magnitude he envisioned would require expertise well beyond his own. And he had just the person in mind. A week before his Paris sermon, Hillis wrote to an old friend in Chicago, one Daniel Hudson Burnham, master planner of the World's Columbian Exposition of 1893 and arguably the most influential architect in the United States at the time. As the exposition's director of works, Burnham had brought in an exclusive cohort of East Coast architects, all practitioners of beaux arts neoclassicism, to design its main buildings—dealing a crippling blow to the pioneering Chicago school, crucible of the modern skyscraper, that Burnham himself had helped found. The aesthetic and visual unity of the "White City" was meant to impart a sanctioned message of civic idealism to a nation swelling with immigrants on the verge of precipitous change. The enormous popularity of the Columbian Exposition—twenty-seven million visitors over a six-month period—helped make academic classicism the style of choice for American civic and institutional buildings for a generation. Burnham's practice boomed as a "City Beautiful" movement swept the nation in the wake of the fair, his firm landing plum jobs like the Flatiron Building in New York and Washington's Union Station. Burnham was in even greater demand as an urban planner. In 1901 he was appointed to the Senate Park Commission, along with Frederick Law Olmsted, Jr., and two colleagues from the World's Fair—Charles Follen McKim and Augustus Saint-Gaudens. The "McMillan Commission," as it became known, applied City Beautiful ideals to draft a plan for Washington and its monumental core, faithful to L'Enfant's original vision for the capital. In 1903, Burnham and his young acolyte, Edward H. Bennett, were hired by a committee of citizens to guide the growth of San Francisco, and—three years later—by the Commercial Club of Chicago to develop a comprehensive plan for that city and its surrounding region.

Hillis and Burnham had been part of the same social circles in Chicago (Central Church, where Hillis was pastor in the 1890s, was later demolished to make way for a Burnham building—the great Marshall Field flagship store). The minister wrote Burnham with great enthusiasm, hopeful that with some professional direction "even in ugly Brooklyn beauty may yet be born."[19] Burnham immediately

Jules Guerin, *View, looking west, of the proposed Civic Center plaza and buildings.* From *Plan of Chicago* (1909).

posted Hillis a copy of his 1909 *Plan of Chicago*, along with a set of lantern slides and notes for a lecture. With these, the minister would introduce New York to the man who turned the hog-butchering, wheat-stacking Windy City into a palace of art and culture. On Sunday, November 5, 1911, Hillis told his congregants that an urban revolution was under way, a "revolt against . . . ugliness and unhealthiness" sweeping the world's cities with "all the power and majesty of a mighty wave, and the beauty of a summer's day." In its wake there was "scarcely a great capital whose rulers are not asking how to arrest the evil within the walls." He described efforts in Paris and London to eliminate "old rookeries and tenements," and then lifted a great folio above the pulpit like a latter-day Moses. "This large book of plates that I hold in my hand," he announced, "represents the work of the most distinguished city builder now living, and perhaps that has ever lived—Daniel H. Burnham." He praised the Chicagoan's earlier leadership of the Senate Park Commission in drafting a new plan for Washington. "Study that plan as you would study a snow-crystal," he counseled, for the city it promised would be "as perfect as a pod plucked from the Tree of Life." It should be distributed throughout the land, "framed and hung on the walls of every public school building in the United States." For this was no mere schema for bureaucrats, but an inspired diagram that "fills the eye and satisfies the imagination," gushed Hillis, "giving one a foretaste and hint of what the new city of God is to be when its walls of jasper and gates of amethyst and pearl ravish the adoring eyes of the pilgrim."[20] Having duly established city planning as God's work—and Burnham as his angel—Hillis outlined a vision for Brooklyn that would have made even the great Chicago planner proud.

While Manhattan was undeniably "the most striking exhibition of what the genius of man can do in two centuries," Hillis cautioned that it was yet an island, with
fixed boundaries that put severe limits on development. However mighty, New
York was but a little "cherry stone . . . carved ever so delicately"; Brooklyn was a
vast tableau whose natural endowments gave it nearly boundless growth potential.
It had all the ingredients for urban greatness. "Modern city building means scope,
horizon, distant elevations, high ground in the center, sloping plains, variegated
shore lines," Hillis argued, "so that the landscape artist or architect can stand off
like an archangel and draw freehand, with room for the elbows." The glacier had
blessed Brooklyn with high ground at Columbia Heights and above the Narrows in
Bay Ridge, and at the north end of Prospect Park and Grand Army Plaza—where,
from the top of the Soldiers' and Sailors' Memorial Arch, a panorama unfolded from
Manhattan to Coney Island. And whereas undeveloped land was virtually nonexistent in Manhattan, much of Brooklyn at the time was still farmland. It was not too
late to secure extensive land for a park system that would be the envy of the world.
To start, Hillis asked people to imagine a great public promenade overlooking the
harbor a stone's throw from Plymouth Church at Columbia Heights. At the time,
nearly all the property on the bluff above Furman Street was in private hands; public access to the sweeping vista was limited to a tiny space no more than sixty feet
wide at the foot of Montague Street. Proposals to condemn properties overlooking
the harbor for a public park had come and gone, handily defeated by the wealth
and power of the residents. Hillis had another idea, one that may sound familiar
to anyone who's been to Brooklyn Heights. "Suppose we take Furman Street," he
ventured, "and build with steel and Portland cement a boulevard one hundred feet
wide, on the level of the gardens in the rear of the Columbia Heights houses. Carry
that boulevard from Joralemon Street north to a street even with the entrance to the
two bridges; let the boulevard sweep to the right down this street to the entrance
of the old Brooklyn Bridge, on to the entrance of the new Manhattan Bridge." This
extraordinary proposal presaged the Brooklyn-Queen Expressway and Brooklyn
Heights Promenade by more than forty years.[21]

And the preacher was just getting started. He then proposed a new civic center
at the junction of Flatbush Avenue and Fulton Street, set in a great circular open
space—a Parisian *rond-point* like a second Grand Army Plaza. Whatever expense
the city incurred in this work would be compensated by the sale of the newly valuable frontage to developers. Next he suggested drawing a great boulevard across
Brooklyn's broad chest by running Kings Highway through Bensonhurst and Dyker
Heights to join Fort Hamilton Parkway. Fourth Avenue would become a tree-lined
parkway, and Shore Road would extend from the Narrows to Coney Island as a
grand "ocean boulevard" at water's edge—a route first discussed in the 1890s that
Moses would eventually build as the Belt Parkway. A system of parks and open
spaces should be established in southern Brooklyn, extending those laid out by
Frederick Law Olmsted a generation earlier. And ancient Gravesend Neck Road
could be transformed into yet another grand thoroughfare, joining Avenue U on
the east and Cropsey Avenue to meet up with Shore Road along Gravesend Bay.
Here he suggested that Brooklyn emulate—and of course outdo—what Chicago

The Preacher of City Planning envisions an early version of the Brooklyn Heights Promenade—"a boule-vard one hundred feet wide, on the level of the gardens in the rear of the Columbia Heights houses." From *Brooklyn Daily Eagle* Development Series, April 26, 1912. Brooklyn Public Library, Brooklyn Collection.

had proposed for its lakefront by laying out "a system of islands and lagoons" from Bensonhurst to Sea Gate, "protected from surf and storm." This blizzard of ideas begged illustration, and the *Brooklyn Eagle* was more than willing to help. Like many American newspapers at the time, it published the Sunday sermons of leading local ministers. But the minister's exegesis on Brooklyn's future was so exhilarating that the editors gave Hillis the front page, too, with a heavily illustrated feature titled "As Brooklyn Would Look under Dr. Hillis' Improvement."[22]

Of course, in the end all this urban designing was but a means to an end: improving the physical city to improve the people within—especially the poor and working classes. This was the Progressive Era, after all. "The new time in city building has come," Hillis avowed; "let us get rid of the tenements, the dark alleys, the parkless wards. We ought ourselves to live to see the time when there shall be playgrounds within walking distance of all our poor children, parks close at hand for the people of every ward, a chance at body building for the little girls who are to be the mothers of our future Brooklyn." Hillis clearly had great empathy for the unfortunate in society. But he cared, too, for society, and was resolute in exposing what he believed to be the costs of doing nothing—a city whose social infrastructure and tax base would be weighed down by "incompetents, intellectual and physical weaklings . . . invalidism, pauperism and insanity." A penny spent now would save dollars and lives later. "We do not want asylums and hospitals for children we have ruined in the end," he expounded; "we want parks, playgrounds, squares, gardens and lagoons, that shall build boys and girls at the beginning." Hillis's sermon, and the generous press coverage it received, launched what quickly became known as the "Brooklyn Beautiful" movement. Borough president Alfred E. Steers had been in the audience and was "almost boyishly enthusiastic" over Hillis's ideas, vowing "to take steps immediately" to make them real. Though he had at his back Brooklyn's most illustrious citizens, Hillis knew that for any of this to happen, it would need the sanction of a respected design professional—Daniel Burnham, for example. In fact, Hillis had vision for Brooklyn enough to spare, but he well knew that Burnham's blessing would immediately grant the whole venture gravitas and legitimacy. The architect was formally invited to Brooklyn two weeks after the Hillis sermon, by a committee of "best men" chaired by Frederic B. Pratt, president of Pratt Institute and the son of its founder. Hillis himself wrote the Chicagoan, coaxing him to accept and apprising him of the groundswell of interest in the borough's future. "What we all want is an opportunity to have you see Brooklyn," Hillis wrote on November 29, "in the hope of impressing our conviction upon you that [it] . . . will offer you the greatest opportunity in the world to build a proper entrance to this American house."[23]

Daniel Hudson Burnham arrived in Brooklyn on Saturday, December 16, 1911, a lion in winter with but six months to live. On the other side of the globe in India it was the last day of the great Coronation Durbar of George V, at which the regent laid the foundation stone for a new imperial capital—New Delhi, the ultimate manifestation of both the British Raj and Burnham's City Beautiful ideals.[24] In Brooklyn it was a dreary, wet day and the Chicagoan was tired—he had arrived late the night before from a meeting of the Fine Arts Commission in Washington. He was greeted at Borough Hall and then bundled off on a lengthy motor tour of the borough. Hillis, Pratt, Alfred T. White, borough president Steers, and park commissioner Michael J. Kennedy accompanied Burnham in the lead car, while following behind were three other automobiles carrying members of the press and the Citizens' Committee that had invited him to the city. Burnham did not even get out of the car at its first stop, indicating only that the elevated rail structure between Tillary and Fulton Streets should be removed to open up views to the Brooklyn Bridge. He was taken to Wallabout Market, expressed disappointment in how the entrance to the Williamsburg Bridge was executed, and was unimpressed by work then under way on a plaza at the foot of the Manhattan Bridge. But he slowly began to revive as the motorcade made its way to East New York, where Burnham showed special interest in Highland Park. They came through Brownsville via Eastern Parkway, which the Chicagoan advised should have been more densely planted with trees—Olmsted's elms having been set out too far apart for an effective sense of enclosure or canopy. The motorcade then headed down Kings Highway to Jamaica Bay and on to Bath Beach and Gravesend Bay. They made a dozen stops in all on the three-hour tour, capped by a climb to the roof of the Brooklyn Museum for a panoramic view of the surroundings.[25]

After the outing came a formal luncheon at the Hamilton Club, Brooklyn's oldest and most august, where nearly two hundred guests had gathered to hear Burnham speak. Those expecting grand prophetic insight may well have been disappointed. Burnham made some remarks on urban improvement generally, avowing that "the bell has rung for a great race in city planning," and then turned to a retrospective on his work and career, illustrated by stereopticon views. He said little about a Brooklyn plan beyond counseling that its scope should comprise not just the borough but—as we saw in chapter 4—*all* of Long Island. He also advised that a permanent committee be formed to lead the effort, composed of "the big men of the borough," with a "big and broad man for your president," and that—however inspired—a plan would sink fast if the public were not rallied to support it. It was Hillis, in a long and reverential tribute to the great planner, who truly roused the audience with a call "to make Brooklyn the City Useful . . . the City Convenient . . . the City Beautiful." Doing so would not only be a good investment, but would "stop the movement of some of our best families to the suburbs." Brooklyn would become the very entrance hall to America—"doorway to the republic . . . portico to the national house"—an urban Cinderella transformed into a city so beautiful "that men might turn their steps thither, as birds may turn toward the fountain and the garden." The Brooklyn press treated Burnham like a prophet, the *Eagle* dedicating four full pages in two sections to his visit and city-planning matters in its Sunday, December 17, edition. On Monday, in place of the usual Sunday sermon, the *Eagle* reprinted Hillis's full Hamilton Club address—"Brooklyn as an Opportunity in City Building." It was no secret that Hillis and the Citizen's Committee wanted to hire Burnham to plan the borough, "to do for Brooklyn," as Hillis had put it in a letter, "what you are doing for Chicago." On December 30, Hillis, Pratt, and Alfred Tredway White met with Burnham in Philadelphia and asked him to prepare "a large and comprehensive plan for Brooklyn and Long Island." Burnham admitted that the opportunity was "attractive and even seductive," but declined—he was too busy. He urged the men to hire instead his trusted understudy, Edward Bennett.[26]

A native of Bristol, England, who had studied at the École des Beaux-Arts in Paris, Bennett was recruited by Burnham to help with a competition for expanding the United States Military Academy at West Point. They worked closely on the San Francisco plan, and soon Burnham came to see the young Englishman as his heir. Though he had little of Burnham's room-filling presence or propensity for self-promotion, Bennett was brilliant in his own right. It was also Bennett, more so than Burnham, who managed the daily work of the great Chicago plan. Burnham told the Brooklyn delegation that their offices were just a floor apart in the Railway Exchange Building, and he often advised Bennett on his work; the elder urbanist would have Bennett's back, in other words. With Burnham's endorsement—and virtual guarantee—Bennett was given the job.[27] He would have to slog through political swamps as extensive as those in Chicago; for Brooklyn, then as now, was not known for easy agreement and mannerly discourse. Burnham had hardly left town when the name-calling began. By Christmas the *New-York Tribune* was gleefully reporting that the Borough Beautiful movement already had "the elements of a fine, all-around rough and tumble fight." Controversy erupted over the siting of key public buildings—a new courthouse, library, police and fire headquarters, municipal offices—mainstays of the civic centers that anchored nearly all City Beautiful plans. The real problem was that several projects had been launched prior to *any* master plan. Two big New York firms—McKenzie, Voorhees & Gmelin; and Lord, Hewlett & Tallant—were already warring over the municipal building commission. Property owners clashed with the city and the American Institute of Architects over the best site for a new courthouse. So did justices of the Kings County Supreme Court, whose first-choice spot for the judicial complex—two blocks of brownstones bounded by Court, State, Clinton, and Livingston streets—was fortunately rejected by the Board of Estimate. McKim, Mead & White's commanding Brooklyn Museum had opened on Eastern Parkway, though only a quarter of the original plan. The nearby Central Library project was also embroiled in controversy. Raymond F. Almirall had just completed a beaux arts design for Grand Army Plaza when an effort was made to move the library to a site opposite the Brooklyn Museum. Almirall's half-built structure languished on Flatbush Avenue for decades until it was razed in 1937 for the present Brooklyn Public Library building.[28]

All this squabbling bored Hillis, eroding his passion for the movement he had fathered. For all his interest in human affairs, the minister had little patience for political infighting or the tumult of the public forum. And, like many brilliant souls, Hillis was better at hatching ideas than seeing them through to implementation. For a time he persevered. In late May 1912 Hillis attended the Fourth National Conference on City Planning in Boston. Speaking at a Boston City Club banquet on its last night—and following Mayor John "Honey Fitz" Fitzgerald, progenitor of the Kennedy clan, to the podium—Hillis repeated his well-honed exegesis on civic beauty and the deterministic function of the built environment. But he argued, too, that beauty was only an outward expression of internal order—an "exterior revelation of soundness and obedience to law on the inside." It was disobedience to the same, he stressed, that bred "ugliness and decay." For much of his speech, Hillis dwelled not on the city proper, but on the moral and physical fitness of its citizens. He admitted being worried about the "physical constitution of the American people, our health, our bodily building up and our mental and spiritual life," and reminded his audience of how the English working classes had "gone all to pieces," rendering them unfit for not only physical labor but "fine thinking." As evidence of America's own degenerating stock of citizens, Hillis pointed to the large number of institutions that had opened for the care of the weak, ill, and insane—asylums and hospitals for "feeble-minded children, for epileptics, for the blind, deaf, lame and halt."[29] Meanwhile, on the other side of the Atlantic, another conference was being planned—this one focused on improving not the habitats of man, but his genes. The First International Eugenics Congress opened on July 24, 1912, at the University of London, chaired by Charles Darwin's son, Leonard, and attended by more than eight hundred delegates—including Winston Churchill, Lord Balfour, and Italian statistician Corrado Gini (of the Gini coefficient). Hillis was not present, but he might as well have been; for not long afterward he began focusing his considerable energies on the stewardship and enhancement of human genetic stock. The minister of improvement had found a new muse.

Herald for the silent-film version of *Damaged Goods*, starring Richard Bennett, 1914. American Film Manufacturing Company.

Hillis was almost certainly at the Fulton Theater on the rainy afternoon of March 14, 1913, the American premier of the Eugène Brieux play, *Les Avariés*. Novelized by Upton Sinclair as *Damaged Goods*, it was a morality tale about a young couple at the outset of married life. The husband learns from his doctor that he has syphilis, contracted in a tryst, but fails to refrain from sexual congress with his wife. Ignorant of her husband's condition, she too is infected and, soon pregnant, gives birth to a syphilitic child who in turn infects his wet nurse. Praised by the *New York Times* as "a highly engrossing and impressive affair," the play—celebrated Broadway actor Richard Bennett played the lead—ended with a lecture on the need for regulating marriage in the interest of public health, its basic message that individual freedom should be subordinate to the interests and welfare of society at large. *Damaged Goods* brought the taboo subjects of sex and venereal disease out of the shadows, generating enormous interest in eugenics—especially among clergy, who approved a lion's share of marriages. In June, Hillis announced that he would lay aside other work to "push the eugenics campaign." He appeared with Richard Bennett at a eugenics forum that month, and invited the actor to speak at Plymouth Church in the fall. He began addressing the subject in lectures and sermons. At the West

Side YMCA just before Thanksgiving, Hillis argued that eugenic marriage laws—prohibiting the union of those deemed unfit to reproduce, including criminals, the insane, and "nervous feeblings"—would make America home to "the finest types of humanity the world has ever seen." As enthusiastic now about eugenics as he had been about the City Beautiful, Hillis looked up another old Midwest acquaintance, John Harvey Kellogg, a medical doctor who ran an institute for holistic healing in Battle Creek, Michigan.[30]

Kellogg was as complex as he was controversial. A macrobiotic vegetarian who enjoyed yogurt enemas, he and his brother had developed a breakfast cereal—by forcing boiled dough between steel rollers and toasting the "flakes"—that brought both men enormous wealth. Kellogg believed that unregulated sexuality was the cause of all human vice and suffering. He waged a relentless campaign against the passions of the human body, treating chronic masturbators with genital cages, spiked penis rings, and carbolic acid applied to the clitoris. He and his wife were themselves celibate; their eleven children were all adopted, two from Mexico.[31] This notwithstanding—and despite having personally treated Sojourner Truth, using skin grafts from his own leg—Kellogg was a committed segregationist who believed the nation's future depended on a comprehensive program of "racial hygiene." In 1906 he established the Race Betterment Foundation with zoologist Charles B. Davenport and the brilliant Yale economist Irving Fisher. How Hillis and Kellogg first met is unknown, but they clearly admired one another (the latter named his youngest son Newell after the minister, and Hillis's daughter, Nathalie, later married a Kellogg). In the summer of 1913, Hillis proposed organizing a national conference on race and breeding—what would become the First National Conference on Race Betterment. He and Kellogg formed its executive committee, along with Fisher, crusading journalist Jacob A. Riis, and Anglo-Irish unionist and member of Parliament Sir Horace Plunkett. Held in Battle Creek in January 1914, the conference tackled questions at the very core of human existence—"race questions, biologic questions . . . whose branches cast their shadows over every phase of human life." Its official mission was as simple as it was disconcerting—"to assemble evidence as to the extent to which degenerative tendencies are actively at work in America."[32]

Despite the presence of many distinguished guests—Booker T. Washington, former Harvard president Charles W. Eliot, conservationist Gifford Pinchot, Melvil Dewey of the Dewey decimal system, educator and suffragist Caroline Bartlett Crane—there was an air of bumpkin artlessness to the conference, like a gaggle of farmhands trying to breed a better human goat. Indeed, as Kellogg put it in his opening address, "We have wonderful new races of horses, cows and pigs. Why should we not have a new and improved race of men?" Topics included the benefits of segregation, raising "better babies," the alarming fecundity of recent immigrants, moral deterioration of women, and the perils of smoke and drink. There were lectures titled "Prostitution and the Cigarette," "The Function of the Dentist in Race Betterment," and "America's Oriental Problem." The most popular talks dealt with conjugal health tests to prevent "vicious selection in marriage." Hillis spoke on "the deterioration of our factory classes," warning that the dissolution of old Puritan bloodlines and the rising tide of immigration meant race extinction—"a Niagara

Banquet at the First National Conference on Race Betterment, Battle Creek, Michigan, which Newell Dwight Hillis conceived and organized with John Harvey Kellogg of breakfast-cereal fame. From *Proceedings of the First National Conference on Race Betterment* (1914).

of muddy waters fouling the pure springs of American life." Blacks, he reasoned, should avoid the urban north for their own good. They did well enough "so long as they live on the Southern plantations," he surmised; but "bring them into the great city, put them into competition with the white race, and they suffer beyond all words." But he blamed affluent whites for the general shredding of America's moral fabric—especially the triumph of "that diseased hag named Lust, that has so long masqueraded as an angel of light." The minister remained hopeful nonetheless, for with new laws and concerted effort, "an elect group, an aristocracy of health" might emerge from the muck, breeding up a new stock of Americans—"taller, stronger, healthier, handsomer."[33]

The Race Betterment conference was a huge success, drawing more than two thousand people to some sessions.[34] Its message reached far beyond Battle Creek, carried by newspapers across the country and to Europe by Pathé Frères. In Brooklyn, the *Eagle* dedicated a two-page spread in its January 19 issue to the conference. In the lead article, Hillis reiterated his call for marriage laws to "eliminate the defectives," and warned that despite the many young sprouts at its base, the mighty elm of nationhood "was dying at the top." The movement Hillis helped launch gathered force in the 1920s, leading to antimiscegenation and compulsory sterilization laws in dozens of states. By the end of the decade eugenics had become widely accepted as a means of dealing with what Margaret Sanger called "the most urgent problem today . . . how to limit and discourage the over fertility of the mentally and physically defective." The Germans heartily concurred; there, the American eugenics movement became the model for systematic Nazi efforts to create an Aryan master race. The 1933 German sterilization law, enacted six months after Hitler became chancellor, virtually duplicated a program to eliminate "degenerate stock" that Harry

Hamilton Laughlin—a close friend of Kellogg's and author of *Eugenical Sterilization in the United States*—had presented at Battle Creek, and that was the template for racial hygiene laws in more than thirty states. Laughlin was so revered by the Germans that the University of Heidelberg granted him an honorary doctorate in 1936. And the admiration was mutual. In 1934, the editors of the august *New England Journal of Medicine* praised Germany as "perhaps the most progressive nation in restricting fecundity among the unfit."[35]

Hillis did not live to see any of this, certainly not the terrible finale of eugenics in the 1940s. Felled by a stroke just before Christmas 1928, he lingered in a coma for nine weeks before dying peacefully on February 25. Hillis had stepped down from the Plymouth pastorate five years earlier, after a quarter century as one of America's most powerful clergymen. In that time he wrote a thousand sermons, delivered thirty-five hundred lectures, and authored more than two dozen books, with a total circulation of a million in 1929. In fact, Hillis had begun to die in spirit years before, a unofficial casualty of the Great War. Hillis was nearly sixty when the United States entered the war in 1917, too old for the front. He offered to serve instead as chaplain for a volunteer fighting force that his old admirer Theodore Roosevelt was recruiting to fight in France—a venture Woodrow Wilson ultimately terminated. That summer Hillis toured the battlefields of France and Belgium, experiencing firsthand the ravages of war. He came back a shell of the radiant and hopeful crusader he once was, a "permanently saddened man." He had journeyed to Europe desperate to disprove the terrible stories of German atrocities, as if his very faith in God and man depended on it. Instead he found a trail of horrors worse than anything he could have imagined, inflicted by a people he had long admired as standard-bearers of Western civilization. Germany! That mighty fountainhead of science, music, and literature, home of Kant, Goethe, and Brahms. "The cold catalogue of German atrocities," he wrote, "makes up the most sickening page in history." Hillis pored over war records in Belgium and France, toured ruined villages in Alsace and Lorraine, saw bombed schools and hospitals, burned cathedrals, orchards with every tree felled. He was left "nauseated, physically and mentally ill." The campaign of devastation had been carried out with the ruthless efficiency of a machine. "For the first time in history," wrote Hillis, "the German has reduced savagery to a science." It would not, of course, be the last.[36]

And thus Newell Dwight Hillis—the unflinching improver who would build the City of God and purge from its realm the poisoned seed of thugs and villains—faced the ultimate test of his creed. Would he now advocate the sterilization of an entire race, of noble Christian Nordics, no less? And his answer was *yes*. Alone now in a Gethsemane of his own making, Hillis wrote one last book, a long and bitter jeremiad brimming with moral outrage. It was titled *The Blot on the Kaiser's 'Scutcheon*, a two-hundred-page tract on the duplicity and barbarism of Germany—that "Judas among nations." His publisher posted a caveat in the front of the book, distancing itself from its pages, cautioning that they were "sparks struck . . . from the anvil of events," penned in haste "on trains, in hotels, in the intervals between public addresses." Its most explosive chapter avowed that the German race must be eliminated. "Society has organized itself against the rattlesnake and the yellow fever," wrote Hillis; "The Boards of Health are planning to wipe out typhoid, cholera and the Black Plague. Not otherwise, lovers of their fellow man have finally become perfectly hopeless with reference to the German people." He cited Tacitus, who wrote of Germanic barbarism two thousand years earlier, and asserted that nothing had changed but the efficacy of their predations. "The rattlesnake is larger," he wrote, "and has more poison in the sac; the German wolf has increased in size, and where once he tore the throat of two sheep, now he can rend ten." He turned to a plan, a draft of which was on his desk as he wrote, calling simply for the extinction of the German people. Grounded in legislation inspired by the state of Indiana's trailblazing 1907 sterilization law, the proposal called for a world conference "to consider the sterilization of the ten million German soldiers, and the segregation of their women." Hillis cheered this final solution; for "when this generation of Germans goes, civilized cities, states and races may be rid of this awful cancer that must be cut clean out of the body of society." It was a grim agenda for a humanist and man of God, but one that—in a terrible twist of irony—might well have spared humanity the horrors of Dachau, Buchenwald, and Auschwitz.[37]

CHAPTER 11

SALT MARSH OF SUNKEN DREAMS

Versailles? That is, indeed, a thought . . .
—EDWARD ALDEN JEWELL

It was at the other end of town, far from the lofty Heights, that the Brooklyn Beautiful movement achieved its greatest victory. Edward Bennett presented his plan at the Brooklyn Academy of Music on December 12, 1913, two years to the day after the celebrated visit of his late partner, Daniel H. Burnham. The report's maps and diagrams were displayed for the public at 180 Montague Street and published in a January 1914 special "City Plan" supplement of the *Brooklyn Eagle*. Though skillful enough, Bennett's plan lacked the originality and grandeur of the Chicago project he and Burnham had collaborated on five years earlier. Some of its key elements—a new civic center in downtown Brooklyn, an institutional complex at Grand Army Plaza, extending Shore Road from Bay Ridge around Gravesend Bay to Coney Island—had been proposed by the Reverend Hillis or others before him. Bennett recommended extending Olmsted's parkway plan, too, by widening several existing thoroughfares, adding medians and multiple rows of trees—Fourth Avenue, Sixty-Fifth Street through Bensonhurst, Kings Highway, Avenue P, and a short section of Nostrand Avenue. From there, a new parkway would run south into the one real diamond of the Brooklyn City Plan—a seventeen-hundred-acre littoral counterpart to Prospect Park. Identified simply as "the marine park," it alone made Bennett's pallid scheme worth the expense.[1]

Bennett did not design the park itself. He showed it only as a green zone stretched across a plexus of radiating avenues, anchored by three baroque *ronds-points*. One was on Flatbush Avenue at the projected crossing of Ralph Avenue; a second at the intersection of Avenue W and Madison Place; and a third at the foot of Knapp Street on Sheepshead Bay, where Sixty-Fifth Street—pushed south from its Avenue P

THE BROOKLYN DAILY EAGLE

CITY PLAN SECTION NEW YORK CITY, SUNDAY, JANUARY 18, 1914 CITY PLAN SECTION

BROOKLYN CITY PLAN

The Story of the Work of the Brooklyn Committee on City Plan, With Maps Embodying the Details of Architect Bennett's Recommendations

"Brooklyn City Plan," special supplement to the *Brooklyn Daily Eagle*, January 18, 1914. Brooklyn Public Library, Brooklyn Collection.

terminus—would meet the Shore Road extension. The marine park would clamp his borough-wide open space system firmly to the shore, achieving at last what Olmsted had attempted a generation earlier with Ocean Parkway at Coney Island. The centerpiece of the new park was the old Strome Kill, whose waters the Gerritsen clan had dammed to power their gristmill two hundred years before. For all its rich history—and notwithstanding the counsel of America's most admired city planners—the storied littoral would almost certainly have been churned into street grid were it not for the two philanthropists who helped bring Burnham and Bennett to Brooklyn: Frederic B. Pratt and Alfred Tredway White. Pratt and White were among Brooklyn's leading men, deeply committed to progressive causes and civic improvement: the former was president of Pratt Institute and the son of its founder; the latter built some of the earliest worker housing in New York City (including the delightful Workingman's Cottages at Warren Place in Cobble Hill and the Home, Tower, and Riverside apartments in Brooklyn Heights). Beginning in 1912, the men began quietly acquiring parcels of land around Gerritsen Creek, eventually accumulating more than 120 acres. In 1920 they attempted to donate their holdings to the city for a park, along with $72,000 in funds to acquire additional land, including the old mill, and to extinguish ancient rights-of-way to the shore.[2]

Incredibly, Mayor John F. Hylan refused to accept the gift, despite a unanimous vote in support by the Board of Estimate. The city ostensibly feared it could not afford the cost of filling the marshy tract in order to make it a functional park, which the shortsighted Hylan, a Tammany drone, was not convinced was even needed in such a thinly settled, still-rural part of the city. Moreover, city officials suspected that Pratt and White had donated the land on behalf of friends in the real estate business. Hylan himself claimed the bequest came with "strings," while commissioner of accounts David Hirshfield bluntly called it "a scheme for enhancing the value of private real estate holdings at the expense of the city." His criticism was not wholly off mark. Much like the Commercial Club of Chicago (which commissioned the Plan of Chicago), the Brooklyn Committee on City Plan was dominated by businessmen committed to the borough's steady growth. One of its most influential members was William M. Calder, a prolific Brooklyn builder who won a seat in the US Senate in 1916 (where he sponsored, among other things, the legislation that created daylight savings time). Calder was a major developer in the southern half of Brooklyn, erecting thousands of homes in Park Slope, Windsor Terrace, Flatbush, and Sheepshead Bay (more on him in chapter 13). Calder had large holdings adjacent to the Pratt and White land, and was among the first to build homes in the Marine Park area. "It is an axiom," he wrote in a leaflet promoting his two-family homes at Coyle Street and Avenue T, "that the building of a park is certain to increase the value of the area adjacent to it." He promised that one day the environs around Gerritsen Creek would be "one of the choicest residential sections of Greater New York."[3]

But the real reason the Pratt-White bequest was refused was politics. The park was gifted to Mayor Hylan's anti-Tammany predecessor and rival, "Boy Mayor" John Purroy Mitchel, whom he defeated in 1917. Mitchel, the city's youngest chief executive, was immortalized eight months later when he fell out of his army plane during a flight-training maneuver in Louisiana. Despite appeals by the press, the Board of

Estimate, and Brooklyn borough president Edward J. Riegelmann, it was not until March 1925—Hylan's last few months in office—that the Pratt-White bequest was finally, fully consummated by the city. The mayor had allowed a political rivalry to keep a major open space from the people of New York City for most of a decade. What finally sprang Hylan into action was fear that his long delay would cost him the Brooklyn vote in the next election. Additional properties were now purchased around the estuary with Pratt-White funds, bringing the park total to 147 acres—a 12 percent increase of open space for park-poor Brooklyn. And this was just the start. Strategic acquisitions at Plum Beach and along Flatbush Avenue fused this land to vast acreage at Barren Island already owned by the city; overnight, the future park grew to over a thousand acres. Suddenly bigger than either Central or Prospect Park, it could become the "greatest Marine Park in the world," shouted the *Brooklyn Eagle*. George Murray Hulbert, president of the city's Board of Aldermen, made a trip to Detroit's Belle Isle Park—one of the few American public parks designed in a formal Italianate style—and came back convinced that "Gerritsen Park . . . could be made a duplicate of Belle Isle and go it one better." As the 1925 Democratic primary neared, Hylan's promises for the city's newest park grew ever more extravagant—it would be "the most varied and delightful playground for the city's populations," a veritable "Garden of Eden for the use of New York's inhabitants in their hours of leisure." But it came too late for Hylan, whose seven years of foot-dragging earned him the distrust and enmity of Brooklyn's well-organized civic groups. The mayor was defeated by Jimmy "Beau James" Walker for the Democratic nomination, losing the borough by just 4,857 votes.[4]

One of the properties acquired in Hylan's rush was the Gerritsen mill and the estate it had been part of for decades—the Brooklyn retreat of William C. Whitney, one of America's wealthiest and most powerful men. A descendant of Puritan settlers, Whitney was educated at Yale and admitted to the New York bar in 1865. He married Flora Payne, daughter of Oliver Hazard Payne and—coincidentally—a distant relative of intrepid airman Calbraith Perry Rodgers. Whitney was later appointed secretary of the navy by President Grover Cleveland, and built immense fortunes in real estate, street railroads, steel, and coal. A man of enormous energy and ambition, Whitney had two great passions in his later life—land and racehorses; and he owned more of each than almost anyone else in the United States. He collected estates up and down the Eastern Seaboard, including a sixty-eight-thousand-acre preserve in the Adirondacks where Gifford Pinchot carried out some of the first experiments in scientific forestry in the United States (much of the land is today the William C. Whitney Wilderness Area around Little Tupper Lake). In his later years, Whitney circled back to New York City, where he built a palatial residence at 871 Fifth Avenue and, in 1899, acquired the Gerritsen spread for breeding thoroughbred horses close to Brooklyn's three great racetracks. Its crown jewel was a palatial Greek-revival manor house that lorded it over the west shore of Gerritsen Creek, like something from the antebellum South that floated in on a proxigean tide. Known as "the finest country house in Kings County," it had been built decades earlier by Stephen H. Herriman—a founder of the Brooklyn, Flatbush and Coney Island Railway Company who had married into the Gerritsen family. Whitney gutted the place to make it his own, seeking solace there after the tragic death of his young second wife, Edith Randolph Whitney. The house was used mainly as a man cave for the Sheepshead Bay racing season. But neither the house nor Whitney's many horses provided succor; a broken man, William Whitney died soon after. Whitney's children—including Harry Payne Whitney, whose immense inheritance helped create the Whitney Museum of American Art (founded in 1931 by Harry's wife, Gertrude Vanderbilt Whitney)—built estates of their own on the fashionable north shore of Long Island. By the time Pratt and White began buying up Gerritsen Creek for the future park, the Whitney land was being used as a children's summer camp by the Brooklyn Tuberculosis Committee. Tragically, in 1937 the city demolished both the Harriman mansion and the Dutch-colonial Gerritsen house nearby, wiping out in a single day three centuries of New York history. The only trace of Whitney's tenure on the estuary today is the population of ring-necked pheasants, descended from his game birds, that still nest among the reeds and native marsh birds.[5]

The city's long-delayed acquisition of the Gerritsen estuary came not a moment too soon; for now a great tide of residential construction—one of the biggest building booms in American history (subject of chapter 13)—swept down Brooklyn to engulf much of the uplands around Gerritsen Creek. Fields cultivated since the 1630s now brought forth a vast crop of mock-Tudor homes. There was one last holdout—an Italian immigrant truck farmer named Frank Buzzio who plowed (alas illegally) the land around Gerritsen Creek with four compatriots and a team of horses. Buzzio and his boys were Brooklyn's last agrarians, at least before the hipster-locavore revolution of recent years. All five were hauled before the authorities for farming public property. Buzzio—"a son of sunny Italy," as one reporter called him—claimed the land was ragweed choked and collecting junk before he plowed it. When it was learned that three of the men were veterans of the Great War, they were not only allowed to continue but commended for making the idle land bear fruit—or at least potatoes and cabbage. But they wouldn't have much longer. Jimmy Walker went on to win the 1925 general election and was sworn into office the following January. Beau James was a parks man, and he understood that Marine Park might make his legacy; he envisioned there the "greatest of a great chain of parks in New York City."[6]

But now a seductive future grabbed the headlines. It came from the fruitful mind of promoter, impresario, and serial entrepreneur Sol Bloom. Bloom was an American original. The self-made son of Jewish immigrants, he amassed a fortune in the music industry while still a teenager. In 1891, just twenty-one years old, he moved to Chicago to take a position as entertainment director for the 1893 World's Columbian Exposition. For a salary of $1,000 a week he was to supervise planning and development of the Midway Plaisance. Daniel Burnham was his boss. He liked the ambitious young man: "You are in complete charge of the Midway," he told Bloom; "Good luck." Bloom was a funhouse-mirror Burnham, his Midway the antithesis of everything the latter's didactic White City stood for—order, unity, civic virtue. It was a mile-long sideshow full of hucksters and oddities, anchored by the first Ferris wheel and lined with scandalous displays of ethnic "types" from Asia and Africa. Bloom's biggest hit was "A Street in Cairo," with snake charmers and fettered camels and a salacious act that introduced Americans to the belly dance. Burnham allowed

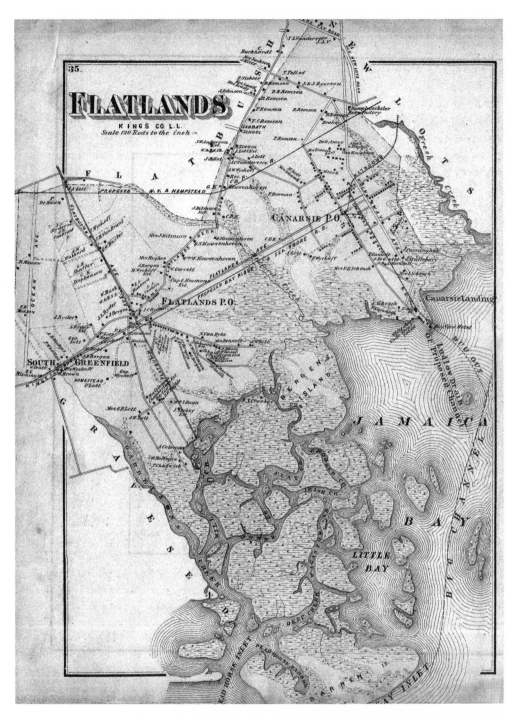

Flatlands, 1873. From F. W. Beers *Atlas of Long Island, New York*. Lionel Pincus and Princess Firyal Map Division, The New York Public Library.

the Midway as a concession to popular taste and because it would pay the bills; he placed it as far as possible from his Court of Honor—literally on the other side of the Illinois Central tracks. Yet the people came—more, in fact, than toured the White City's free exhibits. Bloom's Midway was the most popular attraction of the fair. Bloom later moved to New York to make another fortune, selling sheet music and the Victrola phonograph (he coined the slogan "His Master's Voice"). In 1922 he was talked into running on the Tammany ticket in a special election for the Nineteenth Congressional District. He narrowly won a seat. Two years later, President Coolidge appointed him to the Washington Bicentennial Commission, formed to prepare for the two hundredth anniversary, in 1932, of George Washington's birth. Before long he was chairing the commission. Bloom threw himself into the work: he read books on Washington, visited his ancestral home in England, pored over documents in the British Museum. Bloom bombarded the commission with ideas—plays and theatricals about the great man; Washington busts for every classroom; a full-scale replica of Mount Vernon for Prospect Park; broadcasts of Washingtonia from an antenna—where else?—atop the Washington Monument. One Bloom initiative lives on in our pockets and purses even now—the ubiquitous Washington quarter. But all this was spare change to Bloom's pièce de résistance: a great jubilee to honor Washington, bigger than the Columbian Exposition.[7]

The Washington Bicentennial Exposition of 1932, as he called it, would be staged in Brooklyn—"hallowed theater of his first exploits in the name of liberty"—and on the very acreage that was supposed to become Marine Park. With the élan of a master showman, Bloom outlined a vision for the great fair that captured the imagination of press and public alike. It would be the grandest ever held, with pavilions for forty-six nations, a channel deep enough to accommodate naval ships, and a football stadium for 200,000 spectators—more capacious than any stadium in the world even today. There would be a great skyport to receive flying dignitaries. The fair's parking lot alone—to accommodate a staggering 100,000 automobiles—would require an area the size of Prospect Park. High overhead would be a structure "taller and greater," insisted the *Brooklyn Eagle*, "than either the Woolworth Building or the Eiffel Tower," topped with a searchlight bright enough to be seen in Detroit or Quebec. An "international aviation tour," led by famed pilot Clarence D. Chamberlin—would circle the globe to seed interest among foreign governments. More than 25 million people attended the Columbian Exposition; Bloom promised 100 million in just the first six months—nearly 90 percent of the American population in 1925. The press swooned. The *Brooklyn Eagle* gave Bloom's Washington Expo plan the entire Sunday edition front page on November 8, 1925, while the *New York Times* hailed his proposal "to build a magical city . . . with all the splendor of the Court of Honor at Chicago," and predicted that soon "the structural beauty of Washington Fair by day and its brilliant constellation by night will gleam across the lower bay and far out on the Atlantic" (after all, the writer allowed, "our architects lead the world . . . especially in this matter of dream cities"). Nor would all this be a flash in the pan. Bloom wanted a permanent exposition—"a perpetual monument to Washington's memory." And since Washington was an entrepreneur before he was a statesman, his bicentennial fair would also earn its keep. Bloom pitched it as an entrepôt to advance global commerce and industry, the World Trade Center fifty years before its time. He even envisioned a future Brooklyn Institute of Technology for the site.[8]

As Bloom's Washington Exposition bill went before Congress, Brooklyn's numerous, well-organized civic associations began lobbying on his behalf. An International Exposition Company was formed, with offices at 154 Nassau Street. Former secretary of the World's Columbian Commission John Tilghman Dickinson became an adviser. The president of Columbia University, Nicholas Murray Butler, lent his support, as did the mayor of Miami Beach, Louis Snedigar. The Board of Education was urged to have all city pupils sign a supporting petition, to be flown to Washington by Charles Lindbergh. But the campaign soon fell apart. Backers began squabbling. Bloom's Washington Exposition bill languished in committee. The financial failure of the 1926 Sesquicentennial Exposition in Philadelphia quelled the enthusiasm of investors. Two of the fair's most ardent promoters—Lawson H. Brown and Charles Bang— began soliciting funds even as Bloom's bill was before Congress. When word of this got to Washington, Bloom was forced to sever ties with the very campaign he had inspired. Then Chicago jumped into the fray, announcing plans to mount a Washington Exposition of its own. By now, New Yorkers beyond Brooklyn had bought into the idea of a 1932 fair somewhere in the city. Mayor Walker formed a Greater New York World's Fair Committee, chaired by police commissioner Grover Whalen. The disgraced Brooklyn faction was not invited. Brown and Bang cried foul, accusing Whalen of stealing what had been a Brooklyn idea. But it was not yet Gotham's time, either; Chicago won the round, staging the Century of Progress Exposition in 1933. Despite the worsening Depression, New York forged ahead with plans of its own for a fair—still being called the Washington Exposition as late as October 1935.[9]

Sol Bloom and his daughter Vera aboard ship, 1925. George Grantham Bain Collection, Library of Congress, Prints and Photographs Division.

It would not, however, be held in Marine Park. A powerful new player was on the scene—Robert Moses, first commissioner of the city's unified parks system. Moses was agnostic about the fair but understood it could help fund his dream of transforming one of the city's most blighted landscapes—Flushing's "valley of ashes," invoked by F. Scott Fitzgerald in *The Great Gatsby*. Moses moved mountains, of trash at least, to bring the Washington expo to Flushing. No other city site stood a chance—including Marine Park, despite its many advantages. In the end, it was poetic justice of a sort that Queens should win over Brooklyn: the Corona dumps had been filled mostly with the latter's junk—as Moses himself put it, with "thirty years of the offscourings, the cans, cast-off baby carriages and umbrellas of Brooklyn."[10] When the New York World's Fair finally opened, its centerpiece was not Washington but a pair of abstract forms. But George

James Earle Fraser's monumental sculpture of George Washington, prior to installation on the Central Mall of 1939 New York World's Fair. Manuscripts and Archives Division, The New York Public Library.

was there nonetheless. Not for nothing had Sol Bloom served as a director of the World's Fair Corporation and a member of the United States World's Fair Commission. The impresario may have failed to build his "perpetual monument" in Marine Park, but he made sure that his hero was all over Flushing—there in James Earle Fraser's monumental statue of Washington, sixty-five feet tall and wrapped in a great cape, staring down the fair's Central Mall at the Trylon and Perisphere; there on Julio Kilenyi's official fair medal, with its likeness of the general floating in a cloud. And Bloom made sure, too, that this event otherwise dedicated to "The World of Tomorrow" opened on the 150th anniversary of Washington's inauguration at Federal Hall.

As hope faded for a Washington Exposition in Marine Park, attention turned once again to making it a great urban playground. On January 1, 1928, Brooklyn park commissioner James J. Browne revealed a preliminary plan for Marine Park, promising to banish the "straggling, irregular waterways and swamps abounding in the area," reported the *Eagle*, and build in their place "the finest park and playground in the Nation." The scheme itself was hardly fit for such exalted terms—little more than a golf course and a series of tidal lagoons lashed together with a spaghetti-spill of paths and roads. It had been prepared "under stress and hurry" by department landscape architect Julius V. Burgevin, a former florist from Kingston, New York, who also redesigned Union Square Park and landscaped the Park Avenue Malls. At Pratt-White Field, the portion of Marine Park north of Avenue U, landfilling was well under way along appropriately named Fillmore Avenue, using detritus hauled across Brooklyn from excavation for the Fulton Street subway. A first playground and baseball diamond opened to the public there in August 1930. At the dedication, Walker spoke of Marine Park as one day becoming "the strongest link in the greatest chain of parks in the greatest city in the world." He hoped those in the gathered crowd would "live long enough" to see this dream come true—"I probably won't," he confessed (accurately); "It's a short life for the Mayor, politically and otherwise." That fall, Browne announced plans for a design competition that would draw "the best architects of the country" to design the vast balance of Marine Park. It would be staged in cooperation with the American Society of Landscape Architects and the influential Park Association of New York City. A "special inducement" of $20,000 would be awarded the winning scheme. Bremer W. Pond, a professor of landscape architecture at Harvard University, agreed to supervise it and draft the competition brief. A youthful Gilmore D. Clarke was the society's choice as adviser. Just thirty-nine, Clarke had gained national attention for the innovative motor parkways he was planning in Westchester County, among the first modern highways in the world. But the dilettante mayor—distracted by showgirls and speakeasies, his administration beset with corruption charges—did little to make real his vaunted "chain of parks." By the spring of 1931 the press was getting restless; "Seven Years Pass for Marine Park," pushed the *Eagle*, "but Where Is It?" The competition was on hold because Walker never referred the proposal to the Board of Estimate for approval. With months lost and suspecting that the mayor might well indeed have a short political life, Browne did what any good Tammany commissioner might do—he offered the job of designing Marine Park to a neighbor.[11]

To be fair, Charles Downing Lay was supremely qualified for the job. No other landscape architect in America knew Brooklyn as well, nor possessed his extensive knowledge of Flatlands and the Gerritsen site. Born in Newburgh, New York, in 1877, Lay initially trained as an architect at Columbia University. But he had landscape in his blood—he was a distant relative of the Victorian landscape designer and "apostle of taste" whom we met in chapter 4, Andrew Jackson Downing. Following this muse, Lay quit Columbia for Harvard, where he studied landscape architecture with Frederick Law Olmsted, Jr., and was granted one of the first formal degrees in the field. He practiced in New York with Robert Wheelwright and Henry Vincent Hubbard, and in 1911 won a coveted appointment as consultant to the Parks Department. But Lay was quickly overwhelmed by a lack of staff, equipment, and even base maps of the city's parks. He clashed with the city's eccentric park commissioner, Charles Bunstein Stover—renowned for mysterious vanishing acts—and soon resigned to return to the relative sanctuary of private practice. By the 1920s Lay was one of the deans of the New York landscape profession, with a busy office in the old Architect's Building at 101 Park Avenue. Despite his Hudson valley childhood, he was a committed urbanist with a profound love of cities. In 1926 Lay authored a forgotten classic on the richness and vitality of urban life, *The Freedom of the City*. In it he argued that "the great merit of the city" came from precisely that thing city planners were constantly fretting over—density, crowding, "the immense congregation of people in one small spot." Lay deplored the perennial American urge to make cities more like the country; "A hint of country pleasures may be possible in the city," he wrote,

Marine Park under construction, 1931. Flatbush Avenue and Floyd Bennett Field can be seen at upper left. The vast field of white at top is freshly dredged sand for the Gerritsen Avenue ball fields. Photograph by Fairchild Aerial Surveys, Inc. Collection of the author.

"but they cannot be allowed to interfere with the essential quality of the city, which is congestion."[12]

In its place, Lay loved nature and possessed an especially deep appreciation for the estuarine landscape. "Of the beauty of tidal marshes," he wrote in a 1912 article for *Landscape Architecture*, "no one who has lived near them and watched their changing color with the advance of the seasons can speak too enthusiastically. They come to have a place in the heart which mountain scenery, with all its grandeur and fearfulness, cannot equal. Nowhere except at sea does the sky become so much a part of one's life, and nowhere is there greater beauty of line than in their curving creeks and irregular pools." Unlike most of his contemporaries, Lay also understood the ecological complexity of wetlands. "The tidal marsh," he wrote, "is a delicately balanced organism. It has a flora and fauna of its own, and it depends for its life upon the recurring tides, which bring soil and fertility and moisture for the plants at home there. Equally important . . . is the effect which continual flooding with salt water has in restricting the varieties of plants which grow there; for the grasses and sedges only can endure such hard conditions." Nonetheless, Lay's nuanced appreciation of the marsh landscape never eclipsed his Calvinist sense of utility. The task incumbent on the landscape architect—especially this one, charged with creating a great city park—was "to make the marsh more usable, and at the same time preserve its beauty, or at least give it beauty of another type."[13]

Doing so would not be easy. For one, Browne's sudden job offer enmeshed the genteel Lay in a firestorm of controversy. Nathan Straus, Jr.—heir to the Macy's fortune and head of the Park Association—led the charge, rising from his sickbed to proclaim that such a "makeshift" approach to planning Marine Park was "nothing short of criminal." He called Lay, unfairly, an "inconspicuous man with no outstanding park achievements to his credit." In an open letter to Browne published in the *New York Times*, Straus insisted that a competition was "the only right way to develop the great Marine Park"—the only way to find a designer with the genius and vision to give New York the Marine Park it deserved. That person, he emphasized, "will as surely be revealed by the prize contest for the Marine Park as was Frederick Law Olmsted Sr. by the prize contest for Central Park." Straus implored Browne to reverse his decision. "Every friend of the parks, every friend of a better city," he wrote, "is looking to you to throw open the design contest to a fair field with no favor." But Browne would not budge. Lay was his man, and the mayor—anxious to give work to the city's swelling phalanx of unemployed—agreed. Moreover, reasoned Walker, "We can't expect some man from Kalamazoo to take any genuine interest in Marine Park." Only a local would do, and a diehard at that. "In my opinion," the mayor stated, "one of the requisites must be that the man hired loves New York City." Even Straus could not deny Lay that qualification. For his part, Lay betrayed no qualms about transforming the Gerritsen marshes into a great urban playground, even if he had never taken on a commission of such vast scale. "I believe in the greatness of New York," he wrote, "in its people and in its future, and it is my ambition to design a park worthy of New York."[14]

The press cheered. *New York Times* art critic Edward Alden Jewell swooned over the scale and possibility of Marine Park, praising Lay for having "undertaken the task of supplying a picture for one of the biggest frames in the history of art." Moved by his *Freedom of the City*, Jewell surmised that all who have read Lay's "wise and delightful little book . . . must agree that the Marine Park assignment has come into able hands." Jewell, unlike Lay, saw nothing of value in marshland; to him it was simply a "clean slate" upon which almost any design might be projected. He compared Lay's task to that of creating Central Park, arguing that Marine Park posed the greater challenge. For while Olmsted and Vaux had on-site a surfeit of "plastic materials . . . all at hand," Lay faced the topographic equivalent of a blank sheet of paper—"a flat stretch of land and strand, of marsh and bayou and lagoon." Order and beauty would have "literally to be manufactured," a Herculean task in which "pumps and steam shovels become the artist's brushes." Given this, Jewell speculated, it was unlikely that the architect would "attempt to paint into his picture any ambitious hills and valleys. We need not expect even a hint of the grandiose clipped melodrama of Tivoli's Villa d'Este, the picturesque Baroque of Frascati, Como or Isola Bella. Here will bloom no fabulous Babylonian hanging garden. Versailles? That is, indeed, a thought . . ." Lay evidently leaked his *parti* to Jewell, who reasoned that the French mode—that "stately and charming artificiality that supplied warp and woof for the landscape loom of the Roi Soleil"—was indeed perfect for the "flat country" of Flatlands, even if such a courtly lexicon "might not meet with unqualified favor along the shores of Sheepshead Bay."[15]

Lay submitted his plans to City Hall in October 1931. Months passed before Walker even looked at them; by now Beau James had more urgent matters on his mind. The Seabury Commission was closing in on his police department and law courts, both of which had become Augean stables of corruption on his watch. However enthusiastic the mayor had been about Marine Park, it took a backseat now to political survival. It was not until late February 1932 that Walker finally signed off on Lay's plans and released them to the public. Expectations for Marine Park were sky-high by now, but Lay handily met them all. Everything about his scheme was Brobdingnagian in scale—starting with the plan itself, rendered by Lay in oil on a sweeping nine-by-five-foot canvas. Swelled now to 1,840 acres, the vast pleasure ground would be larger than Central and Prospect parks combined, with room for more than two million people at any one time—most of the population of Brooklyn in 1930. It would feature bowling greens, archery butts, bocce pitches, picnic groves, lacrosse and croquet fields, two hundred tennis courts, eighty baseball diamonds, and three outdoor swimming and wading pools. There would be a skating rink, a zoo, an eighteen-hole golf course, thirty restaurants and cafeterias, a thousand-seat casino with formal gardens, and an open-air theater and a music grove that, together, could accommodate thirty thousand patrons. Public transit access would be via the long-proposed Utica Avenue subway extension, a key part of the so-called Second System. Emerging near Crown Street, the new line was to run down Utica Avenue and hook south at Flatbush Avenue, running from there above Avenue S and ultimately connecting with a similar extension of the Nostrand Avenue line (a later version swung down Flatbush instead to serve Floyd Bennett Field). Circulation within the vast site would be facilitated by thirty miles of walkways and nine miles of road served by circulator buses.[16]

The vast space was organized about a great central armature formed by what had been Gerritsen Creek, now bulkheaded and piled into an extended artificial

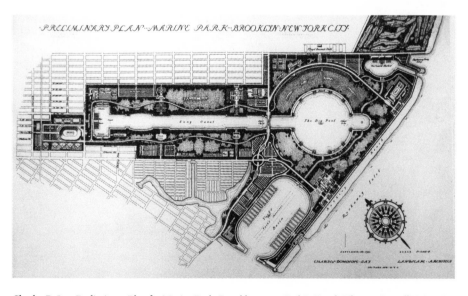

Charles D. Lay, Preliminary Plan for Marine Park, Brooklyn, 1931. Carl A. Kroch Library, Cornell University.

waterway. Two miles from end to end and shaped like a giant banjo, the Long Canal and Big Pool were to accommodate a recreational flotilla including model yachts, racing shells, and the sailing canoes that had become popular in the 1920s. Lay hoped that the canal would be used for Olympic rowing trials, and even secured a tentative commitment from Columbia University to move its crew team there. To the east of the Big Pool was an Outboard Harbor; to the west—just off today's Plumb Beach park—a boat basin with slips and moorings for hundreds of yachts. At the southern-most edge of Marine Park was the sea itself, where a two-mile stretch of new beach on Rockaway Inlet would be anchored by cavernous bathing pavilions—each large enough to handle twelve thousand bathers. Some thirty thousand trees would be planted throughout Marine Park, including quadruple rows of American elms flank-ing the Long Canal. To better compete with the spectacle of Coney Island, Marine would also be New York's first park fully illuminated by electric lights, and thus open well into the night. Lay personally looked forward to nocturnal "carnivals or pageants on the water" that might be staged there. Walker's plum was across Avenue U, in Lay's "Playground." There, the largest football stadium in America was to be erected, with seating for 125,000 spectators—twice the capacity of Yankee Stadium at the time. A proud Irishman, Walker pledged to name the colossus for celebrated Notre Dame coach Knute Rockne, who had recently died in a Kansas plane crash. "Not only will the principal football games of the country be held there," promised Commissioner Browne, "but it will provide a fitting place for the Olympic Games the next time they come to the United States."[17]

This was, all told, no place for idle lounging or the *vita contemplativa*. Marine Park would be a mighty exercise yard for Gotham's teeming masses, a sprawling landscape of athletics, gamesmanship, and competitive sport. It was the grand culmination

Charles D. Lay, aerial perspective of Canoe Harbor at Avenue U, Marine Park, 1931. Carl A. Kroch Library, Cornell University.

of a movement that began in New York in 1906 with the formation of the Playground Association of America. Searching for new ways to fortify immigrant youth against everything from "pauperism" and radical politics to exaggerated sexuality, reformers like Jane Addams, Jacob Riis, Luther Halsey Gulick, and Charles B. Stover came to see "scientific play" as the solution to a gamut of urban ills. As Dominick Cavallo has written, these progressives considered highly structured forms of recreation "a vital medium for shaping the moral and cognitive development of young people." They believed such activities would not only strengthen bodies but—more importantly—impart a sense of moral and civic responsibility by exposing youth to "ideals of cooperation, group loyalty, and the subordination of self." Socialization of this sort was also deemed vital to state and society, for team sports and structured play—especially for adolescents—were considered "an ideal means," writes Cavallo, "of integrating the young into the work rhythms and social demands of a dynamic and complex urban-industrial civilization." The playground movement eventually yielded a whole new form of American open space—what architect-sociologist Galen Cranz has called the Reform Park. In the early years of the twentieth century, parks came to be seen as instruments by which the working classes could be inculcated with democratic values, molded into upstanding American citizens. This was a radical departure from the ideals of the previous generation. The great pleasure grounds of Olmsted and Vaux—Central and Prospect parks—emphasized leisurely promenade and the passive contemplation of nature as elixirs for the ills of urban life. Banned were the very kinds of structured sport and recreation that reformers now deemed essential for citizen building. An ersatz rural landscape in the midst of the city—the old *rus-in-urbe* model—might have fortified Victorians against the presumed moral hazards of the city, but it would never do in a metropolis threatened by "the evils," as Charles W. Eliot put it, "which have arisen from congestion of population." Nor did it seem likely that the poor would be edified and uplifted by mere passing contact with their social betters in the park, as Olmsted had hoped. Parks would now have to deliver a public service, as efficiently as any other infrastructure or utility. As Cranz put it, the urban working classes—men, especially, whom reformers routinely likened to naughty children—were now seen as effectively "incapable of undertaking their own recreation." Men's play must now be as structured and supervised as work in the industrial city. "Deliberate, organized sports," writes Cranz, "would ensure their exposure to a full complement of human experience, acutely needed since office and factory work was perceived as routine and dull."[18]

There were, of course, clear design implications in all this. As the ultimate expression of the reform-era park, Marine Park was as spatially disciplined as the Victorian park was languid and informal. It employed few of the spatial tricks used by Olmsted and Vaux at Prospect Park to cast an illusion of rustic removal from the city—the artful masking of views to surrounding city blocks, gradual revelation of spaces to foster a sense of mystery, provision of a variety of spatial types, from intimate rambles to open meadows, to create a kinesthetic experience of the landscape. Such sleights of hand gave way now to a spatial imperative emphasizing probity and pragmatism; the sensuous curves of Olmsted's Anglo-romantic aesthetic yielded to one of formal

Charles D. Lay, view of Boathouse, Marine Park, 1931. Carl A. Kroch Library, Cornell University.

architectonics and axial symmetry. Lay's own ideal for playgrounds, outlined in a 1912 *Landscape Architecture* article, foretold of his Marine Park scheme. In it he called for a design "without elaborate detail and with no naturalesque planting" and striving for "a sense of beauty through . . . symmetry and order." Likewise, Lay chose for his great people's park a stripped-down version of Renaissance formalism straight out of Versailles. This was spatial machinery that might transform even the roughest immigrant stock into vigorous American citizens. As the *Eagle* approvingly editorialized in March 1932, edifying the masses called for an aesthetic of greater authority and restraint than the languorous informality of Central or Prospect Park. "It is the discipline of the plan, the fact that it isn't hit or miss, which Mr. Lay believes will induce a sense of responsibility in those who use it—a respect for order and decency that is conspicuously absent in the habitués of public amusement parks and beaches." Indeed, the more proximate target of Marine Park's reformist zeal was Coney Island, ground zero of just the sort of moral mayhem and carnality that kept social reformers up at night.[19]

Site work on the great park commenced in the summer of 1931. From July to November, the "curving creeks and irregular pools" that Lay so admired in the estuarine landscape were smothered with up to fourteen feet of sand dredged from the bottom of nearby Rockaway Inlet. The business end of this land-making effort was the mighty *Lake Fithian*, largest and most powerful hydraulic dredge in the world at the time. Converted in 1927 from a cargo vessel built for the Great War, it was used to dredge flood-control cutoffs on the lower Mississippi River and to deepen the Norfolk ship channel before being towed to New York. Essentially a giant sea-vacuum, the dredge's impeller was driven by a three-thousand-horsepower steam engine; an elephantine snout tipped with whirling cutters grubbed about the bottom like a primeval sea monster. Anchored by a pair of "spuds," the crew of fifty-five men swung the colossal bottom-feeder back and forth through a great arc, its snout sucking up slurry and pumping it out at a velocity of twenty feet per second over more than a mile of a segmented pipeline, thirty inches in diameter and floating on

The *Lake Fithian* dredging shoals on the Hooghly River near Calcutta (Kolkata) c. 1959, shortly before its tragic capsizing. Collection of the author.

pontoons. At the other end, an unholy pancake formed as the mud rushed out over the salt grasses and toward the perimeter dike. Overhead, a wheeling, shrieking cloud of gulls gathered to feast on the ejecta, which teemed with upchurned sea life. And then came the snipe—tens of thousands of them, long bills probing the mud for the rich horde below missed by the gulls. The birds were "so thick," reported one old-timer, "that you close your eyes, fire a gun into their midst and bag about 50 . . . It's just too bad that we can't take our shotguns and have a little sport." At night, the *Lake Fithian* could be seen by the glow of its boiler fires, a flat-water *Pequod* reversing the order of sea bottom and salt marsh. The snorting beast worked the bay bottom for four months, twenty-four hours day and night. All told it pumped a total of 2.7 million cubic yards of fill—enough sand to cover 422 football fields three feet deep, fill 828 Olympic-size swimming pools, or make twenty thousand children happy with a sandbox all their own.[20]

It was on a frigid Friday in 1933, six months after corruption finally forced Jimmy Walker out of office (and off to Europe, a Ziegfeld showgirl on his arm), that work finally began on New York's first great park "keynoted to modern recreation needs." Officials at the February 18 groundbreaking at the Whitney mansion included Lay, Commissioner Browne, and Major L. B. Roberts of the Emergency Work Bureau—a military engineer who had led surveying expeditions to central Asia and the Sudan. Shortly after two o'clock, Commissioner Browne climbed aboard a pile driver and shifted a lever to drop the hammer on the first of twelve hundred piles for the bulkhead around Lay's canoe harbor. A great cheer went up from the six hundred workers gathered along the shore, all of whom had recently been unemployed. They

Sewer line construction on Gerritsen Avenue, December 1932, showing vast plain of dredged sand in Marine Park. Photograph by Edgar E. Rutter. Courtesy of Paul Link.

were soon be joined by several thousand more. But the New Deal in New York prior to 1934 was plagued by mismanagement, poor planning, and supply shortages. By the end of the year, a lack of building material and machinery had idled two thousand Civil Works Administration laborers at Marine Park alone. But a new fusion administration took the city's helm in January, led by Mayor Fiorello La Guardia. In one of his first official acts, La Guardia appointed Robert Moses commissioner of the newly unified Parks Department. Moses lost no time getting to work, swinging like a wrecking ball through an agency calcified by years of scandal, corruption, and political favoritism. Insofar as it was the largest parks project in the city, Moses was especially concerned about the situation at Marine Park. There, not surprisingly, his staff found workers milling about campfires, playing dice, and passing around bottles of wine. They had barely enough clothes to ward off the cold wind. Robert Caro described the scene at Gerritsen Creek as "more reminiscent of a French bivouac during the Retreat from Moscow than a park reclamation project." Moses ordered scores of men fired.[21]

It is a public-works axiom that projects inherited from a previous administration live short and bitter lives. If Moses had no tolerance for shovel-leaning laborers, he had less still for the patrician designer whose extravagant scheme they were building. Moses and Lay, it turns out, had a "past." A decade earlier, the landscape architect had opposed Moses's park and parkway plans on Long Island. Lay helped wealthy estate owners force Moses to build a long and costly diversion of the Northern State Parkway around the Wheatley Hills. Lay further alienated Moses by arguing that parkways—the very ligature of the Moses regional vision—were obsolete and "ill adapted to present needs"; for "the chief end of the motorist," he stressed (with prescience, as anyone who's driven the Northern State today well knows), "is to get to his destination . . . he is little interested in the scenery on the way." More fatally still, Lay convinced voters in the town of Hempstead to defeat Moses's first attempt to build Jones Beach, arguing that the oceanfront real estate was far too valuable to be donated to the state of New York—a "princely gift" for which Hempstead would get "nothing at all." Thus it was a very bad turn of luck for Lay that his old nemesis was suddenly in a position of absolute authority over his Marine Park masterpiece. Moses delighted in ridiculing "Landscaper Lay" and his "preposterously formal" Marine Park scheme, boasting that "one of the first things I did was toss this ridiculous plan into the wastebasket and get rid of whatever associations there were with the landscape architect in question." With equal contempt Moses scrapped the Knute Rockne football stadium, dismissing it as an "imitation Roman coliseum." Moses was certain the whole Marine Park saga had been hatched by Senator Calder's real estate cabal, starting with the Pratt and White gift—"widely heralded as a tremendous piece of philanthropy," Moses snarked, but really just "bait to persuade the city to acquire all the surrounding property." At the same time, he was adamant about defending Jamaica Bay, and among his many forgotten environmental victories was ending Sanitation Department plans to use its waters for dumping the city's refuse. He also recognized that Marine Park was a vital part of the citywide park system, and assigned its replanning to his most experienced design consultants—Gilmore D. Clarke and Michael Rapuano.[22]

Clarke, who worked briefly for Lay after graduating from Cornell in 1913, was of course familiar with Marine Park from the Park Association kerfuffle years before. Now responsible for park design throughout the five boroughs, Clarke delegated the Marine Park job to his acolyte, Michael Rapuano. By September 1934 Rapuano had a new plan ready. Moses and Clarke presented it to a packed auditorium at James Madison High School in early September. The Rapuano plan proposed far less draconian alteration of the existing site, and even introduced some of the flowing, romantic forms wholly absent from Lay's disciplined, formal scheme. Ironically, the new plan embraced a strategy of marshland improvement that Lay himself had advocated twenty-five years earlier but abandoned. In his 1912 *Landscape Architecture* essay on tidal marshes, Lay concluded that "complete filling is the most expensive way to treat a marsh, and the least satisfactory"—for both engineering and environmental reasons. He proposed instead "a compromise . . . between filling and draining, by excavating part of the marsh to make ponds or creeks, or lagoons with islands, and filling over the remainder of the marsh with the excavated material. We might call this picturesque ditching."[23] Clarke and Rapuano did precisely this, thus requiring far less bulkheading or landfilling than the earlier scheme. Lay's grand canal was reconfigured into a sinuous waterway cleaved around an island with two golf courses. Much of the tidal marsh ecosystem would remain; so would the old Gerritsen mill, to be restored now as a museum. Other features included an arboretum of native

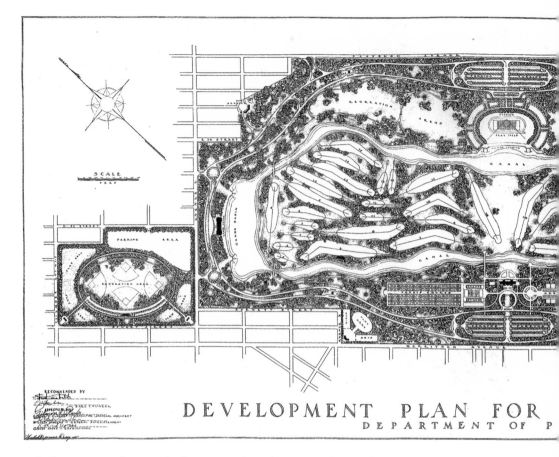

DEVELOPMENT PLAN FOR
DEPARTMENT OF P

Michael Rapuano, Development Plan for Marine Park Brooklyn, 1935. Collection of Marga Rogers Rapuano.

plants and trees and a parkway loop that would enable motorists to drive themselves anywhere in the park; a second and larger motorway—what would later become the Belt Parkway—crossed the site from north to south. Not surprisingly, Knute Rockne stadium was eliminated, leaving only a ghostly impression of itself in an elliptical bicycle and running track north of Avenue U. The two-mile beach Lay had proposed was also dropped; the waters of Rockaway Inlet, Moses argued, were far too polluted for bathing.

Moses also made Marine Park part of his administrative empire, quietly placing it under the auspices of the Marine Parkway Authority (MPA), which—like the Triborough Bridge Authority and the Long Island State Park Commission—he largely controlled. The MPA also included Jacob Riis Park—the city's only true oceanfront park—and a magnificent art-deco lift-span bridge designed by Othmar Ammann to carry Flatbush Avenue over Rockaway Channel. Moses favored these more glamorous projects over the park he had inherited. Both beach and bridge opened in the summer of 1937, well ahead of Marine Park. Riis Park and the Marine Parkway Bridge so depleted MPA funds that Moses was forced yet again to scale back plans for Marine Park. Now even Clarke and Rapuano's "economy scheme" proved too

RINE PARK BROOKLYN
NEW YORK CITY

costly to build. "It is as clear as crystal to me now," Moses wrote in an August 1936 staff memo, "that the plan which we announced in good faith cannot be carried out within any reasonable time, that it is far too expensive and also that its merits . . . are extremely dubious." He even mocked his most trusted landscape architect, whose "academic" plan for Marine Park was "just another case where we were too much influenced by pretty pictures drawn by Gilmore Clarke and some of the other boys." He now directed his more pliant staff designers—Frances Cormier, Allyn Jennings, and Clarence C. Combs (principal designer of Jones Beach)—to come up with yet another scheme for Marine Park. The new plan was as reductive of the Clarke and Rapuano scheme as that one had been of Lay's. Moses instructed his men to simply finish the playing fields north of Avenue U, create a small boat basin by Plum Beach, and lay out a chain of "border developments"—playgrounds, ball fields, basketball courts—along Gerritsen Avenue. "For the rest," he concluded, "I am satisfied that Marine Park should be left largely as it is." Even the golf course would go—for it, too, was "impractical and could not possibly justify the enormous cost of fill and the destruction of a naturally attractive area." Thus after twenty-five years of ambitious plans, the salt marsh prevailed, saved by the otherwise most ruthless builder in American history.[24]

Robert Moses (in white) explains plans for Marine Park to (left to right) Queens borough president George U. Harvey, Brooklyn borough president Raymond V. Ingersoll, and Federal Works Administration supervisor John M. Carmody, 1939. Brooklyn Collection, Brooklyn Public Library.

Perspective rendering of Marine Park by J. MacGilchrist, c. 1940. Parks Photo Archive, New York City Department of Parks and Recreation.

Marine Park Fieldhouse, 1943, by Herbert Magoon and S. L. Snodgrass. This building was to replace a drab temporary structure on Fillmore Avenue that stood until 2008. Magoon had designed bathhouses at Jones Beach State Park, Sunset Pool, and the Crotona Play Center. Parks Photo Archive, New York City Department of Parks and Recreation.

Charles Downing Lay never forgave Robert Moses for scuttling his masterpiece and did his level best to make trouble for the headstrong builder in years to come. Among other things, he helped organize opposition to Moses's ill-conceived plans for a suspension bridge between the Battery and Brooklyn (a crossing eventually realized as the Brooklyn-Battery Tunnel). Lay would never see another commission on the scale of Marine Park, but he got a nice consolation prize for all his labor—a silver medal in the 1936 Berlin Olympics. Jesse Owens might have been the most celebrated participant in the infamous "Hitler games," but it was "Landscape Lay"— not the great track star—who was the first American awarded a medal. Until 1948, art was an official class of competition in the summer Olympiad, and "Designs for Town Planning" was one of several subcategories that also included sculpture, painting, music, and literature ("Lyric," "Dramatic," or "Epic"). Of course, there had to be *some* reference to sport and athletics; this was the Olympics, after all. As the 1936 Art Section entry form put it, "Only works relating to sport will be admitted," while those "representing a human body at rest, without apparent sport character . . . will be excluded." A sprawling monument to fitness and competitive sport, Lay's Marine Park plan certainly met those Olympian standards.[25]

By the 1970s Gerritsen Creek had become a scruffy and scofflaw place, overrun by dirt bikers and scattered with the rusting hulks of stolen cars. There were brush fires almost weekly, set by local teenagers, which the fire department dutifully attempted to quell at great taxpayer cost. The landscape seemed to mirror the city's own bleak chaos and decline in those years. And yet despite its use as an urban dumping ground, the salt marsh retained a certain austere majesty. On autumn afternoons, the teal-blue waters of the tidal inlet would stretch to the horizon, framed

Silver medal of the 1936 Berlin Olympic Games. Cadbury Research
Library—Special Collections, University of Birmingham.

by hillocks bearing a tawny mane of *Phragmites australis*—an enterprising invasive
species that colonized the nutrient-poor fill dumped on the site over the decades,
excluding most native flora and fauna and dramatically altering the natural ecosystem. At high tide, not a trace of Charles Downing Lay's titanic playground can
be seen; but come back when the moon has sucked low the seawater, and rows of
mussel-encrusted pilings emerge revealing the bulkhead line of his canoe harbor and
grand canal. On the shores above, time and space appear to be moving in reverse;
for in recent years the Corps of Engineers and the New York City Parks Department
have reversed a century of environmental degradation by scraping away both the
phragmites and the fill they've colonized—a exercise in ecological restoration much
like a great weeding operation. Tucked beneath a fresh layer of topsoil and planted
with native marsh grasses, the Gerritsen estuary is today one of fifty-one Forever
Wild nature preserves throughout New York City, anchored by the pleasing, low-
slung contours of the Salt Marsh Nature Center. In good time, this marginal place
will again resemble the pristine landscape that Danckaerts and Sluyter once roamed;
that sustained the Leni Lenape for a thousand years before them; that has outlasted
the quondam schemes of dreamers and visionaries alike.

Concrete bulkheading for Charles D. Lay's Long Canal stacked on the east side of Gerritsen Creek in 1988. They were removed a decade later when the Salt Marsh Nature Center was built. Photograph by author.

Gerritsen Creek from the Salt Marsh Nature Center, November 2012. Taken a month after Hurricane Sandy; debris in tree at right indicates high point of storm surge. The taller pilings in back outline the eastern corner of Lay's canoe harbor. Photograph by author.

GRAND CENTRAL OF THE AIR

Not all of Jamaica Bay was as resistant to human will as Gerritsen Creek. At Barren Island just a mile to the east lay an estuarine landscape subjected to seventy-five years of abuse at the hand of man only to be obliterated by one of the largest landfill operations in city history. Even as plans to make the bay a great world harbor fell apart, Barren Island was chosen to become a port of a different sort—for vessels not of the high seas, but of the air. Here on the southernmost edge of the city, New York would build its first municipal airport. Just as the impending opening of the Panama Canal spurred a feverish campaign to maintain the city's primacy as a sea-port, it was an event of global significance that helped kick the Big Apple into the air age—Charles Lindbergh's solo crossing of the Atlantic in May 1927. Lindbergh's flight was an American triumph, but one that vexed many New Yorkers. This was because Lucky Lindy's so-called New York–Paris flight into history was launched not from the mighty metropolis, but from an airfield on Long Island. It should more accurately have been called the Garden City–Paris flight. Lindbergh had nothing against Gotham, of course; it's just that there was no place in New York City proper to take off from. No place *dry*, that is. The very first crossing of the Atlantic by an aircraft—nearly a decade before Lindbergh's—set out from the waters of Jamaica Bay in the spring of 1919 (and included a young naval officer named Richard E. Byrd, whom we shall meet later). This was no stirring "lone eagle" adventure, but a massive naval expedition involving several planes, fifty ships, and hundreds of men. Three Curtiss NC flying boats departed Naval Air Station Rockaway (about where Jacob Riis Park is today) on May 8, making stops on Cape Cod, Nova Scotia, and Newfoundland before heading out over the Atlantic—guided by not only navigational charts but a chain of twenty-two well-lighted navy warships riding at anchor all along the flight path. Only one craft, NC-4, made it to the Azores, and from there to Lisbon and—eventually—Plymouth, England, where the flying boat was met with tremendous fanfare. The aerial crossing was cheered by the London press as "the opening achievement in a new era of transpontine travel." The NC-4's six-man crew, commanded by Albert Cushing Read, was feted on both sides of the Atlantic—and promptly forgotten once Lindbergh made his solo flight.[1]

But the future of aviation was in airports, not flying boats. And that America's largest, most powerful metropolis had no airport to call its own in 1927 was an embarrassment to citizens and civic leaders alike. This was no longer the rude dawn of aviation, when fliers like Kay Stinson and Cal Rodgers could trundle stick-built craft over pasture and sand (their favored field at the Sheepshead Bay Speedway was itself gone, in any case). There were more than four thousand federally sanctioned airfields in the United States by now, and yet none within the limits of the nation's greatest city. Despite Gotham's titanic power, complained Brooklyn, "airplane landings must now be made at isolated aviation fields far out from the city on Long Island and the New Jersey meadows." Clearly something had to be done. Even before the *Spirit of St. Louis* had rolled to a stop at Le Bourget, New Yorkers had begun clamoring for an airfield worthy of their city. And in the weeks and months after Lindbergh's flight, dozens of sites all over town were proposed for the inaugural airfield, ranging in fitness from the ideal to perfectly absurd. Jamaica Bay was consistently in the press for a number of possible sites—all, ironically, on land that was to be created as part of the World Harbor scheme. Governors Island was an early contender, favored by several prominent aviators. It certainly had pedigree: the island had been the launch point for the first airplane flights in New York City—Wilbur Wright's jaunts around the Statue of Liberty and Grant's Tomb during the Hudson-Fulton Celebration of 1909. In a fit of generosity, the Flatbush Chamber of Commerce even suggested "landing places" in *each* of the boroughs, lorded over—of course—by "one large and completely equipped field" in Brooklyn. The Regional Plan Association suggested no fewer than thirty-two airports for the New York metropolitan area![2]

Brooklyn's boosters were loud and effective campaigners for an airfield on their turf. Aviation was all bright and soaring promise, offering redemption of a sort from tenement grit and industrial grime. Here was a chance for Brooklyn to step boldly out from Manhattan's shadow and stake a claim on the future itself. The borough certainly had the land for a modern airfield and could make a lot more at its marshy margins. The ever-ambitious Marine Park Civic Association was first in line, launching a campaign for "Lindbergh Field" on that perennial field of dreams, Marine Park (the "playground" portion between Fillmore Avenue and Avenue U, erstwhile site of Knute Rockne stadium). The old Dreamland site in Coney Island was proposed, vacant ever since a catastrophic 1911 fire. A 116-acre parcel on Gowanus Bay was suggested by star Curtiss airplane designer Harvey C. Mummert, while a "Bay Ridge Airport" was proposed in the Narrows off Shore Road, set on an enormous island of fill stretching from Ninety-Second Street north past the Brooklyn Army Terminal. A similar proposal was made for Gravesend Bay, with runways laid out on a trapezoid of new land between Sea Gate and Bath Beach. Others suggested Stilwell Basin in Coney Island (site of the New York City Transit rail yards) and the east end of Manhattan Beach, today the campus of Kingsborough Community College. But not all Brooklyn airport boosters had their eyes on terra firma: Brooklyn manufacturer Richard Gibbons looked instead to the city's rooftops, proposing that landing accommodations be fixed atop buildings using air rights purchased from owners. He designed an extraordinary articulated steel platform—two hundred feet long and sixty feet wide—that could be rotated into wind and pitched up or down to help launch or land a plane. The deck was equipped with a reversible fan system to "blow away snow in Winter, or as a source of suction to keep a landing plane from bounding after it hits the runway." Gibbons had filed a patent for this "Airplane Receiving Apparatus" years before—in August 1919—and fabricated a scale model at his Columbia Street factory in Red Hook (itself equipped with a "platform for aeros" on the roof). Nine years later he was still at it, aided by a team of engineers (including Harvey Mummert) and testing a prototype in wind tunnels at New York University's short-lived Guggenheim School of Aeronautics.[3]

Of course, choosing a site for New York City's first airport—a vital piece of urban infrastructure—could not be left up to boosters and visionaries, let alone armchair inventors. Even before Lindbergh's flight, the Board of Estimate had asked city engineer Arthur S. Tuttle to evaluate promising airport sites in New York. Tuttle was a highly respected figure in the city, having helped design Brooklyn's waterworks years earlier. He urged officials to think well ahead of present needs, warning that most of the best sites, including Marine Park, were already hemmed in by residential development and offered little capacity for future growth. "A commercial flying field in a city like New York," he cautioned, "is certain to become the most crowded aviation center in the whole United States." Tuttle determined that the most advantageous site in the long run was East Island in Jamaica Bay, the artificial island that was to be created out of the JoCo and Silver Hole marshes as part of the Great Port plan. Tuttle's airport, laid out as a 640-acre square, would have been located just off the southern tip of runway 4L-22R at today's John F. Kennedy Airport. But Mayor Walker, rumored to fear flying, was slow to make a municipal airport a priority of his colorfully corrupt administration. Secretary of commerce Herbert Hoover, convinced that a modern airfield in New York City was vital to the nation's economic health, made it a federal case. He appointed a blue-ribbon board to determine the best site—the Fact-Finding Committee on Suitable Airport Facilities for the New York Metropolitan District. Its location subcommittee, chaired by philanthropist-aviator Harry F. Guggenheim, cast a wide net, soliciting input from business, professional, and civic groups and the public at large. In all, some seventy-two sites across the region were considered. The committee's findings were publicized just before Christmas at a Hotel Astor luncheon, to which Mayor Walker arrived predictably late. Hoover's team divided the city into six "localities," recommending specific airport sites for each. Unobstructed flight paths, availability and cost of land, favorable meteorology, road and rail access, and expansion potential were among the many factors considered. Though it endorsed a total of ten locations (six first- and four second-choice sites), the committee clearly favored building New York's municipal airport in Queens—on still-rural land in Juniper Valley that was nonetheless well served by public transit (the Myrtle Avenue Elevated to the south, Long Island Rail Road to the north). It also commended the city of Newark's recent decision to construct an airfield of its own on Newark Bay—eventually the cause of much grief for partisans of Brooklyn, as we shall see.[4]

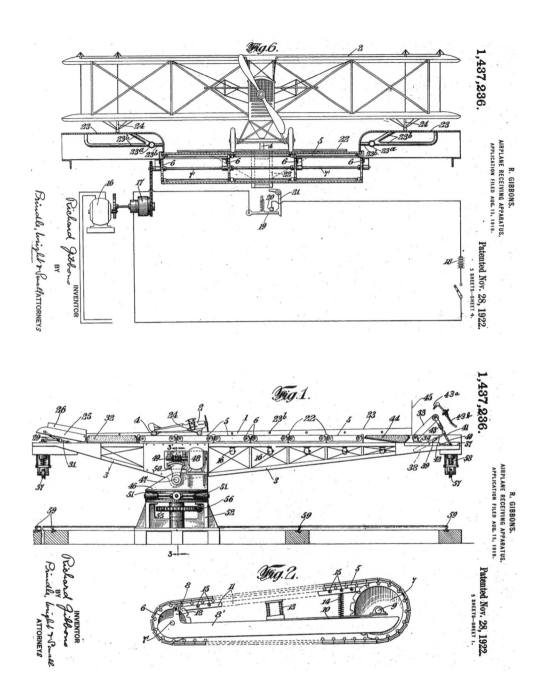

Richard Gibbons, illustration for an "Airplane Receiving Apparatus," 1919. United States Patent Office.

But the Hoover committee was advisory only and had no teeth to force its find-ings; it was up to the Board of Estimate and the mayor's office to make the final decision. Mayor Walker, ambivalent about the whole flying-field matter from the start, refused to set foot in an airplane and ordered his loyal assistant, Charles F. Kerrigan, to look over the sites by air. Ultimately, the decision came down to cost. Building an airport at all but two of the Hoover sites would require purchasing vast holdings from private owners or the federal government—a very expensive proposition. Jamaica Bay, already mostly in municipal hands, moved two sites— East Island and Barren Island—into the pole position. Recall that in 1927 the Great Port of Jamaica Bay was not yet cold in the grave. To make an airport out of either of these wet spots would mean a tremendous amount of fill. Dredging channels for the long-envisioned port was the obvious source. The skyport could help make the seaport, thus killing two infrastructural birds with the proverbial single stone (or clump of sand). Linkage between the schemes also helps explain why responsibility for building and operating the airport was handed not to some glamorous new minis-try of aviation, but to the plodding, old Department of Docks—the very agency that had long sought to make Jamaica Bay the greatest port on the seven seas. But just as Jamaica Bay made little sense for a deepwater harbor, it was also far from ideal for an airport. Both locations were a long haul from lower Manhattan, far from rail or subway connections. East Island did not even yet exist and—once created—would require bridging a thousand-foot channel to join it to the city.[5]

Barren Island was hardly close to town either, but at least it was above water. There, some three hundred acres of level city-owned land were ready to go. An-other five hundred could easily be filled, and all of it was already joined to the city by the recent extension of Flatbush Avenue. Kerrigan's air tour had convinced him that Barren Island was indeed the best site, and he pointed out that an airport there would terminate the new "bee-line automobile route" that ran through the heart of Brooklyn along Flatbush Avenue, connecting to Canal Street over the Manhattan Bridge and the rest of America via the newly opened Holland Tunnel. It was also not beyond the reach of rail and rapid transit; trolleys ran to Avenue U, and as early as 1910 plans had been made to extend the Utica Avenue subway to Flatbush Avenue and Jamaica Bay as part of the port project, while the Long Island Rail Road began looking at a Barren Island spur from its New York Connecting Railroad. And as was not the case at any of the other contending sites, airplanes were already taking off and landing at Barren Island. A twenty-three-year-old self-taught Brooklyn flyer named Paul Rizzo had begun flying an Epps monoplane from a sandy strip of pri-vate land along Flatbush Avenue in 1928. He named it, ambitiously, Barren Island Airport. Rizzo gave airplane rides and took news photographers up over the city. Within a couple of years he had a stable of six aircraft, including a Waco 10 biplane that pioneer wing-walker Ova Kinney often performed on. He was soon joined by a competitor, Charles Krohn, who used a shorter parallel runway and often had to "borrow" a bit of Rizzo's at the last minute to get airborne (leading to a "spite fence" and a lawsuit). On February 2, 1928, the Board of Estimate held a final public hearing on the airport matter. Proponents of the various sites pressed their cases. At one point the room was darkened, and aerial footage of the contending sites was

Paul Rizzo with his Waco 220 biplane at Floyd Bennett Field, c. 1931. Rizzo laid out the first earthen runway at what would later become New York City's first municipal airport. Rudy Arnold Photo Collection, Archives Division, National Air and Space Museum.

screened. When the camera panned briefly to a clutch of Manhattan skyscrapers, the mayor cackled, "Is that a landing field?" To Brooklyn boosters, the airport was no joke. The borough desperately wanted the city's first municipal airfield. The powerful Brooklyn Chamber of Commerce was on hand, along with representatives from booming Flatbush and Flatlands. They were joined by a flotilla of ninety-eight community groups from every corner of the borough. By meeting's end the prized bird was in hand: Barren Island was chosen, by a unanimous vote of the Board of Estimate, to be the city's first official airfield. Brooklynites danced in the street. The *Eagle* joyously proclaimed that the new airport would shape the future of New York City, much the way the Brooklyn Bridge had fifty years earlier. Lord Manahatta would now have to come to lowly Brooklyn to see the future—and to Barren Island, no less! The long-suffering isle of bone broth and stink, the Hades of horsedom, dumped on literally by all of Gotham—Barren Island would now be no less than "New York City's Grand Central of the Air."[6]

The man in charge of this metamorphosis was Clarence D. Chamberlin, appointed the city's aeronautic engineer in June 1928. Chamberlin, largely forgotten today, was one of the most celebrated aviators in the world at the time. He was every bit as skilled a pilot as Charles Lindbergh, who beat him to Paris for the Orteig Prize the year before. Chamberlin held the world flight endurance record—a fifty-one-hour, forty-one-hundred-mile schlep back and forth over Long Island to train himself for the transatlantic flight—and would very likely have beat Lindbergh were

Clarence D. Chamberlin, c. 1927. Leslie Jones Collection, Boston Public Library.

it not for the meddling of his airplane's owner, wealthy Brooklyn scrap-metal man Charles A. Levine. Shortly before Chamberlin and his trusted copilot, Lloyd W. Bertaud, were to take off for Paris, Levine attempted to bump Bertaud and copilot the *Miss Columbia* himself. Bertaud sued; an injunction was issued and the aircraft grounded under police guard at Roosevelt Field. By the time Levine got the order lifted, Lindbergh was well on his way toward Paris and the history books. Chamberlin and Levine finally got airborne two weeks later, landing just short of Berlin after sixty hours of flying in rather grim silence (the two were barely on speaking terms). Chamberlin thus gained the sapless honor of being second to fly across the Atlantic, but the first to fly a passenger—an oddly appropriate distinction for a man chosen to build New York's inaugural civilian airfield. Airport planning and design was a nascent field in 1928. Chamberlin toured Europe to learn what he could from its state-of-the-art airports—Le Bourget in Paris, Berlin's Templehof, and Croydon in South London, first in the world to use air traffic control. Working with a team of Dock Department engineers, Chamberlin drafted plans for the new flying field and personally tested potential sites for its floatplane landing base. He requested $2.75 million to build the airport, to include a series of hangars along Flatbush Avenue, a central administration building with control tower, offices, and passenger hall, two concrete runways—one thirty-one hundred feet and the other four thousand feet long—even grandstands to accommodate up to ten thousand air show spectators.[7]

Sand slurry being pumped from Rockaway Inlet to create Floyd Bennett Field. This photo was taken at the commencement of work on the airfield in June 1928. Cora Bennett, Floyd Bennett's widow, is in group on right. Vehicles in background are on Flatbush Avenue. Henry Meyer Collection, Othmar Library, Brooklyn Historical Society.

Even before Chamberlin's plans were finalized, land making for the airport had begun at Barren Island. Preparing a level platform for the airfield required pumping a mammoth quantity of sand—from Mill Basin and the main shipping channel in Jamaica Bay—to fill the creeks and marsh and raise the ground sixteen feet above mean high tide. By Christmas of 1929, nearly four hundred acres of new land had been made, then covered with clay and topsoil. In a rare and early instance of concern for the natural environment, the *New York Times* ran an article on how construction of the airfield was destroying one of the last great havens on the Atlantic Seaboard for the ancient horseshoe crab. As the dredges pumped sand slurry into the marshes and creeks, "burying beyond escape thousands of little ones . . . hiding in the soft mud," the crabs began an extraordinary mass exodus from Barren Island, moving across the bay bottom in the thousands "like an army of miniature wartime tanks." Atop the new land were stretched two runways, set at right angles and fifty feet wide, doubled to one hundred feet even before the airport opened in a bid for the coveted "A1A" airport rating from the Department of Commerce. The concrete had hardly cured when the first scheduled airline began operations—an hourly New York–Washington run launched in August 1930 with a fleet of three-engined, ten-passenger Stinson Airliners. The Administration Building, which included the airport's control tower, was, oddly, the last major building to go up. Designed in the Georgian revival style popular at the time for institutional buildings, it included a telegraph office, barbershop, newsstand, press and radio rooms, a US Weather Bureau chart room, a dormitory for pilots, and a terraced lounge and restaurant for two hundred patrons. The building was erected by the Longacre Engineering and Construction Company of New York, whose earlier work included Chicago's famed Apollo Theater, the Mayflower Hotel in Washington, and the Ford Motor Company headquarters at Broadway and Fifty-Fourth Street, designed by Albert Kahn. But the Brooklyn airport job was peanuts next to Longacre's biggest project at the time—in the Soviet Union, of all places, where it had won a $25 million contract to erect a series of modern apartment blocks and school buildings around Moscow. Crowds of spellbound Muscovites gathered to watch as Longacre crews broke ground with American steam shovels, tractors, and other equipment. The new airport's improbable Soviet connection curiously foreshadowed a controversy some years later during the Depression involving murals commissioned by the Federal Art Project of the WPA for the Administration Building passenger hall. The Armenian émigré Arshile Gorky had originally been contacted to execute the artwork, and a preparatory gouache for his highly abstract mural—based on collages of photographs taken at the airfield by Wyatt Davis—was exhibited at the Federal Art Gallery in December 1935.[8]

But for reasons unclear, Gorky's work was redirected to Newark Airport, and the Brooklyn commission handed instead to August Henkel and his assistant Eugene Chodorow. The pair labored for three years on the murals—each six feet tall and thirty feet long—which were draped from the second-floor balcony above the lobby. But some saw dark and troubling things on Henkel's canvases: a figure thought to bear a uncanny resemblance to Josef Stalin (it was in fact the French parachutist Franz Reichelt); a Soviet airplane that had made a record-breaking flight from Moscow to California (it was actually an American Vultee); a red star on a navy hangar

Federal Art Project artists August Henkel and Eugene Chodorow working on their doomed murals for the Floyd Bennett Field Administration Building, 1939. Photograph by Sidney M. Friend. Federal Art Project, Photographic Division Collection, Archives of American Art.

(that one "slipped by," Henkel admitted). The Wright brothers were depicted in Soviet peasant garb, according to some. Joseph Rosmarin, a local flight instructor who had flown against Franco's forces during the Spanish Civil War, was painted in nearby. Jessie A. Chamberlin of the Women's International Association of Aeronautics called the murals "outrageous things." "Looks like Russian stuff," grumbled another. The WPA overlord for New York City, Colonel Brehon B. Somervell, came to look and immediately ordered Henkel's murals yanked down and destroyed (three were burned; the fourth was spared but remains lost). When Henkel later refused to sign a mandatory affidavit stating that he was not a Communist or a Nazi, Somervell dismissed him from the Federal Art Project. Henkel fired back with a lawsuit, claiming defamation of character and asserting that he refused to sign only because the demand was a violation of his constitutional rights as an American; "My politics are my own affair," he angrily asserted, "and I do not need to disclose them to any Government agency any more than I would need to tell how I vote in an election." Henkel freely admitted he had leftist sympathies; he had twice campaigned for elected office in Queens as a Socialist candidate. Matters got worse when the *New York Times* revealed that Henkel had once been arrested for his part in an ill-considered ceremony at Bouck White's Church of the Social Revolution, in which the flags of nations were burned in a gesture of universal brotherhood. Henkel burned the American flag, an act that landed him a thirty-day sentence in the city workhouse. Now he received death threats and asked for police protection at his Queens Village home. Rockwell Kent was one of the many artists who came to Henkel's defense, rebuking Somervell's "irresponsible dictatorship" and "wanton destruction of the people's property."[9]

Floyd Bennett in April 1925, about a year before his historic flight to the North Pole with Richard E. Byrd. US Naval History and Heritage Command.

New York City's first municipal airfield would be named for pioneering naval aviator Floyd Bennett. Raised on a hardscrabble farm outside Warrensburg, New York, Bennett picked blackberries as a boy, worked in lumber camps, and trained as an automobile mechanic before opening his own garage in Ticonderoga, New York. With war clouds massing over Europe, Bennett enlisted in the navy at Burlington, Vermont, initially training as a landsman mechanic. He later learned to pilot a Curtiss flying boat at the new air station in Pensacola, Florida, and graduated with the navy's very first class of aviators. In 1925 he was selected by Richard E. Byrd to join a naval aviation detachment with the MacMillan Polar Expedition. Byrd and Bennett were an unlikely pair. A highborn Virginian whose forebears founded the city of Richmond, Byrd was a graduate of the United States Naval Academy with a penchant for bravado. The taciturn Bennett, raised in Adirondack poverty with only an eighth-grade education, was the perfect foil to the impetuous Southerner. Weather in Greenland limited flying on the MacMillan expedition, and its real triumph was demonstrating the utility of shortwave radio for long-range communication (Eugene MacDonald, a naval reservist and founder of Zenith, helped lead the trip). The following year, Byrd organized a polar journey of his own, with backing from Edsel Ford, John D. Rockefeller, and Vincent Astor. A master at self-promotion, he also negotiated lucrative media and publicity contracts, including with Pathé News. He tapped Bennett to fly the expedition's trimotor Fokker F-VII, the *Josephine Ford*, named for Henry Ford's only granddaughter. The airplane would catapult both men to world fame, though not without controversy.[10]

The Byrd Expedition got under way from Brooklyn, where—on April 5, 1926—an enthusiastic crowd of well-wishers gathered at the Navy Yard to see the USS *Chantier* off. The *Josephine Ford* and a smaller chase plane had been disassembled and loaded aboard the repurposed warship, which set sail for Spitzbergen, Norway, shortly after lunch (escorted through the Narrows by Astor's steam yacht, *Nourmahal*). On board was enough coal for a fifteen-thousand-mile journey, six thousand gallons of gasoline for the airplanes, $25,000 worth of navigation instruments, and several tons of expedition supplies—including bulky fur flying parkas each valued at more than $1,000. Fifty men crewed the ship, nearly all volunteers, backed by enough food stores to sustain them for six months at sea. They reached Spitzbergen three weeks later, where the Fokker was reassembled and readied for flight to the North Pole. Just after midnight on May 9—the plane's wooden skis performed better when the ice was frozen hard—Bennett gunned the Fokker's three Wright Whirlwind motors, and the *Josephine Ford* rumbled off into the arctic dark. With Byrd navigating and Bennett at the ship's controls, the men made their way over the ice, communicating against the roar of the motors by hand signals and passed notes. At two minutes after nine o'clock that morning, the men crossed the pole, or very near to it. They limped back to Spitzbergen on two engines, returning exhausted but triumphant some sixteen hours after their departure. Bennett demonstrated extraordinary courage, piloting in conditions that would challenge flyers even today. With an unheated cabin, temperatures plunged to −50°F, making the simplest tasks a torturous challenge. Equally remarkable was Byrd's navigating the tiny craft over six hundred miles of trackless ice. The men returned to Brooklyn as national heroes, feted with that gold standard of American hero worship—a ticker-tape parade down Broadway.[11]

For Bennett, it was the high point of a very short life. In the triumphal aftermath of the polar flight, he and Byrd planned to cross the Atlantic in a bid for the Orteig Prize. Department store magnate Rodman Wanamaker, who had a keen interest in aviation, provided financial backing. But the first flight of their custom-built Fokker F-VII ended badly when the test pilot—the plane's designer, Anthony G. Fokker—crashed the ship in a botched landing. Bennett, a passenger at the time, was seriously injured and never fully recovered. A year later he volunteered to fly an exceedingly hazardous route to bring aid to the German-Irish crew of the *Bremen*, stranded on Greenly Island, Quebec, after becoming the first airplane to cross the Atlantic from east to west. Despite already suffering a fever, he and copilot Bernt Balchen departed from Detroit in a Ford Trimotor. At a supply stop near Murray Bay, he finally yielded the yoke. Balchen pushed on to the *Bremen*; Bennett, now gravely ill with pneumonia, was rushed back to Quebec. Charles Lindbergh flew through a snowstorm to deliver a special serum from New York. But it was too late: the arctic flyer succumbed on April 28, 1928. He was all of thirty-eight.[12] Byrd, who was paraded up Broadway a second time in July 1927 for a transatlantic flight with Balchen, would go on to make several more polar expeditions in coming years, all to the Antarctic. The most celebrated was launched just months after Bennett's death, this time with four ships, three airplanes, nearly a hundred dogs, and 650 tons of supplies. The little fleet was led by the *City of New York*, a repurposed nineteenth-century Norwegian barquentine sealer formerly known as the *Samson* and long suspected—incorrectly—of being the "mystery ship" that failed to aid the stricken RMS *Titanic* in 1912 because it had been hunting illegally off the Grand Banks. Byrd was a Jazz Age blogger; from his expedition base on the Ross Ice Shelf—named "Little America"—he broadcast radio updates to eager fans tuning in across the United States. On November 29, he and Balchen became the first men to fly over the South Pole—in a Ford Trimotor named the *Floyd Bennett*. Returning to New York on June 19, 1930, Byrd was given yet another hero's welcome, with an honorary degree from New York University and an unprecedented (and still unmatched) third ticker-tape parade up Broadway. The following week he presided over a ceremony at Barren Island in which the city's inaugural airfield was named for "the realest man I ever knew"—a man who quite literally propelled Admiral Byrd to world fame. Throngs lined the route of Byrd's motorcade from the Manhattan Bridge to Borough Hall and all along Flatbush Avenue to the airfield, including some 500,000 children given the day off from school for "Brooklyn Aviation Day."[13]

Floyd Bennett Field in 1933, showing original runway layout. The chimney of the old New-York Sanitary Utilization Company plant at Barren Island is in upper right; Dead Horse Bay to lower right. Photograph by Fairchild Aerial Surveys, Inc. Collection of the author.

The Mayor's Committee on Aviation Dinner to the visiting United States Army Air Corps commemorating the dedication of the New York City Municipal Airport

Floyd Bennett Field

May 27th 1931   Hotel Pennsylvania

Mayor's Committee on Aviation invitation to banquet celebrating the dedication of Gotham's first municipal airport, May 27, 1931. Henry Meyer Collection, Othmar Library, Brooklyn Historical Society.

The official opening of Floyd Bennett Field, one year later, was marked by perhaps the greatest spectacle ever staged over New York City. At about 5:45 a.m. on wet and blustery May 23, 1931, a drone of distant motors was heard coming from the north. Tiny specks soon peppered the clouds, as a massive "aerial armada"— the entire First Air Division of the US Army Air Corps—made its way down the Hudson. Hundreds of thousands of New Yorkers assembled in parks and on piers and tenement rooftops to see the mighty show—"the greatest fleet of fighting airplanes," reported the *Times*, "ever gathered under a single command." At the Battery alone, some fifty thousand people craned their necks to see the mighty flying force. First came a lumbering vanguard of bombers, led by a faster plane trailing a plume of white smoke. As these disappeared over the Narrows, many assumed that the show was over. But then the air slowly filled again with the choral roar of radial engines as an extraordinary formation of nearly six hundred aircraft—the largest ever assembled over North America—motored past the city. The planes came in wave after wave for what seemed an eternity—nimble Curtiss pursuit planes, tiny scout planes and observation craft, muscular Boeing fighters, hulking Keystone bombers that skimmed low over the water. Their yellow wings were jewel-like against the mercurial sky, glinting as "long bars of light from the shrouded sun broke through for a minute or so." The Air Corps fleet, drawn from units across the country and crewed by fourteen hundred men, had been launched in phases from several airfields on Long Island, flying across the Sound to Ridgefield, Connecticut, before turning west and staging over Ossining, New York, in a great rotating pinwheel. Once the last planes joined in, groups began peeling off for the run down the Hudson, stacked at interval altitudes "like broad stairs," wrote the *Times*, to save "those in the rear from the propeller wash of comrades just ahead." The entire formation stretched twenty miles long and took a full twenty-two minutes to pass a given point along the route; Charles Lindbergh brought up the rear with the 110th Observation Squadron, his old unit of the Missouri National Guard. From the Battery—where a mock battle was called off owing to squalls and the low ceiling—the planes flew through the Narrows, around Coney Island, and out to sea. The pilots then turned sharply north to make a long low pass over Floyd Bennett Field, roaring "like a swarm of insects out of the mist and clouds over the sea." Remarkably, there was only one mishap the entire day, when an observation plane from the 104th Flying Group was forced to ditch in the Narrows near Owl's Head Park; the pilot and his passenger—*Daily News* photographer E. J. Dowling— were unhurt and quickly rescued.[14]

Not everyone was pleased with the mammoth war game, which cost taxpayers a cool $2 million. Pacifists held maneuvers of their own that day, staging a "Peace Parade" and a series of well-attended lectures at the Battery, where members gathered thousands of petition signatures for the advancement of world peace. Writing in the *Militant*, weekly organ of the Communist League of America, George Clarke warned that the world was heading fast toward another war, and that the airplane would be its chief instrument—not the "obsolete and antiquated battleships" haggled over in disarmament conferences. He blasted the air show as capitalist warmongering in the form of bread-and-circus entertainment, and accused even the pacifists of

Illustration of the "sham battle over New York" that marked the dedication of Floyd Bennett Field. From *Modern Mechanics and Inventions*, July 1931.

collusion—offering little more than "soft and soothing music that lulls the working class into a state of drowsy security." Of course, the armada was emphatically meant to signal to the world America's commitment to building a first-rate air force, even if officials passed it off as a training exercise. The War Department insisted that it was meant "to test and improve tactical theories of the army with respect to aerial defense of our coast line." Army chief of staff Douglas MacArthur contended that the great air rally was no "circus" but a "test of the preparedness of the air branch for warfare" and an "exhibition of the potential resources of the United States as an air power," which must aim to be "too strong in military aviation to be attacked." MacArthur needed political support for the army's planned doubling of its aerial arsenal, which explains why the exercises were broadcast live not just locally but to a vast national audience. New Yorkers could hear the action on WNYC, WOR, and

Curtiss O2C-1 Helldivers from Floyd Bennett Field attacking King Kong, 1933. The Naval Reserve pilots were paid $10 each to "jazz the Empire State Building" and had no idea they would actually be starring in one of Hollywood's greatest films. Pictorial Press Limited / Alamy Stock Photograph.

WABC, while a nationwide network of 150 radio stations carried the transmission coast to coast. Announcers positioned throughout the city handed off the play-by-play as the formations passed overhead, their reports mixed in with bursts of radio traffic between the pilots and ground command.[15]

Those who missed the show got a glimpse of war birds over Gotham two years later in the Hollywood blockbuster *King Kong*. The film's epic final scene, in which darting, diving biplanes attack Kong atop the Empire State Building, was inspired by the 1931 aerial maneuvers over the city. Herb Hirst, location manager for RKO Studios, initially wanted to use navy attack planes based in Long Beach, California, but his request was denied. The studio then contacted the commanding officer of a squadron based at Floyd Bennett Field, leapfrogging the entire naval chain of command. Hirst struck a sweet deal with the unit—in exchange for a measly $100 donation to the Officers' Mess Fund and $10 to each pilot, he got the squadron to fly four Curtiss O2C-1 Helldiver attack planes dangerously close to the world's tallest building. The pilots had little idea what kind of mission they were on, or for whom, and were told only to go up and "jazz the Empire State Building." Sharp-eyed movie fans will spot the Brooklyn squadron's whimsical fuselage insignia in some frames—Mickey Mouse riding a bomb-laden goose past the Statue of Liberty. The final footage was intercut with shots of another squadron of aircraft—Boeing P-12 fighters—along with close-ups of a rather poorly made scale model.[16]

Naval Reserve Air Squadron Curtiss O2C-1 aircraft readied for takeoff, c. 1934. The squadron's insignia featured Mickey Mouse riding a bomb-laden goose past the Statue of Liberty. US Naval History and Heritage Command.

Floyd Bennett Field was the most advanced airport in the world when it opened. Its runways were the world's longest, constructed of steel-reinforced concrete eight inches thick and capable of supporting the heaviest aircraft then in existence. Seaplanes and flying boats had ready access to the water via a ramp on Jamaica Bay, next to the city's old garbage pier, with buoy-marked "runways" in the channel. Floyd Bennett was equipped with the most sophisticated navigation and lighting technology then available, including a floodlight system, installed by Brooklyn's own Sperry Gyroscope Company, and General Electric's mammoth illuminated "NYC" sign and arrow on a hangar rooftop. A 240-foot-long tunnel from the taxiway enabled passengers to disembark and walk directly into the Administration Building. And it was immediately a busy place. By the end of 1931, just seven months after opening, nearly eighteen thousand passengers passed through Floyd Bennett in 25,000 landings. Two years on, landings at the airfield had more than doubled to 51,828. Only Oakland Airport in California was busier, and not by much. But the surging numbers hid an ominous trend. Most of the passengers moving through Floyd Bennett were carried not by scheduled airlines, but rather by private and military craft. Three years after the grand opening, none of the major commercial carriers were offering daily passenger service at Floyd Bennett—nor would any until 1937, when American Airlines began daily flights to Boston (which lasted all of a year). Most commercial passenger traffic was going instead through Newark Airport, because

Newark had an ace-of-spades advantage over the Brooklyn airfield—one that New York officials would struggle mightily to win to the city. Floyd Bennett might be the best airfield in the world, but Newark moved the mails.[17]

Newark Airport began operating in October 1928 and by 1930 was already served by several passenger airlines. This was because it had been designated the official eastern airmail terminus by the United States Post Office Department. Between the end of World War I and 1927, the Post Office operated its own fleet of aircraft, after which it began contracting with commercial operators to carry the nation's airmail. The object was to encourage the development of civilian airlines, as passenger traffic alone was insufficient to keep an operator in business. Transporting airmail subsidized the infant airlines, and so those airports endorsed by the Post Office Department were also the ones that developed the first regular scheduled passenger service. The Department of Commerce had very rigorous standards for airports handling the nation's mail, and Newark Airport had been planned with just these standards in mind. New York, on the other hand, had overlooked them—city officials were so certain their state-of-the-art field in Brooklyn would automatically be made the region's new airmail terminal that they failed to take the Commerce standards seriously. As a result—and for all its modern technology—Floyd Bennett fell short on a number of counts and failed to win the essential Class A1A rating. There was also that little matter of geography. The Brooklyn airport was actually closer by several miles to lower Manhattan than was Newark. But Floyd Bennett was stuck in New York City's deep rural south, where even water and sewer service had only just arrived. Getting the mail there from Manhattan meant a long slow haul by truck across the East River and down the full length of Flatbush Avenue—Brooklyn's ancient, heavily congested Main Street (the Gowanus Expressway and Belt Parkway would not be built for another decade). Skeptics had repeatedly warned of this, to no avail. After the final Board of Estimate vote for Barren Island, the *New York Times* moaned that "as a terminal for air mails Barren Island will hardly be satisfactory." Newark Airport, despite being separated from the city by the Hudson and Newark Bay, was easier to get to and from by both rail and road. Trains had been crossing the Hudson River for twenty years by now, and the North River Tunnels provided a swift rail connection between Newark and Pennsylvania Station and the central post office on Eighth Avenue. In inclement weather, mail at Newark could be easily transferred to trains for delivery by rail—an advantage Floyd Bennett Field wholly lacked. Even more importantly, Newark Airport enjoyed easy motor vehicle access to Manhattan via the Pulaski Skyway and Holland Tunnel.[18]

A variety of increasingly desperate schemes were proposed to overcome the Brooklyn airfield's accessibility handicap and make it easier to reach for both passengers and—crucially—the mails. Some suggested that autogiros could be used to fly parcels directly to the rooftops of Manhattan buildings. An aerial taxi service was launched at Floyd Bennett Field in 1931, running between Jamaica Bay and seaplane docks at West Thirty-First Street and at the foot of Wall Street. There was Richard Gibbons's rooftop landing fields, discussed earlier, which might handle "small ships taxiing cargoes from giant air transports at the airports to the heart of the city." In 1934 a dubious "air train" scheme was tested, city officials hoping it would quite literally put Floyd Bennett Field on Post Office Department maps. It was the brain-child of pilot-entrepreneur J. K. O'Meara, aeronautical engineer Roswell E. Franklin of the University of Michigan, and a Bronx-born haberdasher named Elias Lustig, who made a fortune in men's hats. The Lustig Sky Train, as it was known, consisted of a single "locomotive" airplane towing several Franklin PS-2 glider "cars" filled with sacks of mail (including twelve thousand commemorative cachets for philate-lists). The plan was to take off from Brooklyn, gain altitude (and publicity) circling the city, and then head south for the nation's capital. The third and last glider in the train would cut loose over Philadelphia to land at Camden Airport; the second over Baltimore, bound for Logan Field; and the third over Washington, where—incredibly—it was to "land in the Ellipse between the White House and the new Postoffice Building." The Lustig Sky Train took to the air at Floyd Bennett on the morning of August 2, each glider car loaded with a hundred pounds of mail trucked over from the Newark post office. All went well at first. The Eaglerock locomotive plane "roared down the runway," wrote the *Eagle*; "the three gliders, balancing each on a single wheel and spaced about 200 feet apart, trailed after like the tail of a kite." The crazy train was sighted over Philadelphia just before one o'clock. But headwinds were fierce, forcing the tow plane to land there for more fuel. After the train took off a second time (minus the Philly-bound glider, piloted by Professor Franklin himself), it ran into a massive thunderstorm over Chester, which drove it back to the ground again. The trip was rescheduled for the following day, but press and public alike had already lost interest in what was clearly a bad way to transport either the mail or—as O'Meara had planned—living, breathing passengers. It hardly helped that the whole thing was a Soviet innovation, first tested that May by Rus-sian airmen piloting a three-glider air train eight hundred miles from Moscow to Koktebel in the Crimea. When the Brooklyn air train got back to Floyd Bennett on August 5, hardly anyone was on hand to welcome the pilots home.[19]

Perhaps the most workable—if unusual—solution to the Floyd Bennett mail access problem was Clarence Chamberlin's proposal to construct an underground pneumatic tube that would convey parcels from the airfield to the Brooklyn General Post Office on Tillary Street in all of ten minutes. Such a system had been in use in Manhattan since the 1890s, and later extended over the Brooklyn Bridge. Letters and parcels were placed in large cylindrical canisters, breech-loaded into a launch cannon by "Rocketeers," and sent on their way at an average speed of thirty-five miles per hour. To celebrate the system's opening in October 1897, a cat was coaxed into a canister and sent on a short, harrowing ride to the post office at City Hall (leading some to dub the mail tube system the "cat subway"). To demonstrate just how effective a pneumatic system could be for Floyd Bennett Field, Chamberlin staged a "parcel race" from a building on Varick Street to the old Custom House. The package sent by tube arrived in just over four minutes; the one sent by taxi took twenty-five minutes. In the end, the most obvious solution to the airfield access dilemma would have been by simply extending subway service down Utica Avenue or—better yet—from the Flatbush Avenue terminus of the Nostrand Avenue Line (today's 2 and 5 lines, neither of which makes it past Brooklyn College even now). Doing so would have not only made New York's new airport functionally part of the

Cora Bennett and Mayor Fiorello H. La Guardia with pilot Jack O'Meara at Floyd Bennett Field, August 2, 1934, as the Lustig Sky Train prepares for its first (and only) flight. Times Wide World Photo / New York Times.

city's transportation network, but brought subway service to the entire southeast quadrant of Brooklyn—long (and still) underserved by rapid transit. An express track along this route would likely have made it possible to get from Floyd Bennett Field to Wall Street in under thirty minutes—a whole lot better than a forty-five-minute, $60 cab ride from Kennedy.[20]

The fight for Brooklyn's airfield was kicked up several registers by the city's new mayor, Fiorello H. La Guardia. An experienced aviator himself, La Guardia served in the Army Air Corps with the American Expeditionary Forces in Italy during the First World War, and—as a congressman from East Harlem—had piloted one of the six hundred warplanes that flew over the city in the 1931 aerial armada. Elected mayor on a fusion ticket in 1933, La Guardia refused to accept that Gotham's flagship airfield would be located not in New York City but in the bogs of New Jersey. The mayor was on hand for the launch of the Lustig Sky Train in August 1934, cheering it airborne alongside Floyd Bennett's widow, Cora. Cocksure from his electoral victory, he pushed for the airfield most memorably on a flight back from Panama with his wife on November 24. As the TWA airliner rolled to a stop, La Guardia refused to disembark, pointing out that the destination on his ticket read New York City, not Newark. A parade of airline officials pleaded with him to conform, but he remained in his seat. Eventually the big engines were cranked up and the aircraft—empty but for Fiorello and Marie—took off for Brooklyn, where La Guardia disembarked victoriously.[21] Over the next several years, La Guardia put the full-court press on the

Mayor Fiorello H. La Guardia, an experienced pilot, sits hopefully in the cockpit of a TWA DC-1 mail plane at Floyd Bennett Field, November 1934—one of his many ploys to sway the postmaster general to designate Floyd Bennett Field the airmail hub of greater New York City. La Guardia and Wagner Archives.

issue, calling favors in from Washington and directing every Brooklyn lawmaker to write to the Post Office Department detailing Floyd Bennett Field's advantages over Newark. But unfortunately for the Little Flower, the newly appointed postmaster general of the United States, James A. Farley, was no shrinking violet himself. Farley was a kingmaker with friends in very high places, with a temperament every bit as tenacious and forceful as La Guardia's. He had helped Alfred E. Smith win the governorship in 1918 and played a major role in getting Franklin D. Roosevelt elected president; the postmastership was his reward. It was going to take more than airport antics to convince Farley to pull the airmail rug out from under Newark—where the airlines had made substantial investments in terminals and hangars.

Farley played fair, however, and gave La Guardia more than ample opportunity to make his case for Floyd Bennett Field. In early 1935 he directed his staff to study the situation. Newark officials, led by mayor Meyer C. Ellenstein, held their breath, well aware that New York had the might and money for a long fight. The airlines, meanwhile, delighted in this big row for their hand in marriage; "bargaining with the fears of each of the municipalities," wrote Herbert Kaufman, "the airlines were in a position to extract the most favorable terms from both." On August 24 the verdict came down; the Post Office Department had determined that Newark Airport simply offered "superior advantages" over Floyd Bennett Field, which presented "no . . . substantial saving in the time of handling the mails between the airport and the General Post Office in New York City." New Jersey had won. But La Guardia was not yet ready to accept defeat. He marshaled his forces to attack the issue again, appointing a Committee on Airport Development to lobby Washington (chaired by the inimitable Grover A. Whalen), and announced $3 million in improvements for the Brooklyn airfield. Two new runways were built using funds from the Works Progress Administration; a rotating beacon was erected; the looming hazard of the old New-York Sanitary Utilization Company chimney was felled (see chapter 6); special mail-hauling subway cars were promised for the Nostrand Avenue Line. La Guardia was no fool, of course: even as he continued to fight for Floyd Bennett Field, he also quietly arranged for the city to exercise its option on North Beach Airport in Queens—what would one day become La Guardia Airport. And a good thing, too; for this time Farley himself issued the verdict: Floyd Bennett Field would never be the region's airmail terminus. The Brooklyn dream of a "Grand Central of the Air" thus vanished like ground fog in the sun. It was the biggest public-works defeat of La Guardia's career.[22]

But the very factor that caused Floyd Bennett to fail as a commercial airfield—its remote location on the edge of the sea—made it ideal for experimental aviation. All through the 1930s it served as the launch place and landing pad for an extraordinary number of record-breaking flights. Many of the most celebrated figures in the Golden Age of Aviation were regulars at the Brooklyn field—Wiley Post, Roscoe Turner, Amelia Earhart, Hubert Julian, Laura Ingalls, Jimmy Doolittle, Howard Hughes, Douglas "Wrong Way" Corrigan. Two months after its opening, Hugh Herndon, Jr., and Clyde Pangborn took off from Floyd Bennett Field for Wales in a potbellied Bellanca Skyrocket—the *Miss Veedol*—on a round-the-world journey they hoped would land them the $25,000 prize offered by the *Asahi Shimbum*

A TWA DC-1 refuels at Floyd Bennett Field en route to Los Angeles on a record-breaking flight, May 16, 1935. Rudy Arnold Photo Collection, Archives Division, National Air and Space Museum.

Wiley Post (left) and Harold Gatty with the *Winnie Mae* shortly after their record-breaking flight around the world in July 1931. Post repeated the flight solo two years later. Leslie Jones Collection, Boston Public Library.

newspaper for the first nonstop flight across the Pacific. They were an unlikely pair and quarreled all the way—Herndon was the moneyed son of an oil heiress, a Princeton dropout who could hardly read a compass; Pangborn was a seasoned barnstormer and former mining engineer from the West Coast. Somehow they managed to get across all of Europe and Asia without killing each other, stopping in London, Berlin, Moscow, a small village in what they thought was China (it was Mongolia), and eventually Khabarovsk, Siberia. From there they made the short hop to Tokyo, where they were promptly arrested for lacking visas. Locked up for weeks as suspected spies, they were given a single chance to leave Japan in the *Miss Veedol*. If that failed, the aircraft would be confiscated, and the pair would be sent home on a very long boat ride. They spent their internment productively—planning the transoceanic flight home—only to have their navigation charts stolen by the ultranationalist Kokuryūkai (Black Dragon Society), who wanted a Japanese to win the prize. Herndon and Pangborn finally got airborne again from a beach at Misawa in Aomori Prefecture. The plane was so overloaded with fuel that Pangborn was forced to dump seat cushions and survival gear, and he devised a means to jettison the plane's landing gear after takeoff to reduce weight and drag. Thus humbled, *Miss Veedol* waddled back forty-five hundred miles to the United States. It belly flopped to a stop on the outskirts of Wenatchee, Washington, three days later, making Herndon and Pangborn the first to fly an airplane across the mighty Pacific. The epic journey came to a close when they landed back in Brooklyn on October 18—this time smoothly on a new set of wheels.[23]

On November 14, 1932, a swaggering speed demon named Roscoe Turner roared into the Brooklyn sky on a record-breaking dash to California, making the trip in just under thirteen hours. A Mississippi farm boy, Turner drove an ambulance in World War I and later learned to fly, barnstorming across the country and gaining fame as a Hollywood stunt flyer and air racer. Like many aviators of the time, he had a flair for style, sporting a waxed mustache and often flying with a lion cub named Gilmore (after his oil-company sponsor). An even more colorful denizen of the Brooklyn tarmac was Hubert Fauntleroy Julian, the self-styled "Black Eagle of Harlem." With a clipped Oxford accent and a proclivity for exaggeration, Julian was an adventurer whose life story is a magnificent mash-up of fact and fantasy. Born to a family of cocoa planters in Trinidad, Julian emigrated to Canada as a teenager, where he claimed to have flown for the Canadian Medical Services during World War I. He moved to Harlem in his twenties, appearing one afternoon at Clarence Chamberlin's landing strip in New Jersey. Claiming to be a professional parachutist, he convinced the flyer to take him up for several trial jumps. When he refused to climb out of the open cockpit, Chamberlin suggested jumping off the wing. Back up at altitude, the youth still wouldn't jump; he had borrowed a new type of pack chute and didn't trust it would open. Chamberlin circled and circled, increasingly annoyed at the fuel he was wasting. Finally the flyer waggled the plane and shook his rider free. Julian never did let go of the wing strut, however, which had broken off; now the plane's wings were flapping dangerously loose. When Chamberlin finally landed, Julian was already on the ground—tangled in his cords but smiling, wing strut still in hand. The men became fast friends.[24]

On April 29, 1923, Julian made what was probably the first parachute jump within New York City limits, leaping high over Harlem from an airplane piloted by another African American, Edison McVey. The streets were filled with spectators, for just

Hubert Julian with his Packard-Bellanca J-2 Special *Abyssinia* holding a press conference at Floyd Bennett Field, September 1933. Rudy Arnold Photo Collection, Archives Division, National Air and Space Museum.

before jumping the men had tossed a pair of noise bombs overboard to get attention. Julian floated down dressed in crimson tights and tunic "such as Mephistopheles wears," the *Times* elaborated—aiming for St. Nicholas Park, but landing instead on a tenement roof at 301 West 140th Street (now P.S. 123). He was handed a summons for disorderly conduct but carried triumphantly off by the crowd to Marcus Garvey's Liberty Hall. There he gave a speech urging citizens to support a nearby black-owned department store before it fell into the hands of whites—and, incidentally, "to patronize the eye doctor whose card he carried on his shirt front." Julian made several more jumps over the next six months, selling each to a local merchant whose advertising banner he would display prominently on descent. In September he made a five-thousand-foot jump at the Police Games in Jamaica, Queens, before an audience that included boxer Jack Dempsey and Governor Al Smith. The fun and games ended in November, when another Harlem jump with Chamberlin left him dangling precariously from a police station rooftop. He was hauled in by two patrolmen through a second-floor window. Julian then took up flying, trained by Chamberlin and McVey (there is no evidence he had piloted anything more than his imagination in Canada). Soon he was buzzing Harlem rooftops and parades of the Universal Negro Improvement Association. In 1924 he began soliciting funds for a flight to Liberia, which he advertised by placing the seaplane Chamberlin sold him—the *Ethiopia I*—on the corner of Lenox Avenue and 139th Street. Julian kept putting off the expedition until a federal agent explained that he would be charged with felony mail fraud if he didn't at least *try*.[25]

So on July 4, with hundreds of spectators cheering, the Black Eagle roared mightily down the Harlem River in an aircraft he had never flown before. A pontoon tore off, followed by the other; the plane lurched upward and within minutes plunged into Flushing Bay. It vanished for a moment, but then "bobbed up to float with sudden peacefulness"—words that well described the buoyant and irrepressible Julian. Not long afterward, the flyer was spirited off to Africa by imperial edict—literally—when agents of Ethiopian emperor Haile Selassie recruited him to fly in a coronation extravaganza. The regent was so impressed by the black American that he granted him command of the infant Ethiopian air force. But then Julian flew Selassie's cherished de Havilland Gipsy Moth into a tree, and was promptly expelled. Back in New York and finally a licensed pilot, he began plotting treks across the country or around the world that usually never left the ground. His handsome black diesel-powered Packard-Bellanca J-2 Special, the *Abyssinian*—which he planned to fly to India—became a Floyd Bennett fixture. After Italy invaded Ethiopia, Julian returned to fight the colonial aggressors. He was soon booted again, this time for romancing one of Selassie's daughters. In retaliation he began lecturing on Ethiopian atrocities (as Huberto Juliano) but was revealed to be receiving payments to do so from Italian agents. Ever resilient, Julian later flew Morane-Saulnier fighters for the Finnish air force, and produced at least one "race movie"—*Lying Lips*, released in 1939 and starring James Earl Jones's father, Robert.[26]

The summer of 1933 was an especially busy one at Floyd Bennett Field. At the crack of dawn on July 15, Wiley Post took off on a solo round-the-world flight that would make him one of the most celebrated pilots of his generation. Son of Texas

Hubert Julian with his wife, Essie Marie Gittens, December 1935. New York Daily News / Getty Images.

cotton farmers with little formal schooling and a rap sheet for highway robbery, Post leveraged a near tragedy into a successful flying career. When he lost his left eye in an oil-field accident, he donned an eye patch and used the settlement money to buy an airplane. He shot to fame several years later by winning a major air race from Los Angeles to Chicago. In 1931 he circumnavigated the globe with Australian Harold Gatty. Now he would do it alone. From Brooklyn he flew to Berlin in record time, piloted his way across northern Europe to Moscow, over the Ural Mountains (passing some peaks that were higher than he was able to climb), across Siberia and the Bering Sea, and on to Fairbanks, Edmonton, and—seven days, eighteen hours, and forty-nine minutes later—New York City. When his Lockheed Vega— the *Winnie Mae*—landed back in Brooklyn at midnight on July 22, Post was greeted by seventy-five thousand people, many of whom rushed toward the plane and its spinning propeller. A unit of fifty mounted police had to drive back the crowd, which nonetheless mobbed the weary flyer.[27] The airfield had hardly been quiet while he was away. On the sultry afternoon of July 19, two dozen Savoia-Marchetti S.55 flying boats slowly circled Jamaica Bay and, over the next nineteen minutes, landed like Neptune's tridents in groups of three on Clarence Chamberlin's mile-long seaplane runaway. The twin-engined, double-hulled craft had left Italy two weeks before on an international tour. Leading in a ship marked I-BALB was the aristocratic Italian air minister and self-styled *Garibaldini*, Italo Balbo. An erudite Ferrarese with a penchant for Virgil, he nonetheless came of political age cracking the skulls of labor organizers and socialists in and around Bologna as a young fascist squad leader, and helped organize Mussolini's 1922 March on Rome. For many, the brilliant, charismatic Balbo was the very essence of the "New Italy." So was aviation, which had inspired the Italian futurists and which Mussolini long yearned to link with fascism.

Balbo was a competent enough pilot, but his real genius lay in public relations and political organizing. Appointed air minister by Mussolini in 1926 (largely to keep this potentially dangerous rival occupied), Balbo set about planning the regime's greatest publicity stunt—a series of international "aerial cruises" to strengthen diplomatic ties and showcase Italian air power. He would personally lead them all. The first was a neighborhood stroll around the Mediterranean; the second a disastrous flight down the African coast to Bolama, Guinea-Bissau (where two planes and five men were lost), and across the Atlantic to Brazil. The third expedition—dubbed Crociera Aerea del Decennale to celebrate ten years of Italian fascist rule—was the longest and most symbolic; for it brought Balbo back to the very place that had inspired the expeditions years earlier. It was the sight of the Manhattan skyline seen from an ocean liner in 1928—"the bizarre, colossal outlines of the chaotic metropolis, wrapped in epic curtains of smoke and fog"—that first seized Balbo with the vision of a triumphant flight of Italian airplanes to America. His fleet departed the Italian coastal town of Orbetello on July 1, crossing the Alps "in a majestic formation," wrote biographer Claudio Segré, "that was widely reproduced in photographs, on postcards . . . even on a book jacket." From Amsterdam, the men made landings at Londonerry, Ireland, and Reykjavik, Iceland, before crossing the north Atlantic to Canada. After a stop in Montreal, they headed to Chicago, escorted by a formation of American warplanes that spelled out ITALY in the sky. At Chicago, Balbo was feted with a five-thousand-plate banquet, named "Chief Flying Eagle" by a contingent of Sioux Indians, and granted an honorary degree by Loyola University. One million Chicagoans gathered to bid him farewell several days later as his flying boats roared skyward from Lake Michigan for the thousand-mile trip to New York. Seven hours later they soared down the Hudson in a large V-formation—"like so many great water birds flocking southward in the autumn," gushed a reporter from the *Chicago Tribune*. A battery of guns on Governors Island fired a nineteen-volley salute as the fleet passed overhead on its way to Jamaica Bay. There, as Balbo made landfall on a barge, a Brooklyn girl named Grace Mastelloni swam out to greet him; clambering on board and dripping wet, she stood erect and hailed him with the fascist salute.[28]

As in Chicago, Balbo and his company of a hundred handsome flying men were the darlings of the city for most of a week, honored with banquets and dinners and one of the largest ticker-tape parades yet staged in New York. For the city's many citizens of Italian stock, the Balbo visit was a moment of cultural triumph that came in the darkest year of the Great Depression. It is easy to censure retrospectively the Italian American community for so enthusiastically receiving the Italian aviator. But with the full horrors of fascism as yet unrevealed and World War II still years away, it made sense that Balbo would be regarded as a symbol of hope and resilience to a struggling immigrant people. Until World War II, Italians in America were known mostly as ragpickers and organ-grinders, swarthy aliens with garlic breath

Columbus and Balbo, problematic heros. Portrait photograph by Joseph Stangarone, 1933. Library of Congress, Prints and Photographs Division.

Balbo's fleet of twenty-four Savoia-Marchetti S.55 flying boats over the Hudson en route to Jamaica Bay, July 19, 1933. Collection of the author.

and a penchant for crime—a place in society not unlike that of undocumented Latin American immigrants today. When Balbo stepped ashore at Floyd Bennett Field—with the beard of an Assyrian king and resplendent in his starched whites, onto the very same dock where a generation of Mezzogiorno immigrants had sorted through the city's garbage—it was a victory not only for the Ferrarese aviator but for tens of thousands of New Yorkers of Italian heritage. Balbo understood this well. At a Madison Square Garden welcome rally, one of the high points of his life, he exhorted the Italians of America to be proud of their heritage—Mussolini, he asserted, had "ended the period of humiliations." Balbo had spent two full years planning the North American expedition, and the investment paid off handsomely. The voyage was a political and logistical triumph, and made Balbo's a household name on both sides of the Atlantic. He and his men were hailed like gods when they finally returned to Rome. But it also brought about his demise. Balbo and Mussolini had a tense relationship, clashing over racial laws and Italy's alliance with Nazi Germany. Balbo considered the union with Hitler a strategic blunder, and he vehemently opposed the regime's campaign against the Jews. "Surely," he implored, "we're not going to imitate the Germans!" Paranoid that the popular aviator would one day stage a coup, Mussolini gave him a velvet exit, installing him as governor general of Libya, then an Italian colony. It was there, on a flight back to Tobruk in June 1940, that he was killed when the aircraft he was piloting was shot out of the sky by friendly fire. Many still believe, despite considerable evidence to the contrary, that Mussolini had ordered his death.[29]

Balbo may have been the first fascist flier to cast a shadow on Brooklyn, but he would not be the last. On April 25, 1934, a Brooklyn fly girl named Laura Houghtaling Ingalls touched down at Floyd Bennett Field after an extraordinary seventeen-thousand-mile flight across Central and South America—from Mexico down the coast to Chile, over the Andes to Rio de Janeiro, up to Cuba, and on to New York. It remains the longest solo flight ever made by a woman. Ingalls was the first woman to fly solo across the United States—an accomplishment routinely attributed to Amelia Earhart—and in September 1935 broke Earhart's transcontinental speed record, piloting a Lockheed Orion from Burbank to Brooklyn in thirteen hours, thirty-five minutes. Ingalls was a quixotic figure who flew with a six-shooter, lived in airport hotels, and signed her name with the Roman symbol for Jupiter. Born to a well-off family with a palatial brownstone at 321 Clinton Avenue, she studied music in Paris and Vienna, trained as a nurse, and danced briefly with the troupe of famous Sevillan Maria Montero before following her passion for flight. Recognized as one of the boldest stunt pilots of the era, Ingalls garnered more transcontinental speed records than any other woman. But her moment in the limelight was brief, brought to an end by a shadowy series of events as war loomed again in Europe. Like many Americans in the 1930s, Ingalls was opposed to American military intervention in Europe and—like Charles Lindbergh—became active in the isolationist America First Committee. In September 1939, she was arrested for flying into restricted airspace to "bomb" the White House with peace pamphlets on behalf of the Women's National Committee to Keep the United States Out of War. A bright blip on J. Edgar Hoover's radar, Ingalls was arrested in 1941 by the Federal Bureau of Investigation and charged with being an agent of the German Reich. She had been recruited to infiltrate the American antiwar movement to spread Nazi propaganda by Baron Ulrich von Gienanth, a high official with the German Embassy and a covert Gestapo officer. The celebrated aviatrix, it turned out, was an eager Nazi sympathizer who admired Hitler, read *Mein Kampf*, and—according to her New York plastic surgeon—even wore a swastika pendant. Ingalls was convicted of being a spy and locked up for most of a year at the federal women's prison in Alderson, West Virginia. Her flying career over, she lived out the rest of her life in a secluded California canyon home.[30]

By 1938, Floyd Bennett Field had only about a year left as Gotham's official airport; work on its North Beach replacement was by then well under way. That summer Howard Hughes and a crew of four set off from Brooklyn to circumnavigate the globe in a twin-engine Lockheed, mainly to test new radio and navigation instruments. They ended up setting a new round-the-world record, besting Wiley Post's time by four days. Just days later, a youthful Californian named Douglas Corrigan captured the hearts of millions with one of the most improbable and celebrated flights of the twentieth century. On the morning of July 17, Corrigan ambled off from Floyd Bennett in an aged Curtiss Robin, its door held shut by baling wire. He had filed a flight plan to the West Coast but headed out to sea instead. Some twenty-eight hours later he touched down at an airfield in Dublin, Ireland, claiming to an astonished crowd of airport personnel that he had meant to fly to California. In fact, Corrigan had petitioned federal authorities several times for permission to fly to Ireland but was rejected because his airplane was deemed too rickety. When he returned to New York—by ship this time—an estimated one million New Yorkers cheered "Wrong Way" Corrigan in a ticker-tape parade that eclipsed even the one staged a decade earlier for Charles Lindbergh. "My compass must have been wrong," he ventured, with a winning grin and a twinkle in his eye.[31]

Early rendering of Idlewild Airport, 1945, what would eventually become John F. Kennedy International Airport. New York City Municipal Archives.

PARADISE ON THE OUTWASH PLAIN

When it's nesting time in Flatbush,
We will take a little flat,
    With welcome on the mat
    Where there's room to swing a cat.
I'll hang up my hat, I'll hang up my hat . . .
—JEROME KERN AND P. G. WODEHOUSE

When the six hundred warplanes of Douglas MacArthur's aerial armada rounded the Narrows for Floyd Bennett Field on May 23, 1931, the pilots—future mayor Fiorello La Guardia among them—would have seen off to their left a landscape churned asunder by real estate development on a scale unprecedented in American history. Though stilled briefly by the Depression, a great tide of timber, brick, and mortar had inundated this land tilled since the 1640s, transforming fields of cabbage and corn into a tidy grid of middle-class homes. Much of this metamorphosis occurred in a single decade, and nearly all of it south of the terminal moraine. Housing the multitude, rich and poor, was nothing new for Brooklyn—known for much of its history as the City of Homes. That era effectively began on August 17, 1807, when an erstwhile painter and mechanical genius named Robert Fulton launched the first commercial steamboat. Fulton later established a regular ferry line across the East River from lower Manhattan, making Brooklyn easier to reach than almost any other part of town. The speedy, scheduled service encouraged real estate speculators to buy up the old farms on the heights across the river and subdivide them into lots for sale to prosperous merchants and entrepreneurs. One of them was a former trader and gin-distiller named Hezekiah Beers Pierrepont, who laid out the street grid of Brooklyn Heights and fortified his investment by helping Fulton monopolize East River ferry operations. This, of course, also helped the competition, and there was plenty—Gabriel Furman, Henry Remsen, the brothers John and Jacob Middagh Hicks, all of whom modestly named streets after themselves and their families (or fruit, in the case of delightful Pineapple, Cranberry, and Orange Streets). By the 1830s, the pastoral bluff above the East River was fast becoming America's first commuter enclave. The residential development of Brooklyn was under way. The pace of development jumped in the 1850s, an era of national prosperity fueled by the Gold Rush. Completion of Prospect Park in the early 1870s prompted another surge of development, led by Edwin Clark Litchfield, railroad magnate and dredger of Gowanus Canal whose Italianate mansion is today the Brooklyn headquarters of the New York City Parks Department. The 1883 opening of the Brooklyn Bridge and the long boom of America's railroad age ignited Brooklyn's greatest, most expansive period of development yet. Touring the city in 1886, *Washington Post* columnist Julian Ralph described Brooklyn's growth as "the most amazing thing in this part of the world," dwarfing even "all the tales with which the western borderland has nourished us during the past quarter of a century." Riding the el, he saw "literally miles of dwellings in course of erection in slender rows, in solid squares, in detached units."[1]

Many of these new homes were brownstones. Known to geologists as arkosic sandstone, brownstone is a sedimentary rock that formed in the Late Triassic period—some two hundred million years ago—from alluvial grains of silica, quartz, feldspar, and mica. Over time these particles were cemented together, hardened, and tinted pink by an iron oxide known as hematite. Brooklyn brownstone came first from quarries at Belleville and Newark, New Jersey, that mined the Passaic Formation, a belt of bedrock that arcs up from Pennsylvania across the tristate region. Another source was Portland, Connecticut, across the Connecticut River from Middletown, where as many as fifteen hundred men labored in vast quarry pits reminiscent of a Piranesi etching. Mined, cut, and dressed, the chocolate rock was loaded on river boats like the *Brownstone* bound for Red Hook and Gowanus Creek. The somber stone appealed to a nation in mourning, an era that Lewis Mumford memorably termed the "Brown Decades." "The Civil War shook down the blossoms and blasted the promise of spring," he wrote; "The colours of American civilization abruptly changed . . . browns had spread everywhere: mediocre drabs, dingy chocolate browns, sooty browns that merged into black. Autumn had come." The brownstone townhouse was the archetypal dwelling of an era both melancholic and yet replete with new freedoms and national renewal—and heady economic growth. By 1868 the war-stilled economy roared to life again. New York's population doubled between 1860 and 1890; Kings County's tripled. The homes came in a variety of flavors following the rise and fall of architectural fashion—Greek revival, Italianate, Second Empire, Romanesque, even Gothic. Builders were mostly small and speculative, erecting homes in gangs of three or four, sometimes filling an entire block. Brownstones were expensive at first, but mass production soon brought costs down. Forged metalwork was replaced by cast iron poured into a variety of ornamental molds by manufacturers like G. W. Stilwell's Phenix Iron Works. Terra-cotta replaced carved stone; handworked wood trim was cut instead by mechanized planers, routers, and lathes. Even the price of the namesake stone fell, as steam-powered derricks and saws reduced the labor needed to quarry and

Quarry walls, Portland, Connecticut, 2018. Most of Brooklyn's brownstone came from this flooded mine on the Connecticut River, now the Brownstone Exploration and Discovery Park. Photograph by author.

cut the rock. By the 1880s, a building material once associated with great wealth had moved within reach of a middle-class budget.[2]

One of the ironies of the Brooklyn brownstone is that, on nearly all such buildings, the celebrated rock is only skin deep—chocolate frosting on brick-and-timber cake. This was hardly meant to be deceptive, at least at first; references in the *Brooklyn Eagle* in the 1850s are almost always to "brown-stone-front houses." Even the grandest such structures made no bones about their brick bodies. The plain side wall of Two Pierrepont Place in Brooklyn Heights—recently listed for $40 million, the highest ever for a Brooklyn house—can easily be seen from the street. But as brownstones slid down the economic food chain, class-fretful buyers needed their buildings to make ever more bold statements of status and upward mobility. Builders cranked up the aspirational quotient with motifs redolent of poshness and exclusivity—mammoth cornices, doors so massive they could crush a child's skull, elephantine cast-iron railings, windows big enough to let all passersby see the tasteful appointments within. The fact of the cladding was itself muted. By the 1880s, references to brownstone as mere façade material become scarce. The earnest "brown-stone-front house" is dropped for a speedier shorthand—*brownstone*—a subterfuge of omission that effectively extended the prestigious stone to the entire building. Material had become metaphor. In both the *Eagle* and the *New York Times*, use of the solo "brownstone" was rare before 1890 but jumps afterward, while two-step "brown stone" largely disappears from the *Times* by 1885—just as the most frenzied period of brownstone construction gets under way. Of course, not everyone fell for all this posture and stagecraft. Once he hopped off the el for a closer look, Julian Ralph found Brooklyn's brownstone row houses to be "deceptive, fraudulent, pretentious—mere shells—plated, so to speak, with a coating of brown stone in front and trimmed inside with cheap pine stained like mahogany, so that a poor man may boast a brownstone house . . . so that the clerk may live like the shadow of a millionaire."[3]

Brooklyn's long brownstone afternoon ended almost in the blink of an eye. The cause was a change in architectural tastes brought about by the World's Columbian Exposition of 1893. Its planner, Daniel Burnham (whom we met in chapter 10) handed nearly all the plum building jobs to an elite band of architects trained in the neoclassical manner at Harvard, MIT, and the École des Beaux-Arts. They built an ersatz Roman Forum so brightly illuminated by Edison's new lightbulbs that its glow could be seen a hundred miles away (consuming three times the electricity of all Chicago each night). Burnham's White City burned away Mumford's shades, ending America's long brown day of bereavement. In Brooklyn, very few brownstones were built after 1900. All the rage now were bowfront Renaissance-revival townhouses dressed in white limestone or yellow brick. Demand for the chocolate rock tumbled. The Portland quarries mined $575,000 worth of stone in 1890; by 1908 that figure had fallen to just $56,000. And the city was in the midst of a major building boom at the time! The Newark quarries were abandoned by 1913; those in Portland limped on until a storm-swollen Connecticut River flooded the two-hundred-foot-deep pits during the Great Hurricane of 1938 (the site is now the Brownstone Exploration and Discovery Park). Of course, the brownstone has roared back from the nethers of taste and fashion—a process that began in the 1960s as well-educated young progressives discovered in the soot and grime of old Brooklyn refuge from the anomie and consumerism of Cold War America. Today the Brooklyn brownstone is among the most cherished forms of habitat this side of the Atlantic, and a symbol of the borough as iconic as the Brooklyn Bridge or the parachute jump—perhaps more so. When Absolut Vodka sought a design for the Brooklyn edition of its popular city series, it passed over both landmarks for a brownstone façade (Big Ben was selected for London and the Golden Gate Bridge for San Francisco—not bad company for a house). And though the Brooklyn Bridge may have been sold many times, it's never been the focus of a bidding war like those unleashed whenever a choice brownstone goes on the market.[4]

Gotham's next big building boom got under way in 1903. By the time it ended in late 1916, some 400,000 units of housing in twenty-seven thousand apartment buildings had been added to the city—fully 40 percent of all the apartments in New York at the time. "The new construction," writes historian Robert Fogelson, "was enough to house the population of every American city except Chicago"—and enough, more crucially, to accommodate the continuing surge of newcomers from afar and abroad. The population of Greater New York more than doubled in the thirty years from 1890 to 1920, rising by 72 percent between 1900 and 1910 and by another 85 percent over the subsequent decade. And yet apartments were plentiful—with enough vacancies in 1909 to house the entire District of Columbia. In Brooklyn, the great tide of brick and mortar had mounted the crest of the moraine and appeared

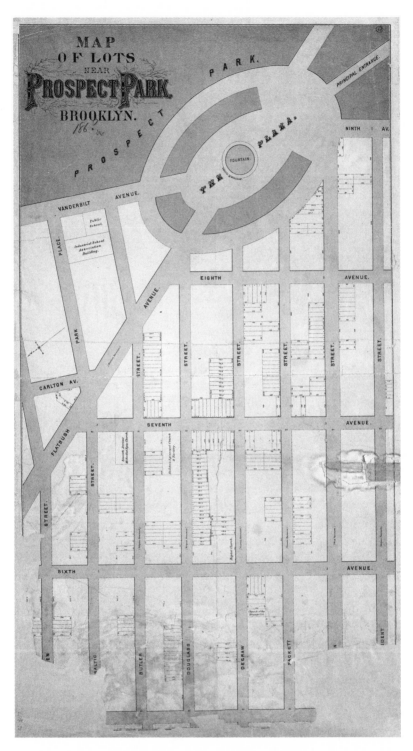

Map of lots in Park Slope west of Grand Army Plaza, c. 1868. Park Slope developed rapidly once construction on the great park got underway. Lionel Pincus and Princess Firyal Map Division, The New York Public Library.

poised to head down the other side. But construction slowed as the situation in Europe worsened and America was dragged into another global conflict. By the time the United States entered the war in April 1917, housing demand in New York was fast catching up with supply. The cost of building supplies had nearly doubled between 1914 and 1919 as material was diverted to the war effort, forcing an end to almost all new construction. Soon much of the city was facing a housing shortage. Things were especially bad in Brooklyn, where the *Eagle* predicted in August 1918 a coming "famine in apartments" and warned that "never before in the history of the real estate market has there been such a scarcity of dwellings for rent." Renters who had had the pick of the litter just a few years before were increasingly at the mercy of rapacious landlords. With the war's end building construction stirred to life, as expected; but the recovery was brief. In all of 1919, just sixty-two apartment houses were erected in all of Brooklyn. The Joint Legislative Committee on Housing, headed by Brooklyn's own Senator Charles C. Lockwood, heard testimony that it had become "well nigh impossible to procure apartments at any price; that families were doubling up; that the health laws of the City of New York were being violated." The cause was twofold: soaring materials and labor costs and a shortage of capital. Money "was very much in demand," writes Fogelson, forcing housers "to compete for loans with other builders, who needed money to put up theaters and other commercial and industrial structures, as well as other businessmen, who needed money to manufacture automobiles and other consumer goods." What loans banks and insurance companies did extend to real estate ventures were substantially less than in the 1903–1916 boom years—falling from 70 to 75 percent of construction costs before the war to just 50 or 60 percent less afterward.[5]

With housing in such short supply, landlords could raise rents with impunity. Some did so rapaciously; most were themselves struggling to keep up with mounting inflation, taxes, and fuel and labor costs. Rent strikes became common. In the prewar years, these had been small and largely limited to the Lower East Side. Now they spread throughout the city. On February 22, 1919, riots erupted in Brownsville when several thousand people gathered to protest the eviction of rent strikers at 1576 Eastern Parkway—and to battle desperate home-seekers who had rushed in to secure the vacated units. Three months later a crowd of five thousand converged to prevent the city marshal and furniture movers from dispossessing three families from a tenement at 387 Williams Avenue. Some strikes were successful. That September, a five-week strike by three thousand tenants near the Navy Yard ended when the B.F.W. Realty Company agreed to reduce a scheduled rent hike and make needed improvements. Joyous renters filled the streets to celebrate as news of the victory spread; "The red-lettered 'Rent Strike' signs that have been posted in every window, and hung from the shoulders of virtually every occupant . . . were flung into the gutter." Most strikes failed, however, as the majority of tenants were too fearful of eviction to partake. Moreover, sympathy for the strikers slackened as anarchist bombings spread and "Red Scare" fears intensified. A threatened May Day action "of overwhelming proportions" in 1920 fizzled after it was condemned by the Brooklyn Tenants Protective Union, which professed "no sympathy with radical Bolshevism" (a promise from Mayor John F. Hylan's Committee on Rent

Profiteering that "any show of violence would be promptly crushed by the police" also played a role). The severe housing shortfall did nothing to foster unity across ethnic and racial lines. In May 1919 the American-African Colonization Association of New York approached the Brownsville Landlords' Protective Association with an offer "to place a colony of 5,000 colored people in the vacant homes of evicted Brownsville tenants," so long as the families were charged "a fairly reasonable rent" and given a five-year lease ("Another color for the Joseph's coat of Brownsville's population," snarked the *Eagle*). The following summer, landlord Jacob B. Felman made good on a threat "to sell his property to negroes" in order to punish striking tenants at 1876 Douglas Street (Strauss Street today). Purchased by a black co-operative, the long-vanished building was the first in Brownsville to be owned by African Americans.[6]

As the housing shortage worsened and rent-strike fever spread, urgent appeals were made to city and state officials for help. When the state legislature convened in January 1920, it was flooded by nearly a hundred housing bills to penalize rent profiteering, slow evictions, and generally give tenants greater protections. Only a dozen of these bills eventually made it to Governor Al Smith's desk, where they were signed into law on April 1. They represented, all told, "the most thorough overhaul of New York's landlord-tenant laws in well over half a century." But Smith, like many legislators, was unconvinced that landlord-tenant laws alone would do much to ease the crisis in New York. "On more than one occasion," writes Fogelson, "he had stressed that the only way to bring down rents was to build houses"—that far more serious than the rent-strike emergency "was the lack of suitable working-men's houses, a longstanding problem that would not be solved by regulating rents or punishing landlords." The city desperately needed to get builders building again. In a special session of the legislature convened by Smith that September, another flood of housing bills was submitted. Ten eventually passed, only one of which—an enabling act known as chapter 949 of the Acts of 1920—was aimed at stimulating residential construction. "Enacted over the opposition of owners of prewar apart-ment houses," Fogelson writes, "the statute allowed the cities, towns, villages, and counties to exempt new residential structures other than hotels from property taxes until January 1, 1932"—so long as construction was completed after April 1, 1920, or begun before April 1, 1922, and finished within two years (or, if currently under way, done by September 27, 1922). In New York City, a first-round chapter 949 ordinance was hotly contested and, despite Mayor Hylan's backing, ultimately defeated by the Board of Aldermen. A revised version, reported out by the Committee on General Welfare, also faced a stormy hearing but fared better, passing by a vote of 42 to 27. Promptly signed by the mayor, the ordinance went to the Board of Estimate, where it faced little opposition and became law on February 25, 1921. The city had wisely added several tweaks to the legislation as it came down from Albany. It limited the amount of the tax exemption to $5,000 to discourage production of high-end homes for the wealthy. In addition, it allowed the exemption to be taken only on a per-room basis ($1,000 per room up to five rooms), not carte blanche for an entire building. City officials "were more interested in securing housing for families than in providing expensive small apartments for individuals," explained Mary Conyngton in the *Monthly Labor Review*, "so they linked the exemption to the rooms, and made sure that no one should secure the maximum remission unless he put up houses or apartments suitable for family use."[7]

Chapter 949 fell like rain upon a thirsty garden. As soon as the tax-exemption statute was enacted in Albany, builders in the city began filing for permits—even before the local tax-exemption ordinance was passed in New York. Once it became law, the housing industry magically jumped to life. Lending institutions that had refused building loans now "opened their coffers," wrote Edward Polak, "and money poured into the mortgage money market." Builders idled for years suddenly had all the work they could handle. Wages in the building trades shot up; labor was back in demand, putting thousands of newly arrived immigrants and African American migrants from the South to work. Skilled laborers and craftsmen began flocking to New York from all over the United States. Dormant quarries, lumber mills, cement plants, and brickyards stirred to life again. Just four weeks after the ordinance was passed, plans were filed for more than 1,000 apartment houses, compared to a mere 190 in the corresponding period the year before. By Christmas, it was clear that a major building boom was under way. More dwellings went up citywide in just the ten months of 1921 following passage of the law than in the previous three years combined, while total expenditures on housing rose from $76 million in 1920 to over $260 million in 1921—an increase of 242 percent. And that was just the start. Construction outlays citywide from 1921 to 1923 were seven times those of the three years prior to the tax exemption. In 1924, a record-breaking 55,000 dwelling units were added to the city—*not* including single- and two-family houses. Manhattan, where almost nothing could be built unless something was first torn down, was relatively unmoved by the building boom. The real action was in the city's still-rural outer boroughs; and nowhere was the frenzy of home construction greater than in outwash Brooklyn. Here, the Cartesian grid of metropolis, perched for a decade on the terminal moraine, rolled down now to the sea.[8]

Land was plentiful and cheap in Brooklyn's southern hemisphere, which was newly tapped into Gotham's pale by extended gas, water, and sewer infrastructure—including a *cloaca maxima* across flood-prone Flatlands rumored to be the largest storm sewer in the world. The so-called Flatbush Relief Sewer was hailed "a triumph of engineering enterprise and skill" no less than the Holland Tunnel, then under construction. The big pipe was officially opened on June 9, 1926, by Mayor Walker in a ceremony at the intersection of Foster Avenue and East Twenty-First Street in Ditmas Park. Electricity set aglow a landscape long lit by candles and gaslight; when utility poles appeared on the southernmost reaches of Flatbush Avenue, the *Eagle* prognosticated "a brilliantly-lighted Broadway at night." Dozens of trolleys

Flatlands sewer main, c. 1905. James A. Kelly Local History Collection, Brooklyn College Library Archives and Special Collections.

and no fewer than four main subway lines—the West End, Culver, Sea Beach, and Brighton Beach—crossed the outwash plain, linking city to sea. Unlike Queens, Brooklyn was familiar ground to anyone who had been to Coney Island. Every year, millions of New Yorkers made their way over the outwash plain on day trips to the beach. Such warm familiarity—happy memories of outings with family and friends—only deepened the rosy glow of the City of Homes. As the boom got under way, the sleepy Bureau of Buildings—an all-Irish shop long stocked by Tammany Hall—was plunged into disarray. Architects awaiting permits or approvals railed against its "backward conditions" and "inability to cope with the growing number of building plans filed." Bribes and hush money passed beneath tables, which might explain why superintendent Thomas P. Flanagan could afford to rent out the entire Orpheum Theater for a bureau staff bash in April 1923.[9]

Builders could hardly keep up with demand, and suppliers were stretched to the limit. Kilns along the Hudson roared night and day to meet the incessant call for bricks. In mid-November 1924, some one hundred brick-laden barges appeared in Gotham's waters, a terra-cotta armada that augured a wild building season to come (the brickmakers sent their wares downriver early to avoid being trapped by ice as the Hudson froze). All told, the fleet carried some forty million bricks—enough to cover 140 football fields or make it a fifth of the way around the equator if placed end to end.[10] That year, construction outlays in the borough were $226 million—a figure that soared in 1925 to $258 million and to $286 million in 1926, the peak of the boom. By 1928, construction spending in the borough was down to $200 million, and shrank to a miserable $74 million in the year following the Wall Street catastrophe of October 1929. The scale and speed of homebuilding in the early 1920s was unlike anything the city had seen before, and drew inevitable comparisons to the speculative mania that gripped Florida at the time ("FLATLANDS SALES RIVAL MIAMI TALES," cried the *Eagle* in 1925).[11] But the Florida land rush was a bubble, burst by the 1926 Miami hurricane and leaving investors with little more than sandy building lots. For all its speculative fever, the Brooklyn housing boom left behind a vast legacy of well-built dwellings, homes for a generation of New Yorkers raised in the tenements of the Lower East Side and eager for a castle of their own.

And castles of a sort they were. Buildings reify society's yearnings as well as its fears, and the residential architecture of the 1920s did just that. The dominant styles then all harkened back to the colonial era or that putative motherland of America, Olde England. Gothic forms were slapped on everything from dormitories to skyscrapers. The neo-Georgian became a style of choice for civic buildings—the Museum of the City of New York and Brooklyn College, for example. A national craze for clapboard colonial-revival homes was set off by Colonial Williamsburg, itself dedicated to a carefully framed set of American traditions. Sears Roebuck marketed mail-order houses named the Lexington and the Jefferson, and was even commissioned to erect a full-scale replica of Mount Vernon above the lake in Prospect Park. Landscaped with boxwoods salvaged from Washington's Hayfield, Virginia, estate (planted by the *pater patriae* himself), the reproduction Mount Vernon was an initiative of Sol Bloom's Washington Bicentennial Commission. Thousands of Brooklyn schoolchildren were dragged through the clapboard shrine until Robert Moses removed it

Perspective rendering of replica Mount Vernon in Prospect Park, 1932; William Smedley, architect. The building was constructed under the auspices of Sol Bloom's George Washington Bicentennial Commission. *Brooklyn Daily Eagle* photographs, Brooklyn Public Library, Brooklyn Collection.

in one of his first official acts as park commissioner.[12] But the most popular style of residential architecture in 1920s New York City reached even further back in time than colonial America—to Tudor England and its medieval vestiges. The Tudor era ended in 1603, decades before the settlement of New Amsterdam. But its architectural traditions lingered on long enough to touch the New World shore, leaving us several extraordinary late-medieval examples on the Atlantic Seaboard—Bacon's Castle in Virginia, for example, and the Judge Corwin and Fairbanks houses in Massachusetts.

What led to all this rifling through the Anglo-architectural attic? As we saw in chapter 3, the country was changing, and many feared that its white, Anglo-Saxon, Protestant charter culture was under siege. For all the progress of the 1920s, it was a conservative, even reactionary decade. The wholesale slaughter of the Great War was still a fresh scar; so too the flu pandemic of 1918. The Russian Revolution sparked fears of Bolshevism, and Prohibition took away the succor of drink. And then there was the matter of immigration. A great tide of newcomers—from Europe and Asia as well as the American South—was rapidly transforming the racial, ethnic, and religious composition of the nation's cities. A hydra-headed nativist movement pushed back hard with violence and intimidation. The Ku Klux Klan was revived as a political force potent enough to hijack the 1924 Democratic National Convention in New York City. Scarier still were pseudoscientific racists like Madison Grant, a Yale-schooled aristocrat and pioneering environmentalist who, like Newell Dwight Hillis, became a committed eugenicist. Grant's 1916 paean to Nordic supremacy, *The*

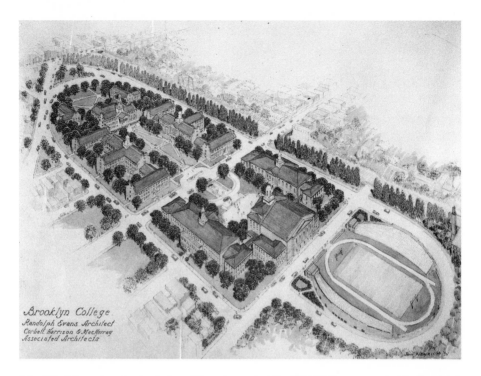

John Wenrich, perspective rendering of Georgian-revival Brooklyn College campus, 1935; Randolph Evans with Corbett, Harrison & MacMurray, architects. Brooklyn College Library Archives and Special Collections.

Passing of the Great Race, was a best seller that helped bring about the draconian immigration laws of the 1920s—including the National Origins and Asian Exclusion acts. Related fears of cultural diminution led Congress to establish the Washington Bicentennial Commission in 1924 (that its chair was a Jewish son of immigrants is a delightful irony). Nominally charged with planning a two-hundredth-birthday bash for George in 1932, the commission's whispered mission was to help cleanse all those immigrants from Sicily and Galicia of unsavory political notions—to impart a bundle of American values to help them "come to understand our principles of liberty . . . our scheme of government."[13]

As with the colonial and Georgian styles, the Tudor revival—Tudorism for short—was likewise born of fears that America's charter culture was weakening in the face of vast immigration. It was "a style for the WASP," writes Gavin Townsend, "a fortress symbol of established Anglo-American lineage at a time when Poles, Slavs, Italians and other 'undesirables' were seemingly flooding the country."[14] Tudorism gained a first foothold in New York around 1910 and quickly became a popular style for single-family homes in the city's posh, lily-white commuter suburbs—Forest Hills Gardens, Bronxville, Riverdale, Scarsdale, Tuxedo Park. It was thus perfectly positioned to spread far and wide with Gotham's next building boom. And the development frenzy unleashed by the tax ordinance did exactly that—it transformed the still-rural landscapes of southern Brooklyn into a stage-set Camelot of steep gables and half-timbered walls, battlements, turrets, and jerkinhead roofs. By the

Harwood Building   Scarsdale, N. Y.

Postcard view, Tudor-revival Harwood Building, Scarsdale, c. 1928. Scarsdale Historical Society.

end of the 1930s, the Tudor-revival row house had become as ubiquitous a feature of Brooklyn's trollyburbs as the Victorian brownstone was of the nineteenth-century neighborhoods north of the moraine. But the politics of the style had changed. In Brooklyn and Queens, Tudorism was an architecture of aspiration, not revanchist yearning for some dewy Anglo past. A style born of xenophobia thus became popular with the very "undesirables"—Jews, Italians, Irish—whose coming helped spawn it in the first place. Trolleyburb strivers were drawn to the Tudor style because it signaled arrival, because it endowed working-class streets with a tiny bit of the polish and grace of Westchester. They were assimilation engines of a sort. The architects and builders of the homes—many of whom were themselves Jewish, Italian, Irish, or Polish—understood well this symbolism. They became expert at distilling the essence of a Riverdale or Bronxville Tudor mansion down to the scale of a small city lot, transforming, in the process, a style for the elite into one for the masses. Thus did "Banker's Tudor" of Scarsdale and Tuxedo Park beget "Teller's Tudor" of Bay Ridge, Flatbush, and Borough Park.

Erecting most of the new homes—single-family dwellings and apartment buildings alike—were scores of relatively small builders. A full accounting of these forgotten shapers of outer-borough New York would fill a telephone book. Louis H. Bossert erected five hundred houses at Utica Avenue and Avenue N; Samuel Bernstein's Lezbern Building Company built forty-two homes on East Twenty-First Street and Neck Road in Gravesend; the oddly named Endocardium Company was active in the vicinity of East Fifty-Second Street and Avenue M in Flatlands. Hyman Selkin built on Flatlands Avenue, Louis Carnadella in Bay Ridge, Louis R. Goldin at Foster Avenue and East Forty-Fifth Street, the Dahl Development Corporation at delightful Dahl Court in Gravesend, the Filloramo Brothers on Avenue D and East

Tudor-revival row houses on northeast corner of Avenue R at East Thirty-Third Street, 1929. Irma and Paul Milstein Division of United States History, Local History and Genealogy, The New York Public Library.

Forty-Eighth Street. E. H. Fritchman's memorably named UONA Home Corporation erected dozens of gumdrop Dutch gable frame houses in Marine Park; the Tudor Homes Corporation focused on nearby Haring Street and Avenue U, and the Wengenroth Company at Avenue T at East Thirty-Sixth Street. Many of these builders slipped under the waves once the Depression got under way. One was Lawrence "Lorry" Rukeyser. Born in Milwaukee to a large family of Jewish immigrants from Liepāja, Latvia (then part of the Russian Empire), Rukeyser made—and lost—a fortune in the construction industry before delving into residential real estate. In 1918, he and partner Generoso Pope—future publisher of the Italian-language daily *Il Progresso*, who helped make Columbus Day a federal holiday—bought out their struggling employer, the Manhattan Sand Company, hit hard by the World War I building slump. Rebranded Colonial Sand and Stone, Rukeyser and Pope's company rode the crest of the 1920s building boom. They supplied gravel, sand, and concrete to thousands of building sites throughout the metropolitan area, from apartment buildings on the Upper West Side to vast row-house projects in Brooklyn and Queens—even the foundation for Yankee Stadium and the runways of Floyd Bennett Field (Rukeyser's daughter, poet and feminist icon Muriel Rukeyser, recalled sneaking up to the rooftops of her father's unfinished Manhattan buildings

with her childhood friend from the Ethical Culture School J. Robert Oppenheimer, who would hold forth on physics as they lay beneath the stars). But the partners began clashing, and Pope—long cozy with mobsters—forced Rukeyser out of the business sometime in 1928. With his vast knowledge and contacts in the building industry, Rukeyser was able to jump quickly into the real estate game on the Flatlands frontier. His Laurye (a portmanteau of his own name) Homes Corporation played its biggest hand in booming Marine Park, where, as we saw in chapter 11, a long-promised playground the size of Central and Prospect parks combined had seeded a frenzy of speculative residential development. Rukeyser had big plans for the Laurye venture, with more than 165 "English Tudor Homes" projected for the blocks in and around East Thirty-Third Street and Fillmore Avenue. The *Brooklyn Eagle* described it as "one of the largest developments of its kind in the history of Brooklyn."[15]

To create his Tudor microcastles Rukeyser chose a Jewish immigrant named Philip Freshmen, whose family had fled the Pale of Settlement first for London and then East New York. Freshmen was by any measure a successful architect, hobnobbing with Irwin S. Chanin, the celebrated apartment designer. Freshmen's commissions included apartment buildings and a hospital in the Bronx, the "perpendicular gothic" Insurance Building at Clinton and Joralemon Streets in Brooklyn Heights, and the original home of St. John's College School of Law at 56 Court Street. But

A Colonial Sand and Stone Mack mixer on a building site, c. 1939. American Truck Historical Society.

like many designers working the busy plains of outwash Brooklyn, Freshmen was quite literally on the margins of a patrician profession dominated by Ivy league elites. And though he did solid work for Rukeyser—Freshmen's houses are among the most sought-after in Marine Park today—the builder's luck ran out even as his bricks were being laid. Less than a year after Rukeyser struck out on his own came the stock market crash of October 1929. Home sales weakened in 1930 but picked up the following summer, a false dawn that encouraged Rukeyser to forge ahead with his Laurye Homes venture. And then came the fall. In September 1931 the *Eagle* reported an ominous "sharp decline" in plans filed at borough building departments. Home sales faltered and then plummeted as the Great Depression spiraled toward its 1933 nadir. Breadwinners lost their jobs; life savings vanished as more than ten thousand banks failed nationwide. By mid-October, foreclosures had become "so common," reported the *Eagle*, "as to constitute a menace to a real estate world already lacking in confidence and a very real peril to a vast list of other securities." Some 128 foreclosed properties in the city were sold in a single week that month, representing nearly $5 million in value. Desperate to sell his remaining Laurye Homes, Rukeyser contacted the Andrew Cone General Advertising Company, a prominent agency whose biggest account at the time was the Empire State Building. Cone ran a series of catchy ads for Rukeyser in the *Brooklyn Eagle* in the fall of 1931. It was money thrown to the wind: the houses failed to sell. He couldn't pay his contractors and before long was being slapped with mechanic's liens from roofers, masons, and carpenters; adman Cone, meanwhile, hauled Rukeyser into bankruptcy court for an unpaid $870 bill.

The next year was worse. Homeowners who had purchased on credit before the crash began defaulting on loans from the New York Title and Mortgage Company, which Rukeyser had backed as a guarantor. By August 1932 the homebuilder had racked up more than $2.2 million in liabilities, a staggering sum for the Great Depression.[16]

Rukeyser was, in the end, small potatoes compared to some players in Brooklyn real estate. One of the first and largest on the scene was Realty Associates, founded in 1901 "to deal in realty," explained director Charles R. Henderson, "and to buy improved real estate in Greater New York on a considerable scale." Unlike most builders in the 1920s, Realty had learned the trade in the previous building boom. Anticipating construction of the BMT Fourth Avenue subway, the company bought the old Backhouse farm in New Utrecht in 1905, laying out streets, installing sewer, water, and gas mains, and platting out

Brooklyn Daily Eagle advertisement for Lawrence Rukeyser's Tudor-revival "Laurye Homes" development, East Thirty-Third Street in Marine Park, 1931.

some five hundred building parcels near today's Maimonides Medical Center. They erected "semi-suburban" two-family row houses in Borough Park, glorious rows of bantam bowfront limestone and brownstone homes on Maple and Midwood streets in Prospect-Lefferts Gardens (for "families who want an entire dwelling without being under the necessity of keeping servants"), semidetached houses on Sullivan Place in Crown Heights and Vista Place in Bay Ridge, and a battery of tenements in Sunset Park for workers at Bush Terminal (which had already assumed "the character of an immense foreign colony," fretted the *Times*, what with all those "Italians and Russian Jews"). By 1909 the company had some two thousand lots and six hundred buildings in its portfolio, with a rent roll of fifteen hundred tenants. Realty's tactics were not always aboveboard. In 1916 it was accused of having "made it a practice for years to create sentiment in favor of the City of New York acquiring properties owned or controlled by them for one purpose or another." That year, Realty director William M. Greve managed to convince the US Department of War to purchase a large parcel it had leased on Rockaway Point (from unlikely owner Southern Pacific Railroad) for a coastal defense installation—the future Fort Tilden. He would later be hauled before the Senate Finance Committee for shorting stocks via a barely concealed Italicized front called Greva Compagnia, and in 1938 caused a scandal by renouncing his American citizenship and emigrating to Liechtenstein, where his vast fortune was safe from the tax man.[17]

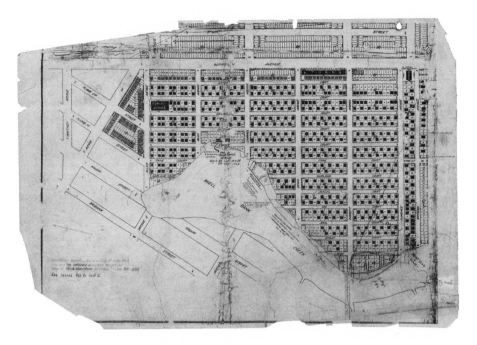

Plan of Gerritsen Estates, c. 1922. New York City Municipal Archives.

That wealth came largely from the thousands of single-family homes Greve erected as president of Realty Associates in the 1920s. His largest single project, launched in the fall of 1922, was a sprawling community of kitten-cute bungalows at Gerritsen Beach, on a spit of filled land along Shellbank Creek. Greve declared that the homes would be built "on the same principle that Henry Ford had developed his automobile—that is, on the basis of strictest economy through standardization of plans." In this, Realty Associates may well have been the first firm in the United States to mass-produce homes, anticipating by a good twenty years an approach that William J. Levitt perfected at Levittown after World War II. Houses were trucked in from the old racetrack rail spur, "all in parts, sashed and ready to be erected over the concrete-cellared foundations." A corps of five hundred laborers erected two dozen of the kit dwellings a month, and by September 1924 some six hundred houses were ready for occupancy at Gerritsen Beach—stick-built boxes on the shifting sand, set in twelve-packs on small blocks (about a third the size of those typical elsewhere in New York City). The houses came in five architectural flavors—all with roughly the same floor area and none costing more than $5,750 (a mere $80,500 today). To emphasize their affordability, Greve advertised the homes as "Ford Houses." When Henry Ford found out about this, he threatened to sue Realty Associates for trademark infringement. Unfazed, Greve simply substituted his own name and kept on building. All told, some fifteen hundred "Greve Houses" were erected at Gerritsen Beach. The company offered its own financing, too; on a $4,950 house, buyers could close with a mere $350 down and a monthly installment of about $65—less than renting. The instant village shot from zero to five thousand residents in eighteen months. It had its own water plant, with 570-foot-deep wells, a 145,000-gallon storage tank,

Long before Levittown: William Greve's "Ford Houses" at Gerritsen Estates, 1924. Brooklyn Public Library, Brooklyn Collection.

and five miles of water main; two churches—St. James and Resurrection; and a community clubhouse provided by Realty Associates (today the Tamaqua Bar and Marina). To meet the needs of its four hundred school-age children, the Board of Education hurriedly erected several portable school structures on Channel Avenue. All the buzz attracted other investors. By 1925, two dozen shops and stores were doing business on its main drag, while celebrated Brooklyn restaurateur Nicholas Satersen commissioned none other than William Van Alen—Brooklyn-born architect of the Chrysler Building—to design a fifteen-hundred-seat "moving picture theater and dance palace" for the corner of Cyrus and Gerritsen avenues. A victim of the Depression, it was never built.[18]

Isolated on the remote margins of the metropolis, linked for years to the rest of town by a single bus line, Gerritsen Beach developed a social fabric as tightly knit as its streets. It had an active civic association, its own chamber of commerce, a Lily of the Valley Garden Club that held annual contests, even its own elected "unofficials"— mayor and cabinet, park commissioner, and commissioner of public welfare. When the city claimed it had no money to deal with a massive sewage backup in Shellbank Creek, the community organized a "pick and shovel army" to cut a six-foot channel across the Plum Island sandbar to Rockaway Inlet, allowing tidal action to flush the waters. Of course, insularity also encouraged illicit deeds; a tight-lipped community with streets dead-ended at the waterfront attracted rumrunners during Prohibition. After a shootout with bootleggers at the foot of Devon Avenue in August 1931, police seized a load of thirty-five hundred bottles of whiskey (twelve hundred promptly vanished as the cops helped themselves to the loot). But the people of Gerritsen Beach took care of their own, forming a Citizens Protective Committee, agitating for emergency milk deliveries during the Depression, and raising money for neighbors in need. Though badly battered by Hurricane Sandy and spoiled by teardowns and mammoth additions, Gerritsen Beach has retained much of its original scale and charm, with perhaps the most picturesque street names in all New York—Melba, Ebony, Dare, Opal, Joval, Dictum, Just. As late as the 1980s there were still commercial trawlers working out of Shellbank Creek, and chickens and horses on one street. Guarded by Brooklyn's last volunteer fire department, Gerritsen Beach remains an extraordinary urban village, a dash of working-class Hibernia on the edge of Gotham.[19]

Aerial view of Shellbank Creek and Gerritsen Beach, looking north from Rockaway Inlet, c. 1929. The Belt Parkway runs along the isthmus in lower half of photo (Plum Beach). Photograph by Air Map Corporation of America. Irma and Paul Milstein Division of United States History, Local History and Genealogy, The New York Public Library.

Greve kept refining his copyrighted Gerritsen Beach model houses and in the summer of 1925 rolled out a larger version—the "Greve S" type—a dwelling "suitable for standardized construction in great quantities." Realty erected a test batch of sixteen on the 3700 block of Quentin Road before building the houses en masse at its Stewart Manor community in Garden City. That December, as work on Gerritsen Beach neared completion, Greve clinched a $3 million deal to buy Brooklyn's last working agricultural landscape—the Flatlands spread settled more than two centuries earlier by Johannes H. Lott. The land was still in the same family, sold to Greve by Jennie M. Suydam—Lott's great-great-great-granddaughter—who retained only a small plot for the Hendrick I. Lott house itself. A once-vast plantation was now down to less than three-quarters of an acre. Ella Suydam, Jennie's daughter, would live in the house until her death in 1989, and the property remained in the Suydam family until purchased by the Historic House Trust on behalf of the New York City Parks Department in 2002.[20] All told, the Lotts and their descendants owned their land for almost 285 years. Where Hendrick's slaves once hoed beans and corn, Realty Associates conjured forth a vast crop of houses. The company graded in miles of cinder streets, laid in a full complement of utilities, and subdivided the new blocks into thousands of lots. Greve christened the new community "Flatbush Centre," and began erecting yet another variant on the "Greve" series, six- and seven-room "duplex and simplex" dwellings that sold for as little as $5,500. Still known in the area as "Realtys," the modest little houses have been spared the teardown tide sweeping across Midwood and other neighborhoods—for now, at least. They remain among Brooklyn's most affordable houses, home now to three generations of New Yorkers and blighted only by the unfortunate conversion of most front yards into carports. Over the next few years, Greve built Realty Associates into a booming conglomerate. The company broke its own sales records in 1925 and again in 1926, selling more than two thousand homes in two years (at one point brokers were moving ten houses a day). Not one for understatement, Greve began billing his company as the "Largest Homebuilders in the World." He may very well have been right.[21]

New York Ave., between Maple and Midwood Sts., Brooklyn

ONLY A FEW LEFT
Remarkable Reduction

$350

CASH

No Additional Payment
When You Move In

Price $8750

10 Years To Pay The Balance

Outstanding Value

This is your **great opportunity** to get a **wonderful home** for **very little money** and on the **easiest possible terms.**

To close out the **few remaining choice homes** in this **successful development** we are offering them to you for **only $350 Cash.** No rent payer can afford to overlook this **remarkable reduction.** The homes are **tapestry brick** in the English Style with **slate roofs** and Colonial iron grill work. Spacious living room, dining room and **well-equipped kitchen** on first floor.

Three large **bedrooms** and tiled bath on second floor. **Automobile driveway.**

A big feature of these fine homes is their situation on **private streets and courts** where **children can play in perfect safety.** Located in one of the **most accessible** sections of Brooklyn, only 15 minutes from **Borough Hall** and 20 minutes from **Wall Street.**

The money you now pay for **rent receipts** will **buy you one of these beautiful** REALTY ASSOCIATES homes.

To Reach Property

Take I.R.T. Subway marked "Flatbush" to Sterling St. Walk three short blocks to Maple St. and one block left to New York Ave. Or take Nostrand Ave. Trolley to Maple St. Representative on premises Daily and Sunday. Write for booklet.

REALTY ASSOCIATES

Largest Homebuilders in the World

162 Remsen St., B'klyn   Phone Triangle 8300

Realty Associates advertisement for row houses with "tapestry brick in the English Style" on New York Avenue in Prospect-Lefferts Gardens. From *Brooklyn Daily Eagle*, July 1926.

Another major Brooklyn builder in the interwar period was the man who gave us daylight saving time and divided the nation into standard time zones—US Senator William M. Calder. Scots-Irish son and grandson of carpenters, Calder grew up on Thirteenth Street in Park Slope and got his start in the building trade working along-side his father as a teenager. He took evening classes in architecture and engineering at Cooper Union and by the 1890s was erecting substantial homes in Williamsburg and Park Slope.[22] Drawn to politics at an early age, Calder became active with the Young Men's Democratic Club and the South Brooklyn Board of Trade, serving on its Committee on Streets and Paving. In 1900 he helped incorporate the Republican Club of Brooklyn's Twelfth Assembly District and one year later was appointed superintendent of buildings by Brooklyn Borough president J. Edward Swanstrom. Cheering the choice, the *Eagle* described Calder as "an experienced builder, an honorable citizen, a man of excellent judgment." When Calder reported to his new office, he found his desk buried under floral tributes from bureau employees worried about their jobs, including an immense horseshoe of roses from the building inspectors. As feared, he promptly began whipping the bumbling bureau into shape. Flowers notwithstanding, Calder fired five inspectors in the first week—part of his plan to "drop undesirable material from the payrolls." He admonished staffers to be "polite and courteous in your treatment of the public," but jealous in the pursuit of compliance and the law. There were new rules for them, too: "Drunkenness will not be tolerated," Calder warned; "To enter a saloon in uniform I will consider a gross breach of the rules. I want you to come here mornings cleanly shaven, shoes shined and with your uniforms carefully brushed." Fire safety was of particular concern to Calder; he banned smoking in the bureau offices, beefed up fire codes for theaters, upgraded tenement fire escapes, and inspected the ruins of a disastrous fire in Atlantic City in April 1902.[23]

His diligence averted at least one tragedy at Coney Island. Shortly before Calder took over as chief, the buildings department had issued entrepreneur Herman O. Moritz a permit for an "aerial coaster" at the Bowery and Kensington Walk. Calder refused to allow Moritz to operate his ride until several safety improvements were put in place. On June 12, 1902, with Coney's summer season wide open, Calder's inspectors arrived to check the ride for approval. After running the empty cars around the track several times, the inspectors boarded to make sure the structure could handle a live load. The car was being winched to the top of a steep incline when the clutch on a sprocket chain gave way, sending the vehicle hurtling down and into Moritz, who was thrown from the track and killed. Coincidentally, Calder played a signal role in bringing a boardwalk to Coney Island. Such an amenity—a "board sidewalk like Atlantic City's"—had been proposed for the beach as early as 1893. A Coney Island Board Walk Association, formed in 1900 by George C. Tilyou and others, tried to build the improvement privately but was opposed by property owners who refused to grant the necessary easements. Edward Marshall Grout— Brooklyn's first borough president and champion of the ill-fated Jamaica Bay port scheme—took up the issue as a way the city might reclaim a waterfront "almost entirely usurped by private parties." But he, too, was defeated by amusement operators expected to help pay for the improvement. The breakthrough came in early

1903, when Calder discovered on topographic maps a long-forgotten street created by the old town of Gravesend, just south of and parallel to Surf Avenue. He proposed that this "Atlantic Avenue" right-of-way be used to construct "a board walk along the ocean front," and to extend to it all streets "now terminating at Surf Avenue"—precisely the configuration eventually realized some twenty years later.[24]

Calder's term as Brooklyn's top building official ended in December 1903, allowing him to get back to his business of brick and mortar. Working on a huge tract on the western edge of Prospect Park, Calder ultimately erected some nine hundred homes in Windsor Terrace, described by the *Eagle* as "one of the most successful home communities in the country," and referred to as Calderville into the 1970s. Many of the homes, such as the bowfront Renaissance-revival row houses at 159–189 Windsor Place, were designed by architect Thomas Bennett, a friend of Calder's who had served as his deputy superintendent at the Department of Building. But politics kept calling. In November 1904 Calder was elected to the US Congress from the Sixth Congressional District; he served for a decade before seeking nomination to the US Senate. Defeated in his first bid, Calder succeeded in 1916, besting his Democratic opponent by 250,000 votes. Calder's senatorial term would hardly be remembered today but for a wartime bill drafted by the National Daylight Saving Association (NDSA). The idea of moving the clocks ahead in spring and back again in fall to make better use of daylight was an old one, and had already been adopted in England and Europe. Benjamin Franklin is generally credited with having first hit on the idea in 1784 while in Paris. Coordinating the workday with the sun, he reasoned, would dramatically reduce the need for artificial light. He rather wildly estimated that Parisians could save sixty-four million pounds of wax, simply "by the economy of using sunshine instead of candles"! But the United States was slow to adopt the idea and struggled even to create standardized time zones (the railroads had established a four-zone system in 1880s, but it was never officially adopted). Led by the NDSA, a national daylight saving movement gathered as the United States entered the Great War. Advocates argued that the added hours of natural light would not only reduce coal consumption, but make more time for healthful recreation and increase food production by giving home gardeners an estimated nine hundred million additional hours nationwide to weed and hoe. Calder and Representative William Borland, a Democrat from Kansas City, took up the cudgel, introducing to Congress the Calder-Borland bill. It was promptly passed by the Senate, approved by the House with amendments, and signed into law by President Woodrow Wilson on March 19 as the Standard Time Act of 1918. At two o'clock in the morning of March 31, the day the new law took effect nationwide, Brooklyn's "champion of daylight saving" was handed the honor of setting forward the big clock below the cupola of Borough Hall.[25]

Calder's timing was flawless. He was elected to the Senate just as the building sector crashed in New York, and—defeated for reelection by a homeopathic physician named Royal S. Copeland in 1922—got back to building just as Brooklyn's greatest real estate boom got under way. Moving his office to Beverley Road, he focused on the borough's newest development frontier—Flatbush and points south on long-rural outwash plain. By 1925 he had erected a phalanx of two dozen apartment

US Senate sergeant at arms Charles Higgins turns the historic Ohio Clock forward an hour for the first Daylight Saving Time, March 1918. William Calder, sponsor of time-change bill, is at left. Photograph by Harris & Ewing. Library of Congress, Prints and Photographs Division.

buildings on Nostrand Avenue at Beverley Road, all the brick row houses on adjacent East Twenty-Ninth Street, and dozens more on Brooklyn Avenue, East Thirty-Fourth, and East Thirty-Fifth streets at Cortelyou Road. Moving south with the tide, Calder snapped up fifty lots on both sides of East Nineteenth between avenues Y and Z in Sheepshead Bay, working with architect J. A. Boyle to "duplicate as near as possible the Calderville development" at Windsor Terrace. By the time the market crashed in October 1929, Calder was the most prolific builder in Brooklyn, having erected some thirty-eight hundred homes across the borough. A deep reserve of cash enabled him to keep going through the Depression—for a while. "Stocks and bonds may go up and down," he saged, "but a well built home and the soil beneath it remain to endure for generations." Calder now turned to land just west of long-delayed Marine Park: "I feel confident," he told a reporter in 1933, "that the completion of Marine Park will mean to Brooklyn what Central Park means to Manhattan."

Walking the talk, he rolled out here his most ambitious venture yet, relocating his office to 2703 Avenue U and building a colony of several hundred gable-spiked Tudor row houses—"Calder's Perfect Homes"—on blocks in and around Avenue T just west of Nostrand Avenue. Designed by Calder himself with interior appointments by his wife, Katherine Harloe Calder, they included basement apartment suites, electric iceboxes, and gas-fired automatic furnaces ("Just think of the house," he regaled, "where the heating plant is controlled by a thermostat"). The homes sported an even more seminal accessory: garages. By now, New Yorkers were falling fast for the automobile, especially in far-flung outer neighborhoods of Brooklyn and Queens beyond the reach of rapid transit and where trolleys were increasingly sluggish and overcrowded. Nationwide, passenger car registrations more than tripled between 1919 and 1929, from 6.8 million to 23 million. In Gotham, Brooklyn led the way, its busy Motor Vehicle Dealers Association holding annual motorcar shows at the Twenty-Third Regiment Armory in Crown Heights, which—as one *Eagle* wag put it—invariably triggered an outbreak of "Motorcargitis" in the borough. There were 150,687 automobiles registered in Brooklyn in 1927, highest of any borough (Manhattan had 106,723, followed by Queens with 96,799).[26]

Advertisement for William Calder's "Perfect 1-Family Brick Homes," *Brooklyn Daily Eagle*, September 1928.

Accommodating the motorcar, in a discrete way beneficial to the urbanism of the street, was the hallmark of Brooklyn's last great builder of the interwar era—Fred C. Trump, father of the contentious forty-fifth president of the United States. Born to Bavarian immigrants in an old-law tenement by the Third Avenue el, Trump—like Calder—knew he wanted to build at a young age. He worked alongside his mother, Elizabeth, to improve a handful of Queens Village building lots left by his father after his death in 1918. He learned all he could apprenticing with local carpenters, took night-school and correspondence courses in drafting and the building trades, and later studied construction management and engineering at Pratt Institute. Trump finished high school in 1923, just in time to grab the tail of the 1920s building boom. The very next year, Elizabeth was advertising homes built by her son on 212th Street in Queens Village, and by 1926 Trump had erected nineteen "beautiful English type homes" of his own design on 199th Street in nearby Hollis ("Be King and Queen in a TRUMP home," shouted his newspaper ads). He contrived a precarious method to finance construction, selling a half-built house to bankroll its completion and start the next one. Because he was not yet twenty-one years old, his mother had to sign for him at his first closing. By 1929, Trump had luxed his operation, erecting upscale stucco-and-stone Tudor homes on rolling, park-like acreage in Jamaica Estates—a setting "so like the aristocratic estates of Old England," gushed the builder in a *Herald* ad, where one could enjoy "the quiet and sturdiness of country—and yet be right in New York City."[27]

With the building industry slowed by the faltering economy, Trump was forced to cool his heels running a supermarket he opened on Jamaica Avenue in Woodhaven—one of the first in New York City (later acquired by the King Kullen chain of Long Island). But the Depression brought new opportunities and opened the door to the neighboring borough. Trump got into Brooklyn real estate by buying up the assets of a failed mortgage and title colossus known as the House of Lehrenkrauss. A German American banking and insurance conglomerate founded in 1878, the firm began trading in what were known as "certificated" mortgages during the great 1920s building boom. "To pay for the residential properties going up all over New York City," writes Trump family chronicler Gwenda Blair, "mortgage banks and title companies began to 'certificate' mortgages—that is, to divide them into shares that were then sold to the general public like so many bonds." The Lehrenkrauss certificates were popular with small investors and continued to pay a respectable return despite the Depression. Then, in early December 1933, the House of Lehrenkrauss became a house of cards. The venerable firm, it was discovered, "had been running a deficit operation for years," writes Blair, "covering expenses and salaries with a haphazard assortment of schemes that included issuing watered stock, writing up mortgages based on either inflated or nonexistent evaluations, selling mortgage certificates worth more than the mortgages they represented, and taking out bank loans against mortgages that had already been certificated." With the Depression holding down its cash flow, the House of Lehrenkrauss soon found itself underwater. To pay its furious creditors, the company's shrinking assets were put on the auction block. Trump and a partner, both outsiders from the wilds of Queens, prevailed against well-heeled, politically well-connected Brooklyn bidders to secure the mortgage-servicing department of the company, which managed a large portfolio of properties on which it held mortgages. One of the Lehrenkrauss assets now controlled by Trump was the Tudor-manse colony of Laurye Homes that Lawrence Rukeyser had begun building in Marine Park. When Rukeyser's operation went belly-up in 1932, his unfinished dwellings were acquired by the Raemore Realty Company, with mortgages guaranteed by the House of Lehrenkrauss. Raemore managed to complete and sell a handful of the homes in spring of 1932. But sales petered out by summer; and when Lehrenkrauss slipped beneath the waves in 1933, Raemore went under with it. Trump lost no time completing the half-built houses; by the end of May 1935 he had sold three properties. Thus was Brooklyn's greatest real estate empire launched at the far-flung corner of East Thirty-Third Street and Fillmore Avenue, on land farmed since the time of Cromwell and Milton.[28]

Trump next built a battery of sixty-five attached "brick bungalow" row houses on a site just north of Kings Highway at Schenectady Avenue in East Flatbush, the first of what would become a Trump staple in the years before World War II. The bungalows made for good urbanism, creating delightfully scaled streetscapes that only improved with time as street trees—nearly always London planes—reached maturity. The typical prewar Trump row house sported a roofline punctuated by gables, black steel-frame casement windows with an occasional pane of leaded glass, a small porch, and "a beach-towel-size swatch of front lawn" raised just enough above the ground-plane to inhibit casual trespass.[29] And, in a departure from the design of the cheaper Realty Associates homes, Trump wisely relegated cars to a common alley behind the dwellings. This not only contributed to the architectural unity of the street, but made on-street parking more plentiful by eliminating that bane of the outer boroughs—driveway curb cuts and the inevitable conversion of front lawns into parking pads. In April 1936 Trump purchased a large parcel from Realty Associates at Cortelyou Road and Albany Avenue, campsite of the Ringling Bros. and Barnum & Bailey Circus that spring. By the Fourth of July, he had four hundred men digging foundations where elephants and camels had trod just months before, and soon erected the first batch of 450 brick bungalows. What sped this and subsequent Trump projects along was a stimulus program initiated by President Franklin D. Roosevelt's new Federal Housing Administration to jump-start the housing sector. In June 1934 Congress passed the National Housing Act, Title II of which authorized the federal government to serve as guarantor of last resort to banks making mortgage loans, thereby assuming much of the risk in a volatile real estate market. Banks could now lend up to 80 percent of the value of a property, up to a limit of $12,800, while the interest rate could not exceed 5 percent. With Uncle Sam thus watching their backs, bankers could "turn on the fiscal spigots, and construction could resume." To assure that it was not backing junk, the FHA issued the first nationwide standards for appraising real estate and assessing the creditworthiness of borrowers, as well as strict guidelines for building design and construction. "Because many areas lacked building codes," writes Blair, "the FHA put together its own minimal standards for key elements like indoor plumbing, fire protection, sewage disposal, lot size and subdivision planning." Trump soon mastered these standards, winning favor with the FHA state director for New York, a Bay Ridge lawyer and Democratic machine operative named Thomas Grace. Impressed by the young man and his plans—and by Trump's expanding network of political friends—Grace authorized $750,000 in mortgage insurance for the circus-ground venture, enabling Trump to take out the huge construction loans necessary to erect the 450 homes.[30]

Thus sheltered under the FHA's big tent, Trump followed the circus—literally. In May 1937 he began erecting a colony of 400 homes at Clarendon and Ralph avenues, with a crew of 350 men working day and night with the aid of floodlights. A year later he had another venture under way closer to Kings Highway, adding 300 more homes to his portfolio. By the spring of 1939, Trump had sold some 700 houses in Flatlands; he was just thirty-four years old. He now set his sights on a large parcel of vacant land near the junction of Utica, Remsen, and East New York avenues in Brownsville. This land, too, had been used—in 1938 and 1939—for the Ringling Bros. and Barnum & Bailey Circus. Here Trump rolled out his largest FHA-backed venture yet, speedily erecting 400 homes. By now he was using principles of mass production similar to those that Greve had pioneered a decade earlier at Gerritsen Beach, earning him the sobriquet "the Henry Ford of housing." By 1940, Fred Trump was the biggest builder in Brooklyn. He erected another 300 homes on East Thirty-Ninth Street and Foster Avenue by Paerdegat Park in East Flatbush, then turned south to Brighton Beach, where he built 200 deluxe dwellings at Corbin Place and Neptune Avenue—this time without FHA backing. And Trump was as ingenious at marketing his homes as he was in constructing and financing them. He set up an elaborate billboard at the 1939 New York World's Fair, seen by hundreds of thousands of visitors, and even took to the sea to sell his wares—in a sixty-five-foot cabin cruiser with

Brick-bungalow row houses by Fred C. Trump, Fillmore Avenue, Marine Park. Photograph by author.

TRUMP HOMES spelled out in ten-foot-tall letters on twin hoardings. The Trump Show Boat first worked the thronged Coney Island strand on July 8, 1939. With the city in the midst of a heat wave, beaches were packed. As the captain drew near the surf, loudspeakers came alive with music, and crewmen began tossing hundreds of inflatable swordfish into the water. Each was stamped with TRUMP HOMES and a figure, from $25 to $250, indicating its value toward a down payment. Like a riot of gulls trailing a laden trawler, swimmers raced into the ship's wake for the bobbing fish. The music was so loud it could be heard a mile off. Hundreds stood at attention when "The Star-Spangled Banner" played; others rushed to the water when the boat began broadcasting "lessons in 'aquacading' or graceful swimming to music." Not everyone was pleased—park commissioner Robert Moses, for example. A hater of carnies, hawkers, and shrills, Moses had a police boat stop the craft and issue the captain tickets for operating in a bathing area, advertising without a license, and violating noise ordinances. Trump suggested Moses join him on board. The Show Boat was back out the next day, cruising the beach while Trump and his buddies fished from the stern—their ears presumably plugged. "Twenty fluke, porgies and weakfish were caught, all while the music was playing," Trump exulted; "When the music stopped playing the fish stopped biting." Moses and Trump played a water-borne game of cat and mouse all that summer and the next, the TRUMP HOMES message reaching countless New Yorkers in the process. At a hearing in September 1940, Judge Jeanette Goodman Brill—first female magistrate in Brooklyn—issued Trump a perfunctory fine before inquiring, sotto voce, whether he still had homes for sale in Flatbush.[31]

"Going South! Wish I could afford to." This 1938 Williamsburgh Savings Bank advertisement refers not to the American South, but to the booming streetcar suburbs of Flatbush and Flatlands. From *Brooklyn Daily Eagle*, February 7, 1938.

Fred Trump went on to erect more than two thousand homes in Brooklyn be-tween 1935 and 1942. Like Greve, Calder, and the long-forgotten scores of small builders before him, Trump helped weave much of the fabric of outer-borough New York City, creating a vast tapestry of bedroom communities far from the centers of commerce and industry. Here were the homes of the great multitude that flocked to Brooklyn all through the interwar years. The decade between 1920 and 1930, the very years of the tax holiday legislation, was the most rapid period of growth in Brooklyn history. The borough's population soared by 577,598 people in those years—more than Washington, New Orleans, or Kansas City at the time. As with Levittown a generation later, the cognoscenti had great fun mocking the mock-Tudor home-scapes of Brooklyn and Queens. George Bowling—protagonist in George Orwell's *Coming Up for Air* (1939)—could well have been returning to once-rural Flatlands when he cringed at the "houses, houses everywhere, little raw red houses . . . semi-detached torture-chambers where the poor little five-to-ten pound-a-weekers quake and shiver . . . with the boss twisting his tail and the wife riding him like the nightmare and the kids sucking his blood like leeches." Critics rightly questioned the suitability of an Old World style like the Tudor for an age of airplanes and penicillin. As Russell Whitehead put it, the Tudor was just "a delicious piece of stage scenery," no different from "the peasant village Marie Antoinette caused to be erected in the Trianon Gar-dens." Lewis Mumford fretted that whenever "a sophisticated age attempts to repro-duce the forms of a simple one . . . the result is bound to be ephemeral." But Mumford was wrong; if anything the Tudorvilles of outwash Brooklyn have endured, still af-fordable and remarkably resistant to all but the most egregious lapses of homeowner taste: stainless-steel railings in place of wrought iron; peach-pink stucco slapped atop perfectly good brick; corrugated awnings from the 1970s, now blackened with mold; black-steel casement windows torn out for cheap double-hung, double-paned vinyl replacements. However inept, these are yet marks of a place suffused with the funk and pulse of life unmediated by the pieties of Historical Significance, far from the Midas of gentrification, undiscovered by the merchants of twee.[32]

The most piercing account of outwash Brooklyn was penned the same year as Orwell's *Coming Up for Air* by brilliant, doomed James Agee, the Tennessee-born, Harvard-dipped wordsmith alcoholic who famously expired in a taxicab on the an-niversary of his father's death forty years earlier. In 1939, Agee was commissioned by *Fortune* to write an article about Brooklyn for a special issue of the magazine on New York City. But the essay he delivered to his editor, "Southeast of the Island: Travel Notes," was deemed "too strong to print" and remained unpublished for nearly thirty years. Agee spent two months at 179 St. James Place in Clinton Hill writing the piece, a smugly merciless portrayal of life and culture in the trolleyburbs of deep-south Brooklyn. No Whitmanic paean to the brotherhood of man, Agee's essay begins by Othering the Brooklynite, as if crossing the East River put him in a foreign land. Here, "in the trolleys, or along the inexhaustible reduplications of the streets of their small tradings and their sleep," wrote Agee, "one comes to notice . . . a curious quality in the eyes and at the corners of the mouths, relative to what is seen on Manhattan Island: a kind of drugged softness or narcotic relax-ation." It was the same look seen in shell-shocked soldiers or "in monasteries and in the lawns of sanitariums." Each action, each building seemed there bound by "a deep taproot of stasis." Brooklyn's storied provincialism—its "absorption in home, the casualness of the measuredly undistinguished . . . is profoundly domesticated, docile and 'stable' a population as one could conceive of, outside England"—was a function of its fateful proximity to Manhattan, whose "mad magnetic energy" sucks the borough of "most of what a city's vital organs are." Brooklyn was thus like no other American city; for "though it has perhaps a 'center,' and hands, and eyes, and feet, it is chiefly no whole or recognizable animal but an exorbitant pulsing mass of scarcely discriminable cellular jellies and tissues; a place where people merely 'live.'" Into the somnolent mass ventured the sanctimonious scribe:

One of Philip Freshmen's "English Tudor Homes" on East Thirty-Third Street. Photograph by author.

> I leave the trolley and walk up a residential street: I have not gone a block before I recognize a silence so powerful and so specialized it has almost a fragrance of its own: it is the silence of having left a street of the open world and of having entered an empty church . . . and there is in the silence an almost Brahmin tranquility, weakening to the senses, and a subtly terrifying quality of suffocation and of the sacrosanct: and in a moment more, standing between these rows of neat homes, I know what this special sanctitude is: that this world is totally dedicated to tame marriages in their first ten years of youth, and that during the sweep of each working day these streets are yielded over to housewives and to young children and infants so entirely, that those who stroll these walks and sit in the sun are cloistral nuns, vestals, made fecund though they are, and govern a world in which returning men are made womanly in an odor of cherished floors, clean cloths, nationally advertised cosmetics, and the sharp stench of babies.

But more than anything it was the sheer scale of Brooklyn that awed Agee, with "continuities so astronomically vast as Paris alone or the suburbs south of Chicago could match." From his morainal perch, the writer peered down upon "a vista of low buildings and side streets of glanded living sufficient to paralyze all conjecture." There seemed, then as now, "simply, far as the eye can strain, no end of Brooklyn," rolling south and forever to the sea-lapped shore.[33]

CHAPTER 14
FIELD OF SCHEMES

. . . as much the pride of Brooklyn as the Piazza San Marco is the pride
of Venice and the Place de la Concorde is the cynosure of Paris.
—**ROBERT MOSES**

Had Rip Van Winkle slept a couple of centuries longer and awakened in Brooklyn
circa 1945, he might well have declared it the mightiest city in the land. Brooklyn
reached its apogee of power and population during World War II and its immediate
aftermath. The war itself was arguably Brooklyn's finest hour. No place in America
contributed more blood, sweat, and toil to defeating the Axis powers—nor more
lives. Some 325,000 Brooklyn men and women served in the armed forces during the
war, 11,500 of whom died; tens of thousands more labored in the borough's booming
defense industry, churning out everything from helmets, searchlights, and bombsights to battleships and ingredients for the atomic bomb (Brazilian monazite sand,
a rare-earth ore, was processed in Bushwick for the Manhattan Project). Brooklyn
was the largest war-staging base in the United States. From the New York Port of
Embarkation, headquartered at the Brooklyn Army Terminal, fully half the troops
that fought in the war sailed overseas—three million in all. A third of all material
and equipment used to defeat the enemy was also directed abroad from there, thirty
million tons out of New York Harbor alone.[1]

Floyd Bennett Field also joined the fight, and long before the United States
formally entered the war. Between January and November 1939, a huge fleet of
Lockheed-Hudson patrol bombers for the Royal Air Force was flown from California to the airfield, where the airplanes—250 in all—were disassembled and crated
for shipment to the British Isles. Flying boats from the base patrolled the coast for
German U-boats, guarding merchant ships and convoys steaming for Great Britain
under the Lend-Lease Program. So vital was the Brooklyn field to keeping Germany

at bay that Nazi agents set up a secret surveillance outpost just a stone's throw from its runways shortly after the British bomber shipments began. From a fishing shack on Gerritsen Creek equipped with powerful binoculars and a shortwave transmitter, agents of the massive Duquesne spy ring kept close tabs on operations at the base. The espionage ring, the largest ever caught on American soil, was broken in June 1941, but not before the spies (thirty-three in all) had spirited off classified plans from Brooklyn's own Sperry Gyroscope Company and—more damaging still—from the Norden Company, whose bombsight was among the most closely guarded military secrets of the war. The same month as the spy ring bust, Floyd Bennett Field was formally acquired by the navy and renamed Naval Air Station–New York. The failed city airport was soon the busiest airfield in America, serving all through the war as a certification and overhaul facility for aircraft, and handling hundreds of transcontinental delivery flights each month as headquarters of the Naval Air Ferry Command and the eastern terminus of the Military Air Transport Service. More than sixty-five hundred personnel were based at Floyd Bennett at the height of the conflict. All told, some forty-six thousand warplanes were tested, certified, and readied for battle in Brooklyn during the war. Among these were a trio of aircraft most credited for the Allied victory in the Pacific air war—Grumman's Long Island–made Avenger torpedo bomber and Hellcat fighter, which outdid the Mitsubishi Zero in speed and agility; and the muscular, gull-winged guardian angel of the Marine Corps grunt, the Connecticut-made Chance-Vought F4U Corsair.[2]

US Coast Guard Sikorsky HNS-1 at Floyd Bennett Field, c. 1949. Rudy Arnold Photo Collection, Archives Division, National Air and Space Museum.

The airfield also trained men and women to fly all these airplanes. In the summer of 1940, students from a dozen colleges and universities in the region—women from Adelphi; men from Brooklyn Polytechnic and Pratt institutes, Brooklyn College, Fordham, Columbia, and New York University—began enrolling in a Civil Aeronautics Authority pilot-training program at the field. Before long, Floyd Bennett was the busiest flight training center on the Eastern Seaboard. When entry requirements were lowered that December to meet soaring demand for aviators, more than a thousand aspiring fliers showed up for testing. By April 1941 some six hundred pilots had already earned their wings at the old airport. The field also became the first helicopter training facility in the world, schooling not only Americans but the first whirlybird pilots in the British army, Royal Air Force, and Royal Navy. So grateful was the crown for its new wings that instructor Frank A. Erickson, a coast guard captain, was granted an honorary knighthood by King George VI. Erikson himself made a number of breakthroughs at the Brooklyn airfield. He was the first to outfit a helicopter for medevac use, to demonstrate that a cable hoist could be effective in air-sea rescue, and—in September 1944—the first to pluck a man by helicopter from a life raft (floating in Jamaica Bay).[3]

These flying credentials were impressive, but they were nothing next to the firepower and muscle Brooklyn unleashed on the seven seas. Opened in 1801, the New York Naval Shipyard on Wallabout Bay—the Brooklyn Navy Yard—had been laying keels since 1817 and launched some of the most fabled ships in American history. The list is long and impressive: the sloop *Vincennes* (1826), first navy vessel to circumnavigate the globe; the *Lexington* (1826), which accompanied Matthew C. Perry

Brooklyn Navy Yard, 1918. US Naval History and Heritage Command.

on his 1854 Japanese expedition; the steam frigate *Niagara* (1853) that laid the first transatlantic cable; the armored cruiser *Maine* (1890) that sank with most of its crew after a mysterious explosion in Havana Harbor, an incident that—blown out of proportion by the press—helped ignite the Spanish-American War; and the battleship *Arizona* (1915), destroyed by a Japanese torpedo at Pearl Harbor, killing more than a thousand crewmen and precipitating America's entry into World War II. The loss of the *Maine* was tragic enough, but the gloves came off in Brooklyn with the sinking of the *Arizona*. Shipbuilding at the yard was already in high gear, where soaring demand for labor opened shop doors for the first time to women in 1942 (twenty thousand applied for the first two hundred jobs). With several hundred buildings and thirty miles of railroad track, the Navy Yard had long been Gotham's largest industrial plant; now it was also its greatest war machine. A city unto itself, its labor force rose to seventy thousand employees in twenty-seven trades and professions. They worked like demons, churning out an astonishing seventeen vessels between 1940 and 1945. These were no little boats but some of the most powerful warships ever built, including five aircraft carriers—the *Bennington, Yorktown, Franklin D. Roosevelt, Kearsarge,* and *Oriskany*—and three immense battleships: the *North Carolina*; the *Iowa* (launched seven months ahead of schedule); and the *Missouri*, last and largest battleship commissioned by the US Navy. It was on this vessel that Japan surrendered on September 2, 1945—poetic closure of a sort: World War II began with the sinking of a Brooklyn ship; it ended on another's deck.[4]

USS *Arizona* on the East River, 1918. Photograph by Robert Enrique Muller. Library of Congress, Prints and Photographs Division.

In the months after V-J Day, Brooklyn was a city in the full flush of life renewed. It was a tough and scrappy town, still the butt of jokes, though mockery of the borough's thick patois and immigrant ways was done a bit more cautiously now—rarely to the face of this polyglot place that had just helped save the world from fascism. And Brooklynites played as hard as they fought and worked. All through the war years, Coney Island was thronged by the largest crowds in its history—despite having its lights dimmed purple and blue to keep German U-boats from silhouetting ships against a glowing skyline. Soldiers and sailors on shore leave spent freely at the beach seeking respite from the war. They came for the girls and the games of chance, and for a thrilling new ride with military roots of its own. In the fall of 1940 George C. Tilyou's eldest son and heir, Edward, brought to Steeplechase Park what would be its most celebrated ride since the namesake horse coaster—a 250-foot-tall, "parachute drop." It was designed by a retired naval air commander, James H. Strong, who had seen primitive timber jump towers in Russia in the 1920s. In 1936 he developed a taller, steel-frame structure with patented safety mechanisms for the US Army, which continues to operate two similar towers at Fort Benning, Georgia. In 1939 Strong created a curvaceous civilian version for the Life Savers Candy Company exhibit at the New York World's Fair. Its twelve twin-seat chairs were winched by motor to the top of the 170-ton tower and released by a "spider" mechanism to free-fall some twenty feet before being slowed in their descent by an opening parachute—itself secured by an array of guide cables. Though there was never a serious accident on the parachute jump, the ride was sensitive to wind and rain, required constant maintenance, and needed several strapping men to handle each chute. A money loser from the start, the jump nonetheless fixed Coney Island on the New York skyline and gave Brooklyn an icon as cherished and enduring as the Eiffel Tower.

The largest crowd to ever descend upon Coney Island's beaches came on the Fourth of July 1955, the zenith of an unforgettable Brooklyn summer. The Brooklyn Dodgers were in Philadelphia that day, giving the Phillies a drubbing in a double-header. The team had brought home the National League pennant five times since 1941 but failed to win a single World Series championship. In each one of their previous division victories—1941, 1947, 1949, 1952, and 1953—the Dodgers were defeated by their perennial crosstown nemeses, the New York Yankees. But this time things were different. Powered by the pitching arms of Don Newcombe and Carl Erskine and the bats of Duke Snider, Carl Furillo, and Roy Campanella (a Most Valuable Player that year), the Dodgers muscled their way to the National League pennant, ending the season thirteen victories ahead of the Milwaukee Braves. On September 28, they once again met their old rivals at Yankee Stadium. Bronx won that day, despite a stunning home-plate steal by Jackie Robinson. But Lady Luck stuck by Brooklyn's side and soon the series was tied at three games apiece. In Game 7 on October 4, Johnny Podres quieted both Yankee bats and Yankee fans with a 2–0 shutout victory. It was the first and only World Series the Brooklyn Dodgers would ever win.[5]

But even as Brooklyn shouted its home team to victory, winds of trouble and change were in the air. The borough's titanic industrial sector was already beginning

Aerial view of Coney Island looking west, April 1930, with Steeplechase Park and pier at center. Photograph by Fairchild Aerial Surveys, Inc. Collection of the author.

to falter, as companies struggled with cramped facilities, worsening traffic conges-tion, rising taxes, escalating utility costs, and infrastructure worn to the bone. Brook-lyn's once-dazzling port facilities were effectively obsolete by 1945, hobbled more than ever by that perennial problem of rail connectivity to mainland America. Its antiquated docks could not berth the increasingly large vessels of the postwar era, and the port was wholly unable to handle containerized shipping—an especially painful irony given that intermodal containerization, as we saw in chapter 9, was first pro-posed in the United States as part of the ill-fated Great Port of Jamaica Bay scheme. Now John Henry Ward's brilliant, neglected idea came back to haunt the very place that inspired it. The end of the war also brought a tsunami of labor trouble. Pressed by the National War Labor Board, America's unions had pledged against striking for the duration of the war (though there were numerous wildcat strikes). With the end of hostilities, however, the gloves came off. Four years of deferred demands by the rank and file, salted by soaring postwar inflation, precipitated a series of crippling union walkouts from coast to coast in 1946. In just the first six months of the year, nearly three million US workers took part in strikes; the Bureau of Labor Statistics called it "the most concentrated period of labor-management strife in the country's history." By year's end, 10 percent of the nation's workforce—4.6 million people—had struck.[6]

In New York, a quarter of a million workers walked off their jobs citywide in 1946 alone. Striking longshoremen paralyzed the docks; communications workers silenced telegraphy for a week; twelve thousand striking Teamsters choked off the flow of goods; even house painters struck, with ten thousand of them laying down their brushes. The most devastating action that year came from an unlikely corner—tugboat operators, thirty-five hundred of whom walked off the job in February. Just how vital these men and their boats were to daily life quickly became evident: Gotham was brought shivering to its knees within days. Schools, factories, libraries, museums, restaurants, and theaters were all ordered closed to save dwindling supplies of coal and heating oil. Sympathy for the men evaporated as the mercury fell. The *New York Times* called the tugboat stoppage "the most drastic disruption in the city's life since the Civil War draft riots," blaming the strikers for "eighteen hours of unparalleled confusion and staggering economic losses." To many, the great postwar strike wave represented a heroic victory for New York City's manual laborers, the men and women whose hands literally helped win the war. "Culturally, socially, and politically, blue-collar workers loomed larger at the end of World War II than at any time before or since," writes historian Joshua B. Freeman, and the "size, strategic importance, and demonstrated power of the working class allowed it to play a major role in determining what kind of city New York would become in the postwar era." What they and union leaders failed to anticipate was the increasing mobility of capital in the postwar era—the growing ability for industry and manufacturing to simply pull up stakes and leave what was becoming a very costly, very complicated town to run a business in. The increasingly contentious, often ugly clashes between labor and management were not the only cause of industry's exodus from Brooklyn after World War II, but for many firms it was an especially compelling one.[7]

One by one, Brooklyn's cornerstone industries began leaving for places with more modern infrastructure, more space, lower taxes, and less militant unions—or no unions at all. At first they went elsewhere in the metropolitan region, then to states where land was dirt cheap and labor unorganized—Virginia, North Carolina, Mississippi, Nevada. Many firms would eventually leave American shores altogether. Others simply shut down, such as the famed Continental Ironworks of Greenpoint, builders of the Civil War ironclad *Monitor*—archrival of the *Merrimack* and hero of the Battle of Hampton Roads. Sperry Gyroscope was one of the first "runaway shops," vacating its Flatbush Avenue headquarters for Nassau County immediately after the war. In 1947 the E. W. Bliss Company—a tool and die works and developer of the first self-propelled torpedo—moved its operations to New Jersey and the Midwest after ninety years in Brooklyn. American Safety Razor, a leading maker of shaving products, departed for Virginia in 1954 after repeated strikes by the United Electrical Workers. Drug giant Squibb pulled up stakes for New Jersey two years later, after a century in Brooklyn. The company was founded in 1858 by Edward Robinson Squibb, a naval ship's surgeon who ran a medical supply depot at the Brooklyn Navy Yard. His first laboratory was on Furman Street, by today's Brooklyn Bridge Park (and just below Squibb Playground at the foot of Middagh Street). Close on Squibb's heels was another giant of industrial Brooklyn—Mergenthaler Linotype, manufacturer of typesetting equipment that revolutionized the printing industry in the 1890s. After seventy-five years and a 114-day strike at its Ryerson Street complex, the company left Brooklyn for Long Island. Labor unrest at the borough's many breweries—a legacy of Brooklyn's once-huge German population—opened

Striking truck drivers prepare to deliver the goods after reaching an accord with the George Ehret Brewery, 1948. The company closed a year later, one of scores of Gotham breweries driven out of business by labor disputes after World War II. Brooklyn Public Library, Brooklyn Collection.

the doors to fatal competition from beyond the Hudson. A citywide walkout of seven thousand brewery workers in 1949, launched at the Rheingold plant in Brooklyn, created a suds gap that was obligingly filled by Anheuser-Busch. Three Brooklyn breweries closed as a result of the walkout; the rest soon followed. Brooklyn had forty-five breweries at the turn of the century, and even after Prohibition shuttered most of these, the borough was still producing 10 percent of all beer in America. By the mid-1970s there wasn't a single brewery left in Brooklyn.[8]

If the dying industrial sector sapped Brooklyn's muscle and wealth, the closure of its beloved newspaper—the *Brooklyn Eagle*—stilled its voice and broke its spirit. Founded in 1841, the *Eagle* had been published without a break for 114 years and was one of New York's oldest and most storied institutions. One of its early editors was none other than Walt Whitman. But the postwar years had been brutal. Circulation was falling, and by 1954 the paper was running in the red. Publisher Frank D. Schroth had nearly sold the entire operation to the *Herald Tribune* the year before, but the deal was dropped owing to fierce union resistance. Schroth fought a pitched battle with his large editorial and office staff—writers, reporters, copyeditors, advertising and circulation managers—who wanted higher wages and more benefits. Then, at midnight on Friday, January 28, 1955, the Newspaper Guild of New York called a strike. Though it was called on behalf of the paper's 315 white-collar employees, the shop floor struck in sympathy; photo engravers, typesetters, press operators, and other "craft union" members all stayed home, making it impossible to publish even a skeleton edition. The strike dragged on all of January and February. By March it was clear the *Eagle* would never fly again. The end came on March 16, when a bitter Schroth declared that he was closing the *Eagle* permanently. He slammed the striking workers and their "malignant" guild for having "silenced forever" the *Eagle* by insisting on wages equal to those at Manhattan's big dailies. The paper's end dealt a stunning blow to Brooklyn. More than 650 people lost their jobs. The *Times* called the *Eagle*'s demise "a civic disaster"; to borough president John Cashmore it was "unthinkable" and a "great misfortune." Brooklyn was now the largest community in America without a paper of its own, "doomed," Schroth lamented, "to be cast in Manhattan's shadow." When the Dodgers beat the Yankees that fall, it was—horror of horrors—the Manhattan press that got to tell the world of sporting Brooklyn's finest hour.[9]

Even if postwar relations between labor and management had been sweetness and light, there were many other daunting problems confronting Brooklyn's industrialists. One of the most vexing was space. Downtown Brooklyn and its industrial zone west of the Navy Yard (today's Dumbo) was overbuilt and terribly congested. The utility infrastructure, much of it dating from before the Civil War, could hardly keep pace with the needs of modern industry. State-of-the-art aircraft instruments were being made on streets paved in the age of clipper ships. What manufacturers needed in the booming postwar era was plenty of flexible space in which to grow—ideally all on the same floor—with ample water and sewer service and an electric grid robust enough to deliver the heavy amperes needed for big machines. Downtown Brooklyn could hardly meet any of these. Neither could it provide easy access to the nation's road and rail networks, a problem that—as we have seen—had long been a thorn in Brooklyn's industrial side. The problem was hardly limited to Brooklyn. There were some thirty-seven thousand manufacturing firms in New York City at the end of the war, mostly small, with just twenty-five workers on average, but together employing close to a million workers—"more manufacturing jobs," writes Freeman, "than Philadelphia, Detroit, Los Angeles, and Boston put together." Just ten years later, forty-two thousand of those jobs were gone. Gotham's industrial age was over; but all was not doom and gloom, for a new service economy was rising. Even as manufacturers closed down, the city gained twenty-eight thousand jobs in banking, law, real estate, and insurance between 1947 and 1955 alone. And while industrial-sector jobs "dropped by 49 percent between 1950 and 1975," writes Suleiman Osman, "employment in finance, insurance, and real estate increased by 25 percent, in services by 52 percent, and in government by 53 percent."[10]

Gotham's age of smokestacks may have been ending, but City Hall did much to hasten its industrial sector to the exit door. Labor strife and lack of space were vexing issues for American Safety Razor, but the straw that broke the company—and sent it packing to Virginia—came in the form of city plans to condemn its vast complex of buildings on Jay and Lawrence streets for an urban renewal project. That fourteen thousand employees—85 percent of them women—lost their jobs when the company left town was particularly egregious given that the city later changed its plans and spared the buildings (they were subsequently occupied by Brooklyn

Polytechnic Institute). It was a drama that played out all over New York as the juggernaut of urban renewal gathered steam. In their efforts to fortify and renew New York, postwar planners helped push out the very businesses New Yorkers needed to stay employed and out of poverty. Urban renewal cleared out urban jobs as rapidly as it did urban blight. As Joel Schwartz revealed in *The New York Approach*, projects on both sides of the East River caused the elimination of some 17,900 jobs by 1955, nearly half of which were in downtown Brooklyn alone, lost to the same urban renewal project that pushed American Safety Razor out. Given the manifold challenges of the postwar period, the very last thing firms needed was the threat of eviction by a city that should have treasured their presence. With so tenuous a foothold, mere rumors could send a firm over the edge. "Once forced to move," writes Freeman, "many companies left the city entirely," while others, "fearing inclusion in a future redevelopment site, refrained from expanding or modernizing their buildings."[11]

For all its good intentions, urban renewal did what the Axis enemy failed to do during the war—pulverize American cities. With the help of the federal government, urban renewal cleared some fifty-seven thousand acres of land nationwide by 1966, displacing more than 300,000 families. It was made possible in large part by Title I of the 1949 Housing Act, which provided vast sums of federal aid to help municipalities eliminate blighted neighborhoods and free valuable center-city land for upscale residential and commercial redevelopment. The objective "was not to wipe out the slums in order to build decent housing and pleasant neighborhoods for low-income families," writes Robert Fogelson; "Rather it was to curb decentralization—to induce the well-to-do to move back to the center by turning slums and blighted areas into attractive residential communities—and, by so doing, to revitalize the central business district to ease the cities' fiscal plight."[12] Redevelopment authorities were formed to carry out this work, armed with broad powers to condemn land and sell or lease it to developers at below-market value (the federal government would pay up to two-thirds of land-clearing costs). Urban blight, the putative enemy, proved conveniently elastic in meaning. The widely used appraisal standards from the American Public Health Association defined blight as a matter of not only substandard buildings but "neighborhood deficiencies, including high population and building density, extensive non-residential land use, inadequate educational and recreational facilities, dangerous traffic, and unsanitary conditions."[13] That effectively described Brooklyn's oldest, poorest, most congested wards—everything from Brooklyn Bridge south to Borough Hall and west to the Navy Yard.

This aging quarter of Gotham sat squarely in the bombsights of that Lord Shiva of urban landscape, Robert Moses. Moses exploited Title I as effortlessly as he had the various New Deal programs to assemble the largest portfolio of urban renewal projects in the United States. "Between 1949 and 1961," writes Sandy Zipp in *Manhattan Projects*, "New York City alone accounted for 32 percent of all construction activity under the federal law." No city would suffer more in the name of urban renewal than New York, and nowhere was the devastation greater than Brooklyn. There, as we will see, Moses carried out the largest, most complex and costliest urban redevelopment program in city history. But Title I was only part of the picture in this frayed and aging part of town. From 1945 to 1965, the vast swath of urban ground south and east of the Brooklyn Bridge endured an unprecedented campaign of metropolitan modernization. Hundreds of structures were blown away to make room for new parks, courthouses, and a variety of civic and institutional buildings. A major arterial, the Brooklyn-Queens Expressway, was punched through the district, hooked up to the Brooklyn and Manhattan bridges with sprawling coils of access ramps. The benighted Sands Street community just west of the Navy Yard was rubbed out to make way for the Farragut Houses, while twenty-two blocks to its south were razed for the Fort Greene Houses—the largest public housing complex ever built in the United States (subject of chapter 15). "No other part of New York," marveled the *Times* in 1955, "has undergone as much outward change since World War II as the area spreading south and east of the Brooklyn Bridge."[14]

Much of this urban upgrading had been schemed, dreamed, and fantasized about decades before Moses came on the scene. Creating a formal open space at the foot of the Brooklyn Bridge—a kind of majestic foyer to Brooklyn—was a perennial subject of debate. Even before the span was completed, calls were made for "a sort of plaza" at Washington and Sands streets, and to extend Flatbush Avenue north from Fulton Street to create a visual axis between Grand Army Plaza and the bridge towers—a grand gesture of linkage straight out of Haussmann's Paris playbook. By 1895, the Brooklyn end of Roebling's bridge was pure chaos—a helter-skelter jumble of tracks and catenary dominated by the looming hulk of the Sands Street depot—a colossal elevated structure, nearly four hundred feet long, that was meant to be temporary but endured for half a century. The depot brought together a Medusan tangle of rapid transit and streetcar lines—several leading over the bridge to Manhattan. With outrigger support columns resembling the legs of a great arachnid, the els extending out from the depot were collectively known as "Brooklyn's Black Spider." There were moral hazards, too, with no fewer than forty saloons within a short walk of the bridge. All told it was "horribile dictu," remarked Brooklyn columnist Cromwell Childe; "If you want to get a New Yorker to invest in Brooklyn real estate," he suggested, "the best method is to blindfold him until you have reached several blocks past the City Hall." Improvement plots came and went like the robins of spring. The delightfully named Tree Planting and Fountain Society of Brooklyn advanced an "ingenious scheme" by Albert E. Parfitt in 1895 to beautify the Brooklyn end of the bridge, promising "a very park like prospect." Not long after, Whitney Warren, one of the architects of Grand Central Terminal, proposed a great circular plaza (discussed in chapter 10) to receive both the Brooklyn and Manhattan bridge ramps and distribute traffic to all points of town via a plexus of radiating avenues. With an obelisk anchoring its center, his Brooklyn-baroque piazza would have pleased Sixtus V, the planner-pope of sixteenth-century Rome.[15]

After 1900, pressure mounted from real estate, business, and civic groups to rid downtown of its unsightly mat of elevated tracks. These groups were well represented in the leadership of the Brooklyn Beautiful movement, which made creating "a proper and dignified entrance" to the borough a priority. One of the first things Daniel Burnham recommended on his 1911 visit with the Brooklyn Committee on City Plan was eliminating the Sands Street train depot to open

The Piazza del Popolo in Brooklyn: Whitney Warren's 1905 plan for an obelisk-anchored baroque plaza with avenues leading to the Brooklyn and Manhattan bridges. New York City Municipal Archives.

Brooklyn Terminal of the Brooklyn Bridge, 1903. Detroit Publishing Company Photographic Collection, Library of Congress, Prints and Photographs Division.

views to the East River bridges. The movement's guiding light—preacher-planner Newell Dwight Hillis—urged city bridge commissioner Arthur J. O'Keeffe to help make this happen. "We have a good deal of pride in our borough," he professed, "but we have been going into Brooklyn through the back door and the kitchen for a great many years." A blue-ribbon commission headed by Frederic B. Pratt in 1913 echoed the sentiment, pressing that "no city can hope to improve and brighten itself and still neglect its front door." O'Keeffe's successor, Frederick J. H. Kracke, committed himself to embellishing that front door, presenting plans to Mayor John Purroy Mitchel for not just a plaza at the bridge terminus but a municipal center in full-blown City Beautiful mode—itself an idea batted around for years. In truth, little could be done until downtown Brooklyn's elevated transit lines were replaced with subways, a process that began in earnest with signing of the Dual Contracts of 1913.[16]

Negotiated by zoning pioneer and Brooklyn Committee executive Edward Murray Bassett, the Dual Contracts vastly expanded subway service throughout the city, establishing the system we know today and giving Gotham a new set of acronyms—IRT, BRT, BMT. As part of the deal, Brooklyn was connected to Manhattan by three new rapid transit tunnels under the East River—infrastructure that made rail service over the Brooklyn Bridge superfluous, thus allowing for removal of the much-loathed Sands Street terminal. But it took another twenty years and the

G. W. Peters, "The New Terminal in Brooklyn of the New York and Brooklyn Bridge." From *Harper's Weekly*, June 15, 1895.

fusion administration of Fiorello La Guardia to bring all this about. Within weeks of his inauguration, La Guardia began negotiating with the BMT to remove the terminal and Fulton Street el, collaborating with newly elected borough president Raymond V. Ingersoll to jump-start the long-stalled bridge plaza. Frederick Kracke, now commissioner of plant and structures, was asked to dust off his 1914 plans. On June 14, 1935, the Board of Estimate voted unanimously in favor of the project. Help came, oddly enough, by way of far-off Bergen Beach, where fraudulent condemnations for the Jamaica Bay port project—the result of "collusive activities by former city officials," including Mayor Jimmy Walker—had cost the city $3.2 million in excess awards. Recovered, the funds "saved in Brooklyn," announced La Guardia, "should be spent in Brooklyn." The money enabled the city to acquire a ten-square-block area between the bridge ramp and Borough Hall. Demolition began within weeks, and by early 1936 the site was cleared of everything but the elevated station and tracks. That August, park commissioner Moses sent a force of two hundred WPA workers to transform the site with lawn, gardens, and shade trees. The first public event planned for the new space was a "community sing" on New Year's Eve 1936, with an appearance by Metropolitan Opera soprano Martha Atwood and song lyrics projected on a Washington Street building façade. Two years later the vast plaza was officially named after the late Brooklyn Heights minister and social reformer S. Parkes Cadman. The honor very nearly went to Brooklyn's famous, flawed abolitionist minister Henry Ward Beecher.[17]

Though the Sands Street depot still loomed heavily over the space, its days were numbered. Demolition of the Fulton Street el, which ran along the plaza's west side, commenced on June 17, 1941, with Mayor La Guardia personally making the first cut

Demolition of BMT Fulton Street elevated at Lafayette Avenue, c. 1940. Collecton of George Conrad.

of steel with a welder's torch. A crowd of three thousand gathered to watch the rusty structure's "tentacles" come down. At a luncheon that afternoon, the Downtown Brooklyn Association toasted its demise; no longer would the el "cast a shadow over the heart of Brooklyn." Fulton Street had long been the flagship of Brooklyn retail, even if encumbered overhead. With the street basking in sunshine for the first time in fifty-three years, the sky was quite literally now the limit: Fulton Street could well become one of the nation's "swank shopping centers." Pratt Institute architecture students offered sketches of what the rejuvenated thoroughfare might look like. There would be shiny buses instead of rattletrap trolleys and streetlights—vowed association president Henry J. Davenport—"similar to those on 5th Ave., Manhattan." For the rest of that summer, Brooklyn delighted in the "mammoth production" staged on its downtown streets as the Fifth Avenue and other sections of elevated track fell. The *Eagle* called the show "Slaying of the Black Spider," and pronounced that as pure spectacle, "Billy Rose or any other Broadway impresario couldn't have done a better job."

> The fiery sting of the acetelyne [*sic*] torches against the antiquated steel structure sends sprays of colorful, glowing sparks downward and keeps the thousands of watchers enthralled in the performance of the iron workers . . . star performers in this show as they scamper along their precarious perches atop the steel trusses, applying the flaming "death ray" to the tentacles of the spiderish framework.[18]

The Sands Street station complex came down at last in 1943, ending its fifty-year run as a "temporary" structure. Cadman Plaza had shed its last encumbrance and was entirely opened to the sky. In a few years only the Myrtle Avenue line—stubbed off at Jay Street—remained of the once-vast network of downtown Brooklyn els.

Removal of all this heavy infrastructure was also a Herculean recycling effort. The section of the Fulton Street el between Court Street and Lafayette Avenue alone yielded three thousand tons of scrap steel. Rumors swirled that the steel was sold to Japan, perhaps destined to be returned in the form of artillery shells. In truth, nearly all of it was purchased for reuse by Bethlehem Steel. Some of it might well have come back to Brooklyn to help build a warship in the Navy Yard.

Removing the dark maze of elevated tracks from downtown Brooklyn had long been seen as an essential first step toward creating a new civic and administrative center at the heart of the borough. As discussed earlier, the idea for a civic center had been batted about since the 1900s and was taken up with particular enthusiasm by Newell Dwight Hillis and his circle of patrician improvement advocates. His Chicago pal, Daniel Burnham, endorsed placing "a proper civic center" between the Brooklyn Bridge and Borough Hall. In an April 1913 letter to Frederic B. Pratt, city comptroller William A. Prendergast avowed that "there should be a civic center in Brooklyn," suggesting he form a committee of citizens to study the problem. Pratt tapped nine of his Brooklyn Beautiful cronies—Alfred T. White and Edward Murray Bassett among them—to spend the next two months drafting a plan. Working closely with Edward Bennett, Pratt's Committee of Ten recommended placing the long-anticipated new Kings County courthouse behind Borough Hall, and a new municipal office building just opposite to the north, on the triangular site occupied

Demolition of blocks around Sands Street and Brooklyn Terminal, August 1937. New York City Municipal Archives.

today by the Korean War Veterans Park. From the air the scheme resembled a great hourglass or bow tie. The *Eagle*'s January 1914 special section on the Brooklyn City Plan featured Bennett's rendering of the projected civic center on the front page.[19]

Of course, not everyone agreed that this was the best way forward. A young New York society architect named Charles S. Peabody proposed an alternative scheme, which the *New York Times* called "daring and original" and treated to a full-page article—the result more likely of Peabody's family connections than of a sudden interest in Brooklyn on the part of the paper (Charles was the nephew of banker and philanthropist George Foster Peabody, benefactor of the Peabody Awards). Charles Peabody was a graduate of Harvard and the École des Beaux-Arts who had designed the Delaware and Hudson train station in Lake George and Mayborn Hall at Vanderbilt University. His civic center proposal featured a single megastructure for both the county courts and borough offices. He placed the courtrooms in a six-story perimeter building wrapping the full block behind Borough Hall and creating a great courtyard from which a twenty-six-story municipal tower rose. He positioned the tower to backstop a visual axis from the Brooklyn Bridge to Borough Hall, anchoring the view of Brooklyn as seen by anyone coming over from Manhattan. The committee rejected Peabody's scheme outright, claiming that combining two separate government entities in a single building—an arranged marriage of sorts—would lead to constant quarrels over management and upkeep. Moreover, Brooklyn was a city of churches and homes, not skyscrapers. "There is," the *Eagle* laconically noted, "opposition to high buildings in Brooklyn." Though a much smaller municipal building was eventually built on the site, not until 1926 would anything in Kings County reach the height of Peabody's Priapus. Senior Brooklyn architect Frank J. Helmle—designer of the Prospect Park Boathouse and the recently restored Hotel Bossert in Brooklyn Heights—delivered the slap-down, berating Peabody's scheme as ill-considered and extravagant: "a Manhattan architect's idea of what Brooklyn needs."[20]

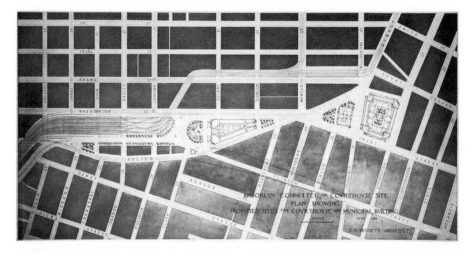

Edward H. Bennett, *Proposed Sites for Courthouse and Municipal Building*, 1913. From "Brooklyn City Plan," special supplement to the *Brooklyn Daily Eagle*, January 18, 1914. Brooklyn Public Library, Brooklyn Collection.

It wasn't until the 1930s that real headway was made on the long-anticipated Brooklyn Civic Center. By now, the City Beautiful generation of Brooklyn improvers had faded from the scene, and it was an outside entity—the Regional Plan Association—that jump-started efforts to revitalize the heart of Brooklyn. The second volume of its landmark *Regional Plan of New York and Its Environs*—the first long-range plan for the metropolitan region—included proposals for a Brooklyn Civic Center. With removal of the elevated lines and creation of the bridge plaza already well under way, the RPA team—led by British town planner Thomas Adams—shifted the entire civic center north of Borough Hall, just as city bridge commissioner Frederick Kracke had suggested years before. They offered two schemes. The first, favored plan called for widening Washington Street (now Cadman Plaza East) into a grand Parisian-style boulevard similar in scale and appointment to Boston's Commonwealth Avenue. The street was chosen because it lined up perfectly with Borough Hall in one direction and the south tower of the Manhattan Bridge in the other, creating a symbolic link between New York's most populous and most powerful boroughs. A formal plaza at the foot of the Brooklyn Bridge anchored the north end of this axis, with grand civic and institutional buildings set in big perimeter blocks just west of Washington Street—where Cadman Plaza and the Korean War Veterans parks are today. The second RPA scheme, clumsy and impractical, drove an axis from Borough Hall down a realigned Liberty Street to a grand municipal tower much like the Municipal Building on Chambers Street.[21]

Though neither of these schemes was adopted, the Regional Plan Association effectively rekindled interest in Brooklyn for a civic center of its own. It also made clear that focusing solely on a grand administrative complex would do little to solve the many interlocking problems in this "least developed and most disordered part of the borough." Adams and his team stressed that downtown Brooklyn should be approached as a whole. "The civic and business center, the residential district of Brooklyn Heights, the approaches to Brooklyn Bridge and the waterfront development on the northern end of the Upper Bay," he wrote, "must be dealt with together in a bold scheme to make Brooklyn's center one of appropriate dignity and distinction."[22] It was Brooklyn's most widely read daily—the *Eagle*—that took up this call. Over the next twenty years it published a barrage of articles and editorials calling for downtown renewal. Leading the crusade was no scion of Anglo-Dutch Brooklyn, but a Dixie transplant named Cleveland Rodgers. Raised by a single mother in Greenville, South Carolina, Rodgers aspired to be a playwright but paid the bills working as a typesetter. He came to New York in 1909 with a panama hat in hand and dreams of Broadway fame, taking a job with the City Club investigating overcrowding on the Third Avenue Elevated. He didn't even have enough money to buy the newspaper, and recalled fishing a copy out of the trash to read about the shooting death of Stanford White.

Rodgers eventually found a job setting linotype at the *Eagle*, and before long was writing drama reviews, articles, and editorials for the paper. He moved from the composing room to the editorial office, becoming associate editor in 1920 and succeeding Arthur M. Howe in the *Eagle*'s top job a decade later. Rodgers had a keen interest in city planning, sparked by a boyhood visit to the 1901 Charleston

LOOKING NEAT BROOKLYN BRIDGE APPROACH FROM COURT MONTAGUE 3 1985-12342 RUTTER

Downtown Brooklyn looking toward the Brooklyn Bridge, 1935. The Fulton Street elevated runs across the left side of image. The Brooklyn General Post Office on Tillary Street, center right, is among the few buildings in this scene that would survive the demolitions of the coming decade—and just barely. New York City Municipal Archives.

Brooklyn-Bridge Plaza - 3-22-38-7294

Same view, 1938. The el and Brooklyn Bridge Terminal at Sands Street would survive for another five years before being cleared to make way for Cadman Plaza. New York City Municipal Archives.

Exposition. "There I glimpsed the possibilities of man-made beauty for the first time," he recalled; "It was a beautiful exposition, Spanish Renaissance buildings with red tile roofs, under clear blue skies." Strings of electric lights came on as the sun dipped behind the moss-bearded oaks, setting aglow the buildings, courts, and colonnades. To Rodgers, the Charleston Exposition was a signal moment in his youthful education: "It gave me the first ideas I ever had of great buildings in landscaped areas." One of the first big stories Rodgers covered as an *Eagle* reporter was the destruction by fire of the old Equitable Assurance Building in lower Manhattan, and its replacement by a forty-two-story tower that obliterated nearly all sunlight from surrounding streets. Outrage over the structure led to the formation of the Committee on the Limitation on the Height and Bulk of Buildings. It was this group, led by Brooklyn's Edward Murray Bassett, that drafted the city's first zoning resolution—"the beginning," wrote Rodgers, "of comprehensive city planning in the United States."[23]

As editor of the *Eagle*, Rodgers had no little sway over the course of civic affairs. But it was his appointment in 1938 to the New York City Planning Commission that gave him real authority to shape the built environment of both Brooklyn and the city at large. The commission was created by the 1936 New York City Charter "to advise and report on all questions affecting the growth of the city." Advisory to the mayor and Board of Estimate, it was charged with drafting the city's master plan, reviewing citywide subdivisions of land and conducting public hearings to gauge public support for and opposition to projects. The first commissioners were appointed two years later, and included Rodgers; Lawrence M. Orton, a Cornell graduate whom Rodgers considered "the best qualified technical planner on the Commission" (he had worked with Thomas Adams at the RPA); Board of Estimate engineer Vernon S. Moon; Edwin A. Salmon, later planning consultant to Brooklyn borough president John Cashmore with expertise in hospitals and health care; and Arthur V. Sheridan, namesake of the Sheridan Expressway. New Dealer Adolf A. Berle, Jr., was the commission's first chair, succeeded shortly after by another of Franklin D. Roosevelt's "Brain Trust," Rexford Guy Tugwell. That Rodgers lacked a background in design or planning was hardly debilitating; rather, it enabled him to maintain an objectivity that transcended the particulars of any one profession. He took to heart Tugwell's remark that the commission's main business was "to think about the City of New York," keeping the big picture in sight when others got lost in the weeds. Rodgers authored the commission's first annual report and later published a book—*New York Plans for the Future* (1943)—about the city's development history and the challenges it faced.[24]

As Brooklyn's voice on the commission, Rodgers did all he could to bring its declining downtown to the promised land of urban renewal. He found his Moses—literally—when Mayor La Guardia appointed the master builder to the planning commission in 1941. Rodgers deeply admired Moses, later authoring a book about him and ghostwriting much of his autobiography; Moses felt similarly about Rodgers, whom he described as "a most valuable public servant." Rodgers's seat on the Planning Commission and bromance with Moses enabled him to move the Brooklyn Civic Center to the very top of New York's postwar public-works agenda. Though

City planning commissioner Cleveland Rodgers (in white) cuts a ribbon, 1939. Robert Moses is second from left; former governor Al Smith on right. Brooklyn Public Library, Brooklyn Collection.

he had formally severed ties to the *Eagle* once he joined the Planning Commission in 1938, Rodgers continued to enjoy a free pass to its editorial page. Thus did "Creation of a Civic Center" become part of a ten-point "Program for Brooklyn" rolled out to mark the newspaper's centennial in October 1941. "It is the conviction of this newspaper," began a piece almost certainly authored by Rodgers, "that nothing would do more to increase the self-respect of Brooklynites and their pride in their home town than the creation of a real civic center of the general type boasted by every other city of any size in the nation." The *Eagle* commissioned a plan of its own for the Cadman Plaza area, prepared by the firm of Slee and Bryson and proposing a rampart of municipal offices, courthouses, and educational buildings on both sides of Cadman Plaza. It was presented in a full-page feature article by state supreme court justice and former chair of the Joint Legislative Committee on Housing Charles C. Lockwood, in which readers were admonished that in order "to regain and maintain its prestige, Brooklyn must plan and act now." Published fatefully on December 7, 1941, the day Japanese forces attacked Pearl Harbor, the plan was completely ignored.[25]

Not until nearly the war's end was anything significant done again on the Brooklyn Civic Center. The catalyst for action this time was not a cluster of new buildings, but an open space—Cadman Plaza, now selected as the site for a memorial to the 11,500 Brooklyn souls lost in the war. Prompted by Moses's call for "one impressive memorial in each borough," *Eagle* publisher Frank Schroth announced a design

Brooklyn War Memorial campaign poster, 1946. Brooklyn Public Library, Brooklyn Collection.

competition for a Brooklyn War Memorial on June 6, 1944—the day of the Normandy invasion and over a year before the war actually ended. The winners of the Brooklyn War Memorial competition were announced in late May 1945. The competition jury—including borough president John Cashmore, Board of Education chief Mary E. Dillon, and Edward C. Blum of the Brooklyn Institute of Arts and Sciences—sorted through some 243 entries from all quarters of the country. But despite a blind review process, the first- and second-place teams were suspiciously dominated by some of Moses's closest confederates.[26] Moses was quietly steering the effort, for he had by now become heavily invested in the future of downtown Brooklyn. Fed up with the bewildering array of plans and proposals advanced for the civic center over the years, he admonished Brooklyn to be "realistic about the future" and stop paying attention to "Buck Rogers" plans by "visionaries with crackpot ideas who would have streamliner landing fields on every corner." But Moses's plans were themselves hardly modest. With the Planning Commission increasingly under his thumb, plans for the Brooklyn Civic Center swelled in scope and scale in step with the titanic Moses ego. No longer was the project about erecting a new municipal center at Cadman Plaza; instead, it expanded to swallow up most of old Brooklyn—from the Columbia Heights waterfront east to Pratt Institute; from the crowded slums of the Navy Yard south to Atlantic Avenue. It would become the largest and most complex project in Moses's long career—"the biggest piece of redevelopment," wrote Lewis Mumford, "the municipality has ever attempted."[27]

The Planning Commission report on the Brooklyn Civic Center, written by Rodgers, was released in March 1945 and made officially part of the city's master plan just weeks before the war memorial competition results were announced. It was based largely on a new study of downtown Brooklyn by Moses's most trusted urban designers—Gilmore D. Clarke and his gifted understudy, Michael Rapuano. Clarke—adviser to the ill-fated Marine Park design competition many years before—was now the most prominent landscape architect in the United States, with an honorary doctorate from Yale and the Architectural League's coveted Gold Medal. Clarke was running a busy practice in the city, chairing the US Commission of Fine Arts and

Proposed cenotaph and reflecting pool at Cadman Plaza, Brooklyn War Memorial competition, 1945.
Brooklyn Public Library, Brooklyn Collection.

also serving as dean of the College of Architecture at Cornell University, spending three days a week in Ithaca. By this time, Moses and Clarke had known each other for twenty-five years. They first met when the latter was supervising construction on the Bronx River Parkway. Moses, then a young staffer with the Bureau of Municipal Research, was sent to investigate a suspected case of corruption—a bridge was being built over a dry meadow near Scarsdale. Moses was led to Clarke, who explained that it was wiser to erect the bridge over dry land and divert water back under it than to build within the existing channel, which would require pumps and coffer dams. When newly elected Mayor La Guardia appointed Moses citywide commissioner of parks in 1934, he made Clarke his consulting landscape architect.[28]

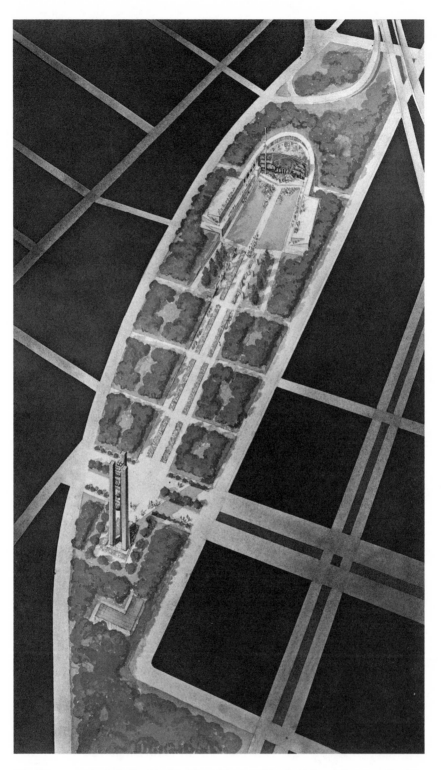

One of the 243 entries in the Brooklyn War Memorial competition for Cadman Plaza, 1945. Brooklyn Public Library, Brooklyn Collection.

Distinguished guests discuss an architectural model for the Brooklyn War Memorial, 1945. Brooklyn Public Library, Brooklyn Collection.

Their ensuing reconstruction of the city's aging parks infrastructure was run more like a military operation than like a public-works project. "Major" Clarke, as he was known, had experience with both. As an officer with the Sixth Engineers of the US Army's Third Division, he had built bridges and roads at the front during World War I. Moses entrusted Clarke with great authority at the Arsenal, the Parks Department's offices in Central Park, giving him veto power over all park design work; no bids or blueprints left the building without Clarke's signature. Clarke was also authorized to hire an officer corps and did so by recruiting to New York the best of his former staff from the Westchester County Park Commission. Well into the 1960s, a plurality of the "Moses Men" could claim a connection to Clarke and Westchester.[29] Michael Rapuano was first among them. A working-class son of Italian immigrants, Rapuano attended Cornell on a football scholarship, graduating in 1926 and winning the Rome Prize in landscape architecture the following year. Clarke recruited Rapuano to Westchester upon his return from the American Academy in Rome in 1930, where the young man quickly became Clarke's aide-de-camp. As he spent more and more time in Washington and Ithaca, Clarke delegated much of his responsibility to Rapuano, deputizing him to head the Parks Department's landscape design team. In this role Rapuano prepared new plans for City Hall, Washington Square, and Madison Square parks, reworked Charles Downing Lay's extravagant scheme for Marine Park, and drafted designs for Orchard Beach, Randall's Island, and Jacob Riis parks. He worked closely with Clarke and Aymar Embury III on the Central Park Menagerie and Prospect

Park Zoo; with M. Betty Sprout on the Central Park Conservatory Garden; and with Clarke and fellow Westchester alumnus Clinton F. Lloyd on the renewal of Riverside Park. Clarke and Rapuano formed a professional partnership in 1939; among their first projects was the master plan for the 1939 New York World's Fair.

It's hardly surprising that Moses would look to this capable pair—on their way to becoming the most influential American landscape architects since the Olmsteds—to realize his vision for downtown Brooklyn. Their first task was to reconfigure the war memorial into something more to Moses's liking. Given the enormous sacrifices made by Brooklyn families for the war effort—no community in America lost more of its own in the conflict—the war memorial project was taken very seriously in Brooklyn. Much of the money for construction came by way of public subscription and from

Perspective rendering of the Brooklyn War Memorial as built, 1949. The last sigh of monumental classicism in New York City, designed by the architects of the Jefferson Memorial and National Gallery of Art in Washington. Parks Photo Archive, New York City Department of Parks and Recreation.

Cadman Plaza and the Brooklyn War Memorial, c. 1958, with the newly planted *boschetto* of London plane trees. Parks Photo Archive, New York City Department of Parks and Recreation.

fund-raising efforts at the neighborhood level and in the borough's innumerable churches, synagogues, and schools. But there was a shortfall, and the project had to be scaled back and started over, allowing Moses to hand it to a team led by Clarke and Rapuano. Not surprisingly, the new scheme was nearly identical to what Clarke and Embury had proposed in their own competition entry—a "great wall facing the Plaza, which may be suitably embellished with sculptural bas-relief."[30] The memorial itself was designed by Otto Eggers and Daniel Higgins, whom Clarke knew well from Washington. Eggers and Higgins were the architects of the Jefferson Memorial and the West Building of the National Gallery of Art, both begun by their late partner, John Russell Pope. Indeed, their Brooklyn memorial would have fit well on the National Mall—an austere classical sarcophagus, clad in limestone and framed by heroic figures representing military victory and family. These were among the final works of New York sculptor Charles Keck, a student of Augustus Saint-Gaudens whose commissions included a likeness of Huey Long in Baton Rouge, the Booker T. Washington Memorial at Tuskegee University, and—in New York—the Alfred E. Smith statue on the Lower East Side and the figurative pylons flanking Columbia University's Broadway gate (he also designed a commemorative plaque to the USS *Maine*, cast from metal salvaged from the ship). It was Rapuano who really made the war memorial a distinguished piece of work. Drawing from his studies of Renaissance spatial design twenty years earlier at the American Academy in Rome, he created at Cadman Plaza one of New York City's finest urban parks. He skillfully adapted a baroque spatial design trick to the trapezoidal site, splaying the sides of the green to manipulate the sense of perspective—creating an illusion of foreshortened or extended depth: from the south end of the space, the war memorial appears to loom just a bit, while the view from its steps toward Borough Hall seems ever so slightly more distant. Rapuano enclosed the space with a great grid of London plane trees, a move itself inspired by Italian precedent—the centuries-old *boschetto* of Oriental planes at the Villa Aldobrandini in Frascati, just outside Rome.

Clarke and Rapuano plan for Brooklyn Civic Center, 1951, showing federal courthouse, relocated Brooklyn High School for Specialty Trades, and the unbuilt Mies van der Rohe scheme for the Concord Village. Parks Photo Archive, New York City Department of Parks and Recreation.

Aerial perspective, Brooklyn Civic Center, 1952. The building adjacent to the post office is today the Theodore Roosevelt Federal Courthouse at 225 Cadman Plaza East. American Red Cross Building at center. Parks Photo Archive, New York City Department of Parks and Recreation.

With its imposing memorial and soaring plane trees, Cadman Plaza was a glorious centerpiece about which to arrange the Brooklyn Civic Center. Moses predicted that it would be "what the great cathedral and opera plazas are to European cities . . . as much the pride of Brooklyn as the Piazza San Marco is the pride of Venice and the Place de la Concorde the cynosure of Paris."[31] Unfortunately, nothing that came afterward matched its high standard. Nor could even this jewel of an open space compensate for the urban design failures of the larger subsequent project. What doomed the civic center was the postwar emphasis on isolated object buildings that ignored the street and did nothing to create the kind of cohesive fabric that even the clunkiest of the earlier City Beautiful schemes—with their block-defining perimeter buildings—took as essential to good urbanism. The civic center devolved into a loose assembly of dull modernist buildings, each more forgettable than the next, all orbiting Cadman Plaza like space junk about a star. The brochure produced for a 1952 exhibition on the Brooklyn Civic Center at Borough Hall unwittingly emphasized the project's greatest failings, featuring on its cover an abstract expressionist plan drawing absent any context, in which the various civic center buildings appear like free-floating architectural flotsam. Of existing buildings in the vicinity, only Borough Hall, the Brooklyn Municipal Building, and Mifflin E. Bell's glorious Romanesque Brooklyn General Post Office—nearly razed by Moses and today home to the US

Bankruptcy Court—are shown. The principal civic center components included a federal complex at Tillary Street and Cadman Plaza East (today occupied by César Pelli's superfortified US District Courthouse, opened in 2006) and—marooned on the north edge of Walt Whitman Park—a small headquarters for the Brooklyn chapter of the American Red Cross, designed by Eggers and Higgins and renovated after 9/11 as the city's new crisis command center. To the east of this was Concord Village, a towers-in-the-park housing cooperative that was originally assigned to one of the pillars of modernism—Mies van de Rohe. On the west side of Cadman Plaza Park, Clarke and Rapuano had themselves recommended a set of well-defined perimeter buildings. But redevelopment of those blocks—filled with hundreds of century-old buildings including the shop in which Walt Whitman typeset *Leaves of Grass*—was not carried out until the mid-1960s. With superblock urbanism then all the rage, it's no surprise that these blocks—the "fruit streets" between Henry Street and Cadman Plaza West—ended up like something torn from a Corbusian sketchbook.

Closer to Borough Hall was the one building everyone hoped would be the flagship of the civic center—the sprawling, $16 million Supreme Court Building. Replacing an earlier courthouse built during the Civil War at the corner of Adams and Joralemon streets, its prime site—fronting Columbus Park and visible for blocks all around—called for an architectural tour de force. And this is what the architects should have delivered; they were, after all, one of the city's top firms—Shreve, Lamb & Harmon—designers of the Empire State Building. Instead they produced a banded gargantua that is neither modernist fish nor beaux arts fowl, whose bleak limestone

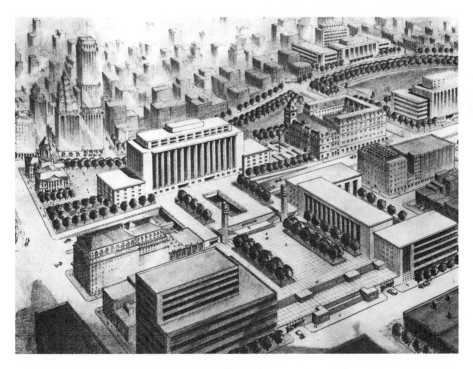

Lorimer and Chiljean plan for Brooklyn Supreme Court plaza, c. 1953. Local History Research Collection, Brooklyn College Library Archives and Special Collections.

façade is relieved by so few windows that it more closely resembles a prison than a hall of justice. It was on the other side of this building, between Adams and Jay streets, that the civic center nearly achieved a second note of grand spatial sensibility. Extending from the Supreme Court Building's rear façade to Jay Street was to be a spacious formal plaza with a parking garage below, flanked to the north by the Welfare Building (demolished) and the Domestic Relations Court at 283 Adams Street (now a public school) and to the south by the civic center's best modernist work, the Board of Transportation Building—"well conceived, straightforward in design," wrote Mumford, "the very model of an efficient office building" (today home to New York University's Center for Urban Science and Progress).[32] Reminiscent of Lincoln Center, this pedestrian-friendly composition was envisioned by two Department of Public Works architects—A. Gordon Lorimer and Victor Chiljean. Mumford cheered it as an example of the kinds of pedestrian gathering places—"human catchment basins," as he called them—that would bring vitality and life to the civic center. By placing Adams Street in an underpass beneath the plaza, their plan fused the core of the civic center to Myrtle Avenue and the populous neighborhoods east of downtown. This was an essential move, for Adams Street had been widened from 60 to 160 feet and was now carrying all motor traffic to and from the Brooklyn Bridge. The once-ordinary street was now a busy ten-lane arterial barrier that threatened to isolate the civic center from its context. Unfortunately, the Adams Street underpass was eliminated, thus piercing the civic center "in defiance," noted Mumford, "of every canon of sound civic design" and nullifying "most of the aesthetic and social qualities this center might have possessed." The underground garage was built, but with a park on its roof rather than a plaza. Never well used, the space was eliminated altogether in 1996 for the Renaissance Plaza redevelopment, which erected an office tower and hotel on the site—the first in the borough since the 1930s (today the New York Marriott at the Brooklyn Bridge).[33]

American Red Cross Building, Eggers & Higgins, architects, 1952. Extensively altered, the structure is today the Emergency Operations Center of the New York City Office of Emergency Management at 165 Cadman Plaza East. New York City Department of Parks and Recreation.

The Brooklyn Civic Center was so vast in scope, so hydra-headed in its administrative and bureaucratic complexity that it seemed to generate political weather all its own. It dragged on for three decades and four mayoral administrations, outlasting not only Moses but nearly all of its most vocal proponents, ultimately becoming a symbol of all the promise and failure of the postwar welfare state. In the end, it yielded not a masterpiece of civic urbanism but a sad Orwellian cluster of unloved institutional buildings, enframed by superblock housing estates and entangled by expressway ramps. In a tragically poetic twist of fate, the Mosaic juggernaut consumed even the extravagant old nest of the *Brooklyn Eagle*—a building designed by George L. Morse and once lauded as "one of America's most perfect newspaper establishments," the aerie from which Cleveland Rodgers had so tirelessly called for the comprehensive renewal of downtown Brooklyn, beckoning the very winds of creative destruction that would sweep it all away.[34]

End of an era: the *Brooklyn Eagle* block falls to the wrecking ball, 1955. Photograph by William M. Schouten. Brooklyn Public Library, Brooklyn Collection.

CHAPTER 15

THE BABYLONISH BRICK KILN

Let us open new streets, clean up the populous neighborhoods
that lack air and daylight, and let the sun's beneficial rays penetrate
everywhere . . . like the light of truth in our hearts.
—NAPOLEON III

A stone's throw from the star-crossed civic center, just south and west of the Brooklyn Navy Yard, were some of the worst slums in all of Gotham—the embattled old Fifth, Eleventh, and Twentieth wards. Life in this vast human rookery, with its tenement-packed streets and cold-water flats, was only a nick better than what Jacob Riis had documented a generation earlier on the Lower East Side. Just below the Navy Yard, from Prince Street east to Carlton Avenue, was a predominantly African American slum known as the "Jungle." Nearly 83 percent of the residential buildings here lacked either central heat or hot water in 1940; well over a hundred had only hall toilets, and some still used century-old outhouses. The area was riven with disease, and scored the highest rates of tuberculosis and infant mortality in the entire city. Life was even harder in the nearby Fifth Ward, where residents lived cheek by jowl with heavy industry that spewed untold toxins into soil, air, and water. The 1939 Federal Writers' Project guidebook to New York City called the Fifth Ward "a shapeless grotesque neighborhood, its grimy cobblestone thoroughfares filled with flophouses, crumbling tenements and greasy restaurants." It was haunted, too, by war crimes and death; for in 1808 a mass grave was found on the west shore of Wallabout Bay containing the remains of some ten thousand Americans who had perished aboard British prison ships during the Revolution. The remains were interred in a crypt—a wall of which was discovered in 2003 at 91 Hudson Avenue—and later moved to the Prison Ship Martyrs' Monument atop Fort Greene Park.[1]

Lost world: High Street looking west from Hudson Avenue, 1926, heart of Brooklyn's vital, embattled Fifth Ward. Everything in this view will eventually be razed for the Farragut Houses. Brown Brothers photograph. Irma and Paul Milstein Division of United States History, Local History and Genealogy, The New York Public Library.

The building stock in the Fifth Ward was among the oldest in Brooklyn, erected between 1818 and the 1830s by speculative builders who filled the marshy western shore of Wallabout Bay to erect sturdy brick Greek revival shop houses. It became known as Vinegar Hill, after a battle site of the Irish Rebellion of 1798, though most people knew the area as "Irishtown." The spiritual centerpiece of the community was St. Ann's Church, at the corner of Front and Gold Streets, sadly razed in 1992 for a parking lot. A modest Gothic structure, it was designed by Patrick C. Keely, an Irish-born architect and neighborhood resident who built some seven hundred churches for working-class parishes up and down the Eastern Seaboard—from St. Joseph Church in New Orleans to Boston's colossal Cathedral of the Holy Cross, still the largest Catholic church in New England. After the Civil War, industry began moving into the area, pushing more affluent residents south to newer neighborhoods and leaving behind the very poor. The streets in and around Hudson Avenue became crammed with a hodgepodge of shops, factories, and slaughterhouses. Storage tanks filled with explosive gas rose alongside crowded tenements. It was an urban planner's nightmare and explains why exclusionary zoning was taken up with such zeal by Progressive Era reformers—something we often forget when we wax rhapsodic on the mixed-use urbanism of prewar America. Vinegar Hill was soon a mob-ruled slum, filled with "ricketty, tumble down houses," noted a journalist in 1873, "and hordes of ragged, unkempt children."[2] It was especially notorious for its gin mills and distilleries. Bootleggers employed gangs of local youths to chase government inspectors off the streets. Even the police dared not enter the area.

Matters reached a breaking point in the fall of 1870, when two thousand federal troops were dispatched from the Navy Yard to administer a dose of law and order. Bedlam ensued, and "for quite a while," reported the *Times*, "a lively time was made by showers of stones and brickbats flying through the air. Every chimney and window seemed to have an enraged distiller behind it, who felt it to be his duty

Tenement at 475 Adelphi Street. Irma and Paul Milstein Division of United States History, Local History and Genealogy, The New York Public Library.

to break the head of at least one soldier." When the commanding officer ordered his men to load their rifles, "the belligerents became like lambs, a little swearing excepted." Mash tubs, vats, and stills were smashed and overturned by the troops, who nonetheless made sure to set aside thirty barrels of rotgut whiskey for their troubles.[3] In time the Fifth Ward Irish gave way to immigrant Italians from the Lower East Side, while a small community of African Americans, established before the Civil War, held its ground on lower Sands Street. It was no paradise of brotherhood. Irish toughs like Jimmy Maroney's River Front Gang battled equally vicious Italian bands for control of neighborhood turf. The very future of that turf itself was tenuous. Rumors had swirled for years that a sister span to the Williamsburg Bridge would annihilate the district. The fears were not unfounded. The East River Bridge Company had indeed been granted a charter in 1892 to take Hudson Avenue over the East River to Grand Street in Manhattan. As explained in an 1893 *Harper's Weekly* article, the Hudson Avenue Bridge would have a clear span of 1,470 feet, with piers between Hudson Avenue and Gold Street in Brooklyn and an entrance at the junction of Myrtle and Hudson avenues. In Manhattan, the bridge would set down in the vicinity of Jackson and Scammel streets (site of the Vladeck Houses today) and run north into Grand Street. Though the company later lost its charter, the specter of a bridge continued to loom over the ward like a sword of Damocles. As late as March 1901, bids were solicited for construction of a tower in Brooklyn to take "bridge No. 3 . . . from Pike Slip, Manhattan, to Hudson Avenue."[4] Residents of the besieged district finally breathed a sigh of relief when the crossing was sited instead at the foot of Adams Street, for what would become the Manhattan Bridge.

Threats came in smaller packages, too, from the legions of rats that swarmed up from the East River at night to diseases long eradicated from the rest of the city. In February 1893, an outbreak of typhus was reported at 31 Front Street—a building "peopled by many Italians of the lower order," grumbled the *Eagle*, "who do not know enough to keep themselves and their surroundings clean." Smallpox outbreaks bedeviled the Navy Yard slums as late as 1902. A decade later, Elizabeth Venable Gaines—a progressive educator at Adelphi College (then still in Clinton Hill)—found that nineteen children had perished on a single street in the Italian ghetto west of the Navy Yard; forty-two others had been blinded, and eighty-nine crippled by disease. This was a place, it seemed, "where babies seemed to be born only to die."[5] Even for adults, life in the Fifth Ward was not easy. Livestock unloaded on the wharves each week were driven bleating and lowing up Hudson Avenue to slaughterhouses at Tillary Street, where the terror-screams of animals created many a vegetarian. Paint, soap, lead, and leather works spewed poison into soil and air. Towering over everything were the four chimneys of Brooklyn Edison's Hudson Avenue station, the largest steam turbine generating plant in the world. Completed in 1927 with a capacity of one million horsepower, it electrified the vast tide of residential development unleashed across Brooklyn and Queens in the Jazz Age. The plant also delivered steam to hundreds of office buildings in lower Manhattan, making vapor-exhaling manhole covers a new part of the Gotham winterscape. It brought no such magic to the streets of the Fifth Ward. When workers purged the boilers, a great drift of ash would fall

Long before Dumbo; looking west over the Fifth Ward, April 1946. The Brooklyn Navy Yard and Hudson
Avenue Generating Station are at right. New York City Housing Authority, La Guardia and Wagner Archives.

silently over the neighborhoods beneath its four-hundred-foot smokestacks. Mothers
would shout across the backyard lots, *"Pull in the wash!"* while children donned
folded newsprint hats and listened as the cinders tinkled down upon their paper
trilbies—black snow from the titanic God of Light.

To many reformers, the foulest toxin in these parts came not from industry but
from the merchants of pleasure and flesh on Sands Street, a gritty gauntlet that
ran from the main gate of the Navy Yard to Washington Street. It bore the name of
the brothers who first platted this part of Brooklyn for development, Comfort and
Joshua Sands. Natives of Cow Neck, Long Island (Sands Point today), the pair made
a dubious fortune selling overpriced provisions to the Continental Army during the
Revolution. After the war, Comfort founded the Bank of New York with Alexander
Hamilton, becoming its first director in 1784. That year he and Joshua acquired part
of the old Rapelje spread west of Wallabout Bay, where they launched a speculative
venture named City of Olympia. They hoped to make its hilly prospect a retreat for
harried New Yorkers. Instead, Connecticut Yankees from New London came, seeking
to establish a shipworks on the bay. The Sands brothers themselves erected warehouses, wharves, and ropewalks to manufacture rigging, laying the groundwork for
what would eventually become the largest military shipyard in North America. In the
years before the Brooklyn Bridge, Sands Street was a fashionable address—many of
Brooklyn's "first families" made it home, worshipping at the Sands Street Methodist

Brooklyn Edison's Hudson Avenue Generating Station, June 1932. Photograph by Fairchild Aerial Surveys, Inc. Collection of the author.

Episcopal Church, among the city's oldest and most prestigious houses of worship. The street turned to commerce with the advent of horsecar service between Fulton Ferry and the Navy Yard gate—then on York Street—a transition accelerated by the opening of the Brooklyn Bridge in 1883. Now Sands Street was the most direct route between the Navy Yard and Manhattan. What sealed its commercial fate was the July 1896 opening of a Sands Street entrance to the Navy Yard, a move prompted by completion of the elevated rail depot at Washington Street. Overnight, Sands Street became a passageway to the city for thousands of sailors on shore leave from the Navy Yard, a street they had to traverse the length of on their way to and from downtown and the trains to Manhattan or Coney Island. Merchants responded nimbly to this new source of steady custom. Naval outfitters opened there, as did luncheonettes and shops that cleaned and tailored uniforms or rented civilian clothes to "jackies" who wished to roam the city less conspicuously. Pawnbrokers lent hard up sailors cash; souvenir shops and photographic galleries provided keepsakes for loved ones back home. When the fleet was in, Sands Street was transformed; "all you could see," one merchant recalled, "was a sea of white hats."[6]

Shore-leave sailors supplied only part of the trade that sustained Sands Street a century ago—at least by day. It was also a vital shopping street for residents of the increasingly polyglot neighborhoods around the Navy Yard. A 1908 survey found four Italian doctors and an equal number of Italian barbers on Sands Street. There

Hudson Avenue looking north toward the Boorum and Pease factory (extant), c. 1946. The older buildings here, which included the grocery store and home of the author's grandparents at 96 Hudson Avenue, were demolished in the early 1960s for P.S. 307. Photograph by John Tambasco.

were German butchers and Jewish tailors, shops catering to the area's large Polish and Lithuanian populations, and an Irish-owned bar on almost every street corner. Immigrants had long flocked to the area for cheap housing and industrial jobs; others came by way of the military installation at its doorstep. The rise of America's blue-water navy at the end of the nineteenth century made the Navy Yard an unintended agent of diversity. A tiny Chinese community—mostly waiters and their families—was centered on the Chinese Association on nearby Bridge Street. A substantial Filipino community flourished closer to Washington Street, seeded by a discriminatory section in the immigration law that barred citizenship to any Filipino except those honorably discharged from the US Navy. Sands Street was soon the main drag of Filipino Brooklyn, "dotted with little restaurants whose walls are painted with gay parrots and scenes from the islands." Small but tenacious, the community held on in the face of urban renewal until its spiritual center—a Roman Catholic church at 209 Concord Street—was demolished for the Brooklyn-Queens Expressway. A small Japanese settlement was established even earlier in and around Sands Street by cooks, valets, and servants of Pacific fleet officers. The community doubled almost overnight when the navy forcibly discharged all Japanese enlisted men as "yellow peril" fears erupted after Japan's victory in the Russo-Japanese War—the first time an Asian nation had defeated a Western power. By 1910 there were several Japanese boardinghouses on Sands Street, two restaurants, and bakeries where "dainty rice and tea cakes" were manufactured, delighted an *Eagle* reporter, "in full view of the street." There was also a Japanese soda shop and candy store, a curio shop, and a purveyor of artificial flowers. A Japanese physician had offices on High Street, and a tattoo artist "of no mean ability" plied his trade nearby.[7]

But there was a darker side to this corridor of noonday commerce. Shopkeepers were squeezed by organized crime and lived in fear of holdups.[8] As twilight descended, the busy thoroughfare became "a dark and almost sinister street"—a rogue's gallery of establishments aimed at the wallets and loins of seamen. There were basement gambling dens, porn shops, brothels male and female, and bars galore—Leo's, Richard's, Tony's Square, Terry Mitchell's. Bar brawls, scuffles, and stabbings were a nightly ritual on Sands Street. Drugs were a problem as early as 1906, when it was revealed that Sands Street pharmacists were selling cocaine even to youths. Coke may have been addictive, but the "whiskey" sold to sailors—especially during Prohibition—was often pure poison. In a single week in December 1921, scores of men were sickened by toxic hooch they bought from local bootleggers. Many awakened hours later, only to find they had been relieved of all their valuables. One man—a fireman on the USS *Pueblo*—died from acute alcohol poisoning, prompting the navy to join police, federal agents, and staff from the Sands Street YMCA to crack down on the lawbreakers. More than anything, however, Sands Street was about sex, in all its forms and variations. Prostitution was right behind keel laying and booze as a force in the local economy, though many women dismissed as whores were probably no more than maritime groupies—"silly girls who follow the navy from port to port" (mostly "from Pennsylvania," offered the *Eagle*, without evidence), who rented rooms in and around Sands Street and would "stay until the sailors depart and then head for the next stop of the fleet."[9]

Campaigns by church and state to combat strumpetry were checked only by the fear that, absent whores to slake their lust, horny sailors would simply start humping each other—as they most surely did. Cruising was as much a part of Sands Street life as the all-night coffee pot. An antivice society investigator in 1917 found Sands Street on a summer night filled with "sex mad" sailors, many of whom "were with other men walking arm in arm," and even kissing. Poet Hart Crane was among the many young men from all classes and quarters of the city who came to Sands Street in search of sexual pleasure, a place he could find lovers far from his circle of Gotham literati—"among men that his friends would never meet." It was a dangerous sport for Crane, and "more than once," writes Evan Hughes, "he came home beaten and bloodied."[10] Gay men were not the only ones who came to savor Sands Street's forbidden fruits. As early as the 1930s, the street had begun to attract tourists, some comparing the "picturesque Brooklyn thoroughfare" to bohemian Greenwich Village. Well-dressed men and women, university cads down from New

Haven or Ithaca would "roll down Sands St. in luxurious automobiles," seeking adventure and titillation. By this time, the street was a mere shadow of its truly wild days during Prohibition or World War I; one writer even went so far as to call it "as tame as Flatbush." The 1939 publication of a Federal Writers' Project guide to New York City further increased the number of young people coming to Sands Street in search of authenticity and ashcan grit.[11]

One of these slum tourists was Carson McCullers. In 1940, the Georgia-born writer moved into a townhouse at 7 Middagh Street that *Harper's Bazaar* editor George Davis had bought to fill with an ersatz family. Between 1940 and 1942 an extraordinary group of artistic and literary souls gathered under its roof—Benjamin Britten, Gypsy Rose Lee, poets W. H. Auden and Chester Kallman, Paul and Jane Bowles, set designer Oliver Smith, even Thomas Mann's son, Klaus. This "rambling society of creative eccentrics," as Caroline Seebohm called them, seemed ordered just the way "the populace once liked to think of artists," observed British poet and playwright Louis MacNeice, then a lecturer at Cornell, "ever so bohemian, raiding the icebox at midnight and eating the cat food by mistake."[12] Anaïs Nin called it February House. Anticipating today's authenticity-seeking hipsters by half a century, McCullers and her housemates would often head to Sands Street after a late, long meal—"a little area as vivacious as a country fair" where the liquor was cheap and "sunburned sailors swagger up and down the sidewalks with their girls." She, of all the Middagh Street crowd, was especially moved by this boulevard of the id and its flamboyant characters. "Some of the women you find there are vivid old dowagers," she wrote in *The Mortgaged Heart* (1955), "who have such names as The Duchess or Submarine Mary."

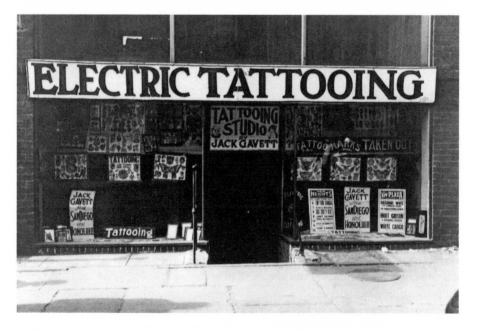

Jack Gavett's tattoo parlor, 59 Sands Street, July 1930. Photograph by Percy Loomis Sperr. Irma and Paul Milstein Division of United States History, Local History and Genealogy, The New York Public Library.

Every tooth in Submarine Mary's head is made of solid gold—and her smile is rich-looking and satisfied. She and the rest of these old habitués are greatly respected. They have a stable list of sailor pals and are known from Buenos Aires to Zanzibar. They are conscious of their fame and don't bother to dance or flirt like the younger girls, but sit comfortably in the centre of the room with their knitting, keeping a sharp eye on all that goes on.

In one bar McCullers was mesmerized by "a little hunchback who struts in proudly every evening, and is petted by everyone," a character who appears in slightly altered form as Cousin Lymon in McCullers's 1951 masterpiece, *The Ballad of the Sad Café*. Sands Street and its tumbledown quarter of cobblestoned blocks running to the East River may have even been the inspiration for *West Side Story*, at least according to Middagh Street denizen and Broadway producer Oliver Smith. Smith often cruised Sands Street and took late-night walks in the quarter with choreographer Jerome Robbins, and his set design for the original production of the theatrical, he once confessed, "was more Brooklyn than Manhattan."[13]

Just five years after Carson McCullers moved to Brooklyn, the whole brave, sad, beautiful urban world west and south of Sands Street and the Navy Yard was—for better or worse—swept into oblivion. The wheels of annihilation were officially set into motion on Thursday, June 27, 1940, a day before city schools closed for the summer. That morning, Mayor La Guardia and Brooklyn borough president John Cashmore met in the Park Avenue apartment of Governor Herbert H. Lehman to see him sign a $20 million state loan to the city for a vast public housing complex, one that would replace "the man-made jungle of the Navy Yard slums . . . one of the worst blighted sections in the entire city" with an austere array of high-rise towers set amidst a field of landscaped lawns. Contracts were let to level the thirty-nine-acre site. All that summer and fall the city worked feverishly to move some sixteen hundred families out of the condemned tenements, shacks, and boarding-houses. Most were rehoused within a four-mile radius of the site—temporarily, at least; they, along with defense workers and navy personnel, would have priority access to a new apartment on the site. The handful of families resisting eviction eventually yielded to "a touch of diplomacy here and a bit of sympathy there," obviating the need for ugly forced removals. Many residents had lived in their homes for decades, and—slum or not—were heartbroken to leave. An elderly barber named Frank Scania had cut hair at 44 Ashland Place for forty-five years, paying the same $13 rent he was charged in 1895; dazed by his impending ouster, Scania lingered until the end, the last holdout in a building erected when Andrew Jackson was president.[14]

As the people moved out, squads of Pied Pipers moved in to deal with residents of a different sort. Razing nearly forty acres of tumbledown shacks and tenements would unleash a biblical plague of vermin. Crack exterminators were called on to kill the legions of rats before they could infest neighboring areas. "As fast as a house is vacated," related the *Eagle*, "the drab angels of death move in." Tasty morsels of meat and fish were left behind, loaded with a toxin made from the ground bulbs of sea onion. How many rats were dispatched is unknown, but extermination work

Men drinking in rear of tenement house at 293 Hudson Avenue, April 1940, one of hundreds of substandard buildings that would soon be cleared for the Fort Greene Houses. New York City Housing Authority, La Guardia and Wagner Archives.

for the smaller Baxter Terrace housing project in Newark killed 500,000 rodents. Demolition began in December, and by early March 1941 more than half of the site's seven hundred-odd structures were gone. Ground was broken on May 6 for the project's pilot phase at Park and North Portland avenues. With customary bluster, Mayor La Guardia hailed the start of the largest low-rent housing project "ever attempted in this or any other country." Invoking the Navy Yard next door, Governor Lehman spoke of good housing as vital to American security; for "housing projects to protect us from the enemy from within," he remarked, "were as essential as battleships to protect us from the enemy from without." Brooklyn borough president John Cashmore likened the project to "the kind of war we like to fight, a war against filth, crime and disease." With a crowd of two thousand looking on, Lehman climbed into the cab of a steam shovel, shifted a lever, and dug its bucket into the terra firma. Aided by "quick-setting cement and floodlights for night work," the thirteen-story building went up fast—too fast, as we will see. The first apartments were ready for occupancy by November, months ahead of schedule.[15]

By this time the rest of the huge project was well under way. Commissions for the thirty-five towers, divided into three "units," went to some of the city's most prominent architects. Wallace K. Harrison and J. André Fouilhoux were lead architects for the first set of buildings. The men had been part of the Rockefeller Center design

team and collaborated on the Trylon and Perisphere, centerpiece of the 1939 New
York World's Fair; Harrison would go on to play a formative role in the creation of the
United Nations Headquarters. Their associates on the Fort Greene job were Rosario
Candela, master craftsman of the Park Avenue apartment, and Albert Mayer, an
architect-engineer who helped found the Housing Study Guild and whose service in
India during the war would lead to a plum commission: planning a new capital city
for the Punjab at Chandigarh. It was only after Mayer backed out of this project—his
partner, Matthew Nowicki, had been killed in a plane crash—that the Chandigarh job
was handed to Le Corbusier, who retained much of Mayer's street grid. Ely Jacques
Kahn, designer of some of Manhattan's most prestigious department stores, led the
team for the second unit of the Fort Greene Houses, while housing reformer and regional planner Clarence S. Stein headed the third. Stein, the most progressive of the
group, had been part of a brilliant gathering of New York intellectuals in the 1920s that
sought to realize in America the ideals of English town planners and social visionaries
Ebenezer Howard and Patrick Geddes. In 1923 he helped found, with Lewis Mumford
and Benton MacKaye, the Regional Planning Association of America, and went on
to design several landmark communities: Sunnyside Gardens and the Phipps Garden
Apartments in Queens, and the celebrated "town for the motor age" at Radburn, New
Jersey, meant to be America's first true Garden City.

By almost every measure, the scale of the Fort Greene Houses was vast. This was
public housing on the order of the Manhattan Project, the single largest such development ever attempted in the United States. Some six thousand tons of steel went
into framing its buildings, nearly the amount used to erect the Eiffel Tower. There

Fort Greene Houses under construction, August 1942. New York City Housing Authority, La Guardia and
Wagner Archives.

were fifty thousand windows and twenty thousand doors in the complex, and its ninety-three elevators boasted a combined lift of nearly a mile. Orders for masonry emptied brickyards from Newburgh to Albany. More than sixteen million bricks were devoured by the project—set end to end, they would form a line from Brooklyn to Mexico City. The surface area of the exterior brick walls alone covered almost two million square feet—more acreage than the site itself. With a projected resident population of over thirteen thousand people, Fort Greene was an instant town, roughly the size of Saratoga Springs, Beacon, or Oneonta at the time. Formal dedication took place in September 1942, with Governor Lehman, Mayor La Guardia, navy admiral E. J. Marquat, and other officials on hand. The ceremonies were broadcast on WNYC.[16] It was a historic moment indeed, for the project's completion marked the arrival of urban design ideology that had been lapping American shores for several years—the tower-in-the-park model that Franco-Swiss modernist Le Corbusier first proposed in the early 1920s. Le Corbusier recoiled at the same conditions of overcrowding and congestion that reformers sought to eliminate in the Fifth Ward. Like many of his generation, he was spellbound by the promise of technology—"the joyous and productive impulse of the new machine-civilisation." It was that most exhilarating of machine-age innovations—the airplane, and the aerial perspective it enabled—that convinced him of the urgent need to sweep away the calcified urban past. For Le Corbusier, flying over Paris was no joyride but a revelation of human failure; spread out below he saw "a spectacle of collapse" that laid bare a damning fact: "that men have built cities for men, not in order to give them pleasure, to content them, to make them happy, *but to make money!*" "*L'avion accuse*," he declared: "The airplane is an indictment. It indicts the city. It indicts those who control the city." Here, Corb resolved, was "proof . . . of the rightness of our desire to alter methods of architecture and town-planning." His mandate rang clear: "Cities, with their misery, must be torn down. They must be largely destroyed and fresh cities built."[17]

It was a seductive call to arms, heeded on both sides of the Atlantic by architects, planners, and developers alike. Traditional forms of urbanism were scrapped almost overnight for a sleek vision of soaring towers in an expansive landscape of parks and motorways. The Fort Greene Houses were a marvel of modernity in the midst of hardscrabble Brooklyn. From atop Fort Greene Park, ramparts aglow in the raking light of a late November afternoon, the Corbusian towers "take on the appearance of a veritable city," rhapsodized an *Eagle* reporter. "But it is a city strangely altered from our usual concepts," he confessed, more like "some strange projection of the future" than anything else in Gotham.[18] More perceptive critics saw the folly of imposing a supranational, one-size-fits-all solution on highly specialized urban problems, willfully ignoring the exigencies of local culture, politics, climate, and site. Corb's machinic urbanism proved antithetical to everything people loved about cities—it was "a frigid megalomaniacally scaled negation," writes Norma Evenson, "of the familiar urban ambient."[19] The most penetrating critique of this utopianist urbanism on Brooklyn soil came, not surprisingly, from the pen of Lewis Mumford. As skeptical of the machine as Le Corbusier was exhilarated by it, Mumford feared that modernity would release "a Pandora's box of mechanical marvels that eventually threatened to absorb all human purposes."[20] The title of a 1950 *New Yorker* essay on the subject—"The Red-Brick Beehives"—says it all. By the time Mumford wrote the piece, a decade after the Fort Greene project broke ground, identical housing estates had popped up all over Gotham. Mumford was troubled by the relentless uniformity of these complexes, as if "arranged by a tidy but too methodical child." He found this extraordinary given that the projects were designed and built by a diversity of actors—the city housing authority, life insurance companies, private developers. "Strange to say," he remarked, "dozens of architectural firms, in free rivalry, produced those masterpieces of regimentation," all seemingly struck from the "same forbidding institutional pattern . . . as if they had all been designed by one mind, carried out by one organization, intended for one class of people, bred like bees to fit into these honeycombs." Though the projects created housing far superior to the slums they replaced, their sterility and "inhuman scale . . . their barrackslike air" troubled him. These were places formed, he feared, not around family or neighborhood but the elevator shaft. "If this new pattern of building becomes more widely imitated," he predicted with great prescience, "it will create urban disabilities that will be more difficult to remove than the old slums."[21]

With the slums of old long gone from New York City, it is easy to forget just how pernicious an evil unregulated urban density once was to planners and city officials. Today, uncoupled from its toxic former associations, density is cheered as a palliative to ills of a different sort—those born of the placeless sprawl of postwar suburbia and the sterilities of single-use zoning. Open space was desperately needed in the heavily congested neighborhoods around the Navy Yard. But so was housing robust

Fort Greene Houses nearing completion, 1942. New York City Municipal Archives.

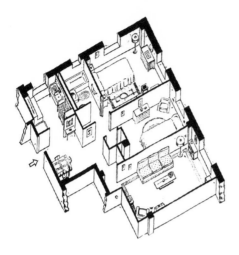

Axonometric rendering of a two-bedroom apartment in the Fort Greene Houses. From *Brooklyn Eagle*, August 16, 1942.

enough to rehouse the thousands of families displaced by slum clearance. Superblock modernism offered a solution to a seemingly unresolvable conundrum: accommodating huge numbers of people while also providing an abundance of open space. The Fort Greene project housed some thirty-five hundred families, more than double the former population on the thirty-nine-acre site. And it did so using a fraction of the land for buildings. Building coverage was over 90 percent in the "Jungle"; the total footprint of the new towers was less than 25 percent. Open space shot from practically zero to nearly thirty acres. It was a victory for all, or so it seemed. For all his qualms about the dehumanizing architecture of the new housing, Mumford—champion of the Garden City—cheered the superblock, calling it "the most important contribution these projects have made to the concept of a new city." Not only was the superblock economical—eliminating "long stretches of street and with unnecessary duplications of water, sewer, and gas mains"—but it kept vehicular traffic away from the living environment, creating "pools of quiet" that enabled residents to "probably sleep better than the inhabitants of most other parts of the city." For Mumford, the Corbusian park saved its towers; for without "generous planting of trees, bushes, and flower beds . . . walks and grass plots and outdoor shelters," buildings like those at Fort Greene justified indeed "Herman Melville's epithet for New York: a Babylonish brick kiln."[22]

The opening of the Fort Greene Houses was greeted with a groundswell of enthusiasm by officials, the downtown business community, and the press. To make sure all went well, the city hired an experienced facilities director—an architect named Frank Dorman—to manage the huge estate. Dorman had previously run the Williamsburg Houses and the Vladeck Houses on the Lower East Side. At his side was a large corps of "trained housing assistants," all women, who would call on tenants "not just to collect the rent, but to discuss with them their problems." Dorman was confident that he and his handpicked staff of sixty could run the Fort Greene Houses "with efficiency and economy," making the complex a model for both city and nation. "We won't have too many problems." Everyone wanted the project to be a resounding success, a showpiece. "Brooklyn will be proud of this splendid civic achievement," foretold the *Eagle* in a sixteen-page Sunday supplement a day before opening on August 17, 1942. It was a Cinderellic metamorphosis indeed: "straggling, sagging rookeries" had been expunged, and in their place was now "comfortable housing for workmen . . . streamlined for happy homemaking." Few could imagine these gleaming towers as anything but a great boon to Brooklyn. "Borough real estate men," the paper reported, "are convinced, they say, that property values in the vicinity of the Fort Greene Houses . . . will be favorably affected by the vast residential development." The well-appointed model unit only confirmed this. Cheerfully didactic, it exuded cleaning-day freshness, vitality, and middle-American values. "In the living room is a divan, two comfortable easy chairs and a chest of drawers," noted the *Eagle*, "which serves as both a console table and a place to store household extras. A scatter rug makes a bright spot against the dark gray asphalt tiling of the floor," while the bed was made up with a "candlewick spread." The baby's nursery was airy and sun splashed, with a crib in one corner, "a gay play rug on the floor and a rocking chair for mother." The apartments all had bathtubs "similar to those in high-rent Forest Hills." Fulton Street retailers salivated at the throngs of new customers needful of housewares

A nice healthful jaunt

will take you from

FORT GREENE HOUSES

to the

HORN & HARDART AUTOMAT
3 Willoughby Street at Fulton

and

RETAIL SHOPS
20 Willoughby Street near Pearl
551 Fulton Street near Bond

Advertisement for Horn and Hardart Automat aimed at residents of the newly opened Fort Greene Houses. From *Brooklyn Eagle*, August 16, 1942.

and provisions of every sort. Every major Brooklyn department store ran an advertisement in the *Eagle* supplement, many featuring handsome white people strolling through the modernist utopia or poring over plans for homemaking. "We salute the exciting development brought by men of vision!" gushed Oppenheim Collins; "We salute our new neighbors who have brought it life and richness!" "We're anxious to meet you," chirped Martins, "eager to welcome you as the old friends we hope you soon will be." "We're practically next door, you know," coaxed Abraham and Straus, "just a few minutes away on your bicycle!" Within a decade, no one would be boasting of such proximities.[23]

Even before the war ended, there were signs that all was not well in this redbrick paradise. The needle barely registered these at first. A beat reporter visiting the Fort Greene Houses just after Thanksgiving 1944 saw that walkways were littered "and windows here and there are broken," but concluded nonetheless that "time has not dealt too unkindly with the greatest thing of its kind in the city." But just that summer there had been clashes between black and white youths on the edges of the vast complex. The fighting started, predictably enough, after the sister of one of the ringleaders was catcalled by a group of black teens. A crowd of more than a hundred white youths from the larger neighborhood gathered that night at the Prison Ship Monument before descending on the housing project to exact random retribution. Armed with clubs and baseball bats, the mob "fanned out in all directions, pushing and shoving Negroes in apparent efforts to instigate fights." Nearly two hundred officers from three precincts responded to the melee. The police were not evenhanded in deploying their nightsticks. The following week, a white Fort Greene resident and community organizer named Belle Sundeen, the office manager of the radical *Daily Worker*, led a twelve-member, biracial "Anti-Discrimination Committee of Tenants of the Fort Greene Houses" to the Brooklyn district attorney's office, pressing for an investigation into reports "that police action had been biased and that Negroes had been unfairly treated."[24]

Despite this, race relations among residents of the Fort Greene Houses were largely positive—at least at first. Whites dominated the complex when it opened and were still a strong majority in 1945, when only 539 of about 3,500 resident families were African American. This is why all those Fulton Street retailers clamored to advertise in the 1942 *Eagle* supplement on the Fort Greene Houses: the folks moving in were mostly middle-class families with steady incomes—not welfare recipients, former sharecroppers from the South, or even displaced residents of the impoverished "Jungle" promised new homes. The outbreak of World War II effectively turned the just-launched Fort Greene project into a military housing facility. Priority for units was given to personnel in the Third Naval District and the army's Second Service Command, headquartered on Governors Island, to women serving with the US Naval Reserve (WAVES), and to workers employed at the Navy Yard and in war-related industry. The change was slow at first, encouraging a too-brief period of seeming harmony and tolerance—a "pleasant neighborliness of races," as the *Eagle* put it. "Here Negro and white toddlers eat and play games together and go through all the pre-school and kindergarten learning routines," a reporter observed of Fort Greene's on-site nursery school. "When asked to come along to the play corner, a small white girl seized a tiny Negro girl by the hand, in an apparently familiar gesture, and they ran in side by side." A variety of tenant organizations had turned the forbidding complex into a real community. There was scouting for boys and girls, a group called "Teen Town," a meeting of men interested in crafts, and support groups for the elderly. At least two outside organizations—the National Negro Congress and American Youth for Democracy—attempted to hold meetings in the project's recreation room but were stopped by the housing authority because of their links to the Communist Party. Residents even published a monthly newsletter—the *Tenant's Voice*.[25]

But as Fort Greene's demographics shifted, the fragile ecology of tolerance and goodwill began to fray. The *Eagle* gamely tried to downplay reports of racial discord, chalking them off as wash-day squabbles common to every American neighborhood. In a painfully forced 1946 piece, columnist Jane Corby insisted that there were "no racial distinctions when it comes to a good, neighborly free-for-all. No racial name-calling. Just clean American fight lingo . . . give and take between racial equals, to be heard up and down any dumbwaiter shaft." By this time, the navy had moved out nearly all of its three hundred-odd families from the Fort Greene Houses. They were replaced in the main by African American families arriving from North Carolina, Virginia, and other Southern states. As the black population rose, white residents began leaving at a faster clip. Some moved elsewhere in Brooklyn; others headed for the suburbs of Queens, Long Island, or New Jersey. Then came an ill-considered policy directive that virtually assured the end of Fort Greene's fragile balance of race and class. In January 1947 the housing authority began serving eviction notices to families earning over $3,000 a year.

The rule was well-meant—space was needed for the many poor families arriving daily from the South and, increasingly, Puerto Rico and the West Indies. But Fort Greene's more prosperous families, black and white, were a stabilizing force in the housing complex; purging them was like pulling the keystone out of an arch. By the 1960s, more than fifty families a year were being evicted for exceeding the income cap. "Those are the families we need to keep," pleaded resident activist Olivette Thompson, "the kind we can't afford to lose."[26]

And so what had been a thriving mixed-race, mixed-income community was transformed almost overnight into a near monoculture of race and class. Housing authority records show that, exclusive of navy personnel, the racial composition of the Fort Greene Houses was 83 percent white and 17 percent black in July 1945. A decade later, the white population was less than 27 percent, while more than 73 percent of residents were either black or Puerto Rican—and many very poor.[27] The income cap had another, even more pernicious effect: it punished success. Residents could keep a unit at Fort Greene only if their household income remained below a certain level. To struggle up the economic ladder was to hazard being thrown to a merciless housing market. "The able, rising families are constantly driven out as their incomes cross the ceiling," noted Harrison E. Salisbury in a 1958 *New York Times* exposé on the complex drawn from his best-selling book, *The Shook-Up Generation*. By excluding high achievers and role-model families, the community was deprived of "the normal quota of human talents needed for self-organization, self-discipline and self-improvement." The rule incentivized inertia, and bent ambition and enterprise toward crime. The result, Salisbury concluded, was "a human catchpool that breeds social ills and requires endless outside assistance." Equally ill-considered were "senseless man-in-the-house welfare regulations," as activist Walter Thabit called them—rules that discouraged women from having in their homes an employed, breadwinning male partner. This took a wrecking ball to traditional family structure, laying the groundwork for the single-parent epidemic that would create a generation of black men raised without a male role model. All this worked against the formation of social capital at the Fort Greene Houses, fostering a climate lethal to a sense of community or love of place. It is no wonder, then, that this showpiece of progressive housing policy was soon beset by a shattering gamut of social problems.[28]

It was during the summer of 1949, with the city besieged for weeks by a terrible heat wave, that crime at the Fort Greene Houses first began making news. On July 11, a delegation of frightened residents led by Fannie Weinstein Bakal, president of the Fort Greene District Civic Association, marched into the Eighty-Eighth Precinct station to beg the police to do something about the escalating number of assaults and burglaries in the complex. Just recently six women had nearly been raped on the grounds, including a grandmother on her way back from the Navy Yard. Bakal led a second delegation to housing authority offices in Manhattan, this time accompanied by five victimized women. A special unit of security guards, she was reminded, had already been deployed at the housing project. But the men were older and poorly trained, and they carried no guns; overwhelmed, they took to patrolling in groups of three. Not a week later two more attempted rapes were reported, including one involving a ten-year-old girl. "Terror stalks the Fort Greene Housing Project these hot, humid nights," hyperbolized the *Eagle*, "when fog rolls through the brick canyons from the East River nearby." Combat veterans from the local post of the American Legion threatened to organize a vigilante committee to fight the crime wave. "I'd just as soon pack a gun myself and guard the place, like we did overseas," exclaimed the post commander; "It's come to that." Faced with a public relations disaster, the Eighty-Eighth Precinct amended its patrol routine to take in the complex; police posts and call boxes were installed at strategic locations. But all this was restricted to the perimeter of the vast housing complex, thanks to the celebrated Corbusian superblock. The police were not permitted to enter housing authority grounds or buildings unless they were responding to a call, or were actively pursuing a suspect. The lack of interior streets kept patrolmen and "prowl cars" on the edges of the vast complex, where their presence had little deterrent effect. The housing authority eventually established an armed force of its own, trained at the city's police academy, but it took until 1958 for it to open a police precinct within a housing project. They put it, not surprisingly, at Fort Greene.[29]

By this time, crime was soaring both in and around the huge complex—muggings, burglaries, gang scuffles, sexual assaults all became commonplace. To be out after dark was to hazard life and limb. In October 1953, police just barely headed off "a bloody gang fight" when some thirty youths gathered at the Carleton Avenue

Jackie Robinson speaking at the dedication of a playground at the Fort Greene Houses, October 1959. New York City Housing Authority, La Guardia and Wagner Archives.

entrance of the Fort Greene Houses "armed with knives, clubs, zip-guns and other makeshift weapons." Early the next year, a twenty-two-year-old mother of four and wife of an army private serving overseas was slashed to death in her bed as her children slept in the next room. By 1958 there were at least two more killings on the project's doorstep—a sailor knifed by a group of teens and the stomping death of a youth by rival gang members. Elevators, the weakest link in a high-rise public housing complex, were a particular problem at Fort Greene. The small-cab lifts, unstaffed and claustrophobic, were traps in which muggers and rapists caught many a woman coming home from a late shift. Typical was a case involving nineteen-year-old Adele Rocco, who was returning to her apartment when a man followed her into the lift, brandished a knife, grabbed her purse, and escaped down the staircase. Sluggish and prone to malfunctions, the lifts could barely manage ordinary use and became total choke points with any surge in traffic. When school let out in the afternoon, for example, dozens of restless teens would gather in the lobby for an interminable wait, inevitably leading to trouble. And then there was the piss and filth. "Most visitors to the Fort Greene Houses in Brooklyn prefer to walk up three or four flights instead of taking the elevator," explained the *Times*; "They choose the steep, cold staircases rather than face the stench of stale urine that pervades the elevators."[30]

Vandalism, too, plagued Fort Greene—mailboxes kicked in, lightbulbs smashed or stolen, fire hoses slashed with knives, hall lights ripped out, tree limbs broken, shrubs and flowers trampled, sitting bench slats cracked, split, and burned. The housing authority and its on-site managers were "seemingly helpless," complained one tenant, "in the face of the constant destruction of project property." Though there's no excusing bad-apple tenants for this behavior, much of the vandalism could have been prevented had Fort Greene's builders made more judicious decisions about design, materials, and construction. The project architects understood the need for toughness and durability, but they also wanted to avoid creating a place so coldly institutional that it resembled a prison or psychiatric hospital. Nor did anybody in 1940 anticipate just how much abuse the model complex would be subjected to. So steel doors were rejected in favor of homey wooden ones, which were quickly carved up. Glass was used in the stair halls and entranceways to foster a sense of transparency and openness, but shattering the costly panes became "one of the forms of amusement for the children in the area," complained housing authority chief Philip J. Cruise; "we have two gangs of men assigned solely to the task of replacing glass." Maintenance staff had their hands full even without the vandalism. War-induced shortages had forced the use of inferior materials and equipment throughout the complex. Walls crumbled, elevator mechanisms rusted to the point of failure, and corroded pipes sprang leaks. Barely fifteen years after Fort Greene opened, all of its plumbing had to be replaced and all the walls plastered afresh. The original cut-rate kitchen appliances were swapped out, elevators were upgraded, wooden doors were replaced with steel, and every last piece of glass was pulled out of stairways and entrances. The *Times* called the $1.3 million upgrade "the biggest home fix-it job" ever undertaken by the housing authority.[31]

To some critics, however, none of this would remedy the real problem at Fort Greene and nearly every other public housing project in the city at the time—the "bureaucratically produced rootlessness," as Michael Harrington put it; the fact that at every turn, life in these places was made to feel provisional and impermanent. One of the fiercest was renowned housing advocate Charles Abrams. Son of a Williamsburg pickle-and-herring merchant, Abrams enjoyed a long career in public service—as a lawyer, urban-planning educator, and United Nations consultant. If anyone could call out the New York City Housing Authority, it was Abrams; he had drafted the legislation to create the agency in 1934 and was its first counsel. For all his faith in the welfare state, Abrams concluded that the trouble with public housing was the lack of any sense of proprietorship on the part of residents. The transitionality and impermanence of such housing fostered a pernicious "squatter attitude" that worked against the formation of communal bonds—breeding vandalism and a host of social ills. The solution, Abrams proposed in 1952, was to sell apartment units to tenants as they achieved financial stability. Ownership would counter the "economic ghetto aspects of public housing," he argued, giving residents "pride and a sense of belonging" and thus helping to eradicate "the slipshod living which is already wrecking new projects like the Fort Greene Houses." Aware of the political storm such a plan would kick up, Abrams offered an alternative: rather than forcing residents out as their incomes rose, simply raise their rents. This would both stabilize the community and raise desperately needed funds for more housing.[32]

But Abrams's advice was not heeded, and the Fort Greene project slowly spiraled into chaos. Born of good intentions but ruined by ill-considered policy, a failed model of urban design, and "blind enforcement of bureaucratic rules," the celebrated city-in-a-city became more feared than the infamous "Jungle" it had replaced. "Nowhere this side of Moscow," wrote Salisbury, "are you likely to find public housing so closely duplicating the squalor it was designed to supplant."[33] The dreary Corbusian housing estates he had toured in the Soviet Union had been replicated in Brooklyn, with "the same shoddy shiftlessness, the broken windows, the missing light bulbs, the plaster cracking from the walls . . . the playgrounds that are seas of muddy clay, the bruised and battered trees, the ragged clumps of grass, the planned absence of art, beauty or taste, the gigantic masses of brick, of concrete, of asphalt, the inhuman genius with which our know-how has been perverted to create human cesspools worse than those of yesterday." Salisbury did not mince his words. He branded New York's postwar housing projects "fiendishly contrived institutions for the debasing of family and community life to the lowest common mean. They are worse than anything George Orwell ever conceived."[34]

In the end it was that most celebrated aspect of the Fort Greene project—its immense, unprecedented scale—that helped turn America's most progressive housing experiment into a modern ghetto. The Fort Greene Houses concentrated far too many desperately poor families in one place, and a relatively isolated place at that. Abrams understood this well, arguing that public housing must be small and scattered, eased rather than forced into the social and physical fabric of the city. Bigness built the battleships and bombs that won the war, but it was no way to create a lasting, resilient urban community. Thirty years before architects and urban planners embraced a small-scale infill approach to public housing, Abrams urged developing vacant lots throughout the city as a wiser alternative to massive—and massively disruptive—slum-clearance projects. Today, the Fort Greene Houses no longer exists, at least administratively. In a desperate effort to ease the scale of the increasingly unmanageable complex, the housing authority divided it down the middle in 1958. The western half was named after former Brooklyn borough president Raymond V. Ingersoll; the eastern half for Walt Whitman. The largest public housing project in American history was split into history.

Aerial view of the Fort Greene Houses looking east, 1958, showing the long-vanished BMT Myrtle Avenue elevated. America's largest public housing complex, it was later split administratively into the Walt Whitman and Raymond V. Ingersoll Houses. New York City Housing Authority, La Guardia and Wagner Archives.

COLOSSUS OF ROADS

In downtown Brooklyn, the real harbinger of things to come was neither the embattled Fort Greene Houses nor that alcazar of postwar liberalism—the long-delayed Brooklyn Civic Center—but rather the asphalt passage between the two. Wholly absent from earlier schemes for the civic center, the Brooklyn-Queens Expressway became a key piece of the downtown renewal plan crafted by Robert Moses, for it was vital to the highway system he had long envisioned for the region. Originally called the Brooklyn-Queens Connecting Highway, the twenty-three-mile motorway drove a path through the city every bit as destructive as the later, more highly publicized Cross Bronx Expressway. By the time construction on the artery was finished in 1950, Gotham's road grid was fully woven into the extensive web of motor parkways built earlier in Westchester and across Long Island. Moses was well on his way to achieving one of his oldest dreams—to "weave together," as he famously put it, "the loose strands and frayed edges of New York's arterial and metropolitan tapestry."[1]

If, as we saw in chapter 4, the parkway was a Brooklyn invention, the modern highway was a product of the Greater New York metropolitan region. The word *highway* itself was first officially used in Kings County, in a document dated June 1654 that made reference to Kings Highway. It was in Westchester County in the early 1920s that the essential elements of modern highway design—limited access, grade-separated crossings, and smooth flowing curves, all enabling the sustained high-speed operation of motor vehicles—first appeared, in the pathbreaking trio of the Bronx, Saw Mill, and Hutchinson River parkways. Progenitors of the American interstates, they were the first roads anywhere designed for the pleasure of the motoring public. The Westchester parkways were studied by engineers from Germany, China, and Australia, replicated throughout North America and around the globe. Indeed, there is not a highway in the world without some of their DNA. In its original form, the parkway was meant to be not a commuter arterial, but rather a scenic reservation threaded with a drive for the leisurely—and exclusive—use of passenger automobiles (buses, like trucks, were prohibited from the start, complicating later claims that parkway bridges were made low on purpose to prevent the nondriving poor from using parks and beaches). The parkway was literally a *way* through a *park*. Like an extruded version of Central Park, it was meant to spirit one away from the city—from the "cramped, confined and controlling circumstances of the streets of the town," as Frederick Law Olmsted put it—by imparting an immersive, almost cinematic sense of travel through a vast pastoral landscape. This was, of course, mostly stagecraft and illusion. In reality, the parkway corridor was just a narrow strip of land, in places just a few hundred feet wide. But it was richly garnished with rustic fences, signs and light standards, and romantic, low-slung bridges dressed with ashlar stone, while off-site scenes disruptive of the pastoral reverie—factories, commercial districts, apartment buildings, adjacent neighborhoods—were artfully screened by berms and lush plantings of trees and shrubs. The parkway was thus both a bold step forward and a nostalgic glance back—the machine age in tweeds or, as Marshall Berman memorably put it, "a kind of romantic bower in which modernism and pastoralism could intertwine."[2]

Equally innovative was the way these early parkways were used to structure a region-wide system of parklands and open space, creating in Westchester County the first park system of the motor age. It was specifically this—the motorway as regional parks-and-recreation infrastructure—that caught the eye of Robert Moses, whom Governor Al Smith had placed in charge of a new statewide parks agency in 1924. Moses modeled both the Long Island State Park Commission and the earlier New York State Council of Parks on the Westchester County Park Commission, and tapped the design genius behind its parks and parkways—Gilmore D. Clarke—to help him develop a sand-and-sea replica of the Westchester system for Long Island. Clarke, as we've seen, first met Moses while supervising construction of the Bronx River Parkway and later planned the Brooklyn Civic Center with partner Michael Rapuano. A decade before Moses brought Clarke to New York City, he tried to recruit the landscape architect to the Long Island State Park Commission. Though Clarke declined the job, he agreed to give lantern-slide presentations about his Westchester work to Long Island civic groups. Clarke later advised Clarence C. Coombs and a fellow veteran of the American Expeditionary Forces, Henry Lee Bowlby, in laying out the first Long Island parkways. He also sent one of his Westchester acolytes—Melvin B. Borgeson—to help draft plans for Jones Beach State Park, on which he was a consultant.[3]

By 1935, with the suburbs north and east of town laced with state-of-the-art motorways, New York struggled to make do with a street grid designed for horse carts and carriages. Traffic congestion was so bad that planners feared for the city's future as an economic powerhouse. For Moses, lacing Gotham with modern parkways, linking the metropolis by road to the nation at large, was a keystone ambition of his career, one that he first unveiled in February 1930 as chairman of the Metropolitan Park Conference—and that he acted on within days of taking office as the first citywide commissioner of parks. The first of these—the Henry Hudson Parkway—linked Manhattan and the Bronx to Westchester County via the Saw Mill Parkway.

Watercolor rendering of the Westchester County Park System, 1928. Westchester County Archives.

A project Moses had dreamed about for decades, work on the road began in early 1934, with the northernmost section opening two years later. Like its Westchester antecedents, the Henry Hudson was much more than just a vehicular thoroughfare. One of the hallmarks of motor parkway design as it evolved in Westchester was the provision of a rich array of leisure and recreation facilities along the route for use by the nonmotoring public—trails, picnic areas, ball fields, playgrounds. For Moses, too, such amenities were vital—at least at first. In his own words, parkways were "long ribbon parks with landscaped edges providing passive and active recreation for all age-groups resident nearby."[4] The southernmost section of the Henry Hudson was especially well endowed in this regard. It was part of a massive overhaul of Olmsted's old Riverside Park—the West Side Improvement—that fused city, park, and motorway into a seamless whole. At Seventy-Ninth Street, Clarke and Rapuano and architect Clinton F. Lloyd created an extraordinary multileveled roundabout—officially the "79th Street Grade Crossing Elimination Structure" (carefully worded to tap federal funds for removing dangerous road-rail intersections). There, parkway access ramps and walking paths were spun around a Romanesque sunken plaza with a fountain in the center and a terrace overlooking the Hudson (today the Boat Basin Café). Elsewhere the Henry Hudson Parkway was padded with playgrounds, ball courts, and athletic fields, all framed by the same Italianate grid of London plane trees that Rapuano used at Cadman Plaza and Bryant parks. The West Side Improvement was highway planning at its best, a splendid union of city, citizenry, and the motorcar.[5]

That high note would be struck again in Brooklyn, though under very different circumstances. It was there that Robert Moses built the most ambitious parkway project of his career—that shoreline route proposed as early as 1911 by Brooklyn's minister of improvement, the Reverend Newell Dwight Hillis, and later urged by the Regional Plan Association as part of a "Parkway Circuit in South Brooklyn." Originally called the Brooklyn-Queens Circumferential Parkway, the thirty-six-mile route would ultimately consist of four signed sections through Brooklyn and Queens—the Shore, Southern, Laurelton, and Cross Island parkways. Moses personally renamed the route the Belt Parkway shortly after construction began in 1938, reportedly because Queens borough president George U. Harvey could neither spell nor pronounce "circumferential." Mayor La Guardia called it "New York's first Ringstrasse," while others favored "Lynque Parkway"—a playful homophone emphasizing the road's linkage of Brook*lyn* and *Que*ens. No road offered more amenities for communities along the route than the Belt Parkway, which is why—along with its fifty-eight bridges—the project cost nearly as much as Hoover Dam. In a letter to Reagan "Tex" McCrary of the *New York Daily Mirror* (who later produced the "American house" display at the 1959 United States Exhibition in Moscow, setting off the Nixon-Khrushchev kitchen debate), Moses described the Belt as "not just an automobile roadway," but "a narrow shoestring park running around the entire city and including all sorts of recreation facilities"—ball fields, basketball courts, and many miles of bike path. He implored one of his superintendents, Allyn R. Jennings, to keep in mind that such "incidental . . . features are just as important as the parkway itself," especially for "people in the neighborhoods along the route, present and future, who do not have automobiles." With this great profusion of

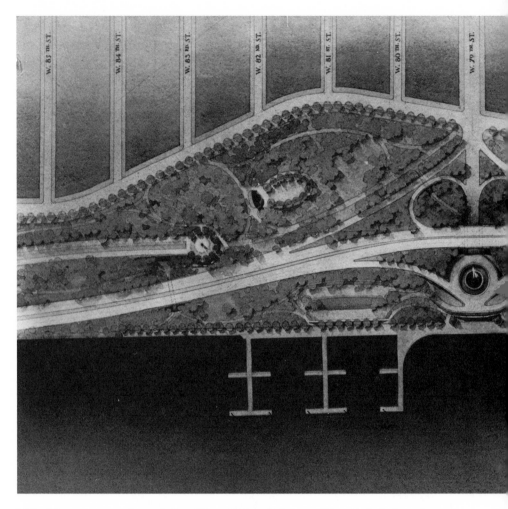

Michael Rapuano, watercolor rendering of Henry Hudson Parkway and Riverside Park, December 1935. This section of Rapuano's immense drawing shows the parkway from West Eighty-Fifth Street to West Seventy-Second Street, including Clinton F. Lloyd's roundabout and fountain court at Seventy-Ninth Street (Boat Basin Café). From *Detail Plans and Estimated Cost of Construction . . . for the West Side Improvement in Riverside Park* (1936). Division of Rare and Manuscript Collections, Cornell University Library.

public amenity—3,550 acres of parkland in all—the Belt Parkway was hailed "the greatest municipal highway venture ever attempted."[6]

However innovative, the Belt was not the first trailblazing thoroughfare in Brooklyn. Nor was it the first conceived as part of a greater park system, or even to be called a *parkway*. As we saw in chapter 4, Olmsted coined the term to describe the three great pleasure drives, based on Haussmann's Parisian boulevards, that he proposed to extrude Prospect Park through still-rural Brooklyn and Queens and even back to Central Park via a bridge at Roosevelt Island.

After World War II, with car sales soaring and a new culture of speed and efficiency in place, the humanism of Olmsted's parkways and the motorways of the 1930s was largely set aside. Long, flowing spiral curves were pulled straight; lushly

planted parkway reservations were pared down to the barest minimum; bike paths, walks, playgrounds, and ball fields were scrapped. Partly this was because, by 1945, the "easy" pieces of the arterial tapestry had all been woven—routes along the shoreline, often on filled land, like the Belt and Henry Hudson, or through farmland, parks, or cemeteries like the Hudson, Interboro (Jackie Robinson), or Grand Central parkways. Connecting up the remaining dots now involved punching through some of the most densely built urban terrain on the Eastern Seaboard—lower Manhattan, the South Bronx, and downtown Brooklyn. The longest and most costly of these—the Brooklyn-Queens Connecting Highway—began with the construction of the Gowanus Parkway prior to World War II. A transitional project, it was meant to extend the Belt Parkway north from Bay Ridge through Sunset Park as part of a grand arterial loop Moses hoped to build through Brooklyn and Queens. But the Gowanus was nothing like the Belt or the earlier scenic motor parkways. Instead, it was up high and arrow-straight, riding atop the steel piers that once carried the BMT Third Avenue Elevated from downtown to Sixty-Fifth Street (and on new supports north of Thirty-Eighth Street). Because the roadbed was much wider

Cover, *Gowanus Improvement*, Triborough Bridge Authority, 1941. Division of Rare and Manuscript Collections, Cornell University Library.

than the railway, hundreds of buildings had to come down on both sides of the street. And while Third Avenue had been shadowed by the el since the 1890s, it flourished nonetheless as the commercial core of Sunset Park's large Scandinavian community. The shade cast by elevated tracks is light dappled and moves with the sun, like that of forest trees. The shade cast by an elevated roadbed is as fixed and unbroken as night. It "buried the avenue in shadow," writes Robert Caro; "and when the parkway was completed, the avenue was cast forever into darkness and gloom." Seduced by Moses's ingenuity in repurposing the old el, the *Times* missed the larger point—that the Gowanus, despite its name, had scuttled nearly every design principle that distinguished the American parkway. "When Commissioner Moses finds the surface of the earth too congested for one of his parkways," it rationalized, "he lifts the road into the air and continues it on its way." New York was, after all, just "too heavily built up for a leisurely, landscaped parkway." Time to get tough with all that silly urbanism cluttering the path of automobiles! And trucks, too: insofar as it was a nominal "parkway," only passenger cars were permitted on the Gowanus, so Moses widened Third Avenue from four to ten lanes to handle all the truck traffic generated by the still-busy industrial waterfront. Within a decade, not only Third Avenue—once home to seven movie theaters, scores of shops, stores, restaurants, and cafés—but much of Sunset Park would be spiraling toward abandonment and blight. Whatever survived was finished off by the late 1950s, when the Gowanus was widened from four to six lanes and officially named what it had been all along—the Gowanus Expressway.[7]

Worse was in store for the older, denser, poorer neighborhoods north of Sunset Park—the large working-class community of South Brooklyn (parts of which were rebranded Carroll Gardens and Cobble Hill as the area began gentrifying in the 1960s). Here a new colossus of roads would be built—not overhead like the Gowanus, but in a mile-long trench down Hicks Street from Hamilton to Atlantic avenues. The Brooklyn-Queens Connecting Highway would extend the Belt-Gowanus system north toward Astoria, eventually joining the Grand Central Parkway to provide "a convenient and rapid connection," explained the *Times*, "between congested Brooklyn districts and popular routes leading to the World's Fair, as well as Long Island parks and seashore."[8] Moses positioned the project as one of four "vital gaps" in the region's arterial system that he sought to fill on Washington's dime. Bending geopolitics to serve his will, he announced a $65 million program of road building on Armistice Day 1940, ostensibly to "facilitate the defense of New York City in war." Left unfilled, Moses argued, these arterial lacunae would invalidate two decades of public works, for all those bridges, tunnels, and parkways built since the 1920s "could not adequately cope with both military and essential civilian requirements in wartime without the four proposed highways." This was a tautology Moses would deploy again and again in the postwar era: unlocking a full return on earlier highway investments required investing in more of the same. Filling these gaps—the Harlem River Drive, a Pelham–Port Chester Express Highway (southern end of the New England Thruway today), and an expressway across lower Manhattan were the others—would open the city to "ponderous units of mobile war machines" and "mass military manoeuvers" while at last realizing Moses's decades-old dream of a fully integrated system of metropolitan arterials. If the city took no action, Moses warned, Gotham might have to choose between food and freedom; for "if the streets are to be kept open for the inhabitants to survive, they cannot be commandeered for military use and defense transportation without disaster." Moses, always shovel-ready, promised that work on all four segments could begin immediately and be done in a year, using round-the-clock shifts and a "speeded-up" condemnation process.[9]

Construction on the BQE came in bursts, with the first section—from Meeker Avenue in Greenpoint over the Kosciuszko Bridge to Queens Boulevard—opening in the fall of 1939. In South Brooklyn, Hicks Street was approved for conversion into a multilane arterial by the City Planning Commission in May 1941. At first it was to be simply widened, from 60 to 160 feet, with twin carriageways separated by a narrow median and flanked by service roads and sidewalks. But an Ocean Parkway it was not; for "it is proposed ultimately," noted commission chair Rexford Tugwell, "to depress the central roadways below the level of the service roadways and to introduce grade separations . . . for express traffic in this highway." Title to some 250 parcels on the west side of Hicks Street was secured by late August, and demolitions began within weeks. Construction on this and other sections of the BQE was halted with America's entry into the war. Not until August 1946 did work begin on a "six-lane depressed highway down the center of widened Hicks Street," with twin twenty-eight-foot service roads, twelve-foot sidewalks, and bridges to carry

The Brooklyn-Queens Connecting Highway (BQE) trenched along Hicks Street in South Brooklyn, showing Union and Sackett street overpasses. Parks Photo Archive, New York City Department of Parks and Recreation.

streets across at Union, Sackett, Kane, and Congress streets. With South Brooklyn thus gutted, how would this python of a motorway cross Brooklyn Heights? In map view the most obvious route was to simply stay the course: continue the BQE in a Hicks Street ditch straight north to the Brooklyn Bridge. Heights residents lived in fear of just this—that Moses would drive his road north and split the gracious old neighborhood like Solomon's baby. And so when surveyors were seen fiddling with theodolites and transit rods on Hicks Street in early September 1942, the neighborhood was set abuzz like a boot-kicked beehive. The *Brooklyn Eagle* called the planned road "shocking," while the *Brooklyn Heights Press* pulled out its biggest font to DENOUNCE EXPRESS HIGHWAY, claiming readers were "shocked beyond recovery." Calmer souls knew that only a fool would incur the huge costs of condemning Hicks Street mansions when an easier route was at hand—around the Heights to the west along the steep Furman Street embankment. Moses understood this better than anyone. Aside from a self-serving quip years later—that he was talked out of going "through the Heights" by borough president Cashmore—there is no evidence that Moses seriously meant to run his road up Hicks Street. At best, the alignment was considered only briefly in the project's early route-vetting stage. As one of Moses's most trusted engineers, Ernest J. Clark, put it, none of the alignment options "except the one around Furman Street" met expressway standards, and most involved cutting through "very expensive property and churches." Furman Street was clearly "the most logical way to go."[10]

Fear and outrage over Hicks Street alignment of Brooklyn-Queens Connecting Highway, *Brooklyn Heights Express*, September 25, 1942. Roy M. D. Richardson Collection, Brooklyn College Library Archives and Special Collections.

Hicks Street would have also been politically costly. This was, after all, no hard-scrabble immigrant district like Red Hook, but a neighborhood as well off as it was well connected. While the glory days of the Heights were past, it still had real power in 1940—the soft-spoken, old-money power of club and boardroom. A list of residents in and around Columbia Heights compiled in April 1943 reads like a page from the social register—Sturgis, Talmadge, Hamilton, Fairbanks, Parke, Hale, Edwards, Atwater, MacKay. There is not a single Jewish, Italian, Irish, Greek, Polish, or Chinese name among them.[11] Moses had already been stung by the moneyed WASPs of Brooklyn Heights. Given his penchant for grudges and Machiavellian nature, it is very plausible that Moses directed his engineers to make a big show of surveying Hicks Street simply to provoke the community—as payback, perhaps, for its role in ending his Brooklyn-Battery Bridge dream several years earlier. Among the well-placed souls he faced in that fight was first lady Eleanor Roosevelt, who twice denounced the Moses span—an "eyesore perpetrated in the name of progress"—in her *New York World-Telegram* "My Day" column, evidently at the behest of friends on the Heights. By playing coy with the truth, Moses gained a strategic advantage as well: threatening the community with the Hicks Street alignment virtually guaranteed that any alternative would be eagerly approved. Introducing Furman Street as an apparent substitute for the dreaded Hicks Street route made Moses seem to be yielding to community will, while Heights residents convinced themselves it was their timely action that saved the day. Indeed, there was virtually no opposition to the "new" alignment, the one Moses almost certainly meant to build all along. "Representatives of a dozen Brooklyn business and civic organizations," the *Times* reported of the sole planning commission hearing on the project on March 10, 1943, "were unanimous in approving the proposed route." Proof that Hicks Street was just a diversion comes by way of a map, published the previous year in the Triborough Bridge Authority's *Gowanus Improvement* brochure, that clearly shows the future BQE running along the Heights waterfront. Even earlier, in a June 1941 *New York Times* article about extending the Gowanus Parkway north, borough president John Cashmore explained that it was "the intention of the city . . . to extend this express highway route . . . to Furman Street and by way of Furman Street to a connection with the Brooklyn, Manhattan and Meeker Avenue bridges."[12]

Given all this, it is poetic justice of a sort that Moses is blamed to this day for having nearly destroyed Brooklyn Heights with his expressway. Heights lore has it that only prompt action on the part of the Brooklyn Heights Association—the venerable body founded by the Reverend Hillis—saved the neighborhood from the same ruination that befell Sunset Park, Red Hook, and the South Bronx. Colorful tales abound, too, of heroics and selflessness on the part of influential Heights residents. One of the most persistent involves the Brooklyn-born typewriter heiress Gladys Underwood James. As the late Heights chronicler Henrik Krogius put it, James organized a "dinner of persuasion" to which she invited Moses and two other local doyennes. At some point in the evening, the good woman trotted out "diagrams and maps" and proceeded to convince the autocratic Moses "that the [Hicks Street] route would be fatal to the neighborhood, and that the highway must be put along Furman Street." But as Krogius later discovered, James was not even a Heights resident until

1948, when she and her husband—Darwin James III—purchased Two Pierrepont Place. In any case, an expressway down Hicks Street was hardly the most extreme proposal floated for Brooklyn Heights in the decade before World War II. That came instead, ironically, not from Demon Moses but from the pious progressives of the Regional Plan Association, who endorsed a mind-boggling scheme by architect Electus Darwin Litchfield in 1931 to remedy the presumed "obsolescence of large numbers of houses on Brooklyn Heights." How? By razing every last structure on all the blocks west of Willow Street—purging in a single pass some of the most magnificent residential architecture on the Eastern Seaboard. In its place would rise a phalanx of three-hundred-foot-tall apartment buildings. Their immense scale would have cowed even Albert Speer. At the base of these towers, Litchfield—president of the Municipal Arts Society and a descendant of Edwin Litchfield, developer of Park Slope—proposed a formal park atop Furman Street, built on a plinth with a four-lane thoroughfare tucked underneath.[13]

This idea for a combined road and promenade at Columbia Heights was not new in 1931. As we saw in chapter 10, the Reverend Hillis had proposed a "boulevard one hundred feet wide, on the level of the gardens in the rear of the Columbia Heights houses" some twenty years before. Though he was the first to envision a joint promenade and drive, plans for a "Harbor View Terrace Park" had circulated at least a decade earlier. Elaborated in a lengthy piece in the May 10, 1903, issue of the *New-York Tribune*, the "imposing park or terrace" above the Furman Street embankment would run from Middagh Street to Joralemon Street and command "an unobstructed view of New-York Harbor." At intervals along its great retaining wall there would be "semi-circular, turretlike stone platforms, like those along Riverside Drive, but more ornamental." Columbia Heights property owners were predictably "not overjoyed with the scheme." Promoters—including the Municipal Arts Society and some two thousand "leading business and professional men of the borough"—attempted to bully the holdouts, warning that failure to build the park "will mean the erection of large apartment houses upon this location within twelve months." Homeowners on Columbia Heights already had a long history of fighting attempted takings in the public interest. As early as 1827, none other than pioneer Heights developer Hezekiah Pierrepont proposed creating "an open promenade for the public . . . from Fulton ferry to Joralemon Street," but his own neighbors quashed the idea. Robert Moses refused to brook such opposition, especially from the rich, and under his autocratic rule the old idea of a Heights promenade was finally made real.[14]

At the March 1943 City Planning Commission hearing, the BQE was presented as a single broad platform elevated above Furman Street at roughly the level of Columbia Heights. Roy M. D. Richardson—Heights Association president and a Wall Street lawyer (who lived at 218 Columbia Heights)—suggested that the road be built instead as "a double-decker . . . covered on top." This would not only require taking less land along the embankment, but "keep to a minimum . . . noise and fumes" while enabling Columbia Heights homeowners to have their backyards "re-created over the covered highway." Moses had a similar scheme in mind, but where Richardson and his neighbors dreamed of private gardens, Moses envisioned

Electus D. Litchfield's solution to the "obsolescence of large numbers of houses on Brooklyn Heights," 1931. The immense podium would replace the warehouses along Furman Street, what is today Brooklyn Bridge Park. From Thomas Adams, *Regional Plan of New York and Its Environs*, vol. 2 (1931).

Section-elevation of cantilevered deck structure looking north at Clark Street, Brooklyn-Queens Connecting Highway (BQE), 1944. Rendering by Julian Michele. Brooklyn Public Library, Brooklyn Collection.

a grand public promenade, from which the breathtaking vista of lower Manhattan could be enjoyed by more than a few well-heeled elites. A full month before the public hearing, his trusted engineering consultants, Andrews and Clark, had prepared plans for an ingenious cantilevered highway structure topped by a deck with room enough for both private gardens and a public promenade. It was a quantum improvement over Litchfield's bloated podium or Hillis's Ocean Parkway on stilts. This idea, too—stacking the highway lanes one above the other—had itself been proposed before. In 1939 site planner Fred W. Tuemmler was retained by the City Planning Commission to prepare drawings for a "Brooklyn-Queens East River Express Highway." His work, published the following year, called for a partly cantilevered stacked highway structure along Furman Street, with the upper road at roughly the level of Columbia Heights but without any promenade or even sidewalks. It was left to a team of Moses consultants—led by Andrews and Clark and backed by the omnipresent Clarke and Rapuano—to recognize that a series of cantilevered decks topped with a promenade would transform a clunky piece of arterial infrastructure into a masterpiece of urban design.[15]

It's long been debated who deserves principal design credit for the cantilevered viaduct and promenade, and every line of inquiry leads to the same conclusion: like all public works of the Moses era, it was the product of many hands and minds. That said, it is probable that Michael Rapuano was the first to envision the highway cover as a grand viewing terrace. This was certainly the contention of Clarke and Rapuano partner Domenico Annese, a veteran of the Long Island State Park Commission who had once worked for Clarence C. Coombs. And it stands to reason; for not only was Rapuano one of the most gifted spatial designers of his generation, but he had

Perspective rendering of Brooklyn-Queens Expressway and Heights Promenade by C. M. Flynn, 1951. Photo Archive, New York City Department of Parks and Recreation.

Michael Rapuano, watercolor section-elevation through the Villa d'Este, Tivoli, c. 1929. Photographic Archive of the American Academy in Rome.

particular expertise in the architectonics of steeply sloping sites. It was Rapuano who helped translate the rugged bluffs below Riverside Drive into a symphony of terraces and platforms, and who—years earlier as a fellow at the American Academy in Rome—spent months studying that masterpiece of cliffside design, the Villa d'Este in Tivoli. Prior to World War II, recipients of the Rome Prize in landscape architecture were required to produce detailed measured drawings of great Renaissance villas. Queen of Italian gardens, the Villa d'Este was an elusive subject, owing to its sheer scale and complexity; wrestling the terraced titan onto paper took hundreds of hours of work in field and at the drawing board. Today a UNESCO World Heritage site, the complex was built in the 1560s by the Ferrarese cardinal Ippolito II d'Este, who had architect Pirro Ligorio erect a palace over an old monastery and transform the hillside below into a fountain-splashed cat's cradle of platforms and promenades. Soaring concrete arches and retaining walls, visible only from the valley below, made the seemingly effortless play of space possible. The gardens inspired a legion of artists over the centuries, from Piranesi to Franz Liszt, and tutored a generation of landscape architects in the mechanics of topography. "There is enough in that one garden," Daniel Burnham observed, "to furnish profitable food for thought to all landscape men in America."[16] Rapuano's exquisite watercolor renderings of the Villa d'Este, completed in 1928, were the basis of the Italian government's later restoration of the garden complex. It requires no great leap of imagination to see the similarities between the Heights promenade and the expansive viewing terrace atop the Villa d'Este, high above the Lazio Plain. Rapuano's hand is evident at a finer scale too. The layout and appointment of the promenade was commissioned to Clarke and Rapuano, where the latter took responsibility for it. Rapuano employed there one of his signature motifs—a scroll or volute—to terminate both north and south ends of the promenade, a design move he had used previously at Bryant Park and Battery Park (neither of which survives).

The Red Hook portion of the Brooklyn-Queens Connecting Highway opened on May 25, 1950, along with the Brooklyn-Battery (Hugh L. Carey) Tunnel—still the longest vehicular tunnel in North America. A caravan of "500 official automobiles" carried dignitaries over the new road from the tunnel ribbon cutting in lower Manhattan to a luncheon at the Hotel Bossert on Montague Street. The Furman Street section—stalled the previous autumn while some three hundred families were relocated from buildings south of Joralemon Street—was finished not long afterward, with the promenade itself opening on October 7, 1950. At a ribbon-cutting ceremony that December (complete with benedictions by a minister, rabbi, and priest) borough president Cashmore called Moses "the modern Leonardo da Vinci." It was hyperbole, to be sure; but Moses had indeed created an extraordinary piece of urban infrastructure here—one that both solved an arterial problem and gave New York one of its finest public spaces. Lewis Mumford, a critic not easily impressed by anything to do with Moses or the motorcar, admitted that the viaduct and promenade "must be counted among the most satisfactory accomplishments in contemporary urban design." Exhausted by the project's more heroic aspects, he focused on an exquisite little space at the foot of Orange Street—the Fruit Street Sitting Area formed by Rapuano's scrolled terminus at the promenade's northern end. Here the great space reached "a breathless architectural climax," wrote Mumford; "From one side of this circle, a reverse spiral leads upward in a ramp to the street. Within the circle, there are benches and trees, all arranged in the same circular pattern, while the stone paving consists of circular bands of contrasting textures—broken stone, hexagonal blocks, cobblestones—forming a complicated pattern with which the eye could play for hours." All this yielded such a "deeply satisfying composition" that Mumford set down his pen, pleasantly spent. "Perhaps it is just as well to leave my account of these great reconstructions at this point," he sighed; "When one has reached a moment of perfection, there is no use pushing any further."[17]

In Brooklyn Heights, the BQE bestowed a great blessing on the city. Elsewhere it took much and gave little in return. The enormous cost of the cantilevered viaduct and promenade was effectively subsidized by poorer communities along the

The highway and the city: perspective rendering of cantilevered highway structure and Brooklyn Heights Promenade by Greville Rickard, 1945. Brooklyn Public Library, Brooklyn Collection.

Robert Moses speaking at dedication of the Brooklyn Heights Promenade and Furman Street section of Brooklyn-Queens Expressway, October 1950. Brooklyn Public Library, Brooklyn Collection.

February House (with pediment) at western end of Middagh Street shortly before demolition, c. 1949. New York City Municipal Archives.

route, which were deprived of much-needed parks and playgrounds as project funds dried up. In the Heights, too, the BQE was hardly evenhanded. Swinging east past the promenade, the road obliterated several blocks of the working-class North Heights at Middagh, Poplar, and Vine streets. Among the casualties was February House, the bohemian rookery made famous by Carson McCullers. Scores of homes were caught in the road's yawning right-of-way, but February House lay directly in the highway's path—as if Moses had purposely tweaked the alignment to blow away the storied den of libertines (the house stood where the BQE's east-bound lanes exit the Columbia Heights underpass, at about the level where Paul Bowles would have had his basement piano). Also sacrificed for the expressway were the "Quaker Row" townhouses—104 to 110 Columbia Heights—erected by James Cromwell Haviland in the 1840s. It was from a window in the last of these that Washington A. Roebling monitored progress of the Brooklyn Bridge after falling victim to Caisson's disease. The homes later came into the possession of Haviland's grandson, Hamilton Easter Field. Born in the Heights, Field studied architecture at Columbia before moving to Europe, where he immersed himself in the Parisian art scene. He befriended many avant-garde artists, including Pablo Picasso, whom he commissioned in 1909 to create an eleven-piece mural for his Brooklyn Heights library—an ensemble that was only partly executed and never installed (one painting, *Nude Woman,* is at the National Gallery of Art; another, *Pipe Rack and Still Life,* is at the Met). Field was later art critic for the *Brooklyn Eagle* and opened a gallery and art school—the Ardsley School of Modern Art—in Quaker Row, joining several of the homes together at the first floor. It became a key venue by which Americans were introduced to European and Japanese modern art. Field's first big show—Important Exhibition of Modern Art: Impressionism, Post Impressionism and Cubism—opened in December 1916, featuring work by Man Ray, Marsden Hartley, and John Marin.[18]

There were other noteworthy tenants in the building and on the street. Not long after Field's death in 1922, poet Hart Crane began renting rooms at 110 Columbia Heights, exulting at what he described as "the finest view in all America." He set up a desk close to Washington Roebling's window, and there began his epic tribute to the span—*The Bridge* (finished, ironically, in a basement apartment up the

Pablo Picasso, *Pipe Rack and Still Life on a Table* (1911). Estate of Pablo Picasso / Artists Rights Society.

street). John Dos Passos moved to the building shortly after Crane, and the pair often dined and drank together at a local Italian eatery in the winter of 1925. It was at 110 Columbia Heights that Dos Passos launched his most celebrated novel, *Manhattan Transfer*. Thomas Wolfe, Asheville-born author of *Look Homeward, Angel*, resided briefly across the street in a building spared by a hair's breadth when the BQE came through. As it plodded on toward the Navy Yard, the expressway consumed hundreds more buildings, mostly homes of common folk and wholly erased from collective memory. Between Jay Street and Hudson Avenue, acres of heavily built land were cleared just to accommodate the coiled ramps joining the BQE to the Brooklyn and Manhattan bridges. This was the last, fatal blow to the old Fifth Ward, a place long bedeviled by the ill winds of improvement and renewal. And it came right on the heels of another convulsive burst of modernity dumped in the neighborhood's lap—the Admiral Farragut Houses.[19]

While not as vast as the earlier Fort Greene project, the Farragut complex obliterated all the blocks around the entrance gate to the Navy Yard—including, for better or worse, notorious Sands Street. The grim fleet of hub-and-spoke towers, set adrift on superblocks, was the work of Alfred T. Fellheimer—a onetime classicist, incredibly, who had helped design Grand Central Station. The project should have been named the Panoptic Houses, given the chilling resemblance of its barbican towers to eighteenth-century English philosopher Jeremy Bentham's scheme for a total-surveillance penitentiary. Making room for the Farragut Houses and the BQE together consumed some forty-five acres of the most heavily built blocks in Brooklyn, displacing scores of families (including my uncle and grandmother) and laying waste to a community that—for all its problems and against all odds— had survived for more than a century. The expressway was elevated now, lifted on pylons after passing beneath the Manhattan Bridge. But it was not lifted much. Riding lower and wider than the Gowanus Expressway, the BQE crushed the life

Perspective rendering of Farragut Houses, 1947. New York City Department of Parks and Recreation.

out of Park Avenue; it was a looming rampart that made everything in its path a dark and forbidding no-man's-land. Every neighborhood touched by the BQE from here to the Queens line was doomed to the same "gyre of destruction" that made Sunset Park a slum years before—including the struggling Fort Greene Houses. As it roared past the Navy Yard, the BQE swung north again, marching through Williamsburg and Greenpoint like a latter-day Sherman's army. Photographs of the newly cleared right-of-way recall scenes of bombed-out Lebanon. This was urban warfare. As Mumford observed, the impact of arterial construction on the fabric of a city was very much like that of "the passage of a tornado or the blast of an atom bomb." A six-lane expressway is wildly out of scale with all but the most industrial cityscapes, and arterials like the Brooklyn-Queens Expressway "must not be thrust," he cautioned, "into the delicate tissue of our cities; the blood they circulate must rather enter through an elaborate network of minor blood vessels and capillaries." But "what is Brooklyn to the highway engineer," Mumford lamented, "except a place to go through rapidly, at whatever necessary sacrifice of peace and amenity by its inhabitants?"[20]

A man with the ego and drive of a Robert Moses is never satisfied. Nor is highway building generally an enterprise with intrinsic closure. Roads can go on forever, and they generate a momentum all their own; build one and suddenly, inevitably, others seem vitally needed. This was especially the case in the postwar era, when Americans were buying cars by the millions and Detroit was the nation's economic polestar. Each completed highway—wide open and traffic free at first—convinced that many more people to take up the wheel, increasing traffic volumes and soon prompting another round of road building. Lewis Mumford was the first to call this ruinous cycle, whereby the remedy "actually expands the evil it is meant to overcome." The highwaymen, he feared, would not stop until that "terminal point" was reached, when all civic life was forced from the city, leaving behind "a tomb of concrete roads and ramps covering the dead corpse."[21] Something more sinister was at work, too. Noting that the limited-access highway made it possible "to go from Coney Island to Buffalo without encountering a traffic light," Mumford conjectured that "once a system like that takes shape, it has an abstract, hypnotic fascination, which leads to the next step of complementing it by a system that will lead the motorist from Washington to Maine with the same smooth facility"—even if this meant scrambling "the living quarters of tens of thousands of people."

> Thus, at a time when our cities can be made livable again only by isolating their residential neighborhoods from through traffic and rebuilding our decaying systems of mass transportation, our public authorities are busily breaking down the structure of neighborhoods and parks and devoting public funds to private transportation and private speculative building.

"As a formula for . . . ruining what is left of our great cities," Mumford concluded, "nothing could be more effective."[22]

In postwar America, a roaring economy, cheap oil, and widespread suburban development made the highway juggernaut nearly unstoppable—and nowhere more so than the New York City of Robert Moses. In the 1930s, motorways were woven

The Brooklyn-Queens Expressway carves a path through Williamsburg, 1958. New York City Municipal Archives.

thoughtfully into the metropolitan fabric; roads served city and citizen. Now Moses and his cadre of engineers began to see the city as little more than an obstacle to a future of seamless, flowing rivers of cars—the very future General Motors presented so seductively in its Futurama exhibit at the 1939 New York World's Fair. What was needed, Moses expounded after winning a GM essay contest on highway building, was the temerity and boldness to drive "modern expressways right through and not merely around and by-passing cities."[23] And Moses was as good as his word. By 1956 he had completed the Prospect and Major Deegan expressways. Work was well under way on the Cross Bronx Expressway, which opened in stages between 1955 and 1963. The Clearview and Van Wyck expressways were completed in the early 1960s, the latter eventually extended north and south to the Whitestone Bridge and John F. Kennedy Airport. The ill-starred Bruckner, last of the Mosaic pythons, dragged on for years—an "indeterminate artery," Ada Louise Huxtable called it, that epitomized the turmoil and paralysis of New York City in the 1970s.[24]

Just as the New Deal paid for the parkways of the 1930s, the postwar expressways were heavily subsidized by another federal initiative—officially the Eisenhower Interstate Highway program. Made law on June 29, the Federal-Aid Highway Act of 1956 was among the most significant pieces of legislation of the twentieth century. It authorized billions in federal funds to help states construct a forty-one-thousand-mile matrix of asphalt—a National System of Interstate and Defense Highways, as Congress called it—that would eventually link up nearly all US cities with populations over fifty thousand. Substantially built in just over a generation, this "greatest and the longest engineered structure ever built" forever changed the lifeways and landscape of the United States.[25] Ironically, Moses was at first opposed to a national highway system, believing it wasteful to run big roads "through many thinly populated sections of the country where no such super-highways are needed."[26] There were trains and planes for cross-country travel. "The only justification for superhighways and parkways," he argued in a 1940 letter to Thomas H. MacDonald of the Bureau of Public Roads, "lies in their close relationship to metropolitan centers and substantial cities."[27] The whole point of this infrastructure, he avowed, was to ease congestion, and congestion was fundamentally an urban problem. But the postwar Moses was very different from the prewar model. Among other things, he changed his tune about a national highway system. Once it became clear that Uncle Sam could help fund his arterial dreams for Gotham, Moses threw his weight behind the Eisenhower interstate program. Most of his postwar expressways were built with huge infusions of federal cash, and all were eventually made part of that sprawling web of asphalt that changed forever the American landscape.

CHAPTER 17

HIGHWAY OF HOPE

Of course, not even Robert Moses got everything he wanted. By the mid-1960s, opposition to urban highways was reaching a fever pitch in many American cities. San Franciscans were the first to push back, stirred into action by a map of proposed routes leaked to the press in 1956. Of the dozen-odd highways planned for the city, it was the Embarcadero Freeway that rankled most, the first section of which—a double-decked monstrosity that severed the city from its magnificent waterfront—opened in 1959. Resistance to any further expressway construction in the Bay Area mounted over the next few years. An antifreeway rally in May 1964 drew some 200,000 people to Golden Gate Park. In Louisiana, an artery Moses had himself recommended building—the Vieux Carré Riverfront Expressway—generated tremendous opposition in what came to be known as the "Second Battle of New Orleans." Well-organized resistance in Boston ended several major highway projects, including the Southwest Expressway and the Inner Belt through Cambridge and Somerville. In New York, Lewis Mumford became a forceful antagonist of the highway lobby, urging Americans to "forget the damned motor car and build cities for lovers and friends." With persuasive eloquence, he argued that monster expressways were not only destroying the delicate fabric of cities but making traffic congestion worse by dumping thousands of cars where there should be few or none. "In short, the American has sacrificed his life as a whole to the motorcar, like someone who, demented with passion, wrecks his home in order to lavish his income on a capricious mistress who promises delights he can only occasionally enjoy."[1]

It was Jane Jacobs who took up the cudgel where Mumford left off with his pen. Though he savaged her *Death and Life of Great American Cities* in a *New Yorker* review ("Mother Jacobs' Home Remedies"), Mumford and Jacobs were strong allies when it came to highways. Jacobs had already battled Moses over plans to extend Fifth Avenue through Washington Square Park and raze a fourteen-block area of her West Village neighborhood for urban renewal. Her most storied fight began in

Jane Jacobs at a meeting of the Committee to Save the West Village, December 1961. Photograph by Phil Stanziola. New York World-Telegram and the Sun Newspaper Photograph Collection, Library of Congress, Prints and Photographs Division.

1962, against an elevated expressway Moses had long planned to plow across lower Manhattan. Like so many projects he brought to fruition, the Lower Manhattan Expressway—or LOMEX, as it was hatefully known—had been recommended decades earlier by the Regional Plan Association, one of five east-west connectors it called for to span the island. The Moses version would run along Broome Street from the Williamsburg Bridge to the Holland Tunnel, conveying traffic between New Jersey and Long Island. At the same time (and contradicting this bypass function), Moses promised that the highway would bring new energy to Manhattan's dying industrial sector. If the BQE was a defense play, LOMEX was an economic stimulus package. The ten-lane expressway, swimming in a 350-foot-wide right-of-way, would have required demolishing some 400 buildings and displaced 2,200 families and 845 shops, stores, and other commercial establishments.[2] It would also have laid waste to the largest concentration of cast-iron architecture in the world, including the magnificent E. V. Haughwout Building at 490 Broadway—a former housewares emporium built with one of the first passenger elevators in the world. The landmarking of this structure by the city's nascent Landmarks Preservation Commission effectively dropped a boulder in Moses's path. Bigger ones were soon to come.

The fate of the Lower Manhattan Expressway was ultimately determined in Brooklyn. Getting across the vast borough had long challenged Moses, to whom it was little more than a congested mess between Manhattan and his beloved Long

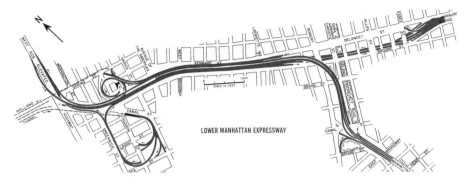

The Lower Manhattan Expressway (LOMEX). From *Future Arterial Program* (Triborough Bridge and Tunnel Authority, 1963).

Island beaches. His maps of Brooklyn slowly filled with dashed lines—planned expressways that would shorten the schlep from city to sand, most of which would become dashed dreams. None of these was more vital to Moses than the Bushwick Expressway. It was proposed by the Regional Plan Association in 1936; Moses called for its construction as early as 1941 and made it part of his infamous 1955 report—*Joint Study of Arterial Facilities*—that laid out a generation's worth of megaroads for the metropolitan area. In its original configuration, the Bushwick Expressway was to run southeast across Brooklyn from the Williamsburg Bridge via Broadway or Bushwick Avenue, bending east at Atlantic Avenue to John F. Kennedy Airport via the broad central median of Conduit Boulevard. A northern link to the Queens Midtown Tunnel was added later, ostensibly to relieve traffic on the Long Island Expressway. It would not be an easy build. Some 4,850 families stood in the way of the original alignment, twice the number impacted by LOMEX and three times the number eventually displaced by the Cross Bronx Expressway. Yet Moses forged ahead, bucking a growing local and national backlash against neighborhood-wrecking road projects. He did so because building the Bushwick Expressway would all but assure his victory in the LOMEX fight. To Moses, LOMEX and the Bushwick Expressway were two segments of the same arterial. In a 1963 report on highway construction, he even referred to the Bushwick route as "an extension of the Lower Manhattan Expressway through the northerly and heretofore neglected sector of Brooklyn."[3] Moses reasoned that if the Bushwick road were built, it would channel such a flood of traffic from Long Island onto lower Manhattan's congested streets that the city would be forced to build LOMEX too. But by the mid-1960s, political winds were blowing strongly against Moses in both city and state. The newly elected Republican mayor, John Vliet Lindsay, had campaigned on a platform that included support for mass transit and an end to LOMEX; for "cities are for people," he said repeatedly on the campaign trail, "not for automobiles."[4] Though he reneged on LOMEX, as we will see, Lindsay was fundamentally opposed to highways and the man who had been imposing them on the city for decades. Now, for the same reasons that Moses wanted to build the Bushwick Expressway, the young mayor sought to kill it. LOMEX without the new link across Brooklyn would feed fatal loads of traffic onto the already-overburdened Brooklyn-Queens and Long Island expressways.

Killing the Bushwick Expressway, Lindsay realized, would make LOMEX a road
to nowhere.

The City Planning Commission, long in the Moses camp, had just that summer
recommended prioritizing another Brooklyn road over the Bushwick project—the
Cross-Brooklyn Expressway. Outraged, Moses demanded that the commission
withdraw the substitution. Commission chairman William F. R. Ballard—a Wagner
appointee and Moses adversary—refused.[5] Unlike nearly every other expressway
in postwar New York, the Cross-Brooklyn actually made sense. Not only would it
provide commercial traffic an alternative to the Brooklyn-Queens Expressway—all
of five years old but already overloaded—but it would "divert a maximum amount of
through traffic," stressed Ballard, "from the congested Manhattan core," channeling
it instead over the newly opened Verrazzano-Narrows Bridge. Equally compelling,
the Cross-Brooklyn would unlock Brooklyn's sprawling southeastern quarter to
industrial development, which the city itself had been promoting for years at its
Flatlands Industrial Park. Launched in January 1959, the project was a last echo of
the manufacturing sector pitched as part of the Jamaica Bay port scheme—and a
late, ultimately futile attempt by Mayor Richard F. Wagner, Jr., to stem the postwar outflow of industry from Brooklyn by providing modern factory space within
city limits.[6] It was an idea so novel at the time that press stories on the Flatlands

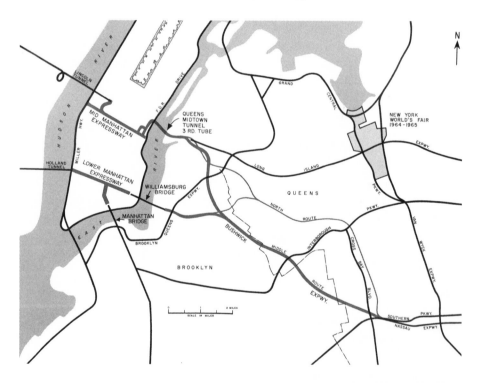

The planned Bushwick Expressway as it was to connect with the Lower and Mid-Manhattan expressways.
Moses described the Bushwick arterial as "an extension of the Lower Manhattan Expressway through
the northerly and heretofore neglected sector of Brooklyn." When the Lindsay administration refused to
approve the Bushwick route, it effectively also killed LOMEX. From *Future Arterial Program* (Triborough
Bridge and Tunnel Authority, 1963).

initiative routinely placed "industrial park" in quotes (North Carolina's Research Triangle Park had yet to open, and the fabled Stanford Industrial Park, birthplace of Silicon Valley, was just several years old). Though the projected zone already had a major tenant—the Brooklyn Terminal Market, opened in 1942 to replace Wallabout Market, razed for a wartime expansion of the Navy Yard—the project floundered for years. Paltry incentives and—especially—the lack of easy access to the regional highway system made finding tenants difficult. Project management changed; a new master plan was solicited. Tishman Realty proposed an innovative multistory live-work industrial village by shopping mall sage Victor Gruen, anchored by the East 105th Street subway station. Instead, the city went with a plodding array of single-story superblocks. The project ultimately shriveled from 680 acres to a mere 96. And even that proved too much: by 1966 not a single shovelful of dirt had been turned. A Lindsay subordinate sent to the site that spring reported finding "a glacier of mouldy mattresses, unsprung sofas and a strange gamut of debris." The much-heralded village of industry had become instead "the most expensive garbage dump in the city."[7]

Sane and an easy build, the Cross-Brooklyn Expressway gained many supporters. The *New York Times* contended that the expressway would "enable a huge volume of traffic to flow from Brooklyn and Long Island to New Jersey and the South," and

Watermelon race at the Brooklyn Terminal Market in Flatlands, 1964. Photograph by Phyllis Twachtman. New York World-Telegram and the Sun Newspaper Photograph Collection, Library of Congress, Prints and Photographs Division.

affirmed that "the City Planning Commission is right in arguing that future highways should not be built where they will pour more automobiles into lower Manhattan." The city's traffic commissioner, Henry A. Barnes—a Moses rival and public transit advocate (when asked once what to do with a car in Manhattan, he said "sell it")—also favored the Cross-Brooklyn road over Bushwick. The matter came to a head on July 6, 1966, when Governor Nelson Rockefeller signed a bill eliminating the Bushwick Expressway "and designating the Cross-Brooklyn expressway . . . in place thereof." The eastern extension of LOMEX was thus stricken from the state's map of arterial projects. When, the following week, a vengeful Moses announced that $40 million in surplus authority funds would be used for highway bridge improvements—money Lindsay had hoped to use for public transit—the new mayor promptly dismissed Moses from his post as the city's arterial coordinator. The great irony here is that the Cross-Brooklyn project was first proposed by Moses himself, and in the same 1955 *Joint Study* that called for the Bushwick Expressway. In that report, a dotted "Cross Brooklyn Expressway" is shown leading east from a great span across the Narrows, twelve lanes wide and nearly three miles long—the future Verrazzano-Narrows Bridge—joining the Bushwick Expressway just past the Queens line near the Belt Parkway and Idlewild Airport.[8]

Both a Narrows crossing and a highway across Brooklyn had been recommended decades earlier by, once again, Thomas Adams and the Regional Plan Association. They were part of a "Metropolitan Loop or belt line highway" proposed in 1928 to facilitate regional freight traffic and "relieve pressure upon the street system of Manhattan"—what Peter Hall called "the first true orbital motorway in the world."[9] For the Brooklyn segment of this great loop, Adams suggested using Eighty-Sixth Street, Kings Highway, and Flatlands Avenue—an alignment that would have gutted neighborhoods from Dyker Heights to East Flatbush. Moses wisely favored instead using a quiet freight rail corridor to get the artery across Brooklyn—the Bay Ridge Branch of the Long Island Rail Road, which arcs across the borough from Brooklyn Army Terminal to East New York (joining there the New York Connecting Railroad). By using an extant transit corridor, the Cross-Brooklyn would have dislodged fewer families or businesses than any other highway in postwar New York. But fixated as he was on LOMEX, Moses put all his eggs in the Bushwick basket. In mid-December 1966, with his power waning fast, Moses begrudgingly agreed to support the Cross-Brooklyn road, but only if his rejected Bushwick Expressway was also built. He armed himself with a report by a trusted Triborough consultant, Blauvelt Engineering, which concluded that the Cross-Brooklyn Expressway was "no substitute for the Bushwick Expressway," and that *both* were necessary to handle projected loads of transborough traffic. Building either road without the other, in other words, would be a waste of taxpayer money.[10]

The Lindsay administration fired back with a study of its own, by the Brill Engineering Corporation, whose principal, former city highways commissioner John T. Carroll, advised that the only fix for "intolerable" traffic conditions in Brooklyn—"the largest community in the country without interior access to an expressway"—was to build the Cross-Brooklyn route as soon as possible. Not only would the road patch borough commerce and manufacturing into the regional

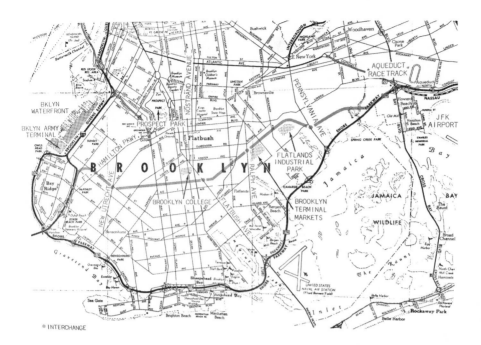

Route of proposed Cross-Brooklyn Expressway (gray line across center). From Brill Engineering Corporation, *Cross Brooklyn Expressway: Benefits for Brooklyn* (1967).

highway network, making Flatlands Industrial Park readily accessible by trucks, but it would take traffic pressure off both the BQE and the Belt Parkway while completing the long-envisioned "southern bypass of New York City's central business areas." Much the same had been said before, of course. But the report also recommended joining the easternmost section of the Cross-Brooklyn Expressway corridor and the New York Connecting Railroad to create "a future high-speed rapid transit link" between John F. Kennedy Airport and Manhattan—a perennial dream of every New Yorker who's had to endure a long, smelly cab ride home from Queens. Brill further counseled the city to acquire the air rights above the new highway for development—an idea first put into practice a decade earlier along the FDR Drive. The busy expressway-rail corridor could be transformed "from an eyesore to a pleasing architectural experience," the report noted, "by the addition of housing, schools, vest-pocket parks, playgrounds and sitting areas along and above the right-of-way."[11]

If Carroll's report was the first to suggest building atop the Cross-Brooklyn artery, it was an exhibit at the Museum of Modern Art that revealed the full potential latent in the Brooklyn air. It was called The New City: Architecture and Urban Renewal, and Mayor Lindsay himself opened it on January 20—just days after receiving the Brill study. Featured were speculative urban design projects by student-practitioner teams from Columbia, Princeton, Cornell, and MIT. Each proposed interventions to create new housing, parks, and neighborhoods. The Columbia group was led by a quintet of young architects—Jaquelin T. Robertson, Richard Weinstein, Giovanni Pasanella, Jonathan Barnett, and Myles Weintraub. They focused on redeveloping

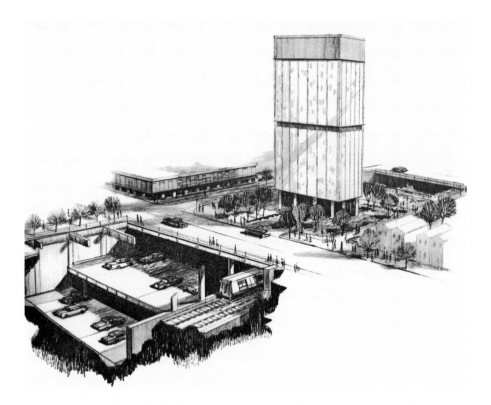

Ilustrative rendering of air-rights development above Cross-Brooklyn Expressway. From Brill Engineering Corporation, *Cross Brooklyn Expressway: Benefits for Brooklyn* (1967).

the Penn Central railroad right-of-way along Park Avenue in Harlem. As any Metro-North rider knows, when trains leaving Grand Central emerge into daylight at Ninety-Seventh Street, first a ponderous brownstone viaduct and then a steel el structure carries them toward the Harlem River. All the grace and elegance of lower Park Avenue is obliterated by this infrastructure, which has long divided the Harlem community. The Columbia team proposed using the air rights above the tracks for a development program to stitch together Harlem's fabric, removing the blight of the tracks while making room for housing and other community amenities.[12]

The MoMA show came at a time of resurgent interest in the future of cities, and in the transformative potential of city design. Jacobs published her searing critique of superblock modernism and the failures of urban renewal in 1961. A whole new field—urban design—was forming out of the ashes of the city-planning profession, self-immolated for having midwifed the disastrous urban renewal program. Architects around the world, weary of orthodox modernism, were exploring urban-architectural systems as heroic in scale as in social ambition. Team 10 and Archigram in Europe and the United Kingdom and the metabolists in Japan experimented with megastructural forms that combined all the functions of the traditional city in exciting new ways. Japanese architect Kenzo Tange's students proposed a city for twenty-five thousand in Boston Harbor in 1959, and an even larger project for Tokyo Bay the following year. In the fall of 1964, Norval White's thesis students at Cooper

Union drafted a bold plan for a network of hyperdense pyramidal towers on Staten Island structured about multimodal transit lines. There was even a "Design-In" on the Central Park Mall, organized by New York University and the Department of Parks. The May 1967 event brought together citizens, architects, and planners committed to applying lessons of political action to the urban crisis. It was a kaleido-scopic affair, with hippies checking out electric cars and geodesic domes to music by the Department of Sanitation Band. Among the many speakers were then council-man Edward Koch and Thomas Hoving, pompous director of the Metropolitan Museum of Art and Lindsay's first commissioner of parks. Lindsay himself gave the closing speech.[13]

For all his patrician airs, Lindsay was a committed urbanist—deeply concerned about New York's built environment and enthusiastic about the potential of archi-tecture and urban design to make the city a better place for all. "We are fast becom-ing a nation of cities, indeed a world of cities," he wrote, "and their problems and promise must occupy the forefront of national concern." Soon after taking office in January 1966, the new mayor called upon Boston Redevelopment Authority chief Edward J. Logue for advice on slum redevelopment, asking him to chair a Study Group on New York Housing and Neighborhood Improvement. Lindsay called the group's report—provocatively titled *Let There Be Commitment*—a "brilliant, penetrating analysis" of the city's housing problems. It concluded that New York needed some 450,000 new apartments, which should be built by a new housing and development agency with authority over all aspects of the planning, design, and construction process. A supplement by architects David A. Crane and Tun-ney F. Lee, Logue associates from Boston, focused specifically on urban design problems facing the city. Lindsay responded by appointing a Task Force on Urban Design charged with envisioning new ways for the city to manage increasingly complex problems of urban development. Chaired by CBS chief William S. Paley, it included I. M. Pei, Robert A. M. Stern, and philanthropist Joan K. Davidson of the J. M. Kaplan Fund. Its report, *The Threatened City*, described New York as blighted by "depressingly blank architecture, arid street scenes and baleful housing condi-tions," and recommended, among other things, appointing "an urban design force of trained professionals of the highest competence" to advise the mayor. Lindsay concurred and in April 1967 assembled an elite advisory corps of architects within the City Planning Commission known as the Urban Design Group. "Design is not a small enterprise in New York City today," he later explained; "In our increasingly crowded, man-shaped urban world, esthetics must now include not only the marble statue in the garden, but the house, the street, the neighborhood and the city, as a cumulative expression of its residents."[14]

The original Urban Design Group, not coincidentally, consisted of the same team of young architects that produced the Park Avenue air-rights scheme for the New City exhibition—Robertson, Barnett, Weinstein, Pasanella, and Weintraub. It was Jaque Robertson who had urged Barnett and the others to seek work in the new administration. As Barnett tells it, all five headed down to City Hall one day to meet with the new chair of the City Planning Commission, Donald H. Elliott. Unbeknownst to them, Elliott's first design advisers, including Norval White and

Mayor John Lindsay speaking at a street rally, 1965. Photograph by Walter Albertin. New York World-Telegram and the Sun Newspaper Photograph Collection, Library of Congress, Prints and Photographs Division.

Elliot Willensky (whose iconic *AIA Guide to New York* had just been published), had just that morning quit in a huff. He needed a new team and decided to take his chances with the eager band at his door.[15] The Urban Design Group came to epitomize Lindsay's penchant for stocking his administration with "bright young people of wit, zeal and imagination." It was all white, all male, and nearly all Yale—hardly a reflection of the city's surging diversity at the time. Nonetheless, the group brought real expertise to what had been a bloated, largely ineffectual city agency—"understaffed, underbudgeted and undertalented," as the *New York Times* put it, with just one architect on payroll. "The planning task and responsibility," Elliott explained, "must be placed in the hands of experts who are at once creative and disciplined, visionary and sure-footed when traversing bureaucratic terrain." Thus by the summer of 1967 John Lindsay had fortified City Hall with more architecture and urban design know-how than any administration since La Guardia's. And it was expertise urgently needed; for the city seemed to be falling apart. "To a New Yorker born and bred such as myself," wrote Allan Temko, longtime architecture critic of the *San Francisco Chronicle*, "the great city at times appears to be spinning towards Mumfordian doom; overgrown, over-congested, ill-managed and ill-kempt, usually sullen, sometimes violent, and scarred by enormous 'gray areas.'"[16]

Few places in New York needed help more desperately than Brooklyn's easternmost neighborhoods of Brownsville and East New York. Never an affluent part of the city, it had been home to working-class Jews and Italians from the Lower East Side who moved there in large numbers once the Williamsburg Bridge opened in 1903. By the 1920s Brownsville was more than 75 percent Jewish, known as the "Jerusalem of America." A progressive hotbed, it regularly elected socialists to the New York State Assembly and was the site of the first birth control clinic in the United States—opened by Margaret Sanger at 46 Amboy Street. It produced scores of Jewish intellectuals—Norman Podhoretz, Isaac Asimov, George Gershwin, and literary critic Alfred Kazin, whose 1951 book, *A Walker in the City*, chronicled the Sutter Avenue world of his youth. To Kazin, Brownsville was "New York's rawest, remotest, cheapest ghetto, enclosed on one side by the Canarsie flats and on the other by the hallowed middle class districts that showed the way to New York." Like so many other Brooklyn neighborhoods, Brownsville and East New York changed rapidly after World War II. African Americans began moving in, driven by rising rents and overcrowding in adjacent Bedford-Stuyvesant; the influx topped twelve hundred people per month by the late 1950s. Many of the new families were desperately poor, some arriving penniless straight from North Carolina, Virginia, and other southern states. Residents blamed social service agencies for sending them the poorest of the poor, making their neighborhoods "the biggest dumping ground for welfare cases in the city." With poverty and despair came crime. Arrests in the Seventy-Third Precinct, spanning Brownsville and Ocean Hill, more than doubled between 1956 and 1966; homicides rose by 200 percent between 1960 and 1967 alone. In December 1966 an elderly tailor named Hyman Getnick was stabbed to death by teenagers for a fistful of dollars. The crime shocked a city still reeling from the Kitty Genovese murder two years earlier. Synagogues were broken into and stripped of anything of value. Pitkin Avenue merchants cowered behind steel gates; many had already been held up or burgled several times. There were violent street fights between blacks and Italians, blacks and Jews, blacks and Puerto Ricans. The clashes peaked in the summer of 1966, leading to an exodus of dozens of families—black and white—and pleas for calm from City Hall.[17]

As African Americans poured into Brownsville and East New York, whites fled—to nearby Canarsie and Mill Basin, or the suburbs of Queens and Long Island. Prejudice and racial animosity were powerful motivating forces, but the real driver was fear—fear of crime, fear of violence, fear of realtor-led blockbusting that could vaporize the value of a family home overnight. Between 1950 and 1960, 38 percent of Brownsville's whites moved out of the area. Its population in 1960 was 43 percent black or Puerto Rican; by mid-decade, that figure had topped 95 percent. Always distant from the centers of culture and commerce in the city, Brownsville was now a kind of quarantine zone, a place that "symbolized the economic, geographic, political and educational isolation of New York's black community." Linden Boulevard became a border of sorts, a "redline" separating the ghetto from still-white Canarsie to the south. "An unspoken assumption existed among Canarsie residents," writes Jerald E. Podair, "that blacks from Ocean Hill–Brownsville would not be permitted to move across Linden Boulevard in appreciable numbers" (Canarsie's pricier real estate effectively assured this). By the time Lindsay became mayor, Brownsville and East New York were plagued by a gamut of social ills—from a welfare rate double the city average (with 75 percent of residents on public assistance) to unemployment five times that of the rest of New York. Drug addiction, juvenile crime, rape, and out-of-wedlock birth rates were all among the highest in the city. But it was the deplorable state of the public schools in Brownsville and East New York that most troubled community leaders and city officials. At the district's new flagship junior high school on Herkimer Street—now John M. Coleman Intermediate School 271—"reading and math scores were among the lowest in the city, with 73 percent of its pupils below grade in reading and 85 percent in math." With discipline poor, attacks on teachers common, and acts of vandalism routine, "it was clear," Podair writes, "that education of a very different sort was taking place in Ocean Hill–Brownsville and the white majority schools of the city."[18]

It was the issue of school quality and segregation in this embattled quarter of Brooklyn that ultimately transformed the Cross-Brooklyn Expressway from a straightforward road play into one of the most promising public works of the 1960s—a Moses-style arterial project leavened with the insurgent idealism of Jane Jacobs and the civil rights movement. In the wake of *Brown v. Board of Education* it was taken on faith that segregated schools were bad, and that integrating classrooms would improve learning outcomes for minority children. "The racial imbalance existing in a school in which the enrollment is wholly or predominantly Negro," argued New York State commissioner of education James E. Allen, Jr., "interferes with the achievement of equality of educational opportunity and must therefore be eliminated."[19] But unlike the South, where blacks and whites were kept separate by

"They want action against hoodlums." East New York mothers and kids rally against street violence at Atlantic Avenue overpass, August 1953. Photograph by Johnny Kruh. Brooklyn Public Library, Brooklyn Collection.

Jim Crow laws, school segregation in the North was largely a function of residential demographics. Schools in predominately white neighborhoods had mostly white student bodies, and vice versa. In Brownsville's District 17, the percentage of white students had fallen from 53 to 17 percent between 1958 and 1966, making racially integrated schools there a virtual impossibility.[20] Integration thus called for a lot more than declaring certain laws unconstitutional. It would require, for example, reconfiguring school-district boundaries, building new schools on community borders, or transporting students twice a day between neighborhoods. Busing, as this last option came to be known, was especially controversial. Conservatives were fundamentally opposed to it, and for progressives it contradicted core values of the local and the grassroots. As the decade wore on, more and more black parents would come to suspect the whole project of integration. After all, the idea that thinning densities of African American students would improve outcomes—that black children could do well only with whites around—was itself intrinsically racist.[21]

In the decade following *Brown*, the Board of Education tried but largely failed to integrate the city's schools, many of which were declining fast in terms of academic performance. It thus fell to the Lindsay administration to reform the nation's largest school system and make it compliant with the 1954 Supreme Court ruling. Sidestepping the integration issue, Lindsay and his advisers focused on improving schools in minority neighborhoods—a goal they believed would best be met by making the monolithic Board of Education more responsive to local community needs. Lindsay appointed an advisory panel to study the matter—chaired, ironically, by former national security advisor McGeorge Bundy, architect of America's disastrous plunge into Vietnam. Now head of the Ford Foundation and a professor of government at Harvard, Bundy and his panel recommended replacing the city's colossal education bureaucracy with a more nimble federation of school districts administered by boards staffed at the community level. The Bundy proposal was fiercely opposed by the Board of Education and the teachers' union, and much diluted by the time its recommendations went off to Albany in the form of a bill. A consortium of parents and civic groups from Brownsville, meanwhile, had been battling the Board of Education over district zoning and school siting since early 1963. For its part, board officials knew well how dire the situation had become in Brownsville and East New York. With class sizes pushing sixty pupils in some schools, new facilities were desperately needed. In response, the board proposed constructing seven new schools across Canarsie, Brownsville, and East New York. The parents feared the new schools would be segregated upon opening, as all were sited well within largely white or black neighborhoods. Drawing on the work of educational sociologist Max Wolff, they called instead for a single campus-like school complex for fifteen thousand pupils at the junction of Canarsie, Brownsville, and East New York—on the very spot, in fact, where the city was trying to launch its star-crossed Flatlands Industrial Park. Wolff—then research director for the Migration Division of the Commonwealth of Puerto Rico—considered southeast Brooklyn ideal for an "educational park" where a vibrant mix of white, black, and brown students would come together as one and ease "the fetters of poverty and discrimination from minority groups and the poor."[22]

Industrial-scale education was not a new idea. As early as 1900, Los Angeles school superintendent Preston Search proposed a two-hundred-acre "school park" for the entire student population, with a farm-like setting to remove pupils from "smoking chimneys and congested urban conditions." Similar plans for school complexes accommodating up to ten thousand pupils were envisioned for Detroit and Glencoe, Illinois, during the Depression, and in the postwar era by officials in New Orleans, Albuquerque, and Pittsburgh. One of the few to become reality was in Fort Lauderdale, where a 546-acre "South Florida Education Park" was proposed for a former naval air field in March 1960. Funded by the Educational Facilities Laboratories of the Ford Foundation and later renamed the Nova Educational Experiment, the facility covered all levels of learning—"from nursery school through the Ph.D."—and was anticipated to establish a pattern for school districts nationally. New York City first began seriously considering education parks at a two-day conference in June 1964 organized by the Board of Education. Held at the Harriman estate near Bear Mountain, it brought school officials from New York and other cities together with experts from the Ford Foundation—led by a Harvard colleague of McGeorge Bundy's, Cyril G. Sargent. In his closing remarks, Sargent noted that while education parks were worth trying "on an experimental or prototype basis" in New York, they were not "a panacea nor a cure-all" for educating urban youth or reducing racial imbalance. Board of Education acting president Lloyd K. Garrison—great-grandson of famed abolitionist William Lloyd Garrison—was amenable to the idea but called for further study. "We laid groundwork here on which we can usefully build," he said at the end of the Harriman meeting; "This is not a matter to be decided overnight."[23]

By September 1965 Garrison and the board had provisionally approved two education parks for New York City, both in the Bronx—one on the former site of Freedomland, a short-lived theme park (today the Northeast Bronx Education Park at Co-op City), and one in Marble Hill, anchored by the future—and ill-fated—John F. Kennedy High School (closed in 2014). But they vetoed the Flatlands park proposed by the Brownsville parents, explaining that it should not be built "until the first two could be appraised for their merits." The parents were outraged, claiming that the board was wielding its construction budget "as an illegal instrument to perpetuate segregation," and that in canceling Flatlands the board was effectively entrenching "an apartheid system in New York." The following May, Brownsville activists led by Harlem minister Milton A. Galamison petitioned state education commissioner James Allen to stop the seven-schools scheme. Allen concurred, restraining the Board of Education from going ahead with its construction plans—temporarily, at least, pending outcome of a hearing on the parents' appeal for a state order to compel the board to establish "a centrally-located educational park . . . that would draw pupils from an ethnically varied population."[24]

Matters reached a head on July 19, 1966, opening day of the long-awaited Flatlands Industrial Park. A large and noisy throng of protesters had gathered, shouting, "Jim Crow Must Go," and denouncing the city for choosing industry over schoolchildren and failing to build the Flatlands education park. Befuddled dignitaries sat before a stage full of worried officials, all anxiously waiting for Mayor Lindsay to arrive. When his black sedan slowly pulled up, they were shocked to see Lindsay get out and walk unescorted into the crowd of demonstrators. "There was a moment of startled silence," reported the *Times*; "Then the chants of anger turned to cheers as a half-dozen burly Negro youths lifted the Mayor to their shoulders and carried him through the throng." The moment was not without effect; for several weeks later the Board of Education reversed itself, announcing that it was now considering an education park in the Brownsville–East New York area. It ultimately proposed a pair of parks, one in East Flatbush and one on the eastern edge of East New York. Both were far from the core of Brownsville–East New York, and purposely so. As Walter Thabit recounted in *How East New York Became a Ghetto*, Board of Education planners "felt that if the parks were in or near white areas, they would have a better chance of being integrated"—a point the Brownsville activists, too, had themselves argued for years. With the board and the parents now at loggerheads, the city that fall commissioned a Connecticut consulting firm, Community Research and Development (CORDE), to decide which of the proposals—the parents' or the Board of Education's—had greater merit.[25]

CORDE pulled together a team of experts for this Solomonic task, led by Cy Sargent and a junior colleague named Allan R. Talbot. Scion of the famed Boston family, Sargent was Bundy's collaborator at the Ford Foundation and a professor at the Harvard Graduate School of Education. He was best known—even notorious—for authoring a controversial 1953 study of the Boston public school system that recommended closing sixty-eight obsolete facilities across the city. A decade later Sargent was asked by Ed Logue, newly appointed head of the Boston Redevelopment Authority, to update the so-called Sargent Report. In his second study (1962), Sargent urged tapping federal urban renewal funds to build scores of new inner-city schools—including a thirty-acre centralized "Campus High School" to which students would come "from every part of the City, of every background, of every intellectual level and every talent." The idea of centralized megaschools had become a hot one by now, especially at Harvard, where the Ford Foundation was funding research on their potential to reduce racial segregation. Logue knew Sargent from his days as redevelopment chief of New Haven, where the latter helped create a school for Logue's lauded Wooster Square renewal project. Sargent intended the facility—now the Harry A. Conte West Hills Magnet School—to serve as a hub of communal life in Wooster Square. The complex was eventually designed by Gordon Bunshaft and Natalie de Blois of Skidmore, Owings & Merrill, and included a senior center, library, auditorium, recreation room, gymnasium, hockey rink, pool, and playground. Allan Talbot had worked closely with both Sargent and Logue at the New Haven Redevelopment Agency and had just published a book on Mayor Richard Lee's efforts to transform New Haven into a "slumless city"—*The Mayor's Game* (1967). The Queens native was already back in town, for Logue had tapped him to serve on his Study Group on New York Housing and Neighborhood Improvement.[26]

Parachuting in, as it were, Talbot and Sargent could see from above what the embattled partisans in the schools fight could not. They immediately realized that both the parents and the Board of Education had overlooked critical demographic and land use data in their respective proposals, both of which "seemed to have been developed in a planning vacuum." Most glaring was a failure to account for the Cross-Brooklyn Expressway, which—extending across the entire district—effectively rendered both plans untenable. As Talbot and Sargent put it, the arterial would "cut through part of one of the sites proposed by the school staff and partially isolate the Flatlands site proposed by the parents." Worse, it would drive a divisive wedge between East Flatbush and Canarsie, Brownsville and East New York. In short, "the huge public investments represented by the expressway and the schools were in direct conflict with each other." To Talbot and Sargent, the situation had all the ingredients for a municipal planning disaster—"a lack of precise demographic data, massive housing construction unrelated to total community planning, unchecked blight . . . and the clash of a highway alignment with school sites." The solution Talbot and Sargent came up with was a stroke of liability-to-asset genius. To them, the old Long Island Rail Road cut seemed to be the one thing that united the disparate neighborhoods from Midwood to East New York. "The line is a landmark," they wrote, "a strong physical symbol shared by each of the five communities . . . the line unites the entire area." What nearly everyone saw as an immutable barrier—not unlike Harlem's Park Avenue viaduct—Talbot and Sargent recognized as a key to renewing East Central Brooklyn. How? By building over it an array of public amenities that would create a shared center of gravity for all the communities along the Cross-Brooklyn Expressway—Midwood, East Flatbush, Canarsie, Brownsville, and East New York. They called it "A Linear City for New York."[27]

Of course, Jack Carroll had already recommended building above the corridor in the Brill report, but only at selected nodes and not as a contiguous megastructure. Moreover, he projected doing so only at the western end of the expressway, through Borough Park, Kensington, and West Midwood—stable, relatively affluent neighborhoods where the city could expect to "reap . . . maximum benefit" from infill development. For Talbot and Sargent, building at the eastern end of the expressway had nothing to do with municipal return on investment; it was an act of intensive care, suturing an urban wound. For decades, expressways had torn apart urban neighborhoods; here, perhaps, was a highway of hope, a road that might heal Gotham's most embattled quarter. Over the rail-and-road core would be six thousand units of housing, shops, and stores, a cultural center, fine arts museum, parks, playgrounds, and recreation facilities—all served by a local "rail bus." First and foremost, however, Linear City was learning infrastructure—a great extruded education park anchored at one end by Brooklyn College and at the other by a new community college. In between would be an array of classroom and performance spaces and specialized facilities for the study of science, technology, and the arts. "In effect, children would be in school once they arrived at stops along the transportation line closest to their homes," the consultants wrote, enabling students to "spend part of or a full day—or perhaps a month—at a humanities, sciences or social sciences center"—all according to individual need or preference. The same facilities could be used in the evening for adult education. Thus—in a complete reversal of what had gone before—this major piece of arterial infrastructure would not lay waste communities but rather "result in a revitalized city within a city . . . stable, environmentally pleasing, and capable of offering the urban dweller conditions for the attainment of his personal aspirations."[28]

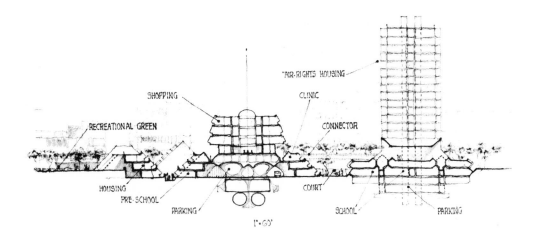

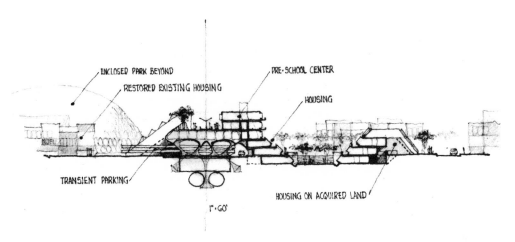

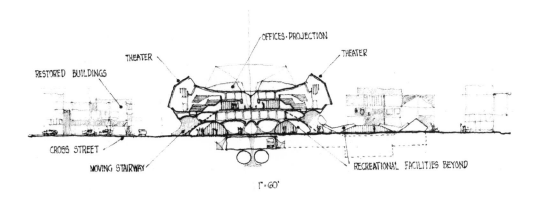

Architectural sections through communal spine of Cross-Brooklyn Expressway, showing housing, recreation facilities, and other civic amenities. From McMillan Griffis Mileto, *Linear City, Brooklyn, New York: Feasibility Study and Planning* (1967).

Lindsay loved it and immediately directed his staff to procure a feasibility study. The firm they commissioned—McMillan Griffis Mileto (MGM)—was itself recommended by Sargent and possessed a wealth of experience in educational facility design. Its principal, Robert S. McMillan, had been a founding partner, with Walter Gropius, of The Architects Collaborative (TAC) and played a lead role on the Pan Am Building, Harvard Graduate Center, and the US Embassy in Athens. He had worked with Sargent on a spectacular plan for the University of Baghdad, complete with dormitories, a shopping center, teaching hospital, and mosque. John H. Griffis, another former Gropius associate, led projects for the Libyan Health Ministry and for the Aga Khan in Sardinia, Kenya, and Ethiopia. The firm's youngest partner, William P. Mileto, was an Italian émigré who had studied at the University of Rome and taught design at Pratt Institute. He, too, had a connection to Cy Sargent, having worked with him, Logue, and Talbot in New Haven. There, Mileto designed an award-winning ensemble of townhouses within the Wooster Square Redevelopment, the Neighborhood Music School on Audubon Street, and the innovative North Quinnipiac Elementary School, with its array of sunken spaces for small-group teaching. An eclectic builder, Mileto spearheaded projects including everything from suburban Connecticut supermarkets to parliamentary buildings in Africa; he even supervised the marble contracts in Italy for the Kennedy Center for Performing Arts. Among them, the MGM principals had designed dozens of school and university buildings in New England, Europe, Africa, and the Middle East, and prepared master plans for the University of Lagos and Pahlavi (now Shiraz) University in Iran. If anyone could build an extended superschool in Brooklyn, it was McMillan, Griffis, and Mileto.[29]

Jane Jacobs meets Robert Moses: perspective rendering showing residential neighborhood along spine of Cross-Brooklyn Expressway. From McMillan Griffis Mileto, *Linear City, Brooklyn, New York: Feasibility Study and Planning* (1967).

For Linear City, the trio envisioned "an integrated complex of buildings and public spaces" arranged along the road-rail spine like notes on a musical staff—with social services facilities, public housing, playgrounds, shopping centers, an industrial park, schools, and an array of suspended pedestrian platforms. All this would be carefully stitched into the surrounding urban fabric, "kept in sympathic harmony with relation to the existing communities" and minimizing "indiscriminate use of high-rise architecture." The linear complex, more than five miles long from end to end, would be "interrupted at key points, touching the ground and laterally expanding in the form of nodular configurations" and in response to the availability of city-owned or derelict land on either side. This was the first American attempt to realize a form of urbanism that had fascinated architects and planners for almost a century. Its earliest iteration came from a Spanish town planner named Arturo Soria y Mata, whose 1882 "Ciudad Lineal" anticipated Ebenezer Howard's more famous Garden City proposal by a decade. Rather than merely "throwing off a planetary system of satellite communities," Soria y Mata's Ciudad was meant to ruralize the urban and urbanize the rural by linking congested city centers to their hinterlands, decanting the former while conveying "the hygenic conditions of country life to the great capital cities." Resembling a giant fishbone, his extruded city was structured about "a single street of 500 metres' width," in and about which would be "trains and trams, conduits for water, gas and electricity, reservoirs, gardens and, at intervals, buildings for different municipal services." The Ciudad could be extended ad infinitum, to "Cadiz and St. Petersburg, or Peking and Brussels," and would resolve "almost all the complex problems that are produced by the massive populations of our urban life." In the 1890s Soria y Mata launched a series of ventures to turn his vision into reality, among them a publication, *La Ciudad Lineal*, that soon evolved into the world's first city-planning journal. A short segment of linear city was eventually built in the suburbs northeast of Madrid, along a boulevard now named Calle de Arturo Soria.[30]

The great prophet of the linear city in America was an Alabama-born inventor named Edgar Chambless. Employed as a patent investigator in New York and reflecting on the flotsam of bad ideas he was forced to sift through, Chambless began "to dream of new conditions"—specifically, of a metropolis that might work a lot better if it were extruded outward into the countryside. "The idea occurred to me," he wrote in 1910, "to lay the modern skyscraper on its side and run the elevators and the pipes and the wires horizontally instead of vertically . . . I had invented Roadtown."

> I would build my city out into the country. I would take the apartment house and all its conveniences and comforts out among the farms by the aid of wires, pipes and of rapid and noiseless transportation. I would extend the blotch of human habitations called cities out in radiating lines. I would surround the city worker with the trees and grass and woods and meadows and the farmer with all the advantages of city life.

Chambless spent the rest of his life searching for a place and a patron to build this "earthscaper." He was a forceful missionary, converting skeptics by the score and even convincing Thomas Edison to donate his patent for cast-in-place concrete

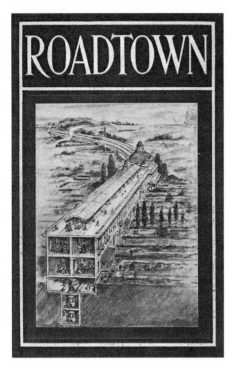

Illustration from the cover of Edgar Chambless, *Roadtown*, 1910.

houses (admittedly not one of his better ideas). Chambless self-published a treatise in 1910, *Roadtown*, a cult classic today among infrastructure junkies (its shortest chapter, "The Servant Problem in Roadtown," is but a single sentence: "There will be no servant problem in Roadtown, as there will be no need for servants"). Julian Hawthorne, in the book's foreword, predicted that—like the biblical Moses—Chambless would "lead us out of our long Egyptian bondage" to urban congestion. The *New York Times* gave the book two glowing reviews, noting that Roadtown would not only be "fire, cyclone, and earthquake proof," but likely do away with "most of the inconveniences of city life, including noise, dust, smoke, streets, horses, trusts, graft, and city employees." Shoppers that fall found generous renderings of "the queer, snakelike metropolis" in store windows all over Manhattan.[31]

Chambless found his ablest evangelist in Milo Hastings, a polymath social reformer and inventor who patented, among other things, a forced-air egg incubator and a health-food snack for children called Weeniwinks. Close friends and onetime roommates, Chambless and Hastings collaborated on several ventures. In December 1916, the latter penned a lengthy tract in the *Sun* proposing Roadtown as the solution to the "blight" caused by the textile industry's incursion into the Fifth Avenue shopping district. He envisioned a great linear Garment City along Newtown Creek, joined to Manhattan via the IRT line (today's 7 train) and extending from Hunters Point Avenue across two hundred acres of vacant "factory flat land . . . where the dead sunflowers now protrude through the untrodden snow." To this production-line metropolis "the makers of clothes may move," wrote Hastings, "and by moving may save both New York and themselves." It could be made high or low, adorned with parks or plazas, configured in a hundred ways—giving "city planners . . . real creative work and not merely a chance to bewail the mistakes of the fathers and to patch expensively that which has been wrongly made by a petty and individualistic generation." It was during the Depression that Chambless came closest to realizing his linear city dream. In March 1933, the *Times* and other news outlets reported that federal officials were seriously considering a roadtown between Baltimore and Washington, and even assigned staff from the Emergency Work Bureau to draw up plans. But Rexford Tugwell's Resettlement Administration chose instead a more conservative alternative for the satellite town of Greenbelt, Maryland. Chambless also nearly convinced the World's Fair Corporation to adopt a linear layout for the fair's Flushing site. The back-to-back rejections broke Chambless, now widowed, ill, and living in a rooming house on West Forty-Ninth Street (across, ironically, from that icon of nonlinearity, Rockefeller Center). On a Sunday morning in May 1936 he came home from church, stuck a tube in his mouth, and turned on the gas; "the Roadtown Man" was dead.[32]

Around the same time federal planners were weighing a Baltimore and Washington linear city, Franco-Swiss architect Le Corbusier published a speculative scheme for the North African port city of Algiers that placed lineal urbanism squarely in the pantheon of the avant-garde. Conceived in protest of the French colonial government's official plan, Corb's Plan Obus was a radical departure from the beaux arts style favored by the regime (though it was just as tone-deaf to Algerian culture, customs, and local climate). It consisted of a monumental business district and civic center on the waterfront, a series of curving residential towers on the heights above the ancient Casbah, and—most memorably—a long serpentine expressway along the coast from which housing units for 180,000 workers were suspended in vast tiers.

"Roadtown" as imagined by *Popular Mechanics*, December 1933, including school complex at lower right.

Corb had first toyed with linear city planning in a speculative scheme for Rio de Janeiro in 1929 and remained fascinated with its possibilities for the rest of his life. During World War II he developed plans for a "Cité Linéaire Industrielle" to solve the inefficiencies of scattered factory development by looking to imperatives of the assembly line—of "alignment, not dispersion"—as a model for modern industrial urbanism. Essentially a chic French edition of the homely Chambless-Hastings Garment City, it nonetheless kept the linear city flame alive long enough to make it back to New York City. At an evening convocation at Columbia University on April 28, 1961—part of a series of events honoring the founders of modern architecture—an aging Le Corbusier gave a speech "devoted exclusively to a presentation of his linear regional plan." It is very likely that in the audience that night were at least some of the young dreamers who gathered about the court of John Lindsay's Camelot.[33]

Plans for Linear City were trotted out in a swirl of publicity on February 25, 1967. Lindsay called it "a dramatic new concept for community development . . . a breakthrough of sweeping significance." Planning commissioner Donald Elliott was confident that the Cross-Brooklyn Expressway would be substantially complete by 1973, while work on the project's schools would begin within two years. The all-important air rights over the tracks would have to be negotiated from the Pennsylvania Railroad, but no one anticipated resistance from the faltering, cash-strapped company. Ten days later, Washington dumped cold water on all this vision making, doubtless to the great pleasure of Robert Moses. The Bushwick Expressway, though canceled by city and state, had never been officially removed from federal interstate highway system maps. Lindsay and his team assumed the Cross-Brooklyn Expressway could simply be substituted for the Bushwick. Officials at the Bureau of Public Roads promptly put the kibosh on such a swap; "the Cross-Brooklyn route," spokesman Warner Siems informed Gotham, "was not an acceptable alternative." Inclusion in the interstate highway network was vital, for then 90 percent of construction costs would be covered by Uncle Sam. The city, on the edge of fiscal disaster, couldn't afford to build a goat path without a massive federal subsidy, let alone America's first linear city. The bureau wanted a whole new proposal if it was to consider the Cross-Brooklyn Expressway at all. Nor were locals all that happy about the futuristic conurbation in their backyard. Lindsay had promised that Linear City would not be built without "continuing consultation" with residents in the affected area. But before the first meeting could be scheduled, howls of protest rose from all sides. Leading the charge was Bertram L. Podell—a Democratic assemblyman later charged with conspiracy (his trial put a young assistant US attorney named Rudolph W. Giuliani, an East Flatbush boy himself, on the front pages for the first time). Podell claimed that 1,042 residents would be displaced by the project (the Bushwick alignment would have dislodged nearly 4,000). "The people of Flatbush," he vowed, "will not permit the Cross-Brooklyn Expressway to go through their homes." And as for the proposed development atop the road, Podell suggested it be called "Carbon Monoxide City." The Reverend Galamison, on the other hand, hitched his hopes to the scheme; "If linear city fails," he said, "all hope for integration is lost." Many in the local black community nonetheless feared that the huge project would be forced upon them without their input or consent.[34]

Lindsay and his team pressed on, quietly winning from federal authorities in April a pledge of partial support for the Cross-Brooklyn Expressway—50 percent of costs—if the route was officially added to the city's arterial system. In a pyramid of Faustian bargains, Lindsay planned to take that pledge to the Tri-State Transportation Commission to beg inclusion of the route in the general highway plan for the metropolitan region. With that in hand he could go back to the Bureau of Public Roads to request reconsideration of the Cross-Brooklyn Expressway as part of the interstate network, thus making it eligible for federal funding. In August he secured a commitment from the state commissioner of education that the new schools planned for Flatlands, Brownsville, and East New York would be made part of Linear City, to include up to twenty thousand students. Excitement mounted for what could be the most progressive few miles of highway in the Western Hemisphere, if not the world. Ada Louise Huxtable, the city's most admired architecture critic, admitted that while the dense urban core must be saved from ill-conceived renewal and expressway plans, it was also "a chamber of horrors for many" that called for bold action on the part of planners. "We need the roads," she wrote; "We need the housing. We need the schools, the industry and the office buildings. But we do not need them in the conventional, city-destroying form that has forced so many thinking and feeling citizens to the barricades." And the seeds of salvation, she pressed, might even be in the very things we fight. "In the superroad, the city-as-a-building, even in the gigantism that we have learned to dread and deplore, may be answers to our problems and challenging solutions to the modern urban dilemma." Huxtable was unconvinced, however, that it could be pulled off. Money was not the issue, she reasoned, nor design or engineering know-how or construction technology. "The real problem is simple, and appalling," she wrote; "In government everything is solidly stacked against getting anything done." A project as vast in scale and scope as Linear City "must cut across all city departments and agencies. A design breakthrough is not enough. An administrative breakthrough is equally necessary." And that, alas, would never come.[35]

By now, Lindsay had fully reversed his prior opposition to the Lower Manhattan Expressway—succumbing to pressure from the construction trade unions and presumably satisfied that, without the Bushwick Expressway, LOMEX would not be overwhelmed with traffic. In January 1967 he remarked that there was "no question that a high-speed multilane highway across lower Manhattan is necessary," flatly contradicting a statement from his office only months before, that the project "never would be built in any form." Fears had been eased in Little Italy by vague promises that the road would be fully underground. But tunneling under Manhattan proved too costly, and in early 1967 city engineers were directed to come up with an alternative plan using a combination of tunnels, open cuts, and surface roads. On March 7, 1968, the Board of Estimate approved the LOMEX project in a 16-to-6 vote. Lindsay called for the immediate construction of both LOMEX and the Cross-Brooklyn Expressway, hailing them both "key and indispensable" to the city's future. A public hearing on LOMEX was then scheduled for April 10 at Seward Park High School on Grand Street. Purely pro forma, it had been hastily planned to evade pending legislation that would require a more rigorous community input process. State and

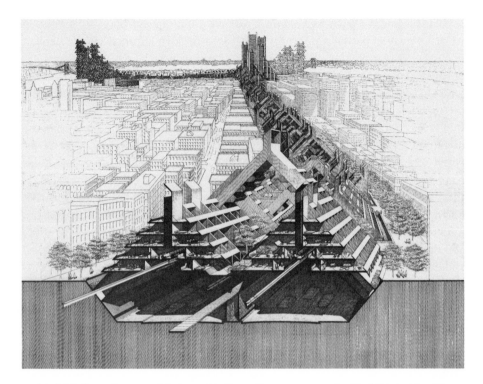

Paul Rudolph, linear city proposal for Lower Manhattan Expressway, 1970. Paul Rudolph Archive, Library of Congress, Prints and Photographs Division.

city officials did not expect many attendees, nor did they count on the presence of one Jane Jacobs among them. In a turn of events now part of Gotham lore, a huge crowd packed the auditorium and grew restless as testifying speakers were summarily cut off for going over the time limit. The protesters began chanting, "We want Jane! We want Jane!" Jacobs rose from her seat, took the microphone, and warned that anarchy would be unleashed if construction of LOMEX went ahead. She then mounted the stage and called upon the crowd to join her. In the ensuing ruckus, the stenographer's tapes spilled to the floor and were gleefully trampled and tossed about by the protesters. "Without the stenographic notes," writes Anthony Flint in *Wrestling with Moses*, "the officials couldn't prove they had satisfied the requirement to gather public input." Grabbing the microphone again, Jacobs shouted, "Listen to this! There is no record! There is no hearing! We're through with this phony, fink hearing!" She was promptly charged with disorderly conduct. "I couldn't have been arrested for a better cause," she later told a reporter.[36]

But the torpedo had found its mark. Opposition to urban expressways of any sort was peaking in the city, an outcry that did not go unheard in Albany. By late April, the New York State Senate had passed legislation nixing the Cross-Brooklyn Expressway from state highway plans. With the bill making its way to the state assembly, Lindsay and Rockefeller made an end run around the legislators, convincing the state Department of Transportation to request inclusion of the Cross-Brooklyn road in the interstate highway system. When news of this broke, Representative

Edna F. Kelly was outraged; a vocal opponent of the project, she accused state and city officials of brokering a clandestine deal that made a mockery of the democratic process. When asked about this, the mayor's office simply responded, "We don't know of any secret agreement." The move paid off; for on June 28, 1968, three federal agencies—Transportation, Housing and Urban Development, and Health, Education, and Welfare—joined in an unprecedented multiparty endorsement of Linear City. Together they pooled several million dollars for studies of the necessary community and educational infrastructure, while the Cross-Brooklyn Expressway was at last made a formal part of the interstate highway system. The Ford Foundation chipped in, too, offering a $100,000 grant for further planning reports. To manage the increasingly complex project, a Linear City Development Corporation would be formed, with representatives from the City Planning Commission, Board of Education, Human Resources Administration, Housing and Development Administration, and both city and state transportation agencies—a herd of cats if ever there was one. Long a neglected backwater of Gotham, the southeastern corner of Brooklyn was poised to become the most prodded, poked, and overplanned place in the city. Linear City was so complex an enterprise, with so many moving parts, that a "Plan for Planning" was deemed necessary just to start. Produced by a youthful Baltimore firm later known as RTKL and featuring an elaborate system of hieroglyphs, three-dimensional "molecular" models abstracting the project anatomy, and piano-roll charts of dizzying complexity, it described Linear City as "an urban laboratory, radical in concept, massive in scale," an experiment validated in its boldness and innovation by the "failure of existing social and physical institutions to adjust thus far to the volcanic forces that are shaking our society." Even a "project historian" was called for, to record the evolution of Linear City from seed to completion, anticipated—incredibly—for 1975.[37]

Linear City would, in fact, never see the light of day. It died on a balmy Saturday afternoon in May 1969, as news of a fatal vote in Albany reached City Hall. State attorney general Lewis J. Lefkowitz had previously ruled that legislative approval was necessary for New York State to accept a federal offer to pay virtually the entire cost of the schools, community centers, libraries, parks, and playgrounds vital to Linear City. By now, Lindsay himself was having serious doubts about the project; just two months earlier he had quietly asked the Board of Education to build the planned Linear City schools elsewhere. The bill seeking approval for the federal funds passed in the state senate; legislators in the assembly, however, hadn't forgotten Lindsay's end run around them the year before. In a rush to vote just before adjournment on Friday, May 2, they voted down the reimbursement bill. Without Washington's help, neither city nor state could ever afford to build all the infrastructure for Linear City, stripped of which the Cross-Brooklyn Expressway would be just another conduit out of town. Convinced its impacts would be "disastrous" to a part of town already severely stressed, Lindsay ordered an immediate halt to the entire project. The tea leaves were easy to read; the age of big urban highways was over. Desperate now for the support of liberal Democrats since losing the Republican primary in June, Lindsay scuttled the two big balls of asphalt chained to his political feet. On July 16, 1969, the mayor announced that both LOMEX and the Cross-Brooklyn Expressway were officially terminated—dead "for all time." Thus a project once promised to unite the embattled, warring communities of southeastern Brooklyn did just that—it joined them in opposition. "I will not," he vowed, "permit a swath of concrete to divide Brooklyn." The summer of 1969 put Americans on the moon, the most complex and costly venture in human history. But it was also the summer of Stonewall and Woodstock, and a season of victory for the partisans of walkability and social justice and human-scaled cities. Just one week before Lindsay's announcement, secretary of transportation John A. Volpe ended plans for the Vieux Carré Expressway that would have gutted the French Quarter, a project Moses had himself proposed twenty years earlier. America's long day of urban highway building was over, and with it went Brooklyn's star-crossed road of hope.[38]

CHAPTER 18

BOOK OF EXODUS

Everybody who's anybody is moving to Babylon.
—PATTY HASSETT

The 1960s left Brooklyn with a lot less than a kumbaya highway stretched across its strife-torn south. A sojourner returning after a decade abroad would have been stunned to find many of the borough's most vital, venerated institutions dead or dying. The fifteen years between 1955 and 1970 were the most convulsive in Brooklyn history, a time of exodus and loss that left the borough a quaking shell of its former self. It was as if the wrecking balls of urban renewal so busy downtown had begun smashing the very temples of Brooklyn life and culture. The presses of the *Brooklyn Eagle* were stilled in 1955, leaving the most opinionated place in America without a mouthpiece of its own. As Pete Hamill has put it, the *Eagle* was never a great paper, but "it had a great function: it helped to weld together an extremely heterogeneous community. Without it, Brooklyn became a vast network of hamlets, whose boundaries were rigidly drawn but whose connections with each other were vague at best, hostile at worst."[1] The timing of the daily's demise was itself extraordinary—folding just seven months before one of the biggest stories of the era: the Dodgers victory over the Yankees in the 1955 World Series. Two years later, almost to the day, the Dodgers themselves were gone. Their storied Flatbush ballpark, Ebbets Field, vanished not long after, cleared for a dreary housing estate. In 1964, just days before Thanksgiving, secretary of defense Robert S. McNamara announced that the 158-year-old Brooklyn Navy Yard would be shuttered, dooming thousands of jobs. That news came on the heels of another bombshell—that Steeplechase Park, last and greatest of Coney Island's storied amusement grounds, would not open again after the 1964 season. Its cavernous Pavilion of Fun—Brooklyn's own Crystal Palace—was purchased by Fred Trump, ostensibly for an apartment complex à la Miami Beach.

On September 21, 1966—after the city denied him the requisite zoning changes (but before the nascent Landmarks Preservation Commission could designate the Pavilion a city landmark)—Trump hosted a boorish "V.I.P. Farewell Ceremony" at which guests were handed bricks to hurl through the great windows. He razed the structure a few weeks later, an act of vandalism that destroyed a memory-palace of the very people who made Trump rich.

By this time, all of Brooklyn seemed "shabby and worn-out," wrote Hamill, "not just in the neighborhood where I grew up, but everywhere . . . The place had come unraveled, like the spring of a clock dropped from a high floor."[2] People were fleeing in droves. Brooklyn's population had climbed steadily for a century, leveling off after World War II and peaking at 2.74 million in 1950—more than the populations of Los Angeles, Detroit, and Philadelphia at the time. The collapse began slowly but accelerated wildly in the 1960s. By the 1970s, the bleakest decade in modern New York history, more than 500,000 people had fled Kings County—a city the size of Atlanta gone in a generation. Precipitating this mass exodus was a Gordian knot of both push and pull forces, many of which were operating with equal ferocity in cities throughout the Northeast at the time. As we have seen, the postwar collapse of Brooklyn industry and resulting loss of tens of thousands of factory jobs yanked the keystone from the borough's economic arch. There were many other factors; race, for one. The influx of large numbers of African Americans from the rural South and Harlem was, to put it gently, not a demographic shift met with joy and open arms by Brooklyn's white ethnic community. They regarded the newcomers with the same skepticism and outright hostility that had been aimed at them a generation before by the Anglo-Dutch elite. And just as the borough's old-line WASPs fled for Westchester and Long Island in the 1920s, so too now did the Irish, Jews, Italians, Greeks, and Poles. The nexus of race, crime, and white flight in New York City is a barbed and hazardous topic, but vital to understanding not just the postwar era but everything that came afterward—including the "discovery" of Brownstone Brooklyn by antiestablishment elites in the 1970s and the wholesale gentrification of once-shunned neighborhoods in the 1990s. In the fields of urban planning and American studies, it has long been an article of faith that racism and bigotry were the chief causes of the postwar flight to the suburbs—a population shift that deprived cities of billions in tax revenue, gutting their coffers and plunging them into a protracted era of fiscal crisis.

There was, to be sure, no shortage of racial hatred in Brooklyn; working- and lower-middle-class whites, especially, resented the influx of African Americans from the South—a demographic shift that began in the 1920s, but reached a fever pitch following World War II. But if racist loathing of the black Other drove some to abandon the old neighborhood, it was the calamitous unraveling of the borough's social fabric in the 1960s—especially the rise of violent crime—that turned what might have been a trickle into a full-scale exodus. In all of New York, crime skyrocketed in the postwar years—a phenomenon that baffled police, politicians, and sociologists alike. To most observers, Gotham at war's end seemed on the verge of a glorious era of peace and prosperity. Civic leaders were convinced that, just as the war had vanquished evil, New York would enter "a new era in which intelligence, education, and the insights of psychology and other social sciences," wrote Roger Starr in *The Rise and Fall of New York City*, "would overcome most behavior problems . . . that full employment would eliminate crime." Few indeed could have seen that, despite a booming national economy and high overall employment, "crime itself would, within twenty-five years, be regarded as New York's most serious problem." The statistics are grim. As Vincent J. Cannato notes in *The Ungovernable City*, between 1955 and 1965 murders citywide "increased 123 percent; robberies 25 percent; assaults 88 percent; and burglaries 31 percent." And it was just the start. From 1960 to 1974, robberies soared by 255 percent, forcible rape by 143 percent, and aggravated assault by 153 percent. There were 58,802 incidents of violent crime in the city in 1965; by 1975 that figure had nearly tripled to 155,187. Murders in the same period shot from 836 citywide to 1,996—an increase of 139 percent. As James Q. Wilson and others pointed out, this upsurge came in spite of President Lyndon B. Johnson's Great Society programs and War on Poverty and an unprecedented array of social welfare initiatives at every level of government. "If in fact crime resulted from poverty," writes Philip Jenkins in *Decade of Nightmares*, "then it should surely have declined, or at least got no worse. Instead, crime rates had risen to historic highs."[3]

Fairly or not, whites blamed the crime explosion on the city's swelling black and brown underclass. In Brooklyn, the African American population more than tripled between 1950 and 1970, rising from about 208,000 to more than 650,000, while the number of Puerto Ricans citywide jumped from 187,420 to 817,712 in the same period. The disappearance of manufacturing jobs, owing to automation as well as factory closures, hit minority communities first and hardest. By the mid-1960s, unemployment among African American men in the eighteen-to-twenty-four age bracket was five times that of white men. The ego-shattering inability of breadwinners to find and hold a job not only mired families in poverty, but spawned a vexing array of social ills—single-parent households, truancy, youth gangs, prostitution, drug addiction. Blacks in the city suffered higher mortality rates than whites, paid more in rent for lower-quality housing, and were forced to contend with lesser schools, while median black household income was just 65 percent that of whites. In Brooklyn, conditions were especially bad in Bedford-Stuyvesant, which shifted from majority white to 85 percent black between about 1945 and 1960. Battered by urban renewal, hemmed in by redlining, and gutted by blockbusting real estate agents, the enormous neighborhood—really a vast assembly of neighborhoods forced under the racialized rubric of "Bed-Stuy"—was terra incognita to most New Yorkers until July 1964, when protests touched off in Harlem by the police shooting of a black student spread to Brooklyn.[4]

Several days of violence and looting ensued, centered on Fulton Street and Nostrand Avenue. Police, pelted with brickbats from rooftops, could do little to quell passions. Equally unsuccessful was the NAACP, whose sound truck was nearly overturned as lawyer George Fleary and other staffers begged for calm while handing out pamphlets exhorting, "Cool It, Baby." Hundreds of shops were gutted and torched by the time peace was restored. Police arrested some 450 protesters; more than a hundred people were injured. The uprisings were the first of the civil rights era, and by summer's end had spread to Rochester, Philadelphia, Jersey City, Paterson,

Clash between police and African American residents on Nostrand Avenue, Bedford-Stuyvesant, July 1964. Photograph by Stanley Wolfson. New York World-Telegram and the Sun Newspaper Photograph Collection, Library of Congress, Prints and Photographs Division.

Elizabeth, and Chicago. The violence rattled Brooklyn and took a toll on racial tolerance throughout the city. For all its liberal, Democratic leanings, the city's white community—along with the majority of blacks—was unyielding when it came to the rule of law and order, concurring with Mayor Wagner's avowal that it must be "absolute, unconditional, and unqualified." In a *New York Times* survey conducted that fall, just weeks before the 1964 presidential election, 93 percent of white New Yorkers reported that the riots "had hurt the Negro cause," while large pluralities in the white ethnic community—61 percent of Irish, 58 percent of Italians, and 46 percent of Jews—felt that the "Negro movement . . . was going too fast." And while just 18 percent of whites citywide expressed support for Republican candidate Barry Goldwater, 27 percent asserted that they "had become more opposed to Negro aims during the last few months."[5]

However offensive to present sensibilities, the blame put on minorities was not wholly misplaced: a study of the 543 solved murder cases in New York City in 1966 revealed that 73 percent had been committed by blacks and Puerto Ricans. But if minorities were committing most of these acts, they were doing so largely within their own communities. An April 1967 article in the *Times*, published in the wake of several high-profile instances of black-on-white violence, showed that "violence against white people by Negroes is relatively infrequent both in New York City and nationally"—that the vast majority of violent crime victims were blacks themselves. Blacks in the inner city "had far more reason to be afraid," writes Adam Shatz; for "they lived in poor areas where crime was more widespread, and where the police were often absent." In Harlem, the *Amsterdam News* complained of "predatory thugs who bring terror to the streets," with a 1968 report by the NAACP denouncing "the reign of criminal terror" and calling for harsher penalties for drug dealing and violent crime, better enforcement of antivagrancy laws, and more cops on the beat. "It is not police brutality," argued the group, "that makes people afraid to walk the streets at night." But perception is nine-tenths of reality, and reports like this did little to dissuade whites from seeing crime in starkly racialized terms. Increasing violence and social chaos "posed a classic case of cognitive dissonance for many whites," writes Michael W. Flamm. "Intellectually, they knew that most blacks were not muggers; emotionally, they could not ignore the sense that most muggers seemed black. Adding to the racial tension and providing human faces to the grim statistics were a dramatic series of high-profile events and a disturbing number of sensational black-on-white crimes." The most widely publicized of these was the March 1964 murder of Kitty Genovese outside her Kew Gardens home at the hands of Winston Moseley—a married African American father of two who later confessed to three other murders—and the rape and murder two months later of a popular Brooklyn schoolteacher, Charlotte Lipsik, by an illiterate teenager who went on to rape and kill an eighty-three-year-old woman in the Bronx before being caught.[6]

The ugly tangle of race and crime turned the very geography of the city plastic, with neighborhoods shape-shifting in response to black advance and white retreat. The boundaries of Bedford-Stuyvesant "progressively enlarged," writes Michael Woodsworth, "to match the spreading radius of black settlement," while nearby Flatbush—a middle-class Jewish district settled by émigrés from Williamsburg and the Lower East Side—contracted in response. A *Times* reporter probing its borders in 1968 was given as many answers as people he asked. "If you really want to know the truth," one resident admitted, "today when people say 'Flatbush' they mean the place where the Negroes aren't." Attitudes on the street contrasted sharply with those in the halls of power and learning, where any linkage between race and crime was sanitized with euphemism and spoken of sotto voce. Indeed, "most liberal political leaders," writes Jenkins, "tended to dismiss concern about violent crime as coded language for racial hatred and white supremacy." Propinquity did nothing to warm whites to their new black neighbors; it had the very opposite effect. This contradicted prevailing social theory at the time, especially Gordon W. Allport's "intergroup contact hypothesis," which posited that tolerance and harmony would increase with proximity. Writing about working-class Italian-Jewish Canarsie a decade later, Jonathan Rieder noted that "physical closeness to blacks widened the moral and social chasm between them." New Yorkers with little daily contact with poor blacks became their greatest champions; those closest to them physically and economically were the most hostile. As Cannato put it, "Enlightened views on race were easy to hold for whites who lived in the comfortable suburbs or in the doorman buildings of Manhattan."[7]

As crime surged in the late 1960s, New Yorkers of every race, class, and ethnicity became prisoners in their own homes. In a December 1968 piece, journalist Michael Stern observed that fear was making people "live ever-larger portions of their lives behind locked doors."

> Feeling themselves besieged by an army of muggers and thieves, they are changing their habits and styles of life, refusing to go out after dark, peering anxiously through peepholes before opening their doors, side-stepping strangers on the streets, riding elevators only in the company of trusted neighbors or friends and spending large sums to secure their homes with locks, bolts, alarms and gates.[8]

Unease pervaded every aspect of life. "The fear is visible," wrote David Burnham in the *Times* in June 1969; "It can be seen in clusters of stores that close early because the streets are sinister and customers no longer stroll after supper for newspapers and pints of ice cream. It can be seen in the faces of women opening elevator doors, in the hurried step of the man walking home late at night from the subway . . . in elaborate gates and locks, in the growing number of keys on everybody's keyrings."[9] The effects on civic life were corrosive. "Since the very purpose of a city is to provide convenient access to the necessities and amenities of industrial civilization," wrote Starr, "it is no exaggeration to say the crime that has emerged in New York City threatens the very existence of the city in its present form." And it wasn't just violent crime but "lesser offenses that make the streets and subways seem outlaw lands. The ordinary rules of civility have been lost." Vandalism, including astonishing eruptions of graffiti that covered entire subway cars, signaled that "the quality of life, despite all the conscious agitation to improve it, has been soiled and damaged in far more crucial ways that none can control." Anticipating the city's "broken window" policing policies by decades, Starr surmised that to ignore low-level offenses "opens the city streets to further testing: If I can get away with this, what may I not do next?"[10] The specter of crime and social collapse was magnified in impact by the chaos being unleashed at the very same time by vast urban renewal and highway projects. These, as we have seen, not only subjected residents to years of noise, dust, and congestion, but forced jobs out of town and eradicated rental housing that, however substandard, was at least cheap. Life in Brooklyn, never easy for those of little means, was fast becoming intolerable.

Nor were these purgative forces operating in a regional vacuum. As crime, racial tensions, escalating taxes and rents, and a deteriorating quality of life began pushing Brooklynites out, equally powerful forces were luring them to suburbs both in town and out. Many moved to the trolleyburbs of Brooklyn and Queens explored in chapter 13; others fled the city altogether, settling in the many new subdivisions then being built in New Jersey, Long Island, and Connecticut. Facilitating the exodus were all those splendidly engineered parkways, bridges, and expressways built by Robert Moses in the 1930s and after the war—the very infrastructure that dislodged as many city dwellers as it convinced to buy a car. Moses had built the roads to put the beaches and parks of Long Island and upstate New York within easy reach of the motoring middle classes. Now they became the taps that ran the population kegs dry. The flush of affluence in the postwar years, combined with cheap and abundant gasoline, created an army of new motorists. Weekend jaunts to "The Island" often involved touring a gleaming new subdivision, where many an urban denizen saw her future. For all its problems, it is unlikely that so many families would have left Brooklyn had not savvy developers like William and Alfred Levitt offered seductively affordable alternatives out beyond the city line. By streamlining supply chains, barring unionized labor, negotiating more flexible building codes, and applying mass production techniques similar to those pioneered by William Greve and Fred Trump, the Levitts were able to build 17,500 homes between 1948 and 1951 that sold for as little as $8,000 (about $80,000 in 2017). Underwriting by Uncle Sam in the form of low-interest home loans made the homes more affordable still. The GI Bill—formally the Servicemen's Adjustment Act of 1944—made available an array of programs and services meant to smooth the transition of soldiers back to civilian life. The most celebrated of these was the tuition support that enabled countless servicemen to attend college, launch a professional career, and thus gain entry to the American middle class. Equally impactful was its provision of loan guarantees to cover the cost of purchasing a home—so long as that buyer was "a member of the Caucasian race," as racist FHA restrictions then required. The legislation, meant to stimulate the economy via the homebuilding industry, offered nothing to those veterans who wished to rent in the city.

The Servicemen's Adjustment Act transformed the housing market overnight, easing the postwar housing crunch and putting home ownership within reach of millions. Prior to World War II, less than half the households in America owned their own homes—a function of the huge down payments then required by lenders (between half and two-thirds of purchase price) as well as mortgage contracts obliging borrowers to pay back loans in less than a decade. Such terms made even buying

Long Island Lighting Company office and appliance store, Levittown, New York, 1953. Gottscho-Schleisner Collection, Library of Congress, Prints and Photographs Division.

a home on credit a privilege of affluence. Many needed no help at all. Between one-quarter and half of all homes sold before the war were purchased in full and free of debt.[11] Uncle Sam changed all this by effectively underwriting projects like Levittown that opened the dream of suburban home ownership to the children of impoverished immigrants. Levittown's cozy Cape Cod homes, bracketed by lawn and garden in front and back, appealed to that perennial American yearning for pastoral tranquility and the elixir of nature—little Monticellos far from the chaos of urban life and the "mobs of great cities," as Thomas Jefferson himself put it. Derided from the start by the intelligentsia, mocked sanctimoniously by Malvina Reynolds and Pete Seeger, the "Little Boxes" of Levittown were nonetheless a proud mark of arrival and acceptance into mainstream America for working-class ethnics whose childhoods had been marred by the Depression, who came of age in a world wracked by war, who yearned for a modicum peace and prosperity and a chance to raise a family. The last thing these children of hardship wanted was yet another crisis—and the slow-motion collapse of Brooklyn's social and physical infrastructure in the 1960s was just that. That their departure helped bring about that very collapse—pulling the tax-base rug out from under Gotham, stripping the city of a stable citizenry—only adds to the multivalent tragedy that was Brooklyn in the postwar era.

The mass exodus of Brooklyn's middle and working classes after World War II sealed the fates of many a borough institution, none more vital to Brooklyn's identity and self-image than its merry band of the diamond, the Brooklyn Dodgers. The club started out in 1883 in the minor leagues, moving to the majors the following year and eventually joining the National League. It was known by almost as many names as it had players—the Grays, Superbas, Bridegrooms, Robins. Not until 1895 did sportswriters and fans alike start calling the team by a name that referred to the ostensible dexterity of locals in dodging Brooklyn's swift, newly electrified streetcars. The Dodgers first played at two different ball fields named Washington Park on the edge of Park Slope, moving to Eastern Park in Brownsville in 1891, and returning seven years later to yet another Washington Park adjacent to the Gowanus Canal (near today's Whole Foods Market on Third Avenue). By then the club was being managed by Charles Ebbets. Son of a bank president, Ebbets quit school to work as a draftsman in the architectural office of John B. Snook, designer of the original Grand Central Depot, and later sold penny novels for a publishing house. He joined the Dodgers organization as a bookkeeper and ticket-taker, but moved up fast; by 1900 he was on his way to majority ownership in the ball club. Ten years later he set out to build a new stadium for the team, the best and most modern in America. The site he chose was in a section of Flatbush known as Pigtown, then only sparsely settled but close to transit and in the path of future growth. Ebbets commissioned the architect son of a Gravesend minister, Clarence Randall Van Buskirk, to design the structure. The new field, which Ebbets modestly named for himself, sported a steel-frame upper deck and roof and a neoclassical façade. Fans entered through a marble rotunda with terrazzo floor over which hung a spider-like bat-and-ball chandelier, which—if ever found—would likely fetch as much as the entire stadium cost in 1913 ($750,000).[12]

Ebbets Field opened auspiciously with an exhibition game on April 5, 1913. Casey Stengel scored the first Brooklyn run; the Dodgers won the game. Fans flocked to the new ballpark; attendance records were broken. In 1916 the Dodgers took home a pennant and did so again in 1920. But in 1925 Charles Ebbets was felled by a heart attack, and his death brought an ill wind. A protracted legal battle over club ownership dragged through the Great Depression, wrecking what had been one of the most financially sound clubs in baseball. Its board of directors feuded constantly; management was inept. Out of luck and out of cash, the Dodgers reached bottom in 1937. "Phone service had been cut off because the bills were not being paid," writes baseball historian Andy McCue; "The team's office was crowded with process servers seeking payment. Ebbets Field was a mass of broken seats, begging for a paint job. Charles Ebbets pride, the beautiful rotunda, was covered with mildew." But then came Leland Stanford MacPhail, an innovator who would transform the club over the next decade. As a college football coach in Ohio, MacPhail had developed the system of penalty hand signals still used today by referees. He later turned the Cincinnati Reds into a profitable baseball franchise by expanding radio broadcasts and introducing night games—the first in the Major Leagues. In Brooklyn, MacPhail hired still-popular Babe Ruth as a coach and named loudmouthed Leo Durocher as manager. He fixed up Ebbets Field and began broadcasting games on radio before either the Yankees or the Giants.[13]

The fans were soon streaming back. Attendance rose 37 percent in 1938. In 1940 the Dodgers led their league in attendance, setting a franchise record of 1.2 million attendees the following year. But the abrasive MacPhail made many enemies and was eased out of the organization by 1942. Replacing him was Branch Rickey, then general manager of the St. Louis Cardinals and the one who had recommended MacPhail to the Dodgers. A religious conservative who had once preached on the temperance circuit, Rickey was a respected figure in baseball—he invented the modern farm system, among other things—but he was not much liked. He was duplicitous, cheap, anti-Catholic, and anti-Semitic. And yet the much-flawed Rickey would make sports history just three years later by recruiting Jackie Robinson to the Dodgers, breaking baseball's color line. With the game in good hands, the directors focused on strengthening its front office. For this, George V. McLaughlin, president of the Brooklyn Trust Company and the ball club's biggest creditor, turned to a young Brooklyn lawyer he had mentored, Walter F. O'Malley. Within a few years Rickey and O'Malley not only were managing all aspects of the Dodger organization, but were majority owners of the club itself. They turned the team into a winner on both field and balance sheet. Rickey scored a moral victory by signing Robinson, but also landed a great player who drew new fans from the borough's growing African American community. O'Malley negotiated innovative branding, royalty, and television deals that boosted the club's bottom line; profits rose steadily each year from 1945 to 1949. On the diamond the team was at the top of its game, scoring two pennant victories between 1946 and 1950 and twice coming close.[14]

If integrating baseball was Rickey's great project, O'Malley's was to build the Dodgers a new ballpark—a matter he began studying as soon as he joined the organization in 1946. Ebbets Field, already past its expected thirty-year life span, was

Jubilant crowd of boys at Ebbets Field, 1954. Photograph by Jules Geller. Public Library, Brooklyn Collection.

fast becoming a maintenance liability and could barely handle the huge crowds the Dodgers were drawing. Seats were splinter prone, bathrooms were obsolete, and parking in the surrounding neighborhood was scattered, scarce, and costly. O'Malley wanted a large modern stadium convenient to public transit but—more vital still—one that could also accommodate the increasing percentage of fans driving to Flatbush to catch a game. O'Malley retained one of the finest engineers in New York, Emil H. Praeger, to develop preliminary plans for a superstadium. Praeger was a Flatbush kid himself, a graduate of Erasmus Hall Academy and the Rensselaer Polytechnic Institute. He was also, like Clarke and Rapuano, part of the Robert Moses brain trust. Moses had appointed him chief engineer of the newly consolidated Parks Department in 1934, where his first job was to conduct an unprecedented survey of the entire city's parks and open spaces. Praeger went on to design the Henry Hudson and Marine Parkway bridges and engineer the reclamation of the Flushing ash dump that Moses claimed as one of his greatest achievements. Praeger's first project with O'Malley—designing a small field for the Dodger spring-training facility in Vero Beach, Florida—allowed the pair to test ideas for a superstadium in Brooklyn. Of course, such a high-profile venture—a modern home for one of the most popular clubs in baseball—drew the attention of many other creative souls. First among them was the media-savvy industrial designer Norman Bel Geddes.[15]

Norman Bel Geddes with Jackie Robinson (left) and Roy Campanella (right), c. 1952. Harry Ransom Center, The University of Texas at Austin.

Bel Geddes had begun his career creating sets for the Metropolitan Opera and gained wide renown for his work on the 1939 New York World's Fair. He first approached O'Malley in 1948, certain that a new Dodger stadium could be the capstone commission of his career. Jumping O'Malley's light, Bel Geddes told reporters in March 1952 that he was already designing a state-of-the-art ballpark for Brooklyn. It would have rubberized seats and vending machines on every third seat back. Teams would play on an early version of Astroturf—"a synthetic substance to replace grass . . . which can be painted any color." There would be seating for fifty-five thousand fans, expandable to ninety thousand for prize fights or conventions. All seats would be oriented toward the pitcher's mound, and none would have an obstructed view. Lighting for night games would be indirect, eliminating glare. Bel Geddes continued working on his ballpark all summer, without O'Malley's approval or even a site upon which to build it. That hardly mattered, for his "All Weather–All Purpose Stadium" was a self-contained spaceship of sport, sealed from both weather and the mean streets of Flatbush. A carapace-like retractable roof would put an end to the hated rain check (which Charlie Ebbets had introduced to New York baseball). A *Collier's* article in September described the complex as designed to counter the impacts of television and suburbia, which together threatened to make the ballpark fan "as extinct as the bison." Bel Geddes was America's most persuasive prophet of automobility, the mastermind behind the General Motors "Futurama" exhibit at the 1939 World's Fair, which envisioned a gleeful technotopian future of skyscraper cities linked by twenty-lane expressways. He understood better than most that the new Dodger stadium would have to be convenient to all those Brooklynites fleeing the city for the sprawling suburbs of Queens and Long Island.[16]

As O'Malley himself remarked, "The public used to come to Ebbets Field by trolley cars, now they come by automobile." The old ballpark had depended on a patchwork of tiny parking lots that could, at best, accommodate seven hundred cars; the Bel Geddes scheme boasted a parking garage for seven thousand. And if easy parking wasn't enough to lure suburbanites off their sofas, there were other amenities never before seen in a ballpark—including a modern shopping center beneath the stands. There, supermarkets, shops, and stores would serve fans as well as local residents, as would playgrounds where mothers "can place their youngsters in the hands of trained young men and women while they shop, or visit the doctor or dentist." Fearful suburbanistas could drive their autos right into the stadium, hand the keys to a parking attendant, and even have the family car serviced while they watched the game. The getaway would be a cinch, too, with an array of lanes to permit "easy loading or unloading of 3,000 taxis, 400 buses, 1,500 private cars in a quarter of an hour." All this seduced even the pragmatic O'Malley, who was soon penning odes of his own to the proposed stadium in the *Eagle*. But the exuberant Bel Geddes proved too much for this cigar-chomping backroom deal maker, whose agitated "No, no, Norman!" was becoming a daily refrain. The Rubicon was likely crossed when the designer insisted that the ball field be engineered to allow "conversion . . . into an artificial lake for motorboat and sailboat shows." For better or worse, the buoyant Bel Geddes was out of the Dodger scene by the end of 1954.[17]

The following April, perhaps feeling this loss, O'Malley wrote to architect Eero Saarinen, asking if he might share "any photographs or technical articles" on Kresge Auditorium—the just-completed thin-shell concrete dome structure that Saarinen had designed for the MIT campus. The next month he read a magazine article on perhaps the only person in America who could outstrip Bel Geddes in scope of vision—the polymath futurist R. Buckminster Fuller, genius of the geodesic dome and the man who gave us the concept of "spaceship earth." O'Malley wrote to Fuller on May 26, relating his ambition to erect a revolutionary all-weather stadium in Brooklyn, capped with a translucent dome. He wanted the stadium to be a game-changer; "I am not interested in just building another baseball park." Fuller responded enthusiastically; the project promised to be the ultimate application of the kind of lightweight self-supporting, lattice-shell structure he had first experimented with at Black Mountain College in 1948 (and just received a patent for). Fuller and his design team had already worked out load calculations for a similar "clearspan enclosure" for the Denver Bears, and just months earlier he was retained by Minneapolis architects Thorshov & Cerny to explore options for enclosing a new Twin Cities ballpark (Metropolitan Stadium, demolished for Mall of America). Fuller proposed for Brooklyn the same "Octetruss" structural system he had recommended for Minneapolis, making possible a vast clearspan roof "skinned with translucent fiberglass petals opening and closing to the sky." Inside, Fuller explained, a canted array of polyester-resin seating boxes—lightweight and "rotatably dumpable for cleaning purposes"—would enclose the field, affording fans "unprecedented altitude and view advantage." Wrapped about the Octetruss exterior, meanwhile, would be "tiered parking balconies" that fans would access via a "spiral drive-yourself-up ramp." Fuller closed his letter suggesting he and O'Malley attend a ballgame together to discuss plans.[18]

In late September, with the World Series just getting under way, O'Malley formally announced that Fuller would be collaborating with the Dodgers on a new stadium. The projected arena, reported the *Times*, would be "circular in shape and covered by a thin plastic dome," 750 feet in diameter and rising to 300 feet above the pitcher's mound—"high enough to cover a thirty-story building." Passively cooled by "natural currents of air circulating beneath the dome," it would be the largest clear-span structure ever built. A dedicated teacher, Fuller made the stadium the focus of a graduate design studio he taught that fall at Princeton University. O'Malley attended a review of their work just before Thanksgiving, marveling at a large-scale model of the stadium, its translucent dome anchored at five points and creating "a pleasant interior effect of the sort one finds in a greenhouse." Inspired by one of Fuller's lectures, Princeton MFA student Theodore W. Kleinsasser decided to make the stadium the subject of an independent master's thesis. A Tennessee native, Kleinsasser had played football at Princeton as an undergraduate, returning to campus after a stint in the army as a paratrooper. Kleinsasser's thesis arena, slightly smaller than Fuller's, was presented on January 21, 1956, to a ten-member jury including O'Malley, Fuller, Praeger, and J. Robert Oppenheimer, father of the Manhattan Project and head of Princeton's Institute for Advanced Study. Perhaps the most memorable feature of Kleinsasser's stadium scheme was a rooftop tramway to carry sightseers across the vast dome—a Sputnik-era recap of the cog railway that was to have inched around huckster-visionary Sam Friede's great Coney Island globe.[19]

Like Friede's fraudulent orb, a state-of-the-art Dodger stadium was destined to remain a figment of dreams and imagination. The real challenge was not the design of the new stadium, but where to put it and how to pay for it. With the Ebbets Field property too small and encumbered to support a modern stadium, O'Malley knew he needed a new site. But he needed help, for he lacked the money to both acquire the land and build a ballpark. Thus, in June 1953, he went to see the almighty Robert Moses, asking—hat in hand—whether urban renewal funds might be used to assemble land for a stadium at the junction of Atlantic and Flatbush avenues, on the site of the Long Island Rail Road's aging depot at Hanson Place. Moses was no fan of professional sports, never much liked Brooklyn, and reviled O'Malley's Tammany-Irish background. He resisted the Dodger owner's overtures from the start. The ensuing battle of wills between the two men—both brilliant, both hard-headed, each long accustomed to getting his own way—has been written about extensively and need not be recounted here.[20] Put simply, Moses refused to apply Title I slum clearance funds to build a stadium for a private ball club, arguing that eminent domain could not be used for anything other than improvements with a clear public purpose. Moses did agree, all the same, that O'Malley's proposed Atlantic-Flatbush site was a good one. It had come into play when the antiquated meat market on Fort Greene Place, just behind the rail depot, was scheduled to close. Situated at a

Princeton architecture student Ted Kleinsasser (right) with (left to right) Emil Praeger, Walter O'Malley, and R. Buckminster Fuller, 1956. Seeley G. Mudd Manuscript Library, Princeton University.

major crossroads, it was easily accessed by road, rail, and subway. It was here that Kleinsasser had sited his thesis stadium—the "Princeton bubble," as Moses called it, "the idea of an ambitious graduate reporting to a rather wild professor." At the final review, O'Malley had asked Kleinsasser—for the benefit of the reporters in the room—whether he had come across any better site "where the stadium could be logically be built." As if rehearsed, the student responded, "No, sir; It's the most magnificent site in the world."[21]

O'Malley's struggle to build a new ballpark in Brooklyn achieved a seeming major victory when an act to create a public benefit corporation—the Brooklyn Sports Center Authority—was signed into law by Governor Averell Harriman in April 1956. Drafted by attorney John P. McGrath and cosponsored by Brooklyn borough president John Cashmore and a somewhat skeptical Mayor Wagner, the bill was aimed at "constructing and operating a sports center . . . at a suitable location in an area bounded by DeKalb Avenue, Sterling Place, Bond Street and Vanderbilt Avenue"—a vast swath of vintage Brooklyn surrounding the rail depot that, in effect, extended the Brooklyn Civic Center urban renewal zone well to the south.[22] Cashmore had, several months earlier, commissioned the ubiquitous Clarke and Rapuano to prepare a redevelopment plan for the area, to which was now tacked the immense task of siting a modern ballpark. Clarke's report, completed in November 1956, made a number of recommendations—relocating the Long Island Rail Road depot, elevating Atlantic Avenue to create a grade-separated crossing at Flatbush, developing the air rights over the adjacent rail yards for housing. But where O'Malley and Kleinsasser had envisioned locating the ballpark on the depot site north of Atlantic Avenue, Clarke and Rapuano recommended instead a site to the south, just west of Flatbush Avenue, atop the Victorian-era homes of hundreds of working-class families.

In light of prevailing wisdom in urban planning and design, the Clarke and Rapuano proposal was a stunningly misguided piece of midcentury modernism, so wholly dismissive of traditional urbanism—architectural diversity, pedestrian scale, delightfully walkable streets—that even Robert Moses thought it was nuts. "The notion that we can declare a large area across Atlantic Avenue a slum is ridiculous," he wrote to McGrath; "We would never get City Planning or federal approval. We would be murdered in Court and by public opinion."[23] Clarke, an otherwise brilliant planner, reasoned—evidently on Emil Praeger's advice—that a stadium for fifty thousand people would never fit on the Long Island Rail Road parcel. He proposed placing it instead, with twin garages and a tangle of access roads, in the space bounded by Flatbush Avenue, Third Avenue, and Prospect Place—a sixty-acre wedge of Park Slope and Boerum Hill including some of the best brownstone blocks

The ill-considered Clarke and Rapuano site for the new Dodger ball field on the edge of Park Slope. From Gilmore D. Clarke and Michael Rapuano, *A Planning Study for the Area Bounded by Vanderbilt Avenue, DeKalb Avenue, Sterling Place and Bond Street in the Borough of Brooklyn* (1956).

in all New York. Home plate would have been in the backyard of 105 Saint Mark's Place, third base near 400 Bergen Street; the outfield wall would have run through LuLu's for Baby and the kitchen of El Viejo Yayo on Fifth Avenue. Of course, in an era before Jane Jacobs nailed her thesis to the cathedral door, architects and planners saw little of value in "obsolete" neighborhoods like this, which Clarke himself described as "one of the more deteriorated sections" in downtown Brooklyn. All told, some eleven hundred buildings in the neighborhood would have been destroyed to make way for the colossal arena, its narrow streets blown out "to a minimum width of 100 feet" and the historic city grid obliterated "to create larger blocks better suited to the present day concept of residential redevelopment"—distended Corbusian superblocks, in other words, one of the great planning mistakes of the twentieth century.[24]

A week or so before the Clarke and Rapuano report was bundled off to the printers—on the morning of October 31, 1956—an icon of Brooklyn life passed into history. "While most of Brooklyn slept," reported the *Herald Tribune*, "the last trolley cars on the last two remaining trolley lines in the borough made their last runs and quietly closed an era of public transportation." It was a very bad sign for Brooklyn baseball; for, as we've seen, the fast electric streetcars—introduced in the 1890s—had given the many-named Brooklyn ball club its most famous appellation: the Brooklyn Trolley Dodgers. The beloved rattletraps had been disappearing from the streets of Gotham for years—and from cities across the country (New Rochelle's last operating streetcar carried a sign that read "Streetcar Named Expire"). The last Manhattan trolleys—the Broadway-Kingsbridge and 125th Street crosstown lines—closed down in late June 1947. Brooklyn's busy crosstown trolleys were pulled out of service in January 1951, replaced by the B61 bus. Those plying Smith Street (B75) and Seventh Avenue (B67) were retired the following month, while service on Flatbush Avenue—the borough's longest trolley line—ended on March 4 (replaced by the B41). The new diesel vehicles, unpopular from the start, had all the magic and romance of a wet mop; "we have never been convinced," the *Times* opined, "that the bus was a fair or completely beneficial exchange." The October 1956 removal of Brooklyn's last trolleys—from Church Avenue and McDonald Avenue—came, appropriately enough, just three weeks after the Yankees beat the Dodgers in the seventh (and final) World Series matchup between the two New York teams. Needless to say, the loss restored to Brooklyn its perennial underdog status.[25]

Ill-considered and ill-timed, the Clarke and Rapuano stadium proposal was fateful for another reason: it fractured the fragile consensus that was forming around the Long Island Rail Road site—one that, against all odds, O'Malley, Cashmore, and even Moses all agreed was the best location for a new ballpark. Now, with a respected planning firm—Moses's own consultants on scores of projects—recommending a wholly different locale, the waters were newly muddied. Moses weighed in publicly on the whole "Dodger rhubarb" in a portentous July 1957 *Sports Illustrated* essay, complaining that professional baseball was "rapidly becoming our No. 1 domestic headache." Claiming to be thoroughly bewildered by the stadium shenanigans—"I am no diagnostician," he professed, "merely a builder of parks and public works"—Moses blamed the mess on the "assorted tribal doctors, medicine and confidence

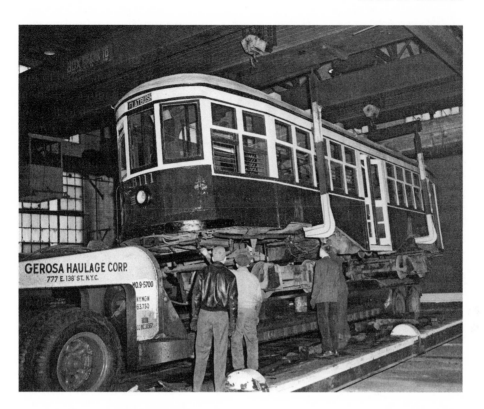

One of Brooklyn's last working trolleys is loaded on a flatbed truck, January 1953. The borough's streetcar system was once the most extensive in North America. This car, No. 8111, served Ocean Avenue and is preserved today at the Shore Line Trolley Museum in East Haven, Connecticut. Photograph by Jules Geller. Public Library, Brooklyn Collection.

men, shills, barkers, swamis and self-anointed pundits" who offered nothing but quack remedies. He described O'Malley's appeal as a sob story full of veiled threats and "embroidered . . . with shamrocks, harps and wolfhounds," and feigned fresh indignation over the proposal that eminent domain be used to assemble land for the ballpark. "From the point of view of constitutionality," he wrote, "Walter honestly believes that he in himself constitutes a public purpose." Moses reserved special vitriol for infidels Clarke and Rapuano. "Instead of directing various city agencies to concentrate on a careful analysis of this site," he crabbed, "a firm of planning consultants turned to an alternative site across Atlantic Avenue which included expensive built-up property and was by no stretch of the imagination a slum." The move "further bedeviled and confused an already difficult problem"—in large measure, of course, because it had infuriated New York's omnipotent master of public works.[26]

In the end, of course, O'Malley left Brooklyn, taking his ball club to that sunny national suburb, Southern California. The Dodgers played their last game at Ebbets Field on September 24, 1957. The team was gone one month later. "If somebody had asked me 10 years ago, 'Which do you think is the most likely to move—the Brooklyn Bridge or the Brooklyn Dodgers,'" quipped Leo Durocher, "I'd have picked the Bridge." The ballpark was sold to a local developer, Marvin Kratter, who pulled

A wheelchair-bound Roy Campanella bids farewell to Ebbets Field, February 1960, shortly before the stadium was razed. Bruce Bennett / Getty Images.

it down for a housing project and spent the rest of his life in repentance. O'Malley became, unfairly, the most hated man in Brooklyn; "Hitler, Stalin and Walter O'Malley," sang the chorus. That changed only with Robert Caro's 1974 publication of *The Power Broker*, which revealed Moses to be the real demon in the Dodger tale. But blame must also be placed, perhaps first, at the feet of Dodger fans themselves. Long "more vociferous than numerous," these were the very souls fleeing Brooklyn in droves after the war—and who would, oblivious to their own role—weep tears for decades for the "beloved Bums" and the Brooklyn of their youth. Ultimately, what propelled the Dodgers out of town was neither O'Malley's duplicity nor Moses's stubbornness, but the loss of their fans. "The dominant issue," writes McCue, "was attendance. Despite the legend of legions of vocal, supportive, and, above all, devoted Brooklyn fans, the evidence is that not enough of them were buying tickets to Ebbets Field at the rate the legend would have predicted." Ticket sales to Dodger ballgames mirrored Brooklyn's falling population. As we have seen, between 1950 and 1955 alone some fifty thousand Brooklyn residents left town, most from the same white working- and middle-class demographic that formed the core of Dodger fandom. While Major League Baseball nationwide underwent a 22 percent decline in game attendance between 1947 and 1956, the Dodgers numbers dropped by a whopping 33 percent in that period—a difference of some 800,000 attendees. "We have given the fans the finest baseball possible in the last nine years," O'Malley grumbled, "and still our attendance declines." Indeed, not even that most elusive of dreams—a Dodger world championship, captured at long last in 1955—would stem the inexorable tide of flight.[27]

The clouds of change above postwar Brooklyn were nowhere more highly charged than over that other landscape of summer delights, Coney Island. There, racial lines were quite literally drawn in the sand that ultimately spelled the doom of that American Tivoli, Steeplechase Park, Brooklyn's oldest and most venerated playground. Though the great weekend crowds of the Depression and war years were long gone, Coney Island did well enough all through the 1950s—despite the steady loss of much of its patron base to the backyards of suburban Long Island and resplendent state parks like Jones Beach. To some extent, the losses were offset by a new source of patrons; arriving African American, Puerto Rican, and West Indian residents were just as excited as whites about Coney Island's famous beach and amusements. And if the expanding regional highway system spirited many old patrons off to the suburbs, it also brought new ones from far away. By the late 1940s, Steeplechase had become an especially popular destination for African Americans from Maryland, Washington, and northern Virginia, where amusement parks were either officially segregated or effectively so. Black church and civic groups would charter buses for day trips to Steeplechase Park, which they knew to be safe not only from bad weather (its great pavilion assured that a long bus trip would not be a wash), but from the rougher aspects of Coney Island. In 1945, one ride operator estimated that there were "nine Negroes to every white" at Coney Island on the Fourth of July, "and all heavy spenders." The profligacy stereotype would be invoked over and over by amusement operators—the very beneficiaries of the alleged extravagance. "Labor Day brought many excursions via busses, mainly from out of town," reported the *Billboard* in 1949, "with the percentage largely in favor of Negro customers"—visitors "gladly welcomed . . . because of their liberal spending." Blacks were drawn, too, by the fact that many of their people worked at the park. African Americans had long been employed as laborers in Coney Island, but Steeplechase was the first to put them in frontline jobs dealing with the public. The first were hired in 1943, many as "Red Coats"—the park's uniformed workers who operated rides, punched tickets, and worked as "platform men" assuring patron safety on rides. As World War II got under way, many more African Americans were brought on to replace workers serving in the military. By the late 1940s, Steeplechase was the largest and most visible employer of African Americans in Coney Island.[28]

In fact, blacks had been part of Coney Island life for well over a century by this time. A hardscrabble community had formed as early as the 1830s in the salt meadows along Coney Island Creek—the "old negro settlement," as it was known, which survived municipal dumping only to be wiped out by a fire in October 1909. As we saw in chapter 5, a more substantial black community evolved in nearby Gravesend and Sheepshead Bay as thoroughbred racing was established there in the 1880s. By the 1920s, in wake of the first Great Migration, African Americans from Harlem began visiting Coney Island in steadily rising numbers. Many first came on church outings, like the one to Steeplechase Park led by the Progressive Mission on Lorimer Street in September 1923—an event noted in the *Chicago Defender*. Black civic organizations also brought large groups down to the island. In 1938 the Harlem-based *Amsterdam News*, New York's leading black daily, led a big outing to Luna Park for three hundred of its paper boys. But though their coin was

Boys, black and white, prepare for a race on the namesake horse coaster at Steeplechase Park, 1910. Hulton Archive / Getty Images.

welcome, African Americans were often treated with resentment and hostility at Coney Island—where racial prejudice was as much a part of daily life as the sand and sea. It didn't help that blacks were often brought in by employment agencies to break strikes by Coney Island's hotel and restaurant workers (whose unions barred blacks). The crass amusements of the midway were a special chamber of racial humiliations. Among the most shameful was a game eventually outlawed by the state legislature during World War I. It featured a "negro who will put his head through a hole in a canvas," explained the *New-York Tribune* in 1911, "that it may become a target for all who will gamble on hitting it with a baseball." Though the human target was able to maneuver somewhat to avoid the ball, "the general effect upon the boys and girls who see it," observed the *Tribune*, was to make "the sport . . . alright so long as it is a negro that is hit." Bam Boula, an African native, toured with an animal troupe until 1910. A popular freak-show attraction at the Palace of Wonders in the late 1920s was a caged "wild man," actually a young African American novelist named Leroy Flynn, who forced himself to endure a daily barrage of racist catcalls to pay the rent.[29]

Though Steeplechase Park prided itself on being a moral octave above the rest of Coney Island, plenty of midway riffraff got through the gates. Shortly after opening day in May 1912, a Steeplechase porter named Aaron Nelson was arrested for lashing out at a group of white men who had been tormenting him. "Maddened by the taunts and insults of the men, Nelson suddenly whipped a knife from his

A young African American couple and their child on a hot day at Steeplechase Park, July 1939. Andrew Herman for Federal Art Project / Museum of the City of New York. 43.131.5.49.

pocket and began to slash out blindly," injuring two and landing himself in prison on charges of felonious assault. Nor was management always innocent. "Race discrimination at George C. Tilyou's famous Steeplechase," reported the *Amsterdam News* in 1927, "continues unabated. Within the last several years numerous complaints have been lodged against this popular amusement enterprise." In July 1920 a Steeplechase bathhouse worker named Jennie Newton refused to sell a ticket to George E. Wibecan, Jr., a nineteen-year-old Brooklyn electrician of mixed African and Danish heritage. Prior to completion of the boardwalk in 1923, nearly every inch of beachfront at Coney Island was private. Access was via bathhouses, where visitors wishing to swim were forced to pay a fee. But Wibecan was the wrong person to cross; he had civil rights in his blood and refused to go quietly. His grandfather was a West Indian immigrant who survived the Draft Riots by hiding in a rowboat at the Brooklyn Navy Yard. His father, a former "ruler" of the Colored Elks of the World and president of the Crispus Attucks Community Council, was a prominent Republican Party leader. Wibecan, Sr., had brought Frederick Douglass to Brooklyn in 1892 and organized the purchase of Harry H. Roseland's painting of the infamous Beecher slave-girl auction—"Pinky"—as a gift of gratitude to Plymouth Church in 1928 (where it still hangs). The younger Wibecan reported the bathhouse matter to the police and then sued Steeplechase Park. Newton was promptly arrested "on a charge of discrimination"—testament to the respect the Wibecan name commanded even in the white community. Though the case was dismissed in court, it galvanized Wibecan's passion for racial justice; he later became active with the NAACP and fought housing discrimination as chair of the Montclair Civil Rights Commission.[30]

The Wibecan incident was just one of many, few of which ever made the news. A story that did took place in the middle of a heat wave in July 1927. Two African American teenagers—Ernest Huggins and his sister Josephine, a student at the Yale School of Music—and an older family friend named Fannie Potter had purchased the standard combination ticket to Steeplechase Park before attempting to rent "carnival suits"—overalls made of coarse fabric meant to protect a patron's clothes from dirt and grease on the rides. The suit vendor refused to serve the trio. Pressed, he sent them to speak to George Tilyou, Jr., son of the founder. Tilyou coolly informed them that a $25 deposit would be required for each suit, not the twenty-five-cent fee charged white patrons. Outraged, Potter returned a week later with a reporter from the *Amsterdam News*; she again sought to rent a carnival suit and was again told by Tilyou that she must first pay the inflated "colored" fee. (Decades later, coincidentally, Josephine Huggins would teach music at the Harry Conte School in New Haven, centerpiece of the Wooster Square renewal project and brainchild of Cy Sargent, father of the Brooklyn Linear City). Fortunately, blatant acts of discrimination like this became infrequent as more and more blacks flocked to Coney Island after the Depression. By the 1940s, Jim Crow had effectively withdrawn to a handful of dark recesses—all spaces of public intimacy where strangers of both sexes were put into close contact with one another.[31]

Integrating such holdouts—swimming pools, dance halls, bathhouses—was a struggle that unfolded in cities across the United States as the civil rights movement got under way. In Biloxi, Mississippi, a riot ensued when protesters staged a "wade-in" on a segregated beach in 1960, prompting the Justice Department to bring suit against the city (federal funds had been used to create the beachfront). Wedgewood Village amusement park in Oklahoma City was integrated in June 1963 after a large demonstration in which fifty people were arrested. Owner Maurice Woods relented only after receiving repeated telephone threats "to kill him and members of his family and to blow up the park." But attendance plunged soon after, convincing Woods to try a harebrained "Black Thursday" plan—integrating the park that one day and restricting admission "only to non-Negro customers" the rest of the week. An incensed NAACP rejected these "spoon-fed days at Wedgewood" and promised to organize new rallies. Demonstrations were staged at Chain of Rocks park in suburban St. Louis and Holiday Hill near Ferguson, Missouri, where blacks were admitted only as part of mixed school groups. In New Orleans, African American parents sued to desegregate municipal playgrounds and recreation centers; the city rejected their pleas, arguing that blacks and whites "co-mingled in large numbers in public parks has definite dangers to the peace and tranquility of the State." For years, the owners of Gwynn Oak Park in Baltimore deflected requests to integrate from the NAACP, the Congress of Racial Equality, and the Maryland Commission on Interracial Problems and Relations. Matters came to a head on the Fourth of July 1963, when a huge rally at the gates was ordered to disperse; nearly three hundred people were arrested, including "clergymen of all three major faiths" (Episcopal priest Daisuke Kitagawa and Bishop Daniel Corrigan were among them). Owner Arthur B. Price defended the white-only policy in real estate terms, claiming that "an impulsive switch would shake values." "I don't condone second-class citizenship," he retorted; "but the road to first-class citizenship is not downhill on a Roller Coaster." The work of integrating erstwhile places of joy was often wretchedly comic: in June 1964 a group of fifty civil rights demonstrators marched into the surf on a segregated public beach in St. Augustine, Florida, an equal number of starchily uniformed state troopers wading in at their heels.[32]

Ugly fears of miscegenation made swimming pools among last redoubts of segregation throughout the United States. As Jeff Wiltse has written in *Contested Waters*, "Although the rationale remained mostly unspoken, northern whites in general objected to black men having the opportunity to interact with white women at such intimate and erotic public spaces. They feared that black men would act upon their supposedly untamed sexual desire for white women by touching them in the water and assaulting them with romantic advances." White resistance was often violent. When a large group of African American men attempted to swim in Pittsburgh's immense new Highland Park pool in August 1931, they were hounded out of the water. "Each Negro who entered," reported the *Post-Gazette*, "was immediately surrounded by whites and slugged or held beneath the water until he gave up." After passage of the 1964 Civil Rights Act, operators outfoxed the new law's "public accommodations" clause by becoming members-only clubs. The owners of Alward Lake Resort in suburban Lansing, Michigan, hauled into court for refusing admission to a group of African American college students, sidestepped the matter by immediately reorganizing as a private club. So did Lakeland Park east of Memphis, which privatized just days after the act was signed into law by President Johnson. Fees were low at Lakeland, but memberships could be purchased only "in person at the park." "You can't buy by mail," related manager Louis M. Garner, for obvious reasons. Fontaine Ferry Park in Louisville, Kentucky, was successfully integrated, except for the pool, which was hurriedly leased to separate management to be operated as a members-only facility. Many pools were simply closed to resist integration. The city manager of Little Rock, Arkansas, preemptively shut the city's two public pools—one white, one "colored"—days before the landmark bill passed the Senate. In Atlanta, residents demanded that the recently integrated pool at Candler Park be shut down, fears of "race mixing" thus taking precedence over the summer fun of their own children (a case of throwing the baby out with the bathwater if ever there was one). Not coincidentally, it was in this era that backyard swimming pools soared in popularity. Only about 2,500 American households owned an in-ground home swimming pool in 1950. The number hit 26,000 by the end of 1955, and 375,000 a decade after that. By 1970 there were some 800,000 residential pools in the United States, a figure that would continue to soar in coming years. "The proliferation of residential swimming pools," writes Wiltse, "represented not simply an abandonment of public space but a profound retreat from public life," accelerating the atomization of American society by reducing opportunities to interact with people of different backgrounds.[33]

At Coney Island, the struggle to integrate dance halls, pools, and other spaces of public intimacy began early. Luna Park was the first target of coordinated action. In July 1940 the Brooklyn Council of the National Negro Congress launched a "determined drive against the alleged discrimination of Negroes" at Luna, where—as the *Amsterdam News* reported—blacks "were admitted to other attractions . . . but were refused admittance to the dance hall." Vowing to fight "any and all discriminatory practices on the island," the committee—led by Frank D. Griffin and Malcolm G. Martin—organized a mass meeting at West Thirtieth Street and Mermaid Avenue. Samuel A. Neuberger, a prominent labor lawyer, then filed suit against Luna Park. The council went after Luna's pool the following summer, charging that management's refusal to admit a group of African American boys was a "Hitler-like action" that would result in another lawsuit. These actions were generally successful at Coney; ride and amusement operators dreaded negative coverage in the city's dozen-odd dailies and quickly backed down. After the war, with so many blacks working at Steeplechase and other attractions, truly segregated spaces became scarce. Steeplechase was soon booking acts specifically aimed at black audiences. Fred Sindell's Cavalcade of Variety often played to packed crowds, with a show "catering for the most part to the Negro element." Racial attitudes had so softened that even poet Langston Hughes could wax forth on Coney Island's vibrant diversity. There, as summer thickened and Gotham sweltered, the beaches grew "crowded with bathers of all nationalities and sizes and shapes with no color line between them," the hot sun "doing its best to make everyone darker." Hughes saw hope even in the loutish midway: "A side show has a colored snake charmer," he wrote in 1947; "the strong man is white as is the fire-eater, the turtle-girl is colored, but a mule-faced boy is white. Democracy is all-inclusive at Coney Island."[34]

There was one last holdout of segregation in Coney island, and it was at that paragon of middle-class respectability, Steeplechase. There, the park's famous swimming pool had become a kind of sanctum sanctorum after World War II—a last redoubt against the churn of societal change. Built on the very site of the Friede Globe Tower, it was the largest saltwater pool in North America, as long as a city block is wide and filled with 160,000 gallons of seawater. It was flanked on either side by simple loggias topped with bleachers (women were prohibited from the west bleacher, as it afforded a clear view of the men's showers and changing rooms). At the head of the pool was an ornate tower modeled loosely on those of the cathedral of Santiago de Compostela in Spain. Originally meant for the newly opened boardwalk, the tower (which also concealed a water tank) was designed by Michael Marlo, an Italian immigrant architect who did extensive work over the years at Steeplechase. The pool was open to daily bathing prior to World War II—admission was fifty cents—but in March 1946 the Tilyou family launched a "season bathing only" policy. Bathers were now required to rent, as individuals or a family, a locker or tiny bathhouse each spring to use the pool. It is not clear whether this was meant to exclude the many

Patrons on an updated version of Sam Friede's old airship tower ride at Steeplechase Park, c. 1945. The great glass-and-steel façade of the Pavilion of Fun, target of Fred Trump's bikini-clad vandals, is in back. Hulton Archive / Getty Images.

blacks who had begun flocking to the park after the war, or was simply a means of raising cash to paint and prep the park well in advance of opening day. The units were not cheap: the 1947 rate for a bathhouse for a couple with two children was $72—nearly $800 in today's dollars. It may also have been a way of regulating behavior at the pool; for troublesome or rowdy guests could be threatened with losing their lease. Whatever the motivation, season bathing was private-club membership by another name; it effectively segregated the pool. Though African Americans can clearly be seen enjoying Steeplechase rides in Pathé newsreels from the 1920s, in footage from the pool's annual Modern Venus bathing-beauty competition in the 1940s and 1950s—and in Reginald Marsh's many photographs of the event at the Museum of the City of New York—not a single black person can be seen among either contestants or the large crowds of onlookers.[35]

The Tilyous and their legendary park manager, James J. Onorato—a man Walt Disney spent a week with and tried to recruit before he launched Disneyland— were untroubled about the implications of the members-only policy, at least at first. Few blacks seemed interested in the pool, which—compared to the jubilant beach scene—appeared stuffy and unwelcoming and was not included on the park's famous combination ticket. It was also filled with the same seawater as the surf, where one could splash about all day for free. The Tilyous also held the view, abhorrent today but common at the time, that blacks did not like to swim, especially in frigid saltwater (the pool was emptied and refilled on Tuesdays and Thursdays, so it never had a chance to warm up). Why stir up trouble with the season bathers, they reasoned, when blacks themselves showed little or no interest in the pool? Of course, it mattered not a whit whether or not African Americans *wanted* to use the pool: that they were prohibited from doing so was all. As the struggle for civil rights came together in the late 1950s, word began circulating that blacks were being barred from the Steeplechase pool. Comity and decorum were declining generally at the park, and the pool crowd was becoming especially rowdy. Season bathers began to crow about the pool's racial exclusivity, infuriating Onorato and the Tilyou family. Onorato was becoming nervous; "I told the Tilyous," he recounted later, "that we were skating on thin ice with our white only policy." On July 9, 1959, following a tip, Bill Leonard of WCBS did a story about "color discrimination" at the pool on his popular evening radio program. Suddenly the whole city knew that Jim Crow was summering at Steeplechase. It was a season of growing scrutiny of discriminatory practices in the city. The very day Leonard's piece aired, the *New York Times* ran a front-page story on how the elite West Side Tennis Club in Forest Hills excluded blacks and Jews from membership, refusing to allow even Nobel laureate and UN official Ralph Bunche and his son to join.[36]

In the early spring of 1964, with the civil rights bill moving through the Senate, the Tilyous decided to preempt a very public integration battle by shutting down the Steeplechase pool. Duly notified on March 15, the season bathers—an increasingly rancorous and insubordinate group—were outraged; some threatened violence. The flush of cash in spring from membership rental fees would surely be missed, but even that hardly compensated for the headaches the pool and its entitled patrons were causing—especially now that the city health department

A precocious little boy surveys the troublesome Steeplechase pool, July 1960. New York Daily News Archive / Getty Images.

was demanding that a costly new filtration system be installed. The great tank was dutifully filled as before, deck and railings painted and prepped, even the Adirondack chairs were set out—all to keep up appearances; the gates remained locked. The stilled, silent water was an omen in a season of bad signs. Just five days after Steeplechase opened for the season on May 2, the last surviving son of George C. Tilyou—Frank S. Tilyou, born at his father's park in 1908 as the Pavilion of Fun neared completion—died in Phoenix after a brief illness. Frank played an active role in park management all his life and changed the Brooklyn skyline by bringing the

Life Savers parachute jump to the boardwalk from the 1939 World's Fair. Shuttling between his home at 35 Prospect Park West and the Flying T Ranch in Scottsdale, he was the linchpin that kept the querulous Tilyou heirs in line. His death threw the family into disarray. In a letter the very next day, May 8, 1964, Jimmy Onorato related to his son that negotiations were already under way to sell the Steeplechase property "for an apartment project." The bombshell news, that the economic rug was about to be pulled out from under Coney Island, was kept secret for months. Meanwhile, attendance boomed. On Sunday, May 24, with the mercury pegging ninety-one degrees, an estimated 900,000 people flocked to Coney Island. It was the largest crowd since the end of the war.[37]

But the pot, long simmering, was about to boil over. The following Saturday—Memorial Day weekend—saw racial unrest throughout the city. "Very bad disorderly crowd," the laconic Onorato confided to his diary on May 30; "hoodlums—trouble in City & riot in Coney Island—bad for business."[38] Gangs of teenagers terrorized passengers on subways and the Staten Island Ferry. A group of twenty black youths that boarded the D train at Stillwell Avenue "beat and robbed white passengers, and smashed windows and light bulbs." At Kings Highway, the motorman stopped the train and called for help. A boy attempting to leave the train was struck on the head with a bottle and knocked unconscious. In the adjoining car a man was similarly assaulted. "He tried to get out when the train doors opened," his wife recounted to a *Times* reporter, "but they dragged him back in and started beating him up." Echoing the Kitty Genovese case just two months earlier, she added that "fellow passengers refused to help him while he was being attacked." The marauders then fled the station, breaking shop windows and pillaging stores on Kings Highway. Residents "poured out into the street and shouted racial epithets," the *Times* reported. The police ultimately arrested a dozen youths, while restraining angry locals "from attacking the teenagers."[39] By mid-July, the whole city was seething with racial tension. Six nights of violence in Harlem and Bedford-Stuyvesant were set off by the July 16 police killing of James Powell. People began avoiding crowded public places. Attendance at Steeplechase plunged. Profits had been declining for years as costs spiraled and more and more people fled to the suburbs of Long Island. But as Labor Day neared, it became clear that the 1964 season would go down as the very worst for Steeplechase in the postwar period. "Violence," observed Onorato, "cut the attendance in half." At a September 24 meeting, Marie Tilyou and the family decided not to open Steeplechase again. It was a day everyone knew was coming. When Onorato closed the park for the season the previous Sunday, he had done so with all the solemnity of a state funeral. Michael Onorato, then a professor at Canisius College, beheld the final moments from afar. "My father placed a long-distance call to me," he recalled, "from an extension phone located at the Eldorado carousel."

> At 7:35 p.m. the closing bell, which was a rescued locomotive bell, signaled the Park's final closing. Then the public address system played "Auf Wiedersehen," "There's No Business Like Show Business," and then "Auld Lang Syne." As the music finished, the bell began to toll slowly for each year of the Park's existence.

With each stroke, the electricians shut down "tier after tier of lights throughout the Park." All became dark and quiet. And then, with Broadway flourish, Onorato had the men throw all the big paddle switches back on for a brief moment, setting the grounds aglow in a last blaze of light before night fell for good. Steeplechase Park, anchor of a playground that touched a million lives and transformed American culture, lay in a darkness broken only by the glow of emergency lights.[40]

Sic transit ludicrum mundi. Fred C. Trump surveys the emptied shell of George C. Tilyou's Pavilion of Fun, what Reginald Marsh called "the last and greatest example of Victorian architecture in the United States." Trump razed the beloved landmark just months after this photo was taken in February 1966, an act of vandalism as tragically shortsighted as the destruction of Pennsylvania Station the year before. Photo by Leroy Jakob. New York Daily News Archive / Getty Images.

UNDER A TUNGSTEN SUN

Everything changes; the light of Brooklyn remains . . . long-shadowed horizontal light, revealer of form, Dutch light, the light of Vermeer, if you will, suffused with the presence of the sea, slanted, immanent, revealing.
—PETE HAMILL

Fred Trump razed the Pavilion of Fun just months after the last of Pennsylvania Station fell to the wrecking ball. The destruction of these icons—unprecedented acts of civic vandalism—formed an axis of loss that spanned the East River and seemed to augur troubled times to come. Most of the mighty train station—Gotham's own Baths of Caracalla—came down in the very months that Steeplechase Park struggled through its final season, its immense granite columns carted off ingloriously to the Secaucus meadows shortly after the Funny Place closed for good in September 1964. A decade later, Brooklyn and the rest of New York City struck bottom. But even then—with muggings rampant, subway cars covered in graffiti, Son of Sam on the loose, and the city teetering on the brink of bankruptcy—a revival was well under way in parts of Brooklyn. Starting in the late 1960s, a trickle of college-educated, young, and mostly white progressives began moving to the borough, lured by the threadbare glory of once-aristocratic precincts like Park Slope and Brooklyn Heights. These children of Woodstock, straining against the status quo, relished the borough's working-class grit. Like Carson McCullers and her February House fellow travelers a generation earlier, they found in Brooklyn's seedy squalor the flowers of authentic urban culture—one that promised respite from the conformities of suburbia and the relentless consumerism of mainstream American society. Here was a place with everything Levittown lacked—a storied past, architectural splendor, racial diversity, down-to-earth folk more or less tolerant of nontraditional lifestyles.

The "brownstoners," as they came to be known, stripped and scraped paint to expose brick walls and original wood trim, reveling in the grandeur of mansions reclaimed from rooming-house ignominy. They developed strong bonds with one another, which in time gelled into a potent political force. Well-organized, well-informed, charged with a Davidian zest to take on Modernity's many Goliaths—highway builders, urban renewal authorities, city planners, city hall—the brownstoners helped institutionalize participatory democracy, neighborhood preservation, and local control of the planning process in New York City.[1] Their patron saints were Rachel Carson, Betty Friedan, and—above all—Jane Jacobs, whose 1961 *Death and Life of Great American Cities* was a shot across the bow of the urban renewal juggernaut that, led by Robert Moses, had been tearing holes in the city's physical and social fabric for decades.[2] The brownstoners changed the map of Brooklyn, coining—with the eager assistance of realtors—evocative new names for the plebian hoods they colonized. Cobble Hill and Carroll Gardens were carved from the Italo-Rican vastness of South Brooklyn; the nebulous *terroir* between Atlantic Avenue and the Gowanus Canal was renamed Boerum Hill, where the newcomers displaced a small community of Mohawk ironworkers from upstate New York. The long-reviled Fifth Ward, a place nobody (my mother, for example) boasted of hailing from—was cleverly rebranded Vinegar Hill, a name from the 1830s when the area was an Irish enclave (recalling a key battle site in the Irish Rebellion of 1798). By 1981, the old manufacturing district next door had caught the eye of a developer named David Walentas, who saw in its vast, largely empty industrial lofts a real estate diamond in the rough. With financial backing from an unlikely source—the Estée Lauder family—Walentas went on a buying spree, snapping up eleven buildings with two million square feet of floor space for a mere $15 million. Most of this was the old Robert Gair Company complex, or "Gairville," birthplace of the mass-produced cardboard box and later home to scores of manufacturers great and small—among them the Heyman Glass Company, where my grandfather worked as a cutter and polisher in Gair Building No. 6 (75 Front Street). Two decades after he first set foot on Fulton Landing, Walentas had single-handedly transformed the deserted industrial zone into America's hottest new neighborhood—Dumbo, for Down Under the Manhattan Bridge Overpass. In 2017 the iconic clock-tower apartment in Gair Building No. 7 (1 Main Street)—*a single unit*—sold for the same sum that bought Walentas nearly a dozen buildings in 1982.[3]

By the early 1990s the gentrification of Brooklyn was officially under way, as creative-class professionals—eased out of Manhattan by skyrocketing rents—snapped up Brooklyn's relatively affordable but rapidly escalating real estate. As the Heights, Park Slope, Fort Greene, and Dumbo all soon Manhattanized beyond the reach of all but the very wealthy, real estate refugees began settling in places farther afield, with progressively less architectural quality and fewer cultural amenities—cheaper, grittier, more "real" precincts far from the stroller-jogging yoga moms of overpriced Park Slope. This new generation of neo-bohemians—the aspiring actors and barista novelistas, but also worker bees of the emerging "symbolic economy": software architects, web designers, sound engineers, bloggers and editors and other content-producing creatives—channeled (at least at first) much the same fiercely

countercultural spirit that drove the brownstoners, even if they rejected their predecessors as old hippie sellouts. They appropriated (with due irony) a "white trash"
aesthetic that has since become synonymous with hipsterdom: tattoos and facial
hair, feed-store ball caps, flannel shirts, and truck-stop sunglasses. The coming of the
hipsters, again mostly well-educated, white, and middle-class, signaled the closing
of a great circle for Brooklyn—the return of a suburban bourgeoisie not, this time,
to the rarefied brownstone districts of the long-vanished Anglo-Dutch elite, but to
immigrant cradle neighborhoods from which some of their very grandparents had
struggled to escape. "Symbolically, in their styles and attitudes," writes Mark Grief,
hipsters "seemed to announce that whiteness and capital were flowing back into the
formerly impoverished city." Their unrelenting search for the bloggably unique—
handcrafted, local, organic, untainted by the filthy fingers of global capital—has, over
the last twenty-five years, produced an almost comical succession of goods, services,
and foods, each briefly curated by an über-cool hipster elite before diffusing to the
masses as yet another must-have marker of membership, another stock item on sale
at Urban Outfitters. For all their avowed animus toward mainstream culture, hipsters
are aggressive shoppers. "The rebel consumer," writes Grief, "is the person who,
adopting the rhetoric but not the politics of the counterculture, convinces himself
that buying the right mass products individualizes him as transgressive." While any
bohemian community has at its core "a very small number of hardworking writers,
artists, or politicos," it inevitably attracts a larger cohort of wannabes, emulators,
and hangers-on. "Hipsterdom at its darkest," writes Grief,

> is something like bohemia without the revolutionary core. Among hipsters,
> the skills of hanging-on—trend-spotting, cool-hunting, plus handicraft skills—
> become the heroic practice. The most active participants sell something—
> customized brand-name jeans, airbrushed skateboards, the most special whiskey,
> the most retro sunglasses—and the more passive just buy it.[4]

More than anything, the hipster quest for cool has been about consuming place. First
Williamsburg, then Bushwick and Greenpoint, later Bed-Stuy and Crown Heights—
these once-shunned neighborhoods seemed to promise insider status for anyone
moving there, entrée into a rarefied club of creative fellow travelers. In the process,
Brooklyn has become both a product and a brand, one synonymous with the batch-
made and the bespoke, the fixed-gear, fair-traded, and cruelty-free. That brand has
now spread around the world—even to many of the very places from which immigrants once came in search of a better life.

Of course, the great irony of gentrification is that newcomers moving to an area
for its character, charm, and individuality set into motion a concatenation of forces—
economic, cultural, political—that ultimately destroy the very qualities that drew them
to the place. Time and again, the unwitting agents of this upscaling are artists, writers,
musicians, and other cash-poor creative types who colonize a place no one else seems
to care or even know about and create—by their very presence alone—a "scene" that
draws others with a ken for music and the arts. Before long come the galleries, cafés,
and pop-up restaurants curated by visiting chefs. Next in are savvy developers like
David Walentas, who buy up undervalued properties and turn them into luxury lofts

for well-heeled professionals with jobs on Wall Street and Madison Avenue. By now, the penniless creatives who set the whole thing off are long gone. This unintended trend seeding is nothing new: it happened in Stockbridge in the Berkshires in the 1890s, Greenwich Village in the 1920s, and Brooklyn Heights in the 1940s. It's what made Wellfleet and Provincetown sought-after summer spots, and what helped turn East Hampton—where Pollock, Motherwell, and de Kooning painted in shacks and Quonset huts—into the toniest place on the Atlantic Seaboard. Similar trajectories have reconfigured the Lower East Side, Tribeca, SoHo, and Chelsea, each now "a smooth, sleek replica of its former self," writes Sharon Zukin, where chain-store banalities like Starbucks and Chipotle sit alongside wine bars with Montepulciano at $18 a glass.[5]

Once a badge of shame, now a point of pride: Brooklyn nativity gentrified at City Point, "largest food, shopping and entertainment destination in the borough." Photograph by author, 2017.

The real motor of gentrification is contemporary society's fevered quest for authenticity, a function of an unsettled, increasingly homogenized world in which all the old bulwarks—neighborhood, tribe, family, faith, nationality—have progressively weakened. "Claiming authenticity," writes Zukin, "becomes prevalent at a time when identities are unstable and people are judged by their performance rather than by their history or innate character." With everything in flux in a globalizing world, authenticity "differentiates a person, a product, or a group from its competitors," conferring "an aura of moral superiority, a strategic advantage that each can use to its own benefit." Today, people of privilege hunger for authenticity the way their class forebears yearned for status and luxury. Because most consumers are content with a simulacrum of the real thing (so long as the stage props are right), authenticity can easily be manufactured—"made up," says Zukin, "of bits and pieces of cultural references: artfully painted graffiti on a shop window, sawdust on the floor of a music bar, an address in a gritty but not too thoroughly crime-ridden part of town." However ersatz, these "fictional qualities of authenticity" have a genuine impact on our urban imaginary, and "a real effect as well on the new cafés, stores, and gentrified places where we like to live and shop." In this sense, authenticity is hardly a neutral aesthetic but a political and economic weapon—a means of controlling "not just the look but the use of real urban places" like shopping streets, neighborhoods, parks, and community gardens. "Authenticity," Zukin concludes, "is a cultural form of power over space that puts pressure on the city's old working class and lower middle class, who can no longer afford to live or work there." Gentrification kills the real McCoy to venerate its taxidermal remains.[6]

Truth may be greater than fiction, but in New York City today manufactured authenticity has rubbed out much of the thing itself. The search for character, color, and uniqueness has cost many a city neighborhood those very things—their essence, their identity, their soul. And the juggernaut shows no sign of slowing. As Manhattan morphs into an isle of the superrich, Brooklyn has become ground zero of gentrification in New York. Like an oil stain on a sheet of newsprint, its upscaled terrain has spread steadily over the last twenty-five years—down into Red Hook and Latino Sunset Park, now even Bay Ridge; south into Kensington and Ditmas Park; east across Crown Heights and even edging into the embattled neighborhoods of Brownsville and East New York. The leading edge of this gentrificant tide is difficult to pin down and requires an almost block-by-block analysis. On a summer evening in 2017, I attempted to do just this—took a break from working on this book to walk Flatbush Avenue from Fulton Street to my deep-south Brooklyn neighborhood of Marine Park. I was hoping to see the light, literally: the warm tungsten light of vintage Edison lightbulbs. I'll confess a deep affection for these retro-style bulbs myself; nearly every room in our home is illuminated by their soft carbon glow, which seems particularly "period appropriate" for a house built in the 1920s. And I'm hardly alone in this. Many people have a penchant for these bulbs, or at least for bars and restaurants basked in their light. Walk around any upscaled part of New York City, and at least half the eating and drinking establishments will be sporting vintage lights in their pendants and chandeliers. My evening walk was meant to test a little hypothesis: that the spread of Edison bulbs across town was effectively a map of gentrification.

It's hardly a coincidence that the Edison phenomenon has closely tracked the revival of urban living—especially the loft culture that blossomed in postindustrial districts like SoHo and Tribeca. After all, vintage tungsten-filament lamps (and their more recent, more sustainable LED equivalents) show best in spare industrial fixtures, not hidden behind a fussy lampshade. It was entrepreneur Bob Rosenzweig who helped ignite this lighting revolution in the 1980s, manufacturing reproduction vintage lightbulbs for collectors and museums. Sales were thin for years, until compact fluorescent (CFL) lamps began replacing incandescents on store shelves. By the mid-aughts, Rosenzweig's bulbs had become all the rage with New York restaurant designers. Then came the 2007 Energy Independence and Security Act, which set new standards for energy consumption that effectively banned most incandescent bulbs. But there were exceptions—among them yellow bug lights, black lights, and "decoratives" such as Edison bulbs. Sales were also helped by the harsh blue-white light of the early CFLs, which could make the coziest home look like a morgue. The appearance or quality of a light source is a function of its color temperature. Measured in Kelvin—a thermodynamic temperature scale with a null point of absolute zero—color temperature is counterintuitive: the lower the temperature, the "warmer" a light appears, and vice versa. Natural daylight—a mixture of sunlight and skylight—runs from about 2,000K at sunrise or sunset to as high as 5,500K when the sun is directly overhead. The temperature of an ordinary incandescent bulb is about 2,700K, while that of a halogen lamp is around 3,000K and a cool-white compact florescent approximately 4,000K.

Tungsten and twee in Prospect-Lefferts Gardens. Photograph by Alyssa Loorya, 2017.

Most people find light of lower color temperature to be warm and intimate—the light of home and snug bistros on Old World streets. Much of this is hardwired in our brains, a function of deep ancestral memories of camp and cooking fires and the cycle of day and night. The high light of noon stimulates us; the autumnal glow of sunset eases us like a glass of wine. Culture, too, plays a role. In China, a brightly lit home was long associated with wealth and luck (demons lurked in dark corners, flushed out with fireworks at Lunar New Year). That illumination was both a status symbol and a ward against evil helps explains why brightly lighted shops and restaurants are still common in China. Most Westerners (and younger Chinese) favor low dim light in a restaurant—light that evokes the ambience of a candlelit dinner. It is no coincidence that the gossamer tungsten glow of an Edison lightbulb delivers a color temperature almost identical to the romantic light of a candle flame. The retro lights are today accurate markers of the upmarket consumerscape, signaling the presence of creative-class tribal space. They offer seeming respite from the buzzing glow of our digital screens, retreat to a curated version of an earlier, simpler, more earnest age. And with our streets increasingly amped up with intense LED light—Brooklyn was the first New York City borough to have its amber sodium-vapor streetlights replaced by LED units—it's hardly surprising that we expect our bars and cafés to provide shelter from the light storm outside.

Brooklyn's original Main Street, Flatbush Avenue, makes a ten-mile plunge from downtown Brooklyn to Floyd Bennett Field. The route has long formed an unspoken boundary between Brooklyn's majority black neighborhoods of Bedford-Stuyvesant, Crown Heights, and East Flatbush, which lie to its east, and the mostly white enclaves of Park Slope, Ditmas Park, and Midwood to its west. My summer evening stroll revealed two dense concentrations of Edison-lit establishments on the avenue. The first, not surprisingly, lay between Grand Army Plaza and Atlantic Avenue, where Flatbush runs past affluent Park Slope. There was a second burst of incandescence from Empire Boulevard to Caton Avenue—in the more recently upscaled neighborhood of Prospect-Lefferts Gardens (where Greenlight Bookstore is the only nonreligious bookstore on Flatbush Avenue south of Prospect Park. My observed density of Edison bulbs, it turns out, aligned precisely with data compiled on real estate heat maps of residential property valuation and listing prices. Areas with the highest concentrations of tungsten were reliably deep within or on the edges of neighborhoods with very expensive housing. In fact, they mapped closely to market valuations of a million dollars or more. Once listing prices dropped below seven digits, at about Beverley Road, the lights disappeared. The last tungsten-bulbed establishment was close by, Forever Ink Bar, at the corner of Duryea Place near the recently restored Kings Theater. This is effectively the outermost line of gentrification in Brooklyn: the lights go out, so to speak, just as white people with plugged earlobes and yoga pants also vanish. From here Flatbush then becomes a teeming bazaar with an island patois, Main Street of one of the largest West Indian communities in the world outside the Caribbean. From Forever Ink to Avenue U (a three-mile run, or nearly half my walk), I found not a single Edison bulb—none in the hundreds of West Indian shops and eateries; none by Brooklyn College; none in the busy blocks through Orthodox Midwood; none as the avenue glides expansively across the quiet residential terrain of Flatlands and Marine Park. It was as if I had tripped an invisible cultural switch.[7]

Here lies one of the great truths of urban life today, not only in Brooklyn but in gentrifying cities around the world: the truly authentic lies far from the places that claim it most insistently—far from the historic districts with their pious, exclusionary

Fluorescent authenticity, Island Buffet, Flatbush Avenue. Photograph by Alyssa Loorya, 2017.

rules about architectural minutiae; from boutiques with all things fair-traded and bespoke; from restaurants with curated chervil and house-made catsup where only the rich can eat. If you seek the real New York, flee the twee and you will have found the city in all its brassy bravado, its loud messy magical heartfelt glory. Look, in other words, beyond the warm light of vintage tungsten (or sustainable LED equivalents) to the cold white glare of coiled CFLs and ceiling-mounted fluorescent tubes—in the Guyanese grills and Dominican bodegas, the Hasidic shuls and African American storefront churches that rock with gospel on Sunday; in the Bangladeshi newsstand or the Chinese take-out with its kitchen-god temple—the harsh unflinching light of reality in our town, where life is still lived unposed and uncurated and close to the bone.

NOTES

INTRODUCTION

1. Only in the last decade have we begun to see substantial works of scholarship on Brooklyn's urban environment. These include Michael Woodsworth's *Battle for Bed-Stuy* (2016); Joseph Alexiou's *Gowanus: Brooklyn's Curious Canal* (2015); Judith Wellman's history of Weeksville, *Brooklyn's Promised Land* (2014); Tarry Hum's study of Sunset Park, *Making a Global Immigrant Neighborhood* (2014); Elizabeth Macdonald's *Pleasure Drives and Promenades* (2012); and Suleiman Osman's *Invention of Brownstone Brooklyn* (2011), arguably the best book yet written about the borough. Earlier works of note include Walter Thabit's *How East New York Became a Ghetto* (2003); Wendell E. Pritchett's *Brownsville, Brooklyn: Blacks, Jews, and the Changing Face of the Ghetto* (2002); and Craig Wilder's *A Covenant with Color: Race and Social Power in Brooklyn* (2001). If Brooklyn as a whole has been off the radar, its southern hemisphere—everything below the terminal moraine, from Bay Ridge to Broadway Junction—is virtual terra incognita. With the exception of several superb books on Coney Island—John F. Kasson's classic *Amusing the Million* (1978), Charlie Denson's *Coney Island: Lost and Found* (2004), and Woody Register's biography of Fred Thompson, *The Kid of Coney Island* (2001), and *Of Cabbages and Kings County: Agriculture and the Formation of Modern Brooklyn* by Marc Linder and Larry Zacharias (1999)—this vast part of New York City has completely escaped scholarly scrutiny.

2. Anton Chekhov, "The Student," in *Ward No. 6 and Other Stories*, ed. David Plante (New York: Barnes & Noble Classics, 2003), 246.

3. Kenneth T. Jackson, introduction to *The Neighborhoods of Brooklyn*, ed. John B. Manbeck (New Haven, CT: Yale University Press, 1998), xxi.

4. James Agee, *Brooklyn Is: Southeast of the Island* (New York: Fordham University Press, 2005), 6.

5. There is an ancient Chinese maxim that expresses well this spatial calculus: *shan gao huangdi yuan*— "The mountains are tall and the emperor is far away." A reference to regions far from the throne that developed cultures of feisty independence, it was famously invoked in the 1980s to explain why Deng Xiaopeng's groundbreaking economic reforms were launched in Guangdong Province, safely far from Beijing.

6. Henry R. Stiles, *History of the City of Brooklyn*, vol. 1 (Brooklyn: published by subscription, 1867), 262.

7. Frederick Law Olmsted and Calvert Vaux, *Observations on the Progress of Improvements in Street Plans* (Brooklyn, NY: Van Anden's Print, 1868), 22–24.

8. Rem Koolhaas, *Delirious New York: A Retroactive Manifesto for Manhattan* (New York: The Monacelli Press, 1994), 31, 75.

9. Robert D. McFadden, "Rockets' Red Glare Marked Birth of Merged City in 1898," *New York Times*, January 1, 1973; Hewitt quoted in David C. Hammack, *Power and Society: Greater New York at the Turn of the Century* (New York: Russell Sage Foundation, 1982), 193.

10. Hammack, *Power and Society*, 192, 197–199, 206, 209–211.

11. Agee, *Brooklyn Is*, 3–5, 8.

12. Truman Capote, "Brooklyn," in *Portraits and Observations* (New York: Modern Library, 2008), 17, 20; "A House on the Heights," in *The Brooklyn Reader*, ed. Andrea W. Sexton and Alice Leccese Powers (New York: Crown Trade Paperbacks, 1994), 27.

13. Pete Hamill, "Brooklyn: The Sane Alternative," *New York*, July 14, 1969.

14. Henry Miller, *Tropic of Capricorn* (London: Flamingo, 1993), 271–272; *Henry Miller: Asleep and Awake*, directed by Tom Schiller (1975).

CHAPTER 1. THE NATAL SHORE

1. For more on Fairchild and his work, see Thomas J. Campanella, *Cities from the Sky: An Aerial Portrait of America* (New York: Princeton Architectural Press, 2001). Also see "Airplane Camera Maps Entire City Clearly in 69 Minutes, Flying 10,000 Feet High," *New York Times*, February 26, 1922; "Air Map of Greater City," *New York Times*, September 30, 1924. The 1924 imagery is readily available today via the New York City GIS website (http://gis.nyc.gov), something we should also thank Sherman Fairchild for: his Fairchild Semiconductor of Mountain View, California, developed the integrated circuits that launched the digital revolution and, in the process, helped create Silicon Valley.

2. Reginald Pelham Bolton, *Indian Paths in the Great Metropolis* (New York: Museum of the American Indian, 1922), 150–151; Frederick Van Wyck, *Keskachauge: Or the First White Settlement on Long Island* (New York: G. P. Putnam's Sons, 1924), 416, 664. Anne-Marie Cantwell, "Penhawitz and Wampage and the Seventeenth-Century World They Dominated," in *Tales of Gotham, Historical Archaeology, Ethnohistory and Microhistory of New York City*, ed. Meta F. Janowitz and Diane Dallal (New York: Springer, 2013). See also Robert Steven Grumet, *Native American Place Names in New York City* (New York: Museum of the City of New York, 1981), 18–19.

3. Van Wyck, *Keskachauge*, 8, 15–18; Daniel Denton, *A Brief Description of New York: Formerly Called New-Netherlands* (London: John Hancock, 1670), 6, in *Proceedings of the Historical Society of Pennsylvania*, ed. John Pennington (Philadelphia: Press of the Historical Society of Pennsylvania), 1:1. Dubois placed the center of the Great Flats at about the intersection of Flatbush Avenue and Avenue J today, and nearby Amersfort Park is probably the only part of the Flats that has never been built on. See Anson Dubois, *A History of the Town of Flatlands* (Brooklyn, NY, 1884).

4. William Cronon, *Changes in the Land* (New York: Hill and Wang, 1983), 51.

5. Timothy Dwight, *Travels in New-England and New-York*, vol. 3 (London: William Baynes and Son, 1828), 305–307.

6. I. N. Phelps Stokes, *The Iconography of Manhattan Island 1498–1909*, vol. 2 (New York: Robert H. Dodd, 1915–1928), 182.

7. Van Wyck, *Keskachauge*, 139. Translation from New York State archivist A.J.F. van Laer, quoted in Edward Van Winkle, *Manhattan, 1624–1639* (New York: Knickerbocker Press, 1916), 27.

8. Jasper Danckaerts and Peter Sluyter, *Journal of a Voyage to New York*, trans. Henry C. Murphy, vol. 1 of *Memoirs of the Long Island Historical Society* (Brooklyn: Long Island Historical Society, 1887), 123–126; Van Wyck, *Keskachauge*, 16, 650.

9. Denton, *A Brief Description of New York*, 5.

10. Van Wyck, *Keskachauge*, 11.

11. See Julius Lopez and Stanley Wisniewski, "The Ryders Pond Site," *Bulletin of the New York State Archeological Association* 53 (November 1971): 2–9; Bolton, *Indian Paths*, 157–160; Van Wyck, *Keskachauge*, 649–650; "Brooklyn Man Has Valuable Lot of Indian Antiquities," *Brookyn Daily Eagle*, March 10, 1901.

12. Robert Juet, *Juet's Journal of Hudson's 1609 Voyage*, transcribed by Brea Barthel from 1625 edition of *Purchas His Pilgrimes* (Albany, NY: New Netherland Museum, 2006), 591; Van Wyck, *Keskachauge*, 625, 632–633.

13. Van Wyck, *Keskachauge*, xiii, 652–665.

14. The deed was sold to a private collector in 2007 by Bloomsbury Auctions for $156,000. See "Dutch Deed Fetches More Than a Handful of Beads," *New York Times*, November 3, 2007.

15. Berthold Fernow, ed., *Documents Relating to the History of the Early Colonial Settlements Principally on Long Island* (Albany, NY: Weed, Parsons and Company, 1883), 2–4; John W. Pirsson, *The Dutch Grants, Harlem Patents and Tidal Creeks* (New York: L. K. Strouse, 1889), 19.

16. Van Wyck, *Keskachauge*, 15, 18–25; Stokes, *Iconography*, 2:185, 201; F. B. O'Callaghan, ed., *Documents Relating to the Colonial History of the State of New-York*, vol. 14; Fernow, *Documents*, 3. Differing European and Native American concepts of land tenure would become a major source of tension and eventual war. See Anne-Marie Cantwell, "Penhawitz and Wampage," in *Tales of Gotham*, 10–11; Reginald Pelham Bolton, *New York City in Indian Possession* (New York: Museum of the American Indian, 1920), 359–361.

17. Peter Ross, *A History of Long Island* (New York: Lewis Publishing, 1902), 310; Van Wyck, *Keskachauge*, 116; Stokes, *Iconography*, 2:235; Van Wyck, *Keskachauge*, 115–117.

18. Lynn Ceci, *The Effect of European Contact and Trade on the Settlement Pattern of Indians in Coastal New York, 1524–1665* (New York: Garland Publishing, 1990), 246.

19. "F. Van Wyck, 82, Antiquarian, Dies," *New York Times*, February 17, 1936; Van Wyck, *Keskachauge*, 664; Reginald Pelham Bolton, *Indian Life Long Ago in the City of New York* (Port Washington, NY: Ira J. Friedman, 1971 [1934]), 144–147; Ceci, *Effect of European Contact*, 231–233.

20. Fernow, *Documents*, 131–132.

21. "Ordinance of the Director and Council of New Netherland regulating the purchase of Indian Lands" (1652), in O'Callaghan, *Laws and Ordinances*, 130–132. See also Fernow, *Documents*, 33.

22. "10 Million Land Claims Slashed to $300,000," *Brooklyn Daily Eagle*, July 31, 1938.

23. Charles Wolley, *A Two-Years' Journal in New York* (Cleveland, OH: Burrows Brothers, 1902 [1701]), 55.

24. Lynn Ceci, "The Value of Wampum among the New York Iroquois: A Case Study in Artifact Analysis," *Journal of Anthropological Research* 38:1 (Spring 1982): 97–98; Ceci, "The Effect of European Contact and Trade on the Settlement Pattern of Indians in Coastal New York, 1524–1665: The Archaeological and Documentary Evidence" (PhD diss., City University of New York, 1977), 86–88; Stuyvesant quoted in Evan T. Pritchard, *Native New Yorkers: The Legacy of the Algonquin People of New York* (San Francisco: Council Oak Books, 2002), 149.

25. J. Thomas Scharf, *History of Westchester County* (Philadelphia: L. E. Preston, 1886), 20; Denton, *A Brief Description of New York*, 6; Gabriel Furman, *Antiquities of Long Island* (New York: J. W. Bouton, 1875), 83, 22; Ross, *History of Long Island*, 19.

26. Danckaerts and Sluyter, *Journal of a Voyage to New York*, 1:130–131.

27. The mill was being restored under the direction of park commissioner Robert Moses and his architectural consultant, Aymar Embury III. Moses had fired scores of laborers working on the site only months before, and it's possible that one of the disgruntled men was the arsonist. Charles A. Ditmas, *Historic Homesteads of Kings County* (Brooklyn, NY: The Compiler, 1909), 95; Maud E. Dilliard, *Old Dutch Houses of Brooklyn* (New York: R. R. Smith, 1945), 25. See also "Plan to Transform Garritsen's Creek," *Brooklyn Daily Eagle*, January 21, 1900; "The Last of the Tide Water Mills," *Weekly Northwestern Miller*, December 11, 1907, 649–650; "Haste Is Vital in Restoring of Gerritsen Mill," *Brooklyn Daily Eagle*, June 29, 1931; "Gerritson's Mill, Old Landmark, to Be Rebuilt," *Brooklyn Daily Eagle*, August 26, 1934; "Pre-Revolutionary Gerritsen Mill Razed by Blaze at Marine Park," *Brooklyn Daily Eagle*, September 4, 1935. On the firing of workers at Marine Park, see Robert A. Caro, *The Power Broker: Robert Moses and the Fall of New York* (New York: Knopf, 1974), 370.

28. Gertrude Lefferts Vanderbilt, *The Social History of Flatbush* (New York: D. Appleton, 1899), 188; Shane White, *Somewhat More Independent* (Athens: University of Georgia Press, 1991), 3–4, 18; Dwight, *Travels in New-England and New-York*, 3:309. Dwight's star has fallen recently owing to his unsavory views on race and for having been an apologist for America's "peculiar institution." See Najah Farley, "Wary of Slave Past, Dwight Hall Mulls Name Change," *Yale Daily News*, September 26, 2001.

29. Vanderbilt, *Social History*, 268; Wilder, *Covenant with Color*, 22; Edgar J. MacManus, *A History of Negro Slavery in New York* (New York: Syracuse University Press, 1966), 11–13, 16–17.

30. Graham Russell Hodges and Alan Edward Brown, eds., *"Pretends to Be Free": Runaway Slave Advertisements from Colonial and Revolutionary New York and New Jersey* (New York: Garland Publishing, 1994), xvii.

31. Médéric Moreau de St. Méry quoted in White, *Somewhat More Independent*, 20; Wilder, *Covenant with Color*, 25–30.

32. Hodges and Brown, *"Pretends to Be Free"*, xxi, xxv; Henry Onderdonk, Jr., *Revolutionary Incidents of Suffolk and Kings Counties* (Brooklyn, NY: Leavitt & Company, 1849), 193, 199.

33. Christopher G. Ricciardi, "Changing through the Century: Life at the Lott Family Farm in the Nineteenth Century Town of Flatlands, Kings County, New York" (PhD diss., Brooklyn College, 2004), 49, 182–184. 1810 US census; 1820 US census; White, *Somewhat More Independent*, xxv, 29, 38.

34. White, *Somewhat More Independent*, 152.

35. Graham Russell Hodges, *Root and Branch: African Americans in New York and East Jersey, 1613–1863* (Chapel Hill: University of North Carolina Press, 1999), 35.

36. White, *Somewhat More Independent*, 152; Gerald Francis De Jong, "The Dutch Reformed Church and Negro Slavery in Colonial America," *Church History* 40:4 (December 1971): 429–430; Godefridus Udemans, *'t Geestelyk Roer van 't Coopmans Schip* (1638), quoted in De Jong, "The Dutch Reformed Church and Negro Slavery," 430; De Jong, 431, 434.

37. "Through a Walk-In Closet in Brooklyn, a Passage to Liberty," *New York Times*, December 28, 2002; Edward Rothstein, "When Slavery and Its Foes Thrived in Brooklyn," *New York Times*, January 16, 2014.

38. "Vanderveer's Mill" (1879), quoted in Vanderbilt, *Social History*, 181. See also "The Destruction of Old Landmarks," *Brooklyn Daily Eagle*, March 6, 1879; Van Wyck, *Keskachauge*, 663, 10; Kathleen G. Velsor, *The Underground Railroad on Long Island* (Charleston, SC: The History Press, 2013), 57–64; Kathleen Velsor,

email message to author, July 9, 2015; William J. Switala, *Underground Railroad in New Jersey and New York* (Mechanicsburg, PA: Stackpole Books, 2006). Lott's Lane was later straightened and named Kimball Road, part of which ran along today's Kimball Street. A portion along East Thirty-Sixth Street on the Hendrick I. Lott House property (now owned by the New York City Department of Parks and Recreation) has been marked with traditional oyster-shell paving.

39. Wellman, *Brooklyn's Promised Land*, 2, 13–14, 19, 43, 80–81; "Born a Slave in Flatbush," *Brooklyn Daily Eagle*, September 18, 1898. Long-vanished Hunterfly Road crossed Flatlands Neck Road near the present intersection of Sutter Avenue and Legion Street in East New York; a tiny portion survives as Hunterfly Place just north of Atlantic Avenue.

40. "Through a Walk-In Closet in Brooklyn, a Passage to Liberty," *New York Times*, December 28, 2002. The definitive account of Lott House archaeology is Chris Ricciardi's 2004 PhD dissertation, "Changing through the Century."

41. Alyssa Loorya, interview with author, July 27, 2015. See also "Remembering Africa under the Eaves," *Archeology*, May/June, 2001; and Brent Staples, "To Be a Slave in Brooklyn," *New York Times*, June 24, 2001.

CHAPTER 2. LADY DEBORAH'S CITY BY THE SEA

1. Arthur Mee, ed., *Berkshire: Alfred's Own Country* (London: Hodder and Stoughton, 1939), 113; James W. Gerard, *Lady Deborah Moody: A Discourse* (New York: F. B. Patterson, 1880), 19; Charles S. Fry and Edward A. Fry, *Abstracts of Wiltshire: Inquisitions Post Mortem, Returned into the Court of Chancery in the Reign of Charles the First* (London: Wiltshire Archaeological and Natural History Society, 1901), 153–155; Alonso Lewis, *The History of Lynn* (Boston: Samuel Dickinson, 1844), 112; Thomas J. Campanella, "Sanctuary in the Wilderness: Deborah Moody and the 1643 Town Plan for Colonial Gravesend," *Landscape Journal* 12:2 (Fall 1993): 106–130; Eric J. Ierardi, *Gravesend: The Home of Coney Island* (Charleston, SC: Arcadia, 2001), 15–18. A. P. Stockwell, "History of the Town of Gravesend," in *The Civil, Political, Professional and Ecclesiastical History and Commercial and Industrial Record of the County of Kings and the City of Brooklyn, New York*, vol. 1, ed. Henry R. Stiles (New York: W. W. Munsell and Company, 1884), 157. Historian Eric Platt of St. Francis College has effectively debunked the old theory that Moody left England in search of religious freedom: "Lady Deborah Moody: Radical Puritan Noblewoman?" (unpublished paper, New York State Association of European Historians Conference, Rochester, October 2013).

2. Darrett B. Rutman, *Winthrop's Boston: A Portrait of a Puritan Town, 1630–1649* (New York: W. W. Norton, 1972), 253; Thomas Lechford, *Plain Dealing, or, Newes from New England* (1641), quoted in Martha Bockée Flint, *Early Long Island: A Colonial Study* (New York: G. P. Putnam's Sons, 1896), 105n. Also see Mrs. Henry W. Edwards, "Lady Deborah Moody," in *Essex Institute Historical Collections*, vol. 31 (Salem, MA: Essex Institute, 1894), 97; Lewis, *History of Lynn*, 112; Gerard, *Lady Deborah Moody*, 14; Rutman, *Winthrop's Boston*, 261; Stockwell, "History of the Town of Gravesend," 157.

3. Edward Johnson, *Wonder-working Providence* (1636), 96; Winthrop in Edwards, "Lady Deborah Moody," 97; Massachusetts *Records*, quoted in Isaac Backus, *A history of New-England, with particular reference to the denomination of Christians called Baptists*, vol. 1 (Boston: Edward Draper, 1777), 126; Cobbett quoted in Flint, *Early Long Island*, 106n; Winthrop in Frederick James Zwierlein, *Religion in New Netherland, 1623–1664* (New York: J. P. Smith, 1910), 168; Winthrop in Rutman, *Winthrop's Boston*, 72.

4. Leo Hershkowitz, "The Troublesome Turk: An Illustration of Judicial Process in New Amsterdam," *New York History* 46:4 (October 1965): 299.

5. Russell Shorto, *The Island at the Center of the World* (New York: Random House, 2005), 86; Saretta G. Hicks, *Documentary History of Gravesend Town and Dame Deborah Moody, 1643–1659*, TMs [photocopy] (Brooklyn, NY: Brooklyn Historical Society, 1964), 7.

6. Washington Irving, "A History of New-York," in *The Complete Works of Washington Irving* (Frankfort: Schmerber, 1835), 153; Ben Kiernan, *Blood and Soil: A World History of Genocide and Extermination from Sparta to Darfur* (New Haven, CT: Yale University Press, 2008), 235. Once word of his behavior reached Holland, Kieft was relieved of his post by the Dutch West India Company and replaced by the redoubtable Peter Stuyvesant. Kieft never made it back home; his ship was wrecked crossing the Atlantic, drowning all aboard.

7. Massachusetts Historical Society, *Winthrop Papers*, vol. 1 (Boston: Historical Society, 1929), 456; Edwards, "Lady Deborah Moody," 98; Stockwell, "History of the Town of Gravesend," 163; Willem Kieft, New Amsterdam, to Moody, Baxter, Hubbard, and others, December 19, 1645, reproduced in *Gravesend Town Records, 1666–1691*, no. 1, handwritten copy, pp. 1–3, Gravesend Collection, vol. 3010, Municipal Archives, City of New York.

8. Baxter quoted in Flint, *Early Long Island*, 111; "horned beast": Shorto, *Island at the Center of the World*, 85–86; "evil language": John E. Stillwell, *Historical and Genealogical Miscellany: Early Settlers of*

New Jersey and Their Descendants, vol. 5 (New York, 1932), 223; Hershkowitz, "The Troublesome Turk," 302. It is possible that van Salee was the first Muslim New Yorker; a splendid copy of the Qu'ran was among his possessions left to a descendant. See Michael A. Gomez, *Black Crescent: The Experience and Legacy of African Muslims in the Americas* (New York: Cambridge University Press, 2005), 131–134.

9. On the back of a 1694 copy of the plan there is a mysterious inscription in the hand of John Emans, clerk of Gravesend from 1688 to 1705. It reads, "I would not any to Admire this plote nor for to thinke it was Lade down by one ho (who) undre stood it not. For he that dus thinke so the ploter ded not know. Allthoughe not founded by ye Grounds of tre (three), yet being ingenus there in he ded it, but only by suposition for after memry." I have never been able to decipher this odd passage, nor have several prominent scholars I've consulted. Harvard theologian Harvey Cox had no idea what it meant, while historian Bernard Bailyn proposed the following loose translation: "The author hopes that anyone who sees the plat will not think it fantastic or written by someone who did not understand the layout. Anyone who thinks that, does not know the situation. It is true, however, that it was written by conjecture, from memory." Bailyn confessed to being completely stumped by "ye Grounds of *tre*," which he noted "may be the key to the whole thing." One possibility is that this refers to the tripod of a surveying instrument, suggesting that the plan was laid out lacking ("not founded by") such an aid. Letter from Bernard Bailyn, Harvard University, to author, May 3, 1993. See *Historical Notes, Gravesend Town*, TMs, p. 1, Gravesend Collection, Municipal Archives, City of New York, and Maud E. Dilliard, *An Album of New Netherland* (New York: Twayne Publishers, 1963), 31.

10. Nathaniel S. Prime, *A History of Long Island: From Its First Settlement by Europeans to the Year 1845* (New York: Robert Carter, 1845), 335–336; Town of Gravesend, *Town Records*, book 3, *Town Meetings, 1656–1705*, handwritten copy, p. 59, Gravesend Collection, vol. 302, Municipal Archives, City of New York; Benjamin F. Thompson, *History of Long Island, containing An Account of the Discovery and Settlement, with Other Important and Interesting Matters to the Present Time* (New York: E. French, 1839), 438, 441 (also see June 6, 1650, in Town of Gravesend, *Town Records*, book 1, *Town Meetings, 1646–1653*, handwritten copy, Gravesend Collection, vol. 300, Municipal Archives, City of New York). Evidence suggests that the radial subdivision took place several years after the initial settlement. The minutes of a town meeting in December 1647 note that "the inhabitants of the towne in general desired that the meadow ground should be laid oute" such that "each man might know his particular portion." See Town of Gravesend, *Town Records, 1666–1691*, no. 1, handwritten copy, p. 33, Gravesend Collection, vol. 3010, Municipal Archives, City of New York; Sylvia Doughty Fries, *The Urban Idea in Colonial America* (Philadelphia: Temple University Press, 1977), 28.

11. Perry Miller quoted in John Archer, "Puritan Town Planning in New Haven," *Journal of the Society of Architectural Historians* 34 (May 1975): 140.

12. Davenport in Archer, "Puritan Town Planning," 146.

13. Albert H. Newman, *A History of the Baptist Churches in the United States* (Philadelphia: American Baptist Publication Society, 1898), 232; Francis J. Bremer, *Building a New Jerusalem: John Davenport, a Puritan in Three Worlds* (New Haven, CT: Yale University Press, 2012), 221–222, 391n; Eaton quoted in Mary Beth Norton, *Founding Mothers & Fathers: Gendered Power and the Forming of American Society* (New York: Random House, 2011), 173; Prime, *History of Long Island*, 334.

14. Edmund Bailey O'Callaghan, *History of New Netherlands*, vol. 2 (New York: D. Appleton, 1855), 455; John W. Reps, *The Making of Urban America* (Princeton, NJ: Princeton University Press, 1992 [1965]), 128–129. See also Anthony N. B. Garvan, *Architecture and Town Planning in Colonial Connecticut* (New Haven, CT: Yale University Press, 1951); Rollin G. Osterweis, *Three Centuries of New Haven, 1638–1938* (New Haven, CT: Yale University Press, 1953); Elizabeth Mills Brown, *New Haven: A Guide to Architecture and Urban Design* (New Haven, CT: Yale University, 1976), 11–12.

15. Cleveland Rodgers, *Brooklyn's First City Planner* (Brooklyn: Kings County Trust Company, 1956), 5; Stockwell, "History of the Town of Gravesend," 161–162; December 26, 1650, in Town of Gravesend, *Town Records*, book 1, *Town Meetings, 1646–1653*, handwritten copy, Gravesend Collection, vol. 300, Municipal Archives, City of New York. The subdivision of Davenport's original nine squares is clearly evident on the 1802 Wadsworth map of New Haven.

16. Stockwell, "History of the Town of Gravesend," 23; Robert Friedmann, *The Theology of Anabaptism: An Interpretation* (Scottsdale, PA: Herald Press, 1973), 81; Prime, *History of Long Island*, 338; Dominie Megapolensis and Drisius (1657) in Stiles, *History of the City of Brooklyn*, 178.

17. Stockwell, "History of the Town of Gravesend," 23; James Bowden, *The History of the Society of Friends in America*, vol. 1 (London; Charles Gilpin, 1850), 319.

18. Bowden, *History of the Society of Friends*, 319.

19. Ibid., 1:312–318, 322–323; Stockwell, "History of the Town of Gravesend," 23; Gertrude Ryder Bennett, *Turning Back the Clock* (Francestown, NH: Marshall Jones Company, 1982), 29; W. Robertson Nicoll, ed., *George Fox's Journal* (London: Isbister and Company, 1903), 424, 431–434; Stockwell, 23–24; Rufus M. Jones, *The Story of George Fox* (New York: The Macmillan Company, 1919), 138.

20. Thompson, *History of Long Island*, 445; Edwin Salter and George C. Beekman, *Old Times in Old Monmouth* (Freehold, NJ: Monmouth Democrat, 1887), 146; Reps, *Making of Urban America*, 158; Jean R. Soderlund, ed., *William Penn and the Founding of Pennsylvania, 1680–1684: A Documentary History* (Philadelphia: University of Pennsylvania Press, 1983), 89n.

21. Fries, *Urban Idea*, 90–92.

22. Ibid., 89–90, 94, 100; Russell Frank Weigley, *Philadelphia: A 300 Year History* (New York: W. W. Norton, 1982), 11; Reps, *Making of Urban America*, 163–165.

23. George Baxter, Richard Gibbons, William Wilkins, James Hubbard, et al., Gravesend, to the Directors of the West Indie Company, September 14, 1651, unpublished letter reproduced in Hicks, *Documentary History*, 71; Furman, *Antiquities of Long Island*, 75; Ross, *History of Long Island*, 365, 359.

24. *New York Colonial Documents*, 14:270, cited in Stokes, *Iconography*, 4:151.

25. *New York Colonial Documents*, 1:550–555, 14:231–232, in Stokes, *Iconography*, 4:144.

26. Martha J. Lamb, *History of the City of New York* (New York: A. S. Barnes, 1877), 183–184; Jacqueline Overton, *Long Island's Story* (Garden City, NY: Doubleday, Doran and Company, 1928), 54.

27. Van Wyck, *Keskachauge*, xviii; Stockwell, "History of the Town of Gravesend," 158; Ross, *History of Long Island*, 357; Arthur Konop, interview with author, May 8, 1992.

CHAPTER 3. DEATH AND THE PICTURESQUE

1. David Hackett Fischer, *Washington's Crossing* (New York: Oxford University Press, 2004), 31–33.

2. Stiles, *History of the City of Brooklyn*, 255–257. The HMS *Rose*, laid down in 1757, had nearly become James Cook's vessel on his first Pacific voyage. Several months before the Battle of Brooklyn, the *Rose* had harassed Rhode Island after the colony declared independence on May 4, 1776. It was to rid Narragansett Bay of the pest that the Continental Navy was created. Though the *Rose* was scuttled at Savannah in 1779, a replica was built in the 1970s using original Royal Navy plans. That ship was later acquired by Fox Studios and altered for use in several films, including *Master and Commander: Far Side of the World* and *Pirates of the Caribbean: On Stranger Tides*, where it appears as the HMS *Providence* (captained by Geoffrey Rush).

3. Charles Francis Adams, "The Battle of Brooklyn," *American Historical Review* 1:4 (July 1896): 651.

4. Ross, *History of Long Island*, 201.

5. Stiles, *History of the City of Brooklyn*, 263.

6. Ten rods is approximately 165 feet.

7. Stiles, *History of the City of Brooklyn*, 265–268.

8. James L. Nelson, *With Fire and Sword: The Battle of Bunker Hill and the Beginning of the American Revolution* (New York: Thomas Dunne Books, 2011), 17.

9. Stiles, *History of the City of Brooklyn*, 274n; William J. Parry, "The Battles of Brooklyn: Memorializing the 'Maryland 400'" (unpublished paper, August 2017); Kenneth T. Jackson, introduction to Manbeck, *Neighborhoods of Brooklyn*, xxi.

10. Adams, "The Battle of Brooklyn," 650, 656; Nelson, *Fire and Sword*, 9.

11. Adams, "The Battle of Brooklyn," 652, 658, 662–663; Stiles, *History of the City of Brooklyn*, 282–290.

12. Nehemiah Cleaveland, *Green-Wood Illustrated* (New York: Robert Martin, 1847), 80; Adams, "The Battle of Brooklyn," 650–651, 664.

13. Ross, *History of Long Island*, 198; Stiles, *History of the City of Brooklyn*, 243, 296.

14. Frank Barnes and Louis Morris, "The 'Maryland 400' at the Cortelyou House, Brooklyn: The Action and the Burial Site" (National Park Service—Region Five, unpublished report, May 20, 1957, 3–5, 10.

15. Thomas W. Field, *The Battle of Long Island* (Brooklyn: Long Island Historical Society, 1869), 200, 202–203.

16. Barnes and Morris, "The 'Maryland 400,' " 14; Stiles, *History of the City of Brooklyn*, 280; Field, *Battle of Long Island*, 203.

17. *New York Herald*, July 29, 1906; Barnes and Morris, "The 'Maryland 400,' " 16, 17n.

18. "Maryland Memorials," *Brooklyn Daily Eagle*, January 10, 1897; "Coal Yard Is Cemetery of Revolutionary Dead," *Brooklyn Daily Eagle*, July 24, 1910; Barnes and Morris, "The 'Maryland 400,' " 17–19.

19. Barnes and Morris, "The 'Maryland 400,' " 20; "Remains of 256 Colonial Soldiers Sought under Cellar of Unused Brooklyn Factory," *New York Times*, January 17, 1957. Kelly's reaction was related to William J. Parry by James O'Halloran, a participant in the 1957 excavation. See Parry, "The Battles of Brooklyn," 11–12.

20. Parry, "The Battles of Brooklyn," 2, 4, 7–8.

21. Edward Howland Tatum, ed., *The American Journal of Ambrose Serle: Secretary to Lord Howe, 1776–1778* (Berkeley: University of California Press, 1940), 91; Joseph Plumb Martin, *A Narrative of Some of the Adventures, Dangers and Sufferings of a Revolutionary Soldier* (Hallowell, ME: Glazier, Masters &

Company, 1830), 97–98; Parry, "The Battles of Brooklyn," 7, 9–11; "Common Council," *Brooklyn Daily Eagle*, March 10, 1846; "Old Brooklyn," *Brooklyn Daily Eagle*, July 14, 1870; Frederick Boyd Stevenson, "How the City Planning Movement, Begun by Brooklyn, Became a Part of the Municipal System of New York," *Brooklyn Daily Eagle*, November 29, 1914. Some eight hundred former slaves from the Carolinas, Georgia, and Virginia participated in General Howe's assault on Brooklyn, including some from Dunmore's original Ethiopian Regiment and very likely others fleeing the slaveholding Dutch plantations of New Utrecht, Gravesend, and Flatlands.

22. Eric Hobsbawm, "Inventing Traditions," in *The Invention of Tradition*, ed. Eric Hobsbawm and Terence Ranger (Cambridge: Cambridge University Press, 1983), 1–4.

23. Justin Burke, "Seeking Brooklyn's Lost Mass Grave," *New York Times*, August 25, 2012.

24. Ibid.

25. Caity Weaver, "Patrick Stewart Will Look Great Forever," *GQ*, February 23, 2017.

26. Elizabeth D. Meade, AKRF, to Philip Perazio, NYS Office of Parks, Recreation and Historic Preservation, Waterford, NY, "End of Phase 2 Fieldwork: Proposed Pre-K at 168 8th Street, Brooklyn, NY (16PR03021) (October 13, 2017).

27. Norman T. Newton, *Design on the Land: The Development of Landscape Architecture* (Cambridge, MA: Belknap Press of Harvard University Press, 1971), 211.

28. John Gorham Coffin (attributed), *Remarks on the Dangers and Duties of Sepulture* (Boston: Phelps and Farnham, 1823), 5, 11; Washington Irving, *The Sketch Book of Geoffrey Crayon, Gent.* (Chicago: Belford, Clarke and Company, 1885 [1819]), 177.

29. Jacob Bigelow, *History of Mount Auburn Cemetery* (Boston: James Munroe and Company, 1860), 1, 11; Nehemiah Cleaveland, *Green-Wood Cemetery: A History of the Institution from 1838 to 1864* (New York: Anderson and Archer, 1866), 31; David B. Douglas, *Exposition of the Plan and Objects of the Green-Wood Cemetery* (New York: Narine and Company, 1839), 11.

30. Douglas, *Exposition*, 11–12n.

31. William Gilpin, *Essays on Picturesque Beauty* (London: Richmond Blamire, 1792), 8.

32. Cleaveland, *Green-Wood Cemetery*, 23, 31; Andrew J. Downing, "Additional Notes on the Progress of Gardening in the United States," *Gardener's Magazine*, March 1841, 146–147; "A Talk about Public Parks and Gardens," *Horticulturalist* 3:4 (October 1848): 157.

33. Cleaveland, *Green-Wood Cemetery*, 23–24; Downing, "A Talk about Public Parks and Gardens," 157.

34. Cleaveland, *Green-Wood Cemetery*, 28; Cleaveland, *Rules and Regulations of the Green-Wood Cemetery* (Brooklyn: Green-Wood Cemetery, 1831), 24.

CHAPTER 4. YANKEE WAYS

1. The epigraph is drawn from "Report of the Landscape Architects" (January 24, 1866), in *Annual Reports of the Brooklyn Park Commissioners 1861–1872* (Brooklyn, NY, 1873), 94; Frederick Law Olmsted, Jr., and Theodora Kimball, eds., *Forty Years of Landscape Architecture: Early Years and Experiences* (New York: G. P. Putnam's Sons, 1922), 77.

2. Ibid., 70–71.

3. Ibid., 46, 62. "The word *sceneric* flows from my pen unbidden," he wrote; "and I venture to let it stand."

4. Ibid., 46, 62, 55–56.

5. Frederick Law Olmsted, Jr., and Theodora Kimball, eds., *Forty Years of Landscape Architecture: Central Park* (New York: G. P. Putnam's Sons and Knickerbocker Press, 1928), 36, 42; Francis R. Kowsky, *Country, Park and City: The Architecture and Life of Calvert Vaux* (New York: Oxford University Press, 1998), 96.

6. Olmsted and Kimball, *Forty Years of Landscape Architecture: Central Park*, 42–46.

7. John Adams, "Defense of the Constitutions of Government of the United States," in *The Works of John Adams*, vol. 4, ed. Charles Francis Adams (Boston: Little, Brown, and Company, 1856), 587–588; Thomas Jefferson, *Notes on Virginia*, vol. 2 of *The Writings of Thomas Jefferson*, ed. Andrew A. Lipscomb (Washington, DC: Thomas Jefferson Memorial Association, 1904), 230, query 19.

8. Andrew Jackson Downing, *Rural Essays*, ed. George W. Curtis (New York: George A. Leavitt, 1869 [1858]); quoted in Jeanne Goode, "Andrew Jackson Downing on Trees," *Arboricultural Journal* 12 (1988): 191; John R. Stilgoe, "Town Common and Village Green in New England: 1620 to 1981," in *On Common Ground*, ed. Ronald L. Fleming (Cambridge: Townscape Institute, 1982), 26.

9. Orville Dewey, *Autobiography and Letters of Orville Dewey*, ed. Mary E. Dewey (Boston: Roberts Brothers, 1883), 28; Richard Berenberg, "Village Improvement Societies in New England, 1850–1900: The Rural Ideal in an Age of Rural Depopulation and Urban Growth" (PhD diss., Harvard University, 1966), 72.

10. Luigi Castiglioni, "Observations on Useful Plants," in *Luigi Castiglioni's Viaggio: Travels in the United States of North America, 1785–1787*, ed. Antonio Pace (Syracuse, NY: Syracuse University Press, 1983), xi–xvi,

459–460; F. André Michaux, *The North American Sylva, or A Description of the Forest Trees of the United States, Canada and Nova Scotia*, vol. 3 (Philadelphia: Dobson and Conrad, 1819), 83–86.

11. Charles Sprague Sargent, "The American Elm," *Garden and Forest*, June 11, 1890, 281; Henry Ward Beecher, *Norwood, or Village Life in New England* (New York: Fords, Howard, & Hulbert, 1888), 4–5; Beecher quoted in *Report of the General Superintendent of Parks* (Cambridge, MA: City of Cambridge, 1894), 76n; Oliver Wendell Holmes, *Elsie Venner: A Romance of Destiny* (Cambridge, MA: Riverside Press, 1891 [1861]), 55–56; Lady Emmeline Stuart Wortley, *Travels in the United States* (New York: 1851), quoted in George Dudley Seymour, *New Haven* (New Haven, CT: Privately printed, 1942), 77–78; Charles Dickens, "American Notes," in *Works of Charles Dickens*, vol. 2 (New York: Sheldon and Company, 1865), 78.

12. Whitney R. Cross, "The Burned-over District," in *The Social and Intellectual History of Enthusiastic Religion in Western New York, 1800–1850* (Ithaca, NY: Cornell University Press, 1950), vii.

13. L. Collins, "Arboriculture," in *The Tree Planting and Fountain Society of Brooklyn: Bulletin No.1* (Brooklyn, NY: Eagle Book and Job Printing Company, 1894), 5; "F. Van Wyck, 82, Antiquarian, Dies," *New York Times*, February 17, 1936.

14. Collins, "Arboriculture," 5; "F. Van Wyck, 82, Antiquarian, Dies," *New York Times*, February 17, 1936; Andrew Jackson Downing, "Shade Trees in Cities," *Horticulturalist* 8 (August 1, 1852): 345–347. Ailanthus was given lasting fame in Betty Smith's 1943 novel *A Tree Grows in Brooklyn*. The London plane, a cross between the American sycamore and the Old World *Platanus orientalis*, has long been New York City's iconic street tree but was not planted in large numbers until the 1930s. See Thomas J. Campanella, "The Roman Roots of Gotham's London Plane," *Wall Street Journal*, July 20, 2011.

15. Henry King Olmsted and George K. Ward, *A Genealogy of the Olmsted Family in America* (New York: A. T. De La Mare Company, 1912), vii; Henry Howe, "New Haven's Elms and Green," a scrapbook of his articles from the *New Haven Daily Morning Journal and Courier* (1883–1884), Sterling Memorial Library, Yale University, 4.

16. Olmsted and Kimball, *Forty Years of Landscape Architecture: Central Park*, 70–71; *An Account of the Dinner by the Hamilton Club to Hon. James S. T. Stranahan* (Brooklyn, NY: Eagle Press, 1889), 17.

17. "Report of the Commissioners of Prospect Park" (February 3, 1860), in *Annual Reports*, 6–10.

18. Ibid., 6–10, 11–17.

19. "Report of Egbert L. Viele (January 15, 1861), in *Annual Reports*, 27–28. Viele claimed a pedigree "back to the Iroquois Nation" in an 1895 *New-York Tribune* article, "Effect of the Building of the Hudson River Bridge" (August 27, 1895). On Viele as amateur naturalist, see "A Glimpse of Nature from My Veranda," *Harper's New Monthly Magazine*, August 1878, 404–411; M. M. Graff, *Central Park, Prospect Park: A New Perspective* (New York: Greensward Foundation, 1985), 111.

20. Richard Henry Savage, "General Egbert Ludovicus Viele," in *Viele 1659–1909: Two Hundred and Fifty Years with a Dutch Family of New York*, ed. Kathlyne Knickerbocker Viele (New York: Tobias A. Wright, 1909), 127–129; on Colonel Charles Hart Olmstead, see Olmsted and Ward, *Genealogy of the Olmsted Family in America*, 286.

21. "Report of the Landscape Architects" (January 24, 1866), in *Annual Reports*, 91–92, 102–103, 98–99; David Schuyler and Jane Turner Censer, eds., *The Papers of Frederick Law Olmsted: The Years of Olmsted, Vaux & Company, 1865–1874* (Baltimore: Johns Hopkins University Press, 1992), 341.

22. "Report of the Landscape Architects" (January 24, 1866), in *Annual Reports*, 93–95; Frederick Law Olmsted, *Public Parks and the Enlargement of Towns* (Cambridge, MA: Printed for the American Social Science Association at the Riverside Press, 1870), 21; "Sixth Annual Report of the Commissioners of Prospect Park" (1866), in *Annual Reports*, 88; "Report of the Landscape Architects" (January 24, 1866), 100–103. The Vaux sketch appears in Graff, *Central Park, Prospect Park*, 115.

23. "First Annual Report of the Commissioners of Prospect Park" (January 28, 1861), in *Annual Reports*, 21; *An Account of the Dinner by the Hamilton Club to Hon. James S. T. Stranahan*, 16–17; "Sixth Annual Report" (1866), in *Annual Reports*, 89.

24. "Report of the Landscape Architects" (1866), in *Annual Reports*, 94, 116–117; "Prospect Park," *Brooklyn Daily Eagle*, November 11, 1870. In a map on p. 29 of *Pleasure Drives and Promenades*, Elizabeth Macdonald outlines a route for this second drive that runs very close to Kings Highway.

25. Olmsted and Vaux, *Observations on the Progress of Improvements in Street Plans*, 22–24.

26. Olmsted and Kimball, *Forty Years of Landscape Architecture: Central Park*, 56; Macdonald, *Pleasure Drives and Promenades*, 23–37. See also Charles E. Beveridge and Carolyn F. Hoffman, eds., *The Papers of Frederick Law Olmsted: Writings on Public Parks, Parkways, and Park Systems* (Baltimore: Johns Hopkins University Press, 1997), 134–141. It was also in Paris that Olmsted appears to have picked up the term *landscape architect*, which was stamped—*Service de l'architecte-paysagiste*—on drawings Alphand shared with him of the Bois de Boulogne. See Charles Waldheim, "Landscape as Architecture," *Harvard Design Magazine* 36 (2013).

27. Beveridge and Hoffman, *Papers of Frederick Law Olmsted*, 134–137, 140–141; "Prospect Park Extension," *Brooklyn Daily Eagle*, January 29, 1868; Macdonald, *Pleasure Drives and Promenades*, 47.

28. "The Eastern Parkway," *Brooklyn Daily Eagle*, March 17, 1874; "Eastern Parkway," *Brooklyn Daily Eagle*, November 16, 1874; "Brooklyn's Chain of Parkways," *Brooklyn Daily Eagle*, December 13, 1896.

29. Frederick Boyd Stevenson, "Nassau County Plans Central Boulevard Route," *Brooklyn Daily Eagle*, June 9, 1912; "Suffolk's Lively Start in Long Island Plan," *Brooklyn Daily Eagle*, February 18, 1912; "Want Four New Roads for Long Island," *New York Times*, July 15, 1923; "Fine Parkway Planned for Queens," *New York Times*, September 21, 1913; "Queens Parkway Project Revived," *New York Times*, September 10, 1922.

30. Beveridge and Hoffman, *Papers of Frederick Law Olmsted*, 137; "Our Albany Correspondence: From Prospect Park to Fort Hamilton," *Brooklyn Daily Eagle*, March 26, 1869; "Brooklyn's Chain of Parkways," *Brooklyn Daily Eagle*, December 13, 1896; Macdonald, *Pleasure Drives and Promenades*, 56–57.

31. "Brooklyn's Chain of Parkways," *Brooklyn Daily Eagle*, December 13, 1896; "Bay Ridge Shore Drive," *New-York Tribune*, June 10, 1894; David Schuyler and Gregory Kaliss, eds., *The Papers of Frederick Law Olmsted: The Last Great Projects, 1890–1895* (Baltimore: Johns Hopkins University Press, 2015), 40–41, 919.

32. "Bay Ridge Shore Drive," *New-York Tribune*, June 10, 1894; "A Sea Side Boulevard," *Brooklyn Daily Eagle*, January 27, 1894; "The Bay Ridge Parkway," *New-York Tribune*, February 24, 1895; "Development of Park System," *New-York Tribune*, August 24, 1902; "Parkways and Boulevards in American Cities," *American Architect and Building News*, October 8, 1898; "Brooklyn's Chain of Parkways," *Brooklyn Daily Eagle*, December 13, 1896; "Mayor Dedicates Eriksson [*sic*] Square," *New York Times*, May 24, 1925.

33. *Report of the Brooklyn Park Commissioners* (Brooklyn, NY, 1880), 45–46; "Parkways and Boulevards in American Cities," *American Architect and Building News*, October 8, 1898; *Twenty-Fifth Annual Report of the Brooklyn Park Commissioners for the Year 1885* (Brooklyn, NY, 1886), 46; "Must Ride on the Cycle Path," *New York Times*, May 5, 1896; Macdonald, *Pleasure Drives and Promenades*, 111–113.

34. Macdonald, *Pleasure Drives and Promenades*, 113; *Thirty-Fourth Annual Report of the Department of Parks* (Brooklyn, NY, 1895), 9; "A Straight Run to the Sea," *New York Times*, August 26, 1894; "The New Bicycle Path, Ocean Parkway," *Scientific American*, August 24, 1895, 120; *Thirty-Fifth Annual Report of the Department of Parks* (Brooklyn, NY, 1896), 21–24; "Will Contest the Order," *New York Times*, May 9, 1896; "Cycle Path's Opening," *New York Times*, June 28, 1896.

35. "Editorial Notes: Public Parks and the Enlargement of Towns," *Putnam's Monthly*, September 1870, 336–337; *Report of the Brooklyn Park Commissioners* (Brooklyn, NY, 1880), 46. The requests for proposals ran in the *Brooklyn Daily Eagle* on October 15 and November 29, 1872.

CHAPTER 5. WHIP, SPUR, AND SADDLE

1. Hicks, *Documentary History*, 7.

2. Stiles, *History of the City of Brooklyn*, 317, 321. Loosley appears to have had two establishments, one—Brooklyn Hall—downtown and the King's Head on the Ascot Heath.

3. "The Robber Baron of New Hampshire," *New England Historical Society* (http://www .newenglandhistoricalsociety.com/the-robber-baron-of-new-hampshire-part-hog-part-shark); Leonard Benardo and Jennifer Weiss, "Street Cred," *New York Times*, February 25, 2007; Leonard Dinnerstein, *Anti-Semitism in America* (New York: Oxford University Press, 1994), 40; http://www.albanylaw.edu/media /user/glc/racing_gaming/there_used_to_be_a_racetrack_but_where11.pdf.

4. Deborah Fulton Rau, "John Pickering Putnam, Visionary in Boston," *Architectura* 22 (February 1992): 109–119; "The Reading," *Locomotive Firemen's Magazine*, August 1889, 681; "The Robber Baron of New Hampshire"; Leonard Benardo and Jennifer Weiss, "Street Cred," *New York Times*, February 25, 2007; Dinnerstein, *Anti-Semitism in America*, 40.

5. http://www.westland.net/coneyisland/articles/earlyhistory2.htm; "Manhattan Beach Hotel Soon to Go," *New York Times*, September 17, 1911; "The New Race Track," *Brooklyn Daily Eagle*, May 9, 1880.

6. "A Pioneer Gone," *Brooklyn Daily Eagle*, January 12, 1884; "Maurice E. McLoughlin, "Tide Helped to Build Old Brighton Baths," *Brooklyn Daily Eagle*, November 6, 1930.

7. "By the Sea," *Brooklyn Daily Eagle*, May 24, 1880; James Walter Smith, "How Buildings Are Moved," *Strand Magazine* 13:78 (June 1897): 689.

8. Steven A. Riess, *The Sport of Kings and the Kings of Crime* (Syracuse, NY: Syracuse University Press, 2011), 49–50; "Racing at Jerome Park," *New York Times*, September 22, 1866.

9. Quoted in Riess, *Sport of Kings*, 52–54.

10. [No title] *New York Times*, May 28, 1885.

11. "The Track to Kill a Horse," *New York Times*, September 21, 1879.

12. "The New Race Track," *Brooklyn Daily Eagle*, May 9, 1880.

13. Riess, *Sport of Kings*, 240; "The New Race Track," *Brooklyn Daily Eagle*, May 9, 1880; Riess, 55–58, 240.

14. Riess, *Sport of Kings*, 56–57; "The Great Suburban," *New-York Daily Tribune*, June 8, 1902.

15. "Electioneer Winner of the Rich Futurity," *New York Times*, September 2, 1906; Riess, *Sport of Kings*, 60; "Proctor Knott's Futurity," *New York Times*, September 4, 1888; "Futurity of 1890," *Los Angeles Herald*, August 30, 1890; Ed Hotaling, *Wink: The Incredible Life and Epic Journey of Jimmy Winkfield* (New York: McGraw-Hill, 2005), 13–14, 23.

16. Jon Sterngass, *First Resorts: Pursuing Pleasure at Saratoga Springs, Newport, and Coney Island* (Baltimore: John Hopkins University Press, 2001); "The Great Suburban," *New-York Daily Tribune*, June 8, 1902. Decades later this sense of community would play a vital role in organizing opposition to city plans to raze the neighborhood for a new high school (what was eventually built nearby as John Dewey High School), standing firm even as a cross was burned in front of the church.

17. Lisa K. Winkler, "The Kentucky Derby's Forgotten Jockeys," Smithsonian.com, April 23, 2009: http://www.smithsonianmag.com/history/the-kentucky-derbys-forgotten-jockeys-128781428; Hotaling, *Wink*, 7–11.

18. Riess, *Sport of Kings*, 50; David Wiggins cited in Steven A. Riess, "The American Jockey, 1865–1910," *Transatlantica* 2 (2011): 6; "Futurity of 1890," *Los Angeles Herald*, August 30, 1890; Hotaling, *Wink*, 15–16.

19. "Negro Jockeys Shut Out," *New York Times*, July 29, 1900; Parmer quoted in Riess, "The American Jockey," 6; Winkler, "The Kentucky Derby's Forgotten Jockeys"; Hotaling, *Wink*, 92, 79–120.

20. Paul W. Rhode and Koleman S. Strumpf, "Historical Presidential Betting Markets," *Journal of Economic Perspectives* 18:2 (Spring 2004): 135–136; Riess, *Sport of Kings,* 40.

21. Riess, *Sport of Kings*, 44, 177; John A. Lapp, "Race Track Gambling," *American Political Science Review* 2:3 (May 1908): 422; Riess, 192–193, 213.

22. Riess, *Sport of Kings*, xii–xiv.

23. "Betting at Sheepshead Bay," *Brooklyn Daily Eagle*, June 27, 1885; Riess, *Sport of Kings*, 74–75.

24. New York State Racing Commission, *Racing Laws, State of New York, and Rules of Racing, 1907* (New York: Hull and Company, 1906), 13–14; Riess, *Sport of Kings*, 304–314.

25. Riess, *Sport of Kings*, 316–317; "Foelker's Trip Ends in Collapse," *New York Times*, June 11, 1908; "Owes Victory to Heroic Foelker," *Boston Daily Globe*, June 12, 1908; "Foelker's Heroism," *Boston Daily Globe*, June 15, 1908.

26. "Police Enjoined in Race Track War," *New York Times*, June 20, 1908; "Keene's Ballot Wins Suburban," *New York Times*, June 20, 1908; Riess, *Sport of Kings*, 320–322; "Secret Bettting in Vogue at Track," *New York Times*, June 21, 1908.

27. "May Sell Brighton Track," *New York Times*, August 9, 1908; Riess, *Sport of Kings*, 323–333.

28. "Closing Day at Sheepshead Bay Brings Out Record Attendance," *Brooklyn Daily Eagle*, July 5, 1910; Riess, *Sport of Kings*, 333–335.

CHAPTER 6. THE ISLE OF OFFAL AND BONES

1. "Lucky B's Burial," *New York Times*, September 6, 1887; "Lucky B Dying," *New York Times*, September 4, 1887; "Golgotha," *Brooklyn Daily Eagle*, August 20, 1877.

2. William Wallace Tooker, *Indian Names of Places in the Borough of Brooklyn* (New York: Francis P. Harper, 1901), 51; Flint, *Early Long Island*, 89; Van Wyck, *Keskachauge*, 13; Dubois, *A History of the Town of Flatlands*, 14; Sarah K. Cody and John Auwaerter, *Cultural Landscape Report for Floyd Bennett Field* (Boston: Olmsted Center for Landscape Preservation, 2009), 22; "Rare Documents Relating to New York," *New York Times*, March 2, 1901. The 1664 Barren Island deed was published for the first time in Dubois's 1884 *History of the Town of Flatlands*, 15.

3. "A Woman's Romantic History," *New York Times*, May 17, 1880; "The Mutiny on the Vineyard," *New York Times*, January 14, 1878. A more elaborate version of the tale, by William H. Stillwell, is cited in Ross, *History of Long Island*, 376–378.

4. "The Prospect at Quarantine—Barren Island and West Bank," *New York Times*, April 30, 1867; "Quarantine on Barren Island," *Brooklyn Daily Eagle*, February 28, 1859; "Barren Island as Quarantine Ground," *Brooklyn Daily Eagle*, April 20, 1859; "Offal Contract," in *Proceedings of the Board of Aldermen of the City of Brooklyn*, vol. 1 (Brooklyn: Bishop and Kelly's Steam Power Presses, 1856), 68; Benjamin Miller, *Fat of the Land* (New York: Four Walls Eight Windows, 2000), 54; Stiles, *Civil, Political, Professional and Ecclesiastical History and Commercial and Industrial Record*, 756; *Gardener's Chronicle and Agricultural Gazette* 37 (September 15, 1855): 617; *International Exhibition, 1862: Reports by the Juries* (London: William Clowes and Sons, 1863), 168. The extract cited in the advertisement is from *Agricultural Gazette* (April 7, 1855).

5. Jessica Wang, "Dogs and the Making of the American State: Voluntary Association, State Power, and the Politics of Animal Control in New York City, 1850–1920," *Journal of American History* 98:4 (March

2012): 1003; "City Dogs," *New York Daily Times*, June 26, 1857; "A Distressed Widow Visits an Up-Town Institution," *New York Times*, August 13, 1855.

6. Joel A. Tarr, "Urban Pollution: Many Years Ago," *American Heritage* 22:6 (October 1971): 65–69; Clay McShane and Joel A. Tarr, *The Horse in the City: Living Machines in the Nineteenth Century* (Baltimore: Johns Hopkins University Press, 2007), 4, 16, 63–67.

7. McShane and Tarr, *The Horse in the City*, 26; "The Terrible Horse Disease," *New York Times*, October 26, 1872; "Excursion to Barren Island," *Brooklyn Daily Eagle*, July 18, 1861.

8. "The Offal in the Bay," *Brooklyn Daily Eagle*, August 19, 1870; "Barren Island," *New York Times*, May 12, 1866; "Befouling the Bay," *New York Times*, September 24, 1870.

9. "The Dog-Catcher Abroad," *New York Times*, June 2, 1881; "Barren Island," *Brooklyn Daily Eagle*, January 30, 1891; "A Large Fire on Barren Island," *New York Times*, April 3, 1879; "Subdued Only by Death," *New York Times*, April 6, 1883; "The Big Elephant Albert Killed," *New York Times*, July 21, 1885; "Jumbo's Funeral Pyre," *New York Times*, September 18, 1885; "A Jumbo House for Coney Island," *New York Times*, February 21, 1884.

10. Thomas Morton, *The New English Canaan* (Boston: Prince Society, 1883), 225; G. Brown Goode, "The Natural and Economical History of the American Menhaden," in US Commission of Fish and Fisheries, *Report of the Commissioner for 1877*, pt. 5 (Washington, DC: Government Printing Office, 1879); 11–13; H. Bruce Franklin, *The Most Important Fish in the Sea: Menhaden and America* (Washington, DC: Island Press, 2007), 15; Benjamin H. Latrobe, "A Drawing and Description of the *Clupea Tyrannus* and *Oniscus Prægustator*," *Transactions of the American Philosophical Society* 5 (1802): 80; C. M. Porter, "Benjamin Henry Latrobe and the Nomenclature of Two American Fishes," *Archives of Natural History* 14:1 (1987): 85–88.

11. Samuel L. Mitchill, "The Fishes of New York," *Transactions of the Literary and Philosophical Society of New York* 1 (1815): 453; Goode, "American Menhaden," 282, 78–79, 2, 192.

12. "Golgotha," *Brooklyn Daily Eagle*, August 20, 1877; Goode, "American Menhaden," 173; Dubois, *A History of the Town of Flatlands*, 15; Franklin, *The Most Important Fish in the Sea*, 6.

13. "Odoriferous," *Brooklyn Daily Eagle*, June 11, 1879; "Golgotha," *Brooklyn Daily Eagle*, August 20, 1877.

14. "Invasion of Barren Island by United States Troops," *New York Times*, February 12, 1874; "New-York's Moonshiners," *New York Times*, February 6, 1880; Rebecca Dalzell, "The Whiskey Wars That Left Brooklyn in Ruins," *Smithsonian*, November 18, 2004; "Melee on Barren Island," *Brooklyn Daily Eagle*, February 10, 1897; "Police for Barren Island," *Brooklyn Daily Eagle*, April 17, 1897; "Golgotha," *Brooklyn Daily Eagle*, August 20, 1877; "'Ruby's' History," *New York Times*, August 9, 1880.

15. "Excursion to Barren Island," *Brooklyn Daily Eagle*, July 18, 1861; "In Raymond Street Jail," *Brooklyn Daily Eagle*, February 19, 1894; "Barren Island," *Brooklyn Daily Eagle*, January 30, 1891.

16. "Befouling the Bay," *New York Times*, September 24, 1870; "Attacking Foul Odors," *New York Times*, August 18, 1888; "Barren Island's Odors," *New York Times*, November 7, 1890; "Testimony in the Matter of the Investigation of Barren Island," in *Eleventh Annual Report of the State Board of Health of New York*, vol. 1 (Albany, NY: James B. Lyon, 1891), 63, 67–68, 155–157; "Barren Island: Its Noxious Vapors Subject to Further Inquiry," *Brooklyn Daily Eagle*, November 25, 1890.

17. "Barren Island," in *Eleventh Annual Report*, 49–50; "Personal Information," *Municipal Engineering* 15:6 (December 1898): 381–382.

18. Miller, *Fat of the Land*, 69–85; "Wastes of a Great City," *New York Times*, September 27, 1896; "The Disposal of City Refuse," *New York Times*, August 23, 1896; "The Barren Island Garbage Reduction Works, Greater New York," *Engineering News* 43:5 (February 1900): 66; "Garbage and Sewage," *New York Times*, July 6, 1907; "The Disposal of City Refuse," *New York Times*, August 23, 1896; Clarence Ashton Wood, "Try Pots and Fish Factories," *Long Island Forum*, March 1946, 53.

19. "Barren Island," *Engineering News* 43:5, 66–68; "To Use New-York Garbage," *New York Times*, September 27, 1896; William W. Locke, "Refuse Disposal," in Z. Taylor Emery, *Report of the Department of Health of the City of Brooklyn for the Year 1896* (City of Brooklyn, 1897), 308–315.

20. Locke, "Refuse Disposal," 313; "Caught in a Garbage Press," *Brooklyn Daily Eagle*, August 16, 1898; "Fatal Explosion on Barren Island," *New York Times*, May 1, 1910; "Harbor Police Heroes at Big Explosion," *Brooklyn Daily Eagle*, May 1, 1910.

21. "Barren Island Nuisance," *Brooklyn Daily Eagle*, August 12, 1897; Locke, "Refuse Disposal," 317; William P. Dixon, "Barren Island Odors," *Brooklyn Daily Eagle*, August 22, 1899; "Barren Island Odors," *Brooklyn Daily Eagle*, September 1, 1897.

22. "Col. Waring a Witness," *Brooklyn Daily Eagle*, September 10, 1897; "Barren Island Nuisance," *Brooklyn Daily Eagle*, August 12, 1897.

23. "Hayes Favors Remsen's Bill," *Brooklyn Daily Eagle*, January 18, 1900; "Local Legislators Ready with Pet Bills," *Brooklyn Daily Eagle*, January 10, 1900; "Removal of Penitentiary," *Brooklyn Daily Eagle*, January 16, 1901; "Remsen Bill Hearing," *Brooklyn Daily Eagle*, April 10, 1900; "To Purify Barren Island," *New York*

Times, January 11, 1898; "To Make an End of Barren Island Odors," *Brooklyn Daily Eagle,* September 3, 1898; "The Barren Island Nuisance," *New York Times,* January 31, 1899; "Rockaway Jubilant," *Brooklyn Daily Eagle,* April 26, 1899; "Barren Island's New Era," *Brooklyn Daily Eagle,* May 8, 1899; "Barren Island's Days Are Numbered Now," *Brooklyn Daily Eagle,* July 25, 1899; "Garbage Crematory Wanted," *New York Times,* December 21, 1899; "Dr. A. H. Doty Favors Cremating Garbage," *Brooklyn Daily Eagle,* December 24, 1899; "Doughty Withdraws Barren Island Bill," *Brooklyn Daily Eagle,* March 14, 1901; "The Problem of 'Final Disposition,'" *New York Times,* September 23, 1904.

24. "$1,500,00 Fire Loss on Barren Island," *New York Times,* May 21, 1906; "Objection to the Rebuilding of Barren Island Plant on the Old Lines," *New York Times,* June 21, 1906; "Garbage on the Beaches," *New York Times,* May 25, 1906; "Refuse Will Be Towed Fifty Miles to Sea," *New York Times,* May 22, 1906; "Reports of Inspectors of Rendering Plants Appointed under Executive Order," in *Twenty-Eighth Annual Report of the State Department of Health of New York,* vol. 2 (Albany, NY: J. B. Lyon Company, 1908), 571; "All the Dead Horses," *New York Times,* November 7, 2000; "Mother of Exiles" is from Emma Lazarus's 1883 sonnet "The New Colossus."

25. "Good Work of School on Barren Island," *Brooklyn Daily Eagle,* August 18, 1901; "Diptheria Is Prevalent," *New York Times,* August 6, 1897; "Diptheria in a School?" *Brooklyn Daily Eagle,* September 16, 1897; "Record of Progress," *Immigrants in America Review* 1:3 (September 1915): 103–104; "Preying upon Helpless Immigrants," *New York Times,* April 14, 1912.

26. Frances A. Kellor, "Immigrants in America: A Domestic Policy," *Immigrants in America Review* 1:1 (March 1915): 53–54; "New Plan for Solving the Immigration Problem," *Brooklyn Daily Eagle,* August 4, 1912; Kellor, "The Immigrant and Preparedness," *Immigrants in America Review* 1:4 (January 1916): 21–22; "Record of Progress," 103–104; "How Children Are Taught in Public Kindergartens," *Brooklyn Daily Eagle,* August 18, 1901; "Good Work," *Brooklyn Daily Eagle,* August 18, 1901; "Barren Island Is Out on a Strike," *New York Times,* April 12, 1913; "Police in Battle with 300 Polacks," *Brooklyn Daily Eagle,* May 17, 1913; "Man Is Shot in Riot on Barren Island," *New York Times,* May 18, 1913; "Strike Riot on Barren Island," *Brooklyn Daily Eagle,* May 18, 1913.

27. "First Auto Trip on Record to Barren Island," *Brooklyn Daily Eagle,* January 27, 1918; "Missionary Found for Barren Island," *Brooklyn Daily Eagle,* November 10, 1918; "All the Dead Horses," *New York Times,* November 7, 2000; "Finds Barren Island Richest Spot on Earth," *Brooklyn Daily Eagle,* June 22, 1930; "Miss Jane Shaw, Educator, Dies," *Brooklyn Daily Eagle,* September 5, 1939.

28. "Heartbreak Settles over Barren Island," *Brooklyn Daily Eagle,* March 14, 1936; "Finds Barren Island Richest Spot on Earth," *Brooklyn Daily Eagle,* June 22, 1930; Letter from Jane F. Shaw to Raymond V. Ingersoll, Brooklyn Borough President, March 22, 1936, Robert Moses Papers, Manuscripts and Archives Division, The New York Public Library; "Acts to End Air Menace," *New York Times,* February 11, 1937; "Chimney to Come Down," *New York Times,* February 17, 1937; "Barren Island Stack Blast to Rain Cement, Not 'Pennies from Heaven,'" *Brooklyn Daily Eagle,* March 11, 1937; "Blast Topples Bennett Field's Stack Nuisance," *Brooklyn Daily Eagle,* March 21, 1937; "Miss Jane Shaw, Educator, Dies," *Brooklyn Daily Eagle,* September 5, 1939.

CHAPTER 7. A HOUSE FOR THE GOD OF SPEED

1. "Meet at Sheepshead Bay," *New York Times,* August 12, 1910; "Makes Trial Flight in a 45-Mile Gale," *Brooklyn Daily Eagle,* August 18, 1910; "Airships Parade at Sheepshead Bay," *New York Times,* August 20, 1910; "Bird-Men Bow to Boreas," *Brooklyn Daily Eagle,* August 22, 1910.

2. The nine-lived aviator was so badly injured in a wreck at Erie, Pennsylvania, a year later that the *New York Times* reported him "Fatally Hurt" and printed his obituary. He lived another thirty-three years. See "Mars Fatally Hurt in Aeroplane Fall," *New York Times,* July 15, 1911; "Bud Mars, 68, Dies; Aviation Pioneer," *New York Times,* July 27, 1944.

3. "Post's Air Feats Thrill Spectators," *New York Times,* August 28, 1910; "Aviators Are Ready to Try for New Laurels," *Brooklyn Daily Eagle,* August 26, 1910.

4. "Back from Flights in the Far East," *New York Times,* June 19, 1911. Later accounts claim Mars took the young Emperor Hirohito up for a ride over Tokyo, but this is not mentioned in any of the news reports at the time.

5. Charlie Wentz, "Who Was Calbraith P. Rogers?" *American Philatelist,* November 2011, 1018.

6. "Souvenir Hunters Worry Rodgers," *Brooklyn Daily Eagle,* September 18, 1911; Eileen F. Lebow, *Cal Rodgers and the Vin Fiz: The First Transcontinental Flight* (Washington, DC: Smithsonian Institution Press, 1989), 87–90; "Rodgers Falls 35 Feet and Gives Up Flight," *Brooklyn Daily Eagle,* September 18, 1911; "Cal P. Rodgers to Continue His Flight, To-Morrow," *Middletown Times-Press,* September 19, 1911.

7. "20,000 See Rodgers Land," *New York Times*, November 6, 1911; Charles S. Wiggin, "The First across the Continent," *Air and Space* 26:4 (September 2011); "Rodgers to Finish Flight To-Day," *New York Times*, November 4, 1911; "Ask President's Help," *New-York Tribune*, January 28, 1912; "Needs of Aviation Confided to Taft," *New York Times*, January 28, 1912; "Aero Club Banqueters Hail Taft with Song," *Sun*, January 28, 1912; Lebow, *Cal Rodgers*, 239; "Fall Kills Aviator," *San Francisco Call*, April 4, 1912.

8. "Race Track Now for Sale," *Brooklyn Daily Eagle*, October 30, 1911; "Historic Race Track Bought for $3,000,000," *Brooklyn Daily Eagle*, December 13, 1911; "Sheepshead Track Offered for Sale," *New York Times*, December 14, 1911; "Macy Employees' Outing," *Brooklyn Daily Eagle*, May 29, 1913; "Brentwood Hero Takes All Honors," *Brooklyn Daily Eagle*, May 31, 1913.

9. "Civic Pride Should Make Speedway Opening Memorable in the History of Brooklyn," *Brooklyn Daily Eagle*, October 1, 1915. Parsons owned one of the finest thoroughbred stables in the United States with H. K. Knapp, namesake of a Brooklyn street that runs through the old Sheepshead Bay racetrack site. A nearby avenue is named after Harkness.

10. "Motor Race Course at Sheepshead Bay," *New York Times*, November 16, 1914; "Sheepshead Track to Have Golf Links," *Brooklyn Daily Eagle*, November 16, 1914; "Sheepshead Bay New Motor Speedway to Cost $3,500,000," *Brooklyn Daily Eagle*, August 29, 1915; "New York Speedway Is Assured," *Motor World*, April 15, 2015; "Big Backers for New York Speedway," *Automobile*, April 16, 1915, 664–665; "World's Largest Sport Arena," *New York Times*, May 2, 1915.

11. "Big Backers for New York Speedway," *Automobile*, April 16, 1915, 664–665; "Boston Opera Company Coming," *Yale Daily News*, February 14, 1914; "'Father' of Yale Bowl Dies in San Francisco," *Yale Daily News*, May 5, 1924; "Autoists Inspect Bay Motordrome," *New York Times*, June 16, 1915; "27 Miles of Seats for New Speedway," *New York Times*, April 25, 1915. Batchelder, who also had a strong interest in aviation, was killed in a 1921 plane crash. Batchelder Street in Brooklyn, close to the old speedway site, bears his name. Koehler's partners in their bid for the speedway job were Lawrence N. Spyr and Robert M. Farrington, architect of the first reinforced-concrete structure in Bogotá, Colombia.

12. "They Know Him in Flatlands," *Brooklyn Daily Eagle*, February 18, 1896; James Baron, "To Fans, Queensboro Bridge Is a Steel Swan," *New York Times*, March 28, 2009; Walter C. Kidney, *Henry Hornbostel: An Architect's Master Touch* (Pittsburgh, PA: Roberts Rinehart, 2002); "World's Largest Sport Arena," *New York Times*, May 2, 1915; "Sheepshead Bay New Motor Speedway," *Brooklyn Daily Eagle*, August 29, 1915; "Grandstand at Sheepshead Bay Speedway, New York, Seats More Than 30,000," *Engineering Record*, October 2, 1915; "Aviation at Speedway," *New York Times*, August 18, 1915.

13. "Sheepshead Bay New Motor Speedway," *Brooklyn Daily Eagle*, August 29, 1915. The brick track at the Indianapolis Motor Speedway was paved over in the 1930s, and only a small strip survives today—the fabled "Yard of Brick" that winners of the Indy 500 make a point of kissing.

14. "Building the Modern Speedway," *Motor*, August 1915, 41–43, 110; "Motor Club Will Open Big Speedway," *New York Times*, August 1, 1915.

15. "$3,500,000 Speedway Formally Opened with Big Parade," *Brooklyn Daily Eagle*, September 19, 1915; "World's Record at Speedway Opening," *New York Times*, September 19, 1915; "Auto Driver Grant Severely Burned," *New York Times*, September 28, 1915. The thirteen-mile length assumes two car lengths between each pair of the two thousand vehicles. The distance from Columbus Circle to the speedway is roughly 13.7 miles.

16. "Yankee Stamina Wins Astor Cup," *Motor* 25:2 (November 1915): 41–47, 122. The cup was featured on the David Letterman show in October 2013, when New Zealand champion Scott Dixon was a guest.

17. "Bombs on Washington," *Brooklyn Daily Eagle*, April 16, 1916; Eileen F. Lebow, *Before Amelia* (Washington, DC: Brassey's, 2002), 189; "Auto Races Aeroplanes," *New York Times*, May 7, 1916.

18. "General O'Ryan Speaks for Big War Show," *New York Times*, May 14, 1916; "Defense Show Open Today," *New York Times*, May 20, 1916; "Wilson May Attend Big Military Show," *New York Times*, May 16, 1916; "Blue Laws Bungle Militia War Game," *New York Times*, May 22, 1916; "Sunday War Show to Take 7 to Court," *New York Times*, May 23, 1916. O'Ryan was a lawyer in civilian life who organzed major demonstrations in support of European Jews in the 1930s.

19. *Los Angeles Times* cited in "The Week," *Nation*, July 6, 1918, 3; "Hot Weather Gossip," *Record*, June 15, 1918; "Telegram from Theodore Roosevelt to Ex-Senator W. P. Jackson on June 8, 1916," in *The Progressive Party: Its Record from January to July, 1916* (New York: Press of The Mail and Express Job Print, 1916), 89; "German-Americans Here Thanked by Kaiser," *Brooklyn Daily Eagle*, February 27, 1916.

20. "Teutons Proclaim Loyalty to America," *New York Times*, June 5, 1916; "America 'First' Is Teutons' Pledge," *Brooklyn Daily Eagle*, June 5, 1916.

21. "$500,000 Raised at Police Games," *New York Times*, September 1, 1918.

22. "World's Largest Sport Arena," *New York Times*, May 2, 1915.

23. "Opera to Aid Italian Earthquake Victims," *New York Times*, July 19, 1919; "Open Air 'Aida' Tomorrow," *New York Times*, August 15, 1919; " 'Aida' Sung before 45,000 Persons in the Open Air at Sheepshead Bay," *New York Herald*, August 17, 1919; "Riot at Speedway as 'Aida' Is Sung by Chorus of 200," *Brooklyn Daily Eagle*, August 17, 1919; "30,000 Hear Gala 'Aida' in the Open," *New York Times*, August 17, 1919. Crowd estimates and the number of performers and musicians vary considerably between these accounts.

24. "Demolish Speedway at Sheepshead Bay for New Home Site," *Brooklyn Daily Eagle*, December 2, 1919; "Selling Speedway Lumber," *Brooklyn Daily Eagle*, February 19, 1920; "Sheepshead Bay Racetrack Sold to Max Natanson," *Brooklyn Daily Eagle*, June 28, 1923; "650-Acre Purchase," *New York Times*, July 1, 1923.

25. "Flatbush Auction Breaks Records," *New York Times*, September 9, 1923; "Broke Sale Records at Sheepshead Bay," *New York Times*, July 4, 1925; "Sheepshead Bay Track Sale Establishes New Auction Record," *New York Times*, July 12, 1925.

CHAPTER 8. THE STEAMPUNK ORB

1. A. P. Stockwell, "History of the Town of Gravesend," in Stiles, *Civil, Political, Professional and Ecclesiastical History and Commercial and Industrial Record*, 171; William H. Stillwell, "History of Coney Island," in ibid., 194.

2. Stillwell in Stiles, 195–203, 209; Harold Coffin Syrett, *The City of Brooklyn, 1865–1898: A Political History* (New York: Columbia University Press, 1944), 183–185.

3. Sterngass, *First Resorts*, 235–237; Kasson, *Amusing the Million*, 34; Edward S. Sears, *Souvenir Guide to Coney Island* (Brooklyn, NY: Megaphone Press, 1905), 3; Syrett, *City of Brooklyn*, 186, 193.

4. Kasson, *Amusing the Million*, 58; Jeffrey Stanton, "Coney Island—Sea Lion Park," https://www .westland.net/coneyisland/articles/sealionpark.htm.

5. Kasson, *Amusing the Million*, 63–66; Albert Bigelow Paine, "The New Coney Island," *Century Magazine*, August 1904, 538, quoted in Kasson, 66.

6. Walter Ehrlich, *Zion in the Valley: The Jewish Community of St. Louis*, vol. I (Columbia: University of Missouri Press, 1997), 155–158; "St. Louis," *Jeweler's Circular*, May 17, 1899; "Giant Aerial Globe," *St. Louis Republic*, March 17, 1901. Minnie Friede would never wed and cared for her father till the end of his life.

7. "Giant Aerial Globe," *St. Louis Republic*, March 17, 1901.

8. "Project for St. Louis Fair," *New York Times*, August 28, 1901; "Cyrus F. Blanke Resigns from Concessions Committee" and "Friede Aerial Globe May Get Concession," *St. Louis Republic*, August 28, 1901) "Wonders of the Friede World's Fair Globe," *St. Louis Republic*, December 22, 1901; "Talk of Plans for the Fried Globe," *St. Louis Republic*, June 22, 1901. The Faust Blend globe advertisement ran in a number of national magazines and newspapers, including the *American Monthly Review of Reviews*.

9. "Book Almanacks," *British Printer* 4:21 (May–June 1891): 100; "Palacio's Design for a Columbus Monument," *Manufacturer and Builder* 23:1 (January 1891): 18; *Picture Magazine* (January–June 1893): 53. I have been unable to determine where the earlier, Madrileño version of the globe—"Proyecto de Monumento á Cristóbal Colón"—was first published.

10. "Wonders of the Friede World's Fair Globe," *St. Louis Republic*, December 22, 1901.

11. "A City in the Clouds," *St. Louis Republic*, November 3, 1901; "Recent Exploits of Science and Invention," *Brooklyn Daily Eagle*, September 5, 1903. Sans Souci, which closed in 1913, was later the site of Frank Lloyd Wright's legendary Midway Gardens.

12. Sears, *Souvenir Guide to Coney Island*, 12.

13. "Decoration Day at Coney Island" (advertisement), *New York Daily Tribune*, May 27, 1906; Friede Globe Tower Company, "Did You See Our Advertisement in Last Sunday's Paper?" (advertisement), *Sun*, January 26, 1906. Friede's office at Steeplechase was initially in Tilyou's just-completed post office building; the company's offices in New York were on the fifteenth floor of 27 William Street.

14. "Friede Tower Fiasco Swallowed $346,000," *Brooklyn Daily Eagle*, August 14, 1909; Samuel M. Friede, *Friede Globe Tower: Built of Steel, 700 Feet High* (New York: self-published, 1906), 3–8, 21–22; "Decoration Day at Coney Island" (advertisement), *New York Daily Tribune*, May 27, 1906. Cleverdon and Putzel are listed as "associated architects" in an advertisement in the *Bridgeport Herald*, February 4, 1906, 4.

15. "Cornerstone Laid for Friede Globe Tower," *Brooklyn Standard Union*, May 31, 1906; "New York Parks," *Billboard*, March 16, 1907, 29; Friede Globe Tower Company, "Friede Globe Tower" (advertisement), *Sun*, September 1, 1906; "First Shaft of Globe Tower," *Brooklyn Daily Eagle*, February 18, 1907.

16. "Coney Island Reserves Out," *New York Times*, March 1, 1907; "New York Parks," *Billboard*, March 16, 1907, 29; "Big Friede Tower Steel Order," *New-York Tribune*, March 31, 1907; "Steel for the Big Tower," *New York Times*, March 31, 1907.

17. "Broker Out of Firm for Believing Wade," *New York Times*, February 24, 1912; "Wade Sues Friede Tower Co.," *New York Sun*, April 9, 1907.

18. "Sheriff Releases Eiffel of Coney," *New York Herald*, April 10, 1907; "Henry Clay Wade Arrested," *New York Times*, April 26, 1907; "Charge Is That Wade Cashed Tilyou Check," *Brooklyn Daily Eagle*, April 26, 1907; "Friede Tower Ex-Treasurer to Jail," *New York Times*, May 30, 1907.

19. "Friede Tower Boomer," *Brooklyn Daily Eagle*, March 21, 1907; "Charges City Job Was Used to Push Stock Sale," *New York Press*, August 13, 1909.

20. Samuel M. Friede, " An Open Letter to the Public," *New-York Daily Tribune*, October 6, 1907; "Tilyou Wins in Friede Case," *New York Clipper*, June 27, 1908. Friede brought a second suit, but after months of litigation and appeals the case was also decided in Tilyou's favor.

21. "Eviction by Dynamite for Friede 'Tower,'" *Brooklyn Daily Eagle*, February 22, 1909; "Dynamite Coney," *Billboard*, March 6, 1909.

22. "Circus by the Sea," *New-York Tribune*, May 3, 1908; "Coney Island Hippodrome Circus," *New York Times*, May 24, 1908; "Gossip of Amusement World," *Brooklyn Daily Eagle*, May 28, 1908; "Circus at Coney Island," *New-York Tribune*, May 24, 1908; "Circus Men Stranded," *New-York Tribune*, June 10, 1908; "Actors in Hard Luck, Stranded at Coney," *Brooklyn Daily Eagle*, June 7, 1908.

23. "Mr. Moore Enlivens Coler Investigation," *Brooklyn Eagle*, August 12, 1909; "Contractor Paid," *Standard Union*, August 25, 1909; "Tilyou Was Pounded by Building Dept.," *Brooklyn Daily Eagle*, August 26, 1909.

24. "No Petty Graft in Langan's Plan," *Brooklyn Eagle*, August 13, 1909; "Coler's Man in Tower Deal," *Sun*, August 13, 1909.

25. "Friede Tower Fiasco Swallowed $346,000," *Brooklyn Eagle*, August 14, 1909; "No Petty Graft in Langan's Plan," *Brooklyn Eagle*, August 13, 1909.

26. "Eviction by Dynamite for Friede 'Tower,'" *Brooklyn Daily Eagle*, February 22, 1909; "Tilyou Was Pounded by Building Dept.," *Brooklyn Daily Eagle*, August 26, 1909. Incredibly, instead of ordering the work stopped, Coler turned to Tilyou and asked what he thought they should do.

27. "An Iridescent Dream," *Brooklyn Daily Eagle*, June 12, 1913. Hinsdale studied at the New York School of Art and trained with Clinton and Russell before establishing a firm of his own in Cleveland in 1904. He designed the Park Lane Villa residential hotel, Agudath B'nai Israel temple, several churches, and numerous homes in Cleveland Heights and Shaker Heights.

28. Milton Berger quoted in Michael P. Onorato, *Another Time, Another World: Coney Island Memories* (Fullerton: M. P. Onorato and California State University—Fullerton Oral History Program, 1988), 35.

29. Sigfried Giedion, *Space, Time and Architecture: The Growth of a New Tradition* (Cambridge, MA: Harvard University Press, 1952), 164–169.

30. "Steeplechase Park Plans," *New York Press*, February 16, 1908; "New Steeplechase Pushed," *New York Press*, March 17, 1908; "Coney Island," *New York Press*, October 11, 1908; "Fortunes Found at Coney Island," *Billboard*, March 21, 1908; "Work on Coney Island Parks Progressing Rapidly," *Billboard*, March 21, 1908.

31. Reginald Wright Kauffman, "Why Is Coney?" *Hampton's Magazine*, January 1909, 224; "Coler's Record Scored by the Evening Post," *Brooklyn Daily Eagle*, October 17, 1909.

CHAPTER 9. PORT OF EMPIRE

1. "If the Coney Creek Is Deepened," *Brooklyn Standard Union*, May 11, 1918; Harry Chase Brearley, *The Problem of Greater New York and Its Solution* (New York: Committee on Industrial Development of the Brooklyn League / Search-Light Book Corporation, 1914), 40–41; "A Vast Project for Transforming New York's Marshlands," *New York Times*, March 13, 1910; New York, New Jersey Port and Harbor Development Commission, *Joint Report with Comprehensive Plan and Recommendations* 1:4 (Albany, NY: J. B. Lyon Company, 1920), 342; Harold A. Caparn, "A Great Water Park in Jamaica Bay, New York," in *Transactions of the American Society of Landscape Architects*, ed. Harold A. Caparn, J. S. Pray, and Downing Vaux (Harrisburg, PA: J. Horace McFarland Company, 1907), 94.

2. Caparn, "A Great Water Park," 92; "Jamaica Bay Port's Savior, Ruston Says," *Brooklyn Standard Union*, December 6, 1928.

3. Cody and Auwaerter, *Cultural Landscape Report for Floyd Bennett Field*, 15–18; Frederick R. Black, *Jamaica Bay: A History* (Washington, DC: National Park Service, 1981), 8–9; Pritchard, *Native New Yorkers*, 433n.

4. Brearley, *Problem of Greater New York*, 42.

5. Joseph Caccavajo, *The Development of Brooklyn and Queens* (Brooklyn, NY: Allied Boards, 1909), 1.

6. Edward M. Grout, *Improvement and Development of Jamaica Bay* (New York: Martin B. Brown Press, 1905), 3–16.

7. Black, *Jamaica Bay*, 23; Phoebe Neidl, "A Brief History of the Gowanus Canal," *Brooklyn Daily Eagle*, April 10, 2012; Stiles, *Civil, Political, Professional and Ecclesiastical History and Commercial and Industrial Record*, 641–644.

8. New York, New Jersey Port and Harbor Development Commission, *Joint Report with Comprehensive Plan and Recommendations*, 11–13; Daniel Bell, *The End of Ideology: On the Exhaustion of Political Ideas in the Fifties* (Glencoe, IL: Free Press, 1960), 178, 188; Wilcox in *Joint Report*, 2. According to Bell, shore-handling costs, which "once were a minor factor in the operation of a boat . . . began to exceed the combined costs of vessel depreciation, crew's wages, insurance, supplies, overhead, maintenance, and fuel oil."

9. George Ethelbert Walsh, "Traffic Congestion in New York," *Cassier's Magazine*, June 1908, 151–158; *Proceedings of the Barge Canal Terminal Commission of the State of New York*, vol. 2 (Albany, NY: J. B. Lyon Company, 1911), 457; "No Pier Extension Ruling Will Aid Brooklyn and L.I.," *Brooklyn Daily Eagle*, March 1, 1911; "As to Herrings on Piers," *Sun*, December 3, 1912.

10. Philip P. Farley, William G. Ford, and John J. McLaughlin, *Report of the Jamaica Bay Improvement Commission* (New York: Martin P. Brown Press, 1907), 6–15; "If the Coney Creek Is Deepened," *Brooklyn Standard Union*, May 11, 1918; Walsh quoted in Brearley, *Problem of Greater New York*, 44.

11. "America Host to the Masters of the World's Commerce," *New York Times*, September 22, 1912; Richard Campanella, *Time and Place in New Orleans* (New Orleans, LA: Pelican Publishing, 2002), 73; Roy G. Finch, *The Story of the New York State Canals* (Albany: State of New York, 1925), 11–17; Noble E. Whitford, *History of the Barge Canal of New York State* (Albany, NY: J. B. Lyon Company, 1922), 5–12, 13–15, 131.

12. "Urges US to Hustle for Panama Trade," *New York Times*, February 18, 1912; "Erie Basin Docks," *New York Times*, September 21, 1913; "State Barge Canal Terminal Opened," *Sun*, October 15, 1919; Whitford, *History of the Barge Canal*, 528; "Jamaica Bay Port Building Plan Boomed," *Long Island Daily Press*, November 18, 1922; Frank M. Williams, *Annual Report of the State Engineer and Surveyor for the Year Ended June 30, 1919* (Albany, NY: J. B. Lyon Company, 1920), 14–18.

13. *Proceedings of the Barge Canal Terminal Commission of the State of New York*, 453; "Jamaica Bay Port Building Plan Boomed," *Long Island Daily Press*, November 18, 1922; Whitford, *History of the Barge Canal*, 434–436; John B. Creighton, "Borough Will Be Factory Centre," *New York Times*, May 3, 1908.

14. "If the Coney Creek Is Deepened," *Brooklyn Standard Union*, May 11, 1918; "Ask $882,910 to Buy Canal Right of Way," *New York Times*, February 3, 1920.

15. Its present outfall is about four thousand feet from the western end of runway 13R-31L, the airport's busiest and one of the longest commercial runways in North America.

16. The first of the alternative routes started at Bergen Basin and moved inland along 130th Street, crossing Rockaway Boulevard just west of Lincoln Street and joining the alignment described above at Liberty Avenue and Remington Street in South Jamaica—about where the Vibes Nightclub stands today. The other led from Cornell Creek across the terminal moraine near Midland Parkway in Jamaica Estates, and on to Flushing Bay via the old Mill Creek valley through Kissena Park.

17. The south tidal lock was to be located just before the canal crossed today's Belt Parkway, in the vicinity of Exit 19; the north lock about where Ederle Terrace stands today in Flushing Meadows Park.

18. Whitford, *History of the Barge Canal*, 415–416.

19. "Proposed Canal across the Island," *New York Times*, May 31, 1908.

20. "Jamaica Bay Work Begins This Spring," *New York Times*, March 17, 1912; "Material for Homes Via New Canal," *Brooklyn Daily Eagle*, November 6, 1915; "Barge Canal to Jamaica Bay Direct," *New York Sun*, November 7, 1915; "Barge Canal Shipment," *New York Times*, November 7, 1915.

21. "A State Scandal," *Evening World*, October 13, 1914.

22. Christopher Gray, "The Columbia Street Grain Elevator," *New York Times*, May 13, 1990.

23. Denton, *A Brief Description of New York*, 5, in *Proceedings of the Historical Society of Pennsylvania*, ed. John Pennington, 1:1 (Philadelphia: Press of the Historical Society of Pennsylvania); Black, *Jamaica Bay*, 22–23; "Answers of Gov. Andros to Enquiries about New York; 1678," in *Documentary History of the State of New-York*, vols. 1–3 (Albany, NY: Weed, Parsons & Co., 1849), 88–92; "Gov. Dongan's Report to the Committee of Trade on the Province of New-York, Dated 22nd February, 1687," in *Documentary History*, 160–161; "Report of His Excellency William Tryon, Esquire," in *Documentary History*, 752.

24. "A Vast Project for Transforming New York's Marshlands," *New York Times*, March 13, 1910; "Ask $882,910 to Buy Canal Right of Way," *New York Times*, February 3, 1920. Cody and Auwaerter suggest that the rapid accumulation of sand may have partly been the result of "jetties, groin fields, and other beach stabilization structures that were created to protect beach-front communities" in the area. See *Cultural Landscape Report for Floyd Bennett Field*, 15–18.

25. John B. Creighton, "Borough Will Be Factory Centre," *New York Times*, May 3, 1908.

26. John H. Ward, *Trinity Freight Terminal in the City of New York* (New York: Waterfront Investments, 1919), 3–4, 23–25.

27. Dongan, 1687, in *Documentary History*, 151–153; John B. Creighton, "Borough Will Be Factory Centre," *New York Times*, May 3, 1908; Harold A. Caparn, "A Great Water Park in Jamaica Bay, New York," *Transactions of the American Society of Landscape Architects*, 93.

28. "Jamaica Bay Improvements," *Long Island Daily Press*, April 12, 1921; "Jamaica Bay Work Starts," *Brooklyn Daily Eagle*, June 7, 1921.

CHAPTER 10. THE MINISTRY OF IMPROVEMENT

1. "Purchase of a Slave in Plymouth Church," *Brooklyn Eagle*, February 6, 1860.

2. Ira W. Henderson, "Newell Dwight Hillis: An Appreciation," n/d, Box 8, Newell Dwight Hillis Papers (1883–1964), Othmer Library Archives and Manuscripts, Brooklyn Historical Society.

3. Peter Clark MacFarlane, "Newell Dwight Hillis: The Preacher Who Is Conspiring to Make Brooklyn Beautiful," *Collier's* 49:18 (July 20, 1912): 21; Benjamin B. Warfield, "The Making of the Westminster Confession," *Presbyterian and Reformed Review* 45 (January 1901): 282; "Dr. Hillis May Quit the Presbytery," *New York Times*, March 28, 1900.

4. "Robert A. Van Wyck Dies in Paris Home," *New York Times*, November 16, 1918; "The Responsibility of People for the City's Government and Rulers," *Brooklyn Daily Eagle*, October 28, 1901.

5. "Rev. Dr. Hillis Speaks on Tammany Hall," *New York Times*, October 28, 1901; "The Responsibility of People for the City's Government and Rulers," *Brooklyn Daily Eagle*, October 28, 1901; "Mark Twain and Seth Low Speak," *New York Times*, October 30, 1901.

6. "Dr. Lyman Abbott Discusses the Negro," *New York Times*, July 5, 1903; "Dr. Abbott on the Negro," *New York Times*, May 24, 1901.

7. "Grover Cleveland on Negro Problem," *New York Times*, April 15, 1903.

8. "Dr. Hillis Demands Vote for the Negro," *New York Times*, May 18, 1903; Emmett J. Scott, *Booker T. Washington: Builder of a Civilization* (Garden City, NY: Doubleday, Page & Company, 1917), 125–126; "Hillis Would Make Bed for Booker Washington," *Brooklyn Daily Eagle*, May 22, 1903.

9. "Dr. Hillis Plans a Tunnel to Relieve the Bridge," *Brooklyn Daily Eagle*, March 7, 1902.

10. "'To Hades on a Brooklyn Car,'" *New York Herald*, May 2, 1903; "Masked Dancers in the Dance of Life," *Evening Telegram*, May 13, 1903; "Brooklyn and East Side War over Bridge Loop," *New York Times*, June 16, 1906; "Charge Graft in Plan for an Elevated Loop," *New York Times*, February 27, 1905; "Hoots and Cat-Calls at Bridge Loop Hearing," *New York Times*, January 4, 1907; "Denounce Transit Board," *New York Times*, January 17, 1907. Bassett, vice-chairman of the Brooklyn Committee on City Plan, authored New York City's first zoning ordinance in 1916.

11. Stuart Meck and Rebecca C. Retzlaff, "A Familiar Ring: A Retrospective on the First National Conference on City Planning (1909)," *Planning and Environmental Law* 61:4 (April 2009): 3–10; "To Avoid Congestion, Brooklyn Must Act Now," *Brooklyn Daily Eagle*, April 7, 1908; *The Report of the New York City Improvement Commission* (New York: Kalkhoff Company, 1907), 20–21; William C. Hudson, "Planning a Grand Gateway to Brooklyn," *Brooklyn Daily Eagle*, May 23, 1909.

12. "Ideals for Our Own City," *Brooklyn Daily Eagle*, May 30, 1909.

13. Ibid.; "Life in the Great City," *Brooklyn Daily Eagle*, September 20, 1909. Lamb's famous essay "The Londoner" (1802) mocked the gentry's enchantment with rural life, claiming that a crush of theatergoers in Drury Lane gave him "ten thousand sincerer pleasures, than I could ever receive from all the flocks of silly sheep that ever whitened the plains of Arcadia." See *The Works of Charles Lamb*, vol. 4 (London: Edward Moxon, 1855), 159–161.

14. "Ideals for Our Own City," *Brooklyn Daily Eagle*, May 30, 1909.

15. "Heights Demand Heard for Better Transit," *Brooklyn Daily Eagle*, February 3, 1910; "Heights Demands Rights," *New York Times*, February 6, 1910; "Brooklyn's Future Development Plan," *New York Times*, April 9, 1911. The Clark Street tunnel to Brooklyn, begun in 1914, was engineered by Clifford Milburn Holland, who later designed the first tunnel to New Jersey.

16. "Permanent Committee Formed to Work with City Officials," *New York Times*, February 4, 1912; "Boston—1915 Program for 1911," *New Boston*, July 1911, 83–85; see also Lawrence W. Kennedy, *Planning the City upon A Hill* (Boston: University of Massachusetts Press, 1992), 123–125; "Dr. Hillis on the Great Strike," *Brooklyn Daily Eagle*, October 16, 1911.

17. "MacMonnies' arch" is the Soldiers and Sailors Memorial Arch in Grand Army Plaza, with sculptural groups designed by Frederick W. MacMonnies.

18. "Dr. Hillis' Sermon—What Can Be Learned from France," *Brooklyn Daily Eagle*, October 30, 1911. Hillis was incensed that the mayor had just nixed a proposal to erect a National Academy of Design gallery in Bryant Park. Opposition to the plan was led by Charles N. Lowrie, a Yale-trained engineer who, as president of the American Society of Landscape Architects from 1910 to 1912, fought several high-profile battles to keep Tammany Hall from usurping park land for building projects. See "National Academy after Another Park," *New York Times*, December 25, 1910.

19. Newell Dwight Hillis to Daniel H. Burnham, October 23, 1911, Daniel H. Burnham Collection (1836–1946), Ryerson and Burnham Archives, Ryerson and Burnham Library, The Art Institute of Chicago.

20. "A More Beautiful City," *Brooklyn Daily Eagle*, November 6, 1911.

21. Ibid.

22. "See a Beautified Brooklyn Ahead," *New York Times*, November 30, 1911; "As Brooklyn Would Look under Dr. Hillis' Improvement," *Brooklyn Daily Eagle*, November 6, 1911.

23. "A More Beautiful City," *Brooklyn Daily Eagle*, November 6, 1911; "Citizens Approve Rev. Dr. Hillis' Plan," *Brooklyn Daily Eagle* (n.d.); "As Brooklyn Would Look under Dr. Hillis' Improvement," *Brooklyn Daily Eagle*, November 6, 1911; Newell Dwight Hillis to Daniel H. Burnham, November 29, 1911, Daniel H. Burnham Collection (1836–1946), Ryerson and Burnham Archives.

24. Christopher Hussey, *The Life of Sir Edwin Lutyens* (1953), in Peter Hall, *Cities of Tomorrow* (Oxford: Blackwell, 1988), 184.

25. "May Put Brooklyn in Burnham's Hands," *New York Times*, December 17, 1911; "Chicago Architect Aid in Move to Beautify Brooklyn," *Herald Tribune*, December 17, 1911; "For a 'Brooklyn Beautiful,'" *Sun*, December 17, 1911.

26. "Permanent Committee for Laying Out Great Development Plan for Brooklyn," *Brooklyn Daily Eagle*, December 17, 1911; Frederick Boyd Stevenson, "Daniel H. Burnham, a Leader in City Planning," *Brooklyn Daily Eagle*, December 17, 1911; "Planning to Make Brooklyn a City Beautiful," *New York Times*, February 4, 1912; "Brooklyn's Unique Opportunity," *Brooklyn Daily Eagle*, December 18, 1911; Newell Dwight Hillis to Daniel H. Burnham, December 9, 1911, Daniel H. Burnham Collection (1836–1946), Ryerson and Burnham Archives.

27. Report enclosed with letter from Newell Dwight Hillis to Daniel H. Burnham, January 9, 1912, Ryerson and Burnham Archives; David L. A. Gordon, "The Other Author of the 1908 Plan of Chicago," *Planning Perspectives* 25:2 (April 2010): 229–230.

28. "Brooklyn City Plan," *Brooklyn Daily Eagle*, January 18, 1914; "May Fight over Beauty," *New-York Tribune*, December 24, 1911.

29. *Proceedings of the Fourth National Conference on City Planning* (Cambridge, MA: Harvard University Press, 1912), 198–210. The Boston City Club was founded by Brandeis and Filene as part of their Boston 1915 effort, modeled on the Commercial Club of Chicago, sponsor of the 1909 *Plan of Chicago*.

30. "Brieux Play Acted," *New York Times*, March 15, 1913; "Fifth Avenue Churches to Take Up Eugenics," *Sun*, June 6, 1913; "Pastors for Eugenics," *New York Times*, June 6, 1913; "Dr. Hillis on Eugenics," *New York Times*, November 24, 1913; Christine Rosen, *Preaching Eugenics*: Religious Leaders and the American Eugenics Movement (New York: Oxford University Press, 2004), 88. See also Upton Sinclair, *Damaged Goods: The Great Play "Les Avariés" of Brieux* (Philadelphia: The John C. Winston Company, 1913).

31. According to the 1900 Federal Census, John and Ella Kellogg had eleven children, including a boy named Ricardo, age eight (who became a dentist at the sanitarium), and a daughter, Teressita, age six, both born in Mexico. Newell, the youngest, was born in 1895. All eleven are listed as "parentage unknown."

32. Emily F. Robbins, ed., *Proceedings of the First National Conference on Race Betterment* (Battle Creek, MI: Race Betterment Foundation, 1914), 1–2. The title page of the *Proceedings* quoted Herbert Spencer: "To be a good animal is the first requisite to success in life, and to be a Nation of good animals is the first condition of national prosperity."

33. "Needed—A New Human Race," *Brooklyn Daily Eagle*, January 19, 1914; Robbins, *Proceedings*, 350–355.

34. Rosen, *Preaching Eugenics*, 90. The organizer's large Central Committee included Charles W. Eliot, president emeritus of Harvard University, Charles B. Davenport, founder of the Eugenics Record Office in Cold Spring Harbor, and conservationist and father of the US Forest Service Gifford Pinchot. Of all the colleges in the northeastern states, only Cornell sent representatives to the conference—Walter F. Willcox, who taught the first course on statistics at Cornell, and Arthur W. Gilbert, a professor of plant breeding at the New York State College of Agriculture. See Robbins, *Proceedings*, xi–xiv.

35. Newell Dwight Hillis, "Dangers of the American Physique," *Brooklyn Daily Eagle*, January 19, 1914; Margaret Sanger, "The Eugenic Value of Birth Control Propaganda," *Birth Control Review* 5:10 (October 1921); Robbins, *Proceedings*, 592; Andrew Goliszek, *In the Name of Science: A History of Secret Programs, Medical Research, and Human Experimentation* (New York: Macmillan, 2003), 88.

36. Newell Dwight Hillis, *Murder Most Foul!* (London: Field and Queen, 1917), 3–4.

37. Newell Dwight Hillis, *The Blot on the Kaiser's 'Scutcheon* (New York: Fleming H. Revell Company, 1918), 10, 56–59.

CHAPTER 11. SALT MARSH OF SUNKEN DREAMS

1. Bennett was not the first to see the value of a park in this location, but he was the first to feature it prominently in a plan. The 1907 *Report of the New York City Improvement Commission* recommended that

"Paerdegat Basin and the basin of Garretson Creek . . . be reserved for park purposes." It was also the first to envision the circumferential drive that both Hillis and Bennett proposed, and that would eventually become the Belt Parkway. See *The Report of the New York City Improvement Commission* (New York: The Kalkhoff Company, 1907), 20–21.

2. Constance Rosenblum, "A Building with a Heart of Gold," *New York Times*, December 9, 2011.

3. Edward Murray Bassett, *The Gift of Gerritsen Park to the City of New York* (pamphlet, 1935, Brooklyn Collection, Brooklyn Public Library); "Hirshfield Warns against New Park," *New York Times*, May 17, 1923; *Marine Park and Its Influence on Realty Values* (brochure, c. 1930, Charles Downing Lay Papers, 1898–1956, Division of Rare and Manuscript Collections Library, Cornell University).

4. "Jamaica Bay Park, Gift to City of White and Pratt, Awaits Signature of Mayor," *Brooklyn Daily Eagle*, July 2, 1922; Carl Wilhelm, "Greatest Marine Park in the World Is Planned by City along Ocean Front with Gerritsen Park and Basin as the Center," *Brooklyn Daily Eagle*, March 30, 1924; "Marine Park, with Two-Mile Waterfront and 1,240 Acres of Scenic Beauty, Will Be One of City's Most Popular Playgrounds within a Few Years," *Brooklyn Daily Eagle*, August 9, 1925.

5. Mark D. Hirsch, *William C. Whitney: Modern Warwick* (New York: Dodd, Mead, 1948), 584; "Plan to Transform Garretson's Creek," *Brooklyn Daily Eagle*, January 2, 1900; Ditmas, *Historic Homesteads of Kings County*, 37; "Old Whitney Mill Built Back in 1500, Civic Body Claims," *Brooklyn Daily Eagle*, August 28, 1927. A lesser structure from the Whitney estate—often confused with the demolished manor house—was moved to 2356 Burnett Street, where it still stands, clad in vinyl siding and guarded by cast stone lions.

6. "Italian Plants Vegetables Where Municipal Fathers Were to Build Rival of Detroit's Belle Isle," *Brooklyn Daily Eagle*, April 27, 1926; "Farmer-Squatters Permitted to Stay at Marine Park," *Brooklyn Daily Eagle*, April 28, 1926; "Walker Dedicates Marine Park Field," *New York Times*, August 28, 1930.

7. Sol Bloom, *The Autobiography of Sol Bloom* (New York: G. P. Putnam's Sons, 1948), 120, 215.

8. "World Exposition in Brooklyn Park Sought by Bloom," *Brooklyn Daily Eagle*, March 1, 1926; "Bloom Outlines World Fair Here to Congressmen," *Brooklyn Daily Eagle*, December 18, 1925; "Chamber of Commerce Outlines Great Plans for Boro Betterment," *Brooklyn Daily Eagle*, January 8, 1926; "Ask Walker's Aid," *New York Times*, February 1, 1928; "Chamberlin Aviation Chief of Washington Exposition," *Brooklyn Daily Eagle*, June 24, 1928; "A Washington Fair," *New York Times*, December 6, 1925; "Wants World Fair on Jamaica Bay," *New York Times*, December 1, 1925; "Sol Bloom Defends World's Fair Plans," *New York Times*, August 10, 1928; "Two Officials Quit 1932 Fair Campaign," *New York Times*, February 25, 1928; George Boochever, "A Permanent World's Fair," *New York Times*, March 1, 1928. The searchlight was a figment of Bloom's imagination: curvature of the earth would curtail the distance even a very powerful light could be seen. My line-of-sight calculations, assuming a 1,110-foot tower (twice the 555 feet of the Washington Monument), would limit the beam's visibility to some fifty miles at best.

9. "Joe Guider Was Daddy of City World's Fair," *Brooklyn Daily Eagle*, June 11, 1937; "Flatbush United for World's Fair," *Brooklyn Daily Eagle*, February 24, 1928; "Sol Bloom Defends World's Fair Plans," *New York Times*, August 10, 1928; "Marine Park World's Fair Hope Doomed," *Standard Union*, August 21, 1929.

10. Robert Moses, *The Saga of Flushing Meadow* (New York: Triborough Bridge and Tunnel Authority, 1966).

11. "Park Commissioner Browne Proposes 30 to 50 Millions Expenditure on Elaborate Layout of Marine Park," *Brooklyn Daily Eagle*, January 1, 1928; "Urge Contest to Fix Marine Park Plan," *Brooklyn Daily Eagle*, October 1, 1930; "Walker Dedicates Marine Park Field," *New York Times*, August 28, 1930; "Notables Attend Formal Opening of Marine Park," *Brooklyn Daily Eagle*, August 28, 1930; "Seven Years Pass for Marine Park, but Where Is It?" *Brooklyn Daily Eagle*, April 28, 1931. Burgevin served as Parks Department landscape architect for fourteen years, until his death in June 1934. He had been hit by a truck several weeks earlier while crossing Jerome Avenue in the Bronx. See "J. V. Burgevin Dead of Auto Injuries, *New York Times*, June 7, 1934. The original bronze plaque noting Pratt and White's gift was restored and affixed to the new Marine Park field house in 2014.

12. "C. D. Lay Named Park Architect," *New York Times*, August 11, 1911; Charles A. Birnbaum and Robin Karson, *Pioneers of American Landscape Design* (New York: McGraw-Hill, 2000), 221–223; Charles D. Lay to Board of Park Commissioners, May 1, 1913, Charles Downing Lay Papers, 1898–1956, Division of Rare and Manuscript Collections Library, Cornell University; Charles Downing Lay, *The Freedom of the City* (New York: Duffield and Company, 1926), 8, 46. Also see "Stover Again Loses His Park Architect," *New York Times*, May 2, 1913. The colorful Stover was not the easiest commissioner to get along with. Lay's predecessor, Samuel Parsons, had also resigned after a series of clashes with him.

13. Charles Downing Lay, "Tidal Marshes," *Landscape Architecture* 2:3 (April 1912): 101–102.

14. "Straus to Quit Sick Bed for Park Fight," *Brooklyn Daily Eagle*, April 6, 1931; "Lay, Surprise Architect, Has No Park Plans," *Brooklyn Daily Eagle*, March 26, 1931; "Park Contest Plea Pressed by Straus," *New York Times*, April 27, 1931; "Walker Favors Lay as Park Designer," *New York Times*, May 13, 1931; "Wants Group to

Aid Lay on Marine Park," *New York Times*, June 7, 1931. Straus demanded that Browne appoint an advisory committee drawn from the American Society of Landscape Architects to supervise Lay's work, arguing that "no one man is big enough or far-seeing enough" for such a huge project.

15. "Art to Transform Marshes into a Great Marine Park," *New York Times*, June 21, 1931.

16. "Architect Completes Marine Park Plans," *Brooklyn Daily Eagle*, February 25, 1932; "Design Completed for Marine Park," *New York Times*, February 25, 1932; "Plans Marine Park as World's Biggest," *New York Times*, February 26, 1932; "Sees 5 Million Annual Yield in Marine Park," *Brooklyn Daily Eagle*, February 26, 1932; "Plans for Marine Park Shown," *New York Sun*, February 25, 1932. The Utica Avenue subway extension is noted in "Huge Stadium Planned for Rockne Field Here to Seat 100,000 for Big Football Games," *New York Times*, October 17, 1931. Commissioner Browne promptly hung Lay's vast canvas in his office at the Brooklyn parks headquarters in the Litchfield villa; it has since been lost.

17. "Design Completed for Marine Park," *New York Times*, February 25, 1932; O. R. Pilat, "Marine Park Is New Front Door to Boro," *Brooklyn Times-Union*, March 10, 1932; "Huge Stadium Planned," *New York Times*, October 17, 1931.

18. Dominick Cavallo, *Muscles and Morals: Organized Playgrounds and Urban Reform, 1880–1920* (Philadelphia: University of Pennsylvania Press, 1981), 2–4; Charles W. Eliot, "Welfare and Happiness in Works of Landscape Architecture," *Landscape Architecture* 1:3 (April 1911): 147. There was no little irony in the new obsession with programmed play; as Cranz notes, "the substitute for the loss of the traditional creative satisfactions of work was to specialize recreation in the same way that work is specialized rather than to try to reunite human activites." See Galen Cranz, *The Politics of Park Design: A History of Urban Parks in America* (Cambridge, MA: MIT Press, 1982), 62.

19. Charles Downing Lay, "Playground Design," *Landscape Architecture* 2:2 (January 1912): 64; "Marine Park," *Brooklyn Daily Eagle*, March 13, 1932.

20. "Marine Park Made Paradise for Snipe," *Brooklyn Daily Eagle*, August 3, 1931. Snipe are notoriously difficult to shoot, hence the origin of "sniper" to describe a marksman of particular skill. The twenty-seven-hundred-ton *Lake Fithian* was built in 1919 by the Globe Shipbuilding Company of Superior, Wisconsin, for the United States Shipping Board, one of scores of "Lakers" built to haul material during World War I. It was later acquired by the New Orleans and South American Steamship Company and used on the first direct steamship line between New Orleans and the west coast of South America, sailing via the Panama Canal to Ecuador, Peru, and Chile. The vessel was sold in 1926 to William Clifford, who had just patented a technique for converting ordinary freight vessels into hydraulic or cutter-suction dredges. The reborn *Lake Fithian*, launched in 1927, may have been converted specifically for flood-control work on the Mississippi and was likely also used to create Jones Beach State Park. It was later acquired by Société française d'entreprises de dragages et de travaux publics and Amsterdamse Ballast Maatschapij (ABM) of the Netherlands, which operated it on the Suez Canal until Egypt nationalized the waterway (triggering the Suez Crisis and the second Arab-Israeli War). In 1958 AMB began operating the dredge on a World Bank–funded project to eliminate shoals on the Hooghly River below Calcutta. On the night of November 18, 1960, a powerful tidal bore swung the aged vessel around on its moorings; as it leaned, the boilers broke free and fell, causing the vessel to capsize. Most of the fifty-odd men on board escaped, but twelve Dutch and five Indian crew members were trapped and drowned. The river quickly silted over the wreck, which was not recovered for months. See *Tenth Annual Report of the United States Shipping Board* (Washington, DC: General Printing Office, 1926), 90; "Ramp met 'Lake Fithian' is niet helemaal een geheim . . ." *De Waarheid*, December 17, 1960.

21. "Marine Park Lagoon Started," *Brooklyn Daily Eagle*, February 17, 1933; "Huge Marine Park Begun in Brooklyn," *Brooklyn Daily Eagle*, February 17, 1933; Charles Downing Lay, "City Generous in Marine Park Unemployment Aid," *Brooklyn Daily Eagle*, October 26, 1933; "Lack of Material Holding Up Work at Marine Park," *Brooklyn Daily Eagle*, January 14, 1934; Caro, *The Power Broker*, 363, 370. The acting mayor, John P. O'Brien, and borough president Henry Hesterberg chose to attend instead a more photogenic affair—the opening of a new bascule bridge across Coney Island Creek.

22. Robert Moses, *Is There Any Reason to Suppose They Are Right Now?* (New York: Triborough Bridge Authority, June 3, 1939), 2–3, Box 1, Robert Moses Papers, Manuscripts and Archives Division, New York Public Library; Charles Downing Lay, *A Park System for Long Island: A Report to the Nassau County Committee* (privately printed, February 1925), 8–10, 16; Charles Downing Lay and David Dows, *The Nassau County Committee and State Parks on Long Island* (Glen Head, NY: The Nassau County Committee, October 1925), 5–6; Robert Moses to John A. Hefferman, July 8, 1938, Box 97, Robert Moses Papers, Manuscripts and Archives Division, New York Public Library; Moses to Thomas P. Smith, Jr., July 12, 1940, Parks Department General Files, New York City Municipal Archives; Robert Moses quoted in letter from Eugene S. McQuade to W. Earle Andrews, November 25, 1935, Box 97, Robert Moses Papers, Manuscripts and Archives Division, New York Public Library (McQuade was chairman of the Greenpoint Community Council); Robert Moses to Thomas P. Smith, Jr., July 12, 1940, Parks Department General Files, New York City Municipal Archives.

23. Charles Downing Lay, "Tidal Marshes," *Landscape Architecture* 2:3 (April 1912): 104.

24. "New Plans Ready for Marine Park," *New York Times*, September 7, 1934; "Plan for Proposed Marine Park Development," *Brooklyn Daily Eagle*, September 24, 1934; Robert Moses, memo to Allyn Jennings, August 27, 1936, Box 97, Robert Moses Papers, Manuscripts and Archives Division, New York Public Library.

25. "Entry Form for the Art Competition and Exhibition of the XIth Olympiad, Berlin," Art Section XI Olympiad Berlin, 1936, Charles Downing Lay Papers, 1898–1956, Division of Rare and Manuscript Collections Library, Cornell University. See also "New Yorker Wins Olympic Medal for Marine Park Landscape Plan," *New York Times*, August 1, 1936.

CHAPTER 12. GRAND CENTRAL OF THE AIR

1. "London Gives Read and Crew of NC-4 a Great Reception," *New York Times*, June 2, 1919.

2. "Boro Real Estate Men Will Push Plans for City Airport," *Brooklyn Daily Eagle*, July 3, 1927; "Canarsie Site for Airport Has 200-Acre Field," *Brooklyn Daily Eagle*, September 25, 1927; "Governors Island Favored as Municipal Airport Site," *Brooklyn Daily Eagle*, August 1, 1927; "Proposes Landing Field in Each Boro," *Brooklyn Daily Eagle,* August 10, 1927; Herbert Kaufman, *Gotham in the Air Age* (Washington, DC: Committee on Public Administration Cases, 1950), 11.

3. "Three Sites Are Urged for City Airport," *Brooklyn Daily Eagle*, July 13, 1927; "Dreamland Park, Red Hook Urged as Airport Sites," *Brooklyn Daily Eagle*, August 21, 1927; "Boro Real Estate Men Will Push Plans for City Airport," *Brooklyn Daily Eagle*, July 3, 1927; "Canarsie Site for Airport Has 200-Acre Field," *Brooklyn Daily Eagle*, September 25, 1927; *Report of the Fact-Finding Committee on Suitable Airport Facilities for the New York Metropolitan District* (Washington, DC, 1927); "New Device for Landing Airplanes," *New York Times*, November 11, 1928; Richard Gibbons, "Airplane-receiving apparatus," U.S. Patent 1,437,236, filed August 15, 1919; "Brooklyn Building with Airplane Landing," *New York Times*, June 22, 1919; "New Device Enables Planes to Land on Top of Buildings," *Brooklyn Daily Eagle*, February 3, 1924. A later magazine article—"Airplane Field for Tall City Buildings," *Mechanics and Handicraft*, October 1937, 47—credits another Brooklynite, J. Herbert Jones, with an identical structure, though his name appears in none of the earlier accounts.

4. "Tuttle Favors East Island as City's Airport," *Brooklyn Daily Eagle*, July 11, 1927; "Outlook Bright for Municipal Airport," *Brooklyn Daily Eagle*, May 22, 1927; Patrick W. Sullivan, "Floyd Bennett Field" (unpublished paper, St. Francis College, 1964), 4; "Hoover Report Names Five Sites for City Airports," *Brooklyn Daily Eagle*, December 20, 1927; "Brooklyn Likely to Have Airport on Flatbush Avenue," *Brooklyn Daily Eagle*, December 15, 1927.

5. "Pick Barren Island for City Airport," *New York Times*, December 29, 1927; "City Votes Airport on Barren Island," *New York Times*, February 3, 1928.

6. "Industrial Boom in Flatbush Seen," *Brooklyn Daily Eagle*, December 3, 1927; "Great Benefits in Utica Avenue Line," *New York Times*, October 9, 1910; "Officials Discuss Railroad Spur to New City Airport," *Brooklyn Daily Eagle*, February 9, 1928; "Court Told of First Airport Spite Fence," *Brooklyn Daily Eagle*, October 6, 1930; "Mill Basin Site for Airport Gets Civic Council O.K.," *Brooklyn Daily Eagle*, September 27, 1927; "Brooklyn's Air Terminal," *Brooklyn Daily Eagle*, May 23, 1931. Rizzo went on to a distinguished career as a military aviator. He later trained the first generation of New York City Police Department pilots and taught aviation mechanics with the Board of Education for many years. I had the pleasure of meeting Rizzo quite by chance at Floyd Bennett Field in the early 1990s, while he was meeting with National Park staff. Though in his nineties by then, he was still fit and active.

7. "Chamberlain Named as City's Air Engineer," *New York Times*, June 5, 1928; Wolfgang Saxon, "Charles A. Levine, 94, Is Dead," *New York Times*, December 18, 1991; "$2,750,000 Is Asked for City's Airport," *New York Times*, October 9, 1928.

8. "City Ready to Build Airport Hangars," *New York Times*, December 23, 1929; "Haven of Horseshoe Crabs Destroyed by City Airport," *New York Times*, January 27, 1929; "Floyd Bennett Field Grows from Sand Waste," *New York Times*, July 20, 1930; Porter R. Blakemore and Dana C. Linck, *Historic Structures Report, Historical Data Section, Floyd Bennett Field, Gateway National Recreation Area*, vol. 1 (National Park Service, Denver Service Center, unpublished report, 1981), 74–111; "Precast Ornamental Concrete Units Beautify Theater," *Engineering World*, November 1921, 319; Jeffrey W. Cody, *Exporting American Architecture* (London: Routledge, 2003), 108; "Work Is Under Way on Russian Housing," *New York Times*, July 7, 1929; Walter Duranty, "New Yorkers Get $25,000,000 Moscow Job to Construct Modern Apartments," *New York Times*, March 2, 1929; Matthew Spender, *From a High Place: A Life of Arshile Gorky* (Berkeley: University of California Press, 2000), 134, 145–149.

9. "Painter of Murals to Sue Somervell," *New York Times*, July 10, 1940; "Too Much 'Red' in Airport Murals," *Brooklyn Daily Eagle*, July 8, 1940; David R. George, "Artist Denies Murals Were Red," *Brooklyn*

Daily Eagle, July 9, 1940; "1916 Case Is Recalled," *New York Times*, July 12, 1940; "Begins Court Fight on New Districts," *Brooklyn Daily Eagle*, June 8, 1916; "White Gets 30 Days . . . for Desecrating Flag," *Brooklyn Daily Eagle*, March 15, 1917; "Airport Muralist Asks Police Guard," *Brooklyn Daily Eagle*, July 13, 1940; Rockwell Kent, "Those Rejected Murals," *New York Times*, July 27, 1940.

10. Cora L. Bennett, *Floyd Bennett* (New York: W. F. Payson, 1932), 1–12; Sheldon Bart, *Race to the Top of the World* (Washington, DC: Regnery History, 2013), 276–281; John H. Bryant and Harold N. Cones, *Dangerous Crossings: The First Modern Polar Expedition, 1925* (Annapolis, MD: Naval Institute Press, 2000). Floyd and Cora Bennett lived at the just-opened Patrician Court apartments, across from Prospect Park at 239 Ocean Avenue.

11. "Byrd Explorers Packed," *Brooklyn Daily Eagle*, April 5, 1926; Raimund E. Goerler, ed., *To the Pole: The Diary and Notebook of Richard E. Byrd, 1925–1927* (Columbus: Ohio State University Press, 1998), 41–79. The first Byrd polar expedition was controversial from the start. The race to the pole had pitched a number of very ambitious, competitive souls against each other, and it's hardly surprising that there would be questions raised as to who really got there first.

12. Goerler, *To the Pole*, 97–102; Bennett, *Floyd Bennett*, 138–149.

13. "Byrd Dedicates Bennett Air Field," *New York Times*, June 27, 1930.

14. "50,000 at Battery View Air Spectacle," *New York Times*, May 24, 1931; "Great Air Armada Thrills Millions," *New York Times*, May 24, 1931; "Air Show Dedicates Floyd Bennett Field," *New York Times*, May 24, 1931; "Air Fleet Saves New York from Imaginary Foes," *Chicago Tribune*, May 24, 1931; "Army Plane Falls, 2 Saved from Bay," *New York Times*, May 24, 1931.

15. "50,000 at Battery View Air Spectacle," *New York Times*, May 24, 1931; "Back of the Air Maneuvers," *Militant* 4:11 (June 1931): 8; "597 Planes Pass over the City in 22 Minutes," *New York Times*, May 24, 1931; "The Army Air Manoeuvres," *New York Times*, May 25, 1931; "Nation Hears Story of Flight over City," *New York Times*, May 24, 1931.

16. Lawrence H. Suid, *Guts & Glory: The Making of the American Military Image in Film* (Lexington: University Press of Kentucky, 2002), 52–53.

17. Blakemore and Linck, *Historic Structures Report*, 99, 118, 127; Cody and Auwaerter, *Cultural Landscape Report for Floyd Bennett Field*, 63, 67, 69.

18. Kaufman, *Gotham in the Air Age*, 14; "A Barren Island Airport," *New York Times*, February 4, 1928.

19. Clinton L. Mosher, "Plan Docks for Sea Planes," *Brooklyn Daily Eagle*, March 11, 1928; "World's First Roof-Top Landing Field to Link Downtown Brooklyn with Barren Island Airport," *Brooklyn Daily Eagle*, February 12, 1928; " 'Air Train' Ready to Fly from Here," *New York Times*, July 24, 1934; "First Air Train Hops, Gliders Carrying Mail," *Brooklyn Daily Eagle*, August 2, 1934; "Head Winds Balk First 'Sky Train,' " *New York Times*, August 3, 1934; "Air-Mail Train Reaches Washington, Day Late," *New York Herald Tribune*, August 4, 1934.

20. Megan Garber, "That Time People Sent a Cat through the Mail," *Atlantic*, August 13, 2013; "Stages Test to Show Air Mail Tube Need," *New York Times*, January 30, 1930. It has taken me only about twenty-five minutes to get from the Flatbush Avenue terminus near Brooklyn College to the Wall Street Station on the 5 train (Lexington Avenue Express), and that's making eleven stops along the way. An airport express from Floyd Bennett Field, making a single stop at, say, Atlantic Avenue, would take no more time than that. Sadly, both the Nostrand Avenue and Utica Avenue subway extensions remain mere pipe dreams, although Mayor Bill de Blasio briefly revived the latter—to the joy of many in Flatlands—in the spring of 2015. See Emma G. Fitzsimmons, "Mayor de Blasio Revives Plan for a Utica Avenue Subway Line," *New York Times*, April 22, 2015.

21. Kaufman, *Gotham in the Air Age*, 16.

22. Ibid., 20–22; "Let's Land in Brooklyn," *Brooklyn Daily Eagle*, August 26, 1938; "Bennett Field Will Be Made Finest Airport," *Brooklyn Daily Eagle*, September 12, 1935; "Farley Again Bars City Airport Plea," *New York Times*, March 22, 1936.

23. Edward T. and Robert L. Heikell, *One Chance for Glory* (Bloomington, IN: AuthorHouse, 2014); "Clyde Pangborn and Hugh Herndon, Jr.: First to Fly Nonstop across the Pacific," *Aviation History*, June 12, 2006.

24. Morris Markey, "The Black Eagle," *New Yorker*, July 11, 1931, 22–23.

25. "Harlem Sees Devil Drop from the Sky," *New York Times*, April 30, 1923; "Smith and Dempsey Swap Compliments," *New York Times*, September 16, 1923; "Negro in Parachute Hits Police Station," *New York Times*, November 6, 1923; Jill D. Snider, "Great Shadow in the Sky," in *The Airplane in American Culture*, ed. Dominick A. Pisano (Ann Arbor: University of Michigan Press, 2003), 131.

26. "Negro Aviator Recovering," *New York Times*, July 6, 1924; Morris Markey, "The Black Eagle," *New Yorker*, July 18, 1931, 20–25; "Negro Trains for Air Trip," *New York Times*, February 28, 1931; "Negro Plans

Ocean Flight," *New York Times*, September 9, 1933; David Shaftel, "The Black Eagle of Harlem," *Air & Space*, December 2008; Snider, "Great Shadow in the Sky," 126–133.

27. Rebecca Maksel, "Wiley Post's Historic Around-the-World Flight," *Air & Space*, July 16, 2013; "75,000 Greet Post; Break Police Line," *New York Times*, July 23, 1933.

28. Italo Balbo, *Stormi in volo sull'oceano* (Milan: A. Mondadori, 1931), 14–15, quoted in Claudio G. Segré, *Italo Balbo: A Fascist Life* (Berkeley: University of California Press, 1987), 215; "'1,000,000 in Chicago Bid Balbo Good-Bye," *New York Times*, July 19, 1933; Segré, 48–52, 215–225, 230–245; "Balbo Armada Arrives in N. Y. from Chicago," *Chicago Tribune*, July 20, 1933.

29. Segré, *Italo Balbo*, 247–248, 277, 346.

30. "Aviatrix Missed Stop but Captured Record," *Florida Times-Union*, April 14, 1999; Glen Jeansonne, *Women of the Far Right: The Mothers' Movement and World War II* (Chicago: University of Chicago Press, 1996), 68–69; "Laura Ingalls Held as Reich Agent," *New York Times*, December 19, 1941; "Indictment Voted for Laura Ingalls," *New York Times*, December 24, 1941.

31. Howard Mingos, ed., *The Aircraft Year Book for 1939* (New York: Aeronautical Chamber of Commerce of America, 1939), 467, 160–161, quoted in Tony P. Wrenn, *General History of the Jamaica Bay, Breezy Point, and Staten Island Units, Gateway National Recreation Area* (National Park Service, unpublished report, 1975), 32; Robert McG. Thomas Jr., "Douglas Corrigan, 88, Dies; Wrong-Way Trip Was the Right Way to Celebrity as an Aviator," *New York Times*, December 14, 1995.

CHAPTER 13. PARADISE ON THE OUTWASH PLAIN

1. Julian Ralph, "The City of Brooklyn," *Buena Vista Democrat*, February 17, 1887. This was a reprint of "Brooklyn's Growth, Some Interesting Facts about New York's Sister City," *Washington Post*, October 18, 1886, cited in Osman, *The Invention of Brownstone Brooklyn*, 29–30.

2. "Here All Stone Is Brown," *New York Times*, August 12, 1894; Lewis Mumford, *The Brown Decades* (New York: Harcourt, Brace and Company, 1931), 5.

3. Julian Ralph, "The City of Brooklyn," *Buena Vista Democrat*, February 17, 1887.

4. Alison C. Guinness, "The Portland Brownstone Quarries," *Chronicle of the Early American Industries Association* 55:3 (September 2002): 95; "Portland Put Its Stamp on an Era," ConnecticutHistory.org, http://connecticuthistory.org/portland-puts-its-stamp-on-an-architectural-era/.

5. Robert M. Fogelson, *The Great Rent Wars: New York, 1917–1929* (New Haven, CT: Yale University Press, 2013), 18, 20, 22–25; Edward Polak, "The NY Tax Exemption Law," in *Report of the National Tax Relief Convention*, ed. Emil O. Jorgensen (Chicago: Manufacturers and Merchants Federal Tax League, 1924), 25–32; Fogelson, 27–28.

6. "Rent Riots Rage in Brownsville," *Brooklyn Daily Eagle*, February 23, 1919; "'Evicted' Tenants Move Right Back," *Brooklyn Daily Eagle*, May 29, 1919; "Settle Rent Strike; Big Reductions Won by 3,000 Tenants," *Brooklyn Daily Eagle*, September 7, 1919; "Brownsville Tells Hilley It Will Not Have May Day Strike," *Brooklyn Daily Eagle*, April 27, 1920; "Big Colony of Negroes in Brownsville, Newest Project in Rent 'Strike,'" *Brooklyn Daily Eagle*, May 30, 1919; "Douglas St. House Is Sold to Negroes," *Brooklyn Daily Eagle*, June 2, 1920.

7. Fogelson, *Rent Wars*, 156–157, 166, 172, 194–195, 357–359; Mary Conyngton, "Effect of the Tax-Exemption Ordinance in New York City on Housing," *Monthly Labor Review* 14:4 (April 1922): 23–32.

8. Polak, "The NY Tax Exemption Law," 25–32; Conyngton, "Effect of the Tax-Exemption Ordinance," 23–32; Mason Gaffney, "The Resurgence of New York City after 1920: Al Smith's 1920 Tax Reform Law and Its Aftermath" (unpublished paper, Department of Economics, University of California–Riverside (2001), 3; Fogelson, *Rent Wars*, 388.

9. "By Way of Reminder," *Brooklyn Daily Eagle*, June 12, 1926; "Mayor Helps Open Flatbush Sewer; Is Largest in the World," *Brooklyn Daily Eagle*, June 10, 1926; "3,000 Acres of Flatlands Salt Marshes, Filled In by Federal Government, Have Become $50,000,000 'Gold Mine' to City in Land Boom," *Brooklyn Daily Eagle*, September 20, 1925; "Boro Architects Ask Betterment of Buildings Bureau," *Brooklyn Daily Eagle*, April 29, 1922; "Building Bureau Has Theater Party," *Brooklyn Daily Eagle*, April 25, 1923.

10. "Heavy Brick Supply for Winter Demand in New York City," *Brooklyn Daily Eagle*, November 16, 1924.

11. "Flatlands Sales Rival Miami Tales of Realty Boom," *Brooklyn Daily Eagle*, April 5, 1925.

12. The fate of the structure remains a mystery. "CWA Workers Raze 'Mount Vernon' As Builders Try to Raise Its Cost," *Brooklyn Daily Eagle*, February 23, 1934.

13. *Report of the United States George Washington Bicentennial Commission*, vol. 5 (Washington, DC: George Washington Bicentennial Commission, 1932), 600; *History of the George Washington Bicentennial*

Celebration, vol. 3 (Washington, DC: George Washington Bicentennial Commission, 1932), 239. For what it's worth, the commission also insisted that it was Washington—not Dolly Madison—who first introduced America to ice cream.

14. Gavin E. Townsend, "The Tudor House in America: 1890–1930" (PhD diss., University of California, Santa Barbara, 1986), 248–249.

15. "Rukeyser, Headed Colonial Sand," *New York Times*, May 28, 1958; Alan M. Wald, *Exiles from a Future Time* (Chapel Hill: University of North Carolina Press, 2002), 300; "Active Home Buying Near Marine Park," *Brooklyn Daily Eagle*, September 20, 1931.

16. "Jewish Charity Enlarged by Club of Boro Realty Men," *Brooklyn Daily Eagle*, May 17, 1925; "Project 12-Story Skyscraper for Insurance Trade," *Brooklyn Daily Eagle*, October 4, 1925; "Sharp Decline in Plans Filed at Bureaus," *Brooklyn Daily Eagle*, September 27, 1931; "Scores Growing Foreclosures as Menace to Realty Values," *Brooklyn Daily Eagle*, October 18, 1931; "Bankruptcy Proceedings," *New York Times*, December 5, 1931; "Bankruptcy Proceedings," *New York Times*, August 27, 1932.

17. "Large Realty Concern Formed," *New York Times*, November 3, 1901; W. G. Morrisey, "South Brooklyn's Rapid Development," *New York Times*, April 23, 1911; "Opening of New Era for Brooklyn Realty," *New York Times*, November 7, 1909; "Building New Community," *New York Times*, October 24, 1909; "To Build Many Houses," *New York Times*, May 25, 1919; "Improved Types of Two-Family Dwellings," *New York Times*, October 25, 1908; "Says 'City Defense' Is a Realty Scheme," *New York Times*, April 1, 1916; "Oppose U. S. Purchase," *New York Times*, August 13, 1916; "William Greve Tells of Short Accounts," *Brooklyn Daily Eagle*, April 23, 1932; "Greve, Money Baron, Renounces Citizenship for Tax-Free Haven," *Brooklyn Daily Eagle*, July 17, 1938. The company's Midwood and Maple Street row houses are between Bedford and Rogers avenues; the Sullivan Place homes are on the south side between Rogers and Nostrand avenues. Vista Place is between Sixty-Eighth Street and Bay Ridge Avenue.

18. "Brooklyn Acreage for Small Homes," *New York Times*, May 6, 1923; "Plan 200 Homes at Gerritsen Beach to Start in Week," *Brooklyn Daily Eagle*, September 7, 1924; "Ford Wants His Name Kept for His Own Use," *New York Times*, March 13, 1925; "Ford Puts Ban on Use of Name," *Brooklyn Daily Eagle*, March 13, 1925; "Brooklyn Co. Has Its Biggest Year," *New York Times*, December 13, 1925; "Plan Theater for Gerritsen Beach to Cost $100,000," *Brooklyn Daily Eagle*, January 20, 1924; "New Church at Gerritsen Beach Plans Parish Group," *Brooklyn Daily Eagle*, September 28, 1924; "Hundreds of Small Homes," *New York Times*, March 29, 1925; "Building Many Brooklyn Homes," *New York Times*, October 7, 1923.

19. "Gerritsen Beach to Install Mayor," *Brooklyn Daily Eagle*, September 17, 1935; "Creek Diggers Cheer as First Boat Uses Cut," *Brooklyn Daily Eagle*, December 11, 1933; "Sixteen Indicted in Recent Raid at Gerritsen Beach," *Brooklyn Daily Eagle*, August 27, 1931.

20. It is managed today by the Friends of the Lott House.

21. "New Home Development in Flatbush Center Section," *Brooklyn Daily Eagle*, August 23, 1925; "Old Flatbush Farm in $3,000,000 Deal to Be Developed," *Brooklyn Daily Eagle*, December 13, 1925; "Rapid Changes in Flatbush Centre," *New York Times*, February 7, 1926; "Flatbush Centre Sales," *New York Times*, October 24, 1926; "Brooklyn Co. Has Its Biggest Year," *New York Times* December 13, 1925; "Realty Associates Set Company Record," *New York Times*, July 11, 1926; "Realty Associates Close a Record Year," *New York Times*, December 5, 1926.

22. Some of Calder's early work includes the Renaissance revival apartment houses at 256–262 Twelfth Street, 336–346 Fourteenth Street, and 496–506 Eleventh Street, along with the adjacent commercial building at 369 Seventh Avenue—home of chef Dale Talde's eponymous restaurant.

23. "Two Good Appointments," *Brooklyn Daily Eagle*, December 31, 1901; "Five Dismissals by Calder," *Brooklyn Daily Eagle*, January 7, 1902; "Calder Talks to Employes [sic]," *Brooklyn Daily Eagle*, January 15, 1902.

24. "Killed by His Aerial Slide," *Brooklyn Daily Eagle*, June 13, 1902; "What Is Taking Place at Gravesend," *Brooklyn Daily Eagle*, March 19, 1893; Coney's Board Walk," *Brooklyn Daily Eagle*, October 2, 1900; "Board Walk Is Proposed for Island's Water Front," *Brooklyn Daily Eagle*, September 7, 1900; "Board Walk Plan Rejected," *Brooklyn Daily Eagle*, January 10, 1901; "Board Walk for Coney Is Supt. Calder's Plan," *Brooklyn Daily Eagle*, March 2, 1903.

25. "Calder Company Successful in Flatbush Field," *Brooklyn Daily Eagle*, January 6, 1924; "Calder Company to Move," *Brooklyn Daily Eagle*, August 29, 1923; David Prerau, *Seize the Daylight: The Curious and Contentious Story of Daylight Saving Time* (New York: Thunder's Mouth Press, 2005), xiii, 88–90; "Ushering in the New Time," *Brooklyn Daily Eagle*, March 30, 1918.

26. "Calder Firm Launches New Building Program," *Brooklyn Daily Eagle*, January 4, 1924; "Calder Buys Sheepshead Bay Plot for Home Colony," *Brooklyn Daily Eagle*, March 5, 1926; "Real Estate Secure While Stocks Decline," *Brooklyn Daily Eagle*, October 18, 1931; "Calder Sees Marine Park as Realty Value Maker," *New York Herald Tribune*, April 9, 1933; "Calder Designs Model Dwelling in Development," *Brooklyn Daily Eagle*, February 10, 1929; "Brooklyn Builder Learned His Trade from Ground Up," *Brooklyn Daily*

Eagle, March 17, 1929; Louis De Casanova, "Motorcar Show Brings a New Epidemic to Town," *Brooklyn Daily Eagle*, March 5, 1922. Most of Calder's Marine Park homes are within the area bounded by Avenue S, Nostrand Avenue, Avenue U, and East Twenty-Seventh Street; he built another large group closer to the park itself, on Coyle and Bragg streets (the model houses were 2005, 2038, and 2056 Coyle Street). Calder might be the only Brooklyn developer to have received an honorary doctorate, from George Washington University in 1945.

27. Gwenda Blair, *The Trumps* (New York: Simon & Schuster, 2000), 119–121. The advertisements are from the *Brooklyn Daily Eagle* (September 13, 1924; October 17, 1927; March 25, 1928) and *New York Herald Tribune* (March 22, 1931, and October 19, 1930).

28. Blair, *The Trumps*, 106–107; "Will Complete Development," *New York Herald Tribune*, May 5, 1935; "Three Flatbush Homes Sold," *New York Herald Tribune*, May 26, 1935.

29. Blair, *The Trumps*, 151.

30. "Trump Syndicate Plans Brooklyn Bungalows," *New York Herald Tribune*, April 24, 1936; "Circus Grounds Acquired as Site for 450 Homes," *New York Herald Tribune*, July 4, 1936; Blair, *The Trumps*, 141, 144, 149–150.

31. "Trump Works 2 Shifts on New Brooklyn Colony," *New York Herald Tribune*, May 23, 1937; "Mass Building Lowering Cost, Builder Finds," *Brooklyn Eagle*, January 29, 1939; "Circus Ground in Flatbush Is Sold for Homes," *New York Herald Tribune*, May 28, 1939; "Plans to Finish Brighton Beach Project July 1," *New York Herald Tribune*, December 15, 1940; "Show Boat Tells Bathers about Trump Flatbush Homes," *Brooklyn Eagle*, July 16, 1939; "Trump Does It in 'Big Way,' Even to Collecting Tickets," *Brooklyn Eagle*, July 13, 1939; "Trump to Continue Boat Campaign," *Brooklyn Eagle*, September 3, 1939; "Builder Fined for Violation, Then Handed a 'Home Prospect,'" *Brooklyn Eagle*, September 8, 1940.

32. "Borough Had Big Growth in Past Decade," *Brooklyn Daily Eagle*, December 28, 1930; George Orwell, *Coming Up for Air* (New York: Harcourt, Brace and Company, 1950 [1939]), 102; Russell F. Whitehead, "Current Country House Architecture: The Pendulum of Design Swings," *Architectural Record*, November 1924, 386, quoted in Townsend, *The Tudor House in America*, 255–256; Lewis Mumford, "American Architecture of Today," *Architecture*, June 1928, 301.

33. Agee, *Brooklyn Is*, 48–49, 3–5, 8, 25–26, 7.

CHAPTER 14. FIELD OF SCHEMES

1. "The Firstest and the Mostest," *Brooklyn Eagle*, December 9, 1945.

2. "Big Plane Order Rushed," *New York Times*, November, 1939; "Operated from Shack," *Brooklyn Eagle*, July 2, 1941; Cody and Auwaerter, *Cultural Landscape Report for Floyd Bennett Field*, 101–104.

3. "Flight Training," *New York Times*, January 23, 1941; "Training Plan Grows," *New York Times*, October 13, 1940; "626 Civilian Fliers on Rolls of Schools at Floyd Bennett," *Brooklyn Eagle*, April 6, 1941. https://www.history.navy.mil/browse-by-topic/wars-conflicts-and-operations/world-war-ii/1944/vignette--frank-erickson.html.

4. "First Women Hired in Navy Yard Shops," *New York Times*, September 14, 1942; "Navy Yard Payroll Is Triple Peak," *Brooklyn Eagle*, April 13, 1941.

5. It was only the second Series defeat for the New York Yankees since 1926.

6. Quoted in Samuel Rosenberg, *American Economic Development since 1945: Growth, Decline and Rejuvenation* (New York: Palgrave Macmillan, 2002), 66; Joshua B. Freeman, *Working-Class New York: Life and Labor since World War II* (New York: The New Press, 2001), 4.

7. Freeman, *Working-Class New York*, 4–6; "City Shutdown Ended As Fuel Crisis Eases," *New York Times*, February 13, 1946; Amy Mittelman, *Brewing Battles: A History of American Beer* (New York: Algora Publishing, 2008), 141. Freeman, 7.

8. "Shipping News and Notes," *New York Times*, October 20, 1949; "Brewery Workers Ordered to Strike," *New York Times*, April 1, 1949; "Brewery Concern Buys in Brooklyn," *New York Times*, April 1, 1948; Freeman, *Working-Class New York*, 152–154; Arthur Gregg Sulzberger, "When Brooklyn Brewed the World," *New York Times*, July 10, 2009.

9. "Walkout Is Begun at Eagle by Guild," *New York Times*, January 29, 1955; "Strikebound Eagle Shut Permanently," *New York Times*, March 17, 1955.

10. Freeman, *Working-Class New York*, 8, 10; Raymond Vernon, "Production and Distribution in the Large Metropolis," *Annals of the American Academy of Political and Social Science* 314 (November 1957): 25; Osman, *The Invention of Brownstone Brooklyn*, 10. Jobs in the nascent service sector—banking, law, real estate, insurance—rose by twenty-eight thousand between 1947 and 1955.

11. Joel Schwartz, *The New York Approach: Robert Moses, Urban Liberals and Redevelopment of the Inner City* (Columbus: Ohio State University Press, 1993), 238–239; Freeman, *Working-Class New York*, 149.

12. Robert M. Fogelson, *Downtown: Its Rise and Fall, 1880–1950* (New Haven, CT: Yale University Press, 2001), 378.

13. Quintin Johnstone, "The Federal Urban Renewal Program," *University of Chicago Law Review* 25 (1958): 303.

14. Samuel Zipp, *Manhattan Projects: The Rise and Fall of Urban Renewal in Cold War New York* (London: Oxford University Press, 2010), 164; Charles Grutzner, "Our Changing City; Downtown Brooklyn Glistens," *New York Times*, July 18, 1955.

15. "It is the manifest destiny of Flatbush Avenue," reasoned the *Eagle* in 1877, "to be opened through to the entrance to the Bridge"—a prophecy eventually realized when Flatbush Avenue Extension was opened to the Manhattan Bridge in 1909. See "Flatbush Avenue: Its Extension to the Bridge," *Brooklyn Daily Eagle*, December 8, 1877; Franklin Matthews, "The Brooklyn Terminal Station of the Brooklyn Bridge," *Harper's Weekly*, June 15, 1895, 557; "Against More Saloons," *Brooklyn Daily Eagle*, November 26, 1894; "Cromwell Childe, "The Looker On," *Brooklyn Daily Eagle*, August 24, 1895; "Plans for the Bridge Plaza," *Brooklyn Daily Eagle*, July 31, 1895.

16. William C. Hudson, "Planning a Grand Gateway to Brooklyn," *Brooklyn Daily Eagle*, May 23, 1909; "Not a Voice against Brooklyn Bridge Plaza," *Brooklyn Daily Eagle*, January 6, 1912; Frederic B. Pratt, ed., *Down Town Brooklyn: A Report to the Comptroller of the City of New York on Sites for Public Buildings* (Brooklyn, NY: Borough of Brooklyn, 1913), 9.

17. Inclement weather forced the "songfest" indoors to Borough Hall. "Bridge Plaza Plan Definitely in Sight," *Brooklyn Daily Eagle*, February 28, 1935; "Brooklyn Bridge Plaza Voted by City" and "Plaza Plans Agitated for Half Century," *Brooklyn Daily Eagle*, June 14, 1935; "Conway Sets Aside Beach Land Grab," *Brooklyn Daily Eagle*, April 12, 1935; "Landscaping of Plaza Is Begun by WPA Men," *Brooklyn Daily Eagle*, August 20, 1936; "Singing Good Time on Plaza," *Brooklyn Daily Eagle*, December 30, 1936.

18. "'L' Falls Fast, with Boro Hall Sector Cleared," *Brooklyn Eagle*, June 17, 1941; "S.R.O. Sign Out on Fulton Street," *Brooklyn Eagle*, June 18, 1941.

19. Pratt, *Down Town Brooklyn*, 9; "Brooklyn City Plan," *Brooklyn Daily Eagle*, January 18, 1914.

20. "New Plan Suggested for Brooklyn's Civic Centre," *New York Times*, March 22, 1914; "Peabody Civic Plan Strongly Opposed," *Brooklyn Daily Eagle*, March 23, 1914.

21. Thomas Adams, *The Building of the City* (New York: Regional Plan of New York and Its Environs, 1931), 474–478.

22. Ibid., 475–476.

23. *Reminiscences of Cleveland Rodgers*, transcript of an oral history conducted 1950 by Owen Bombard, Columbia Center for Oral History, Columbia University, 1950, 25, 55–57, 59, 85–87.

24. Ibid., 206; Cleveland Rodgers, *New York Plans for the Future* (New York: Harper & Brothers, 1943), 148–151; *Reminiscences*, 198.

25. "Moses Regrets Loss of Rodgers from City Planning Commission," *Brooklyn Eagle*, December 28, 1951; "Point-by-Point Discussion of Program for Brooklyn," *Brooklyn Eagle*, January 12, 1942; Charles C. Lockwood, "Borough Authority Urged to Create Civic Center," *Brooklyn Eagle*, December 7, 1941.

26. These included architect Aymar Embury II and landscape architects Gilmore D. Clarke and Stuart Constable. Clarke and Embury placed second, while Constable and a young sculptor named Elisabeth Gordon (E. Gordon Chandler) were awarded the first-place prize of $5,000. They proposed a trio of formal buildings with a memorial court anchored by a figural piece that Gordon had made for an unrealized Pearl Harbor memorial—a melancholic youth whose outstretched arms were strapped with "the man-made wings of airpower."

27. "Boro to Get Civic Center, Moses Says," *Brooklyn Eagle*, February 17, 1944; Lewis Mumford, "The Sky Line: From Blight to Beauty—I," *New Yorker*, April 25, 1953.

28. City Planning Commission, *Master Plan of Brooklyn Civic Center and Downtown Area* (City of New York, May 9, 1945); *Reminiscences of Gilmore D. Clarke*, transcript of an oral history conducted 1959, Columbia Center for Oral History, Columbia University, 1959.

29. They included, among others, Leslie G. Holleran, Ernest J. Clark, Clinton F. Lloyd, Jay Downer, Edmund F. Passarelli, and Allyn R. Jennings.

30. Walter B. Gunnison, "War Memorial Winners," *Brooklyn Eagle*, May 27, 1945.

31. Charles Grutzner, "Our Changing City; Downtown Brooklyn Glistens," *New York Times*, July 18, 1955.

32. Mumford, "The Sky Line: From Blight to Beauty—I."

33. Lewis Mumford, "The Sky Line: From Blight to Beauty—II," *New Yorker*, May 9, 1953.

34. Moses King, *King's Views of New York* (New York: Sackett & Wilhelms Company, 1903), 68. The bronze eagle was moved to the Brooklyn Public Library at Grand Army Plaza, where it sits in a window alcove above the entrance lobby.

CHAPTER 15. THE BABYLONISH BRICK KILN

1. "Award Contracts for Demolition on Fort Greene Site," *Brooklyn Eagle*, November 5, 1940; "Cite Necessity for Navy Yard Housing Plan," *Brooklyn Eagle*, April 13, 1939; "Navy Yard 'Jungle' Doomed by New Housing Contract," *Brooklyn Eagle*, June 28, 1940; Federal Writers' Project, *New York City Guide* (New York: Random House, 1939), 450; Jim O'Grady, "What Remains of the Day," *New York Times*, December 13, 2003.

2. "The Navy Yard," *Brooklyn Daily Eagle*, May 16, 1873.

3. "Enforcing the Laws," *New York Times*, November 3, 1870.

4. Barnet Phillips, "The Williamsburg Bridge," *Harper's Weekly*, May 20, 1893, 472; "A Third Bridge for Brooklyn," *Brooklyn Daily Eagle*, November 30, 1898; "Hudson Avenue Bridge," *Brooklyn Daily Eagle*, April 4, 1899; "Bids for Tower Foundation," *Brooklyn Daily Eagle*, March 11, 1901.

5. "Typhus in Brooklyn," *Brooklyn Daily Eagle*, February 13, 1893; "Adelphi College Has a Scientific Exhibit of Baby Week," *Brooklyn Daily Eagle*, May 14, 1916.

6. There were several small hills in the vicinity, only one of which—today's Fort Greene Park—remains. See Stiles, *History of the City of Brooklyn*, 389; Edwin G. Burrows and Mike Wallace, *Gotham: A History of New York City to 1898* (London: Oxford University Press, 1999), 272; Landmarks Preservation Commission, *Vinegar Hill Historic District Designation Report—LP-1952* (City of New York, 1997, prepared by Donald G. Presa), 5; "Changes on Sands St. in Last Thirty Years," *Brooklyn Daily Eagle*, June 7, 1908; "Naval Life's Bright Side," *New York Times*, July 12, 1896; Michael Faiella quoted in Ellen M. Snyder-Grenie, *Brooklyn! An Illustrated History* (Philadelphia: Temple University Press, 2004), 159.

7. "Sinful Sands Street Really Just a Sissy," *Brooklyn Daily Eagle*, October 26, 1935; Jean Piper, "100,000 Filipinos in U. S.; 1,000 in Brooklyn," *Brooklyn Daily Eagle*, July 1, 1928; "Changes on Sands St. in Last Thirty Years," *Brooklyn Daily Eagle*, June 7, 1908.

8. One of the most brazen occurred on February 23, 1921, when two men clubbed jeweler Irving Solowey in his shop at 125 Sands Street. They chose the wrong shopkeeper to victimize: as the thieves looted his safe (containing $40,000 worth of merchandise), Solowey grabbed a handgun from behind the counter and began shooting. The ensuing gunfight blasted out the store window, leaving one of the attackers dead. "Hold-Up Man Dying by Jeweler's Shot," *New York Times*, February 24, 1921.

9. Margaret Mara, "Down in the Old Neighborhood," *Brooklyn Eagle*, March 21, 1952; "Brooklyn Annoyed by Cocaine Stories," *Brooklyn Daily Eagle*, January 13, 1907; "Navy Joins Fight on Sands St. Rum," *New York Times*, December 12, 1921; "Sinful Sands Street," *Brooklyn Daily Eagle*, October 26, 1935.

10. Quoted in George Chauncey, *Gay New York* (New York: Basic Books, 1995), 82; Evan Hughes, *Literary Brooklyn: The Writers of Brooklyn and the Story of American City Life* (New York: Henry Holt, 2011), 65–66.

11. "Sinful Sands Street," *Brooklyn Daily Eagle*, October 26, 1935.

12. Seebohm and MacNeice quoted in Neil Powell, *Benjamin Britten: A Life for Music* (New York: Henry Holt and Company, 2013), 187–188.

13. Carson McCullers, "Brooklyn Is My Neighbourhood," in *The Mortgaged Heart: Selected Writings* (New York: Houghton Mifflin, 2005 [1971]), 218–219; Smith quoted in Hughes, *Literary Brooklyn*, 176–177.

14. "Navy Yard 'Jungle' Doomed by New Housing Contract," *Brooklyn Eagle*, June 28, 1940; "It's Brooklyn Not Britain and Rubble of Demolition Spells Housing Progress," *Brooklyn Eagle*, March 3, 1941; "Century-Old Building Is Doomed by Project," *Brooklyn Eagle*, November 17, 1940.

15. "Rats Face Blitzkrieg in Slum Housing Raid," *Brooklyn Eagle*, January 12, 1941; "Clearing Housing Site," *New York Times*, February 28, 1941."Governor Starts Ft. Greene Housing," *New York Times*, May 7, 1941; "Fort Greene Houses Put Brooklyn in Lead in Slum Clearance," *Brooklyn Eagle*, May 7, 1941. "Wallabout Houses for Navy Families to Open Next Month," *Brooklyn Eagle*, October 28, 1941. The building begun on May 6, the only one north of Park Avenue, was originally the Wallabout Houses.

16. "$20,363,000 Homes in Kings Dedicated," *New York Times*, September 10, 1942.

17. Le Corbusier, *Aircraft* (Milan: Abitare Segesta, 1996 [1935]), 5–12.

18. "Fort Greene Houses," *Brooklyn Eagle*, November 25, 1944.

19. Norma Evenson, *Le Corbusier: The Machine and the Grand Design* (New York: George Braziller, 1969), 7.

20. Eugene Halton, *The Great Brain Suck: And Other American Epiphanies* (Chicago: University of Chicago Press, 2008), 242.

21. Lewis Mumford, "The Red-Brick Beehives," *New Yorker*, May 6, 1950, 92–98.

22. Ibid., 92–98.

23. "Meet Mr. Dornam, Manager of Buildings," "Woolin, Builder of Homes, Not Content with Houses," "Borough Values Are Boosted; Neighborhood Is Improved," "Furniture Problem Solved in Model Flats," "No Showers, Plenty of Baths," *Brooklyn Eagle*, August 16, 1942.

24. "Fort Greene Houses," *Brooklyn Eagle*, November 25, 1944; "Extra Cops Out to Crush Boro Street Clashes," *Brooklyn Eagle*, June 17, 1944; "2 Youths Admit Roles in Boro Race Clashes," *Brooklyn Eagle*, June 18, 1944; "Heffernan Promises Probe of Fort Greene Race Clash," *Brooklyn Eagle*, June 22, 1944.

25. "Tabulation of Tenant Data—Statistical Sheets," Series 8, Box 63E2, Folder 3, New York City Housing Authority Collection, La Guardia and Wagner Archives, La Guardia Community College; "Charges Half of Negroes in Boro Are Poorly Housed," *Brooklyn Eagle*, April 11, 1946; "Lamb Denies Communist Associations," *Broadcasting—Telecasting*, April 25, 1955, 76; "Meeting Bans Fought," *New York Times*, May 28, 1947; Jane Corby, "Racial Prejudice? What's That?" *Brooklyn Eagle*, January 13, 1946.

26. Jane Corby, "Racial Prejudice? What's That?" *Brooklyn Eagle*, January 13, 1946; "Admits Plans to Evict 10% at Ft. Greene," *Brooklyn Eagle*, January 27, 1947; William Robbins, "Brooklyn Neighbors Win a Housing Battle," *New York Times*, April 14, 1968.

27. "Charts of Racial Distribution," Series 11, Box III, Folders 19–21, New York City Housing Authority Collection, La Guardia and Wagner Archives, La Guardia Community College.

28. Harrison E. Salisbury, " 'Shook' Youngsters Spring from the Housing Jungles," *New York Times*, March 26, 1958; Thabit, *How East New York Became a Ghetto*, 41.

29. "Fort Greene Housing Tenants Plead to Cops," *Brooklyn Eagle*, July 11, 1949; "Vigilantes Set to Fight Crime at Ft. Greene," *Brooklyn Eagle*, July 17, 1949; "Fort Greene Houses Given More Police," *Brooklyn Eagle*, July 30, 1949; "Police Head's Timely Move to Check Ft. Greene Crime," *Brooklyn Eagle*, August 1, 1949; "27 Police Added by Housing Unit," *New York Times*, July 15, 1958; Phillip J. Cruise to William Peer, February 22, 1957, Series 1, Box 65C8, Folder 6, New York City Housing Authority Collection, La Guardia and Wagner Archives, La Guardia Community College.

30. "Alert Cops Avert Zip-Gun Gang War," *Brooklyn Eagle*, October 17, 1953; "GI's Wife, Mother of 4, Is Slashed to Death," *Brooklyn Eagle*, January 24, 1955; "Knife Bandit Robs Girl," *Brooklyn Eagle*, June 30, 1952; "Girl Waylaid in Lift, Beats Off Attack," *Brooklyn Eagle*, May 22, 1951; Cruise to Peer, February 22, 1957, New York City Housing Authority Collection; Harrison E. Salisbury, " 'Shook' Youngsters," *New York Times*, March 26, 1958.

31. "Reveals Vandalism in Housing Projects," *Brooklyn Eagle*, August 27, 1954; Cruise to Peer, February 22, 1957, New York City Housing Authority Collection; "Ft. Greene Houses to Be Renovated," *New York Times*, February 10, 1957; "Fort Greene Houses Refitted by City," *New York Times*, February 4, 1958.

32. Harrington quoted in Osman, *The Invention of Brownstone Brooklyn*, 172; Dwight MacDonald, "Charles Abrams: A Biography" (1975), Charles Abrams Papers, 1923–1970, Division of Rare and Manuscript Collections, Carl A. Kroch Library, Cornell University; Murray Illson, "Charles Abrams, Worldwide Housing Expert, Dies," *New York Times*, February 23, 1970; Dan Noonan and Leslie Hanscom, "Offers Plan to Sell Public Housing Projects to Tenants," *Brooklyn Eagle*, December 9, 1952.

33. Harrison E. Salisbury, " 'Shook' Youngsters," *New York Times*, March 26, 1958.

34. Harrison E. Salisbury, *The Shook-Up Generation* (New York: Harper & Row, 1958), 75.

CHAPTER 16. COLOSSUS OF ROADS

1. Quoted in Marshall Berman, *All That Is Solid Melts into Air: The Experience of Modernity* (New York: Penguin Books, 1982), 301.

2. Ibid., 302.

3. *Reminiscences of Gilmore D. Clarke*, transcript of an oral history conducted 1959, Columbia Center for Oral History, Columbia University, 1959, 53–54; Newton, *Design on the Land*, 569; "Melvin B. Borgeson, 66, Dies; A Government Airport Planner," *New York Times*, November 23, 1963.

4. Robert Moses, "If I Had a Magic Wand" (1939), Robert Moses Papers, Manuscripts and Archives Division, New York Public Library.

5. It was not without serious environmental impact; Moses devised a brilliant, Machiavellian, maneuver to finance the project, which involved routing the parkway through pristine woodland in Inwood Hill. See Caro, *The Power Broker*, 525–552.

6. Adams, *Building of the City*, 490; "Circumferential Loses to 'Belt' as Highway Name," *New York Times*, December 18, 1938; "Kings-Queens Road Has a 'Dedication,' " *New York Times*, December 11, 1938; Robert Moses to Reagan McCrary, December 3, 1938, Box 97, Moses Papers, New York Public Library; Memo from Robert Moses to Allyn Jennings, September 17, 1938, Box 97, Moses Papers, New York Public Library; "58 Miles of Park Bicycle Paths Urged as WPA Project by Moses," *New York Times*, August 9, 1938; "Belt Road to Open to Traffic Today," *New York Times*, June 29, 1940.

7. Caro, *The Power Broker*, 520–523.

8. George Mathieu, "New Brooklyn-Queens Highway to Open in Fall," *New York Times*, April 23, 1939.

9. "$65,000,000 Roads Proposed by Moses for City's Defense," *New York Times*, November 11, 1940; "Roads for Defense," *New York Times*, November 11, 1940.

10. City Planning Commission, meeting minutes (No. 10), May 7, 1941, Series I, Box 2, Folder 29, Roy M. D. Richardson Papers, Archives and Special Collections, Brooklyn College; "City Gets Land for Widening of Hicks Street," *Brooklyn Eagle*, August 27, 1941; "Start of Work Ordered on New Highway Link," *Brooklyn Eagle*, April 18, 1949; "Plan for Express Highway through Heights Is Shocking," *Brooklyn Eagle*, September 19, 1942; "Heights Residents Unanimously Veto Proposed Project," *Brooklyn Heights Press*, September 25, 1942; "Brooklyn Heights Promenade Opens; Moses Praised," *Brooklyn Eagle*, October 8, 1950; Ernest J. Clark quoted in Henrik Krogius, *The Brooklyn Heights Promenade* (Charleston, SC: The History Press, 2011), 75.

11. List of residents is appended to a letter from Roy Richardson on Brooklyn Heights Association stationery, April 21, 1943; Series I, Box 2, Roy M. D. Richardson Papers, Archives and Special Collections, Brooklyn College.

12. Eleanor Roosevelt, "My Day," *New York World-Telegram*, April 5, 1939 and May 13, 1939; "Highway Hearing Ends," *New York Times*, March 11, 1943; "City to Act Today on Hicks St. Work," *New York Times*, June 26, 1941. Moses made the "friends on the Heights" claim in *Public Works: A Dangerous Trade* (New York: McGraw-Hill, 1970).

13. Krogius, *The Brooklyn Heights Promenade*, 73–74; Adams, *Building of the City*, 482–490. Litchfield is perhaps best known for planning Yorkship Village, a 225-acre new town in Camden, New Jersey, meant to provide housing for shipyard workers during World War I (renamed Fairlawn in 1922).

14. "A More Beautiful City," *Brooklyn Daily Eagle*, November 6, 1911; "A Harbor View Park," *New-York Tribune*, May 10, 1903; Stiles, *Civil, Political, Professional and Ecclesiastical History and Commercial and Industrial Record*, 130.

15. Roy M. D. Richardson to multiple recipients, April 21, 1943; Series I, Box 2, Roy M. D. Richardson Papers, Archives and Special Collections, Brooklyn College; *A Proposal for a Brooklyn-Queens East River Express Highway* (New York: Department of City Planning, Division of Master Plan, 1940).

16. Thomas J. Campanella, "Art at the Scale of Landscape," *Wall Street Journal*, September 17–18, 2011, C13.

17. "Boro-Battery Tunnel Opens," *Brooklyn Eagle*, May 25, 1950; "Last Link of Boro Hts. Promenade Dedicated," *Brooklyn Eagle*, December 8, 1951; Lewis Mumford, "The Sky Line: From Blight to Beauty II," *New Yorker*, May 9, 1953.

18. "Roebling House Where Bridge Builder Lived Will Be Demolished," *Brooklyn Eagle*, January 22, 1947; *Brooklyn Life*, March 26, 1916, 124; Doreen Bolger, "Hamilton Easter Field and His Contribution to American Modernism," *American Art Journal* 20:2 (1988): 87, 98; William Rubin, *Picasso and Braque: Pioneering Cubism* (New York: Museum of Modern Art, 1989), 63–69.

19. Hughes, *Literary Brooklyn*, 61–62, 71, 168, 171–172; Sherill Tippins, *February House* (New York: Houghton Mifflin, 2005), 173; Virginia Spencer Carr, *Dos Passos: A Life* (Evanston, IL: Northwestern University Press, 1984), 199.

20. Lewis Mumford, *The Highway and the City* (New York: Harcourt, Brace & World, 1963), 220, 236–237.

21. Ibid., 238.

22. Ibid., 220.

23. Robert Moses, *Working for the People* (New York: Harper and Brothers, 1956), 203.

24. Ada Louise Huxtable, *Will They Ever Finish Bruckner Boulevard?* (New York: Macmillan, 1970), xvii.

25. Tom Lewis, *Divided Highways* (New York: Penguin, 1999), ix.

26. Moses to Frederick C. Cranford, February 21, 1938, Box 97, Moses Papers, New York Public Library.

27. Moses to Thomas H. MacDonald, August 21, 1940, Box 98, Moses Papers, New York Public Library.

CHAPTER 17. HIGHWAY OF HOPE

1. Lewis Mumford, *My Works and Days: A Personal Chronicle* (New York: Harcourt Brace Jovanovich, 1979); Mumford, *The Highway and the City*, 235.

2. Anthony Flint, *Wrestling with Moses* (New York: Random House, 2011), 146.

3. Robert Moses, *Future Arterial Program: New York City* (New York: Triborough Bridge and Tunnel Authority, 1963), 15.

4. Ian Volner and Matico Josephson, "He Is Fresh and Everyone Else Is Tired—Part II," *Triple Canopy*, May 2009, https://www.canopycanopycanopy.com.

5. "Planning Unit Rebuffs Moses on Roads in Capital Budget," *New York Times*, January 1, 1966.

6. In the end, some 200,000 manufacturing jobs would disappear on Wagner's mayoral watch. See Freeman, *Working-Class New York*, 150.

7. Not until 1969 did the first building in the Flatlands Industrial Park finally open, a 130,000-square-foot plastics plant at 101–01 Avenue D erected by Arthur Ratner, a developer whom the city later dragged into court on charges of fraud and racketeering. The park is today known as the Flatlands Fairfield Industrial Business Zone. Charles G. Bennett, "An Industrial Park for Brooklyn Nears Reality with New Layout," *New York Times*, August 20, 1965; Homer Bigart, "Industrial Park Spelled D-U-M-P," *New York Times*, March 30, 1966; Thomas W. Ennis, "Industrial Park Near in Brooklyn," *New York Times*, June 19, 1966; "First Building for the Flatlands Industrial Park," *New York Times*, September 24, 1967; Joseph P. Fried, "Park Opens for Industry in Brooklyn," *New York Times*, January 12, 1969.

8. Paul O'Neil, "Keep 'Em Rolling—to the Final Jam," *Life*, November 13, 1964; *McKinney's Session Laws of New York*, vol. 1 (New York: West Publishing, 1966), 2285–2287; "Road in Brooklyn Called Essential," *New York Times*, July 2, 1965; "Battle of the Planners," *New York Times*, July 6, 1965; "Barnes Backs Road across Brooklyn," *New York Times*, July 8, 1965; "Barnes Gives Plans for an Expressway Crossing Brooklyn," *New York Times*, September 16, 1965; Joseph C. Ingraham, "Lindsay Removes Moses from Post as Road Planner," *New York Times*, July 13, 1966.

9. *The Graphic Regional Plan—Atlas and Description* (New York: Regional Plan of New York and Its Environs, 1929), 214–219, 221; Peter Hall in *Orbital Motorways*, ed. D. Bayliss (London: Thomas Telford, 1990), 3.

10. Murray Illson, "Moses Now Urges Two Expressways in Brooklyn," *New York Times*, December 14, 1966; Charles G. Bennett, "Link Is Favored across Brooklyn," *New York Times*, February 23, 1967.

11. John T. Carroll et al., *Cross Brooklyn Expressway: Benefits for Brooklyn* (New York: Brill Engineering Corporation, 1967).

12. *The New City: Architecture and Urban Renewal* (New York: Museum of Modern Art, 1967), 30–35.

13. Murray Schumach, "Designers and Politicians Gather on the Mall to Explore City Ills," *New York Times*, May 12, 1967.

14. John V. Lindsay, foreword, in Jonathan Barnett, *Urban Design as Public Policy* (New York: Architectural Record Books, 1974); Steven V. Roberts, "Housing Report Gets High Praise," *New York Times*, October 8, 1966; "Lindsay Creates Agency to Direct Fight on Slums," *New York Times*, November 23, 1966; John Kifner, "Architect Named to Planning Body," *New York Times*, May 14, 1967; Mayor's Task Force on Urban Design, *The Threatened City: A Report on the Design of the City of New York* (New York: Department of City Planning, 1967), 47; "Lindsay Appoints City Design Panel," *New York Times*, October 8, 1967. Logue was eventually lured to New York by Nelson Rockefeller to head the Urban Development Corporation. In the fall of 1967, Lindsay formed another blue-ribbon committee—the nine-member Urban Design Council—chaired again by Paley and including socialite Brooke Astor, Whitney M. Young, Jr., of the National Urban League, I. M. Pei, Philip Johnson, and urban planner Chester A. Rapkin, who was then spearheading efforts to preserve and rezone SoHo (a name he coined).

15. It didn't hurt that Robertson was from a patrician family with strong ties to the new mayor. His father, Walter S. Robertson, was John Foster Dulles's right-hand man at the State Department, where he helped craft the fateful policy of nonrecognition of the People's Republic of China; his mother was a close friend of Lindsay's mother-in-law, Mary Hawes. Jonathan Barnett, interview with author, November 11, 2016, Philadelphia; Donald H. Elliott, interview with author, December 14, 2016, New York City.

16. Robert D. McFadden, "John V. Lindsay, Mayor and Maverick, Dies at 79," *New York Times*, December 21, 2000; "Design of the City," *New York Times*, February 13, 1967; John Kifner, "Architect Named to Planning Body," *New York Times*, May 14, 1967; Temko in Mayor's Task Force on Urban Design, *The Threatened City* (1967), n.p.

17. Manbeck, *Neighborhoods of Brooklyn*, 41; Alfred Kazin, *A Walker in the City*, in *Writing New York: A Literary Anthology*, ed. Phillip Lopate (New York: Washington Square Press, 1998), 733; Jerald E. Podair, *The Strike That Changed New York* (New Haven, CT: Yale University Press, 2002), 17; Jonathan Randal, "Brownsville: Neighborhood of Poverty and Strife," *New York Times*, July 17, 1966; John P. Callahan, "Sharp Rise in Crime Alarms Brownsville," *New York Times*, July 8, 1967; "Brownsville Tailor Stabbed to Death after $4 Robbery," *New York Times*, December 2, 1966; "Brownsville Synagogue Vandalized," *New York Times*, August 5, 1967; "40 Negroes Leave Brooklyn Homes," *New York Times*, July 20, 1966; "Brooklyn Unrest Worries Lindsay," *New York Times*, July 30, 1966.

18. Podair, *The Strike That Changed New York*, 17–19.

19. Allen quoted in Vincent J. Cannato, *The Ungovernable City: John Lindsay and His Struggle to Save New York* (New York: Basic Books, 2001), 270.

20. Cannato, *Ungovernable City*, 631n.

21. Diane Ravitch makes a similar point in *The Great School Wars: A History of the New York City Public Schools* (Baltimore: Johns Hopkins University Press, 1974), 268.

22. Max Wolff, "The Educational Park," *American School and University*, July 1964, 9.

23. Cyril G. Sargent and Allan R. Talbot, "A Linear City for New York," in *A Report on the Education Park* (Wilton, CT: CORDE Corporation, 1967), 7–9; Thabit, *How East New York Became a Ghetto*, 160–161; "'Under One Roof,'" *New York Times*, May 14, 1961; Leonard Buder, "Parley Explores Education Parks," *New York Times*, June 25, 1964.

24. M. A. Farber, "7 School Plans Protested Here," *New York Times*, June 21, 1966; Leonard Buder, "Delay Is Ordered on 7 City Schools," *New York Times*, June 29, 1966.

25. Douglas Robinson, "Mayor Walks Alone into Angry Crowd and Draws Cheers," *New York Times*, July 20, 1966; Leonard Buder, "City Considering New School Park," *New York Times*, August 16, 1966; Thabit, *How East New York Became a Ghetto*, 161. Thabit's date of September 1965 for the Board of Education's two-park Brooklyn plan is incorrect; it was 1966. He may have confused this with the board's 1965 approval of the two Bronx education parks.

26. "Some Information on the Size and Location of the Campus High School for Boston" (unpublished fact sheet, Boston, Metropolitan Council for Educational Opportunity, 1966); Joseph M. Cronin, *Reforming Boston Schools, 1930–2006* (New York: Palgrave Macmillan, 2011), 58; Allan R. Talbot, interview with author. November 14, 2016, New York City.

27. Sargent and Talbot, "A Linear City for New York," 70. Talbot and Sargent's Linear City proposal was illustrated with renderings by David Crane and Baltimore architect Peter Paul.

28. Ibid., 71–73, 78.

29. "U. S. Architects Are Helping Iraq," *New York Times*, November 7, 1965; *American Architects Directory* (New York: R. R. Bowker, 1970), 622; McMillan Griffis Mileto: architects, planners (portfolio of work), 1967.

30. George R. Collins, "The Linear City," in *AYB11: The Pedestrian in the City*, ed. David Lewis (London: Paul Elek, 1965), 204–205.

31. Edgar Chambless, *Roadtown* (New York: Roadtown Press, 1910), 19–20, 89; "Chambless's Dream City," *New York Times*, September 19, 1910; "'Roadtown': A New Idea," *New York Times*, October 1, 1910.

32. Milo Hastings, "How a Great Garment City Might Be Built," *Sun*, December 24, 1916; "A One-Line City Plan to Avoid Congestion," *New York Times*, March 19, 1933; "An Invention Ten Miles Long," *Popular Mechanics* 60:6 (December 1933): 845–848; "Moving Big Cities to the Country Is Aim of 'Roadtown' Housing Plan," *Kingston Daily Freeman*, September 15, 1933; "City Plan Expert Ends Life by Gas," *New York Times*, June 1, 1936. On Greenbelt as "the alternate to a Washington-Baltimore Roadtown," see Roadtown Research Files, Series B, Folder B036, The George Collins Collection on Linear City Planning, Special Collections, Frances Loeb Library, Graduate School of Design, Harvard University.

33. F. Sherry McKay, "Negotiating Modernity: Representing Algiers, 1930–1942" (PhD diss., University of British Columbia, 1994); Brian Ackley, "Le Corbusier's Algerian Fantasy," *Bidoun* 6 (Winter 2006); Jacques Quiton, ed., *The Ideas of Le Corbusier on Architecture and Urban Planning* (New York: George Braziller, 1981), 111; Collins, "The Linear City," 212.

34. Seth S. King, "Linear City Asked in Brooklyn Plan," *New York Times*, February 26, 1967; Maurice Carroll, "Brooklyn Road Plan Halted by Lindsay," *New York Times*, May 4, 1969; Carroll, "U. S. Rejects Lindsay Proposal for a Cross-Brooklyn Highway," *New York Times*, March 8, 1967; Peter Kihss, "City Still Seeking Road in Brooklyn," *New York Times*, March 9, 1967; Steven V. Roberts, "First Steps Taken toward Creation of 'Linear City,'" *New York Times*, November 13, 1967.

35. James F. Clarity, "U. S. Aid Is Quietly Pledged for Cross Brooklyn Expressway," *New York Times*, April 26, 1967; Archibald C. Rogers et al., *Linear City and Cross Brooklyn Expressway: "Plan for Planning" Report* (Baltimore: Rogers, Taliaferro, Kostritsky, Lamb, 1967), 7; Ada Louise Huxtable, "How to Build a City, If You Can," *New York Times*, March 12, 1967.

36. Clayton Knowles, "New Plans Prepared for Downtown Expressway," *New York Times*, March 28, 1967; Seth S. King, "Board of Estimate Votes Expressway across Manhattan," *New York Times*, March 8, 1968; Charles G. Bennett, "Mayor Asks Prompt Start for 2 Expressways Here," *New York Times*, April 2, 1968; Flint, *Wrestling with Moses*, xii–xv.

37. Richard L. Madden, "State Asks Cross-Brooklyn Road," *New York Times*, May 7, 1968; Madden, "U. S. Agrees to Aid Lindsay Proposal for a Linear City," *New York Times*, May 7, 1968; Rogers, *Linear City and Cross Brooklyn Expressway*, 9–10, 18–19, 24. To head the Linear City Development Corporation, Lindsay chose George Zeidenstein, a young Harvard lawyer just back from the Peace Corps who would go on to a distinguished career in international development.

38. David K. Shipler, "Mayor Asks School Site Changes Because of Linear City 'Delays,'" *New York Times*, February 7, 1969; "Lindsay Rebutted by Lefkowitz on Linear City Program Delays," *New York Times*, February 11, 1969; Maurice Carroll, "Brooklyn Road Plan Halted by Lindsay," *New York Times*, May 4, 1969; Carroll, "Mayor Drops Plans for Express Roads across 2 Boroughs," *New York Times*, July 17, 1969; Ada

Louise Huxtable, "Politics of Expressways, *New York Times*, July 17, 1969; Michael Stern, "Lower Manhattan Happy That Road Is 'Dead,'" *New York Times*, July 18, 1969; "Construction Halted," *New York Times*, July 19, 1969; Glen Fowler, "Planners' Confrontation Defeats an Expressway," *New York Times*, July 13, 1969.

CHAPTER 18. BOOK OF EXODUS

1. The epigraph is from "After Era of Stability, Flatbush Yields to Change," *New York Times*, February 14, 1968; Pete Hamill, "Brooklyn: The Sane Alternative," *New York*, July 14, 1969.

2. Ibid.

3. Roger Starr, *The Rise and Fall of New York City* (New York: Basic Books, 1985), 104, 113; Cannato, *Ungovernable City*, 525; Philip Jenkins, *Decade of Nightmares: The End of the Sixties and the Making of Eighties America* (New York: Oxford University Press, 2006), 135.

4. Michael W. Flamm, *In the Heat of the Summer: The New York Riots of 1964 and the War on Crime* (Philadelphia: University of Pennsylvania Press, 2016), 48.

5. Ibid., 175–177; Fred Powledge, "Poll Shows Whites in City Resent Civil Rights Drive," *New York Times*, September 21, 1964.

6. Cannato, *Ungovernable City*, 527; Sidney E. Zion, "Interracial Assaults," *New York Times*, April 18, 1967; Adam Shatz, "Out of Sight, Out of Mind," *London Review of Books* 39:9 (May 4, 2017); Michael Stern, "Fear Soars with Rate of Crime," *New York Times*, December 11, 1968; Cannato, *Ungovernable City*, 528; Flamm, *In the Heat of the Summer*, 64; Robert D. McFadden, "Winston Moseley, Who Killed Kitty Genovese, Dies in Prison at 81," *New York Times*, April 4, 2016; Irving Spiegel, "400 Pay Respect to Slain Teacher," *New York Times*, June 1, 1964; Robert Alden, "Youth, 17, Admits to Slaying 2 Women," *New York Times*, September 22, 1964.

7. Woodsworth, *Battle for Bed-Stuy*, 13; "After Era of Stability, Flatbush Yields to Change," *New York Times*, February 14, 1968; Jenkins, *Decade of Nightmares*, 138; Jonathan Rieder, *Canarsie: The Jews and Italians of Brooklyn against Liberalism* (Cambridge, MA: Harvard University Press, 1985), 66; Cannato, *Ungovernable City*, 393.

8. Michael Stern, "Fear Soars with Rate of Crime," *New York Times*, December 11, 1968.

9. David Burnham, "The Changing City: Crime on the Rise," *New York Times*, June 3, 1969.

10. Starr, *The Rise and Fall of New York City*, 116–117.

11. George S. Masnick, "Home Ownership and Social Inequality in the United States," in *Home Ownership and Social Inequality in a Comparative Perspective*, ed. Karin Kurz (Palo Alto, CA: Stanford University Press, 2004), 307–308.

12. Andy McCue, *Mover and Shaker: Walter O'Malley, the Dodgers, and Baseball's Westward Expansion* (Lincoln: University of Nebraska Press, 2014), 26–28; Susanne Spellen, "Walkabout: The Architect, the Baseball Stadium and a Really Bad Couple of Years," *Brownstoner*, June 25, 2015), http://www.brownstoner .com/history/walkabout-the-architect-the-baseball-stadium-and-a-really-bad-couple-of-years/.

13. McCue, *Mover and Shaker*, 32, 34.

14. Ibid., 34–36, 38–42.

15. Michael Shapiro, *The Last Good Season: Brooklyn, the Dodgers, and Their Final Pennant Race Together* (New York: Doubleday, 2003), 35; "Emil Praeger, 81, Engineer, Is Dead," *New York Times*, October 17, 1973.

16. "New Ebbets Field to Have Hot Dogs and Hot Seats," *New York Times*, March 6, 1952; Tom Meany, "Baseball's Answer to TV," *Collier's*, September 27, 1952, 60–62.

17. Brooklyn National League Baseball Club, press release, August 17, 1955, Walter O'Malley: The Official Website, https://www.walteromalley.com/en/biography/reference/Introduction/view-all. "O'Malley Stresses Need for Arena," *Brooklyn Eagle*, October 1, 1952; Meany, "Baseball's Answer to TV," 60–62.

18. Walter O'Malley to Eero Saarinen, April 18, 1955, Walter O'Malley: The Official Website, https://www.walteromalley.com/en/historic-documents/Business-Correspondence/092454---060255; Walter O'Malley to Buckminster Fuller, May 26, 1955, Walter O'Malley: The Official Website, https://www.walteromalley.com/en/historic-documents/Business-Correspondence/092454---060255; Buckminster Fuller to Walter O'Malley, June 14, 1955, Walter O'Malley: The Official Website, https://www.walteromalley.com/en/historic-documents/Business-Correspondence/092454---060255.

19. "Dodger Stadium Study Set," *New York Times*, September 30, 1955; "Stadium with Dome Studied by Dodgers," *New York Times*, October 1, 1955; "O'Malley Views Stadium Model," *New York Herald Tribune*, November 23, 1955; "Dodger Head Hails Studies Made for Domed Stadium," *New York Times*, November 23, 1955; "Student Designs a Stadium for Dodgers," *New York Times*, January 22, 1956; Frank Tinsley, "A Dome Grows in Brooklyn," *Mechanix Illustrated*, July 1956. Peter O'Malley and Roland Seidler have suggested that O'Malley's own thirty-two-foot-long greenhouse at his Amityville home, where he and his wife grew exotic orchids, may have primed his interest in a translucent roof.

20. The best accounts, in addition to Andy McCue's *Mover and Shaker*, are Robert E. Murphy, *After Many a Summer: The Passing of the Giants and Dodgers and a Golden Age in New York Baseball* (New York: Union Square Press, 2009), and Shapiro, *The Last Good Season*.

21. Moses quoted in "Biography: Putting Their Domes Together," Walter O'Malley: The Official Website, https://www.walteromalley.com/en/biography/reference/Putting-Their-Domes-Together; "Student Thesis Envisions Indoor Dodger Stadium," *New York Herald Tribune*, January 22, 1956.

22. Charles J. Mylod, Robert E. Blum, and Chester A. Allen., *Interim Report of Brooklyn Sports Center Authority* (November 15, 1956), 1.

23. Robert Moses to John P. McGrath, April 23, 1956, Box 100, Robert Moses Papers, Manuscripts and Archives Division, New York Public Library; Murphy, *After Many a Summer*, 155–156.

24. Gilmore D. Clarke and Michael Rapuano, *A Planning Study for the Area Bounded by Vanderbilt Avenue, DeKalb Avenue, Sterling Place and Bond Street in the Borough of Brooklyn, New York, New York* (New York: Clarke and Rapuano, 1956).

25. "Manhattan to Lose Last Trolley Sunday," *New York Times*, June 25, 1947; "Buses to Replace Trolleys Sunday," *Brooklyn Eagle*, January 25, 1951; "Flatbush Trolley Line to End Sunday," *Brooklyn Eagle*, March 2, 1951; "An Era of Trolleys Ends in Brooklyn," *New York Herald Tribune*, November 1, 1956; "The Last Trolley Car," *New York Times*, April 5, 1957. On New Rochelle, see "Last Trolley Ends It All," *Brooklyn Eagle*, December 17, 1950.

26. Robert Moses, "Robert Moses on the Battle of Brooklyn," *Sports Illustrated*, July 22, 1957.

27. Leo Durocher, "Los Angeles Will Love the Dodgers!" *New York Herald Tribune*, March 9, 1958; McCue, *Mover and Shaker*, 32, 120.

28. "Coney Island, N.Y.," *Billboard*, July 21, 1945; "Coney Island, N.Y.," *Billboard*, September 17, 1949; Michael P. Onorato, email messages to author, May 31, 2017, and June 2, 2017; Michael P. Onorato, ed., *Steeplechase Park, Coney Island, NY, The Diary of James J. Onorato, 1928–1964*, vol. 2 (Bellingham, WA: Pacific Rim Books, 2000), 104–105.

29. "Many Persons Made Ill by Hart's Garbage Plan," *Brooklyn Daily Eagle*, October 23, 1900; "Cared for by Neighbors," *Brooklyn Daily Eagle*, October 18, 1909; "The Dreamland Fire," *New-York Tribune*, May 28, 1911; "Brooklyn Notes," *Chicago Defender*, September 8, 1923; "Amsterdam News Gives Picnic for 300 Boys," *New York Amsterdam News*, September 3, 1938; "Waiters' Strike Dies Hard," *New-York Tribune*, June 23, 1912; "The Talk of the Day," *New-York Tribune*, November 6, 1911; "Barkers Bark and Hot Dogs Sizzle When Coney Opens with a Bang," *New-York Tribune*, May 20, 1917; "Ballyhoo Bam Boula Too Free with Bruin," *New-York Tribune*, August 14, 1916; "Bottle Thrown by Wild Man of Coney Island Injures Two," *New York Herald Tribune*, August 8, 1927.

30. "Negro Held for Stabbing," *New-York Tribune*, May 27, 1912; "Meet Discrimination at Coney Island," *New York Amsterdam News*, July 20, 1927; "George E. Wibecan," *Brooklyn Daily Eagle*, July 19, 1912; "Negroes Seek Pinky Picture for Church," *Brooklyn Daily Eagle*, May 27, 1928; "Wibecan Loses Suit," *Chicago Defender*, July 31, 1920.

31. "Meet Discrimination at Coney Island," *New York Amsterdam News*, July 20, 1927.

32. "Integration Has Setbacks," *Amusement Business*, July 13, 1963; "Integration Front Booming," *Amusement Business*, August 17, 1963; "Gwynn Oak Integrates," *Amusement Business*, August 3, 1963; "Negroes March on Okla. Fun Park," *Amusement Business*, July 6, 1963; "Integration Has Setbacks," *Amusement Business*, July 13, 1963; "Gwynne Oak: 'Progress' Makes Dilemma," *Amusement Business*, July 20, 1963; "Race Issues at Park Pools," *Amusement Business*, July 4, 1964. Gwynn Oak Park eventually opened to African Americans in a settlement negotiated by the future vice president Spiro T. Agnew; it closed in 1973.

33. Jeff Wiltse, *Contested Waters: A Social History of Swimming Pools in America* (Chapel Hill: University of North Carolina Press, 2007), 124, 126; "Gwynn Oak Integrates," *Amusement Business*, August 3, 1963; "Mich. Racial Case Dissolves," *Amusement Business*, September 28, 1963; "Memphis Park 'Private Club,'" *Amusement Business*, July 18, 1964; Wiltse, 183, 199–201.

34. "Charges Dancehall Bars All Negroes," *Amsterdam News*, July 27, 1940; "Coney Island Dance Hall Faces Suit," *Chicago Defender*, August 3, 1940; "Negro Congress Fights Coney Island Jim Crow," *Chicago Defender*, August 23, 1941; "Coney Island, N.Y.," *Billboard*, June 11, 1955, 57; Langston Hughes, "Here to Yonder: This Summer," *Chicago Defender*, August 9, 1947.

35. See, for example, Grantland Rice, *Canned Thrills*, produced by John L. Hawkinson (New York: Pathé Pictures, 1928) and *Let's Go Coney! Island* (London: British Pathé, 1932).

36. Michael P. Onorato, email message to author, June 22, 2017; Onorato, *Another Time, Another World*, 48, 58; *The Diary of James J. Onorato, 1928–1964*, 4:106; Philip Benjamin, "Color Line Bars Bunche and Son from Forest Hills Tennis Club," *New York Times*, July 9, 1959.

37. *The Diary of James J. Onorato, 1928–1964*, 4:376; Michael P. Onorato, email message to author, June 22, 2017; "Frank S. Tilyou of Coney Island," *New York Times*, May 9, 1964; James J. Onorato to

Michael P. Onorato, May 8, 1964, in *Steeplechase Park and the Decline of Coney Island: An Oral History*, ed. Michael P. Onorato (Bellingham, WA: Pacific Rim Books, 2003), 44; Robert Trumbull, "Beaches Popular on 91-Degree Day," *New York Times*, May 25, 1964.

38. *The Diary of James J. Onorato, 1928–1964*, 4:387.

39. Emanuel Perlmutter, "Gangs on Subway Terrorize Riders," *New York Times*, June 1, 1964.

40. James J. Onorato to Michael P. Onorato, September 25, 1964, in Onorato, *Steeplechase Park and the Decline of Coney Island*, 47; Onorato, *Another Time, Another World*, xi–xii.

EPILOGUE. UNDER A TUNGSTEN SUN

1. The epigraph is drawn from Pete Hamill, "A New Day Dawns," *New York Magazine*, April 21, 1986. As noted earlier, the best account of Brooklyn's early gentrification is Osman's *The Invention of Brownstone Brooklyn*.

2. Jane Jacobs, *The Death and Life of Great American Cities* (New York: Vintage Books, 1961); Harvey Molotch, "The City as a Growth Machine: Toward a Political Economy of Place," *American Journal of Sociology* 82:2 (September 1976).

3. Gabriel Sherman, "The Flying Walentases," *New York*, June 17, 2014.

4. Mark Grief, "What Was the Hipster?" *New York*, October 25, 2010.

5. Sharon Zukin, *Naked City: The Death and Life of Authentic Urban Places* (New York: Oxford University Press, 2010), x.

6. Ibid., x–xiii.

7. There was just one exception, and a partial one at that—a cozy Caribbean wine bar near Ditmas Avenue called Sip Unwine, but their pendants used regular incandescent bulbs rather than the retro Edison style.

SELECTED BIBLIOGRAPHY

Adams, Charles Francis, ed. *The Works of John Adams*. Vol. 4. Boston: Little, Brown, and Company, 1856.

Adams, Thomas. *The Building of the City*. New York: Regional Plan of New York and Its Environs, 1931.

Agee, James. *Brooklyn Is: Southeast of the Island*. New York: Fordham University Press, 2005.

Alexiou, Joseph. *Gowanus: Brooklyn's Curious Canal*. New York: New York University Press, 2015.

Backus, Isaac. *A history of New-England, with particular reference to the denomination of Christians called Baptists*. Boston: Edward Draper, 1777.

Barnes, Frank, and Louis Morris. "The 'Maryland 400' at the Cortelyou House, Brooklyn, NY: The Action and the Burial Site." National Park Service—Region Five, unpublished report, May 20, 1957.

Barnett, Jonathan. *Urban Design as Public Policy*. New York: Architectural Record Books, 1974.

Bart, Sheldon. *Race to the Top of the World*. Washington, DC: Regnery History, 2013.

Beecher, Henry Ward. *Norwood, or Village Life in New England*. New York: Fords, Howard & Hulbert, 1888.

Bennett, Cora L. *Floyd Bennett*. New York: W. F. Payson, 1932.

Bennett, Gertrude Ryder. *Turning Back the Clock*. Francestown, NH: Marshall Jones Company, 1982.

Berenberg, Richard. "Village Improvement Societies in New England, 1850–1900: The Rural Ideal in an Age of Rural Depopulation and Urban Growth." PhD diss., Harvard University, 1966.

Berman, Marshall. *All That Is Solid Melts into Air: The Experience of Modernity*. New York: Penguin Books, 1982.

Beveridge, Charles E., and Carolyn F. Hoffman, eds. *The Papers of Frederick Law Olmsted: Writings on Public Parks, Parkways, and Park Systems*. Baltimore: Johns Hopkins University Press, 1997.

Bigelow, Jacob. *History of Mount Auburn Cemetery*. Boston: James Munroe and Company, 1860.

Black, Frederick R. *Jamaica Bay: A History*. Washington, DC: National Park Service, 1981.

Blair, Gwenda. *The Trumps*. New York: Simon & Schuster, 2000.

Blakemore, Porter R., and Dana C. Linck. *Historic Structures Report, Historical Data Section, Floyd Bennett Field, Gateway National Recreation Area*. Vol. 1. National Park Service, Denver Service Center, unpublished report, 1981.

Bloom, Sol. *The Autobiography of Sol Bloom*. New York: G. P. Putnam's Sons, 1948.

Bolton, Reginald Pelham. *Indian Life Long Ago in the City of New York*. Port Washington, NY: Ira J. Friedman, 1971 [1934].

———. *Indian Paths in the Great Metropolis*. New York: Museum of the American Indian, 1922.

———. *New York City in Indian Possession*. New York: Museum of the American Indian, 1920.

Bowden, James. *The History of the Society of Friends in America*. Vol. 1. London: Charles Gilpin, 1850.

Brearley, Harry Chase. *The Problem of Greater New York and Its Solution*. New York: Committee on Industrial Development of the Brooklyn League / Search-Light Book Corporation, 1914.

Bremer, Francis J. *Building a New Jerusalem: John Davenport, a Puritan in Three Worlds*. New Haven, CT: Yale University Press, 2012.

Bryant, John H., and Harold N. Cones. *Dangerous Crossings: The First Modern Polar Expedition, 1925*. Annapolis, MD: Naval Institute Press, 2000.

Burrows, Edwin G., and Mike Wallace. *Gotham: A History of New York City to 1898*. London: Oxford University Press, 1999.

Caccavajo, Joseph. *The Development of Brooklyn and Queens*. Brooklyn, NY: Allied Boards, 1909.

Campanella, Thomas J. *Cities from the Sky: An Aerial Portrait of America*. New York: Princeton Architectural Press, 2001.

Cannato, Vincent J. *The Ungovernable City: John Lindsay and His Struggle to Save New York*. New York: Basic Books, 2001.

Capote, Truman. *Portraits and Observations*. New York: Modern Library, 2008.

Caro, Robert A. *The Power Broker: Robert Moses and the Fall of New York*. New York: Knopf, 1974.

Carroll, John T., et al. *Cross Brooklyn Expressway: Benefits for Brooklyn*. New York: Brill Engineering Corporation, 1967.

Cavallo, Dominick. *Muscles and Morals: Organized Playgrounds and Urban Reform, 1880–1920*. Philadelphia: University of Pennsylvania Press, 1981.

Ceci, Lynn. "The Effect of European Contact and Trade on the Settlement Pattern of Indians in Coastal New York, 1524–1665: The Archaeological and Documentary Evidence." PhD diss., City University of New York, 1977.

———. *The Effect of European Contact and Trade on the Settlement Pattern of Indians in Coastal New York, 1524–1665*. New York: Garland Publishing, 1990.

Chambless, Edgar. *Roadtown*. New York: Roadtown Press, 1910.

Chauncey, George. *Gay New York*. New York: Basic Books, 1995.

Clarke, Gilmore D., and Michael Rapuano. *A Planning Study for the Area Bounded by Vanderbilt Avenue, DeKalb Avenue, Sterling Place and Bond Street in the Borough of Brooklyn, New York, New York*. New York: Clarke and Rapuano, 1956.

Cleaveland, Nehemiah. *Green-Wood Cemetery: A History of the Institution from 1838 to 1864*. New York: Anderson and Archer, 1866.

———. *Green-Wood Illustrated*. New York: Robert Martin, 1847.

Cody, Sarah K., and John Auwaerter. *Cultural Landscape Report for Floyd Bennett Field*. Boston: Olmsted Center for Landscape Preservation, 2009.

Cranz, Galen. *The Politics of Park Design: A History of Urban Parks in America*. Cambridge, MA: MIT Press, 1982.

Cronon, William. *Changes in the Land*. New York: Hill and Wang, 1983.

Danckaerts, Jasper, and Peter Sluyter. *Journal of a Voyage to New York*. Translated by Henry C. Murphy. Vol. 1 of *Memoirs of the Long Island Historical Society*. Brooklyn, NY: Long Island Historical Society, 1887.

Denson, Charles. *Coney Island: Lost and Found*. Berkeley, CA: Ten Speed Press, 2004.

Denton, Daniel. *A Brief Description of New York: Formerly Called New-Netherlands*. London: John Hancock, 1670.

Dickens, Charles. "American Notes." In *Works of Charles Dickens*, vol. 2. New York: Sheldon and Company, 1865.

Dilliard, Maud E. *An Album of New Netherland*. New York: Twayne Publishers, 1963.

———. *Old Dutch Houses of Brooklyn*. New York: R. R. Smith, 1945.

Ditmas, Charles A. *Historic Homesteads of Kings County*. Brooklyn, NY: The Compiler, 1909.

Douglas, David B. *Exposition of the Plan and Objects of the Green-Wood Cemetery*. New York: Narine and Company, 1839.

Downing, Andrew Jackson. *Rural Essays*. New York: George A. Leavitt, 1869 [1858].

Dwight, Timothy. *Travels in New-England and New-York*. Vol. 3. London: William Baynes and Son, 1828.

Ehrlich, Walter. *Zion in the Valley: The Jewish Community of St. Louis*. Columbia: University of Missouri Press, 1997.

Evenson, Norma. *Le Corbusier: The Machine and the Grand Design*. New York: George Braziller, 1969.

Farley, Philip P., William G. Ford, and John J. McLaughlin. *Report of the Jamaica Bay Improvement Commission*. New York: Martin P. Brown Press, 1907.

Fernow, Berthold, ed. *Documents Relating to the History of the Early Colonial Settlements Principally on Long Island*. Albany, NY: Weed, Parsons and Company, 1883.

Field, Thomas W. *The Battle of Long Island*. Brooklyn, NY: Long Island Historical Society, 1869.

Fischer, David Hackett. *Washington's Crossing*. New York: Oxford University Press, 2004.

Flamm, Michael W. *In the Heat of the Summer: The New York Riots of 1964 and the War on Crime*. Philadelphia: University of Pennsylvania Press, 2016.

Flint, Martha Bockée. *Early Long Island: A Colonial Study*. New York: G. P. Putnam's Sons, 1896.

Fogelson, Robert M. *Downtown: Its Rise and Fall, 1880–1950*. New Haven, CT: Yale University Press, 2001.

——. *The Great Rent Wars: New York, 1917–1929*. New Haven, CT: Yale University Press, 2013.

Franklin, H. Bruce. *The Most Important Fish in the Sea: Menhaden and America*. Washington, DC: Island Press, 2007.

Freeman, Joshua B. *Working-Class New York: Life and Labor since World War II*. New York: The New Press, 2001.

Friede, Samuel M. *Friede Globe Tower: Built of Steel, 700 Feet High*. New York: self-published, 1906.

Friedmann, Robert. *The Theology of Anabaptism: An Interpretation*. Scottsdale, PA: Herald Press, 1973.

Fries, Sylvia Doughty. *The Urban Idea in Colonial America*. Philadelphia: Temple University Press, 1977.

Fry, Charles S., and Edward A. Fry. *Abstracts of Wiltshire: Inquisitions Post Mortem, Returned into the Court of Chancery in the Reign of Charles the First*. London: Wiltshire Archaeological and Natural History Society, 1901.

Furman, Gabriel. *Antiquities of Long Island*. New York: J. W. Bouton, 1875.

Garvan, Anthony N. B. *Architecture and Town Planning in Colonial Connecticut*. New Haven, CT: Yale University Press, 1951.

Gerard, James W. *Lady Deborah Moody: A Discourse*. New York: F. B. Patterson, 1880.

Giedion, Sigfried. *Space, Time and Architecture: The Growth of a New Tradition*. Cambridge, MA: Harvard University Press, 1952.

Gilpin, William. *Essays on Picturesque Beauty*. London: Richmond Blamire, 1792.

Goerler, Raimund E., ed. *To the Pole: The Diary and Notebook of Richard E. Byrd, 1925–1927*. Columbus: Ohio State University Press, 1998.

Goliszek, Andrew. *In the Name of Science: A History of Secret Programs, Medical Research, and Human Experimentation*. New York: Macmillan, 2003.

Gomez, Michael A. *Black Crescent: The Experience and Legacy of African Muslims in the Americas*. New York: Cambridge University Press, 2005.

Graff, M. M. *Central Park, Prospect Park: A New Perspective*. New York: Greensward Foundation, 1985.

Grout, Edward M. *Improvement and Development of Jamaica Bay*. New York: Martin B. Brown Press, 1905.

Grumet, Robert Steven. *Native American Place Names in New York City*. New York: Museum of the City of New York, 1981.

Hall, Peter. *Cities of Tomorrow*. Oxford: Blackwell, 1988.

Halton, Eugene. *The Great Brain Suck: And Other American Epiphanies*. Chicago: University of Chicago Press, 2008.

Hammack, David C. *Power and Society: Greater New York at the Turn of the Century*. New York: Russell Sage Foundation, 1982.

Hicks, Saretta G. *Documentary History of Gravesend Town and Dame Deborah Moody, 1643–1659*, TMs [photocopy]. Brooklyn, NY: Brooklyn Historical Society, 1964.

Hillis, Newell Dwight. *The Blot on the Kaiser's 'Scutcheon*. New York: Fleming H. Revell Company, 1918.

Hirsch, Mark D. *William C. Whitney: Modern Warwick*. New York: Dodd, Mead, 1948.

Hobsbawm, Eric, and Terence Ranger, eds. *The Invention of Tradition*. Cambridge: Cambridge University Press, 1983.

Hodges, Graham Russell. *Root and Branch: African Americans in New York and East Jersey, 1613–1863*. Chapel Hill: University of North Carolina Press, 1999.

Hodges, Graham Russell, and Alan Edward Brown, eds. *"Pretends to Be Free": Runaway Slave Advertisements from Colonial and Revolutionary New York and New Jersey*. New York: Garland Publishing, 1994.

Hotaling, Ed. *Wink: The Incredible Life and Epic Journey of Jimmy Winkfield*. New York: McGraw-Hill, 2005.

Hughes, Evan. *Literary Brooklyn: The Writers of Brooklyn and the Story of American City Life*. New York: Henry Holt, 2011.

Hum, Tarry. *Making a Global Immigrant Neighborhood*. Philadelphia: Temple University Press, 2014.

Huxtable, Ada Louise. *Will They Ever Finish Bruckner Boulevard?* New York: Macmillan, 1970.

Irving, Washington. *The Complete Works of Washington Irving*. Frankfort: Schmerber, 1835.

——. *The Sketch Book of Geoffrey Crayon, Gent.* Chicago: Belford, Clarke and Company, 1885 [1819].

Jacobs, Jane. *The Death and Life of Great American Cities*. New York: Vintage Books, 1961.

Janowitz, Meta F., and Diane Dallal, eds. *Tales of Gotham, Historical Archaeology, Ethnohistory and Microhistory of New York City*. New York: Springer, 2013.

Jenkins, Philip. *Decade of Nightmares: The End of the Sixties and the Making of Eighties America*. New York: Oxford University Press, 2006.

Jones, Rufus M. *The Story of George Fox*. New York: The Macmillan Company, 1919.

Jorgensen, Emil O., ed. *Report of the National Tax Relief Convention*. Chicago: Manufacturers and Merchants Federal Tax League, 1924.

Juet, Robert. *Juet's Journal of Hudson's 1609 Voyage*. Transcribed by Brea Barthel from 1625 edition of *Purchas His Pilgrimes*. Albany, NY: New Netherland Museum, 2006.

Kasson, John F. *Amusing the Million: Coney Island at the Turn of the Century*. New York: Farrar, Straus and Giroux, 1978.

Kaufman, Herbert. *Gotham in the Air Age*. Washington, DC: Committee on Public Administration Cases, 1950.

Kiernan, Ben. *Blood and Soil: A World History of Genocide and Extermination from Sparta to Darfur*. New Haven, CT: Yale University Press, 2008.

King, Moses. *King's Views of New York*. New York: Sackett & Wilhelms Company, 1903.

Koolhaas, Rem. *Delirious New York: A Retroactive Manifesto for Manhattan*. New York: The Monacelli Press, 1994.

Kowsky, Francis R. *Country, Park and City: The Architecture and Life of Calvert Vaux*. New York: Oxford University Press, 1998.

Krogius, Henrik. *The Brooklyn Heights Promenade*. Charleston, SC: The History Press, 2011.

Lamb, Martha J. *History of the City of New York*. New York: A. S. Barnes, 1877.

Lay, Charles Downing. *The Freedom of the City*. New York: Duffield and Company, 1926.

Le Corbusier. *Aircraft*. Milan: Abitare Segesta, 1996 [1935].

Lewis, Alonso. *The History of Lynn*. Boston: Samuel Dickinson, 1844.

Linder, Marc, and Larry Zacharias. *Of Cabbages and Kings County: Agriculture and the Formation of Modern Brooklyn*. Iowa City: University of Iowa, 1999.

Lipscomb, Andrew A., ed. *Notes on Virginia*. Vol. 2 of *The Writings of Thomas Jefferson*. Washington, DC: Thomas Jefferson Memorial Association, 1904.

Lopate, Phillip, ed. *Writing New York: A Literary Anthology*. New York: Washington Square Press, 1998.

Macdonald, Elizabeth. *Pleasure Drives and Promenades: A History of Frederick Law Olmsted's Brooklyn Parkways*. Chicago: Center for American Places at Columbia College, 2012.

MacManus, Edgar J. *A History of Negro Slavery in New York*. New York: Syracuse University Press, 1966.

Manbeck, John B., ed. *The Neighborhoods of Brooklyn*. New Haven, CT: Yale University Press, 1998.

Martin, Joseph Plumb. *A Narrative of Some of the Adventures, Dangers and Sufferings of a Revolutionary Soldier*. Hallowell, ME: Glazier, Masters & Company, 1830.

Mayor's Task Force on Urban Design. *The Threatened City: A Report on the Design of the City of New York*. New York: Department of City Planning, 1967.

McCue, Andy. *Mover and Shaker: Walter O'Malley, the Dodgers, and Baseball's Westward Expansion*. Lincoln: University of Nebraska Press, 2014.

McCullers, Carson. *The Mortgaged Heart: Selected Writings*. New York: Houghton Mifflin, 2005 [1971].

McShane, Clay, and Joel A. Tarr. *The Horse in the City: Living Machines in the Nineteenth Century*. Baltimore: Johns Hopkins University Press, 2007.

Mee, Arthur, ed. *Berkshire: Alfred's Own Country*. London: Hodder and Stoughton, 1939.

Michaux, F. André. *The North American Sylva, or A Description of the Forest Trees of the United States, Canada and Nova Scotia*. Vol. 3. Philadelphia: Dobson and Conrad, 1819.

Miller, Benjamin. *Fat of the Land*. New York: Four Walls Eight Windows, 2000.

Miller, Henry. *Tropic of Capricorn*. London: Flamingo, 1993.

Mittelman, Amy. *Brewing Battles: A History of American Beer*. New York: Algora Publishing, 2008.

Morton, Thomas. *The New English Canaan*. Boston: Prince Society, 1883.

Moses, Robert. *Future Arterial Program: New York City*. New York: Triborough Bridge and Tunnel Authority, 1963.

———. *The Saga of Flushing Meadow*. New York: Triborough Bridge and Tunnel Authority, 1966.

———. *Working for the People*. New York: Harper and Brothers, 1956.

Mumford, Lewis. *The Brown Decades*. New York: Harcourt, Brace and Company, 1931.

———. *The Highway and the City*. New York: Harcourt, Brace & World, 1963.

Murphy, Robert E. *After Many a Summer: The Passing of the Giants and Dodgers and a Golden Age in New York Baseball*. New York: Union Square Press, 2009.

Nelson, James L. *With Fire and Sword: The Battle of Bunker Hill and the Beginning of the American Revolution*. New York: Thomas Dunne Books, 2011.

Newton, Norman T. *Design on the Land: The Development of Landscape Architecture*. Cambridge, MA: Belknap Press of Harvard University Press, 1971.

Nicoll, W. Robertson, ed. *George Fox's Journal*. London: Isbister and Company, 1903.

Norton, Mary Beth. *Founding Mothers & Fathers: Gendered Power and the Forming of American Society*. New York: Random House, 2011.

O'Callaghan, Edmund Bailey. *History of New Netherlands*. Vol. 2. New York: D. Appleton, 1855.

————. *Laws and Ordinances of New Netherland, 1638–1674.* Albany, NY: Weed, Parsons and Company, 1868.

Olmsted, Frederick Law. *Public Parks and the Enlargement of Towns.* Cambridge, MA: Printed for the American Social Science Association at the Riverside Press, 1870.

Olmsted, Frederick Law, and Calvert Vaux. *Observations on the Progress of Improvements in Street Plans.* Brooklyn, NY: Van Anden's Print, 1868.

Olmsted, Frederick Law, Jr., and Theodora Kimball, eds. *Forty Years of Landscape Architecture: Early Years and Experiences.* New York: G. P. Putnam's Sons, 1922.

————, eds. *Forty Years of Landscape Architecture: Central Park.* New York: G. P. Putnam's Sons and Knickerbocker Press, 1928.

Olmsted, Henry King, and George K. Ward. *A Genealogy of the Olmsted Family in America.* New York: A. T. De La Mare Company, 1912.

Onderdonk, Henry, Jr. *Revolutionary Incidents of Suffolk and Kings Counties.* Brooklyn, NY: Leavitt & Company, 1849.

Onorato, Michael P. *Another Time, Another World.* Fullerton: M. P. Onorato and California State University—Fullerton Oral History Program, 1988.

————, ed. *Steeplechase Park and the Decline of Coney Island: An Oral History.* Bellingham, WA: Pacific Rim Books, 2003.

————, ed. *Steeplechase Park, Coney Island, NY: The Diary of James J. Onorato, 1928–1964.* Bellingham, WA: Pacific Rim Books, 2000.

Orwell, George. *Coming Up for Air.* New York: Harcourt, Brace and Company, 1950 [1939].

Osman, Suleiman. *The Invention of Brownstone Brooklyn: Gentrification and the Search for Authenticity in Postwar New York.* London: Oxford University Press, 2011.

Osterweis, Rollin G. *Three Centuries of New Haven, 1638–1938.* New Haven, CT: Yale University Press, 1953.

Overton, Jacqueline. *Long Island's Story.* Garden City, NY: Doubleday, Doran and Company, 1928.

Pace, Antonio, ed. *Luigi Castiglioni's Viaggio: Travels in the United States of North America, 1785–1787.* Syracuse, NY: Syracuse University Press, 1983.

Pirsson, John W. *The Dutch Grants, Harlem Patents and Tidal Creeks.* New York: L. K. Strouse, 1889.

Pisano, Dominick A., ed. *The Airplane in American Culture.* Ann Arbor: University of Michigan Press, 2003.

Podair, Jerald E. *The Strike That Changed New York.* New Haven, CT: Yale University Press, 2002.

Pratt, Frederic B., ed. *Down Town Brooklyn: A Report to the Comptroller of the City of New York on Sites for Public Buildings.* Brooklyn, NY: Borough of Brooklyn, 1913.

Prime, Nathaniel S. *A History of Long Island: From Its First Settlement by Europeans to the Year 1845.* New York: Robert Carter, 1845.

Pritchard, Evan T. *Native New Yorkers: The Legacy of the Algonquin People of New York.* San Francisco: Council Oak Books, 2002.

Pritchett, Wendell. *Brownsville, Brooklyn: Blacks, Jews, and the Changing Face of the Ghetto.* Chicago: University of Chicago Press, 2002.

Quiton, Jacques, ed. *The Ideas of Le Corbusier on Architecture and Urban Planning.* New York: George Braziller, 1981.

Ravitch, Diane. *The Great School Wars: A History of the New York City Public Schools.* Baltimore: Johns Hopkins University Press, 1974.

Register, Woody. *The Kid of Coney Island: Fred Thompson and the Rise of American Amusements.* New York: Oxford University Press, 2001.

Reps, John W. *The Making of Urban America.* Princeton, NJ: Princeton University Press, 1992 [1965].

Ricciardi, Christopher G. "Changing through the Century: Life at the Lott Family Farm in the Nineteenth Century Town of Flatlands, Kings County, New York." PhD diss., Brooklyn College, 2004.

Rieder, Jonathan. *Canarsie: The Jews and Italians of Brooklyn against Liberalism.* Cambridge, MA: Harvard University Press, 1987.

Riess, Steven A. *The Sport of Kings and the Kings of Crime.* Syracuse, NY: Syracuse University Press, 2011.

Robbins, Emily F., ed. *Proceedings of the First National Conference on Race Betterment.* Battle Creek, MI: Race Betterment Foundation, 1914.

Rodgers, Cleveland. *New York Plans for the Future.* New York: Harper & Brothers, 1943.

Rogers, Archibald C., et al. *Linear City and Cross Brooklyn Expressway: "Plan for Planning" Report.* Baltimore: Rogers, Taliaferro, Kostritsky, Lamb, 1967.

Rosen, Christine. *Preaching Eugenics: Religious Leaders and the American Eugenics Movement.* New York: Oxford University Press, 2004.

Rosenberg, Samuel. *American Economic Development since 1945: Growth, Decline and Rejuvenation.* New York: Palgrave Macmillan, 2002.

Ross, Peter. *A History of Long Island*. New York: Lewis Publishing, 1902.

Rutman, Darrett B. *Winthrop's Boston: A Portrait of a Puritan Town, 1630–1649*. New York: W. W. Norton, 1972.

Salisbury, Harrison E. *The Shook-Up Generation*. New York: Harper & Row, 1958.

Scharf, J. Thomas. *History of Westchester County*. Philadelphia: L. E. Preston, 1886.

Schuyler, David, and Jane Turner Censer, eds. *The Papers of Frederick Law Olmsted: The Years of Olmsted, Vaux & Company, 1865–1874*. Baltimore: Johns Hopkins University Press, 1992.

Schuyler, David, and Gregory Kaliss, eds. *The Papers of Frederick Law Olmsted: The Last Great Projects, 1890–1895*. Baltimore: Johns Hopkins University Press, 2015.

Schwartz, Joel. *The New York Approach: Robert Moses, Urban Liberals and Redevelopment of the Inner City*. Columbus: Ohio State University Press, 1993.

Sears, Edward S. *Souvenir Guide to Coney Island*. Brooklyn, NY: Megaphone Press, 1905.

Segré, Claudio G. *Italo Balbo: A Fascist Life*. Berkeley: University of California Press, 1987.

Sexton, Andrea W., and Alice Leccese Powers, eds. *The Brooklyn Reader*. New York: Crown Trade Paperbacks, 1994.

Shapiro, Michael. *The Last Good Season: Brooklyn, the Dodgers, and Their Final Pennant Race Together*. New York: Doubleday, 2003.

Shorto, Russell. *The Island at the Center of the World*. New York: Random House, 2005.

Sinclair, Upton. *Damaged Goods: The Great Play "Les Avariés" of Brieux*. Philadelphia: The John C. Winston Company, 1913.

Soderlund, Jean R., ed. *William Penn and the Founding of Pennsylvania, 1680–1684: A Documentary History*. Philadelphia: University of Pennsylvania Press, 1983.

Spender, Matthew. *From a High Place: A Life of Arshile Gorky*. Berkeley: University of California Press, 2000.

Starr, Roger. *The Rise and Fall of New York City*. New York: Basic Books, 1985.

Sterngass, Jon. *First Resorts: Pursuing Pleasure at Saratoga Springs, Newport, and Coney Island*. Baltimore: Johns Hopkins University Press, 2001.

Stiles, Henry R., ed. *The Civil, Political, Professional and Ecclesiastical History and Commercial and Industrial Record of the County of Kings and the City of Brooklyn, New York*. Vol. 1. New York: W. W. Munsell and Company, 1884.

———. *History of the City of Brooklyn*. Vol. 1. Brooklyn, NY: published by subscription, 1867.

Stokes, I. N. Phelps. *The Iconography of Manhattan Island 1498–1909*. Vol. 2. New York: Robert H. Dodd, 1915–1928.

Suid, Lawrence H. *Guts & Glory: The Making of the American Military Image in Film*. Lexington: University Press of Kentucky, 2002.

Switala, William J. *Underground Railroad in New Jersey and New York*. Mechanicsburg, PA: Stackpole Books, 2006.

Tatum, Edward Howland, ed. *The American Journal of Ambrose Serle: Secretary to Lord Howe, 1776–1778*. Berkeley: University of California Press, 1940.

Thabit, Walter. *How East New York Became a Ghetto*. New York: New York University Press, 2003.

Thompson, Benjamin F. *History of Long Island, containing An Account of the Discovery and Settlement, with Other Important and Interesting Matters to the Present Time*. New York: E. French, 1839.

Tippins, Sherill. *February House*. New York: Houghton Mifflin, 2005.

Tooker, William Wallace. *Indian Names of Places in the Borough of Brooklyn*. New York: Francis P. Harper, 1901.

Townsend, Gavin E. "The Tudor House in America: 1890–1930." PhD diss., University of California, Santa Barbara, 1986.

Vanderbilt, Gertrude Lefferts. *The Social History of Flatbush*. New York: D. Appleton, 1899.

Van Wyck, Frederick. *Keskachauge: Or the First White Settlement on Long Island*. New York: G. P. Putnam's Sons, 1924.

Velsor, Kathleen G. *The Underground Railroad on Long Island*. Charleston, SC: The History Press, 2013.

Viele, Kathlyne Knickerbocker, ed. *Viele 1659–1909: Two Hundred and Fifty Years with a Dutch Family of New York*. New York: Tobias A. Wright, 1909.

Wald, Alan M. *Exiles from a Future Time*. Chapel Hill: University of North Carolina Press, 2002.

Wallace, Mike. *Greater Gotham*. New York: Oxford University Press, 2017.

Ward, John H. *Trinity Freight Terminal in the City of New York*. New York: Waterfront Investments, 1919.

Wellman, Judith. *Brooklyn's Promised Land: The Free Black Community of Weeksville, New York*. New York: New York University Press, 2014.

White, Shane. *Somewhat More Independent*. Athens: University of Georgia Press, 1991.

Whitford, Noble E. *History of the Barge Canal of New York State*. Albany, NY: J. B. Lyon Company, 1922.

Wilder, Craig Steven. *A Covenant with Color: Race and Social Power in Brooklyn*. New York: Columbia University Press, 2001.

Williams, Frank M. *Annual Report of the State Engineer and Surveyor for the Year Ended June 30, 1919*. Albany, NY: J. B. Lyon Company, 1920.

Wiltse, Jeff. *Contested Waters: A Social History of Swimming Pools in America*. Chapel Hill: University of North Carolina Press, 2007.

Winkle, Edward Van. *Manhattan, 1624–1639*. New York: Knickerbocker Press, 1916.

Wolley, Charles. *A Two-Years' Journal in New York*. Cleveland, OH: Burrows Brothers, 1902 [1701].

Woodsworth, Michael. *Battle for Bed-Stuy: The Long War on Poverty in New York City*. Cambridge, MA: Harvard University Press, 2016.

Wrenn, Tony P. *General History of the Jamaica Bay, Breezy Point, and Staten Island Units, Gateway National Recreation Area*. National Park Service, unpublished report, 1975.

Zipp, Samuel. *Manhattan Projects: The Rise and Fall of Urban Renewal in Cold War New York*. London: Oxford University Press, 2010.

Zukin, Sharon. *Naked City: The Death and Life of Authentic Urban Places*. New York: Oxford University Press, 2010.

Zwierlein, Frederick James. *Religion in New Netherland, 1623–1664*. New York: J. P. Smith, 1910.

INDEX

Note: Page numbers in italic type indicate illustrations.